THE RUSSIAN EDITION WAS PRINTED
IN ACCORDANCE WITH A DECISION
OF THE NINTH CONGRESS OF THE R.C.P. (B.)
AND THE SECOND CONGRESS OF SOVIETS
OF THE U.S.S.R.

ИНСТИТУТ МАРКСИЗМА-ЛЕНИНИЗМА ПРИ ЦК КПСС

В. И. ЛЕНИН

СОЧИНЕНИЯ

Издание четвертое

ГОСУДАРСТВЕННОЕ ИЗДАТЕЛЬСТВО
ПОЛИТИЧЕСКОЙ ЛИТЕРАТУРЫ
МОСКВА

V. I. LENIN

COLLECTED WORKS

VOLUME
2
1895-1897

PROGRESS PUBLISHERS
MOSCOW 1972

TRANSLATED FROM THE RUSSIAN
EDITED BY GEORGE HANNA

First printing 1960
Second printing 1963
Third printing 1972

Printed in the Union of Soviet Socialist Republics

11-17-78

CONTENTS

———

ILLUSTRATIONS

PREFACE

Volume two contains Lenin's works of the 1895-97 period. The first group of works in the volume, namely, *Frederick Engels, Draft and Explanation of a Programme for the Social-Democratic Party, The Tasks of the Russian Social-Democrats,* and *The Heritage We Renounce*—is devoted to an elaboration of the tasks of the Russian Marxists as far as their programme, tactics and organisation are concerned.

A considerable part of the present volume is made up of Lenin's economic writings directed against the Narodniks: *A Characterisation of Economic Romanticism, The Handicraft Census of 1894-95 in Perm Gubernia and General Problems of "Handicraft" Industry, Gems of Narodnik Project-Mongering,* etc.

The third group contains agitational works by Lenin—the pamphlets *Explanation of the Law on Fines Imposed on Factory Workers,* and *The New Factory Law,* the leaflets *To the Working Men and Women of the Thornton Factory* and *To the Tsarist Government,* and the article *What Are Our Ministers Thinking About?*

In 1897 and 1898, when preparing the legally published editions of *A Characterisation of Economic Romanticism,* Lenin was compelled, because of the censorship, to replace the words "Marxist theory" by "modern theory"; to replace "Marx" by "a well-known German economist," and "this socialism" by "this doctrine," etc. For the 1908 edition, Lenin either corrected a considerable number of these expressions in the text or explained them in footnotes. In the second and third Russian editions of the *Collected Works* these corrections of Lenin's were given as footnotes. In the present edition they have been included in the text itself.

In the previous editions of V. I. Lenin's *Collected Works* the text of *The Tasks of the Russian Social-Democrats* was taken from a copy of Lenin's manuscript. The copy contains slips of the pen and other mistakes by the copier. In the present edition the text of the pamphlet published in 1902, which was read and corrected by Lenin, has been used.

FREDERICK ENGELS

Written in autumn 1895
First published in 1896
in the miscellany *Rabotnik*,[1]
No. 1-2

Published according
to the text in *Rabotnik*

V. I. LENIN
1897

ПРОЛЕТАРІИ ВСѢХЪ СТРАНЪ, СОЕДИНЯЙТЕСЬ!

РАБОТНИКЪ

№. №. 1 и 2.

НЕПЕРІОДИЧЕСКІЙ СБОРНИКЪ

Съ портретомъ Фридриха Энгельса.

Изданіе „Союза Русскихъ Соціальдемократовъ".

ЖЕНЕВА
Типографія „Союза Русскихъ Соціальдемократовъ".
1896

The title-page of the *Rabotnik* miscellany in which
Lenin's obituary, *Frederick Engels*, was first published.
1896

> What a torch of reason ceased to burn,
> What a heart has ceased to beat! [2]

On August 5 (new style), 1895, Frederick Engels died in London. After his friend Karl Marx (who died in 1883), Engels was the finest scholar and teacher of the modern proletariat in the whole civilised world. From the time that fate brought Karl Marx and Frederick Engels together, the two friends devoted their life's work to a common cause. And so to understand what Frederick Engels has done for the proletariat, one must have a clear idea of the significance of Marx's teaching and work for the development of the contemporary working-class movement. Marx and Engels were the first to show that the working class and its demands are a necessary outcome of the present economic system, which together with the bourgeoisie inevitably creates and organises the proletariat. They showed that it is not the well-meaning efforts of noble-minded individuals, but the class struggle of the organised proletariat that will deliver humanity from the evils which now oppress it. In their scientific works, Marx and Engels were the first to explain that socialism is not the invention of dreamers, but the final aim and necessary result of the development of the productive forces in modern society. All recorded history hitherto has been a history of class struggle, of the succession of the rule and victory of certain social classes over others. And this will continue until the foundations of class struggle and of class domination—private property and anarchic social production—disappear. The interests of the proletariat demand the destruction of these foundations, and therefore the conscious class struggle of the organised workers must be directed against them. And every class struggle is a political struggle.

These views of Marx and Engels have now been adopted by all proletarians who are fighting for their emancipation.

But when in the forties the two friends took part in the socialist literature and the social movements of their time,
they were absolutely novel. There were then many people,
talented and without talent, honest and dishonest, who,
absorbed in the struggle for political freedom, in the
struggle against the despotism of kings, police and priests,
failed to observe the antagonism between the interests of
the bourgeoisie and those of the proletariat. These people
would not entertain the idea of the workers acting as an
independent social force. On the other hand, there were
many dreamers, some of them geniuses, who thought that
it was only necessary to convince the rulers and the governing classes of the injustice of the contemporary social
order, and it would then be easy to establish peace and general well-being on earth. They dreamt of a socialism without struggle. Lastly, nearly all the socialists of that time
and the friends of the working class generally regarded the
proletariat only as an *ulcer*, and observed with horror how
it grew with the growth of industry. They all, therefore,
sought for a means to stop the development of industry and
of the proletariat, to stop the "wheel of history." Marx
and Engels did not share the general fear of the development of the proletariat; on the contrary, they placed all
their hopes on its continued growth. The more proletarians
there are, the greater is their strength as a revolutionary
class, and the nearer and more possible does socialism become. The services rendered by Marx and Engels to the working class may be expressed in a few words thus: they taught
the working class to know itself and be conscious of itself,
and they substituted science for dreams.

That is why the name and life of Engels should be known
to every worker. That is why in this collection of articles,
the aim of which, as of all our publications, is to awaken
class-consciousness in the Russian workers, we must give
a sketch of the life and work of Frederick Engels, one of the
two great teachers of the modern proletariat.

Engels was born in 1820 in Barmen, in the Rhine Province
of the kingdom of Prussia. His father was a manufacturer.
In 1838 Engels, without having completed his high-school
studies, was forced by family circumstances to enter a commercial house in Bremen as a clerk. Commercial affairs did

not prevent Engels from pursuing his scientific and political education. He had come to hate autocracy and the tyranny of bureaucrats while still at high school. The study of philosophy led him further. At that time Hegel's teaching dominated German philosophy, and Engels became his follower. Although Hegel himself was an admirer of the autocratic Prussian state, in whose service he was as a professor at Berlin University, Hegel's *teachings* were revolutionary. Hegel's faith in human reason and its rights, and the fundamental thesis of Hegelian philosophy that the universe is undergoing a constant process of change and development, led some of the disciples of the Berlin philosopher—those who refused to accept the existing situation —to the idea that the struggle against this situation, the struggle against existing wrong and prevalent evil, is also rooted in the universal law of eternal development. If all things develop, if institutions of one kind give place to others, why should the autocracy of the Prussian king or of the Russian tsar, the enrichment of an insignificant minority at the expense of the vast majority, or the domination of the bourgeoisie over the people, continue for ever? Hegel's philosophy spoke of the development of the mind and of ideas; it was *idealistic*. From the development of the mind it deduced the development of nature, of man, and of human, social relations. While retaining Hegel's idea of the eternal process of development,* Marx and Engels rejected the preconceived idealist view; turning to life, they saw that it is not the development of mind that explains the development of nature but that, on the contrary, the explanation of mind must be derived from nature, from matter.... Unlike Hegel and the other Hegelians, Marx and Engels were materialists. Regarding the world and humanity materialistically, they perceived that just as material causes underlie all natural phenomena, so the development of human society is conditioned by the development of material forces, the productive forces. On the development of the productive forces depend the relations into which

* Marx and Engels frequently pointed out that in their intellectual development they were much indebted to the great German philosophers, particularly to Hegel. "Without German philosophy," Engels says, "scientific socialism would never have come into being."[3]

men enter with one another in the production of the things required for the satisfaction of human needs. And in these relations lies the explanation of all the phenomena of social life, human aspirations, ideas and laws. The development of the productive forces creates social relations based upon private property, but now we see that this same development of the productive forces deprives the majority of their property and concentrates it in the hands of an insignificant minority. It abolishes property, the basis of the modern social order, it itself strives towards the very aim which the socialists have set themselves. All the socialists have to do is to realise which social force, owing to its position in modern society, is interested in bringing socialism about, and to impart to this force the consciousness of its interests and of its historical task. This force is the proletariat. Engels got to know the proletariat in England, in the centre of English industry, Manchester, where he settled in 1842, entering the service of a commercial firm of which his father was a shareholder. Here Engels not only sat in the factory office but wandered about the slums in which the workers were cooped up, and saw their poverty and misery with his own eyes. But he did not confine himself to personal observations. He read all that had been revealed before him about the condition of the British working class and carefully studied all the official documents he could lay his hands on. The fruit of these studies and observations was the book which appeared in 1845: *The Condition of the Working Class in England.* We have already mentioned what was the chief service rendered by Engels in writing *The Condition of the Working Class in England.* Even before Engels, many people had described the sufferings of the proletariat and had pointed to the necessity of helping it. Engels was the *first* to say that the proletariat is *not only* a suffering class; that it is, in fact, the disgraceful economic condition of the proletariat that drives it irresistibly forward and compels it to fight for its ultimate emancipation. And the fighting proletariat *will help itself.* The political movement of the working class will inevitably lead the workers to realise that their only salvation lies in socialism. On the other hand, socialism will become a force only when it becomes the aim of the *political* struggle of the working *class*. Such are the main ideas of Engels' book on the condition of the working class in England, ideas which have now been adopted by all thinking and fighting proletarians, but which at that time were entirely new. These ideas were set out in a book written in absorbing style and filled with most authentic and shocking pictures of the misery of the English proletariat. The book was a terrible indictment of capitalism and the bourgeoisie and created a profound impression. Engels' book began to be quoted everywhere as presenting the best picture of the condition of the modern proletariat. And, in fact, neither before 1845 nor after has there appeared so striking and truthful a picture of the misery of the working class.

It was not until he came to England that Engels became a socialist. In Manchester he established contacts with people active in the English labour movement at the time and began to write for English socialist publications. In 1844, while on his way back to Germany, he became acquainted in Paris with Marx, with whom he had already started to correspond. In Paris, under the influence of the French socialists and French life, Marx had also become a socialist. Here the friends jointly wrote a book entitled *The Holy Family, or Critique of Critical Critique.* This book, which appeared a year before *The Condition of the Working Class in England,* and the greater part of which was written by Marx, contains the foundations of revolutionary materialist socialism, the main ideas of which we have expounded above. "The holy family" is a facetious nickname for the Bauer brothers, the philosophers, and their followers. These gentlemen preached a criticism which stood above all reality, above parties and politics, which rejected all practical activity, and which only "critically" contemplated the surrounding world and the events going on within it. These gentlemen, the Bauers, looked down on the proletariat as an uncritical mass. Marx and Engels vigorously opposed this absurd and harmful tendency. In the name of a real, human person—the worker, trampled down by the ruling classes and the state—they demanded, not contemplation, but a struggle for a better order of society. They, of course, regarded the proletariat as the force that is capable of waging this struggle and that is interested in it. Even before the appearance of *The Holy Family*, Engels had published in Marx's and Ruge's *Deutsch-Französische Jahrbücher*[4] his "Critical Essays on Political Economy,"[5] in which he examined the principal phenomena of the contemporary economic order from a socialist standpoint, regarding them as necessary consequences of the rule of private property.. Contact with Engels was undoubtedly a factor in Marx's decision to study political economy, the science in which his works have produced a veritable revolution.

From 1845 to 1847 Engels lived in Brussels and Paris, combining scientific work with practical activities among the German workers in Brussels and Paris. Here Marx and Engels established contact with the secret German Communist League,[6] which commissioned them to expound the main principles of the socialism they had worked out. Thus arose the famous *Manifesto of the Communist Party* of Marx and Engels, published in 1848. This little booklet is worth whole volumes: to this day its spirit inspires and guides the entire organised and fighting proletariat of the civilised world.

The revolution of 1848, which broke out first in France and then spread to other West-European countries, brought Marx and Engels back to their native country. Here, in Rhenish Prussia, they took charge of the democratic *Neue Rheinische Zeitung*[7] published in Cologne. The two friends were the heart and soul of all revolutionary-democratic aspirations in Rhenish Prussia. They fought to the last ditch in defence of freedom and of the interests of the people against the forces of reaction. The latter, as we know, gained the upper hand. The *Neue Rheinische Zeitung* was suppressed. Marx, who during his exile had lost his Prussian citizenship, was deported; Engels took part in the armed popular uprising, fought for liberty in three battles, and after the defeat of the rebels fled, via Switzerland, to London.

Marx also settled in London. Engels soon became a clerk again, and then a shareholder, in the Manchester commercial firm in which he had worked in the forties. Until 1870 he lived in Manchester, while Marx lived in London, but this did not prevent their maintaining a most lively interchange of ideas: they corresponded almost daily. In this correspondence the two friends exchanged views and discoveries and continued to collaborate in working out scientific socialism. In 1870 Engels moved to London, and their joint intellectual life, of the most strenuous nature, continued until 1883, when Marx died. Its fruit was, on Marx's side, *Capital*, the greatest work on political economy of our age, and on Engels' side, a number of works both large and small. Marx worked on the analysis of the complex phenomena of capitalist economy. Engels, in simply written works, often of a polemical character, dealt with more general scientific problems and with diverse phenomena of the past and present in the spirit of the materialist conception of history and Marx's economic theory. Of Engels' works we shall mention: the polemical work against Dühring (analysing highly important problems in the domain of philosophy, natural science and the social sciences),* *The Origin of the Family, Private Property and the State* (translated into Russian, published in St. Petersburg, 3rd ed., 1895),[10] *Ludwig Feuerbach* (Russian translation and notes by G. Plekhanov, Geneva, 1892),[11] an article on the foreign policy of the Russian Government (translated into Russian in the Geneva *Sotsial-Demokrat*, Nos. 1 and 2),[12] splendid articles on the housing question,[13] and finally, two small but very valuable articles on Russia's economic development (*Frederick Engels on Russia*, translated into Russian by Zasulich, Geneva, 1894).[14] Marx died before he could put the final touches to his vast work on capital. The draft, however, was already finished, and after the death of his friend, Engels undertook the onerous task of preparing and publishing the second and the third volumes of *Capital*. He published Volume II in 1885 and Volume III in 1894 (his death prevented the preparation of Volume IV).[15] These two volumes entailed a vast amount of labour. Adler, the Austrian Social-Democrat, has rightly remarked that by publishing volumes II and III of *Capital* Engels erected a majestic monument to the genius who had been his friend, a monument on which, without intending it, he indelibly carved his own name. Indeed

---

* This is a wonderfully rich and instructive book.[8] Unfortunately, only a small portion of it, containing a historical outline of the development of socialism, has been translated into Russian (*The Development of Scientific Socialism*, 2nd ed., Geneva, 1892).[9]

these two volumes of *Capital* are the work of two men: Marx and Engels. Old legends contain various moving instances of friendship. The European proletariat may say that its science was created by two scholars and fighters, whose relationship to each other surpasses the most moving stories of the ancients about human friendship. Engels always—and, on the whole, quite justly—placed himself after Marx. "In Marx's lifetime," he wrote to an old friend, "I played second fiddle."[16] His love for the living Marx, and his reverence for the memory of the dead Marx were boundless. This stern fighter and austere thinker possessed a deeply loving soul.

After the movement of 1848-49, Marx and Engels in exile did not confine themselves to scientific research. In 1864 Marx founded the International Working Men's Association,[17] and led this society for a whole decade. Engels also took an active part in its affairs. The work of the International Association, which, in accordance with Marx's idea, united proletarians of all countries, was of tremendous significance in the development of the working-class movement. But even with the closing down of the International Association in the seventies, the unifying role of Marx and Engels did not cease. On the contrary, it may be said that their importance as the spiritual leaders of the working-class movement grew continuously, because the movement itself grew uninterruptedly. After the death of Marx, Engels continued alone as the counsellor and leader of the European socialists. His advice and directions were sought for equally by the German socialists, whose strength, despite government persecution, grew rapidly and steadily, and by representatives of backward countries, such as the Spaniards, Rumanians and Russians, who were obliged to ponder and weigh their first steps. They all drew on the rich store of knowledge and experience of Engels in his old age.

Marx and Engels, who both knew Russian and read Russian books, took a lively interest in the country, followed the Russian revolutionary movement with sympathy and maintained contact with Russian revolutionaries. They both became socialists after being *democrats*, and the democratic feeling of *hatred* for political despotism was exceedingly strong in them. This direct political feeling, combined with a profound theoretical understanding of the connection between political despotism and economic oppression, and also their rich experience of life, made Marx and Engels uncommonly responsive *politically*. That is why the heroic struggle of the handful of Russian revolutionaries against the mighty tsarist government evoked a most sympathetic echo in the hearts of these tried revolutionaries. On the other hand, the tendency, for the sake of illusory economic advantages, to turn away from the most immediate and important task of the Russian socialists, namely, the winning of political freedom, naturally appeared suspicious to them and was even regarded by them as a direct betrayal of the great cause of the social revolution. "The emancipation of the workers must be the act of the working class itself"—Marx and Engels constantly taught.[18] But in order to fight for its economic emancipation, the proletariat must win itself certain *political* rights. Moreover, Marx and Engels clearly saw that a political revolution in Russia would be of tremendous significance to the West-European working-class movement as well. Autocratic Russia had always been a bulwark of European reaction in general. The extraordinarily favourable international position enjoyed by Russia as a result of the war of 1870, which for a long time sowed discord between Germany and France, of course only enhanced the importance of autocratic Russia as a reactionary force. Only a free Russia, a Russia that had no need either to oppress the Poles, Finns, Germans, Armenians or any other small nations, or constantly to set France and Germany at loggerheads, would enable modern Europe, rid of the burden of war, to breathe freely, would weaken all the reactionary elements in Europe and strengthen the European working class. That was why Engels ardently desired the establishment of political freedom in Russia for the sake of the progress of the working-class movement in the West as well. In him the Russian revolutionaries have lost their best friend.

Let us always honour the memory of Frederick Engels, a great fighter and teacher of the proletariat!

EXPLANATION OF THE LAW
ON FINES IMPOSED
ON FACTORY WORKERS [19]

Written in autumn 1895
First published in
pamphlet form,
St. Petersburg, 1895

Published according to
the 1895 edition checked
with the 1897 edition

ОБЪЯСНЕНІЕ

ЗАКОНА

О

ШТРАФАХЪ, ВЗИМАЕМЫХЪ

СЪ

рабочихъ на фабрикахъ и заводахъ.

Типографія К. Н. Субботина, Екатерин. ул. д. Калинина.
1895.

I
WHAT ARE FINES?

If we were to ask a worker whether he knows what fines are, the question would very likely astonish him. How can he not know what fines are, when he constantly has to pay them? What is there to ask about?

However, it only seems that there is nothing to ask about. Actually, most workers do not properly understand fines.

It is usually thought that a fine is a payment made to the employer for damage done to him by the worker. That is not true. A fine and compensation for damage are two different things. If a worker does some damage to another worker, the latter may demand compensation for the damage (e.g., for a piece of cloth which has been spoiled), but cannot fine him. Similarly, if one factory owner does damage to another (e.g., fails to deliver goods on time), the latter can demand compensation, but he cannot fine the first factory owner. Compensation for damage is demanded of an equal, whereas a fine can only be imposed on a subordinate. Hence, compensation for damage must be claimed in court, whereas a fine is imposed by the employer out of court. A fine is sometimes imposed when the employer has suffered no damage: e.g., a fine for smoking. A fine is a penalty, and not compensation for damage. If a worker, let us say, is careless while smoking and burns the employer's cloth, the employer not only fines him for smoking, but in addition makes a deduction for the burnt cloth. This example clearly shows the difference between a fine and compensation for damage.

Fines are not imposed to compensate for damage but to establish discipline, i.e., to secure subordination

of the workers to the employer, to force the worker to fulfil the employer's orders, to obey him during working hours.
The law on fines in fact says that a fine is a "monetary penalty imposed by the factory management on its own authority
with a view to the maintenance of order." And the amount
of the fine depends, therefore, not on the amount of the
damage, but on the extent of the worker's misdemeanour:
the greater the misdemeanour, the greater the disobedience
to the employer or departure from the employer's demands,
the greater the fine. If anybody goes to work for an employer, it is clear that he loses his freedom; he must obey
his employer, and the employer may punish him. The peasant serfs worked for landlords, and the landlords punished
them. The workers work for capitalists, and the capitalists
punish them. The only difference is that formerly it was
a man's back that suffered, whereas now it is his purse.

It will perhaps be objected that joint work by a mass
of workers at a mill or factory is impossible without discipline: order is needed on the job, somebody has to see
that order is kept and that those who violate it are punished. Hence—we shall be told—fines are imposed not because the workers are not free, but because joint work requires order.

The objection is quite groundless, although at first
sight people may be misled by it. It is only put forward
by people who wish to conceal from the workers that they
are not free agents. Order is certainly necessary wherever
work is done jointly. But is it necessary that people who
work should be subordinated to the tyranny of the factory
owners, i.e., of people who do not work themselves and who
are only strong because they have taken hold of all the machines, instruments and materials? Joint work cannot be
done unless there is order, unless all submit to it; but work
can be done in common without subordinating the workers
to the factory owners. Joint work does, indeed, require
that there is supervision to ensure the maintenance of order,
but it does not at all require that the power to supervise
others should always be vested in the one who does not work
himself, but lives on the labour of others. Hence it can be
seen that fines are imposed not because people work together, but because, under the present capitalist system, all

working folk possess no property: all the machines, instruments, raw materials, land, and bread belong to the rich. The workers have to sell themselves to them so as not to starve. Once, however, they have sold themselves, they are of course obliged to subordinate themselves to them and suffer punishment at their hands.

Every worker desirous of understanding what fines are should be clear on this point. He must know this so as to refute the usual (and very mistaken) argument that fines are necessary since without them joint work is impossible. He must know this, so as to be able to explain to every worker the difference between a fine and compensation for damage, and why fines mean that the workers are not free, that they are subordinated to the capitalists.

II

HOW WERE FINES IMPOSED FORMERLY AND WHAT GAVE RISE TO THE NEW LEGISLATION ON FINES?

The fines laws were introduced recently, only nine years ago. Before 1886 there were no such laws at all. Factory owners were able to impose fines for what they pleased and to any extent they wished. They did so on a monstrous scale and collected enormous sums for themselves out of it. Fines were sometimes imposed simply "at the employer's discretion," without the reason for the fine being given. Fines occasionally amounted to *as much as half the earnings* of the worker, so that the latter gave up to the employer fifty kopeks out of every ruble earned in the shape of fines. There were cases when extra fines, over and above the ordinary ones, were imposed; for example, 10 rubles for leaving the factory. Whenever the employer's affairs were in a bad way, he would have no scruple about reducing wages, despite the existence of a contract. He would compel the foremen to be stricter in fining and in rejecting work done which had just the same effect as reducing the worker's wages.

The workers long tolerated all this oppression, but as more and more big mills and factories, particularly weaving mills, were built, forcing out the small establishments and hand weavers, the workers' indignation at the tyranny and oppression mounted. Some ten years ago there was a *hitch* in the affairs of the merchants and factory owners, what is called a crisis: goods were left on their hands; the factory owners suffered losses and began to increase fines with still greater energy. The workers, whose earnings were small enough as it was, could not bear the additional oppression, with the result that workers' revolts took place in the Moscow, Vladimir and Yaroslavl gubernias. That was in 1885-86. Their patience exhausted, the workers stopped work and wreaked terrible vengeance on their oppressors, wrecking factory premises and machinery, sometimes setting fire to them, attacking managerial personnel, etc.

One of the most remarkable of these strikes was at the well-known Nikolskoye Mill belonging to Timofei Savvich Morozov (in the township of Nikolskoye, near Orekhovo Station on the Moscow-Nizhni Novgorod Railway). From 1882 onwards Morozov started reducing wages, and by 1884 there had been five reductions. At the same time fines were imposed with increasing severity, amounting in the whole mill to almost a quarter of the earnings (24 kopeks in fines for every ruble earned), and in the case of some workers to a half their earnings. To cover up these disgraceful fines, the mill office in the year preceding the outbreak did the following: workers who had been fined to the extent of half their earnings were discharged, but were given their jobs back again sometimes on the same day, together with new pay-books. In this way books that contained records of outrageous fines were destroyed. Where workers were absent without leave, deductions were made at the rate of 3 days' pay for each day's absence; for smoking, the fine amounted to 3, 4 or 5 rubles each time. Their patience exhausted, the workers struck work on January 7, 1885, and over several days wrecked the factory foodstore, foreman Shorin's home and several other factory buildings. This terrific outbreak of some ten thousand workers (up to 11,000 were affected) greatly frightened the government, and was immediately followed by the appearance on the scene in Orekhovo-Zuyevo of troops, the Governor, a prosecutor from Vladimir, and one from Moscow. During negotiations with the strikers, the crowd presented the management with "conditions drawn up by the workers themselves." In these the workers demanded that fines imposed from Easter 1884 onwards be refunded, that thenceforward fines should not exceed 5% of earnings, i.e., should not amount to more than 5 kopeks per ruble earned, and that for one day's absence without permission the fine should not exceed one ruble. Further, the workers demanded a return to the wage rates of 1881-82, they demanded that the employer pay for idle days for which he was to blame, that 15 days' clear notice be given before dismissal, and that goods produced be accepted by the management in the presence of witnesses from among the workers, etc.

This huge strike made a very great impression on the government, which saw that when the workers act in unison they constitute a dangerous force, particularly when the mass of the workers, acting in concert, advance their demands directly. The employers also sensed the workers' strength and became more careful. The newspaper *Novoye Vremya*,[20] for example, published the following report from Orekhovo-Zuyevo: "The significance of last year's outbreak" (i.e., the outbreak at Morozov's in January 1885) "is that it immediately changed the old order in the factories, both in Orekhovo-Zuyevo and its environs." That is to say, not only the owners of the Morozov mill had to change the abominable system when the workers jointly demanded its abolition, but even the neighbouring mill owners agreed to concessions, out of fear of outbreaks taking place at their factories, too. "The main thing," stated the same newspaper, "is that a more human attitude to the workers has now been established, something that previously distinguished few of the factory managers."

Even *Moskovskiye Vedomosti*[21] (this newspaper always supports the employers and blames the workers themselves for everything) understood the impossibility of retaining the old system and had to admit that arbitrary fining is an "evil that leads to disgraceful abuses," that "factory stores are downright robbery," that therefore a law and regulations concerning fines must be introduced.

The tremendous impression created by this strike was further heightened as a result of the trial of several workers. For violent behaviour during the strike, for attacking a military patrol (some of the workers were arrested during the strike and locked in a building, but they broke down the door and made off), 33 workers were brought to trial. This took place in Vladimir in May 1886. The jury found all the accused not guilty, since the testimony of the witnesses, including the owner of the mill, T. S. Morozov, manager Dianov and many of the weavers, shed light on all the abominable oppression to which the workers had been subjected. This verdict of the court was a direct condemnation not only of Morozov and his managers but of the old factory system as a whole.

The alarm and fury of the supporters of the mill owners was thoroughly aroused. The very same *Moskovskiye Vedomosti,* which after the outbreak had admitted the iniquity of the old system, now took a very different line. "The Nikolskoye Mill," it asserted, "is one of the best mills. The workers' relation to the factory is not a feudal or a compulsory one at all; they come voluntarily and leave without hindrance. Fines—but fines are essential in the mills; without them the workers would get out of hand, and you might as well close the mill." All the blame, it asserted, lay with the workers themselves, who were "profligate, drunken and careless." The verdict of the court could only "corrupt the masses of the people."* "But it is dangerous to joke with the masses of the people," ejaculated *Moskovskiye Vedomosti.* "What must the workers think, following the not-guilty verdict of the Vladimir court? The news of this decision spread like lightning through the whole of this manufacturing area. Our correspondent, who left Vladimir immediately after the announcement of the verdict, heard of it at all the stations...."

Thus, the employers tried to scare the government by saying that if one concession were made to the workers, the next day they would demand another.

* The employers and their supporters have always considered that if the workers begin to think about their conditions, begin to work for their rights and join forces in resisting the abominations and oppression of the employers, it is all nothing but "corruption." It is, of course, an advantage to the employers if the workers give no thought to their conditions and have no understanding of their rights.

But the workers' outbreaks were even more frightening, and so the government had to make concessions.

In June 1886 a new fines law appeared, which indicated in what cases the imposition of fines was permissible, specified the maximum fines, and laid it down that the fines must not go into the employer's pocket, but must go to cover the needs of the workers themselves.

Many workers are not aware of this law, while those who are, imagine that the relief gained in the matter of fines is the handiwork of the government, and that thanks for this relief should be accorded to the authorities. We have seen that this is wrong. Despite the iniquity of the old factory system, the authorities did absolutely nothing to bring relief to the workers until the latter began to revolt against it, until the workers in their fury went so far as to start wrecking the factories and machinery, setting fire to goods and materials, and attacking managers and mill owners. *Only then did the government get scared and make concessions.* For the easing of their lot the workers should thank not the authorities but their comrades who worked for and secured the abolition of this disgraceful treatment.

The history of the outbreaks of 1885 shows us what a colossal force is the workers' united protest. All that is required is to ensure that this force is used more consciously, that it is not wasted on wreaking vengeance on some particular factory owner, on wrecking some hated factory, that the whole force of this indignation and this hatred is directed against all factory owners combined, against the entire *class* of them, that it is expended on regular and persistent struggle against them.

Let us now make a detailed examination of our fines legislation. To acquaint ourselves with it, we must examine the following questions: 1) In what cases or on what grounds does the law permit the imposition of fines? 2) What, according to the law, should be the size of the fines? 3) What procedure for imposing fines is laid down in the law? i.e., who, according to the law, may fix the fine? May an appeal be lodged against it? What arrangements must be made to acquaint the worker in advance with the list of fines? How must the fines be recorded? 4) On what must fines be expended according to the law? Where is the money kept? How is it expended on the workers' needs, and on what needs? Finally, the last question, 5) Does the fines law cover all workers?

When we have examined all these questions, we shall know not only what a fine is, but also all the particular rules and detailed regulations of Russian legislation on fines. And the workers need to know this, so that their reaction to each case of unjust fining may be an informed one, so that they may be able to explain to their comrades why there is injustice of one kind or another—whether because the factory management are violating the law, or because the law itself contains such unjust regulations—and so that they may be able accordingly to choose a suitable form of struggle against oppression.

III

ON WHAT GROUNDS MAY THE FACTORY OWNER IMPOSE FINES?

The law says that the grounds for imposing fines, i.e., the misdemeanours for which the factory owner is entitled to fine workers may be the following: 1) defective work; 2) absenteeism; 3) offences against good order. "No penalties," says the law, "may be imposed on other grounds."* Let us examine more closely each of these three grounds separately.

The first ground is defective work. The law states that "defective work is considered to be the production by the worker, through negligence, of defective articles and damage done by him when working to materials, machinery or other instruments of production." The words "through negligence" should be remembered. They are very important. A fine may be imposed, accordingly, only for negligence. If the article proves to be of low quality not because of the worker's negligence, but because, for example, the em-

---

* The law that we are speaking of is Rules for Industry, which is included in Part Two, Volume 11 of the Russian Code of Laws. The law is stated in various articles, which are numbered. Fines are dealt with in articles 143, 144, 145, 146, 147, 148, 149, 150, 151 and 152.

ployer has supplied poor material, then the employer has no right to impose a fine. It is necessary that the workers should well understand this, and, if a fine is imposed for defective work, where the defect is due not to the worker's fault, or his negligence, they must lodge a protest, because to impose a fine in that case is a direct violation of the law. Let us take another example: the worker is doing his job at a lathe near an electric bulb. A piece of iron flies off, hits the bulb and smashes it. The employer imposes a fine "for damage of materials." Has he the right to do so? No, he has not, because it was not through negligence that the worker smashed the bulb: the worker is not to blame that the bulb was not protected at all against bits of iron, which are always flying off when work is in progress.*

The question now arises, does this law adequately protect the worker? Does it protect him against the employer's arbitrary conduct and the unjust imposition of fines? Of course not, because the employer decides at his discretion whether the article is of good or bad quality; fault-finding is always possible, it is always possible for the employer to increase fines for defective work and through their medium get more work done for the same pay. The law leaves the worker unprotected, and gives the employer a loophole for oppressing him. Clearly the law is partial, has been drawn up to the employers' advantage and is unjust.

How should the worker be protected? The workers have shown that long ago: during the 1885 strike the weavers at Morozov's Nikolskoye Mill advanced, among other demands, the following: "that the good or bad quality of articles be established when they are handed in, in case of disagreement, with witnesses from among the operatives working close at hand, all this to be recorded in the goods receipt book." (This demand was recorded in an exercise-book filled up "by general agreement of the workers" and handed in from the crowd to the prosecutor during the strike. The contents of the exercise-book were read out in court.) This demand is

---

* There was a case of that sort in St. Petersburg, in the port (New Admiralty), where the Harbourmaster, Verkhovsky, is well known for his oppression of the workers. After a strike he replaced fines for breaking bulbs by deductions for broken bulbs from all the workers in the shop. Obviously, these deductions are just as illegal as the fines.

quite a fair one, because there can be no other way of avert-
ing the employer's arbitrary conduct than to bring in
witnesses when a dispute arises about quality, the witnesses
without fail having to come from the workers' ranks: foremen or clerks would never dare to oppose the employer.

The second ground for the imposition of fines is absenteeism. What does the law call absenteeism? "Absenteeism,"
states the law, "as distinct from unpunctuality or unauthorised quitting of work, is failure to appear at work for not
less than one half of the working day." The law considers that
unpunctuality or unauthorised quitting of work is, as we shall
soon see, an "offence against good order," and the fine, therefore, is a smaller one. If the worker is several hours late
coming to the factory, but arrives before midday, this will
not be absenteeism, but merely an offence against good order; if, however, he only arrives at midday, then it is absenteeism. Similarly, if the worker quits work without permission after midday, i.e., is away for several hours, this
will be an offence against good order, but if he leaves for a
full half-day it is absenteeism. The law states that if the
worker is absent for more than three days consecutively or
for more than six days all told in a month, the employer is
entitled to discharge him. The question arises, is absence for
half or the whole of a day always to be considered absenteeism?
No. Only when there are no valid reasons for non-appearance at work. Valid reasons for non-appearance are enumerated in the law. They are as follows: 1) "loss of liberty
by the worker." That is to say, if the worker, for example,
is arrested (on orders of the police or by sentence of a magistrate), the employer is not entitled when dismissing the worker
to fine him for absenteeism, 2) "unexpected loss of property due
to a serious accident," 3) "fire," 4) "flood." E.g., if a worker
during the spring thaws cannot get across the river, the employer is not entitled to fine him, 5) "sickness which makes it
impossible for the worker to leave home" and 6) "death or
severe illness of parents, husband, wife or children." In all
these six cases the worker is considered to have a valid excuse
for non-appearance. But to avoid being fined for absenteeism,
the worker has to produce evidence: they will not take his
word for it in the office that he had a valid excuse for not
appearing at work. A certificate should be secured from the

doctor (in case of sickness, for example) or from the police (in case of fire, etc.). If a certificate cannot be obtained at once, it should be submitted later, and a demand made that no fine be imposed, and if it already has been, that it be cancelled.

Regarding these rules about valid reasons for non-appearance, it should be noted that they are as severe as if they applied to soldiers in barracks, and not to free men. They have been copied from those governing non-appearance in court: if anybody is accused of a crime, he is summoned by the investigator, and, as the accused, he is obliged to appear. Non-appearance is only permitted in precisely the same cases as those in which workers are permitted to absent themselves.* That is to say, the attitude of the law is just as strict to workers as it is to all sorts of swindlers, thieves, etc. Everybody understands why the rules about appearance in court are so strict; it is because the prosecution of crime concerns the whole of society. The failure, however, of a worker to appear at his place of work does not concern the whole of society, but only a single employer, and what is more, one worker can easily be replaced by another to prevent a stoppage of work. Which means that there was no need for the laws to have the strictness of military law. The capitalists, however, do not confine themselves to depriving the worker of all his time, so that he may work in the factory; they also want to deprive him of his will, of all interests and thoughts other than those connected with the factory. The worker is treated as though he were not a free man. That is why such fault-finding, bureaucratic rules, reminiscent of barrack life, are drawn up. For example, we have just seen that the law recognises the "death or severe sickness of parents, husband, wife or children" to be a valid reason for non-appearance. It says that in the law on appearance in court. Exactly the same is said in the law about the worker's appearance at work. That is to say, if, for example, the worker's sister, and not his wife, dies, he must not dare to miss a day's work, must not dare to spend time on funeral arrangements: his time belongs not to

---

* Except in the one case of "fire," which is not mentioned in the law about the summoning of accused persons.

himself, but to the employer. As to burial, the police may
deal with it—no need to bother about that. According to
the law on appearance in court, the interests of the family
must yield place to the interests of society, for which the
prosecution of criminals is necessary. According to the law
on appearance at work, the interests of the worker's family
must yield place to the interests of the employer, who must
have his profits. And after this, the fine gentlemen who
draw up, execute and support such laws, dare to accuse the
workers of not valuing family life!...

Let us see whether the law on fines for absenteeism is
a fair one. If the worker stays away from work for a day or
two, that is considered absenteeism, and he is punished
accordingly, and if he is away for more than three consecutive days he may be dismissed. Well, and if the employer
stops the job (e.g., for lack of orders) or provides work
only five days a week, instead of the established six? If
the workers really possessed rights equal to those of the
employers, then the law should be the same for the employer
as for the worker. If the worker stops work, he loses
his pay and pays a fine. So then, if the employer arbitrarily stops the job, he should, firstly, have to pay the worker
his full wage for the whole period that the factory is at
a standstill, and, secondly, he should be liable to be fined.
But neither is laid down in the law. This example clearly
confirms what we said previously about fines, namely that
they signify the enslavement of the workers by the capitalist, they signify that the workers constitute a lower class
without rights, condemned throughout their lives to work
for the capitalists and to create their wealth, receiving
in return a mere pittance that is insufficient to make life
even tolerable. There can be no question of the employers
paying fines for arbitrarily stopping jobs. But they
do not even pay the workers their wages when work
is stopped through no fault of theirs. That is a most outrageous injustice. The law only contains the rule that the
contract between the employer and the worker ceases
"where there is a stoppage of work at the factory for more
than 7 days, due to fire, flood, boiler explosion, or similar
cause." The workers should strive to get a rule adopted
making it obligatory on the factory owners to pay them wages

during stoppages of work. This demand was publicly advanced by the Russian workers on January 11, 1885, during the well-known strike at T. S. Morozov's mill.* The exercise-book of workers' demands contained the following point: "that the deduction for absenteeism shall not exceed one ruble, and the employer shall pay for days idle through his fault, e.g., when machinery is stopped or undergoing repairs, in which connection each idle day to be recorded in the pay-book." The workers' first demand (that the fine for absenteeism shall not exceed one ruble) was implemented, becoming part of the fines law of 1886. The second demand (that the employer pay for days idle through his fault) was not implemented and the workers still have to fight for its adoption. To ensure that the struggle for this demand is a success, all workers should clearly understand the injustice of the law, should clearly understand what must be demanded. In each separate case when some factory is at a standstill and the workers get no wages, they should raise the question of the injustice of it, they should insist that so long as the contract with the employer has not been annulled, the latter is obliged to pay for each day, they should report the matter to the inspector, whose explanation will confirm to the workers the point that in fact the law does not deal with this matter and will give rise to discussion of the law by the workers. They should appeal to the courts when the possibility exists, requesting the exaction of payment of wages from the employer, and, finally, advance general demands for payment for idle days.

The third ground for the imposition of a fine is "offences against good order." According to the law, such offences include the following 8 cases: 1) "unpunctuality or unauthorised quitting of work" (we have already indicated the dif-

---

* It should be noted that at that time (1884-85) cases of factory stoppages through no fault of the workers were quite frequent, as there was a commercial and industrial crisis: the mill owners could not dispose of their stocks, and they tried to cut down production. For example, in December 1884 the big Voznesenskoye Mill (Moscow Gubernia, near Talitsa Station on the Moscow-Yaroslavl Railway) cut down the working week to 4 days. The workers, who were on piece rates, met this with a strike that ended at the beginning of January 1885 in a concession from the owner.

ference between this and absenteeism); 2) "failure to observe on the factory premises the established rules regarding fire precautions, in those cases where the factory
management, by virtue of Note 1 to Article 105, do not
consider it necessary to annul the contract of hire concluded with the workers." This means that where the
worker violates the rules regarding fire precautions, the law
gives the employer the choice of either fining the worker
or of dismissing him ("to annul the contract of hire," as
the law says); 3) "failure to observe cleanliness and tidiness
on the factory premises"; 4) "breaking of silence while
work is in progress by noisiness, shouting, bawling, quar-
relling, or fighting"; 5) "disobedience." It should be noted of
this point that the employer has the right to fine the worker
for "disobedience" only when the latter has not fulfilled a
legitimate request, i.e., one based on the contract. If
some arbitrary demand is made, not based on the contract
between the worker and the employer, then no fine may be
imposed for "disobedience." Suppose the worker is doing a
job at piece rates. The foreman tells him to drop the job
and do another one. The worker refuses. In that case, to fine
the worker for disobedience would be wrong since he con-
tracted to do one particular job and, since he is on piece
rates, for him to transfer to another would mean working
for nothing; 6) "appearance at work drunk"; 7) "organisation
of unauthorised games for money (cards, pitch and toss,
etc.)" and 8) "failure to observe factory regulations." These
regulations are drawn up by the owner of each factory or
mill and are confirmed by the factory inspector. Extracts
from them are printed in the pay-books. The workers should
read these regulations and know them, so as to check whether fines imposed on them for violation of factory regulations are legitimate or not. These regulations must be distinguished from the law, which is the same for all mills
and factories; internal regulations differ for each factory.
The law is endorsed or annulled on the authority of the
tsar; factory regulations, by the factory inspector. Hence,
if these regulations prove to be oppressive to the workers
their annulment may be secured by appeal to the inspector
(should he refuse to take action, an appeal may be
lodged with the Factory Board). To show the need for

distinguishing between the law and factory regulations, let us take an example. Suppose a worker is fined for failure to put in an appearance on a holiday or to work overtime at the demand of the foreman. Is such a fine proper or not? To answer this question we have to know the factory regulations. If they say nothing about the worker's being obliged, on demand, to work overtime, then the fine is unlawful. If, however, the regulations state that the worker is obliged, on demand of the management, to appear on holidays or to work overtime, then the fine will be a legitimate one. To secure the annulment of this obligation, the workers must not direct their complaint against the fines, but demand that the factory regulations be amended. All the workers must be unanimous in this, and then, if they act together, they will be able to get the above regulations cancelled.

IV
HOW BIG MAY FINES BE?

We now know all the cases in which the law permits the fining of workers. Let us see what the law says about the size of the fines. The law does not fix one level for all factories. It only sets a maximum. This maximum is indicated separately for each of the three cases where fines may be imposed (defective work, absenteeism and offences against good order). For absenteeism the maximum fines are the following: under time rates, not more than six days' earnings (reckoning fines for the whole month), that is to say, in the course of one month fines for absenteeism cannot be imposed to the amount of more than six days' earnings.* If, however, payment is by the piece, then the maximum fine for absenteeism is 1 ruble per day and not more than a total of 3 rubles per month. Moreover, where the worker does not put in an appearance, he forfeits his pay for all the time missed. Further, the maximum fine for offences against good order is one ruble for each separate violation.

* The maximum fine for one day's absenteeism under time rates is not indicated. All that is said is: "corresponding to the worker's wages." The exact size of the fines, as we shall soon see, is displayed in each factory in a table of penalties.

Finally, as regards fines for defective work, no maximum is indicated in the law at all. One more maximum is indicated, a general one embracing all fines: for non-appearance, offences against good order, and defective work combined. All these penalties combined "shall not exceed *one-third* of the earnings to which the worker is actually entitled on payday." In other words, if, say, 15 rubles are due to the worker, fines may not, according to the law, amount to more than 5 rubles—for all violations, absenteeism and defects combined. If more than that amount in fines has accumulated, the employer must reduce them accordingly. In that case, however, the law gives the owner another right, namely, that of cancelling the contract where the fines total more than one-third of the worker's earnings.*

These regulations concerning maximum fines are, it must be said, too severe on the worker, and protect the employer at his expense. Firstly, the law permits too high a level of fines, amounting to as much as one-third of earnings. This is a disgracefully high level. Let us compare this maximum with well-known cases of particularly big fines. The factory inspector of Vladimir Gubernia, Mr. Mikulin (who has written a book about the new law of 1886), speaks of the high level of factory fines before the law was adopted. Fines were heaviest in the weaving industry, and the heaviest fines at a weaving mill amounted to 10%, i.e., *one-tenth of the workers' earnings*. The factory inspector of Vladimir Gubernia, Mr. Peskov, in his report** cites the following examples of particularly heavy fines. The heaviest of them was one of 5 rubles 31 kopeks, out of earnings totalling 32 rubles 31 kopeks. This equals 16.4% (16 kopeks per ruble), i.e., just *less than a sixth of the earnings*. That fine was called a heavy one, and not by the worker, but by the inspector. Yet our law permits fines to be *twice* as heavy, to amount to *one-third of earnings*, or $33^1/_3$ kopeks per

_____

* The worker who considers this cancellation of the contract to be wrong, may appeal to the courts, but the period during which such an appeal may be lodged is a very short one—one month (counting, of course, from the day of dismissal).

** The first report for 1885. Only the first reports of factory inspectors were printed, the government having immediately stopped further printing. The state of affairs in the factories must have been wonderful, if they were afraid of a description of it being published.

ruble! Evidently, no more or less decent factory has imposed such fines as are permitted by our laws. Let us take the data on fines at T. S. Morozov's Nikolskoye Mill before the strike of January 7, 1885. The fines at this mill were heavier, according to witnesses, than at the surrounding mills. They were so outrageous that 11,000 workers completely lost their patience. We shall very likely not err if we take this mill as an example of one where fines were outrageous. But how heavy were the fines there? Foreman weaver Shorin testified in court, as we have already stated, that fines amounted to anything up to half the earnings, and, generally speaking, ran from 30% to 50%, from 30 to 50 kopeks per ruble. But in the first place, this testimony was not confirmed by precise data; and, secondly, it relates either to specific cases or to one workshop. When the strikers were tried, some data on fines were read out in court. The earnings (monthly) and fines of 17 workers were cited: the earnings totalled 179 rubles 6 kopeks, while the fines totalled 29 rubles 65 kopeks. This means 16 kopeks in fines per ruble earned. The biggest fine of all these 17 cases was 3 rubles 85 kopeks out of 12 rubles 40 kopeks earnings. This equals $31^1/_2$ kopeks per ruble, and is at any rate less than what is permitted by our law. It is better, however, to take the data for the whole factory. Fines imposed in the year 1884 were heavier than in previous years and amounted to $23^1/_4$ kopeks per ruble (this was the highest figure: the fines constituting from $20^3/_4$ to $23^1/_4$ per cent of earnings). So then, at a factory which became notorious for its abominably high fines, these were at any rate lower than those permitted by Russian law!... There's no gainsaying that the workers are well protected by such a law! The strikers at Morozov's demanded that "fines should not exceed 5% of earnings; furthermore, the worker must be warned about bad work and be called in not more than twice a month." The fines permitted by our legislation can only be compared with the interest drawn by usurers. It is hardly likely that any employer will dare to pile up fines to that extent; the law allows it, but the workers will not permit it.*

---

* One cannot but note in this regard that Mr. Mikhailovsky, formerly Chief Factory Inspector of the St. Petersburg area, considers it quite proper to call this law "a truly philanthropic reform,

What distinguishes our laws on the size of fines is not only their abominable oppressiveness but also their gross injustice. If the fine is too big (more than one-third), the employer may cancel the contract; the worker, however, is not given a similar right, i.e., the right to leave the factory if fines are imposed on him to such an amount that they exceed a third of his earnings. It is clear that the law is only concerned about the factory owner, as though fines are due only to the fault of the workers. Actually, however, everybody knows that the factory owners frequently impose fines without the workers being to blame at all, e.g., in order to speed up the workers. The law only protects the factory owner against the bad worker, but does not protect the worker against the all too oppressive employer. In the latter case, therefore, the workers have nobody to turn to for protection. They must take thought for themselves and for the struggle against the employers.

V
WHAT IS THE PROCEDURE FOR IMPOSING FINES?

We have already stated that by law fines are imposed "on the authority" of factory managements "themselves." Regarding appeals against their instructions the law says that "there is no appeal against fines imposed on the workers by factory managers. If, however, on visiting a factory, officials of the Factory Inspectorate discover from the statements of workers that fines have been imposed on them in contravention to the requirements of the law, the manager shall be prosecuted." This provision, as you see, is very unclear and contradictory.

---

which does supreme honour to the Russian Imperial Government's concern for the working classes." (This view is expressed in the book on Russian manufacturing industry published by the Russian Government for the Chicago World Fair of 1893.) Such is the concern of the Russian Government!!! Before the law was adopted, when there was no law at all, there were avaricious employers who robbed the workers of 23 kopeks per ruble. Yet the law in its concern for the workers says: do not retain more than $33\frac{1}{3}$ (thirty-three and a third) kopeks per ruble! But thirty-three kopeks without the third can be retained now by law. "A truly philanthropic reform" indeed!

On the one hand, the worker is told that there can be no appeal against a fine imposed. Yet on the other hand he is told that the workers may "make statements" to the inspector about fines imposed "in contravention to the law." Anybody who has not had occasion to acquaint himself with Russian laws may ask what is the difference between "to make a statement about unlawful action" and "to appeal against unlawful action"? There is none, but the purpose of this pettifogging provision of the law is very clear: the law is meant to curtail the worker's right to appeal against unfair and unlawful fining by factory owners. Now if a worker should complain to an inspector about a fine unlawfully imposed, the inspector could reply that "the law does not permit appeals against fining." Are there many workers acquainted with this tricky law who could reply in turn: "I am not appealing, I am merely making a statement"? Inspectors are appointed for the express purpose of ensuring the observance of the laws regulating the relations between workers and employers. It is the duty of inspectors to accept all statements concerning the non-observance of the law. The inspector, according to regulations (see Instructions to Factory Inspectorate Officials,[22] endorsed by the Minister of Finance), must have reception days, not less than one a week, on which to give oral explanations to persons requiring them; furthermore, an announcement of these days must be displayed in each factory. Thus, if the workers know the law and are determined not to permit any departures from it, then the trickery of the law now referred to will be in vain, and the workers will be able to secure the observance of the law. Are they entitled to the return of fines paid, if these were wrongly imposed? The common-sense answer should, of course, be "yes." The employer must surely not be allowed to fine the worker wrongly and to refuse to return money wrongly exacted. It turns out, however, that when the law was discussed in the Council of State,[23] it was *deliberately* decided to be silent on this point. The members of the Council of State found that to afford the workers the right to demand the return of wrongly exacted money "will lower in the workers' eyes the importance with which it is intended to endow the factory manager, with a view to maintaining order among

the workers." That is how statesmen judge the workers!
If a factory owner has wrongly penalised a worker, the latter
should not be given the right to demand the return of his
money. But why deprive the worker of his money? Because
complaints "will lower the importance of the managers"!
That is to say, "the importance of the managers" and "the
maintenance of order in the factories" are only based on the
workers not knowing their rights and "not daring" to complain against those in charge, even if they violate the law!
So the statesmen are positively afraid lest the workers take
it into their heads to see to the proper imposition of fines!
The workers should thank the members of the Council of
State for their forthrightness in showing them what the
workers may expect of the government. The workers must
show that they consider themselves human beings just as
much as the factory owners do, and that they have no intention
of allowing themselves to be treated as dumb cattle. Therefore the workers must make it their duty not to let a single
case of wrongful fining pass without appeal, and unfailingly
present a demand for the return of their money—either to
the inspector, or, in case of his refusal, to the courts. Even
if the workers achieve nothing, either from the inspectors,
or from the courts, their efforts will still not be in vain,
but will open the eyes of the workers, and will show
them how our laws treat the workers' rights.

So then, we now know that fines are imposed on the managers' "own authority." But at each factory the fines may
be of different amounts (since the law merely indicates the
maximum above which fines may not be imposed) and there
may be different factory regulations. That is why the law
requires that all violations liable to fines, and the measure
of the fine for each violation be indicated in advance
in the *table of penalties*. This table is drawn up by each
factory owner separately, and is endorsed by the factory
inspector. It must be displayed, according to law, in each
workshop.

To render possible a check on whether fines are being imposed properly, and in what number, it is necessary that
all the fines without exception be properly recorded. The
law requires that fines must be recorded in the worker's
pay-book "not later than three days following the date of

imposition." This record must indicate, first, the grounds for the imposition of the fine (i.e., for what the fine has been imposed—for defective work and for exactly what work, for absenteeism, or for violating regulations, and exactly which), and, secondly, the amount of the penalty. The registration of fines in the pay-book is necessary to enable the workers to check whether fines are properly imposed and to enter an appeal in good time in case of any illegal action. Further, the fines must all be recorded in a special book with numbered pages which has to be kept in each factory to make it possible for all fines to be checked by the Inspectorate.

In this regard it may not be superfluous to say a couple of words about appeals against factory owners and inspectors, since the bulk of the workers do not know how to appeal and to whom. According to the law, appeals against any violations of the law at a factory should be addressed to the factory inspector. He is obliged to accept verbal and written complaints. Should the factory inspector fail to meet the request, a statement may be addressed to a senior inspector, who is also obliged to have reception days for hearing statements. In addition, the senior inspector's office must be open *daily* for persons who need to make inquiries or to receive explanations or to make statements (see Instructions to Factory Inspectorate Officials, p. 18). Appeals against the inspector's decision may be addressed to the Gubernia Factory Affairs Board.* The time limit for these appeals, as provided by law, is one month counting from the day the inspector announces his decision. Further, appeals against decisions of the Factory Board may be made to the Minister of Finance, the time limit being the same.

As you see, the law contains the names of many people to whom appeals may be addressed. And the right to appeal belongs alike to the factory owner and the worker. The only trouble is that this protection is merely a paper one. The

---

* Who constitute the Factory Board? The Governor, the Prosecutor, the Chief of the Police Administration, the Factory Inspector and *two factory owners*. If we were to add the prison governor and the officer commanding the Cossacks, we would have all the officials who give effect to "the concern of the Russian Imperial Government for the working classes."

factory owner is fully able to present his appeals—he has time to spare, funds to get a lawyer's services, etc., and that is why the factory owners really present appeals against the inspectors, go all the way to the minister and have already secured preferential treatment of various kinds. As far as the worker is concerned, however, this right to present appeals is merely a paper one. First of all, he has no time to make the round of the inspectors and offices. He works and is fined for "absenteeism." He lacks the money to obtain a lawyer's services. He does not know the laws, and therefore cannot stand up for his rights. The authorities, on the other hand, not only do nothing to acquaint the workers with the laws, but on the contrary try to hide them from the workers. To anybody who refuses to believe this we shall cite the following regulation from the Instructions to Factory Inspectorate Officials (these instructions were endorsed by the minister and explain the rights and duties of factory inspectors): "All explanations to the owner of an industrial establishment, or to the manager of same, relating to cases of violation of the law and to obligatory regulations published in pursuance of it are made by the factory inspector, but only in the absence of the worker."* There you have it. If the factory owner violates the law, the inspector must not dare speak to him of it *in the presence of the workers*—the minister forbids it! Otherwise the workers may perhaps really get to know the law and start demanding that it be put into effect! Small wonder that *Moskovskiye Vedomosti* wrote that that would be nothing but "corruption"!

Every worker knows that appeals, especially against the inspector, are almost completely beyond his reach. Of course, we do not wish to say that the workers should not appeal: on the contrary, whenever any possibility at all exists, they should certainly lodge appeals, because only in that way will the workers get to know their rights and learn to understand in whose interests the factory laws are written. All we wish to say is that appeals cannot secure any serious and general improvement in the workers' conditions. To achieve that

---

* Note to Article 26 of the Instructions.

only one way exists, namely, that the workers unite to uphold their rights, to combat oppression by the employers, and to win more decent earnings and shorter working hours.

VI
WHAT, ACCORDING TO LAW, SHOULD THE FINES BE SPENT ON?

Let us now turn to the last question concerning fines. How are the fines spent? We have already said that before 1886 the money went into the pockets of the factory owners. But this system resulted in such a mass of abuses, and exasperated the workers to such a degree that the employers themselves began to appreciate the need for abolishing it. At some factories the practice arose spontaneously of using the fines to pay benefits to the workers. For example, at that same Morozov mill the established practice even before the 1885 strike was that fines for smoking and for bringing vodka on the premises should go towards benefits for the crippled and fines for defective work, to the employer.

The new law of 1886 laid down the general rule that fines must not go into the employer's pocket. It states that "penalties imposed on the workers go in each factory to form a special fund in the charge of the factory management. This fund may be used, by permission of the inspector, only for the needs of the workers themselves, according to regulations published by the Minister of Finance in agreement with the Minister of Internal Affairs." So then, fines, according to law, must only go to meet the needs of the workers themselves. The fines are the workers' own money, deductions from their earnings.

The regulations for the expenditure of the fines fund mentioned in the law were only issued in 1890 (December 4), i.e., a total of 3½ years after the promulgation of the law. The regulations state that the fines are expended, *in the main*, on the following needs of the workers: "a) on grants to workers who have become totally incapacitated or who have temporarily lost the ability to work because of illness." At the present time workers who have been injured are usually without any means of subsistence. In order to take the factory owner to court they usually live at the expense of the lawyers who are in charge of their case and who, in return for the sops they give to the workers, get the bulk of the compensation awards. And if the worker is only likely to get a small compensation through the court, he will not even find a lawyer. In such cases use should always be made of the fines money; if the worker gets a grant from the fines fund he will manage somehow for a time and will be able to secure the services of a lawyer to conduct his case against the employer, without his poverty driving him out of the clutches of the employer into those of the lawyer. Workers who lose their jobs through sickness should also secure grants from their fines fund.*

In interpretation of this first point of the regulations, the St. Petersburg Factory Board decided that grants should be made on the basis of a doctor's certificate, to the extent of not more than half the previous earnings. Let us note in parenthesis that the St. Petersburg Factory Board adopted this decision at its session of April 26, 1895. The interpretation was accordingly given 4½ years after the issue of the regulations, while the regulations were made 3½ years after issue of the law. Consequently, *eight years in all were required merely for the law to be adequately interpreted*!! How many years will now be required for the law to become generally known, and to be actually applied?

Secondly, disbursements from the fines fund are made "b) for grants to working women in the last period of pregnancy and who have ceased work 2 weeks before confinement." According to the interpretation of the St. Petersburg Factory Board, disbursements must only be made during a period of 4 weeks (two before and two after confinement) and to the extent of half the previous earnings.

Thirdly, grants are made "c) where property is lost or damaged due to fire or other misfortune." According to the interpretation of the St. Petersburg Board, a police certificate is presented as evidence in such cases and the size of the

---

* It stands to reason that the fact of securing a grant from the fines fund does not deprive the worker of the right to demand compensation from the employer in case, for example, of injury.

grant must not exceed two-thirds of a half-year's earnings (i.e., four months' earnings).

Fourthly, and finally, grants are made "d) for burial." According to the interpretation of the St. Petersburg Board, these grants are made only in the case of workers who were employed and died at the factory in question, or of their parents and children. The amount of the grants is from 10 to 20 rubles.

Such are the four cases mentioned in the regulations in which grants are made. But the workers have the right to receive grants in other cases, too: the regulations state that grants are made "in the main" in those 4 cases. The workers are entitled to receive grants for all sorts of requirements, and not only for those enumerated. The St. Petersburg Board in its interpretation of the regulations concerning fines (this interpretation is hung up in factories) also says that "the allocation of grants in all other cases is made by permission of the Inspectorate," and the Board added that grants should under no circumstances reduce the factory's disbursements on various institutions (e.g., schools, hospitals, etc.) and compulsory expenditures (e.g., on keeping premises occupied by the workers in proper repair, on medical aid, etc.). This means that the making of grants from the fines fund does not entitle the factory owner to consider this an expenditure of his own; it is not his expenditure but that of the workers themselves. The factory owner's disbursements must remain as before.

The St. Petersburg Board laid down one more regulation— "the total regular grants made must not exceed one half of the annual receipts from fines." Here a distinction is made between regular grants (which are made over a definite period, for example, to a sick or injured person) and lump-sum grants (which are made once, e.g., for burial or in case of fire). In order to leave funds for lump-sum grants, the regular grants must not exceed half the total fines.

How can grants be got from the fines fund? The workers must, according to the regulations, apply for grants to the employer, who makes them by permission of the inspector. If the employer refuses, an appeal should be made to the inspector, who may award a grant on his own authority.

The Factory Board may allow reliable employers to make small grants (of up to 15 rubles) without requesting the inspector's permission.

Fines to a total of 100 rubles are kept in the employer's possession, while larger sums are placed in a savings bank.

Should any factory close down, the fines fund is transferred to the gubernia general workers' fund. It is not stated in the regulations how this "workers' fund" (about which the workers do not and cannot know anything) is expended. It should, we are told, be kept in the State Bank "pending further instructions." If even in the capital it required 8 years for regulations to be made about the disbursement of the fines funds at the different factories, more than a dozen years will very likely be required before regulations are devised for the disbursement of the "gubernia general workers' fund."

Such are the regulations concerning the disbursement of the fines money. As you see, they are distinguished by their extreme complexity and intricacy; no wonder, therefore, that to this day the workers are almost totally unaware of their existence. This year (1895) notices about these regulations are being put up at the factories of St. Petersburg.* The workers themselves must now try to make these regulations generally known, must ensure that the workers learn to view grants from the fines fund properly— not as sops from the owners, not as charity, but as their own money made up of deductions from their earnings and disbursed only to meet their needs. The workers have every right to demand that this money be distributed to them.

Regarding these regulations we must speak, firstly, of how they are applied, and of what inconveniences and what abuses arise. Secondly, we must see whether they have been drawn up fairly, and whether they adequately uphold the interests of the workers.

---

* Thus, in St. Petersburg it was only in 1895 that steps were taken to implement the fines law of 1886. Yet Mr. Mikhailovsky, the Chief Inspector, whom we mentioned above, said in 1893 that the law of 1886 "is now being scrupulously put into effect." This little example shows us what an impudent lie is contained in the Chief Factory Inspector's book, intended as it is to acquaint the Americans with the Russian factory system.

As to the application of the regulations we must point first of all to the following interpretation given by the St. Petersburg Factory Board: "If at any particular moment no fines money is available ... the workers may not present any claims to the factory managements." The question, however, arises: how will the workers know whether or not fines money is available, and if it is, how much there is of it? The Factory Board argues as though the workers know this— yet it has taken no trouble to let the workers know the state of the fines fund, nor has it obliged the factory owners to hang up notices about the fines money. Does the Factory Board really imagine that it is sufficient for the workers to learn about it from the employer, who will drive applicants away when there is no fines money in hand? That would be disgraceful because the employers would then treat workers desirous of receiving grants as though they were beggars. The workers must ensure that at each factory an announcement is displayed monthly about the state of the fines fund, indicating how much cash is in hand, how much has been received in the past month, and how much has been expended and "on what items." Otherwise the workers will not know how much they can get; they will not know whether the fines fund can meet all their requirements or only part of them, in which case it would be fairest to choose the most urgent items. Some of the best organised factories have themselves introduced such announcements: in St. Petersburg, I think, it is done at the Siemens and Halske works and at the government cartridge factory. If every time the worker has a discussion with the inspector, he insistently draws attention to this and urges the need for displaying a notice, the workers as a whole will certainly secure the adoption of it everywhere. Further, it would be very convenient for the workers if printed forms* were available at factories for applications for grants from the fines fund. Such forms have been introduced, for example, in Vladimir Gubernia. It is not easy for the worker himself to put the whole

---

* That is to say, forms on which the application is already printed, blank spaces being left in which to write the name of the factory, the grounds for the application, address, signature, etc.

application in writing, and what is more he won't know
how to write all that is required, whereas the form contains
all items, and all he has to do is to fill in a few words in
the blank spaces. If forms are not introduced, many workers
will have to get clerks to write their applications for them, and
this involves expenditure. Of course, the applications may,
according to the regulations, be oral; but, firstly, the worker
has in any case to get the police or doctor's certificate required by the regulations (where an application form is used,
the certifying statement is recorded on the form itself),
and, secondly, where the application is oral, some employer
will perhaps refuse to reply, whereas he is obliged to reply
to one made in writing. Applications made to the factory
office on printed forms will deprive them of the men-
dicant character which the employers try to attach to them.
Many factory owners are particularly dissatisfied with
the fact that the fines money — according to the law —
goes not into their pockets, but to serve the needs of the
workers. That is why many dodges and devices have been
invented for bamboozling the workers and inspectors and
evading the law. As a warning to the workers we shall
mention a few such devices.

Some factory owners have not recorded fines as such but as
money issued to the worker. The worker is fined a ruble, but
the record made in the book says that he has been issued
a ruble. When deducted from the pay this ruble remains
in the employer's pocket. That is not just evasion of the
law, it is downright cheating, fraud.

Other factory owners do not record fines for absenteeism;
instead they do not credit the worker with all his days
worked, i.e., if, say, the worker absents himself one day
in the week, he is not credited with five days' work, but
with four, the wage of one day (which should have been a
fine for absenteeism and should have gone to the fines fund)
going to the employer. This again is sheer fraud. Incidentally let us note that the workers are quite helpless against
such fraud,* because they are not told of the state of the fines
fund. Only if detailed monthly notices are posted (in-

---

* That such fraud is practised is related by none other than Mr.
Mikulin, the *Factory Inspector* of Vladimir Gubernia, in his book
about the new law of 1886.

dicating the number of fines imposed each week in each separate workshop) can the workers see to it that the fines really go to the fines fund. Indeed, who will see to it that all these records are correct, if not the workers themselves? The factory inspectors? But how is the inspector to discover that such and such a figure has been fraudulently entered into the book? Mr. Mikulin, a factory inspector, in dealing with such fraud, remarks:

"In all such cases it was exceedingly difficult to discover the abuses, if there was no direct reference to same in the shape of workers' complaints." The inspector himself admits his inability to discover fraud if the workers do not point it out. And the workers cannot do so if the factory owners are not obliged to put up notices about fines imposed.

Still other factory owners have invented more convenient methods of duping the workers and evading the law, methods so cunning and underhanded as to make it difficult to find fault with them. Many cotton mill owners in Vladimir Gubernia applied for the inspector's endorsement of two or even three rates instead of only one for each kind of cotton cloth; in a footnote to the list it was stated that weavers producing cloth that is faultless are paid the top rate, those producing cloth that is faulty are paid rate No. 2, while cloth that is considered damaged is paid for at the lowest rate.* It is clear why this cunning arrangement was invented: the difference between the top and bottom rates went into the owner's pocket, while the difference actually meant a penalty for defective work and therefore should have gone into the fines fund. This was clearly a gross evasion of the law, and not only of the fines law, but also of the law on rate endorsement; the rate is endorsed so as to prevent the employer arbitrarily altering the wages, whereas if not one, but several rates exist, he obviously is given the fullest license.

The factory inspectors saw that such rates were "*evidently* aimed at evading the law" (all this is related by the self-same Mr. Mikulin in the above-mentioned book); neverthe-less, they "*considered they had no right*" to oppose the respected factory-owning "gentlemen."

* Such rates are in operation in some St. Petersburg mills; for example, it is stated that for such and such a quantity of cloth the worker gets from 20 to 50 kopeks.

Why, of course. It is no easy matter opposing the owners (not one, but several employers simultaneously hit on this way of doing things!). But suppose the workers, and not "Messrs." the Mill Owners, tried to evade the law? It would be interesting to know whether there would be a single factory inspector throughout the Russian Empire who would "*consider he had no right*" to oppose the workers in an attempt to evade the law.

Thus, these two- and three-storey rates were endorsed by the Factory Inspectorate and put into operation. It turned out, however, that Messrs. the Mill Owners, who invent ways of evading the law, and Messrs. the Inspectors, who do not consider they have the right to hinder the owners in their good intention, are not alone in their interest in the rate problem ... the workers, too, are interested. The workers proved to lack that gentle tolerance of the mill owners' knavish tricks, and "considered they had the right" to prevent these mill owners from swindling them.

These rates, Mr. Inspector Mikulin tells us, "aroused such dissatisfaction among the workers that it was one of the chief causes of the violent disorders which broke out and *required* the intervention of armed force."

That's the sort of thing which is going on! At first they "considered they had no right" to prevent Messrs. the Mill Owners from violating the law and bamboozling the workers—but when the workers, indignant at these iniquities, revolted, armed force was "required"! But why was this armed force "required" against the workers, who were upholding their *lawful* rights, and not against the mill owners, who were obviously violating the law? At all events, it was only after the workers revolted that "rates of this kind were abolished by order of the Governor." The workers stood their ground. The law was not introduced by Messrs. the Factory Inspectors, but by the workers themselves, who had shown that they would not permit anybody to slight them and would stand up for their rights. "Subsequently," relates Mr. Mikulin, "the Factory Inspectorate refused to endorse such rates." Thus the workers taught the inspectors to give effect to the law.

It was, however, only the Vladimir mill owners who were taught that lesson. Yet factory owners are the same everywhere, whether they are in Vladimir, Moscow, or St. Petersburg. The attempt of the Vladimir mill owners to circumvent the law was a failure, but the method they devised not only remained, but was even improved on by a certain St. Petersburg factory owner of genius.

What was the method of the Vladimir mill owners? It was that of not using the word fine, but of replacing it by other words. If I say that the worker, in case of defective work, gets a ruble less, that will be a fine, and it will have to go into the fines fund. But if I say that, in case of defective work, the worker is paid at a lower rate, then that will not be a fine, and the ruble will land in my pocket. That was how the Vladimir mill owners argued, but the workers rebuffed them. One can argue in a slightly different way, too. One can say: where work is defective the worker will be paid *without* bonus; then again this will not be a fine, and the ruble will land in the employer's pocket. That is the line of argument devised by Yakovlev, the artful owner of a St. Petersburg engineering works. He says the following: you will get a ruble a day, but if you are not guilty of any misdemeanours, absenteeism, incivility, or defective work, you will get a "bonus" of 20 kopeks. If, however, a misdemeanour does take place, the employer deducts twenty kopeks, and, of course, puts them in his pocket—because, after all, it is "bonus" money and not a fine. All laws indicating what are the misdemeanours for which penalties may be imposed, and in what measure, and how they should be spent on the workers' needs, are non-existent so far as Mr. Yakovlev is concerned. The laws refer to "fines," and he is dealing with "bonuses." The astute factory owner continues to this day to swindle the workers by his pettifogging tricks. The St. Petersburg Factory Inspector very likely also did "*not consider he had the right*" to prevent this evasion of the law. Let us hope that the workers of St. Petersburg will not lag behind those of Vladimir and will teach the inspector and the factory owner how to observe the law.

To show what huge sums of money are collected out of the fines, let us quote reports on the size of fines funds in Vladimir Gubernia.

Grants began to be distributed there in February 1891. By October 1891, grants had been made to 3,665 persons to a total of 25,458 rubles 59 kopeks. By October 1, 1891, the fines fund totalled 470,052 rubles 45 kopeks. Incidentally, reference should be made to another of the uses to which the fines fund is put. At a certain factory the fines fund amounted to 8,242 rubles 46 kopeks. The factory went bankrupt, and the workers were left to face the winter without food or work. Then grants totalling 5,820 rubles of this fund were distributed among the workers, of whom there were as many as 800.

From October 1, 1891, to October 1, 1892, fines totalling 94,055 rubles 47 kopeks, were imposed, while grants made to 6,312 persons amounted to only 45,200 rubles 52 kopeks. The grants were distributed as follows: 208 persons were given monthly disability pensions to a total of 6,198 rubles 20 kopeks, that is to say an average annual grant of 30 rubles per person (these beggarly grants are made while tens of thousands of rubles, fines money, are lying unused!). Further, in connection with loss of property 1,037 persons were given a total of 17,827 rubles 12 kopeks, an average of 18 rubles per person. Expectant mothers received 10,641 rubles 81 kopeks, in 2,669 cases, an average of 4 rubles (that is, for three weeks, one before confinement and two after). Sickness grants were made to 877 workers to a total of 5,380 rubles 68 kopeks, an average of 6 rubles. Funeral grants totalled 4,620 rubles—to 1,506 workers (3 rubles each), and miscellaneous—532 rubles 71 kopeks to 15 persons.

Now we have fully acquainted ourselves with the fines regulations and with the way these regulations are applied. Let us see whether the regulations are fair, and whether the workers' rights are adequately protected.

We know that the law states that the fines money does not belong to the employer, and that it can only go to serve the workers' needs. Regulations dealing with the expenditure of the money had to be endorsed by the ministers.

What, however, came of the regulations? The money is collected from the workers and is expended on their needs—but the regulations do not even state that the employers are obliged to inform the workers of the state of the fines fund. The workers do not possess the right to elect representatives, who will see to the proper flow of money into the fines fund, and who will accept applications from workers and distribute grants. The law states that grants are made "by permission of the inspector," but according to the regulations issued by the ministers, it turns out that applications for grants have to be addressed to the *employer*. But why should applications be made to the employer? Surely the money is not the employer's, but the workers', made up of deductions from their earnings. The employer himself has no right to touch this money: if he spends it, he is responsible for doing so, as for misappropriation and embezzlement, just as if he has spent somebody else's money. The reason the ministers issued these regulations is apparently because they wanted to do a service to the employers: now the workers have *to ask* the employer for grants, just as if they were asking for doles. True, if the employer refuses, the inspector may allocate the grant himself. But then the inspector himself does not know the facts—and he will be told by the owner that the worker is such and such a kind of person, that he does not deserve a grant, and the inspector will believe the owner.* And then, are there many workers who will bother to address complaints to the inspector, losing working time to visit him, and writing applications and so forth? Actually, thanks to the ministerial regulations, we only get a new form of workers' dependence on the employers. The employers are enabled to victimise those workers with whom they are dissatisfied, maybe for refusing to take things lying down: by rejecting a worker's application the employer will certainly cause him lots of extra trouble, and maybe succeed in depriving him of a grant altogether. On the other hand, the

---

* In the printed application for grants which, as we have said, was circulated to the factories by the Vladimir Factory Board and which constitutes the implementation of the "regulations" that is most suitable for the workers, we read: "the factory office testifies to the signature and the contents of the application, and adds that in its opinion, the applicant deserves a grant of such and such a sum."

That is to say, the office can always write, without giving any explanation, that "in its opinion" the applicant does not deserve a grant.

Grants will not be got by those who are in need of them, but by those who, "in the employers' opinion, deserve them."

employer may allow quite big grants to be made to those workers who curry favour with him and kowtow to him, and who act as informers on their workmates even in cases where other applications would be rejected. Instead of abolishing the workers' dependence on the employers in the matter of fines, we get a new dependence, which splits the workers and creates the servile and the go-getter types. And then, take note of the awful red tape that, according to the regulations, surrounds the receipt of grants: on each occasion the worker requiring a certificate has to approach a doctor, who will very likely give him a rough reception, or the police, who do nothing without bribes. Let us repeat, the law says nothing about that; it has been established by the ministerial regulations, which have obviously been drawn up to suit the factory owners, and which are clearly aimed at supplementing dependence on the employers with the dependence of the workers on officials, at barring the workers from all participation in the expenditure on their needs of the fines money taken from themselves, and at weaving a web of senseless formalities that stupefies and demoralises* the workers.

To give the employer the right to authorise the making of grants from the fines money is a crying injustice. The workers must strive for the legal right to choose deputies who shall see that the fines go into the fines fund, receive and check workers' applications for grants, and report to the workers about the state of the fines fund and its expenditure. At those factories where deputies now exist, they should pay attention to the fines money and demand that they be given all data relating to the fines, and that they should accept workers' applications and deliver them to the management.

VII
DO THE FINES LAWS APPLY TO ALL WORKERS?

The fines laws, like most other Russian laws, do not apply to all factories, do not apply to all workers. When it issues a law, the Russian Government is always afraid that

---

* Splits, creates servility, and develops bad habits.

it will hurt the gentlemen who own the factories, is afraid that the network of cunning office regulations and officials' rights and duties will clash with some other office regulations (and we have countless numbers of them), with the rights and duties of some other officials, who will be terribly hurt if some new official bursts into their domain, and will consume barrels of official ink and mounds of paper on correspondence about "departmental delimitation." For that reason a law is rarely introduced in this country for the whole of Russia at once, without exceptions, without cowardly delays, without ministers and other officials being permitted to depart from the law.

All this particularly affected the fines law, which, as we have seen, aroused such dissatisfaction among the capitalist gentlemen, and was only adopted under the pressure of portentous workers' revolts.

Firstly, the fines law only covers a small part of Russia.* This law was issued, as we have said, on June 3, 1886, and became operative as from October 1, 1886, *in only three gubernias*, those of St. Petersburg, Moscow, and Vladimir. *Five years* later the law was extended to Warsaw and Petrokov gubernias (June 11, 1891). Then, *three years* still later it was extended to 13 more gubernias (of the Central gubernias—Tver, Kostroma, Yaroslavl, Nizhni-Novgorod, and Ryazan; of the Ostsee gubernias[24]—Estland and Lifland; of the Western gubernias—Grodno and Kiev; and of the Southern gubernias—Volhynia, Podolsk, Kharkov and Kherson)—according to the law of March 14, 1894. In 1892 the fines regulations were extended to cover private ironworks and mines.

The rapid development of capitalism in the south of Russia, and the tremendous development of mining is bringing together masses of workers there, and compelling the government to hurry.

The government is evidently very slow in abandoning the old factory system. And it should be noted that it is

---

* This law is part of the so-called "special regulations concerning the relations between factory owners and workers." These "special regulations" only cover "localities marked by a considerable development of factory industry," to which we shall refer below in the text.

abandoning that system only under the pressure of the workers: the growth of the working-class movement and the strikes in Poland caused the extension of the law to the Warsaw and Petrokov gubernias (the town of Lodz is in Petrokov Gubernia). The huge strike at the Khludov Mill, Yegoryevsk Uyezd, Ryazan Gubernia, immediately resulted in the law being extended to Ryazan Gubernia. The government evidently also does "not consider it has the right" to deprive Messrs. the Capitalists of the right to un-controlled (arbitrary) fining until the workers themselves interfere.

Secondly, the fines law, like all the factory inspection regulations, does not cover crown and government establish-ments. Government factories have their own chiefs "con-cerned with the welfare" of the workers, people whom the law does not wish to bother with fines regulations. Indeed, why supervise government factories, when the factory chief is an official himself? The workers can complain about him to himself. Small wonder that among these chiefs of govern-ment factories one can find such mischief-makers as, for example, the St. Petersburg Harbourmaster, Mr. Verkhovsky.

Thirdly, the regulations concerning fines funds spent on the workers themselves do not cover workers employed in the shops of those railways which have pensions or savings and mutual benefit funds. The fines are paid into these funds.

All these exceptions still seemed insufficient and so the law contains the decision that the ministers (of Finance and of Internal Affairs) have the right, on the one hand, "to remove unimportant factories from subordination" to these regulations "where really necessary" and, on the other hand, to extend the operation of these regulations to "im-portant" artisan establishments.

Thus, not only did the law instruct the minister to draw up the fines money regulations—it also gave the min-isters the right to free some factory owners from subordina-tion to the law! Such is the extent of our law's kindness to the factory-owning gentry! In one of his interpretations the minister states that he only frees such factory owners regarding whom the Factory Board "*is certain that the owner of the establishment will not transgress the workers' inter-*

ests." The factory owners and inspectors are such close boon companions that they take each other's word. Why burden the factory owner with regulations, when he "gives the assurance" that he will not transgress the workers' interests? Now, what if the worker should try to require of the minister or the inspector that he be released from the regulations, after "giving the assurance" that he will not transgress the factory owner's interests? Such a worker would very likely be considered insane.

That is called "the possession of equal rights" by the workers and the factory owners.

As to the extension of the fines regulations to important artisan establishments, these regulations, so far as is known, have hitherto (in 1893) only been applied to distribution offices which supply warp to home-working weavers. The ministers are in no hurry to extend the operation of the fines regulations. The entire mass of workers doing jobs at home for employers, big stores, etc., continue under the old conditions, totally subordinate to the tyranny of the employers. It is more difficult for these workers to join forces, to arrive at agreement as to their needs, to undertake a common struggle against oppression by the employers— that is why no attention is paid to them.

VIII
CONCLUSION

We have now acquainted ourselves with our fines laws and regulations, with all this exceptionally complicated system that frightens the worker away with its dryness and unattractive official language.

We can now return to the question raised at the outset, to that of fines being a product of capitalism, i.e., of such a social order under which the people are divided into two classes, the owners of the land, machines, mills and factories, materials and supplies—and those who have no property, and who therefore have to sell themselves to the capitalists and work for them.

Has it always been the case that workers in the service of an employer have had to pay him fines for all sorts of defects?

In small establishments—for example, among the urban artisans or workers—no fines are imposed. There is no complete alienation of the worker from the master, they live and work together. The master does not dream of introducing fines, because he himself keeps an eye on the job and can always force the correction of what he does not like.

But such small establishments and trades are gradually disappearing. The handicraftsmen and artisans, and also the small peasants, cannot withstand the competition of the big factories and big employers who use improved instruments and machines and combine the labour of masses of workers. That is why we see that handicraftsmen, artisans and peasants are increasingly being ruined, and are becoming workers in factories, are abandoning their villages and migrating to the towns.

At the big factories the relations between the employer and the workers are quite unlike those in the small workshops. The employer is so far above the worker in wealth and social status that a veritable abyss lies between them, and frequently they do not even know one another and have nothing in common. The worker has no opportunity of making his way into the employers' ranks: he is doomed to remain impoverished for all time, working for rich men whom he does not know. Instead of the two or three workers employed by the small master there are now masses of workers, who come from various localities and constantly replace one another. Instead of separate instructions from the master, general regulations appear that are made obligatory for all workers. The former constancy of the relations between master and worker disappears: the master sets no great store by the worker at all, because he can always easily find another one among the crowd of unemployed ready to hire themselves to anybody. Thus, the power of the employer over the workers increases, and the employer makes use of this power, resorting to fines in order to drive the worker into the narrow confines of factory work. The worker has to submit to this new limitation of his rights and of his earnings, because he is now helpless against the employer.

And so fines appeared on earth not very long ago— together with the big factories, together with large-scale capitalism, together with the complete split between the rich masters and the ragged workers. Fines are the result of the complete development of capitalism and the complete enslavement of the worker.

However, this development of the big factories and intensification of pressure by the employers brought still other consequences in their train. The workers, totally helpless as against the factory owners, began to understand that utter disaster and poverty awaited them if they continued to be divided. The workers began to understand that there was only one means of saving themselves from the starvation and degeneration that capitalism held in store for them— and that was to join forces in order to fight the factory owners for higher wages and better living conditions.

We have seen what disgraceful oppression of the workers our factory owners resorted to in the eighties, how they turned fines into a means of lowering the workers' wages and did not confine themselves to just reducing rates. The oppression of the workers by the capitalists reached its apex.

But this oppression evoked the workers' resistance. The workers rose up against their oppressors and were victorious. The terrified government conceded their demands and hastened to issue a law regulating fines.

That was a concession to the workers. The government imagined that by issuing the fines laws and regulations, by introducing grants from the fines money it would immediately satisfy the workers and make them forget their common workers' cause, their struggle against the factory owners.

However, such hopes of the government, which poses as the protector of the workers, will not be justified. We have seen how unjust the new law is to the workers, how small are the concessions to the workers by comparison with even the demands advanced by the Morozov strikers; we have seen how loopholes were left everywhere for mill owners anxious to violate the law, how grants regulations that supplement the employers' tyranny with that of the officials were drawn up in the employers' interests.

When this law and these regulations are put into effect, when the workers acquaint themselves with them and begin to learn from their clashes with the managements how the law oppresses them, then they will begin steadily to realise that they are in a position of dependence. They will understand that only poverty has compelled them to work for the rich and to be content with crumbs for their heavy labour. They will understand that the government and its officials are on the side of the factory owners, and that the laws are drawn up in such a way as to make it easier for the employer to oppress the worker.

And the workers will appreciate, finally, the point that the law does nothing to improve their status, so long as the workers' dependence on the capitalists continues to exist, because the law will always be partial to the capitalist employers, because the latter will always succeed in devising ruses for evading the law.

Once they have understood this, the workers will see that only one means remains for defending themselves, namely, to join forces for the struggle against the factory owners and the unjust practices established by the law.

GYMNASIUM FARMS
AND CORRECTIVE GYMNASIA[25]

(RUSSKOYE BOGATSTVO)[26]

The solution to the problem of capitalism in Russia proposed by the Narodniks and represented latterly most strikingly by *Russkoye Bogatstvo* has long been known. While not denying the existence of capitalism, for they are compelled to admit its development, the Narodniks consider our capitalism not to be a natural and necessary process crowning the age-long development of commodity economy in Russia, but an accident, a phenomenon not firmly rooted and merely indicative of a departure from the path prescribed by the nation's entire historical life. "We must," say the Narodniks, "choose different paths for the fatherland," leave the capitalist path and "communalise" production, making use of the existing forces of the "whole" of "society," which, so they say, is already beginning to be convinced that there is no basis for capitalism.

Obviously, if a different path may be chosen for the fatherland, if the whole of society is beginning to understand the need for this, then the "communalising" of production presents no great difficulties and requires no preparatory historical period. One has only to draw up a plan of such communalisation and to convince the appropriate persons of its feasibility—and the "fatherland" will turn from the mistaken path of capitalism to the road of socialisation.

Everybody understands how tremendously interesting a plan must be that promises such radiant perspectives; that is why the Russian public should be very thankful to Mr. Yuzhakov, one of the regular contributors of *Russkoye Bogatstvo*, for having undertaken the job of drawing up such a plan. In the May issue of *Russkoye Bogatstvo* we find his article "Educational Utopia," with the sub-heading "Plan for Nation-Wide Compulsory Secondary Education."

What connection has this with the "communalising" of production?—the reader will ask. The most direct connection, since Mr. Yuzhakov's plan is a very broad one. The author plans to set up in every volost a gymnasium embracing the entire male and female population of school age (from 8 to 20 years, and to a maximum of 25 years). Such gymnasia should be productive associations that engage in farming and moral undertakings, that by their labour not only maintain the population of the gymnasia (which, according to Mr. Yuzhakov, constitutes *a fifth* of the entire population), but additionally provide resources for the maintenance of the *entire child population*. The detailed account made by the author for a typical volost gymnasium (or "gymnasium farm," or "agricultural gymnasium") shows that all in all the gymnasium will maintain *over a half of the entire local population*. If we bear in mind that each such gymnasium (20,000 dual, i.e., 20,000 male and 20,000 female gymnasia, are projected for Russia) is provided with land and means of production (it is intended to issue $4^1/_2$ per cent government-guaranteed Zemstvo[27] bonds with $^1/_2$ per cent redemption per annum)—then we shall understand how truly "enormous" the "plan" is. Production is socialised for a total of half the population. At one blow, then, a different path is chosen for the fatherland! And that is achieved "without any expenditure (sic!) on the part of the government, Zemstvo, or people." It "may seem a utopia only at first sight," but actually it is "far more feasible than nation-wide elementary education." Mr. Yuzhakov testifies that the financial operation required for this "is no chimera or utopia," and is achieved not only, as we have seen, without expenditure, without any expenditure, but even without any change in the "established educational plans"!! Mr. Yuzhakov quite justly remarks that "all this is of no little importance when one wishes not to confine oneself to an experiment, but to achieve really nation-wide education." He says, it is true, that "I have not set myself the aim of drawing up a working plan," but he does give us the proposed number of male and female pupils per gymnasium, an estimate of the manpower required to maintain the entire population of the gymnasia and enumerations of the pedagogical and administrative staffs, and indicates both the rations in kind for gymnasia members and the salaries in cash for tutors, doctors, technicians and craftsmen. The author makes a detailed calculation of the number of working days required for agricultural pursuits, the amount of land needed for each gymnasium, and the financial resources needed to get them installed. He provides, on the one hand, for members of national minorities and sects who cannot enjoy the blessings of nation-wide secondary education, and, on the other hand, for persons excluded from the gymnasia because of bad conduct. The author's calculations are not confined to one typical gymnasium. Not at all. He raises the issue of establishing all the 20,000 dual gymnasia and indicates how to get the land required for this and how to secure a "satisfactory contingent of tutors, administrators and managers."

One can understand the enthralling interest of such a plan, an interest that is not only theoretical (evidently, the plan for communalising production drawn up so concretely is intended to finally convince all sceptics and to demolish all who deny the feasibility of such plans), but also genuinely practical. It would be strange if the supreme government paid no attention to the project for organising nation-wide compulsory secondary education, particularly when the author of the proposal definitely asserts that the thing can be done "without any expenditure" and "will meet with obstacles not so much from the financial and economic circumstances of the task, as from the cultural circumstances," which, however, are "not insuperable." Such a project directly concerns not only the Ministry of Public Education, but equally the Ministry of Internal Affairs, the Ministry of Finance, the Ministry of Agriculture, and even, as we shall see below, the War Ministry. The projected "corrective gymnasia" will, most likely, have to go to the Ministry of Justice. There can be no doubt that the rest of the ministries will also be interested in the project, which, in Mr. Yuzhakov's words, "will answer all the above-enumerated requirements (i.e., of education and maintenance) and, very likely, many others too."

We are therefore certain that the reader will not complain if we set about a detailed examination of this very striking project.

Mr. Yuzhakov's chief thought is the following: no studies whatever take place in the summer time, which is devoted to agricultural work. Further, pupils, on graduating the gymnasium, are left to work there for some time; they do winter work and are used for industrial jobs that supplement agricultural work and enable each gymnasium by its own labours to maintain all the pupils and workers, the entire teaching and administrative staff and to cover expenditure on education. Such gymnasia, Mr. Yuzhakov justly remarks, would be large agricultural artels. This last expression does not, by the way, leave the slightest doubt about our being right in regarding Mr. Yuzhakov's plan as the first steps in the Narodnik "communalisation" of production, as part of the new path that Russia is to choose so as to avoid the vicissitudes of capitalism.

"At the present time," argues Mr. Yuzhakov, "the pupils are graduated from the gymnasium at the age of 18 to 20, and occasionally there is a delay of one or two years. Under compulsory education ... the delay will become still more widespread. People will be graduated later, while the three senior classes will be made up of the 16- to 25-year age groups, if 25 years becomes the age limit, after reaching which they must leave without finishing the course. Thus, if we bear in mind the additional contingent of adult fifth-class pupils one may boldly consider about one-third of the pupils in the gymnasium to be ... of working age." Even if the proportion is reduced to one quarter, the author calculates further, by adding to the eight gymnasium classes the two classes for preparatory elementary school (illiterate eight-year-old children would be admitted), we would still get a very large number of workers who, assisted by semi-workers, could cope with the summer work. But the "ten-class gymnasium farm," Mr. Yuzhakov remarks justly, "necessarily requires a certain contingent of winter workers." Where are they to be got? The author proposes two solutions: 1) the hire of workers ("some of the more deserving of whom might be given a share in the proceeds"). The gymnasium farm should be a profitable undertaking and be able to pay for such hire. But the author "considers another solution of greater importance": 2) those who have finished the gymnasium course will be obliged to work to cover the expenditure on their tuition and their keep while in the junior classes. That is their "direct duty," adds Mr. Yuzhakov—a duty, of course, only for those who cannot pay the cost of tuition. It is they who will constitute the necessary contingent of winter workers and the supplementary contingent of summer workers.

Such is the first feature of the projected organisation that is to "communalise" one-fifth of the population into agricultural artels. It already enables us to see what sort of different path for the fatherland will be chosen. Wage-labour, which at the present time serves as the only source of livelihood for people who "cannot pay the cost of tuition" and living, is replaced by compulsory unpaid labour. But we must not be disturbed by that: it should not be forgotten that in return the population will enjoy the blessings of universal secondary education.

To proceed. The author projects separate male and female gymnasia, intending to adopt the prejudice prevalent on the European continent against coeducation, which actually would be more rational. "Fifty pupils per class or 500 for all the ten classes, or 1,000 per gymnasium farm (500 boys and 500 girls) will be quite a normal composition" for an average gymnasium. It will have 125 "pairs of workers" and a corresponding number of semi-workers. "If I mention," says Yuzhakov, "that this number of workers is capable of cultivating the 2,500 dessiatines of land under cultivation in Malorossiya* for example, everybody will understand what a tremendous force is provided by the labour of the gymnasium"!...

But in addition to these workers there will be "regular workers," who "work off" their education and keep. How many of them will there be? The number graduated annually will be 45 pupils, male and female. A third of the pupils will undergo military service for a period of three years (now a quarter do so. The author raises this number to one-third by cutting down the length of service to three years). "It will only be fair to place the remaining two-thirds in

---

* The Ukraine.—*Ed.*

similar conditions, i.e., in keeping them at the gymnasium to work off the cost of their education, and of the education of their comrades who have been called to the colours. All the girls may also be retained for the same purpose."

The pattern of the new system, arranged for the fatherland that has chosen a different path, is assuming increasingly clear outlines. Now all Russian citizens are obliged to undergo military service and, since the number of persons of military age is larger than the number of soldiers required, the latter are chosen by lot. In communalised production the recruits will also be selected by lot, but as for the rest, it is proposed "to place them in the same conditions," i.e., to make it obligatory for them to spend three years in service, not military, it is true, but doing work in the gymnasium. They have to work off the cost of keeping their comrades who have been called to the colours. Have all to do so? No. Only those who cannot pay the cost of the tuition. The author has already advanced this proviso above, and below we shall see that for people who are able to pay for tuition, he plans separate gymnasia altogether, of the old type. Why, the question arises, does the keep of comrades called to the colours have to be worked off by those who cannot pay the cost of tuition? and not by those who can? The reason is very understandable. If the gymnasium pupils are divided into paying and non-paying, it is evident that the contemporary structure of society will not be affected by the Reform; that is quite well understood by Mr. Yuzhakov himself. In that case, it is understandable that the state's general expenditure (on the soldiers) will be borne by those who are without the means of livelihood,* just as they bear it now in the shape, for example, of indirect taxes, etc. In what way is the new system different? In the fact that nowadays those who have no resources can sell their labour-power, while under the new system they will be *obliged* to work *gratis* (i.e., for their keep alone). There cannot be the slightest doubt that Russia will thus avoid all the vicissitudes of the capitalist system. Hired labour, which contains the threat of the "ulcer of the

---

* Otherwise the domination of the former over the latter would not be maintained.

proletariat" is driven out and makes way for ... unpaid compulsory labour.

And there is nothing surprising in the fact that people placed in relationships in which labour is compulsory and unpaid should find themselves in conditions corresponding to these relationships. Just listen to what we are told by the Narodnik ("friend of the people") immediately after the foregoing:

"If marriages are allowed between young people who have finished the course and remain at the gymnasium for three years; if separate premises are arranged for the family workers; and if the profits of the gymnasium allow them to be given at least a modest allowance in cash and kind when they leave it, then such a three years' stay there will be far less burdensome than military service...."

Is it not obvious that such advantageous conditions will impel the population to bend every effort to gain admittance to the gymnasia? Judge for yourselves: firstly, they will be permitted to marry. True, according to the now existing civil legislation such permission (from the authorities) is not required at all. But bear in mind that these will be *gymnasium pupils*, *male* and *female*, true, as old as 25 years, but still gymnasium pupils. If university students are not permitted to marry, could gymnasium pupils be permitted to do so? And what is more, the permission will depend on the school authorities, consequently, on people with a higher education: obviously, there are no grounds for fearing abuses. Those who graduate the gymnasium and remain as regular workers there, are, however, no longer pupils. Nevertheless, they too, people between 21 and 27 years of age, have to obtain permission to marry. We cannot but recognise that the new path selected by the fatherland involves some curtailment of the civil rights of Russian citizens, but, after all, it must be admitted that the blessings of universal secondary education cannot be acquired without sacrifices. Secondly, separate premises will be provided for family workers, probably no worse than the cubicles now inhabited by factory workers. And thirdly, the regular workers get a "modest allowance" for this. Undoubtedly, the population will prefer the advantages of a quiet life under the wing of the authorities to the turmoils of capitalism, will prefer them to such a degree that some workers will stay permanently at the gymnasium (very likely out of gratitude for being allowed to marry): "The small contingent of regular workers, who remain at the gymnasium altogether and associate (sic!!) themselves with it, supplements these labour forces of the gymnasium farm. Such are the possible and by no means utopian labour forces of our agricultural gymnasium."

Have mercy on us! What is there "utopian" in all this? Regular unpaid workers, who have "associated themselves" with their masters, by whom they are permitted to marry— just ask any old peasant, and he will tell you from his own experience that all this is quite feasible.

(To be continued.) *

Written in autumn 1895
Published in the newspaper
Samarsky Vestnik,
No. 254, November 25, 1895.
Signed: K. T—in

Published according
to the text in
Samarsky Vestnik

---

* No continuation followed in the newspaper *Samarsky Vestnik.*— *Ed.*

TO THE WORKING MEN AND WOMEN
OF THE THORNTON FACTORY[28]

Working men and women of the Thornton Factory!

November 6th and 7th should be memorable days for all of us.... The weavers, by their solid resistance to the employer's pressure have proved that at a difficult moment there are still people in our midst who can uphold our common interests as workers, that our worthy employers have not yet succeeded in turning us for all time into the miserable slaves of their bottomless purses. Let us, then, comrades, stand firm and steadfast and carry on to the very end, let us remember that we can improve our conditions only by our common and concerted efforts. Above all, comrades, don't fall into the trap so cunningly prepared for you by Messrs. Thornton. They reason as follows: "There is a hitch now in disposing of our goods, so that if we keep to our previous working conditions we shall not get the profits we got previously.... And we are not ready to take anything less.... So then, we'll have to tighten up on the workers, let them shoulder the cost of the bad prices on the market.... But the job has to be done cleverly and not in any old way, so that the worker, in the simplicity of his mind, will not understand what sort of a titbit we are preparing for him.... If we tackle all of them at once, they will all rise up at once, and we shan't be able to handle them, so we shall first dupe those miserable weavers, and then the others won't get away.... We are not accustomed to restrain ourselves in dealing with these creatures, and what for, anyhow? New brooms sweep cleaner here...." So then, the employers, who are so full of concern for the worker's well-being, want to quietly and steadily impose on the workers of all departments what they have already imposed on the weavers.... That is why, if we all remain indifferent to the fate of the weaving sheds, we shall dig with our own hands a pit into which we, too, shall soon be thrown. Latterly the weavers have been earning, in round figures, 3 rubles 50 kopeks a fortnight, and during the same period families of seven have contrived somehow to live on 5 rubles, and families consisting of husband, wife and child on 2 rubles in all. They have sold the last of their clothes and used up the last coppers they earned by their hellish labour at a time when their benefactors, the Thorntons, were adding millions to the millions they already had. To crown it all ever-new victims of the employers' avarice have been thrown out on the streets before their eyes, and the pressure has been regularly increased with the most heartless cruelty.... Without any explanation, they have started mixing noils[29] and clippings with the wool, which slows the job down terribly; delays in getting the warp have increased as though inadvertently; finally, they have begun without ado to introduce short time, and now the pieces have to be five instead of nine schmitz[30] long, so that the weaver has to fuss around longer and oftener in obtaining and fixing the warps, for which, as is known, not a kopek is paid. They want to wear our weavers down, and the earnings of 1 ruble 62 kopeks per fortnight, which have already begun to appear in the pay-books of some of the weavers, may, in the near future, become general in the weaving sheds.... Comrades, do you, too, want to see the day when you get this sort of kindness from the employers? If not, if, finally, your hearts have not entirely turned to stone in face of the suffering of poor folks like yourselves, rally solidly round our weavers, let us put forward our common demands, and on every suitable occasion let us wrest better conditions from our oppressors. Workers of the spinning sheds, don't delude yourselves about the stability and slight increase in your earnings.... After all, almost two-thirds of your number have already been dismissed, and your better earnings have been purchased at the cost of the starvation of your own spinners who have been thrown out of work. This again is a cunning trick of the employers and is not difficult to understand if you only count how much was earned by the entire mule-spinning department previously, and how much now. Workers of the new dyeing department! Twelve rubles a month, all told, is what you now earn, at the cost of $14^1/_4$ hours' daily work, saturated from head to foot with the murderous fumes of dyes! Pay attention to our demands: we also want to end the illegal deductions made from you due to your foreman's inefficiency. Labourers, and all un-skilled workers generally! Do you really expect to retain your 60-80 kopeks a day, when the skilled weaver has to content himself with 20 kopeks a day? Comrades, don't be blind, don't swallow the employers' bait, stand up for one another more firmly, otherwise it will go badly for all of us this winter. We must all keep a most watchful eye on the employers' manoeuvres aimed at reducing rates, and with all our strength resist every tendency in this direction for it spells ruin for us.... Turn a deaf ear to all their pleadings about business being bad: for them it only means less profit on their capital, for us it means starvation and suffering for our families who are deprived of their last crust of stale bread. Can there be any comparison between the two things? They are now putting pressure on the weavers first of all, and we must secure:

1) an increase in weavers' rates to their spring level, i.e., by about 6 kopeks per schmitz;

2) that the weavers, too, be brought under the law which says that the worker must be told how much he can earn on a job before he begins it. Let the rates list, bearing the factory inspector's signature, exist not only on paper, but in reality, as required by law. For weaving, for example, the existing rates should be accompanied by information about the quality of the wool, the quantity of noils and clippings in it, and there should be an estimate of the time required for preparatory work;

3) that the working time be so distributed that we do not stand idle through no fault of our own; now, for example, things are so arranged that on each piece the weaver loses a day waiting for warp, and since the piece is becoming almost half its former size, the weaver will suffer a double loss, regardless of the rates list. If the boss wants to rifle our earnings this way, let him do so outright, in such a

manner that we definitely know what he wants to squeeze out of us;

4) that the factory inspector sees to it that there is no trickery about the rates, that there are no double rates. That means, for example, that the rates list should not contain two different rates for one and the same kind of article. only with different names. For example, we got 4 rubles 32 kopeks a piece for weaving Bieber, and only 4 rubles 14 kopeks for Ural,[31]—yet as far as work goes isn't it one and the same thing? A still more impudent piece of trickery is the double price given for goods of one denomination. That way Messrs. Thornton dodged the fines laws, which state that a fine may only be imposed for such damage as results from the worker's carelessness and that the deduction has to be recorded in his pay-book under the heading "fines" not later than three days after it is imposed. A strict record has to be kept of all the fines, the total sum of which is not to go into the employer's pocket, but must be used to cover the needs of the workers of the factory concerned. With us, however—we have but to look at our books—there are empty spaces, there are no fines, and one might think our employers are the most kind-hearted of all. Actually, however, due to our lack of knowledge, they dodge the law and easily fix things to suit themselves.... We are not fined, you see, yet deductions are made from us, the smaller rate being paid and as long as two rates have existed, a smaller and a bigger one, there has been nothing at all to cavil at, they have kept on deducting the money and putting it into their own pockets;

5) that in addition to introducing a single rate, let each deduction be registered in the fines column, with an indication of why it is made.

Then wrong fining will be obvious, less of our work will be done for nothing, and there will be a drop in the number of disgraceful things being done now, as, for example, in the dyeing department, where the workers' earnings are lower on account of the foreman's inefficiency, which cannot, according to law, be a reason for non-payment of labour, since there can be no question here of the worker's carelessness. And haven't all of us had deductions for which we are not in the least to blame?

6) we demand that the payment we make for lodgings be on the pre-1891 level, that is to say, one ruble per person per month, because our earnings being what they are we positively have nothing to pay the two rubles with, and in any case, what for?... For the filthy, smelly, crowded kennel always in danger of fire? Don't forget, comrades, that all over St. Petersburg it is considered enough to pay a ruble a month, and that only our considerate bosses are not satisfied with that—so we must force them here, too, to cut down their greed. In defending these demands, comrades, we are not rebelling at all; we are merely demanding that we be given what all the workers of other factories now enjoy by law, the return of what has been taken from us by those who placed all their hopes on our inability to uphold our own rights. Let us, then, show on this occasion that our "benefactors" are mistaken.

Written and first published
in a mimeographed edition
in November 1895

Published according
to the text of the leaflet,
checked with the text
in the miscellany *Rabotnik*,
No. 1-2 (1896)

WHAT ARE OUR MINISTERS
THINKING ABOUT?[32]

Written at the end of 1895
for the newspaper *Rabocheye Dyelo*
First published in 1924

Published according to a copy
found in the archives
of the Police Department

Minister of Internal Affairs Durnovo wrote a letter to Procurator General of the Holy Synod Pobedonostsev. The letter, numbered 2603, was written on March 18, 1895, and bears the inscription "strictly confidential." The minister, therefore, wanted the letter to remain a strict secret. But there proved to be people who do not share the minister's views that Russian citizens should not know the government's intentions, with the result that a handwritten copy of this letter is now circulating everywhere.

What did Mr. Durnovo write to Mr. Pobedonostsev about?

He wrote to him about the Sunday schools. The letter reads: "Information secured during recent years goes to show that, following the example of the sixties, politically unreliable individuals and also a section of the student youth of a certain trend, are endeavouring to enter the Sunday schools as teachers, lecturers, librarians, etc. This concerted attempt, which cannot be inspired by a desire to earn money since the duties in such schools are undertaken gratis, proves that the activity above indicated, on the part of anti-government elements, constitutes a legal means of struggle against the system of state and public order existing in Russia."

That is how the minister argues. Among educated people there are those who want to share their knowledge with the workers, who want their knowledge to be of benefit not to themselves alone, but to the people—and the minister immediately decides that there are "anti-government elements" here, i.e., that it is conspirators of some kind who are inciting people to enter the Sunday schools. Could not the desire to teach others really arise in the minds of some educated people without incitement? But the minister is disturbed because the Sunday-school teachers get no salaries. He is accustomed to the spies and officials in his service only working for their salaries, working for whoever pays them best, whereas all of a sudden people work, render services, teach, and all ... gratis. Suspicious! thinks the minister, and sends spies to explore the matter. The letter goes on to say: "It is established from the following information" (received from spies, whose existence is justified by the receipt of salaries) "that not only do persons of a dangerous trend find their way into the teachers' ranks, but often the schools themselves are under the unofficial direction of a whole group of unreliable persons, who have no connection at all with the official personnel, who deliver lectures in the evenings and give lessons to the pupils on the invitation of the men and women teachers they themselves have installed there.... The fact that outside people are allowed to give lectures offers full scope for the infiltration of persons from frankly revolutionary circles as lecturers."

So then, if "outside people," who have not been endorsed and examined by priests and spies, want to give lessons to workers—that is downright revolution! The minister regards the workers as gunpowder, and knowledge and education as a spark; the minister is convinced that if the spark falls into the gunpowder, the explosion will be directed first and foremost against the government.

We cannot deny ourselves the pleasure of noting that in this rare instance we totally and unconditionally agree with the views of His Excellency.

Further in his letter the minister cites "proofs" of the correctness of his "information." Fine proofs they are!

Firstly, "a letter of a Sunday-school teacher whose name has still not been ascertained." The letter was confiscated during a search. It refers to a programme of history lectures, to the idea of the enslaving and emancipation of the social estates, and reference is made to the revolt of Razin and of Pugachov.[33]

Evidently these latter names scared the good minister so much that he very likely had a nightmare of peasants armed with pitchforks.

- The second proof:

"The Ministry of Internal Affairs is in possession of a programme, privately received, for public lectures in a Moscow Sunday school on the following points: 'The origin of society. Primitive society. The development of social organisation. The state and what it is needed for. Order. Liberty. Justice. Forms of political structure. Absolute and constitutional monarchy. Labour—the basis of the general welfare. Usefulness and wealth. Production, exchange and capital. How wealth is distributed. The pursuit of private interest. Property and the need for it. Emancipation of the peasants together with the land. Rent, profit, wages. What do wages and their various forms depend on? Thrift.'

"The lectures in this programme, which is undoubtedly unfit for an elementary school, give the lecturer every opportunity gradually to acquaint his pupils with the theories of Karl Marx, Engels, etc., while the person present on behalf of the diocesan authorities will hardly be in a position to detect the elements of Social-Democratic propaganda in the lectures."

The minister is evidently very much afraid of the "theories of Marx and Engels," if he notices "elements" of them even in the sort of programme where not a trace of them is to be seen. What did the minister find "unfit" in it? Very likely the problem of the forms of political structure and the constitution.

Just take any geography textbook, Mr. Minister, and you will find those problems dealt with there! May adult workers not know the things that children are taught?

But the minister places no reliance on persons from the Diocesan Department: "They will very likely fail to understand what is said."

The letter ends with an enumeration of the "unreliable" teachers at the parish Sunday school of the Moscow mill of the Prokhorov Textile Company, the Sunday school in the town of Yelets and the proposed school in Tiflis. Mr. Durnovo advises Mr. Pobedonostsev to undertake "a detailed check

of the individuals permitted to take classes in the schools."
Now, when you read the list of teachers, your hair stands on
end: all you get is ex-student, again an ex-student, and
still again an ex-student of Courses for Ladies. The minister would like the tutors to be ex-drill sergeants.

It is with particular horror that the minister says that
the school in Yelets "is situated beyond the river Sosna,
where the population is mainly the common" (o horror!)
"and working people, and where the railway workshops are."

The schools must be kept as far away as possible from the
"common and working people."

Workers! You see how mortally terrified are our ministers
at the working people acquiring knowledge! Show everybody, then, that no power will succeed in depriving the
workers of class-consciousness! Without knowledge the workers are defenceless, with knowledge they are a force!

DRAFT AND EXPLANATION
OF A PROGRAMME
FOR THE SOCIAL-DEMOCRATIC
PARTY[34]

Written in prison in 1895-96
First published in 1924

The *Draft Programme* is published according to the manuscript written in invisible ink between the lines of *Nauchnoye Obozreniye*,[35] No. 5, 1900 and the *Explanation of the Programme*, according to a hectographed notebook

DRAFT PROGRAMME

A. 1. Big factories are developing in Russia with ever-growing rapidity, ruining the small handicraftsmen and peasants, turning them into propertyless workers, and driving ever-increasing numbers of the people to the cities, factory and industrial villages and townlets.

2. This growth of capitalism signifies an enormous growth of wealth and luxury among a handful of factory owners, merchants and landowners, and a still more rapid growth of the poverty and oppression of the workers. The improvements in production and the machinery introduced in the big factories, while facilitating a rise in the productivity of social labour, serve to strengthen the power of the capitalists over the workers, to increase unemployment and with it to accentuate the defenceless position of the workers.

3. But while carrying the oppression of labour by capital to the highest pitch, the big factories are creating a special class of workers which is enabled to wage a struggle against capital, because their very conditions of life are destroying all their ties with their own petty production, and, by uniting the workers through their common labour and transferring them from factory to factory, are welding masses of working folk together. The workers are beginning a struggle against the capitalists, and an intense urge for unity is appearing among them. Out of the isolated revolts of the workers is growing the struggle of the Russian working class.

4. This struggle of the working class against the capitalist class is a struggle against all classes who live by the labour of others, and against all exploitation. It can only end

in the passage of political power into the hands of the working class, the transfer of all the land, instruments, factories, machines, and mines to the whole of society for the organisation of socialist production, under which all that is produced by the workers and all improvements in production must benefit the working people themselves.

5. The movement of the Russian working class is, according to its character and aims, part of the international (Social-Democratic) movement of the working class of all countries.

6. The main obstacle in the struggle of the Russian working class for its emancipation is the absolutely autocratic government and its irresponsible officials. Basing itself on the privileges of the landowners and capitalists and on subservience to their interests, it denies the lower classes any rights whatever and thus fetters the workers' movement and retards the development of the entire people. That is why the struggle of the Russian working class for its emancipation necessarily gives rise to the struggle against the absolute power of the autocratic government.

B. 1. The Russian Social-Democratic Party declares that its aim is to assist this struggle of the Russian working class by developing the class-consciousness of the workers, by promoting their organisation, and by indicating the aims and objects of the struggle.

2. The struggle of the Russian working class for its emancipation is a political struggle, and its first aim is to achieve political liberty.

3. That is why the Russian Social-Democratic Party will, without separating itself from the working-class movement, support every social movement against the absolute power of the autocratic government, against the class of privileged landed nobility and against all the vestiges of serfdom and the social-estate system which hinder free competition.

4. On the other hand, the Russian Social-Democratic workers' party will wage war against all endeavours to patronise the labouring classes with the guardianship of the absolute government and its officials, all endeavours to retard the development of capitalism, and consequently the development of the working class.

5. The emancipation of the workers must be the act of the working class itself.

6. What the Russian people need is not the help of the absolute government and its officials, but emancipation from oppression by it.

C. Making these views its starting-point, the Russian Social-Democratic Party demands first and foremost:

1. The convening of a Zemsky Sobor made up of representatives of all citizens so as to draw up a constitution.

2. Universal and direct suffrage for all citizens of Russia who have reached 21 years of age, irrespective of religion or nationality.

3. Freedom of assembly and organisation, and the right to strike.

4. Freedom of the press.

5. Abolition of social estates, and complete equality of all citizens before the law.

6. Freedom of religion and equality of all nationalities. Transfer of the registration of births, marriages and deaths to independent civic officials, independent, that is, of the police.

7. Every citizen to have the right to prosecute any official, without having to complain to the latter's superiors.

8. Abolition of passports, full freedom of movement and residence.

9. Freedom of trades and occupations and abolition of guilds.

D. For the workers, the Russian Social-Democratic Party demands:

1. Establishment of industrial courts in all industries, with elected judges from the capitalists and workers, in equal numbers.

2. Legislative limitation of the working day to 8 hours.

3. Legislative prohibition of night work and shifts. Prohibition of work by children under 15 years of age.

4. Legislative enactment of national holidays.

5. Application of factory laws and factory inspection to all industries throughout Russia, and to government factories, and also to handicraftsmen who work at home.

6. The Factory Inspectorate must be independent and not be under the Ministry of Finance. Members of industrial

courts must enjoy equal rights with the Factory Inspectorate in ensuring the observance of factory laws.

7. Absolute prohibition everywhere of the truck system.

8. Supervision, by workers' elected representatives, of the proper fixing of rates, the rejection of goods, the expenditure of accumulated fines and the factory-owned workers' quarters.

A law that all deductions from workers' wages, whatever the reason for their imposition (fines, rejects, etc.), shall not exceed the sum of 10 kopeks per ruble all told.

9. A law making the employers responsible for injuries to workers, the employer being required to prove that the worker is to blame.

10. A law making the employers responsible for maintaining schools and providing medical aid to the workers.

E. For the peasants, the Russian Social-Democratic Party demands:

1. Abolition of land redemption payments[36] and compensation to the peasants for redemption payments made. Return to the peasants of excess payments made to the Treasury.

2. Return to the peasants of their lands cut off in 1861.

3. Complete equality of taxation of the peasants' and landlords' lands.

4. Abolition of collective responsibility[37] and of all laws that prevent the peasants from doing as they will with their lands.

EXPLANATION OF THE PROGRAMME

The programme is divided into three main parts. Part one sets forth all the tenets from which the remaining parts of the programme follow. This part indicates the position occupied by the working class in contemporary society, the meaning and significance of their struggle against the employers and the political position of the working class in the Russian state.

Part two sets forth the *Party's aim,* and indicates the Party's relation to other political trends in Russia. It deals with what should be the activity of the Party and of all class-conscious workers, and what should be their attitude to the interests and strivings of the other classes in Russian society.

Part three contains the Party's practical demands. This part is divided into three sections. The first section contains demands for nation-wide reforms. The second section states the demands and programme of the working class. The third section contains demands in the interests of the peasants. Some preliminary explanations of the sections are given below, before proceeding to the practical part of the programme.

A 1. The programme deals first of all with the rapid growth of big factories, because this is the main thing in contemporary Russia that is completely changing all the old conditions of life, particularly the living conditions of the labouring class. Under the old conditions practically all the country's wealth was produced by petty proprietors, who constituted the overwhelming majority of the population. The population lived an immobile life in the villages, the greater part of their produce being either for their own consumption, or for the small market of neighbouring villages which had little contact with other nearby markets. These very same petty proprietors worked for the landlords, who compelled them to produce mainly for their consumption. Domestic produce was handed over for processing to artisans, who also lived in the villages or travelled in the neighbouring areas to get work.

But after the peasants were emancipated, these living conditions of the mass of the people underwent a complete change: the small artisan establishments began to be replaced by big factories, which grew with extraordinary rapidity; they ousted the petty proprietors, turning them into wage-workers, and compelled hundreds and thousands of workers to work together, producing tremendous quantities of goods that are being sold all over Russia.

The emancipation of the peasants destroyed the immobility of the population and placed the peasants in conditions under which they could no longer get a livelihood from the patches of land that remained in their possession. Masses of people left home to seek a livelihood, making for the factories or for jobs on the construction of the railways which connect the different corners of Russia and carry the output

of the big factories everywhere. Masses of people went to
jobs in the towns, took part in building factory and commercial premises, in delivering fuel to factories, and in
preparing raw materials for them. Finally, many people
were occupied at home, doing jobs for merchants and factory
owners who could not expand their establishments fast
enough. Similar changes took place in agriculture; the landlords began to produce grain for sale, big cultivators from
among the peasants and merchants came on the scene, and
grain in hundreds of millions of poods began to be sold
abroad. Production required wage-workers, and hundreds of
thousands and millions of peasants, giving up their tiny
allotments, went to work as regular or day labourers for the
new masters engaged in producing grain for sale. Now it is
these changes in the old way of life that are described by the
programme, which says that the big factories are ruining the
small handicraftsmen and peasants, turning them into
wage-workers. Small-scale production is being replaced
everywhere by large-scale, and in this large-scale production
the masses of the workers are just hirelings employed for
wages by the capitalist, who possesses enormous capital,
builds enormous workshops, buys up huge quantities of
materials and fills his pockets with all the profit from this
mass-scale production by the combined workers. Production
has become capitalist, and it exerts merciless and ruthless
pressure on all the petty proprietors, destroying their immobile life in the villages, compelling them to travel from one
end of the country to the other as ordinary unskilled labourers, selling their labour-power to capital. An ever-increasing part of the population is being separated once and for
all from the countryside and from agriculture, and is concentrating in the towns, factory and industrial villages and
townlets, forming a special propertyless class of people, a
class of hired proletarian workers, who live only by the sale
of their labour-power.

These are what constitute the tremendous changes in
the country's life brought about by the big factories—
small-scale production is being replaced by large-scale,
the petty proprietors are turning into wage-workers.
What, then, does this change mean for the whole of the work-

ing population, and where is it leading? This is dealt with further in the programme.

A 2. Accompanying the replacement of small- by large-scale production is the replacement of small financial resources in the hands of the individual proprietor by enormous sums employed as capital, the replacement of small, insignificant profits by profits running into millions. That is why the growth of capitalism is leading everywhere to the growth of luxury and riches. A whole class of big financial magnates, factory owners, railway owners, merchants, and bankers has arisen in Russia, a whole class of people who live off income derived from money capital loaned on interest to industrialists has arisen; the big landowners have become enriched, drawing large sums from the peasants by way of land redemption payments, taking advantage of their need of land to raise the price of the land leased to them, and setting up large beet-sugar refineries and distilleries on their estates. The luxury and extravagance of all these wealthy classes have reached unparalleled dimensions, and the main streets of the big cities are lined with their princely mansions and luxurious palaces. But as capitalism grew, the workers' conditions became steadily worse. If earnings increased in some places following the peasants' emancipation, they did so very slightly and not for long, because the mass of hungry people swarming in from the villages forced rates down, while the cost of foodstuffs and necessities continued to go up, so that even with their increased wages the workers got fewer means of subsistence; it became increasingly difficult to find jobs, and side by side with the luxurious mansions of the rich (or on city outskirts) there grew up the slums where the workers were forced to live in cellars, in overcrowded, damp and cold dwellings, and even in dug-outs near the new industrial establishments. As capital grew bigger it increased its pressure on the workers, turning them into paupers, compelling them to devote all their time to the factory, and forcing the workers' wives and children to go to work. This, therefore, is the first change towards which the growth of capitalism is leading: tremendous wealth is accumulating in the coffers of a small handful of capitalists, while the masses of the people are being turned into paupers.

The second change consists in the fact that the replacement of small- by large-scale production has led to many improvements in production. First of all, work done singly, separately in each little workshop, in each isolated little household, has been replaced by the work of combined labourers working together at one factory, for one landowner, for one contractor. Joint labour is far more effective (productive) than individual, and renders it possible to produce goods with far greater ease and rapidity. But all these improvements are enjoyed by the capitalist alone, who pays the workers next to nothing and appropriates all the profit deriving from the workers' combined labour. The capitalist gets still stronger and the worker gets still weaker because he becomes accustomed to doing some one kind of work and it is more difficult for him to transfer to another job, to change his occupation.

Another, far more important, improvement in production is the introduction of *machines* by the capitalist. The effectiveness of labour is increased manifold by the use of machines; but the capitalist turns all this benefit against the worker: taking advantage of the fact that machines require less physical labour, he assigns women and children to them, and pays them less. Taking advantage of the fact that where machines are used far fewer workers are wanted, he throws them out of the factory in masses and then takes advantage of this unemployment to enslave the worker still further, to increase the working day, to deprive the worker of his night's rest and to turn him into a simple appendage to the machine. Unemployment, created by machinery and constantly on the increase, now makes the worker utterly defenceless. His skill loses its worth, he is easily replaced by a plain unskilled labourer, who quickly becomes accustomed to the machine and gladly undertakes the job for lower wages. Any attempt to resist increased oppression by the capitalist leads to dismissal. On his own the worker is quite helpless against capital, and the machine threatens to crush him.

A 3. In explaining the previous point, we showed that on his own the worker is helpless and defenceless against the capitalist who introduces machines. The worker has at all costs to seek means of resisting the capitalist, in order to defend himself. And he finds such means in *organisation*. Helpless on his own, the worker becomes a force when organised with his comrades, and is enabled to fight the capitalist and resist his onslaught.

Organisation becomes a necessity for the worker, now faced by big capital. But is it possible to organise a motley mass of people who are strangers to one another, even if they work in one factory? The programme indicates the conditions that prepare the workers for unity and develop in them the capacity and ability to organise. These conditions are as follows: 1) the large factory, with machine production that requires regular work the whole year round, completely breaks the tie between the worker and the land and his own farm, turning him into an absolute proletarian. The fact of each farming for himself on a patch of land divided the workers and gave each one of them a certain specific interest, separate from that of his fellow worker, and was thus an obstacle to organisation. The worker's break with the land destroys these obstacles. 2) Further, the joint work of hundreds and thousands of workers in itself accustoms the workers to discuss their needs jointly, to take joint action, and clearly shows them the identity of the position and interests of the entire mass of workers. 3) Finally, constant transfers of workers from factory to factory accustom them to compare the conditions and practices in the different factories and enable them to convince themselves of the identical nature of the exploitation in all factories, to acquire the experience of other workers in their clashes with the capitalist, and thus enhance the solidarity of the workers. Now it is because of these conditions, taken together, that the appearance of big factories has given rise to the organisation of the workers. Among the Russian workers unity is expressed mainly and most frequently in strikes (we shall deal further with the reason why organisation in the shape of unions or mutual benefit societies is beyond the reach of our workers). The more the big factories develop, the more frequent, powerful and stubborn become the workers' strikes; the greater the oppression of capitalism and the greater the need for joint resistance by the workers. Strikes and isolated revolts of the workers, as the programme states, now constitute the.

most widespread phenomenon in Russian factories. But, with the further growth of capitalism and the increasing frequency of strikes, they prove inadequate. The employers take joint action against them: they conclude agreements among themselves, bring in workers from other areas, and turn for assistance to those who run the machinery of state, who help them crush the workers' resistance. Instead of being faced by the one individual owner of each separate factory, the workers are now faced by the *entire capitalist class* and the government that assists it. The entire *capitalist class* undertakes a struggle against the entire *working class*; it devises common measures against the strikes, presses the government to adopt anti-working-class legislation, transfers factories to more out-of-the-way localities, and resorts to the distribution of jobs among people working at home and to a thousand and one other ruses and devices against the workers. The organisation of the workers of a separate factory, even of a separate industry, proves inadequate for resisting the entire capitalist class, and joint action by the *entire working class* becomes absolutely necessary. Thus, out of the isolated revolts of the workers grows the struggle of the entire working class. The struggle of the workers against the employers turns into a *class struggle*. All the employers are united by the one interest of keeping the workers in a state of subordination and of paying them the minimum wages possible. And the employers see that the only way they can safeguard their interests is by joint action on the part of the entire employing class, by acquiring influence over the machinery of state. The workers are likewise bound together by a common interest, that of preventing themselves being crushed by capital, of upholding their right to life and to a human existence. And the workers likewise become convinced that they, too, need unity, joint action by the entire class, the working class, and that to that end they must secure influence over the machinery of state.

A 4. We have explained how and why the struggle between the factory workers and the employers becomes a class struggle, a struggle of the working class—the proletarians—against the capitalist class—the bourgeoisie. The question arises, what significance has this struggle for the entire people and for all working people? Under the contemporary conditions, of which we have already spoken in the explanation of point 1, production by wage-workers increasingly ousts petty economy. The number of people *who live by wage-labour* grows rapidly, and not only does the number of regular factory workers increase, but there is a still greater increase in the number of peasants who also have to search for work as wage-labourers, in order to live. At the present time, work for hire, work for the capitalist, has already become the most widespread form of labour. The domination of capital over labour embraces the bulk of the population not only in industry, but also in agriculture. Now it is this exploitation of wage-labour underlying contemporary society that the big factories develop to the utmost. All the methods of exploitation used by all capitalists in all industries, and which the entire mass of Russia's working-class population suffers from, are concentrated, intensified, made the regular rule right in the factory and spread to all aspects of the worker's labour and life, they create a whole routine, a whole system whereby the capitalist sweats the worker. Let us illustrate this with an example: at all times and places, anybody who undertakes work for hire, rests, leaves his work on a holiday if it is celebrated in the neighbourhood. It is quite different in the factory. Once the factory management has engaged a worker, it disposes of his services just as it likes, paying no attention to the worker's habits, to his customary way of life, to his family position, to his intellectual requirements. The factory drives the employee to work when it needs his labour, compelling him to fit in his entire life with its requirements, to tear his rest hours to pieces, and, if he is on shifts, to work at night and on holidays. All the imaginable abuses relating to working time are set into motion by the factory and at the same time it introduces its "rules," its "practices," which are obligatory for every worker. The order of things in the factory is deliberately adapted to squeezing out of the hired worker all the labour he is capable of yielding, to squeezing it out at top speed and then to throwing him out! Another example. Everybody who takes a job, undertakes, of course, to submit to the employer, to do everything he is ordered. But when anybody hires himself out on a temporary job, he does not surrender his will at all; if he finds his employer's demands wrong or excessive, he leaves him. The factory, on the other hand, demands that the worker surrender his will altogether; it introduces discipline within its walls, compels the worker to start or to stop work when the bell rings, assumes the right itself to punish the worker, and subjects him to a fine or a deduction for every violation of rules which it has itself drawn up. The worker becomes part of a huge aggregate of machinery. He must be just as obedient, enslaved, and without a will of his own, as the machine itself.

Yet another example. Anybody who takes a job has frequent occasion to be dissatisfied with his employer, and complains about him to the court or a government official. Both the official and the court usually settle the dispute in the employer's favour, support him, but this promotion of the employer's interests is not based on a general regulation or a law, but on the subservience of individual officials, who at different times protect him to a greater or lesser degree, and who settle matters unjustly in the employer's favour, either because they are acquaintances of his, or because they are uninformed about working conditions and cannot understand the worker. Each separate case of such injustice depends on each separate clash between the worker and the employer, on each separate official. The factory, on the other hand, gathers together such a mass of workers, carries oppression to such a pitch, that it becomes impossible to examine every separate case. General regulations are established, a law is drawn up on relations between the workers and the employers, a law that is obligatory for all. In this law the promotion of the employer's interests is backed up by the authority of the state. The injustice of individual officials is replaced by the injustice of the law itself. Regulations appear, for example, of the following type: if the worker is absent from work, he not only loses wages, but has to pay a fine in addition, whereas the employer pays nothing if he sends the workers home for lack of work; the employer may dismiss the worker for using strong language, whereas the worker cannot leave the job if he is similarly treated; the employer is entitled on his own authority to impose fines, make deductions or demand that overtime be worked, etc.

All these examples show us how the factory intensifies the exploitation of the workers and makes this exploitation universal, makes a whole "*system*" of it. The worker now has to deal, willy-nilly, not with an individual employer and his will and oppression, but with the arbitrary treatment and oppression he suffers from the entire employing class. The worker sees that his oppressors are not some one capitalist, but the entire capitalist class, because the system of exploitation is the same in all establishments. The individual capitalist cannot even depart from this system: if, for example, he were to take it into his head to reduce working hours, his goods would cost him more than those produced by his neighbour, another factory owner, who makes his employees work longer for the same wage. To secure an improvement in his conditions, the worker now has to deal with the entire social system aimed at the exploitation of labour by capital. The worker is now confronted not by the individual injustice of an individual official, but by the injustice of the state authority itself, which takes the entire capitalist class under its protection and issues laws, obligatory for all, that serve the interests of that class. Thus, the struggle of the factory workers against the employers inevitably turns into a struggle against the entire capitalist class, against the entire social order based on the exploitation of labour by capital. That is why the workers' struggle acquires a social significance, becomes a struggle on behalf of all working people against all classes that live by the labour of others. That is why the workers' struggle opens up a new era in Russian history and is the dawn of the workers' emancipation.

What, however, is the domination of the capitalist class over the entire mass of working folk based on? It is based on the fact that all the factories, mills, mines, machines, and instruments of labour are in the hands of the capitalists, are their private property; on the fact that they possess enormous quantities of land (of all the land in European Russia, more than one-third belongs to landed proprietors, who do not number half a million). The workers possess no instruments of labour or materials, and so they have to sell their labour-power to the capitalists, who only pay the workers what is necessary for their keep, and place all the surplus produced by labour in their pockets; thus they pay for only part of the working time they use, and appropriate the rest. The entire increase in wealth resulting from the combined labour of the masses of workers or from improvements in production goes to the capitalist class, while the workers, who toil from generation to generation, remain property-less proletarians. That is why there is only one way of ending the exploitation of labour by capital, and that is to abolish the private ownership of the instruments of la-bour, to hand over all the factories, mills, mines, and also all the big estates, etc., to the whole of society and to con-duct socialist production in common, directed by the workers themselves. The articles produced by labour in common will then go to benefit the working people themselves, while the surplus they produce over and above their keep will serve to satisfy the needs of the workers themselves, to secure the full development of all their capabilities and equal rights to enjoy all the achievements of science and art. That is why the programme states that the struggle between the working class and the capitalists can end only in this way. To achieve that, however, it is necessary that political power, i.e., the power to govern the state, should pass from the hands of a government which is under the influence of the capitalists and landowners, or from the hands of a govern-ment directly made up of elected representatives of the cap-italists, into the hands of the working class.

Such is the ultimate aim of the struggle of the working class, such is the condition for its complete emancipation. This is the ultimate aim for which class-conscious, organ-ised workers should strive; here in Russia, however, they still meet with tremendous obstacles, which hinder them in their struggle for emancipation.

A 5. The fight against the domination of the capitalist class is now being waged by the workers of all European countries and also by the workers of America and Australia. Working-class organisation and solidarity is not confined to one country or one nationality: the workers' parties of different countries proclaim aloud the complete identity (solidarity) of interests and aims of the workers of the whole world. They come together at joint congresses, put forward common demands to the capitalist class of all countries, have established an international holiday of the entire organised proletariat striving for emancipation (May Day), thus welding the working class of all nationalities and of all countries into one great workers' army. The unity of the workers of all countries is a necessity arising out of the fact that the capitalist class, which rules over the workers, does not limit its rule to one country. Commercial ties between the different countries are becoming closer and more extensive; capital constantly passes from one country to another. The banks, those huge depositories that gather capital together and distribute it on loan to capitalists, begin as national institutions and then become international, gather capital from all countries, and distribute it among the capitalists of Europe and America. Enormous joint-stock companies are now being organised to set up capitalist enterprises not in one country, but in several at once; international associations of capitalists make their appearance. Capitalist domination is international. That is why the workers' struggle in all countries for their emancipation is only successful if the workers fight jointly against international capital. That is why the Russian worker's comrade in the fight against the capitalist class is the German worker, the Polish worker, and the French worker, just as his enemy is the Russian, the Polish, and the French capitalists. Thus, in the recent period foreign capitalists have been very eagerly transferring their capital to Russia, where they are building branch factories and founding companies for running new enterprises. They are flinging themselves greedily on this young country in which the government is more favourable and obsequious to capital than anywhere else, in which they find workers who are less organised and less capable of fighting back than in the West, and in which the workers' standard of living, and hence their wages, are much lower, so that the foreign capitalists are able to draw enormous profits, on a scale unparalleled in their own countries. International capital has already stretched out its hand to Russia. The Russian workers are stretching out their hands to the international labour movement.

A 6. We have already spoken of how the big factories carry capital's oppression of labour to the highest pitch, how they establish a whole system of methods of

exploitation; how the workers, in their revolt against capital, inevitably arrive at the need to unite all workers, at
the need for joint struggle by the entire working class. In
this struggle against the capitalist class, the workers come
up against the general laws of the state, which protect the
capitalists and their interests.

But then, if the workers are strong enough to force concessions from the capitalists, to resist their attacks by joint
action, they could also, by their unity, influence the
laws of the state, and secure their alteration. That is what
the workers of all other countries are doing. The Russian
workers, however, cannot exert direct influence on the
state. The conditions of the Russian workers are such that
they are deprived of the most elementary civil rights. They
must not dare to gather together, to discuss their affairs
together, to organise unions, to publish statements; in other words, the laws of the state have not only been drawn up
in the interests of the capitalist class, but they frankly deprive the workers of all possibility of influencing these laws
and of securing their alteration. The reason this happens
is that in Russia (and in Russia alone of all European countries) the absolute power of an autocratic government continues to this day, that is, a system of state exists under
which laws that are obligatory for the entire people may be
issued by the tsar alone, at his discretion, while only officials appointed by him may give effect to them. The citizens are not allowed to take any part in issuing laws, in
discussing them, in proposing new or in demanding the repeal of old laws. They have no right to demand of officials
an account of their activity, to check their activity, and to
prosecute them. Citizens do not even possess the right to
discuss affairs of state: they must not dare to organise meetings or unions without the permission of those same officials. The officials are thus irresponsible in the full sense of
the term; they constitute a special caste, as it were, placed
above the citizens. The irresponsibility and arbitrary conduct of the officials, and the fact that the population itself
is inarticulate, give rise to such scandalous abuse of power
by officials and such a violation of the rights of the common
people as are hardly possible in any European country.

Thus, according to law, the Russian Government has absolute authority, and is considered to be quite independent, as it were, of the people, standing above all social estates and classes. If, however, that were really the case, why should the law and the government in all conflicts between the workers and the capitalists take the side of the capitalists? Why should the capitalists meet with ever-growing support as their numbers and their wealth grow, whereas the workers meet with ever-increasing resistance and restriction?

Actually the government does not stand above classes, it protects one class against the other, protects the propertied class against the propertyless, the capitalists against the workers. An absolute government could not rule such a huge country if it did not give all sorts of privileges and favours to the propertied classes.

Although the government, according to law, possesses absolute and independent power, actually the capitalists and landowners possess thousands of means of influencing the government and affairs of state. They have their own social-estate associations—noblemen's and merchants' societies, chambers of trade and manufactures, etc.—recognised by law. Their elected representatives either become officials outright, and take part in governing the state (for example, marshals of the nobility), or are given posts in government institutions of every kind: for example, the law provides for factory owners to participate in factory courts (the chief authority over the Factory Inspectorate), to which they elect their representatives. But they do not confine themselves to this direct participation in ruling the state. In their societies they discuss laws of state, draft bills, and the government usually consults them on each issue, submits draft bills to them with a request for their views.

The capitalists and landed proprietors organise all-Russian congresses, where they discuss their affairs and devise various measures of benefit to their class, and on behalf of all the landed nobility, or of the "merchants of all Russia," petition for the adoption of new laws and for the amendment of old ones. They can discuss their affairs in the newspapers, for however much the government hampers the press with its censorship, it would never dare think of depriving the propertied classes of the right to discuss their affairs. They have all sorts of ways and means of approaching the top representatives of the governmental authorities, they can more easily discuss the arbitrary conduct of lower officials, and can easily secure the repeal of particularly oppressive laws and regulations. And while there is no country in the world where there are so many laws and regulations, such unexampled police supervision by the government, a supervision that extends to all sorts of petty details and robs every undertaking of its individuality, there is no country in the world where these bourgeois regulations are so easily violated and where these police laws are circumvented so easily by just the gracious assent of the supreme authorities. And this gracious assent is never refused.[38]

B 1. This is the most important, the paramount, point of the programme, because it indicates what should constitute the activity of the Party in defending the interests of the working class, the activity of all class-conscious workers. It indicates how the striving for socialism, the striving for the abolition of the age-old exploitation of man by man, should be linked up with the popular movement engendered by the living conditions created by the large-scale factories.

The Party's activity must consist in promoting the workers' class struggle. The Party's task is not to concoct some fashionable means of helping the workers, but to join up with the workers' movement, to bring light into it, to assist the workers in the struggle they themselves have already begun to wage. The Party's task is to uphold the interests of the workers and to represent those of the entire working-class movement. Now, what must this assistance to the workers in their struggle consist of?

The programme says that this assistance must consist, firstly, in developing the workers' class-consciousness. We have already spoken of how the workers' struggle against the employers becomes the class struggle of the proletariat against the bourgeoisie.

What is meant by workers' class-consciousness follows from what we have said on the subject. The workers' class-consciousness means the workers' understanding that the only way to improve their conditions and to achieve their emancipation is to conduct a struggle against the capitalist and factory-owner class created by the big factories. Further, the workers' class-consciousness means their understanding that the interests of all the workers of any particular country are identical, that they all constitute one class, separate from all the other classes in society. Finally, the class-consciousness of the workers means the workers' understanding that to achieve their aims they have to work to influence affairs of state, just as the landlords and the capitalists did, and are continuing to do now.

By what means do the workers reach an understanding of all this? They do so by constantly gaining experience from the very struggle that they begin to wage against the employers and that increasingly develops, becomes sharper, and involves larger numbers of workers as big factories grow. There was a time when the workers' enmity against capital only found expression in a hazy sense of hatred of their exploiters, in a hazy consciousness of their oppression and enslavement, and in the desire *to wreak vengeance* on the capitalists. The struggle at that time found expression in isolated revolts of the workers, who wrecked buildings, smashed machines, attacked members of the factory management, etc. That was the *first*, the initial, form of the working-class movement, and it was a necessary one, because hatred of the capitalist has always and everywhere been the first impulse towards arousing in the workers the desire to defend themselves. The Russian working-class movement has, however, already outgrown this original form. Instead of having a hazy hatred of the capitalist, the workers have already begun to understand the antagonism between the interests of the working class and of the capitalist class. Instead of having a confused sense of oppression, they have begun to distinguish *the ways and means* by which capital oppresses them, and are revolting against various forms of oppression, placing limits to capitalist oppression, and protecting themselves against the capitalist's greed. Instead of wreaking vengeance on the capitalists they are now turning to the fight for concessions, they are beginning to face the capitalist class with one demand after another, and are demanding improved working conditions, increased wages, and shorter working hours. Every strike concentrates all the attention and all the efforts of the workers on some particular aspect of the conditions under which the working class lives. Every strike gives rise to discussions about these conditions, helps the workers to appraise them, to understand what capitalist oppression consists in in the particular case, and what means can be employed to combat this oppression. Every strike enriches the experience of the entire working class. If the strike is successful it shows them what a strong force working-class unity is, and impels others to make use of their comrades' success. If it is not successful, it gives rise to discussions about the causes of the failure and to the search for better methods of struggle. This transition of the workers to the steadfast struggle for their vital needs, the fight for concessions, for improved living conditions, wages and working hours, now begun all over Russia, means that the Russian workers are making tremendous progress, and that is why the attention of the Social-Democratic Party and all class-conscious workers should be concentrated mainly on this struggle, on its promotion. Assistance to the workers should consist in showing them those most vital needs for the satisfaction of which they should fight, should consist in analysing the factors particularly responsible for worsening the conditions of different categories of workers, in explaining factory laws and regulations the violation of which (added to the deceptive tricks of the capitalists) so often subject the workers to double robbery. Assistance should consist in giving more precise and definite expression to the workers' demands, and in making them public, in choosing the best time for resistance, in choosing the method of struggle, in discussing the position and the strength of the two opposing sides, in discussing whether a still better choice can be made of the method of fighting (a method, perhaps, like addressing a letter to the factory owner, or approaching the inspector, or the doctor, according to circumstances, where direct strike action is not advisable, etc.).

We have said that the Russian workers' transition to such struggle is indicative of the tremendous progress they have made. This struggle places (leads) the working-class movement on to the high road, and is the certain guarantee of its further success. The mass of working folk learn from this struggle, firstly, how to recognise and to examine one by one the methods of capitalist exploitation, to compare them with the law, with their living conditions, and with the interests of the capitalist class. By examining the different forms and cases of exploitation, the workers learn to understand the significance and the essence of exploitation as a whole, learn to understand the social system based on the exploitation of labour by capital. Secondly, in the process of this struggle the workers test their strength, learn to organise, learn to understand the need for and the significance of organisation. The extension of this struggle and the increasing frequency of clashes inevitably lead to a further extension of the struggle, to the development of a sense of unity, a sense of solidarity—at first among the workers of a particular locality, and then among the workers of the entire country, among the entire working class. Thirdly, this struggle develops the workers' political consciousness. The living condition of the mass of working folk places them in such a position that they do not (cannot) possess either the leisure or the opportunity to ponder over problems of state. On the other hand, the workers' struggle against the factory owners for their daily needs automatically and inevitably spurs the workers on to think of state, political questions, questions of how the Russian state is governed, how laws and regulations are issued, and whose interests they serve. Each clash in the factory necessarily brings the workers into conflict with the laws and representatives of state authority. In this connection the workers hear "political speeches" for the first time. At first from, say, the factory inspectors, who explain to them that the trick employed by the factory owner to defraud them is based on the exact meaning of the regulations, which have been endorsed by the appropriate authority and give the employer a free hand to defraud the workers, or that the factory owner's oppressive measures are quite lawful, since he is merely availing himself of his rights, giving effect to such and such a law, that has been endorsed by the state authority that sees to its implementation. The political explanations of Messrs, the Inspectors are occasionally

8*

supplemented by the still more beneficial "political explanations" of the minister,[39] who reminds the workers of
the feelings of "Christian love" that they owe to the factory
owners for their making millions out of the workers' labour.
Later, these explanations of the representatives of the state
authority, and the workers' direct acquaintance with the
facts showing for whose benefit this authority operates, are
still further supplemented by leaflets or other explanations
given by socialists, so that the workers get their political
education in full from such a strike. They learn to understand not only the specific interests of the working class,
but also the specific place occupied by the working class in
the state. And so the *assistance* which the Social-Democratic Party can render to the class struggle of the workers
should be: to develop the workers' class-consciousness
by assisting them in the fight for their most vital
needs.

The second type of *assistance* should consist, as the programme states, in promoting the organisation of the workers.
The struggle we have just described necessarily requires
that the workers be organised. Organisation becomes necessary for strikes, to ensure that they are conducted with
great success, for collections in support of strikers, for
setting up workers' mutual benefit societies, and for
propaganda among the workers, the distribution among
them of leaflets, announcements, manifestoes, etc. Organisation is still more necessary to enable the workers to defend
themselves against persecution by the police and the gen-
darmerie, to conceal from them all the workers' contacts
and associations and to arrange the delivery of books,
pamphlets, newspapers, etc. To assist in all this—such is
the Party's second task.

The third consists in indicating the real aims of the struggle, i.e., in explaining to the workers what the exploitation of labour by capital consists in, what it is based on,
how the private ownership of the land and the instruments
of labour leads to the poverty of the working masses, compels them to sell their labour to the capitalists and to yield
up gratis the entire surplus produced by the worker's labour
over and above his keep, in explaining, furthermore, how
this exploitation inevitably leads to the class struggle be-

tween the workers and the capitalists, what the conditions of this struggle and its ultimate aims are—in a word, in explaining what is briefly stated in the programme.

B 2. What is meant by these words: the struggle of the working class is a political struggle? They mean that the working class cannot fight for its emancipation without securing influence over affairs of state, over the administration of the state, over the issue of laws. The need for such influence has long been understood by the Russian capitalists, and we have shown how they have been able, despite all sorts of prohibitions contained in the police laws, to find thousands of ways of influencing the state authority, and how this authority serves the interests of the capitalist class. Hence it naturally follows that the working class, too, cannot wage its struggle, cannot even secure a lasting improvement of its lot unless it influences state authority.

We have already said that the workers' struggle against the capitalists will inevitably lead to a clash with the government, and the government itself is exerting every effort to prove to the workers that only by struggle and by joint resistance can they influence state authority. This was shown with particular clarity by the big strikes that took place in Russia in 1885-86. The government immediately set about drawing up regulations concerning workers, at once issued new laws about factory practices, yielded to the workers' insistent demands (for example, regulations were introduced limiting fines and ensuring proper wage payment); in the same way the present strikes (in 1896) have again caused the government's immediate intervention, and the government has already understood that it cannot confine itself to arrests and deportations, that it is ridiculous to regale the workers with stupid sermons about the noble conduct of the factory owners (see the circular issued by Finance Minister Witte to factory inspectors. Spring 1896). The government has realised that "organised workers constitute a force to be reckoned with" and so it already has the factory legislation under review and is convening in St. Petersburg a Congress of Senior Factory Inspectors to discuss the question of reducing working hours and other inevitable concessions to the workers.

Thus we see that the struggle of the working class against the capitalist class must necessarily be a political struggle. Indeed, this struggle is already exerting influence on the state authority, is acquiring political significance. But the workers' utter lack of political rights, about which we have already spoken, and the absolute impossibility of the workers openly and directly influencing state authority become more clearly and sharply exposed and felt as the working-class movement develops. That is why the most urgent demand of the workers, the primary objective of the working-class influence on affairs of state must be *the achievement of political freedom*, i.e., the direct participation, guaranteed by law (by a constitution), of all citizens in the government of the state, the guaranteed right of all citizens freely to assemble, discuss their affairs, influence affairs of state through their associations and the press. The achievement of political freedom becomes the *"vital task of the workers"* because without it the workers do not and cannot have any influence over affairs of state, and thus inevitably remain a rightless, humiliated and inarticulate class. And if even now, when the workers are only just beginning to fight and to close their ranks, the government is already hastening to make concessions to the workers, in order to check the further growth of the movement, there can be no doubt that when the workers fully close their ranks and unite under the leadership of one political party, they will be able to compel the government to surrender, they will be able to win political freedom for themselves and the entire Russian people!

The preceding parts of the programme indicated the place occupied by the working class in contemporary society and the contemporary state, what is the aim of the struggle of the working class, and what constitutes the task of the Party that represents the workers' interests. Under the absolute rule of the government there are not, nor can there be openly functioning political parties in Russia, but there are political trends which express the interests of other classes and which exert influence over public opinion and the government. Hence, in order to make clear the position of the Social-Democratic Party, it is necessary now to indicate its attitude towards the remaining political trends in Russian society, so as to enable the workers to determine who may be their ally and to what extent, and who their enemy. That is indicated in the two following points of the programme.

B 3. The programme declares that the workers' allies are, firstly, all those social strata which oppose the absolute power of the autocratic government. Since this absolute rule is the main obstacle to the workers' fight for their emancipation, it naturally follows that it is in the direct interest of the workers to support every social movement against absolutism (absolute means unlimited; absolutism is the unlimited rule of the government). The stronger the development of capitalism, the deeper become the contradictions between this bureaucratic administration and the interests of the propertied classes themselves, the interests of the bourgeoisie. And the Social-Democratic Party proclaims that it will support all strata and grades of the bourgeoisie who oppose the absolute government.

It is infinitely more to the workers' advantage for the bourgeoisie to *influence* affairs of state *directly*, than for their influence to be exerted, as is the case now, through a crowd of venal and despotic officials. It is far more advantageous to the workers for the bourgeoisie to *openly* influence policy than, as is the case now, to exert a *concealed* influence, concealed by the supposedly all-powerful "independent" government, which is called a government "by the grace of God," and hands out "its graces" to the suffering and industrious landlords and the poverty-stricken and oppressed factory owners. The workers need *open struggle* against the capitalist class, in order that the entire Russian proletariat may see for whose interests the workers are waging the struggle, and may learn how to wage the struggle properly; in order that the intrigues and aspirations of the bourgeoisie may not be hidden in the ante-rooms of grand dukes, in the saloons of senators and ministers, and in departmental offices barred to the public, and in order that they may come to the surface and open the eyes of all and sundry as to who really inspires government policy and what the capitalists and landlords are striving for. And so, down with everything that hides the present influence of the capitalist class, and our support for any representative of the bourgeoisie who *comes out* against the bureaucracy, the bureaucratic administration, against the absolute government! But, while proclaiming its support for every social movement against absolutism, the Social-Democratic Party recognises that it does not separate itself from the working-class movement, because the working class has its specific interests, which are opposed to the interests of all other classes. While rendering support to all representatives of the bourgeoisie in the fight for political freedom, the workers should remember that the propertied classes can only be their allies for a time, that the interests of the workers and the capitalists cannot be reconciled, that the workers need the abolition of the government's absolute rule only in order to wage an open and extensive struggle against the capitalist class.

Further the Social-Democratic Party proclaims that it will render support to all who rise up against the class of the privileged landed nobility. The landed nobility in Russia are considered to be the first estate in the land. The remnants of their feudal power over the peasants weigh down the masses of the people to this day. The peasants continue to make land redemption payments for emancipation from the power of the landlords. The peasants are still tied to the land, in order that the landed gentry may not suffer any shortage of cheap and submissive farm labourers. Rightless and treated as juveniles, the peasants to this day are at the mercy of officials who look after their own pockets and interfere in peasant life so as to ensure that the peasants make their redemption payments or pay quit-rent to the feudal landlords "punctually," that they do not dare to "shirk" working for the landlords, do not dare, for example, to leave the district and so perhaps compel the landlords to hire outside workers, who are not so cheap or so oppressed by want. The landlords keep millions, tens of millions of peasants in their service, enslaving them and keeping them without rights, and in return for their display of prowess in this sphere enjoy the highest privileges of state. The landed nobility are the principal holders of the highest posts in the state (what is more, by law the nobility, as a social estate, enjoy priority in the civil service); the aristocratic landlords are closest to the Court and more directly and easily than anybody else influence government policy in their own direction. They

utilise their close connections with the government to plun-
der the state coffers and to secure out of public funds gifts
and grants that run into millions of rubles, sometimes in
the shape of huge estates distributed for services, at other
times in the shape of "concessions." *

---

* The hectographed text in the notebook in the possession of the
Institute of Marxism-Leninism, Central Committee of the C.P.S.U.,
breaks off here.—*Ed.*

TO THE TSARIST GOVERNMENT[40]

This year, 1896, the Russian Government has already made two announcements to the public on the workers' struggle against the factory owners. In other countries such announcements are no rarity—there they do not hide what is going on in the country, and the press freely publishes items about strikes. In Russia, however, the government fears more than the plague publicity for factory practices and incidents. It banned the publication of strike news in the press, it forbade factory inspectors to publish their reports, and it even put a stop to the hearing of strike cases in the ordinary courts open to the public; in a word, it took all measures to make a strict secret of all that was going on in the factories and among the workers. And of a sudden, all the devices of the police burst like soap bubbles, and the government itself was compelled to speak out openly of the fact that the workers were engaged in a struggle against the factory owners. What caused this change? In 1895 workers' strikes were particularly numerous. Yes, that is quite true, but strikes also took place previous to this, yet the government succeeded in preventing the secret becoming known, and the mass of the workers as a whole were kept in the dark about the strikes. The present strikes are much bigger than the previous ones and are concentrated in one area. Yes, that is quite true, but strikes as big as these also took place previously, in 1885-86, for example, in Moscow and Vladimir gubernias. Yet the government held out and refused to say a word about the workers' struggle against the employers. What, then, has made it talk this time? The fact is that this time the socialists have assisted the workers, have helped them to explain their case, to spread the news about it everywhere, both among the workers and among the public, to formulate the workers' demands exactly, to show everybody how dishonest the government is, and what brute violence it employs. When the government saw that it was becoming quite ridiculous to keep silent, since the strikes were common knowledge, it also fell into line behind the rest. The socialist leaflets called the government to account, and the government appeared and gave its account.

Let us see what sort of an account it was.

At first the government tried to avoid doing so openly and publicly. One of the ministers, Minister of Finance Witte, sent out a circular to the factory inspectors, in which he called the workers and the socialists "the worst enemies of public order," advised the factory inspectors to try to scare the workers, to assure them that the government would forbid the employers to make concessions, to tell them of the employers' good motives and noble intentions, of how concerned the employers are about the workers and their needs, and of how full the employers are of "good sentiments." Of the strikes themselves the government said nothing, it said not one word about the cause of the strikes, about the facts of abominable oppression and violation of the law by the employers, and about the aims of the workers; in a word, it simply *misrepresented* all the strikes that took place in the summer and autumn of 1895, tried to get away with hackneyed stock phrases about violent and "illegal" actions by the workers, although the workers committed no violence. It was only the police who resorted to violence. The minister wanted to keep the circular a secret, but the very officials to whom he entrusted it failed to keep the secret, and so the circular made the rounds of the public. Then it was printed by the socialists. Whereupon the government, seeing that as usual it had been made a fool of with its "open secrets," had it published in the press. That, as we have already stated, was the government's answer to the summer and autumn strikes of 1895. In the spring of 1896, however, strikes broke out again, on a much bigger scale.[41] The rumours about them were supplemented by socialist leaflets. At first the government maintained a cowardly silence, waiting to see how the matter would end, and then, when the workers' revolt had died down, it belatedly made public its bureaucratic wisdom, as it would a delayed police protocol. On this occasion it had to speak out openly, and what is more, to do so collectively. Its announcement appeared in issue No. 158 of *Pravitelstvenny Vestnik*.[42] On this occasion it could not misrepresent the workers' strikes as previously. It had to tell the full story, to give the facts of the employers' oppressive measures and make known the workers' demands; it had to admit that the workers had behaved "decently." Thus the workers taught the government to give up lying in the vile manner of the police; when they rose up en masse, when they employed leaflets to make their case public, they compelled it to admit the truth. That was a great success. The workers will now know what is their only means of getting a public statement of their needs, of letting the workers throughout Russia know of their struggle. The workers will know now that the government's lies are only refuted by the united struggle of the workers themselves to secure their rights and by their class-consciousness. When the ministers had spoken about the events they started inventing excuses, they proceeded to assert in their statement that the strikes were only caused by "the peculiarities of cotton-spinning and thread production." Indeed! And not by the peculiarities of the whole of Russian *production*, not by the peculiarities of the Russian political system, which permits the police to hound and to seize peaceful workers who are defending themselves against oppression? Why, then, good ministers, did the workers snatch up, read and ask for more leaflets which did not deal with cotton and threads at all, but with the rightless position of Russian citizens and the arbitrary and brutal conduct of a government which fawns on the capitalists. No, this new excuse is perhaps worse, viler than the one with which Finance Minister Witte tried to settle matters in his circular by placing all the blame on "agitators." Minister Witte argues about the strike just like any police official who has had his palm greased by the factory owners: agitators came, runs the explanation, and a strike broke out. Now, when all the ministers saw a strike of 30,000 workers, they began to think, and finally came to the conclusion that strikes do not break out because socialist agitators come on the scene, but that socialist agitators come on the scene because strikes break out, because the workers' struggle breaks out against the capitalists. The ministers now assert that the socialists subsequently "joined" the strikes. That is a good lesson for Finance Minister Witte. Be careful, Mr. Witte, learn the lesson well! Learn to get clear in advance about the cause of the strike, learn to examine the workers' demands and not the reports of your police rats, whom you yourself have not a bit of faith in. The ministers tell the public that it was only "ill-intentioned persons" who tried to give the strikes a "criminally political character," or as they say in one passage, a "social character" (the ministers wanted to say a socialist character, but, whether from ignorance or from bureaucratic cowardice, said social, the result being an absurdity: socialist means that which supports the workers in the struggle against capital, whereas social simply means public. How can a strike be given a social character? Why, it's just the same as giving ministers ministerial rank!). That is amusing! The socialists give strikes a political character! Why, before any socialists did, the government itself took all possible measures to give the strikes a political character. Did it not set about seizing peaceful workers, just as though they were criminals? Did it not arrest and deport them? Did it not send spies and provocateurs all over? Did it not arrest all who fell into its hands? Did it not promise to help the factory owners in order that they might not yield? Did it not persecute workers for simply collecting money in aid of the strikers? The government itself was ahead of everybody else in explaining to the workers that the war they were waging against the factory owners must inevitably be a war against the government. All that the socialists had to do was to confirm this and publish it in leaflet form. That is all. The Russian Government, however, had already had an extensive experience in the art of dissembling, and the ministers tried to keep silent about the methods by which our government "gave the strikes a political character"; it told the public the dates of the socialists' leaflets. But why did it not tell the dates of the orders issued by the City Governor and other bashi-bazouks for the arrest of peaceful workers, putting the troops under arms, the dispatch of spies and provocateurs? They gave details to the public about the number of leaflets issued by the socialists; why did they give no details about the number of workers and socialists seized, about the number of ruined families, the number deported or imprisoned without trial? Why? Because even the Russian ministers, devoid as they are of all shame, are wary of telling the public about such bandit exploits. Peaceful workers who stood up for their rights and defended themselves against the factory owners' tyranny had the entire strength of the state power, with police and troops, gendarmes and public prosecutors, hurled against them; workers who held out on their own coppers and those of their comrades, the British, Polish, German and Austrian workers—had aimed against them the entire strength of the state treasury, which promised assistance to the poor factory owners.

The workers were not united. They were unable to arrange collections, to enlist the help of other cities and other workers, they were hounded everywhere, they had to yield to the entire strength of state authority. The ministerial gentlemen are rejoicing that the government has achieved victory.

A fine victory! The entire strength of the government, the entire wealth of the capitalists—against thirty thousand peaceful, penniless workers! The ministers would be wiser if they waited before boasting of such a victory; their boasting really reminds one very much of that of the policeman, who brags about having got away from the strike *un*hurt.

The "incitements" of the socialists were ineffective, triumphantly declares the government to soothe the capitalists. Why, is our reply to this, no incitements could have created one-hundredth part of the impression created on all St. Petersburg, all Russian workers by the government's conduct in this affair! The workers saw through the government's policy of keeping silent about the workers' strikes and of misrepresenting them. The workers saw how their united struggle forced the abandonment of hypocritical police lies. They saw whose interests were safeguarded by the government, which promised assistance to the factory owners. They understood who was their real foe when they, who were not violating law and order, had the troops and police sent against them, just as though they were the country's enemies. However much ministers may talk of the struggle being a failure, the workers see how the factory owners everywhere have quietened down, and know that the government is already calling the factory inspectors together to discuss what concessions should be made to the workers, for it sees that concessions are necessary. The strikes of 1895-96 have not been in vain. They have been of tremendous service to the Russian workers, they have shown them how to wage the struggle for their interests. They have taught them to understand *the political situation and the political needs of the working class.*

November 1896.

> *The League of Struggle for the Emancipation of the Working Class.*[43]

Written in prison in autumn 1896
Mimeographed in November 1896

Published according
to the text of the leaflet

A CHARACTERISATION
OF ECONOMIC ROMANTICISM
(SISMONDI AND OUR NATIVE SISMONDISTS)[44]

Written in spring 1897

First published in the magazine *Novoye Slovo*,[45] issues 7-10, April-July 1897. Signed: K. T—n

Reprinted in the miscellany *Economic Studies and Essays* by Vladimir Ilyin, 1898

Published according to the text of the miscellany *Economic Studies and Essays*, checked with the text in *Novoye Slovo* and that in the miscellany *The Agrarian Question* by VI. Ilyin, 1908

The cover of *Novoye Slovo* in which Lenin's *Characterisation of Economic Romanticism* and *About a Certain Newspaper Article* were printed. 1897

Reduced

The Swiss economist Sismondi (J.-C.-L. Simonde de Sismondi), who wrote at the beginning of the present century, is of particular interest in considering a solution of the general economic problems which are now coming to the forefront with particular force in Russia. If we add to this. that Sismondi occupies a special place in the history of political economy, in that he stands apart from the main trends, being an ardent advocate of small-scale production and an opponent of the supporters and ideologists of large-scale enterprise (just like the present-day Russian Narodniks), the reader will understand our desire to outline the main features of Sismondi's doctrine and its relation to other trends—both contemporary and subsequent—in economic science. A study of Sismondi is today all the more interesting because last year (1896) an article in *Russkoye Bogatstvo* also expounded his doctrine (B. Ephrucy: "The Social and Economic Views of Simonde de Sismondi." *Russkoye Bogatstvo*, 1896, Nos. 7 and 8).*

The contributor to *Russkoye Bogatstvo* states at the very outset that no writer has been "so wrongly appraised" as Sismondi, who, he alleges, has been "unjustly" represented, now as a reactionary, then as a utopian. The very opposite is true. Precisely *this* appraisal of Sismondi is quite correct. The article in *Russkoye Bogatstvo*, while it gives an accurate and detailed account of Sismondi's views, pro-

---

* Ephrucy died in 1897. An obituary was published in *Russkoye Bogatstvo*, March 1897.

vides a completely. incorrect picture of his theory,* idealises the very points of it in which he comes closest to the
Narodniks, and ignores and misrepresents his attitude to
subsequent trends in economic science. Hence, our exposition
and analysis of Sismondi's doctrine will at the same time
be a criticism of Ephrucy's article.

CHAPTER I

THE ECONOMIC THEORIES OF ROMANTICISM

The distinguishing feature of Sismondi's theory is his
doctrine of revenue, of the relation of revenue to production
and to the population. The title of Sismondi's chief work is:
*Nouveaux principes d'économie politique ou de la richesse dans
ses rapports avec la population* (Seconde édition. Paris,
1827, 2 vol. The first edition was published in 1819)—
*New Principles of Political Economy, or Wealth in Rela-
tion to Population.* This subject is almost identical with
the problem known in Russian Narodnik literature as the
"problem of the home market for capitalism." Sismondi
asserted that as a result of the development of large-scale
enterprise and wage-labour in industry and agriculture,
production inevitably outruns consumption and is faced
with the insoluble task of finding consumers; that it cannot
find consumers within the country because it converts
the bulk of the population into day labourers, plain workers,
and creates unemployment, while the search for a foreign
market becomes increasingly difficult owing to the entry
of new capitalist countries into the world arena. The reader
will see that these are the very same problems that occupy
the minds of the Narodnik economists headed by Messrs.
V.V. and N. —on.[46] Let us, then, take a closer look at
the various points of Sismondi's argument and at its scientific significance.

---

* It is quite true that Sismondi was not a socialist, as Ephrucy
states at the beginning of his article, repeating what was said by
Lippert (see *Handwörterbuch der Staatswissenschaften*, V. Band, Arti-
kel "Sismondi" von Lippert, Seite 678) (*Dictionary of Political Science*,
Vol. V, article by Lippert entitled "Sismondi," p. 678.—*Ed.*).

I
DOES THE HOME MARKET SHRINK
BECAUSE OF THE RUINATION OF THE SMALL PRODUCERS?

Unlike the classical economists, who in their arguments had in mind the already established capitalist system and took the existence of the working class as a matter of course and self-evident, Sismondi particularly emphasises the ruination of the small producer—the process which led to the formation of the working class. That Sismondi deserves credit for pointing to this contradiction in the capitalist system is beyond dispute; but the point is that as an economist he failed *to understand* this phenomenon and covered up his inability to make a consistent analysis of it with "pious wishes." In Sismondi's opinion, the ruination of the small producer proves that the home market shrinks.

"If the manufacturer sells at a cheaper price," says Sismondi in the chapter on "How Does the Seller Enlarge His Market?" (ch. III, livre IV, t. I, p. 342 et suiv.),* "he will sell more, because the others will sell less. Hence, the manufacturer always strives to save something on labour, or on raw materials, so as to be able to sell at a lower price than his fellow manufacturers. As the materials themselves are products of past labour, his saving, in the long run, always amounts to the expenditure of a smaller quantity of labour in the production of the same product." "True, the individual manufacturer tries to expand production and not to reduce the number of his workers. Let us assume that he succeeds, that he wins customers away from his competitors by reducing the price of his commodity. What will be the 'national result' of this?... The other manufacturers will introduce the same methods of production as he employs. Then some of them will, of course, have to discharge some of their workers to the extent that the new machine increases the productive power of labour. If consumption remains at the same level, and if the same amount of labour is performed by one-tenth of the former number of hands, then the income of this section

---

* All subsequent quotations, unless otherwise stated, are taken from the above-mentioned edition of *Nouveaux Principes*.

of the working class will be curtailed by nine-tenths, and all forms of its consumption will be reduced to the same extent.... The result of the invention—if the nation has no foreign trade, and if consumption remains at the same level— will consequently be a loss for all, a decline in the national revenue, which will lead to a decline in general consumption in the following year" (I, 344). "Nor can it be otherwise: labour itself is an important part of the revenue" (Sismondi has wages in mind), "and therefore the demand for labour cannot be reduced without making the nation poorer. Hence, the expected gain from the invention of new methods of production is nearly always obtained from foreign trade" (I, 345).

The reader will see that in these words he already has before him all that so-familiar "theory" of "the shrinkage of the home market" as a consequence of the development of capitalism, and of the consequent need for a foreign market. Sismondi very frequently reverts to this idea, linking it with his theory of crises and his population "theory"; it is as much the key point of his doctrine as it is of the doctrine of the Russian Narodniks.

Sismondi did not, of course, forget that under the new relationships, ruination and unemployment are accompanied by an increase in "commercial wealth," that the point at issue was the development of large-scale production, of capitalism. This he understood perfectly well and, in fact, asserted that it was the growth of capitalism that caused the home market to shrink: "Just as it is not a matter of indifference from the standpoint of the citizens' welfare whether the sufficiency and consumption of all tend to be equal, or whether a small minority has a superabundance of all things, while the masses are reduced to bare necessities, so these two forms of the distribution of revenue are not a matter of indifference from the viewpoint of the development of *commercial wealth* (richesse commerciale).* Equality in consumption must always lead to the expansion of the producers' market, and inequality, to the *shrinking of the market*" (de le [le marché] resserrer toujours davantage) (I, 357).

---

* Italics here and elsewhere are ours, unless otherwise stated.

Thus, Sismondi asserts that the home market shrinks owing to the inequality of distribution inherent in capitalism, that the market must be created by equal distribution. But how can this take place when there is *commercial wealth*, to which Sismondi imperceptibly passed (and he could not do otherwise, for if he had done he could not have argued about the *market*)? This is something he does not investigate. How does he prove that it is possible to preserve equality among the producers if commercial wealth exists, *i.e.*, competition between the individual producers? He does not prove it at all. He simply decrees that that is what *must occur*. Instead of further analysing the contradiction he rightly pointed to, he begins to talk about the undesirability of contradictions in general. "It is possible that when small-scale agriculture is superseded by large-scale and more capital is invested in the land a larger amount of wealth is distributed among the entire mass of agriculturists than previously" ... (i.e., "it is possible" that the home market, the dimension of which is determined after all by the absolute quantity of *commercial* wealth, has expanded—expanded along with the development of capitalism?).... "But for the nation, the consumption of one family of rich farmers plus that of fifty families of poor day labourers is not equal to the consumption of fifty families of peasants, not one of which is rich but, on the other hand, not one of which lacks (a moderate) a decent degree of prosperity" (une honnête aisance) (I, 358). In other words: perhaps the development of capitalist farming does create a home market for capitalism. Sismondi was a far too knowledgeable and conscientious economist to deny this fact; but—but here the author drops his investigation, and for the "nation" of commercial wealth directly substitutes a "nation" of peasants. Evading the unpleasant fact that refutes his petty-bourgeois point of view, he even forgets what he himself had said a little earlier, namely, that the "peasants" became "farmers" thanks to the development of commercial wealth. "The first farmers," he said, "were simple labourers.... They did not cease to be peasants.... They hardly ever employed day labourers to work with them, they employed only servants (des domestiques), always chosen from among their equals, whom they treated as equals, ate with them at the same table ... constituted one class of peasants" (I, 221). So then, it all amounts to this, that these patriarchal muzhiks, with their patriarchal servants, are much more to the author's liking, and he simply turns his back on the changes which the growth of "commercial wealth" brought about in these patriarchal relationships.

But Sismondi does not in the least intend to admit this. He continues to think that he is investigating the laws of commercial wealth and, forgetting the reservations he has made, bluntly asserts:

"Thus, as a result of wealth being concentrated in the hands of a small number of proprietors, *the home market shrinks increasingly* (!), and industry is increasingly compelled to look for foreign markets, where great revolutions (des grandes révolutions) await it" (I, 361). "Thus, the home market cannot expand except through national prosperity" (I, 362). Sismondi has in mind the prosperity of the people, for he had only just admitted the possibility of "national" prosperity under capitalist farming.

As the reader sees, our Narodnik economists say the same thing word for word.

Sismondi reverts to this question again at the end of his work, in Book VII *On the Population*, chapter VII: "On the Population Which Has Become Superfluous Owing to the Invention of Machines."

"The introduction of large-scale farming in the countryside has in Great Britain led to the disappearance of the class of peasant farmers (fermiers paysans), who worked themselves and nevertheless enjoyed a moderate prosperity; the population declined considerably, but its consumption declined more than its numbers. The day labourers who do all the field work, receiving only bare necessities, do not by any means give the same encouragement to urban industry as the rich peasants gave previously" (II, 327). "Similar changes also took place among the urban population.... The small tradesmen, the small manufacturers disappear, and one big entrepreneur replaces hundreds of them who, taken all together, were perhaps not as rich as he. Nevertheless, taken together they were bigger consumers than he. The luxury he indulges in encourages industry far less than the moderate prosperity of the hundred households he has superseded" (ibid.).

The question is: what does Sismondi's theory that the home market shrinks with the development of capitalism amount to? To the fact that its author, who had hardly attempted to look at the matter squarely, avoided analysing the conditions that belong to capitalism ("commercial wealth" plus large-scale enterprise in industry and agriculture, for Sismondi does not know the word "capitalism." Identity of concepts makes this use of the term quite correct, and in future we shall simply say "capitalism"), and replaced an analysis by his own petty-bourgeois point of view and his own petty-bourgeois utopia. The development of commercial wealth and, consequently, of competition, he says, should leave intact the average, uniform peasantry, with its "moderate prosperity" and its patriarchal relations with its farm servants.

It goes without saying that this innocent desire remained the exclusive possession of Sismondi and the other romanticists among the "intelligentsia"; and that day after day it came into increasing conflict with the reality that was developing the contradictions of which Sismondi was not yet able to gauge the depth.

It goes without saying that theoretical political economy, which in its further development* joined that of the classical economists, established precisely what Sismondi wanted to deny—that the development of capitalism in general, and of capitalist farming in particular, does not restrict the home market, but *creates* it. The development of capitalism proceeds simultaneously with the development of commodity economy, and to the extent that domestic production gives way to production for sale, while the handicraftsman is superseded by the factory, a market is created for *capital*. The "day labourers" who are pushed out of agriculture by the conversion of the "peasants" into "farmers" provide labour-power for capital, and the farmers are purchasers of the products of industry, not only of articles of consumption (which were formerly produced by the peas-

---

* This refers to Marxism. (Author's footnote to the 1908 edition.—*Ed.*)

ants at home, or by village artisans), but also of instruments
of production, which could not remain of the old type after
small farming had been superseded by large-scale farming.*
The last point is worth emphasising, for it is the one that
Sismondi particularly ignored when, in the passage we have
quoted, he talked about "consumption" by peasants and
farmers as if only *personal* consumption (the consumption
of bread, clothing, etc.) existed and as if the purchase
of machines, implements, etc., the erection of buildings,
warehouses, factories, etc., were not also consumption, except
that it is of a different kind, i.e., *productive consumption*,
consumption by capital and not by people. And again we must
note that it is precisely this mistake, which, as we shall
soon see, Sismondi borrowed from Adam Smith, that our
Narodnik economists took over in toto.**

II

SISMONDI'S VIEWS ON NATIONAL REVENUE AND CAPITAL

The arguments adduced by Sismondi to prove that capitalism is impossible and that it cannot develop are not
confined to this. He also drew the same conclusions from
his revenue theory. It must be said that Sismondi took
over in its entirety Adam Smith's labour theory of value
and three forms of revenue: rent, profit and wages. Here
and there he even attempts to group together the first
two forms of revenue and contrast them to the third: thus,
he sometimes combines them and opposes them to wages (I,
104-05); sometimes he even uses the term mieux-value
(surplus-value) to describe them (I, 103). We must not,
however, exaggerate the importance of this terminology as,
we think, Ephrucy does when he says that "Sismondi's theory

---

* Thus, simultaneously the elements of both variable capital
(the "free" worker) and constant capital are formed; the means of
production from which the small producer is freed pertain to the
latter.
** Ephrucy says nothing at all concerning this part of Sismondi's
doctrine—the shrinking of the home market as a result of the development of capitalism. We shall see again and again that he left out what
is most typical of Sismondi's *viewpoint* and of the attitude of Narodism
towards his doctrine.

stands close to the theory of surplus-value" (*Russkoye Bogatstvo*, No. 8, p. 41). Properly speaking, Sismondi did not advance a single step beyond Adam Smith, who also said that rent and profit are "deductions from the produce of labour," the share of the value which the worker adds to the product (see *An Inquiry into the Nature and Causes of the Wealth of Nations*, Russian translation by Bibikov, Vol. I, chap. VIII: "Of the Wages of Labour," and chap. VI: "Of the Component Parts of the Price of Commodities"). Nor did Sismondi go further than this. But he tried to link up this division of the newly-created product into surplus-value and wages with the theory of the social revenue, the home market and the realisation of the product in capitalist society. These attempts are extremely important for an appraisal of Sismondi's scientific significance, and for an understanding of the connection between his doctrine and that of the Russian Narodniks. It is therefore worth while analysing them in greater detail.

In everywhere pushing into the forefront the question of revenue, of its relation to production, to consumption and to the population, Sismondi was also naturally obliged to analyse the theoretical basis of the concept "revenue." And so at the very beginning of his work we find three chapters devoted to the question of revenue (l. II, ch. IV-VI). Chapter IV, entitled "How Revenue Originates from Capital," deals with the difference between capital and revenue. Sismondi begins straight away to deal with this subject in relation to the whole of society. "Inasmuch as each works for all," he says, "what is produced by all must be consumed by all.... The difference between capital and revenue is material for society" (I, 83). But Sismondi has a feeling that this "material" difference is not as simple *for society* as it is for the individual entrepreneur. "We are approaching," he makes the reservation, "the most abstract and most difficult problem of political economy. The nature of capital and that of revenue are constantly interwoven in our minds: we see that *what is revenue for one becomes capital for another*, and the same object, in passing from hand to hand, successively acquires different names" (I, 84), i.e., is called "capital" at one moment and "revenue" at another. "But to confuse them," asserts

Sismondi, "is ruinous" (leur confusion est ruineuse, p. 477). "The task of distinguishing between the capital and revenue of society is as important as it is difficult" (I, 84).

The reader has probably noticed wherein lies the difficulty which Sismondi speaks of: if the revenue of the individual entrepreneur is his profit, which he spends on various kinds of articles of consumption,* and if the revenue of the individual worker is his wages, can these two forms of revenue be added together to form the "revenue of society"? What, then, about those capitalists and workers who produce machines, for example? Their product exists in a form that cannot be consumed (i.e., consumed personally). It cannot be added to articles of consumption. These products are meant to serve as capital. Hence, while being the *revenue* of their producers (that is, that part which is the source of profit and wages) they become the *capital* of their purchasers. How can we straighten out this confusion, which prevents us from defining the concept of social revenue?

As we have seen, Sismondi merely approached the question and at once shrank from it, limiting himself to stating the "difficulty." He says plainly that "usually, three kinds of revenue are recognised: rent, profit and wages" (I, 85), and then goes on to expound Adam Smith's doctrine concerning each. The question of the difference between the capital and the revenue of society remained unanswered. The exposition now proceeds without any strict division between social revenue and individual revenue. But Sismondi reverts once again to the question he abandoned. He says that, as there are different kinds of revenue, so there are "different kinds of wealth" (I, 93), namely, *fixed capital*—machines, implements, etc., *circulating capital*—which, unlike the former, is consumed quickly and changes its form (seed, raw materials, wages) and, lastly, *revenue from capital*, which is consumed without being reproduced. Here it is not important to us that Sismondi repeats all the mistakes Adam Smith made in the theory of fixed and circulating capital, that he confuses these categories, which

---

* To be more exact: that *part* of profit which is not used for accumulation.

belong to the process of circulation, with the categories which spring from the process of production (constant and variable capital). What interests us is Sismondi's theory of revenue. And on this question, he draws the following conclusion from the division of wealth into three kinds that has just been made.

"It is important to note that these three kinds of wealth go similarly into consumption; for everything that has been produced is of value to man only insofar as it serves his needs, and these needs are satisfied only by consumption. But fixed capital serves this purpose indirectly (d'une manière indirecte); it is consumed slowly, helping man to reproduce what serves for his consumption" (I, 94-95), whereas circulating capital (Sismondi already identifies it with variable capital) is converted into the "worker's consumption fund" (I, 95). It follows, therefore, that, as distinct from individual consumption, there are two kinds of social consumption. These two kinds differ very greatly. What matters, of course, is not that fixed capital is consumed slowly, but that it is consumed without forming revenue (a consumption fund) for any class of society, that it is not used personally, but productively. But Sismondi fails to see this, and realising that he has again strayed from the path* in quest of the difference between social capital and revenue, he helplessly exclaims: "This movement of wealth is so abstract, it requires such considerable attention to grasp it fully (pour le bien saisir), that we deem it useful to take the simplest example" (I, 95). And indeed, he does take the "simplest" example: a single farmer (un fermier solitaire) harvested a hundred sacks of wheat; part of the wheat he consumed himself, part went for sowing, and part was consumed by the workers he hired. Next year he harvested two hundred sacks. Who is to consume them? The farmer's family cannot grow so quickly. Using this extremely ill-chosen example to show the difference between

---

* Sismondi had only just separated *capital* from *revenue*. The first goes to production, the second to consumption. But we are talking about society, and society also "consumes" fixed capital. The distinction drawn falls to the ground, and the social-economic process which transforms "capital for one" into "revenue for another" remains unexplained.

fixed capital (seed), circulating capital (wages) and the farmer's consumption fund, Sismondi says:

"We have seen three kinds of wealth in an individual family; let us now examine each kind in relation to the whole nation and see how the national revenue can result from this distribution" (I, 97). But all he says after this is that in society, too, it is necessary to reproduce the same three kinds of wealth: fixed capital (and Sismondi emphasises that a certain amount of labour has to be expended on it, but he does not explain how fixed capital will exchange for the articles of consumption required by both the capitalists and the workers engaged in this production); then come raw materials (Sismondi isolates these especially); then the workers' maintenance and the capitalists' profit. This is all we get from chapter IV. Obviously, the question of the national revenue remained open, and Sismondi failed to analyse, not only distribution, but even the *concept* of revenue. He immediately forgets the theoretically extremely important reference to the need to reproduce also the fixed capital of society; and in his next chapter, in speaking of the "distribution of the national revenue among the different classes of citizens" (ch. V), he goes straight on to speak of three kinds of revenue and, combining rent and profit, he says that the national revenue consists of two parts: profit from wealth (i.e., rent and profit in the proper sense) and the workers' means of subsistence (I, 104-05). He says, moreover, that:

"Similarly, the annual product, or the result of all the work done by the nation during the year, consists of two parts: one is ... the profit that comes from wealth; the other is the capacity to work (la puissance de travailler) which is assumed to equal the part of wealth for which it is exchanged, or the means of subsistence of those who work.... Thus, the national revenue and the annual product balance each other and represent equal magnitudes. The entire annual product is consumed in the course of the year, but partly by the workers, who, giving their labour in exchange, turn the product into capital and reproduce it, and partly by the capitalists, who, giving their revenue in exchange, destroy it" (I, 105).

Thus, Sismondi simply thrusts aside the question of distinguishing between national capital and revenue, which he himself so definitely considered to be extremely important and difficult, and forgets entirely what he had said a few pages previously! And then he does not see that by thrusting this question aside, he reduced the problem to utter absurdity: how can the annual product be totally consumed by the workers and capitalists in the shape of revenue, if production needs capital, or, to be more exact, means and instruments of production? They have to be produced, and they are produced every year (as Sismondi himself has only just admitted). And now all these instruments of production, raw materials, etc., are suddenly discarded and the "difficult" problem of the difference between capital and revenue is settled by the absolutely incongruous assertion that the annual product equals the national revenue.

This theory, that the entire product of capitalist society consists of two parts—the workers' part (wages, or variable capital, to use modern terminology) and the capitalists' part (surplus-value), is not peculiar to Sismondi. It does not belong to him. He borrowed it in its entirety from Adam Smith, and even took a step backward from it. The whole of subsequent political economy (Ricardo, Mill, Proudhon and Rodbertus) repeated this mistake, which was disclosed only by the author of *Capital*, in Part III of Volume II. We shall expound the principles underlying his views later on. At present let us observe that this mistake is repeated by our Narodnik economists. It is of special interest to compare them with Sismondi, because they draw from this fallacious theory *the very same conclusions that Sismondi himself drew**: the conclusion that surplus-value cannot be realised in capitalist society; that social wealth cannot be expanded; that the foreign market must be resorted to *because* surplus-value cannot be realised within the country; and lastly, that crises occur because the product, it is alleged, cannot be realised through consumption by the workers and the capitalists.

---

* And which were prudently avoided by the other economists who repeated Adam Smith's mistake.

III

SISMONDI'S CONCLUSIONS FROM THE FALLACIOUS THEORY OF TWO PARTS OF THE ANNUAL PRODUCT IN CAPITALIST SOCIETY

To give the reader an idea of Sismondi's doctrine as a whole, we shall first state the most important conclusions which he draws from this theory, and then deal with the manner in which his chief error is rectified in Marx's *Capital*.

First of all, Sismondi draws from Adam Smith's fallacious theory the conclusion that production must correspond to consumption, that production is determined by revenue. He goes on reiterating this "truth" (which proves his complete inability to understand the nature of capitalist production) throughout the whole of his next chapter, chapter VI: "The Mutual Determination of Production by Consumption, and Expenditure by Revenue." Sismondi directly applies the ethics of the frugal peasant to capitalist society, and sincerely believes that in this way he has corrected Adam Smith's doctrine. At the very beginning of his work, when speaking about Adam Smith in the introductory part (Book I, *History of Science*), he says that he "supplements" Smith with the proposition that "consumption is the sole aim of accumulation" (I, 51). "Consumption," he says, "determines reproduction" (I, 119-20), "the national expenditure must regulate the national revenue" (I, 113), and the whole of the work is replete with similar assertions. Two more characteristic features of Sismondi's doctrine are directly connected with this: firstly, disbelief in the development of capitalism, failure to understand that it causes an ever-increasing growth of the productive forces and denial that such growth is possible—in exactly the same way as the Russian romanticists "teach" that capitalism leads to a waste of labour, and so forth.

"Those who urge unlimited production are mistaken," says Sismondi (I, 121). Excess of production over revenue causes over-production (I, 106). An increase in wealth is beneficial only "when it is gradual, when it is proportionate to itself, when none of its parts develops with excessive rapidity" (I, 409). The good Sismondi thinks that "disproportionate" development is not development (as our Narodniks also do); that this disproportion is not a law of the present system of social economy, and of its development, but a "mistake" of the legislator, etc.; that in this the European governments are artificially imitating England, a country that has taken the wrong path.* Sismondi wholly denies the proposition which the classical economists advanced, and which Marx's theory wholly accepted, namely, that capitalism develops the productive forces. In fact, he goes to the length of regarding all accumulation as being possible only "little by little," and is quite unable to explain the process of accumulation. This is the second highly characteristic feature of his views. The way he argues about accumulation is extremely amusing:

"In the long run, the total product of a given year always exchanges only for the total product of the preceding year" (I, 121). Here accumulation is wholly denied: it follows that the growth of social wealth is impossible under capitalism. The Russian reader will not be very much surprised by this assertion, because he has heard the same thing from Mr. V. V. and from Mr. N. —on. But Sismondi, was, after all, a disciple of Adam Smith. He has a feeling that he is saying something utterly incongruous, and he wants to correct himself:

"If production grows gradually," he continues, "then annual exchange causes only a slight loss (une petite perte) each year, while at the same time improving the conditions for the future (en même temps qu'elle bonifie la condition future). If this loss is slight and well distributed, everybody will bear it without complaint.... If, however, the discrepancy between the new production and the preceding one is great, capital perishes (sont entamés), suffering is caused, and the nation retrogresses instead of progressing" (I, 121). It would be difficult to formulate the fundamental thesis of romanticism and of the petty-bourgeois view of capitalism more vividly and more plainly than is done in

---

* See for example, II, 456-57, and many other passages. Later we shall quote specimens of them, and the reader will see that even in their mode of expression our romanticists, like Mr. N. —on, differ in no way from Sismondi.

the above tirade. The more rapid the process of accumulation, *i.e.*, the excess of production over consumption, the better, taught the classical economists, who, though they were not clear about the process of the social production of capital, and though they were unable to free themselves from Adam Smith's mistaken view that the social product consists of two parts, nevertheless advanced the perfectly correct idea that production creates a market for itself and itself determines consumption. And we know also that Marx's theory, which recognised that the more rapid the growth of wealth, the fuller the development of the productive forces of labour and its socialisation, and *the better the position of the worker*, or as much better as it can be under the present system of social economy, took over this view of accumulation from the classical economists. The romanticists assert the very opposite, and base all their hopes on the feeble development of capitalism; they call for its *retardation*.

Further, the failure to understand that production creates a market for itself leads to the doctrine that surplus-value cannot be realised. "From reproduction comes revenue, but *production in itself is not yet revenue*: it acquires this name" (ce nom! Thus the difference between production, i.e., the product, and revenue lies only in the word!) "and functions as such (elle n'opère comme telle) only after it is realised, after each article produced finds a consumer who has the need or the desire for it" (qui en avait le besoin ou le désir) (I, 121). Thus, the identification of revenue with "production" (i.e., with all that is produced) leads to the identification of realisation with *personal* consumption. Sismondi has already forgotten that the realisation of such products as, for example, iron, coal, machines, etc., the realisation of means of production in general, takes place in a different way, although he had been very close to this idea earlier. The identification of realisation with *personal* consumption naturally leads to the doctrine that it is *surplus-value* that the capitalists cannot realise, because, of the two parts of the social product, wages are realised through workers' consumption. And indeed, Sismondi reached this conclusion (subsequently amplified in greater detail by Proudhon and constantly repeated by our

Narodniks). In controversy with MacCulloch, Sismondi makes the allegation that the latter (in expounding Ricardo's views) does not explain the realisation of profit. MacCulloch had said that, with the division of social labour, one branch of production provides a market for another: the producers of bread realise their commodities in the product of the producers of clothing and vice versa.* "The author," says Sismondi, "presupposes labour without profit (un travail sans bénéfice), reproduction which only replaces the *workers'* consumption" (II, 384, Sismondi's italics) ... "he leaves nothing for the master ... we are investigating what becomes of the excess of the workers' production over their consumption" (ibid.). Thus, we find that this first romanticist already makes the very definite statement that the capitalists cannot realise *surplus-value*. From this proposition Sismondi draws the further conclusion—again the very same as that drawn by the Narodniks—that *the very conditions of realisation* make it necessary *for capitalism to have a foreign market*. "As labour itself is an important component of revenue, the demand for labour cannot be reduced without making the nation poorer. Hence, the expected gain from the invention of new methods of production nearly always relates to *foreign trade*" (I, 345). "The nation which is the first to make some discovery is able, for a considerable time, to expand its market in proportion to the number of hands that are released by each new invention. It employs them forthwith to produce that larger quantity of products which its invention enables it to produce more cheaply. But at last the time will come when the whole civilised world forms a single market, and it will no longer be possible to acquire new purchasers in any new nation. Demand in the world market will then be a constant (précise) quantity, for which the different

---

* See supplement to *Nouveaux Principes*, 2nd ed., Vol. II: "Eclaircissements relatifs à la balance des consommations avec les productions" ("Explanations Relative to the Balance of Consumption and Production."—*Ed.*), where Sismondi translates and disputes the essay by Ricardo's disciple (MacCulloch) published in the *Edinburgh Review* entitled "An Inquiry into the Question as to Whether the Power to Consume Always Grows in Society Simultaneously with the Power to Produce."[47]

industrial nations will compete against each other. If one nation supplies a larger quantity of products, it will do so to the detriment of another. The total sales cannot be increased except by an increase in general prosperity, or by the transfer of commodities, formerly the exclusive possession of the rich, to the sphere of consumption by the poor" (II, 316). The reader will see that Sismondi presents the very doctrine that our romanticists have learned so well, namely, that the foreign market provides *the way out of the difficulty* of realising the product in general, and surplus-value in particular.

Lastly, this same doctrine that national revenue and national production are identical led to Sismondi's theory of crises. After what has been said above, we need scarcely quote from the numerous passages in Sismondi's work which deal with this subject. His theory that production must conform to revenue naturally led to the view that crises are the result of the disturbance of this balance, the result of an excess of production over consumption. It is evident from the passage just quoted that it is this discrepancy between production and consumption that Sismondi regarded as the main cause of crises; and in the forefront he placed the underconsumption of the masses of the people, the workers. This explains why Sismondi's theory of crises (which Rodbertus also adopted) is known in economic science as an example of the theories which ascribe crises to underconsumption (Unterkonsumption)..

IV

WHEREIN LIES THE ERROR OF ADAM SMITH'S
AND SISMONDI'S THEORIES OF NATIONAL REVENUE?

What is the fundamental error that led Sismondi, to all these conclusions?

Sismondi took over his theory of national revenue and of its division into two parts (the workers' and the capitalists') bodily from Adam Smith. Far from adding anything to Adam Smith's theses, he even took a step backward and omitted Adam Smith's attempt (albeit unsuccessful) to substantiate this proposition theoretically. Sismondi appears not to notice how this theory contradicts that of production in general. Indeed, according to the theory which deduces value from labour, the value of a product consists of three components: the part which replaces the raw materials and instruments of labour (constant capital), the part which replaces wages, or the maintenance of the workers (variable capital), and "surplus-value" (Sismondi calls it mieux-value). Such is the analysis of the individual product in terms of value made by Adam Smith and repeated by Sismondi. The question is: how can the *social* product, which is the sum-total of *individual* products, consist only of the two latter parts? What has become of the first part—constant capital? As we have seen, Sismondi merely beat about the bush on this question, but Adam Smith gave an answer to it. He asserted that this part exists independently only in the individual product. If, however, we take the aggregate social product, this part, in its turn, resolves itself into wages and surplus-value— of precisely those capitalists who produce this constant capital.

But in giving this answer Adam Smith did not explain why, when resolving the value of constant capital, say of machines, he again leaves out the constant capital, i.e., in our example, the iron out of which the machines are made, or the instruments used up in the process, etc.? If the value of each product includes the part which replaces constant capital (and all economists agree that it does) then the exclusion of that part from any sphere of social production whatever is quite arbitrary. As the author of *Capital* pointed out, "when Adam Smith says that the instruments of labour resolve themselves into wages and profit, he forgets to add: *and into that constant capital* which is used up in their production. Adam Smith simply sends us from Pontius to Pilate, from one line of production to another, from another to a third,"[48] failing to notice that this shifting about does not alter the problem in the least. Smith's answer (accepted by all the subsequent political economists prior to Marx) is simply an evasion of the problem, avoidance of the difficulty. And there is indeed a difficulty here. It lies in that the concepts of capital and revenue cannot be directly transferred from the individual product to the social product. The economists admit this when they say that from the social point of view what is "capital for one becomes revenue for another" (see Sismondi, as quoted above). This phrase, however, *formulates* the difficulty but does not solve it.*

The solution is that when examining this question from the social point of view, we must no longer speak of products in general, irrespective of their material forms. Indeed, we are discussing the social revenue, i.e., the product which becomes available for consumption. But surely not all products can be consumed through *personal consumption*: machines, coal, iron, and similar articles are not consumed personally, but productively. From the individual entrepreneur's point of view this distinction was superfluous: when we said that the workers would consume variable capital, we assumed that on the market they would acquire articles of consumption with the money the capitalist had paid them, the money which he, the capitalist, had received for the machines made by the workers. Here the exchange of machines for bread does not interest us. But from the social point of view, this exchange cannot be *assumed*: we cannot say that the entire capitalist class which produces machines, iron, etc., sells these things, and in this way realises them. The whole question is *how* realisation takes place—*that is*, the replacement of all parts of the social product. Hence, the point of departure in discussing social capital and revenue—or, what is the same thing, the realisation of the product in capitalist society— must be the distinction between two entirely different types of social product: *means of production* and *articles of consumption*. The former can be consumed only productively, the latter only personally. The former can serve *only* as capital, the latter must become revenue, i.e., must be destroyed in consumption by the workers and capitalists. The former go entirely to the capitalists, the latter are shared between the workers and the capitalists.

---

* We give here only the *gist* of the new theory which provides this solution, leaving ourselves free to present it in greater detail elsewhere. See *Das Kapital*, II. Band, III. Abschnitt.[49] (For a more detailed exposition, see *The Development of Capitalism*, chap. I.)[50]

Once this difference is understood and we rectify the error made by Adam Smith, who left its constant part (i.e., the part which replaces constant capital) out of the social product, the question of the realisation of the product in capitalist society becomes clear. Obviously, we cannot speak of wages being realised through consumption by the workers, and surplus-value through consumption by the capitalists, and *nothing more*.* The workers can consume wages and capitalists surplus-value only when the product consists of articles of consumption, i.e., only in one department of social production. They cannot "consume" the product which consists of means of production: this *must be exchanged for articles of consumption*. But for which part (in terms of value) of the articles of consumption can they exchange their product? Obviously, only for the *constant part* (constant capital), since the other two parts constitute the consumption fund of the workers and capitalists who produce articles of consumption. By realising the surplus-value and wages in the industries which produce means of production, this exchange thereby realises the constant capital in the industries which produce articles of consumption. Indeed, for the capitalist who manufactures, say, sugar, that part of the product which is to replace constant capital (i.e., raw materials, auxiliary materials, machines, premises, etc.) exists in the shape of *sugar*. To realise this part, he must receive corresponding *means of production* in return for it. The realisation of this part will therefore consist in exchanging the *article of consumption* for products which serve as *means of production*. Now the realisation of only one part of the social product, namely, the constant capital in the

---

* That is just how our Narodnik economists Messrs. V.V. and N. —on reason. Above we deliberately dealt in great detail with Sismondi's wandering around the question of productive and personal consumption, of articles of consumption and means of production (Adam Smith came even closer to distinguishing between them than Sismondi did). We wanted to show the reader that the *classical* representatives of this fallacious theory *felt* that it was unsatisfactory, saw the contradiction in it, and made attempts to extricate themselves. But our "original" theoreticians not only see nothing and feel nothing, but know nothing about either the theory or the history of the question they prate about so zealously.

department which manufactures means of production, remains unexplained. This is partially realised by part of the
product going back again into production in its natural form
(for example, part of the coal produced by a mining firm
is used to produce more coal; the grain obtained by farmers
is used for seed, and so forth); and partly it is realised by
exchange between individual capitalists in the same department: for example, coal is needed for the production
of iron, and iron is needed for the production of coal. The
capitalists who produce these two products realise by mutual
exchange that part of their respective products which replaces their constant capital.

This analysis (which, we repeat, we have summarised
in the most condensed form for the reason given above)
solved the difficulty which all the economists felt when
they formulated it in the phrase: "capital for one becomes
revenue for another." This analysis revealed the utter fallacy
of reducing social production solely to personal consumption.

We can now proceed to examine the conclusions drawn
by Sismondi (and the other romanticists) from his
fallacious theory. But first let us quote the opinion of Sismondi expressed by the author of the above analysis, after
a most detailed and comprehensive examination of Adam
Smith's theory, to which Sismondi added absolutely nothing,
merely leaving out Adam Smith's attempt to justify his
contradiction:

"Sismondi, who occupies himself particularly with the
relation of capital to revenue, and in actual fact makes
the peculiar formulation of this relation the differentia
specifica of his *Nouveaux Principes*, did not say *one* scientific word" (author's italics), "did not contribute one iota
to the clarification of the problem" (*Das Kapital*, II, S. 385,
1-te Auflage).[51]

V

ACCUMULATION IN CAPITALIST SOCIETY

The first erroneous conclusion from the fallacious theory
relates to accumulation. Sismondi did not in the least
understand capitalist accumulation, and in his heated

controversy on this subject with Ricardo truth was really
on the side of the latter. Ricardo asserted that production
creates a market for itself, whereas Sismondi denied this,
and based his theory of crises on this denial. True, Ricardo was also unable to correct the above-mentioned fundamental mistake of Adam Smith, and, therefore, was unable to solve the problem of the relation between social
capital and revenue and of the realisation of the product
(nor did Ricardo set himself these problems); but he in-
stinctively characterised the quintessence of the bourgeois
mode of production by noting the absolutely indisputable
fact that accumulation is the excess of production over
revenue. From the viewpoint of the modern analysis that
is how matters stand. Production does indeed create a
market for itself: production needs means of production,
and they constitute a special department of social production, which occupies a certain section of the workers, and
produces a special product, realised partly within this
same department and partly by exchange with the other
department, which produces articles of consumption. Accumulation is indeed the excess of production over revenue
(articles of consumption). To expand production (to "accu-
mulate" in the categorical meaning of the term) it is first
of all necessary to produce means of production,* and for
this it is consequently necessary to expand that department
of social production which manufactures means of production, it is necessary *to draw into it* workers who immediately
present a demand for articles of consumption, too. Hence,
"consumption" develops *after* "accumulation," or *after* "production"; strange though it may seem, it cannot be otherwise in capitalist society. Hence, the rates of development
of these two departments of capitalist production do not
have to be proportionate, on the contrary, they must
inevitably be disproportionate. It is well known that the law
of development of capital is that constant capital grows faster

---

* We would remind the reader how Sismondi approached this;
he distinctly singled out these means of production for an individual
family and tried to do the same for society, too. Properly speaking,
it was Smith who "approached," and not Sismondi, who only related
what Smith had said.

than variable capital, that is to say, an ever larger share of newly-formed capital is turned into that department of the social economy which produces means of production. Hence, this department necessarily grows faster than the department which manufactures articles of consumption, i.e., what takes place is exactly that which Sismondi declared to be "impossible," "dangerous," etc. Hence, products for personal consumption occupy an ever-diminishing place in the total mass of capitalist output. And this fully corresponds to the historical "mission" of capitalism and to its specific social structure: the former is to develop the productive forces of society (production for production); the latter precludes their utilisation by the mass of the population.

We can now fully appraise Sismondi's view of accumulation. His assertion that *rapid* accumulation leads to disaster is absolutely wrong and is solely the result of his failure to understand accumulation, as are his repeated statements and demands that production must not outstrip consumption, because consumption determines production. Actually, the very opposite is the case, and Sismondi simply turns his back on reality in its specific, historically determined form and substitutes petty-bourgeois moralising for an analysis. Particularly amusing are Sismondi's attempts to clothe this moralising in a "scientific" formula. "Messrs. Say and Ricardo," he says in his preface to the second edition of *Nouveaux Principes*, "came to believe ... that consumption had no other limits than those of production, whereas actually it is limited by revenue.... They should have warned producers that they must count only on consumers who have a revenue" (I, XIII).* Nowadays, such naïveté only raises a smile. But are not the writings of our contemporary romanticists, like Messrs. V.V. and N. —on, replete with the same sort of thing? "Let the banking entrepreneurs ponder well" ... over whether they will find a market for their commodities (II, 101-02).

---

* As we know, on this question (as to whether production creates a market for itself) the modern theory fully agrees with the classical economists, who answered this question in the affirmative, *in opposition* to romanticism, which answered it in the negative. "*The real barrier* of capitalist production is *capital itself*" (*Das Kapital*, III, I, 231).[52]

"When it is assumed that the aim of society is to increase wealth, the aim is always sacrificed for the means" (II, 140). "If, instead of expecting an impetus from the demand created by labour" (i.e., an impetus to production from the workers' demand for products), "we expect it to come from preceding production, we shall be doing almost the same thing as we would do to a clock if, instead of turning back the wheel that carries the chain (la roue qui porte la chainette), we turn back another wheel—we would thereby break the whole machine and stop it" (II, 454). Sismondi says that. Let us now hear what Mr. Nikolai —on has to say. "We have overlooked the factors due to which this development" (i.e., the development of capitalism) "is taking place; we have also forgotten the aim of all production ... an extremely fatal blunder..." (N. —on, *Sketches on Our Post-Reform Social Economy*, 298). Both these authors talk about capitalism, about capitalist countries; both reveal their complete inability to understand the essence of capitalist accumulation. But would one believe that the latter is writing seventy years after the former?

An example which Sismondi quotes in chapter VIII: "The Results of the Struggle to Cheapen Production" (Book IV, *Of Commercial Wealth*) vividly demonstrates how failure to understand capitalist accumulation is linked up with the error of reducing all production to the production of articles of consumption.

Let us assume, says Sismondi, that the owner of a manufactory has a circulating capital of 100,000 francs, which brings him 15,000, of which 6,000 represent interest on capital and are paid to the capitalist, and 9,000 constitute the profit obtained by the manufacturer as the entrepreneur. Let us assume that he employs the labour of 100 workers, whose wages total 30,000 francs. Further, let there be an increase in capital, an expansion of production ("accumulation"). Instead of 100,000 francs the capital will be=200,000 francs invested in fixed capital and 200,000 francs in circulating capital, making a total of 400,000 francs; profit and interest=32,000 + 16,000 francs, for the rate of interest has dropped from 6% to 4%. The number of workers employed has doubled, but wages have dropped from 300 francs to 200 francs, hence, making a

total of 40,000 francs. Thus, production has grown fourfold.*
And Sismondi counts up the results: "revenue," or "consumption," in the first case amounted to 45,000 francs (30,000
wages + 6,000 interest + 9,000 profit); it is now 88,000 francs
(40,000 wages + 16,000 interest + 32,000 profit). "Production has increased fourfold," says Sismondi, "but consumption has not even doubled. *The consumption of the
workers who made the machines should not be counted. It
is covered by the 200,000 francs* which have been used for
this purpose; it is already included in the accounts of another
manufactory, where the facts will be the same" (I, 405-06).

Sismondi's calculation shows a diminution of revenue
with an increase in production. The fact is indisputable.
But Sismondi does not notice that the example he gives de-
feats his own theory of the realisation of the product in
capitalist society. Curious is his observation that the consumption of the workers who made machines "should not
be counted." Why not? Because, firstly, it is *covered* by
the 200,000 francs. Thus, capital is transferred to the department which manufactures *means of production*—this
Sismondi does not notice. Hence, the "home market," which
"shrinks," as Sismondi says, does not consist solely of
articles of consumption, but also of *means of production*.
These means of production constitute a special product
which is *not* "realised" by *personal consumption*; and the
more rapidly accumulation proceeds, the more intense, consequently, is the development of that department of capitalist production which manufactures products not for personal
but for productive consumption. Secondly, answers Sismondi,
it is the workers of the other manufactory, where the facts
will be the same (où les mêmes faits pourront se représent-

---

* "The first result of competition," says Sismondi, "is a reduction
in wages and at the same time an increase in the number of workers"
(I, 403). We shall not dwell here on Sismondi's wrong calculation:
he calculates, for example, that profit will be 8 per cent on fixed
capital and 8% on circulating capital, that the number of workers
rises in proportion to the increase of circulating capital (which he
cannot properly distinguish from variable capital), and that fixed
capital goes entirely into the price of the product. In the present
case all this is unimportant, because the conclusion arrived at is correct: a diminution in the share of variable capital in the total capital, as a necessary result of accumulation.

er). As you see, Sismondi repeats Adam Smith in sending the reader "from Pontius to Pilate." But this "other manufactory" also consumes *constant capital*, and its production also provides a market for that department of capitalist production which manufactures means of production! However much we shift the question from one capitalist to another, and then to a third—this department does not disappear, and the "home market" does not reduce itself just to articles of consumption. Therefore, when Sismondi says that "this calculation refutes ... one of the axioms that has been most insisted upon in political economy, namely, the freer competition, the more profitable the development of industry" (I, 407), he does not notice that "this calculation" also refutes what he himself says. It is an undisputed fact that by displacing workers the introduction of machines worsens their conditions; and it is indisputably to Sismondi's credit that he was one of the first to point to this. But this does not in the least prevent his theory of accumulation and of the home market from being absolutely incorrect. His own calculation clearly indicates the very phenomenon which Sismondi not only denied but even turned into an argument against capitalism, when he said that accumulation and production must correspond to consumption, otherwise a crisis will ensue. His calculation shows, precisely, that accumulation and production *outstrip* consumption, and that it cannot be otherwise, for accumulation takes place mainly through means of production which do not enter into "consumption." What seemed to Sismondi to be simply an error, a contradiction in Ricardo's doctrine—that accumulation is excess of production over revenue—actually corresponds in full to reality and expresses the contradiction inherent in capitalism. This excess is *necessary* for all accumulation, which opens a new market *for means of production without correspondingly expanding the market for articles of consumption, and even contracting this market.* Furthermore,

---

* From the above analysis it automatically follows that such a case is also possible, depending upon the proportion in which the new capital is divided up into a constant and a variable part, and the extent to which the diminution of the relative share of the variable capital affects the old industries.

in rejecting the theory of the advantages of free competition, Sismondi does not notice that, together with groundless optimism, he throws overboard the undoubted truth that free competition *develops the productive forces of society*, as is again evident from his own calculation. (Properly speaking, this is only another way of expressing the same fact that a special department of industry is created which manufactures means of production, and that this department develops with particular rapidity.) This development of the productive forces of society without a corresponding development of consumption is, of course, a contradiction, but the sort of contradiction that exists in reality, that springs from the very nature of capitalism, and that cannot be brushed aside by means of sentimental phrases.

But this is just how the romanticists try to brush it aside. And to give the reader no grounds for suspecting us of levelling unsupported charges against contemporary economists in connection with the mistakes of such an "obsolete" author as Sismondi, let us quote a little sample of the writings of that "modern" author Mr. N. —on. On page 242 of his *Sketches* he discusses the development of capitalism in the Russian flour-milling industry. Referring to the appearance of large steam flour-mills with improved implements of production (since the seventies about 100 million rubles have been spent on reconstructing the flour-mills) and with a more than twofold increase in the productivity of labour, the author describes this phenomenon as follows: "the flour-milling industry has not developed, it has merely become concentrated in large enterprises"; he then applies this description to *all* industries (p. 243) and draws the conclusion that "in all cases without exception, a mass of workers are displaced and find no employment" (243), and that "capitalist production has developed at the expense of the people's consumption" (241). We ask the reader: does this argument differ in any way from Sismondi's argument just quoted? This "modern" author registers two facts, those very facts which, as we have seen, were used by Sismondi, and brushes both these facts aside with exactly the same sentimental phrase. Firstly, the example he gives shows that capitalism develops through the means of production. This means that capitalism develops the productive forces of society. Secondly, his example shows that this development proceeds along the specific road of contradictions that is typical of capitalism: there is a development of production (an expenditure of 100 million rubles constitutes a home market for products realised by non-personal consumption) without a corresponding development of consumption (the people's food deteriorates), i.e., what we have is production for the sake of production. And Mr. N. —on thinks that this contradiction will vanish from life if he, with old Sismondi's naïveté, presents it merely as a contradiction in doctrine, merely as "a fatal blunder": "we have forgotten the aim of production"!! What can be more characteristic than the phrase: "has not developed, it has *merely* become concentrated"? Evidently, Mr. N. —on knows of a capitalism in which development *could proceed otherwise* than by *concentration*. What a pity he has not introduced us to this "original" capitalism, which was unknown to all the political economists who preceded him!

VI

THE FOREIGN MARKET AS THE "WAY OUT
OF THE DIFFICULTY" OF REALISING SURPLUS-VALUE

Sismondi's next error, which springs from his fallacious theory of social revenue and the product in capitalist society, is his doctrine that the product in general, and surplus-value in particular, cannot possibly be realised, and that consequently it is necessary to find a foreign market. As regards the realisation of the product in general, the foregoing analysis shows that the "impossibility" is due entirely to the mistaken exclusion of constant capital and means of production. Once this error is corrected, the "impossibility" vanishes. The same, however, must be said in particular about surplus-value: this analysis explains how it too is realised. There are no reasonable grounds whatever for separating surplus-value from the total product so far as its realisation is concerned. Sismondi's (and our Narodniks') assertion to the contrary is simply a misunderstanding of the fundamental laws of realisation in general, an inability to divide the product into three (and not two) parts in terms of value, and into two kinds in terms of material form (means of production and articles of consumption). The proposition that the capitalists cannot consume surplus-value is merely a vulgarised repetition of Adam Smith's perplexity regarding realisation in general. Only *part* of the surplus-value consists of articles of consumption; the other part consists of means of production (for example, the surplus-value of the ironmaster). The "consumption" of *this latter* surplus-value is effected *by applying it to production*; the capitalists, however, who manufacture products in the shape of means of production do not consume surplus-value, but *constant capital* obtained by exchange with other capitalists. Hence, the Narodniks too, in arguing that surplus-value cannot be realised, ought logically to admit that constant *capital* also cannot be realised—and in this way they would safely go back to Adam.... It goes without saying that such a return to the "father of political economy" would be a gigantic step forward for writers who present us with old errors in the guise of truths they have "arrived at by themselves."...

But what about the foreign market? Do we deny that capitalism needs a foreign market? Of course not. But the question of a foreign market has *absolutely nothing to do with the question of realisation*, and the attempt to link them into one whole merely expresses the romantic wish to "retard" capitalism, and the romantic inability to think logically. The theory which has explained the question of realisation has proved this up to the hilt. The romanticist says: the capitalists cannot consume surplus-value and therefore must dispose of it abroad. The question is: do the capitalists supply foreigners with products gratis, or do they throw them into the sea? They sell them—hence, they receive an equivalent; they export certain kinds of products—hence, they import other kinds. If we speak of the realisation of the social product, we thereby exclude the circulation of money and assume only the exchange of products for products, since the problem of realisation consists in analysing the *replacement* of all parts of the social product in terms of value and in terms of material form. Hence, to commence the argument about realisation

and to end it by saying that they "will market the product
for money" is as ridiculous as answering the question about
realising constant capital in the shape of articles of consumption by saying: "they will sell." This is simply a gross
logical blunder: people wander away from the question of
the realisation of the aggregate social product to the viewpoint of the individual entrepreneur, who has no other
interest than that of "selling to the foreigner." To link
foreign trade, exports, with the question of realisation
means evading the issue, merely *shifting* it to a wider
field, *but doing nothing towards clearing it up.** The problem
of realisation will not be made one iota clearer if, instead
of the market of one country, we take the market of a certain group of countries. When the Narodniks assert that
the foreign market is "the way out of the difficulty"**
which capitalism raises for itself in the realisation of the
product, they merely use this phrase to cover up the sad
fact that for them "the foreign market" is "the way out
of the difficulty" into which they fall owing to their failure
to understand theory.... Not only that. The theory which
links the foreign market with the problem of the realisation
of the aggregate social product not only reveals a failure to
understand this realisation, but, in addition, reveals an
*extremely superficial understanding of the contradictions
inherent in this realisation.* "The workers will consume wages,
but the capitalists cannot consume surplus-value." Ponder
over this "theory" from the point of view of the foreign market.
How do we know that "the workers will consume wages"?
What grounds have we for thinking that the products
intended by the entire capitalist class of a given country
for consumption by all the workers of that country will
really *equal their wages in value* and will replace them,

---

* This is so clear that even Sismondi was conscious of the need
to disregard foreign trade in analysing realisation. "To trace these
calculations more exactly," he says on the point about production
corresponding to consumption, "and to simplify the question, we have
hitherto completely excluded foreign trade; we have presupposed
an isolated nation; human society itself is such an isolated nation,
and whatever relates to a nation without foreign trade is equally
true of the human race" (I, 115).

** N. —on, p. 205.

that there will be no need for a foreign market for *these* products? There are absolutely no grounds for thinking so, and actually it is not so at all. Not only the products (or part of the products) which replace surplus-value, but also those which replace variable capital; not only products which replace variable capital, but also those which replace constant capital (forgotten by our "economists" who also forget their kinship ... with Adam); not only products that serve as articles of consumption but also those that serve as means of production—all these products are realised in the same way, in the midst of "difficulties," in the midst of continuous fluctuations, which become increasingly violent as capitalism grows, in the midst of fierce competition, which *compels* every entrepreneur to strive to expand production unlimitedly, to go beyond the bounds of the given country, to set out in quest of new markets in countries not yet drawn into the sphere of capitalist commodity circulation. This brings us to the question of why a capitalist country needs a foreign market. Certainly not because the product cannot be realised at all under the capitalist system. That is nonsense. A foreign market is needed because it is *inherent* in capitalist production to strive for *unlimited* expansion— unlike all the old modes of production, which were limited to the village community, to the patriarchal estate, to the tribe, to a territorial area, or state. Under all the old economic systems production was every time resumed in the same form and on the same scale as previously; under the capitalist system, however, this resumption in the same form becomes *impossible*, and *unlimited* expansion, perpetual progress, becomes the law of production.*

Thus, different conceptions of realisation (more exactly, the understanding of it, on the one hand, and complete misunderstanding of it by the romanticists, on the other) lead to two diametrically opposite views on the significance of the foreign market. For some (the romanticists), the foreign market is an indication of the "difficulty" which capitalism *places in the way of* social development. For others, on the contrary, the foreign market shows how

---

* Cf. Sieber, *David Ricardo, etc.*, St. Petersburg, 1885, p. 466, footnote.

capitalism *removes* the difficulties of social development provided by history in the shape of various barriers—communal, tribal, territorial and national.*

As you see, the difference is only one of the "point of view."... Yes, "only"! The difference between the romanticist judges of capitalism and the others is, in general, "only" one of the "point of view,"—"only" that some judge from the rear, and the others from the front, some from the viewpoint of a system which capitalism is destroying, the others from the viewpoint of a system which capitalism is creating.**

The romanticists' wrong understanding of the foreign market usually goes hand in hand with references to the "specific features" of the international position of capitalism in the given country, to the impossibility of finding markets, etc.; the object of all these arguments is to "dissuade" the capitalists from seeking foreign markets. Incidentally, we are not being exact in saying "references," for the romanticist gives us no actual analysis of the country's foreign trade, of its progress in the sphere of new markets, its colonisation, etc. He has no interest whatever in studying the actual process and in explaining it; all he wants is a *moral condemnation of this process*. So that the reader can convince himself of the complete identity between this moralising of contemporary Russian romanticists and that of the French romanticist, we shall quote some specimens of the latter's arguments. We have already seen how Sismondi warned the capitalists that they would find no market. But this is not all he asserted. He also claimed that "the world market is already sufficiently supplied" (II, 328) and argued that it was impossible to proceed along the capitalist path, that it was necessary to choose another path.... He assured the British employers that capitalism would not be able to give jobs to all the agricultural labourers displaced by capitalist farming (I, 255-56). "Will those to whom the agriculturists are sacri-

---

* Cf. later: *Rede über die Frage des Freihandels* (Karl Marx, *On Free Trade.*— Ed.).

** I am speaking here only of the appraisal of capitalism and not of an understanding of it. In the latter respect the romanticists, as we have seen, stand no higher than the classical economists.

ficed derive any benefit from it? Are not the agriculturists
the nearest and most reliable consumers of English manufactures? The cessation of their consumption would strike
industry a blow more fatal than the closing of one of the
biggest foreign markets" (I, 256). He assured English farmers that they would not be able to withstand the competition of the poor Polish peasant, whose grain costs him
almost nothing (II, 257) and that they were menaced by
the even more frightful competition of Russian grain from
the Black Sea ports. He exclaimed: "The Americans are
following the new principle: to produce without calculating
the market (produire sans calculer le marché), and to produce as much as possible," and here is "the characteristic
feature of United States' trade, from one end of the country
to the other—an excess of goods of every kind over what
is needed for consumption ... constant bankruptcies are
the result of this excess of commercial capital which cannot
be exchanged for revenue" (I, 455-56). Good Sismondi! What
would he say about present-day America—about the
America that has developed so enormously, thanks to the
very "home market" which, according to the romanticists'
theory, should have "shrunk"!

VII

CRISIS

Sismondi's third mistaken conclusion, drawn from the wrong
theory which he borrowed from Adam Smith, is the theory
of crises. Sismondi's view that accumulation (the growth of
production in general) is determined by consumption, and
his incorrect explanation of the realisation of the aggregate
social product (which he reduces to the workers' share and the
capitalists' share of revenue) naturally and inevitably led to
the doctrine that crises are to be explained by the discrepancy between production and consumption. Sismondi
fully agreed with this theory. It was also adopted by Rodbertus, who formulated it somewhat differently: he explained crises
by saying that with the growth of production the workers'
share of the product diminishes, and wrongly divided the
aggregate social product, as Adam Smith did, into wages and
"rent" (according to his terminology "rent" is surplus-value,

i.e., profit and ground-rent together). The scientific analysis of accumulation in capitalist society* and of the
realisation of the product undermined the whole basis of
this theory, and also indicated that it is precisely in the
periods which precede crises that the workers' consumption
rises, that underconsumption (to which crises are allegedly
due) existed under the most diverse economic systems,
whereas crises are the distinguishing feature of only one
system—the capitalist system. This theory explains crises
by another contradiction, namely, the contradiction between
the social character of production (socialised by capitalism) and the private, individual mode of appropriation.
The profound difference between these theories would seem
to be self-evident, but we must deal with it in greater
detail because it is the Russian followers of Sismondi who
try *to obliterate* this difference and to confuse the issue.
The two theories of which we are speaking give totally
different explanations of crises. The first theory explains
crises by the contradiction between production and
consumption by the working class; the second explains
them by the contradiction between the social character
of production and the private character of appropriation.
Consequently, the former sees the root of the phenomenon *outside of* production (hence, for example, Sismondi's
general attacks on the classical economists for ignoring
consumption and occupying themselves only with production); the latter sees it precisely in the conditions of production. To put it more briefly, the former explains crises
by underconsumption (Unterkonsumption), the latter by
the anarchy of production. Thus, while both theories explain crises by a *contradiction* in the economic system itself, they differ entirely on the nature of the contradiction.
But the question is: does the second theory deny the fact
of a contradiction between production and consumption,

---

* The mistaken conception of "accumulation of individual capital"
held by Adam Smith and the economists who came after him is connected with the theory that the total product in capitalist economy
consists of two parts. It was they who taught that the accumulated
part of profit is spent entirely on wages, whereas actually it is spent
on: 1) constant capital and 2) wages Sismondi repeated this mistake
of the classical economists as well.

does it deny the fact of underconsumption? *Of course not.* It fully recognises this fact, but puts it in its proper, subordinate, place as a fact that only relates to one department of the whole of capitalist production. It teaches us that this fact cannot explain crises, which are called forth by another and more profound contradiction that is fundamental in the present economic system, namely, the contradiction between the social character of production and the private character of appropriation. What, then, should be said of those who, while they adhere essentially to the first theory, cover this up with references to the point that the representatives of the second theory note the existence of a contradiction between production and consumption? Obviously, these people have not *pondered over* the essence of the difference between the two theories, and do not properly understand the second theory. Among these people is, for example, Mr. N. —on (not to speak of Mr. V. V.). That they are followers of Sismondi has already been indicated in our literature by Mr. Tugan-Baranovsky (*Industrial Crises*, p. 477, with the strange reservation relative to Mr. N. —on: "evidently"). But in talking about "the shrinking of the home market" and "the decline in the people's consuming capacity" (the central points of his views), Mr. N. —on, nevertheless, refers to the representatives of the second theory who *note* the fact of the contradiction between production and consumption, the fact of underconsumption. It goes without saying that such references merely reveal the ability, characteristic in general of this author, to cite inappropriate quotations and nothing more. For example, all readers who are familiar with his *Sketches* will, of course, remember his "citation" of the passage where it says that "the labourers as buyers of commodities are important for the market. But as sellers of their own commodity—labour-power—capitalist society tends to keep them down to the minimum price" (*Sketches*, p. 178), and they will also remember that Mr. N. —on wanted to deduce from this both "the shrinkage of the home market" (ibid., p. 203 et al.) and crises (p. 298 et al.). But while quoting this passage (which, as we have explained, proves nothing), our author, moreover, *leaves out the end* of the footnote from which his quotation was taken. This quotation was from a *note inserted in the manuscript* of Part II of Volume II of *Capital*. It was inserted "for future amplification" and the publisher of the manuscript put it in as a footnote. *After the words quoted above, the note goes on to say:* "*However, this pertains to the next part*,"* i.e., to the third part. What is this third part? It is precisely the part which contains a criticism of Adam Smith's theory of two parts of the aggregate social product (together with the above-quoted opinion about Sismondi), and an analysis of "the reproduction and circulation of the aggregate social capital," i.e., of the realisation of the product. Thus, in confirmation of his views, which are a repetition of Sismondi's, our author quotes a note that pertains "to the part" which refutes Sismondi: "to the part" in which it is shown that the capitalists *can* realise surplus-value, and that to introduce foreign trade in an analysis of realisation is absurd....

Another attempt to obliterate the difference between the two theories and to defend the old romanticist nonsense by referring to modern theories is contained in Ephrucy's article. Citing Sismondi's theory of crises, Ephrucy shows that it is wrong (*Russkoye Bogatstvo*, No. 7, p. 162); but he does so in an extremely hazy and contradictory way. On the one hand, he repeats the arguments of the opposite theory and says that national demand is not limited to articles of direct consumption. On the other hand, he asserts that Sismondi's explanation of crises "points to only one of the many circumstances which hinder the distribution of the national product in conformity with the demand of the population and with its purchasing power." Thus, the reader is invited to think that the explanation of crises is to be found in "distribution," and that Sismondi's mistake was only that he did not give a full list of the causes which hinder this distribution! But this is not the main thing.... "Sismondi," says Ephrucy, "did not confine himself to the above-mentioned explanation. Already in the first edition of *Nouveaux Principes* we find a highly enlightening chapter entitled 'De la connaissance du marché.'**

---

* *Das Kapital*, II. Band, S. 304.[53] Russ. trans., p. 232. Our italics.
** "About Knowledge of the Market."—*Ed.*

In this chapter Sismondi reveals to us the main causes that disturb the balance between production and consumption" (note this!) "with a clarity that we find among only a few economists" (ibid.). And quoting the passages which say that the manufacturer cannot know the market, Ephrucy says: "Engels says almost the same thing" (p. 163), and follows this up with a quotation saying that the manufacturer cannot know the demand. Then, quoting some more passages about "other obstacles to the establishment of a balance between production and consumption" (p. 164), Ephrucy assures us that "these give us the very explanation of crises which is becoming increasingly predominant"! Nay, more: Ephrucy is of the opinion that "on the question of the causes of crises in the national economy, we have every right to regard Sismondi as the founder of the views which were subsequently developed more consistently and more clearly" (p. 168).

But by all this Ephrucy betrays a complete failure to understand the issue! What are crises? Overproduction, the production of commodities which cannot be realised, for which there is no demand. If there is no demand for commodities, it shows that when the manufacturer produced them he did not know the demand. The question now arises: is this indication of the condition which makes crises possible an explanation of the crises? Did Ephrucy really not understand the difference between stating the possibility of a phenomenon and explaining its inevitability? Sismondi says: crises are possible, because the manufacturer does not know the demand; they are inevitable, because under capitalist production there can be no balance between production and consumption (i.e., the product cannot be realised). Engels says: crises are possible, because the manufacturer does not know the demand; they are inevitable, but certainly not because the product cannot be realised at all. For it is not true: the product can be realised. Crises are inevitable because the collective character of production comes into conflict with the individual character of appropriation. And yet we find an economist who assures us that Engels says "almost the same thing"; that Sismondi gives the "very same explanation of crises"! "I am therefore surprised," writes Ephrucy, "that Mr. Tugan-Baranovsky ... lost sight of this most important and valuable point in Sismondi's doctrine" (p. 168). But Mr. Tugan-Baranovsky did not lose sight of anything.* On the contrary, he pointed very exactly to the fundamental contradiction to which the new theory reduces matters (p. 455 et al.), and explained the significance of Sismondi, who at an earlier stage indicated the contradiction which reveals itself in crises, but was unable to give it a correct explanation (p. 457—Sismondi, before Engels, pointed to the fact that crises spring from the contemporary organisation of the economy; p. 491—Sismondi expounded the conditions which make crises possible, but "not every possibility becomes a fact"). Ephrucy, however, completely misunderstood this, and after lumping everything together he is "surprised" that what he gets is confusion! "True," says the economist of *Russkoye Bogatstvo*, "we do not find Sismondi using the terms which have now received universal right of citizenship, such as 'anarchy of production,' 'unplanned production' (Planlosigkeit); but the substance behind these terms is noted by him quite clearly" (p. 168). With what ease the modern romanticist restores the romanticist of former days! The problem is reduced to one of a difference in terms! Actually, the problem boils down to the fact that Ephrucy does not understand the meaning of the terms he repeats. "Anarchy of production," "unplanned production"—what do these expressions tell us? They tell us about the contradiction between the social character of production and the individual character of appropriation. And we ask every one who is familiar with the economic literature we are examining: did Sismondi, or Rodbertus, recognise this contradiction? Did they deduce crises from this contradiction? No, they did not, and could not do so, because *neither of them had any understanding of this contradiction.* The very idea that the criticism of capitalism cannot be based on phrases

---

* In *The Development of Capitalism* (pp. 16 and 19) (see present edition, Vol. 3, *The Development of Capitalism in Russia*, chap. I, section VI.—*Ed.*) I have already noted Mr. Tugan-Baranovsky's inexactitudes and errors which subsequently led him to go right over to the camp of the bourgeois economists. (Author's footnote to the 1908 edition.—*Ed.*)

about universal prosperity,* or about the fallacy of "circulation left to itself," ** but must be based on the character of the evolution of production relations, was absolutely alien to them.

We fully understand why our Russian romanticists exert every effort to obliterate the difference between the two theories of crises mentioned. It is because fundamentally different attitudes towards capitalism are most directly and most closely linked with the theories mentioned. Indeed, if we explain crises by the impossibility of realising products, by the contradiction between production and consumption, we are thereby led to deny reality, the soundness of the path along which capitalism is proceeding; we proclaim this path to be a "false one," and go out in quest of "different paths." In deducing crises from this contradiction we are bound to think that the further it develops *the more difficult* will be the way out of the contradiction. And we have seen how Sismondi, with the utmost naïveté, expressed exactly this opinion when he said that if capital accumulated slowly it was tolerable; but if it accumulated rapidly, it would become unbearable.—On the other hand, if we explain crises by the contradiction between the social character of production and the individual character of appropriation, we thereby recognise that the capitalist road is real and progressive and reject the search for "different paths" as nonsensical romanticism. We thereby recognise that the further this contradiction develops *the easier* will be the way out of it, and that it is the development of this system which provides the way out.

As the reader sees, here, too, we meet with a difference in "points of view."...

It is quite natural that our romanticists should seek

---

* Cf. Sismondi, loc. cit., I, 8.
** Rodbertus. Incidentally, let us mention that Bernstein, who, in general, is restoring the prejudices of bourgeois political economy, has introduced confusion into this problem too by asserting that Marx's theory of crises does not differ very much from the theory of Rodbertus (*Die Voraussetzungen*, *etc.* Stuttg. 1899, S. 67) (E. Bernstein, *The Premises of Socialism and the Tasks of Social-Democracy*. Stuttgart, 1899, p. 67.—*Ed.*), and that Marx contradicts himself by recognising the ultimate cause of crises to be the limited consumption of the masses. (Author's footnote to the 1908 edition.—*Ed.*)

theoretical confirmation of their views. It is quite natural that their search should lead them to the old rubbish which Western Europe has discarded long, long ago. It is quite natural that, feeling this to be so, they should try to renovate this rubbish, some times by actually embellishing the romanticists of Western Europe, and at others by smuggling in romanticism under the flag of inappropriate and garbled citations. But they are profoundly mistaken if they think that this sort of smuggling will remain unexposed.

With this we bring to a close our exposition of Sismondi's *basic* theoretical doctrine, and of the chief theoretical conclusions he drew from it; but we must make a slight addition, again relating to Ephrucy. In his other article about Sismondi (a continuation of the first), he says: "Still more interesting (than the theory on revenue from capital) are Sismondi's views on the different kinds of revenue" (*Russkoye Bogatstvo*, No. 8, p. 42). Sismondi, he says, like Rodbertus, divides the national revenue into two parts: "one goes to the owners of the land and instruments of production, the other goes to the representatives of labour" (ibid.). Then follow passages in which Sismondi speaks of such a division, not only of the national revenue, but of the aggregate product: "The annual output, or the result of all the work done by the nation during the year, also consists of two parts," and so forth (*Nouveaux Principes*, I, 105, quoted in *Russkoye Bogatstvo*, No. 8, p. 43). "The passages we have quoted," concludes our economist, "clearly show that Sismondi fully assimilated (!) the very same classification of the national revenue which plays such an important role in the works of the modern economists, namely, the division of the national revenue into revenue from labour and non-labour revenue—arbeitsloses Einkommen. Although, generally speaking, Sismondi's views on the subject of revenue are not always clear and definite, we nevertheless discern in them a consciousness of the difference that exists between private revenue and national revenue" (p. 43).

The passage quoted, say we in answer to this, clearly shows that Ephrucy has fully assimilated the wisdom of the German textbooks, but in spite of that (and, perhaps, just because of it), he has completely overlooked the theoretical difficulty of the question of national revenue as distinct from individual revenue. Ephrucy expresses himself very carelessly. We have seen that in the first part of his article he applied the term "modern economists" to the theoreticians of one definite school. The reader would be right in thinking that he is referring to them this time too. Actually, however, the author has something entirely different in mind. It is now the German Katheder-Socialists[54] who figure as the modern economists. The author's defence of Sismondi consists in closely identifying his theory with theirs. What is the theory of these "modern" authorities that Ephrucy quotes? That the national revenue is divided into two parts.

But this is the theory of Adam Smith and not of the "modern economists"! In dividing revenue into wages, profit and rent (Book I, chap. VI of *The Wealth of Nations*; Book II, chap. II), Adam Smith opposed the two latter to the former precisely as non-labour revenue; he called them both deductions from the produce of labour (Book I, chap. VIII) and challenged the opinion that profit is also wages for a special kind of labour (Book I, chap. VI). Sismondi, Rodbertus and the "modern" authors of German textbooks simply repeat Smith's doctrine. The only difference between them is that Adam Smith was aware that he was not quite successful in his efforts to separate the national revenue from the national product; he was aware that by excluding constant capital (to use the modern term) from the national product after having included it in the individual product, he was slipping into a contradiction. The "modern" economists, however, in repeating Adam Smith's mistake, have merely clothed his doctrine in a more pompous phrase ("classification of the national revenue") and lost the awareness of the contradiction which brought Adam Smith to a halt. These methods may be scholarly, but they are not in the least scientific.

VIII

CAPITALIST RENT AND CAPITALIST OVERPOPULATION

We continue our survey of Sismondi's theoretical views. All his chief views, those which distinguish him from all other economists, we have already examined. The others either do not play such an important role in his general theory, or are deduced from the preceding ones.

Let us note that Sismondi, like Rodbertus, did not agree with Ricardo's theory of rent. While not advancing a theory of his own, he tried to shake Ricardo's theory with arguments that were, to say the least, feeble. In this he acts as the pure ideologist of the small peasant; it is not so much a refutation of Ricardo as a complete rejection of the application of the categories of commodity economy and of capitalism to agriculture. In both respects his point of view is extremely characteristic of the romanticists. Chapter XIII of Book III* deals with "Mr. Ricardo's ground-rent theory." Stating at once that Ricardo's doctrine completely contradicts his own theory, Sismondi advances the following objections: the general level of profit (on which Ricardo's theory is based) is never established, there is no free movement of capital in agriculture. In agriculture we must discern the intrinsic value of the product (la valeur intrinsèque), which does not depend upon market fluctuations and provides the owner with a "net product" (produit net), the "labour of nature" (I, 306). "The labour of nature is a power, the source of the net product of the land regarded intrinsically" (intrinsèquement) (I, 310). "We regarded rent (le fermage), or more correctly, the net product, as originating directly from the land for the owner's benefit; it takes no share either from the farmer or the

---

* His very system of exposition is characteristic: Book III treats of "territorial wealth" (richesse territoriale), of wealth in the shape of land, i.e., of agriculture. The next book, Book IV, treats of "commercial wealth" (de la richesse commerciale), of industry and commerce. As though the produce of the land, and land itself, have not also become commodities under the rule of capitalism! For this reason, there is no harmony between these two books. Industry is dealt with only in its capitalist form as it existed in Sismondi's time. Agriculture, however, is described in the form of a motley enumeration of all sorts of systems of exploiting the land: patriarchal, slave, half-crop, corvée, quit-rent, capitalist farming and emphyteutic (the granting of land on a perpetual hereditary lease). The result is utter confusion: the author gives us neither a history of agriculture, for all these "systems" are unconnected, nor an analysis of agriculture under capitalist economy, although the latter is the real subject of his work, and though he speaks of industry only in its capitalist form.

consumer" (I, 312). And this repetition of the old physio-
cratic prejudices concludes with the moral: "In general,
in political economy, one should guard against (se défier)
absolute assumptions, as well as against abstractions"
(I, 312)! There is really nothing to examine in such a "theory," since Ricardo's brief remark about the "labour of
nature" is more than enough.* It is simply a refusal to
analyse and a gigantic step back compared with Ricardo.
Here, too, the romanticism of Sismondi is quite clearly
revealed, for he hastens to condemn the process, but is
afraid to touch it with an analysis. Note that he does not
deny the fact of agriculture developing on capitalist lines
in England, of the peasants there being displaced by capitalist farmers and day labourers, and of things developing in the same direction on the Continent. He simply
turns his back on these facts (which he was in duty bound
to examine since he was discussing capitalist economy) and
prefers talking sentimentally of the advantages of the patriarchal system of exploiting the land. Our Narodniks behave
in exactly the same way: none of them have attempted
to deny the fact that commodity economy is penetrating
into agriculture, that it must produce a radical change
in the social character of agriculture; but at the same time
none of them, in discussing the capitalist economy, raise
the question of the growth of commercial farming, pre-
ferring to make shift with moralising about "people's production." Since we are confining ourselves for the moment
to an analysis of Sismondi's theoretical economy, we shall
postpone a more detailed examination of this "patriarchal
exploitation" to a later occasion.

Another theoretical point around which Sismondi's exposition revolves is the doctrine of population. Let us

---

* Ricardo, *Works*, Sieber's (Russian) translation, p. 35: "Does
nature do nothing for man in manufactures? Are the powers of wind
and water, which move our machinery, and assist navigation, nothing?
The pressure of the atmosphere and the elasticity of steam, which
enable us to work the most stupendous engines—are they not the
gifts of nature? To say nothing of the effects of the matter of heat
in softening and melting metals, of the decomposition of the atmosphere in the process of dyeing and fermentation. There is not a manufacture which can be mentioned, in which nature does not give her
assistance to man, and give it too, generously and gratuitously."

note Sismondi's attitude towards the Malthusian theory, and towards the surplus population created by capitalism.

Ephrucy assures us that Sismondi agrees with Malthus only on the point that the population can multiply with exceeding rapidity, and be the cause of terrible suffering. "Beyond this they are poles apart. Sismondi puts the whole population problem on a socio-historical basis" (*Russkoye Bogatstvo*, No. 7, p. 148). In this formula, too, Ephrucy completely obscures Sismondi's characteristic (namely, petty-bourgeois) point of view and his romanticism.

What does this mean—"to put the population problem on a socio-historical basis"? It means studying the law of population of each historical system of economy separately, and studying its connection and interrelation with the given system. Which system did Sismondi study? The capitalist system. Thus, the contributor to *Russkoye Bogatstvo* assumes that Sismondi studied the capitalist law of population. There is a grain of truth in this assertion but only *a grain*. And as Ephrucy did not think of trying to discover what was lacking in Sismondi's argument about population, and as Ephrucy asserts that "here Sismondi is the predecessor of the most outstanding modern economists" * (p. 148), the result is exactly the same sort of embellishment of the petty-bourgeois romanticist as we saw in respect of the questions of crises and of national revenue. Wherein lies the similarity between Sismondi's doctrine and the new theory on these problems? In that Sismondi indicated the contradictions inherent in capitalist accumulation. This similarity Ephrucy noted. Wherein lies the difference between Sismondi's doctrine and the new theory? Firstly, in that it did not advance the scientific analysis of these contradictions one iota, and in some respects even took a step back compared with the classical economists; and secondly, in that he covered up his own inability to make an analysis (partly his unwillingness to do so) with petty-bourgeois moralising about the need for balancing national revenue

---

* Incidentally, we make the reservation that we cannot know for certain whom Ephrucy has in mind when he speaks of "the most outstanding modern economist," the representative of a certain school which is absolutely alien to romanticism, or the author of the bulkiest Handbuch.

with expenditure, production with consumption, and so forth. This difference Ephrucy *did not note* on a single one of the points mentioned, and thereby totally misrepresented Sismondi's real significance and his relation to the modern theory. We see exactly the same thing on the present problem. Here, too, the similarity between Sismondi's view and the modern theory is limited to *an indication of the contradiction*. And here, too, the difference lies in the absence of a scientific analysis and in the substitution of petty-bourgeois moralising for the analysis. Let us explain this.

The development of capitalist machine industry since the end of the last century led to the formation of a surplus population, and political economy was confronted with the task of explaining this phenomenon. Malthus, as we know, tried to explain it by attributing it to natural-historical causes; he denied absolutely that it sprang from a certain, historically determined system of social economy and simply shut his eyes to the contradictions revealed by this fact. Sismondi indicated these contradictions and the displacement of the population by machines. This is indisputably to his credit, for in the period in which he wrote this was new. But let us see what his attitude towards this fact was.

In Book VII (*On the Population*), chapter VII speaks particularly "on the population which has become superfluous owing to the invention of machines." Sismondi states that "machines displace men" (p. 315, II, VII), and at once asks whether the invention of machines is a boon or a bane to a nation. It goes without saying that the "answer" to this question for all countries and all times whatever, and not for a capitalist country, is a most meaningless piece of banality: it is a boon when "consumers' demand exceeds the population's means of production" (les moyens de produire de la population) (II, 317), and a bane "when production is quite sufficient for consumption." In other words: Sismondi notes the contradiction, but this merely serves as a pretext for arguing about some abstract society in which there are no longer any contradictions, and to which the ethics of the thrifty peasant can be applied! Sismondi makes no attempt to analyse this contradiction, to examine how it arises, what it leads to, etc., in the existing capitalist society. On the contrary, he uses this contradiction merely as material for his moral indignation against such a contradiction. Beyond this the chapter tells us absolutely nothing about this theoretical problem, and contains nothing but regrets, complaints and innocent wishes. The displaced workers were consumers ... the home market shrinks ... as regards the foreign market, the world is already sufficiently supplied ... if the peasants were moderately prosperous, this would be a better guarantee of a market ... there is no more amazing and terrible example than England, which is being followed by the Continental countries—such is the moralising we get from Sismondi, instead of an analysis of the phenomenon! His attitude towards the subject is exactly the same as that of our Narodniks. The Narodniks also confine themselves to stating the fact of a surplus population, and use it merely as a reason to voice lamentations about and complaints against capitalism (cf. N. —on, V. V., and others). Sismondi makes no attempt even to analyse the relation between this surplus population and the requirements of capitalist production, neither do our Narodniks ever set themselves such a problem.

The scientific analysis of this contradiction revealed the absolute falsity of this method. The analysis showed that surplus population, being undoubtedly a contradiction (along with surplus production and surplus consumption) and being an inevitable result of capitalist accumulation, is at the same time *an indispensable component part* of the capitalist machine.* The further large-scale industry de-

---

* As far as we know, this point of view about the surplus population was first expressed by Engels in *Die Lage der arbeitenden Klasse in England* (1845) (*The Condition of the Working Class in England.—Ed.*). After describing the ordinary industrial cycle of English industry the author says:

"From this it is clear that English manufacture must have, at all times save the brief periods of highest prosperity, an unemployed reserve army of workers, in order to be able to produce the masses of goods required by the market in the liveliest months. This reserve army is larger or smaller, according as the state of the market occasions the employment of a larger or smaller proportion of its members. And if at the moment of highest activity of the market the agricultural districts ... and the branches least affected by the general prosperity temporarily supply to manufacture a number of workers, these

velops the greater is the fluctuation in the demand for workers, depending upon whether there is a crisis or a boom
in national production as a whole, or in any one branch of it.
This fluctuation is a law of capitalist production, which
could not exist if there were no surplus population (i.e.,
a population exceeding capitalism's *average* demand for
workers) ready at any given moment to provide hands for
any industry, or any factory. The analysis showed that a
surplus population is formed in all industries into which
capitalism penetrates—and in agriculture as well as in industry—and that the surplus population exists in different
forms. There are three chief forms*: 1) *Floating overpopulation.* To this category belong the unemployed workers in
industry. As industry develops their numbers inevitably
grow. 2) *Latent overpopulation.* To this category belong
the rural population who lose their farms with the development of capitalism and are unable to find non-agricultural
employment. This population is always ready to provide
hands for any factory. 3) *Stagnant overpopulation.* It has
"extremely irregular" employment, under conditions below
the average level.[57] To this category belong, mainly, people
who work at home for manufacturers and stores, including
both rural and urban inhabitants. The sum-total of all these
strata of the population constitutes the *relative surplus population,* or *reserve army.* The latter term distinctly shows what
population is referred to. They are the workers needed by
capitalism for the *potential* expansion of enterprises, but
who can never be regularly employed.

Thus, on this problem, too, theory arrived at a conclusion diametrically opposed to that of the romanticists.
For the latter, the surplus population signifies that capitalism is impossible, or a "mistake." Actually, the oppo-

---

are a mere minority, and these too belong to the reserve army, with
the single difference that the prosperity of the moment was required
to reveal their connection with it."[55]

It is important to note in the last words that the part of the *agricultural* population which turns temporarily to industry is regarded
as belonging to the reserve army. This is precisely what the modern
theory has called the *latent* form of the surplus population (see Marx's
Capital).[56]

* Cf. Sieber's *David Ricardo, etc.,* pp. 552-53. St. Petersburg,
1885.

site is the case: the surplus population, being a necessary concomitant of surplus production, is an indispensable attribute to the capitalist economy, *which could neither exist nor develop without it.* Here too Ephrucy totally misrepresented the issue by saying nothing about this thesis of the modern theory.

A mere comparison of these two points of view is sufficient to enable one to judge which of them our Narodniks adhere to. The chapter from Sismondi's work dealt with above could with every right figure in Mr. N. —on's *Sketches on Our Post-Reform Social Economy.*

While noting the formation of a surplus population in post-Reform Russia, the Narodniks have never raised the issue of capitalism's need of a reserve army of workers. Could the railways have been built if a permanent surplus population had not been formed? It is surely known that the demand for this type of labour fluctuates greatly from year to year. Could industry have developed without this condition? (In boom periods it needs large numbers of building workers to erect new factories, premises, warehouses, etc., and all kinds of auxiliary day labour, which constitutes the greater part of the so-called outside non-agricultural employments.) Could the capitalist farming of our outlying regions, which demands hundreds of thousands and millions of day labourers, have been created without this condition? And as we know, the demand for this kind of labour fluctuates enormously. Could the entrepreneur lumber merchants have hewn down the forests to meet the needs of the factories with such phenomenal rapidity if a surplus population had not been formed? (Lumbering like other types of hired labour in which rural people engage is among the occupations with the lowest wages and the worst conditions.) Could the system, so widespread in the so-called handicraft industries, under which merchants, mill owners and stores give out work to be done at home in both town and country, have developed without this condition? In all these branches of labour (which have developed mainly since the Reform) the fluctuation in the demand for hired labour is extremely great. Yet the degree of fluctuation in this demand determines the dimensions of the surplus population *needed* by capitalism.

The Narodnik economists have nowhere shown that they are familiar with this law. We do not, of course, intend to make an examination of the substance of these problems here.* This does not enter into our task. The subject of our article is West-European romanticism and its relation to Russian Narodism. In this case, too, this relation is the same as in all the preceding cases: on the subject of surplus population, the Narodniks adhere entirely to the viewpoint of romanticism, which is diametrically opposite to that of the modern theory. Capitalism gives no employment to displaced workers, they say. This means that capitalism is impossible, a "mistake," etc. But it does not "mean" that at all. Contradiction does not mean impossibility (Widerspruch is not the same as Widersinn). Capitalist accumulation, i.e., real production for the sake of production, is also a contradiction. But this does not prevent it from existing and from being the law of a definite system of economy. The same must be said of all the other contradictions of capitalism. The Narodnik argument we have quoted merely "means" that the Russian intelligentsia have become deeply imbued with the vice of using empty phrases to get over all these contradictions.

Thus, Sismondi contributed absolutely nothing to the *theoretical analysis* of overpopulation. But how did he regard it? His view is a queer combination of petty-bourgeois sentiment and Malthusianism. "The great vice of the present social organisation," says Sismondi, "is that a poor man can never know what demand for labour he can count upon" (II, 261), and Sismondi sighs for the times when "the village shoemaker" and the small peasant knew the exact amount of their revenues. "The more a poor man is bereft of all property, the more is he in danger of falling into error concerning his revenue and of contributing to the formation of a population (contribuer à accroître une population...) which, being out of proportion to the demand for labour, will not find means of subsistence" (II, 263-64). You see: this ideologist of the petty bourgeoisie is not satisfied with wanting to retard the whole of social development for

---

* That is why we do not deal here with the very original circumstance that Narodnik economists, as grounds for *not counting* all these very numerous workers, advanced the fact that they are not registered.

the sake of preserving the patriarchal relationships of a semi-barbarous population. He is ready to prescribe any device you please for crippling human nature, as long as it helps to preserve the petty bourgeoisie. Here are several more excerpts, which leave no doubt about this last point:

The weekly payment of wages at the factory to the semi-pauperised worker has accustomed the latter to look no further into the future than the next Saturday: "this has blunted his moral qualities and sense of sympathy" (II, 266), which, as we shall see in a moment, consist of "connubial prudence"!... "The more his family becomes a burden upon society the more it will grow; and the nation will suffer (gémira) from the burden of a population which is out of proportion (disproportionnée) to its means of subsistence" (II, 267). Preserve small property at all costs—such is Sismondi's slogan—even at the cost of reducing the standard of living and of distorting human nature! And Sismondi, who, with the air of a statesman, has told us when an increase in the population is "desirable," devotes a special chapter to attacking religion for having failed to condemn "imprudent" marriages. Once his ideal—the petty bourgeois—is affected, Sismondi becomes more Malthusian than Malthus himself. "Children who are born only for poverty are also born only for vice," says Sismondi, admonishing religion. "Ignorance in matters concerning the social system has induced them" (the representatives of religion) "to strike chastity from the list of virtues that are proper to marriage, and has been one of the constantly operating causes which destroy the naturally established balance between the population and its means of subsistence" (II, 294). "Religious morality should teach people that having produced a family, it is their duty to live no less chastely with their wives than celibates with women who do not belong to them" (II, 298). And Sismondi, who, in general, lays claim to the title not only of a theoretician in political economy, but also to that of wise administrator, immediately proceeds to calculate that "producing a family" requires "in general, and on the average, three births," and he advises the government "not to deceive the people with the hope of an independent status which will permit them to

raise a family when that illusory institution (cet établisse-
ment illusoire) leaves them at the mercy of suffering,
poverty and death" (II, 299). "When the social organisation did not separate the labouring class from the class
which owned some property, public opinion alone was enough
to avert the scourge (le fléau) of poverty. For the agriculturist to sell the heritage of his fathers and for the artisan to squander his small capital has always been regarded as something shameful.... But under the system at
present prevailing in Europe ... people who are condemned never to possess any property can feel no shame whatever at being reduced to pauperism" (II, 306-07). It
would be difficult to express more vividly the stupidity and
hard-heartedness of the small proprietor! Here Sismondi
changes from the theoretician into the practical counsellor,
who preaches the morals which, we know, are practised
with such success by the French peasant. This is not only
Malthus, but Malthus deliberately cut to the measure of the
petty bourgeois. Reading these chapters of Sismondi's,
one cannot help recalling the passionately angry invec-
tive of Proudhon, who argued that Malthusianism was
the preaching of the connubial practice of ... a certain
unnatural vice. *

IX

MACHINES IN CAPITALIST SOCIETY

Related to the problem of surplus population is that
of the significance of *machines* in general.

Ephrucy dilates upon Sismondi's "brilliant observations" concerning machines, and asserts that "to regard him
as an opponent of technical improvements is unjust" (No. 7,
p. 155), that "Sismondi was not an enemy of machines and
inventions" (p. 156). "Sismondi repeatedly stressed the idea
that machines and inventions are not in themselves harmful
to the working class, but become so only because of the conditions of the existing system of economy, under which an

---

* See supplement to the Russian translation of Malthus' *Essay
on Population* (Bibikov's translation, St. Petersburg, 1868). Excerpt
from Proudhon's essay *On Justice*.

increase in the productivity of labour leads neither to an increase in working class consumption nor to a reduction of working hours" (p. 155).

All these observations are quite correct. But again, *this* appraisal of Sismondi is a wonderfully vivid revelation of how the Narodnik absolutely failed *to understand the romanticist*, to understand the *point of view* on capitalism specific to romanticism, and the radical difference between this point of view and that of scientific theory. The Narodnik could not understand this, because Narodism itself has not gone beyond romanticism. But while Sismondi's observations concerning the contradictory nature of the capitalist employment of machines marked a great step forward in the 1820s, it is quite unpardonable today to confine oneself to such a primitive criticism and not to see its narrow petty-bourgeois character.

In this respect (i.e., in respect of the difference between Sismondi's doctrine and the modern theory)* Ephrucy keeps firmly to his own ground. He cannot even present the problem. He says that Sismondi saw the contradiction, and rests content with that; as if history had not shown the most diverse ways and means of criticising the contradictions of capitalism. In saying that Sismondi did not regard machines as being harmful in themselves, but harmful in their operation under the present social system, Ephrucy does not even see what a primitive, superficially sentimental point of view he expresses in this one argument alone. Sismondi did indeed inquire: are machines harmful, or not? And he "answered" the question with the maxim: machines are useful only when production is commensurate with consumption (cf. quotations in *Russkoye Bogatstvo*, No. 7, p. 156). After all that has been said above, there is no need for us to prove here that such an "answer" is nothing more nor less than substituting a petty-bourgeois utopia for a scientific analysis of capitalism. Sismondi cannot be blamed for not having made such an analysis. Historical services are not judged by the contributions historical personalities *did not make* in respect of modern

---

* We have already repeatedly seen that Ephrucy tried *everywhere* to draw this comparison between Sismondi and the modern theory.

requirements, but by *the new contributions they did make* as compared with their predecessors. Here, however, we are judging neither Sismondi nor his primitive, sentimental point of view, but the economist of *Russkoye Bogatstvo*, who to this day does not understand the difference between this point of view and the modern one. He does not understand that to bring out this difference he should not have asked whether Sismondi was an enemy of machines or not, but whether Sismondi understood the significance of machines under the capitalist system, whether he understood the role played by machines as *a factor of progress under this system*? Had the economist of *Russkoye Bogatstvo* done that, he might have noted that Sismondi, owing to his *petty-bourgeois, utopian* point of view, *could not even raise* such questions, and that what distinguishes the new theory is that it does raise and answer them. In that case Ephrucy might have understood that by substituting the question of the conditions under which machines can, in general, be "profitable" and "useful" for that of the historical role played by machines in existing capitalist society, Sismondi naturally arrived at the theory that capitalism and the capitalist employment of machines were "dangerous" and urged the necessity of "retarding," "moderating" and "regulating" the growth of capitalism, and, as a consequence, he became a *reactionary*. The fact that Sismondi's doctrine fails to understand the historical role of machines as a factor of progress is one of the reasons for the modern theory regarding it as *reactionary*.

We shall not here, of course, expound the modern theory (i.e., Marx's theory) of machine production. We refer the reader to, say, the above-mentioned study by N. Sieber, chapter X: "Machines and Large-Scale Industry," and particularly chapter XI: "An Examination of the Theory of Machine Production."* We shall merely give the gist of it in briefest outline. It boils down to two points: first, to a historical analysis, which established the place machine pro-

---

* "To tell the truth," says Sieber at the beginning of this chapter, "the theory of machines and of large-scale industry outlined here, represents such an inexhaustible source of new thinking and original research, that if anybody took it into his head to weigh up the relative merits of this theory in full he would have to write almost a whole book on this subject alone" (p. 473).

duction occupies as one of the stages in the development of capitalism, and the relation of machine industry to the preceding stages (capitalist simple co-operation and capitalist manufacture); secondly, to an analysis of the part played by machines under capitalist economy, and in particular, to an analysis of the changes which machine industry effects in all the conditions of life of the population. On the first point, the theory established that machine industry is only one stage (namely, the highest) of capitalist production, and showed how it arose out of manufacture. On the second point, the theory established that machine industry marks gigantic progress in capitalist society not only because it increases the productive forces enormously and socialises labour throughout society,* but also because it destroys the manufactory division of labour, compels the workers to go from occupations of one kind to others, completes the destruction of backward patriarchal relationships, particularly in the rural districts,** and gives a most powerful impetus to the progress of society, both for the reasons stated and as a consequence of the concentration of the industrial population. This progress, like the progress capitalism makes in every other field, is accompanied by the "progress" of contradictions, i.e., by their intensification and expansion.

Perhaps the reader will ask: what interest is there in examining Sismondi's views on such a universally known question and in such a brief reference to the modern theory, with which everybody is "familiar," and with which everybody "agrees"?

Well, to see what this "agreement" looks like we shall take Mr. N.—on, the most prominent Narodnik economist, who claims that he strictly applies the modern theory. In his *Sketches*, it will be remembered, Mr. N.—on sets himself as one of his special tasks the study of the capital-

---

* Comparing "associated labour" in the village community and in capitalist society that has machine industry, Sieber quite rightly observes: "There is approximately the same difference between the 'component' of a village community and the 'component' of society with machine production as there is, for example, between *the unit* 10 and *the unit* 100" (p. 495).

** Sieber, op. cit., p. 467.

isation of the Russian textile industry, the characteristic feature of which is precisely that it employs machines on the biggest scale.

The question is: what is Mr. N. —on's point of view on this subject: the point of view of Sismondi (whose viewpoint, as we have seen, he shares on very many aspects of capitalism), or the point of view of modern theory? Is he, on this important subject, a romanticist or ... a realist*?

We have seen that the first thing that distinguishes the modern theory is that it is based on a historical analysis of the development of machine industry from capitalist manufacture. Did Mr. N. —on raise the problem of the development of Russian machine industry? No. True, he did say that it was preceded by work in the home for the capitalist, and by the hand-labour "factory" **; but he not only failed to explain the relation of machine industry to the preceding stage, he even failed to "notice" that it was wrong in scientific terminology to apply the term *factory* to the *preceding stage* (production by hand in the home or in the capitalist's workshop), which should undoubtedly be described as *capitalist manufacture.* ***

Let the reader not think that this "omission" is unimportant. On the contrary, it is of enormous importance. Firstly, Mr. N. —on thereby identifies *capitalism with machine industry.* This is a gross mistake. What constitutes the importance of the scientific theory is that it cleared up the real place of machine industry as *one of the stages* of capitalism. If Mr. N. —on shared the point of

---

* The word "realist" was used here instead of the word *Marxist* exclusively for censorship reasons. For the same reason, instead of referring to *Capital,* we referred to Sieber's book, which summarised Marx's *Capital.* (Author's footnote to the 1908 edition.—*Ed.*)

** P. 108. Quoted from *Statistical Returns for Moscow Gubernia,* Vol. VII, Part III, p. 32 (the statisticians here summarise Korsak's *Forms of Industry*): "Since 1822 the very organisation of industry has undergone a complete change—instead of being independent handicraft producers, the peasants are becoming merely the performers of several operations of large-scale factory production and only receive wages."

*** Sieber quite rightly indicated that the ordinary terminology (factory, works, etc.) is unsuitable for scientific research, and urged the need for drawing a distinction between machine industry and capitalist manufacture: p. 474.

view of *this theory*, could he have depicted the growth and
victory of *machine industry* as *"the struggle between two
economic forms"*: between some unknown "form based on the
peasantry's ownership of instruments of production"* and
"capitalism" (pp. 2, 3, 66, 198 et al.), whereas, in fact,
we see *a struggle between machine industry and capitalist
manufacture*? Mr. N. —on says not a word about this
struggle; although this replacement of *one form of capitalism
by another* took place, on his own showing, precisely in
the textile industry, the sphere of his special study
(p. 79), Mr. N. —on misrepresented it, calling it the replacement of "people's production" by "capitalism." Is it not
evident that at bottom the problem of the *actual* development of machine industry did not interest him in the least,
and that the term "people's production" covers up a utopia
entirely to the taste of Sismondi? Secondly, if Mr. N.— on
had raised the question of the historical development
of Russian machine industry, could he have spoken of
"implanting capitalism" (pp. 331, 283, 323 et al.), basing
his case on facts of governmental support and assistance—
facts which have also occurred in Europe? The question
is: is he copying Sismondi who also talked in exactly the
same way about "implanting," or is he copying the representative of the modern theory who studied the replacement
of manufacture by machine industry? Thirdly, if Mr. N.—on
had raised the problem of the historical development of
the forms of capitalism in Russia (in the textile industry),
could he have ignored the existence of capitalist manufacture in the Russian "handicraft industries"**? And if he
had *really* followed theory and attempted to apply a scientific analysis to at least a small corner of this production—

---

* N. —on, p. 322. Does this differ even one iota from Sismondi's
idealisation of patriarchal peasant economy?
** We assume that there is no need here to prove this commonly
known fact. It is sufficient to recall the Pavlovo metalworkers, the
Bogorodsk leather and the Kimry boot and shoe trade, the hat-
making district of Molvitino, the Tula accordion and samovar trades,
the Krasnoye Selo and Rybnaya Sloboda jewelry trade, the Semyonov
spoon trade, the horn trade in "Ustyanshchina," the felt trade in Semyonov Uyezd, Nizhni-Novgorod Gubernia, etc. We are quoting
from memory; if we made an investigation of handicraft industries,
we could prolong this list to infinity.

which is also "people's production"—what would have become of this picture of Russian social economy, daubed in cheap and inartistic Suzdal style, which depicts a nebulous "people's production" and an isolated from it "capitalism" which embraces only a "handful" of workers (p. 326 et al.)?

To sum up: On the first point which distinguishes the modern theory of machine industry from the romantic theory, Mr. N. —on *can on no account be regarded as a follower of the former*, for he does not even realise the need to present the question of the rise of machine industry as *a special stage of capitalism*, and is silent about the existence of capitalist manufacture, the stage of capitalism which preceded that of the machines. Instead of an historical analysis, he palms off the utopia of "people's production."

The second point relates to the modern theory of the changes brought about in social relations by machine industry. Mr. N.—on did not even attempt to examine this problem. He complained a great deal about capitalism and deplored the appearance of the factory (exactly as Sismondi did), but he did not even attempt to study the change in social conditions brought about by the factory.* To do that it would have been necessary to compare machine industry with *the preceding stages*, which Mr. N. —on does not refer to. Similarly, the viewpoint of the modern theory on machines as a factor of progress in *present-day capitalist society* is also totally alien to him. Here, too, he did not even present the question,** *nor could he do so*, for this question can arise only out of a historical study of the replacement of *one form of capitalism* by another, whereas according to Mr. N. —on "capitalism" tout court*** replaces ... "people's production."

If, *on the basis of Mr. N. —on's "study" of the capitalisation of the textile industry in Russia*, we were to ask: how does Mr. N. —on regard machines?—we could re-

---

* We ask the reader not to forget that the scientific meaning of this term is not the same as the ordinary one. Science limits its application exclusively to large-scale machine industry.

** As has been done, for example, by A. Volgin, *The Substantiation of Narodism in the Works of Mr. Vorontsov (V. V.).* St. Petersburg, 1896.

*** Simply.—*Ed.*

ceive no other reply than that with which we are already familiar from Sismondi's work. Mr. N. —on admits that machines increase the productivity of labour (not to do so is more than he dare!)—just as Sismondi did. Mr. N. —on says that it is not machines that are harmful, but the capitalist employment of them—just as Sismondi did. Mr. N. —on believes that in introducing machines "we" have lost sight of the fact that production must correspond to "the people's consuming capacity"—just as Sismondi did.

And that is all. Mr. N. —on does not believe anything more. He will not hear of the problems that have been raised and solved by modern theory, because he did not even attempt to examine either the historical succession of different forms of capitalist production in Russia (using, say, the example of the textile industry that he chose), or the role of machines as a factor of progress under the *present* capitalist system.

Thus, on the question of machines—this supremely important question of theoretical political economy—Mr. N. —on also shares Sismondi's point of view. Mr. N. —on *argues exactly like a romanticist*, which, of course, does not prevent him from quoting and quoting.

This applies not to the example of the textile industry alone, but to all Mr. N. —on's arguments. Take, say, the above-mentioned example of the flour-milling industry. Mr. N. —on pointed to the introduction of machines only as an excuse for the sentimental lamentation that this increase in the productivity of labour did not correspond to the "people's consuming capacity." As regards the changes in the social system which machine industry introduces in general (and has actually introduced in Russia), he did not even think of analysing them. The question of whether the introduction of these machines is a progressive step in present-day capitalist society is something quite incomprehensible to him.*

What we have said about Mr. N. —on applies *a fortiori***

---

* The text contains an outline criticism of Mr. N. —on's views based on Marx's theory; this I subsequently completed in *The Development of Capitalism*. (Author's footnote to the 1908 edition.—*Ed.*)

** All the more.—*Ed.*

to the other Narodnik economists: on the question of machines, Narodism to this day adheres to the viewpoint of petty-bourgeois romanticism and replaces an economic analysis by sentimental wishes.

X
PROTECTION

The last theoretical problem that interests us in Sismondi's system of views is that of protection. No little space is devoted to this problem in *Nouveaux Principes*, but there it is examined mostly from the practical aspect, in connection with the anti-Corn-Laws movement in Britain. We shall examine this latter problem later on, for it includes other, broader problems. What interests us here at the moment is only Sismondi's *point of view* on protection. What is of interest in this problem is not a new economic concept of Sismondi's, that has not been discussed, but his understanding of the relation between "economics" and the "superstructure." Ephrucy assures the readers of *Russkoye Bogatstvo* that Sismondi was "one of the first and most talented forerunners of the modern historical school," that he was "opposed to the isolation of economic phenomena from all other social factors." "The view is expressed in the works of Sismondi that economic phenomena must not be isolated from other social factors, that they must be studied in connection with facts of a socio-political character" (*Russkoye Bogatstvo*, No. 8, pp. 38-39). Well, we shall see from the example we have taken, how Sismondi understood the connection between economic and socio-political phenomena.

"The prohibition of imports," says Sismondi in the chapter "Of Customs" (l. IV, ch. XI), "is as unwise and as ruinous as the prohibition of exports: it was invented in order to give the nation manufacture, something it did not yet possess; and it cannot be denied that for nascent industry it is on a par with the most powerful encouragement bonus. This manufacture produces, perhaps, scarcely one-hundredth part of a certain kind of goods consumed by the nation: one hundred buyers will have to compete with each other to obtain commodities from the sole vendor, and the ninety-nine to whom he refuses to sell will have to make shift with contraband goods. In that case, the nation's loss will be equal to one hundred, and its gain equal to one. No matter how much the nation may gain from this new manufacture, there can be no doubt that this gain will be too small to justify such great sacrifice. One could always find less wasteful means of stimulating such manufacture to activity" (I, 440-41).

You see how simply Sismondi solves this problem: protection is "unwise" because the "nation" stands to lose by it!

What "nation" does our economist speak of? What economic relations does he connect the given socio-political fact with? He takes no definite relations, he argues *in general*, about a nation as it *should be, according to his conception of what should be*. And as we know, this conception of what should be is based on the exclusion of capitalism and on the reign of small independent production.

But it is utterly absurd to associate a socio-political factor which belongs to a given economic system, and to it alone, with some imaginary system. Protection is a "socio-political factor" of capitalism, but Sismondi does not associate it with capitalism, he associates it with some nation *in general* (or with a nation of small independent producers). He could, perhaps, have associated protection with, say, the Indian village community, and have obtained a still more striking example of its "folly" and "ruination"; but this "folly" would again have been that of his association and not of protection. Sismondi makes a childish calculation to show that protection is profitable to a very few at the expense of the masses. There is no need to do so, for this is already evident from the very concept protection (whether it takes the form of a direct subsidy or the form of eliminating foreign competitors makes no difference). That protection expresses a social contradiction is beyond dispute. But are there no contradictions in the economic life of the system which created protection? On the contrary, it is full of contradictions, and Sismondi himself indicated these contradictions throughout his book. Instead of *deducing* this contradiction from those of the economic system which he himself indicated, Sismondi *ignores* economic contradictions and reduces his argument to totally meaningless "innocent wishes." Instead of associating this institution which, according to him, benefits a small group, with the position occupied by this group in the country's economy, and with the interests of this group, he associates it with the abstract principle of the "common weal." We see, therefore, that, contrary to Ephrucy's assertion, Sismondi does *isolate* economic phenomena from the rest (by regarding protection apart from the economic system) and has *no conception of the connection* between economic and socio-political facts. The tirade we have quoted contains *all* that he, as a theoretician, could contribute to the problem of protection: all the rest is merely a paraphrase of this. "It is doubtful whether governments fully realise what price they pay for this gain" (the development of manufacture) "and what frightful sacrifices they impose upon the consumers" (I, 442-43). "The governments of Europe wanted to violate nature" (faire violence à la nature). Which nature? Is it the nature of capitalism that protection "violates"? "The nation was forced, in a way (en quelque sorte), into false activity" (I, 448). "Some governments have gone to the length of paying their merchants in order to enable them to sell more cheaply; the stranger this sacrifice and the more it contradicts the simplest calculation, the more it is ascribed to high politics.... The government pays its merchants at the expense of its subjects" (I, 421), and so on and so forth. This is the kind of argument Sismondi treats us to! In other parts of his work, as if drawing the conclusion from these arguments, he calls capitalism "artificial" and "implanted" (I, 379, opulence factice), "a hothouse product" (II, 456) and so forth. Starting out by substituting innocent wishes for an analysis of the given contradictions, he reaches the point of positively distorting reality to suit those wishes. According to him capitalist industry, which is so zealously "supported," is feeble, without a basis, and so forth, it does not play a predominant role in the country's economy and, *consequently*, this predominant role is played by small-scale production, and so forth. The undoubted and indisputable fact that protection was created only by a definite economic system, and by the definite contradictions of that system, that it expresses the real interests of a real class, which plays the *predominant* role in the national economy, is reduced to nothing, even to its opposite, by means of a few sentimental phrases! Here is another specimen (concerning the protection of agriculture—I, 265, chapter on the Corn Laws):

"The English would have us believe that their big farms are the only means of improving agriculture, that is to say, of providing themselves with a greater abundance of agricultural produce at a cheaper price—actually, however, they do the opposite, they produce at a higher price."...

This passage, which so strikingly reveals the romanticist way of arguing that the Russian Narodniks have taken over in its entirety, is wonderfully characteristic! The development of capitalist farming and the technical progress connected with it are depicted as a deliberately introduced system: the English (i.e., the English economists) would have us believe that this system is the only means of improving agriculture. Sismondi wants to say that "there could be" other means of improving agriculture besides capitalist farming, i.e., again "there could be" in some abstract society, but not in the real society of a definite historical period, in the "society" based on commodity production of which the English economists speak, and of which Sismondi too should have spoken. "Improvement of agriculture, *that is to say*, providing themselves" (the nation?) "with a greater abundance of produce." Not "that is to say," at all. Improvement of agriculture and improved food for the masses are by no means the same thing; that the two will not coincide, is not only possible, it is inevitable under the economic system which Sismondi so zealously wants to avoid. For example, an increase in potato cultivation may signify an increase in labour productivity in agriculture (introduction of root crops) and an increase in surplus-value, simultaneously with a deterioration of the workers' food. It is another example of the habit of the Narodnik—that is to say, the romanticist—to dismiss the contradictions of real life with phrases.

"Actually," continues Sismondi, "these farmers, who are so rich, so intelligent and so much supported (secondés)

13*

by all scientific progress, and whose horses are so fine,
whose hedges so solid and whose fields so thoroughly
cleared of weeds, cannot compete against the wretched Polish
peasant, ignorant, crushed by slavery, who seeks consola-
tion only in drink, and whose agriculture is still in the
infant stage of the art. The corn harvested in central Poland, after paying freight for many hundreds of leagues
by river, by land and by sea, and after paying import duties amounting to 30 and 40 per cent ad valorem, is still
cheaper than the corn of the richest counties of England"
(I, 265). "The English economists are amazed at this contrast." They refer to taxes and so forth. But this is not
the point. "The system of exploitation itself is bad, it
rests on a dangerous foundation.... Lately, all writers have
presented this system as an object worthy of our admiration,
but we, on the contrary, must study it well in order to
avoid imitating it" (I, 266).

Really, how infinitely naïve is this romanticist, who
presents English capitalism (commercial farming) as a mistaken system of the economists, who imagines that the "amazement" of the economists who shut their eyes to the contradictions of commercial farming is a sufficiently strong
argument *against* the farmers! How superficial is his understanding; instead of seeking an explanation of
economic processes in the interests of different groups,
he looks for it in the errors of economists, authors and governments! Good Sismondi wants to prick the conscience of
the English and also of the continental farmers and put them
to shame in order to discourage them from "imitating" such
"bad" systems!

Do not forget, incidentally, that this was written seventy years ago, that Sismondi was witnessing the first
steps of these, as yet, totally new phenomena. *His* naïveté
is excusable, for even the classical economists (his contemporaries) no less naïvely regarded these new phenomena as
the product of the eternal and natural qualities of human
nature. But, we ask, have our Narodniks added even one
original word to Sismondi's arguments in their "objections"
to capitalism developing in Russia?

Thus, Sismondi's arguments about protection show that
the historical point of view was totally alien to him. In-

deed, he argues quite abstractly, exactly like the eighteenth-century philosophers and economists, differing from
them only in proclaiming the society of small independent
producers and not bourgeois society to be normal and natural. Hence, he understands nothing of the connection between
protection and a definite economic system; and he disposes
of this contradiction in the socio-political sphere with
sentimental phrases about "the false," "the perilous," the
mistaken, the unwise, etc., similar to those with which he
disposed of the contradictions in economic life. Hence, he
draws an extremely superficial picture of the matter and
presents the problem of protection and Free Trade as one
of the "wrong" or the "right" path (i.e., to use his terminology, the problem of capitalism, or the non-capitalist
path).

Modern theory has fully exposed these delusions, by
revealing the connection between protection and a definite
historical system of social economy, between protection
and the interests of the predominant class in that system
which enjoy the support of governments. It showed that
protection or Free Trade is an issue *between* entrepreneurs
(sometimes between the entrepreneurs of different countries, sometimes between different factions of entrepreneurs
in a given country).

Comparing these two points of view on protection with
the attitude towards it adopted by the Narodnik economists,
we find that here too they fully share the romanticist
viewpoint and associate protection not with a capitalist
country, but with some abstraction, with "consumers" tout
court, and proclaim it to be the "mistaken" and "unwise"
support of "hothouse" capitalism, and so forth. On the subject, for example, of duty-free imports of agricultural machines, which cause conflict between industrial and agricultural entrepreneurs, the Narodniks, *of course*, stand solidly for the agricultural ... entrepreneurs. We do not want
to say that they are wrong. But it is a question of fact,
a question concerning the present historical moment, a
question as to which faction of the entrepreneurs expresses
the more general interests of the development of capitalism. Even if the Narodniks are right, it is certainly not because the imposition of customs duties signifies

"artificial" "support for capitalism," whereas the lifting of such duties signifies support for an "age-old" people's industry, but simply because the development of agricultural capitalism (which needs machines), by accelerating the extinction of medieval relationships in the rural districts and the creation of a home market for industry, signifies a wider, freer and more rapid development of capitalism in general.

We foresee one objection to this classing of the Narodniks with the romanticists on this question. It will probably be said that here it is necessary to make special mention of Mr. N. —on, who, after all, openly says that the problem of Free Trade and protection is a capitalist problem, and says so more than once, and who even "quotes."...
Yes, yes, Mr. N. —on even quotes! But if we are shown this passage from his *Sketches* we shall cite *other passages* in which he proclaims that to give support to capitalism is to "implant" it (and this in his "Summary and Conclusions"! pp. 331, 323 and also 283), and states that the encouragement of capitalism is "a fatal blunder" because "we have overlooked," "we have forgotten," "our minds have been obscured," and so forth (p. 298. Compare this with Sismondi!). How can this be reconciled with the assertion that support for capitalism (with export bonuses) is "one of the numerous contradictions with which our economic life teems*; this one, like all the rest, owes its existence to the form which all production is assuming" (p. 286)? Note: *all production*! We ask any impartial person: what is the point of view of this author, who proclaims support of "*the form which all production is assuming*" to be a "blunder"? Is it the point of view of Sismondi, or of scientific theory? Here, too (as on the subjects we examined above), Mr. N. —on's "quotations" turn out to be irrelevant, clumsy interpolations, which do not in the least express a real conviction that these "quotations" are applicable to Russian reality. Mr. N. —on's "quotations" from modern theory are window-

---

* In the same way as *Sketches* "teem" with exhortations to "us," with the exclamations "we," and similar phrases, which ignore these contradictions.

dressing and can only mislead the reader. It is an awkward-
ly worn "realist" costume under which the thoroughbred
romanticist hides. *

XI
SISMONDI'S PLACE IN THE HISTORY OF POLITICAL ECONOMY

We are now familiar with all of Sismondi's main propositions relating to economic theory. Summing up, we see
that, everywhere, Sismondi remains absolutely true to himself, that his point of view remains unchanged. On the one
hand, on all points he differs from the classical economists
in that he indicates the contradictions of capitalism. On
the other hand, on no point is he able (or willing) to extend the analysis of the classical economists, and therefore
confines himself to a sentimental criticism of capitalism
from the viewpoint of the petty bourgeois. This substitution of sentimental complaints and lamentations for a scientific analysis results in his conception being extremely
superficial. Modern theory accepted his references to the
contradictions of capitalism, subjected them to a scientific analysis, and on all points reached conclusions
which radically differ from Sismondi's, and for that reason
lead to a diametrically opposite point of view concerning
capitalism.

In *A Critique of Some of the Propositions of Political
Economy* (*Zur Kritik*,[59] Russ. trans., Moscow, 1896) Sismondi's place in the history of the science is described as
follows:

"Sismondi is no longer labouring under Boisguillebert's
idea that labour which creates exchange value is adulterated

---

* We have a suspicion that Mr. N. —on regards these "quotations"
as a talisman which protects him from all criticism. It is difficult
otherwise to explain the fact that, on hearing from Messrs. Struve
and Tugan-Baranovsky that his doctrine had been compared with
Sismondi's, Mr. N. —on, in one of his articles in *Russkoye Bogatstvo*
(1894, No. 6, p. 88), "quoted" the opinion of a representative of the
modern theory who describes Sismondi as a petty-bourgeois reactionary and utopian.[58] Evidently, he is profoundly convinced that by
means of such a "quotation" he "refuted" the comparison made between
himself and Sismondi.

by money; but just as Boisguillebert denounced money, so does Sismondi denounce large industrial capital" (p. 36).

The author wants to say: Just as Boisguillebert superficially regarded barter as a natural system and was up in arms against money, which was to him an "extraneous element" (p. 30, ibid.), so Sismondi regarded small-scale production as a natural system and was up in arms against big capital, which he regarded as an extraneous element. Boisguillebert did not understand the inseparable and natural connection between money and commodity exchange, did not understand that he was contrasting two forms of "bourgeois labour" as extraneous elements (ibid., pp. 30-31). Sismondi failed to understand the inseparable and natural connection between big capital and small independent production, failed to understand that these are two forms of commodity economy. Boisguillebert "is up in arms against bourgeois labour in one form while, utopian-like, he praises it in another" (ibid.). Sismondi is up in arms against big capital, i.e., against commodity economy in one form, its most developed form, while, utopian-like, he praises the small producer (especially the peasantry), i.e., commodity economy in another form, its rudimentary form.

"In Ricardo," continues the author of the *Critique*, "political economy reached its climax, after recklessly drawing its ultimate conclusions, while Sismondi supplemented it by impersonating its doubts" (p. 36).

Thus, the author of the *Critique* reduces the significance of Sismondi to the fact that he *raised the question* of the contradictions of capitalism, and thereby set the task of making a further analysis. The author we have quoted regards all the independent views of Sismondi, who also wanted *to answer* this question, as unscientific and superficial, and as reflecting his reactionary petty-bourgeois point of view (see the above-quoted opinions, and one quoted below in connection with a "quotation" by Ephrucy).

Comparing Sismondi's theory with Narodism, we find on nearly all points (except his repudiation of Ricardo's theory of rent and his Malthusian admonitions to the peasants) an astonishing similarity, which sometimes goes as far as identity of terms. The Narodnik economists fully share Sismondi's point of view. We shall be still more convinced of this later, when we pass from theory to Sismondi's views on practical problems.

And lastly, as regards Ephrucy, on no point has he given a correct appraisal of Sismondi. Pointing to Sismondi's emphasis on, and condemnation of, the contradictions of capitalism, Ephrucy was quite unable to understand either the sharp difference between his theory and the theory of scientific materialism, or that the romanticist and scientific points of view on capitalism are diametrically opposite. The fellow feeling of the Narodnik for the romanticist, their touching unanimity, prevented the author of the essays in *Russkoye Bogatstvo* from correctly characterising this classical representative of romanticism in economic science.

We have just quoted the opinion on Sismondi that "he impersonated the doubts" of classical political economy. But Sismondi did not think of confining himself to this role (which gives him an honourable place among the economists). As we have seen, he tried to solve the doubts, but did so very unsuccessfully. Not only that. His accusation against the classical economists and their science was not that they halted before an analysis of the contradictions, but that they employed wrong methods. "The old science does not teach us either to understand or avert" new disasters (I, XV), says Sismondi in the preface to the second edition of his book, and he does not explain this fact by indicating that the analysis made by this science is incomplete and inconsistent but by claiming that it "plunged into abstractions" (I, 55: the new disciples of Adam Smith in England plunged [se sont jetés] into abstractions, forgetting about "man") and was "proceeding along a wrong path" (II, 448). What is the charge levelled by Sismondi against the classical economists which permits him to draw this conclusion?

"The economists, the most celebrated of them, devoted too little attention to consumption and to the market" (I, 124).

This accusation has been repeated innumerable times since Sismondi's day. It has been deemed necessary to separate "consumption" from "production" as a special department of the science; it has been said that production depends upon natural laws, whereas consumption is determined by distribution, which depends upon the will of man, and so on, and so forth. It is common knowledge that our Narodniks hold the same views and put distribution in the forefront.*

What meaning is there to this accusation? It is based solely on an extremely unscientific conception of the very subject of political economy. Its subject is not by any means "the production of material values," as is often claimed (that is the subject of technology), but the social relations between men in production. Only by interpreting "production" in the former sense can one separate "distribution" from it, and when that is done, the "department" of production does not contain the categories of historically determined forms of social economy, but categories that relate to the labour process in general: usually, such empty banalities merely serve later to obscure historical and social conditions. (Take, for example, the concept of capital.) If, however, we consistently regard "production" as social relations in production, then both "distribution" and "consumption" lose all independent significance. Once relations in production have been explained, both the share of the product taken by the different classes and, consequently, "distribution" and "consumption" are *thereby* explained. And vice versa, if production relations remain

---

* It goes without saying that Ephrucy did not miss the opportunity to praise Sismondi for this as well. "The important thing in Sismondi's doctrine," we read in *Russkoye Bogatstvo*, No. 8, p. 56, "is not so much the various special measures which he proposed, as the general spirit which permeates the whole of his system. Contrary to the classical school, he lays special emphasis on the interests of distribution and not on those of production." In spite of his repeated "references" to the "modern" economists, Ephrucy did not understand their theory at all, and continued to busy himself with the sentimental nonsense which distinguishes the primitive critique of capitalism. Here, too, our Narodnik wants to save himself by comparing Sismondi with "many prominent representatives of the historical school"; and so you see, "Sismondi went further" (ibid.), and Ephrucy is quite content with that! "Went further" than the German professors—what more do you want? Like all the Narodniks, Ephrucy tries to lay the main emphasis on the point that Sismondi criticised capitalism. The economist of *Russkoye Bogatstvo* evidently has no idea that capitalism can be criticised in different ways, that it can be criticised from both the sentimental and the scientific point of view.

unexplained (for example, if the process of the production of the aggregate social capital is not understood), all arguments about consumption and distribution turn into banalities, or innocent, romantic wishes. Sismondi was the originator of such arguments. Rodbertus also talked a lot about the "distribution of the national product," and Ephrucy's "modern" authorities even formed special "schools," one of the principles of which was to pay special attention to distribution.* But none of these theoreticians of "distribution" and "consumption" were able to solve even the fundamental problem of the difference between social capital and social revenue; all continued to grope in the contradictions before which Adam Smith had come to a halt.** The problem was solved only by the economist who never singled out distribution, and who protested most vigorously against the "vulgar" arguments about "distribution" (cf. Marx's criticism of the Gotha Programme quoted by P. Struve in his *Critical Remarks*, p. 129, epigraph to chapter IV).⁶⁰ Not only that. The very solution of the problem consisted of an analysis of the *reproduction* of social capital. The author did not make a special problem of either consumption or distribution, but both were fully explained after the analysis of *production* had been carried to its conclusion.

"... Scientific analysis of the capitalist mode of production demonstrates ... that the distribution relations essentially coincident with these production relations are their opposite side, so that both share the same historically

---

* Ingram quite rightly likens Sismondi to the "Katheder-Socialists" (p. 212, *A History of Political Economy*, Moscow, 1891) when he naïvely observed: "...We are ready (!!) to admit Sismondi's view of the state as a power ... charged also with the mission of extending the benefits of the social union and of modern progress as widely as possible through all classes of the community" (215). What profundity distinguishes these "views" of Sismondi's we have already seen in the case of protection.

** See, for example, R. Meyer's article "Income" in *Handwörterbuch der Staatswissenschaft* (Russian translation in the collection of articles entitled *Promyshlennost* [*Industry*]), which reveals the hopeless confusion in the arguments of the "modern" German professors on this subject. It is curious that R. Meyer, who refers directly to Adam Smith and mentions in his bibliography *the very chapters* of Volume II of *Capital* which contain a complete refutation of Smith, makes no mention of this in the text.

transitory character." "The wage presupposes wage-labour, and profit—capital. These definite forms of distribution thus presuppose definite social characteristics (Charaktere) of production conditions, and definite social relations of production agents. The specific distribution relations are thus merely the expression of the specific historical production relations." ... "Every form of distribution disappears with the specific form of production from which it is descended and to which it corresponds."

"The view which regards only distribution relations as historical, but not production relations, is, on the one hand, solely the view of the initial, but still handicapped (inconsistent, befangen) criticism of bourgeois economy. On the other hand, it rests on the confusion and identification of the process of social production with the simple labour-process, such as might even be performed by an abnormally isolated human being without any social assistance. To the extent that the labour-process is solely a process between man and Nature, its simple elements remain common to all social forms of development. But each specific historical form of this process further develops its material foundations and social forms" (*Capital*, Vol. III, 2, pp. 415, 419 and 420, German original).[61]

Sismondi was no more fortunate in attacks of another sort against the classical economists, attacks which occupy still more space in his *Nouveaux Principes*. "The new disciples of Adam Smith in England plunged into abstractions, forgetting about man..." (I, 55). For Ricardo "wealth is everything and men nothing" (II, 331). "They" (the economists who advocate Free Trade) "often sacrifice men and real interests to an abstract theory" (II, 457), and so forth.

How old these attacks are, and yet how new! I have in mind their renewal by the Narodniks, who have made such a noise over the frank admission that the capitalist development of Russia is her real, actual and inevitable development. Have they not repeated the same thing in different keys when shouting about "apologetics of the money power," about "social-bourgeois character," and so forth?[62] The remark addressed to the sentimental critics of capitalism in general is applicable to them to an *even greater extent* than to Sismondi: Man schreie nicht zu sehr über den Zynismus! Der Zynismus liegt in der Sache, nicht in den Worten, welche die Sache bezeichnen! But do not make an outcry at the cynicism of it. The cynicism is in the facts and not in the words which express the facts.[63]

"To an even greater extent," we say. This is because the West-European romanticists did not have before them a scientific analysis of the contradictions of capitalism, because they were the first to indicate these contradictions, because they denounced (in "plaintive words," incidentally) the people *who did not see* these contradictions.

Sismondi violently attacked Ricardo for drawing all the conclusions from his observations and study of bourgeois society with ruthless frankness: he noted frankly both the existence of production for production and the transformation of labour-power into a commodity similar to any other commodity and the fact that the net revenue, that is, the amount of profit, is the only thing of importance to "society."* But Ricardo spoke the absolute truth: *actually everything is exactly as he says*. If this truth seemed to Sismondi to be a "base truth," he should not have sought for the causes of this baseness in Ricardo's theory at all, and should not have directed his attacks at "abstractions"; the exclamations he addressed to Ricardo belong entirely to the sphere of "the deception which exalts us."

---

* Ephrucy, for example, repeats with an important air Sismondi's sentimental phrases about an increase in the net revenue of the entrepreneur not being a gain for the national economy, and so forth, and reproaches him merely for having "realised" this "not quite clearly yet" (p. 43, No. 8).
Would you not like to compare with this the results of the scientific analysis of capitalism:
The gross income (Roheinkommen) of society consists of wages+profit+rent. The net income (Reineinkommen) is surplus-value.
"Viewing the income of the whole society, national income consists of wages plus profit plus rent, thus, of the gross income. But even this is an abstraction to the extent that the entire society, on the basis of capitalist production, bases itself on the capitalist standpoint and thereby considers only the income resolved into profit and rent as net income" (III, 2, 375-76).[64]
Thus, the author fully sides with Ricardo and his definition of the "net income" of "society," sides with the very definition which evoked Sismondi's "celebrated objection" (*Russkoye Bogatstvo*, No. 8, p. 44): "What? Wealth is everything and men nothing?" (II. 331). In modern society—yes, certainly.

Well, what about our modern romanticists? Do they think of denying the reality of the "money power"? Do they think of denying that this power is omnipotent not only among the industrial population, but also among the agricultural population of any "village community" and of any remote village you like? Do they think of denying that there is a necessary connection between this *fact* and commodity economy? They have not even attempted to subject this to doubt. They simply try not to talk of it. They are afraid of calling things by their real names.

We fully understand their fear: the frank admission of reality would completely cut the ground from under the sentimental (Narodnik) criticism of capitalism. It is not surprising that they so ardently rush into battle before they have had time to clean the rusty weapon of romanticism. It is not surprising that they are unscrupulous in their methods and want to present hostility towards *sentimental* criticism as hostility towards criticism in general. After all, they are fighting for their right to existence.

Sismondi even tried to elevate his sentimental criticism to the plane of *a special method of social science*. We have already seen that he did not reproach Ricardo with bringing his objective analysis to a halt when faced with the contradictions of capitalism (such a reproach would have been justified), but reproached him for the *objectivity* of his analysis. Sismondi said that Ricardo "forgets about man." In his preface to the second edition of *Nouveaux Principes* we find the following tirade:

"I deem it necessary to protest against the customary methods, so often superficial, so often false, of judging a work relating to the social sciences. The problem which they have to solve is incomparably more complex than all the problems of the natural sciences; at the same time it appeals as much to the heart as it does to the mind" (I, XVI). How familiar to the Russian reader is this idea of contrasting the natural sciences to the social sciences, and of the latter appealing to the "heart"!* Sismondi here expresses the very ideas

* "Political economy is not simply a science of calculation (n'est pas une science de calcul) but a moral science.... It achieves its object only when the feelings, needs, and passions of men are taken into consideration" (I, 313). These sentimental phrases which Sismondi

which were to be "newly discovered" several decades later
in the far east of Europe by the "Russian school of sociologists" and figure as a special "subjective method in sociology." ... Sismondi, like our native sociologists, of
course appeals "to the heart as well as to the mind."* But we
have already seen that on all the most important problems, the "heart" of the petty bourgeois triumphed over the
"mind" of the economist theoretician.

POSTSCRIPT **

That the appraisal given here of the sentimental Sismondi in relation to scientifically "objective" Ricardo is
correct, is fully confirmed by the opinion Marx expressed
in the second volume of *Theories of Surplus-Value*,
which appeared in 1905 (*Theorien über den Mehrwert*, II.
B., I. Th., S. 304 u. ff. "Bemerkungen über die Geschichte
der Entdeckung des sogenannten Ricardoschen Gesetzes").***
Contrasting Malthus as a wretched plagiarist, a paid advocate of the rich and a shameless sycophant, to Ricardo as a
man of science, Marx said:

---

and the Russian sociologists of the subjective school who utter exactly
the same exclamations regard as new conceptions of social science,
actually show that criticism of the bourgeoisie was still in an infantile,
primitive state. Does not a scientific analysis of contradictions, while
remaining a strictly objective "calculation," provide firm ground
for understanding "the feelings, needs and passions," and the passions not of "men" in general—that abstraction to which both the
romanticist and the Narodnik ascribe a specifically petty-bourgeois
content—but of *the men of definite classes*? The point is, however,
that Sismondi *could not theoretically refute* the economists, and therefore confined himself to sentimental phrases. "Utopian dilettantism
was forced to make theoretical concessions to any more or less learned
defender of the bourgeois order. In order to allay the consciousness
of his own impotence that was rising within him, the utopian consoled himself by reproaching his opponents with objectivity: let us
admit that you are more learned than I, but in return I am kinder"
(Beltov, p. 43).[65]

    * As if the "problems" which arise from the natural sciences do
not also appeal to the "heart"!

    ** This postscript was written for the 1908 edition.—*Ed.*

    *** *Theories of Surplus-Value*, Vol. II, Part I, p. 304, et seq.
"Notes on the History of the Discovery of the So-Called Ricardian
Law."[66]—*Ed.*

"Ricardo regards the capitalist mode of production as the most advantageous for production in general, as the most advantageous for the creation of wealth, and for his time Ricardo is quite right. He wants *production for the sake of production*, and he is right. To object to this, as Ricardo's sentimental opponents did, by pointing to the fact that production as such is not an end in itself, means to forget that production for the sake of production is nothing more nor less than the development of the productive forces of mankind, i.e., *the development of the wealth of human nature as an end in itself.* If this end is set up in contrast to the welfare of individuals, as Sismondi did, it is tantamount to asserting that the development of the whole human race must be *retarded* for the sake of ensuring the welfare of individuals, that, consequently, no war, we shall say for example, can be waged, because war causes the death of individuals. Sismondi is right only in opposition to those economists who *obscure* this antagonism, deny it" (S. 309). From his point of view Ricardo has every right to put the proletarians on a par with machines, with commodities in capitalist production. "Es ist dieses stoisch, objektiv, wissenschaftlich," "this is stoicism, this is objective, this is scientific" (S. 313). It goes without saying that this appraisal applies only to a definite period, to the very beginning of the nineteenth century.

CHAPTER II

THE CHARACTER OF THE ROMANTICISTS' CRITICISM OF CAPITALISM

We have already dealt sufficiently with Sismondi's "mind." Let us now take a closer look at his "heart." Let us attempt to collect all the references to his *point of view* (which we have studied till now only as an element touching on theoretical problems), to his *attitude* towards capitalism, to his social sympathies, to his conception of the "socio-political" problems of the period in which he was active.

I

THE SENTIMENTAL CRITICISM OF CAPITALISM

The distinguishing feature of the period in which Sismondi wrote was the rapid development of *exchange* (money economy, to use modern terminology), which was manifested with particular sharpness after the remnants of feudalism were destroyed by the French Revolution. Sismondi unambiguously condemned this development and growth of exchange, denounced "fatal competition," called upon the "government to protect the population from the consequences of competition" (ch. VIII, l. VII), and so forth. "Rapid exchanges corrupt the good faith of the people. Constant concern for selling at a profit cannot but lead to attempts to demand too high a price and to cheat, and the harder life becomes for the one who gains his livelihood by constant exchanges, the more he is tempted to resort to cheating" (I, 169). Such was the naïveté required to attack money economy in the way our Narodniks attack it! "... Commercial wealth is only of secondary importance in the economic system; and land wealth (territoriale) which provides the means of subsistence must increase first. The whole of that numerous class which lives by commerce must be called upon to participate in the fruits of the earth only to the extent that these fruits exist; it" (this class) "must grow only to the extent that this produce grows" (I, 322-23). Has Mr. N. —on, who fills page after page with complaints about the growth of commerce and industry outpacing the development of agriculture, taken even one step beyond this patriarchal romanticist? These complaints of the romanticist and of the Narodnik merely testify to a complete *misunderstanding* of capitalist economy. *Can there be* a capitalism under which the development of commerce and industry *does not* outpace agriculture? Why, the growth of capitalism is the growth of commodity economy, *that is to say*, of a social division of labour which *separates* from agriculture one branch of the processing of raw materials after another, breaking up the *single* natural economy in which the production, processing and consumption of these raw materials were combined. That is why capitalism *always and everywhere* signifies a *more rapid* development of commerce and industry than of agriculture, a *more rapid* growth of the commercial and industrial population, a *greater* weight and importance of commerce and industry in the social economic system as a whole.* *Nor can it be* otherwise. By repeating such complaints, Mr. N. —on proves again and again that in his economic views he has not gone beyond superficial, sentimental romanticism. "This unwise spirit of enterprise (esprit d'entreprise), this excess of trading of every kind, which causes so many bankruptcies in America, is due, without a doubt, *to* the increase in the number of banks and to the ease with which illusory credit takes the place of real property" (fortune réelle) (II, 111), and so forth endlessly. Why did Sismondi attack money economy (and capitalism)? What does he offer in place of it? Small independent production, the natural economy of the peasants in the countryside, artisan production in the towns. Here is what he says of the former in the chapter headed "Of Patriarchal Agriculture" (ch. III, l. III, "De l'exploitation patriarcale"— the patriarchal exploitation of the land. Book III treats of "territorial" or land wealth):

"The first owners of land were themselves tillers, all the field work was done by the labour of their children and their servants. No social organisation** guarantees more happiness and more virtue to the most numerous

---

* As capitalism develops, agriculture, always and everywhere, *lags behind* commerce and industry, it is always subordinate to them and is exploited by them, and it is always *drawn* by them, only later on, onto the path of capitalist *production*.

** Note that Sismondi—exactly like our Narodniks—at once transformed the peasants' independent economy into a "social organisation." Obvious juggling. What is it that links together these peasants from different localities? The division of social labour and the commodity economy that superseded feudal ties. We at once see the elevation of one division of the commodity-economy system to utopian heights and the failure to understand the other divisions. Compare this with what Mr. N. —on says on p. 322: "The form of industry based on the ownership of the instruments of production by the peasantry." Mr. N. —on does not even suspect that this ownership of the instruments of production by the peasantry is—historically and logically—*the starting-point* of that same *capitalist* production!

class of the nation, a larger prosperity (opulence) to all, greater stability to the public order.... In those countries where the farmer is the owner (où le fermier est propriétaire) and where the produce belongs entirely (sans partage) to the people who perform all the work, i.e., in those countries whose agriculture we call patriarchal, we see at every step signs of the tiller's love for the house in which he lives, for the land which he tills.... Work itself is a pleasure to him.... In those happy countries where agriculture is patriarchal, the particular nature of every field is studied, and this knowledge is passed on from father to son.... Large-scale farming, directed by richer men, will perhaps rise above prejudice and routine. But knowledge (l'intelligence, i.e., knowledge of agriculture) will not reach the one who works and will be badly applied.... Patriarchal economy improves the morals and character of that numerous section of the nation which has to do all the work in the fields. Property cultivates habits of order and frugality, constant abundance destroys the taste for gluttony (gourmandise) and intemperance.... Entering into exchange almost exclusively with nature he" (the tiller) "has less reason than any industrial worker to distrust men and to resort to the weapon of dishonesty against them" (I, 165-70). "The first farmers were simple labourers; they themselves performed the bulk of the agricultural work; they kept the size of their enterprises commensurate with the working capacity of their families.... They did not cease to be peasants: they themselves followed the plough (tiennent eux-mêmes les cornes de leur charrue); they themselves tended their cattle, both in the fields and in the barns, they lived in the pure air and got accustomed to constant labour and to modest food, which create sturdy citizens and stalwart soldiers.* They hardly ever employed day labourers to work with them, but only servants (des domestiques), always chosen from among their equals, whom they treated as equals, who ate with them at the same table, drink the same wine and wear the same kind of

---

* Reader, compare with these honeyed grandmother's tales the statements of the "progressive" publicist of the late nineteenth century whom Mr. Struve cites in his *Critical Remarks*, p. 17.[67]

clothes as they did. Thus, the farmers and their servants constituted one class of peasants, inspired by the same feelings, sharing the same pleasures, subjected to the same influences and bound to their country by the same ties" (I, 221).

Here, then, you have the famous "people's production"! Let it not be said that Sismondi does not understand the need to unite the producers: he says plainly (see below) that "he too" (like Fourier, Owen, Thompson and Muiron) "wants association" (II, 365). Let it not be said that he stands for *property*: on the contrary, he places the weight of emphasis on small economy (cf. II, 355) and not upon small property. It goes without saying that this idealisation of small peasant economy looks different under different historical and social conditions. But there can be no doubt that it is small peasant economy that is glorified by both romanticism and Narodism.

Similarly, Sismondi idealises primitive artisan production and guilds.

"The village shoemaker, who is at once merchant, factory owner and worker, will not make a single pair of shoes without an order" (II, 262), whereas capitalist manufacture, not knowing the demand, may suffer bankruptcy. "Undoubtedly, from both the theoretical and the factual standpoint, the institution of guilds (corps de métier) prevented, and was bound to prevent, the formation of a surplus population. It is also beyond doubt that such a population exists at the present time, and that it is the necessary result of the present system" (I, 431). Many more excerpts of a similar nature could be quoted, but we shall postpone our examination of Sismondi's practical recipes until later. Here let us confine ourselves to what we have quoted in order to probe Sismondi's point of view. The arguments we have quoted may be summed up as follows: 1) money economy is condemned for destroying the small producers' security and the close relations among them (in the shape of the nearness of the artisan to his customers, or of the tiller to other tillers, his equals); 2) small production is extolled for ensuring the independence of the producer and eliminating the contradictions of capitalism.

Let us note that both these ideas constitute an essen-

tial part of Narodism,* and endeavour to probe their meaning.

The criticism of money economy by the romanticists
and the Narodniks amounts to the following: it points to
the fruits of that economy—individualism** and antagonism (competition), and also the producer's insecurity and
the instability of the social economy.***

First about "individualism." Usually, the contrast is
made between the association of the peasants in a given
community, or of the artisans (or the handicraftsmen) of
a given craft, and capitalism, which destroys the ties that
bind them, and puts competition in their place. This argument is a repetition of the typical error of romanticism,
namely: the conclusion that since capitalism is torn by
contradictions it is not a *higher form of social organisation.*
Does not capitalism, which destroys the medieval village
community, guild, artel and similar ties, substitute others
for them? Is not commodity economy already a *tie* between the producers, a tie established by the *market?****
The antagonistic character of *this tie*, which is full of
fluctuations and contradictions, gives one no right to deny
its existence. And we know that it is the development
of contradictions that with ever-growing force reveals the
strength of this tie, *compels* all the individual elements
and classes of society to strive to unite, and to unite no
longer within the narrow limits of one village community,

---

* On this question, too, Mr. N. —on is guilty of such a heap
of contradictions that one can choose from them *any number* of propositions in no way connected with each other. But there can be no
doubt about his idealisation of peasant economy by the use of the
hazy term "people's production." A haze is a particularly suitable
atmosphere in which to don all sorts of disguises.

** Cf. N. —on, p. 321, in f. (in fine—at the end.—*Ed.*) and
others.

*** Ibid., 335. P. 184: capitalism "robs of stability." And many
others.

**** "In actual fact, *society, association* are denominations which
can be given to every society, to feudal society as well as to bourgeois society, which is association founded on competition. How
then can there be writers, who, by the single word *association,*
think they can refute competition?" (Marx, *Das Elend der Philosophie.*)[68] Sharply criticising the sentimental condemnation of competition, the author plainly stresses its *progressive aspect,* its driving
force, which promotes "technical progress and social progress."

or of one district, but to unite all the members of the given class *in a whole nation* and even in different countries. Only a romanticist, with his reactionary point of view, can deny the existence of these ties and their deeper importance, which is based on the common role played in the national economy and not upon territorial, professional, religious and other such interests. If arguments of this kind earned the name of romanticist for Sismondi, who wrote at a time when these new ties engendered by capitalism were still in the embryo, all the more do our Narodniks deserve such an estimation; for *today*, the enormous importance of these ties can only be denied by those who are totally blind.

As regards insecurity and instability, and so forth, that is the same old song we dealt with when discussing the foreign market. Attacks of this kind betray the romanticist who fearfully condemns precisely that which scientific theory values most in capitalism: its inherent striving for development, its irresistible urge onwards, its inability to halt or to reproduce the economic processes in their former, rigid dimensions. Only a utopian who concocts fantastic plans for spreading medieval associations (such as the village community) to the whole of society can ignore the fact that it is the "instability" of capitalism that is an enormously progressive factor, one which accelerates social development, draws larger and larger masses of the population into the whirlpool of social life, compels them to ponder over its structure, and to "forge their happiness" with their own hands.

Mr. N. —on's phrases about the "instability" of capitalist economy, about the lack of proportion in the development of exchange, about the disturbance of the balance between industry and agriculture, between production and consumption, about the abnormality of crises, and so forth, testify beyond all doubt to the fact that he still shares the viewpoint of *romanticism* to the full. Hence, the criticism of European romanticism applies *word for word* to his theory too. Here is the proof:

"Let us hear what old Boisguillebert says:

"'The price of commodities,' he says, 'must always be *proportionate*; for it is such mutual understanding alone

that can enable them to reciprocally give birth to one another.... As wealth, then, is nothing but this continual intercourse between man and man, craft and craft, etc., it is
a frightful blindness to go looking for the cause of misery
elsewhere than in the cessation of such traffic brought
about by a disturbance of proportion in prices.'

"Let us listen also to a modern* economist:

"'The great law as necessary to be affixed to production,
that is, the law of *proportion*, which alone can preserve the
continuity of value.... The equivalent must be guaranteed.... All nations have attempted, at various periods of
their history, by instituting numerous commercial regulations and restrictions, to effect, in some degree, the object here explained.... But the natural and inherent selfishness of man ... has urged him to break down all such
regulations. Proportionate Production is the realisation
of the entire truth of the Science of Social Economy'
(W. Atkinson, *Principles of Political Economy*, London, 1840,
pp. 170 and 195).

"Fuit Troja!** This true proportion between supply and
demand, which is beginning once more to be the object of
so many wishes, ceased long ago to exist. It has passed
into the stage of senility. It was possible only at a time
when the means of production were limited, when the movement of exchange took place within very restricted bounds.
With the birth of large-scale industry this true proportion
had to (musste) come to an end, and production is inevitably compelled to pass in continuous succession
through vicissitudes of prosperity, depression, crisis, stagnation, renewed prosperity, and so on.

"Those who, like Sismondi, wish to return to the true
proportion of production, while preserving the present basis
of society, are reactionary, since, to be consistent, they
must also wish to bring back all the other conditions of
industry of former times.

"What kept production in true, or more or less true,
proportions? It was demand that dominated supply, that
preceded it. Production followed close on the heels of con-

---

* Written in 1847.
** Troy is no more!—*Ed.*

sumption. Large-scale industry, forced by the very instruments at its disposal to produce on an ever-increasing scale, can no longer wait for demand. Production precedes consumption, supply compels demand.

"In existing society, in industry based on individual exchange, anarchy of production, which is the source of so much misery, is at the same time the source of all progress.

"Thus, one or the other: either you want the true proportions of past centuries with present-day means of production, in which case you are both reactionary and utopian.

"Or, you want progress without anarchy: in which case, in order to preserve the productive forces, you must abandon individual exchange" (*Das Elend der Philosophie*, S. 46-48).[69]

The last words apply to Proudhon, with whom the author is polemising, thus formulating the difference between his own viewpoint and the views both of Sismondi and of Proudhon. Mr. N. —on would not, of course, approximate to either one or the other in *all* his views.* But look into the content of the passage given. What is the main thesis of the author we have quoted, his basic idea, which brings him into irreconcilable opposition to his predecessors? Undoubtedly, it is that he places the question of the instability of capitalism (which *all these three* authors admit) on a *historical* plane and regards this instability as a *progressive factor*. In other words: he recognises, firstly, that existing capitalist development, which proceeds through disproportion, crises, etc., is *necessary development*, and says that the very character of the means of production (machines) gives rise to the desire for an unlimited expansion of production and the constant anticipation of demand by supply. Secondly, he recognises *elements of progress* in this development, which are: the development of the productive forces, socialisation of labour within the bounds of the whole of society, increased mobility of the population and the growth of its consciousness, and so forth. These two points ex-

---

* Although it is a big question as to *why* he would not do so. Is it not only because these authors raised problems on a wider plane, having in mind the existing economic system in general, its place and significance in the development of the whole of mankind, and did not limit their outlook to *one country*, for which one may supposedly invent a *special* theory?

haust the difference between him and Sismondi and Proudhon, who agree with him in indicating the "instability" of capitalism and the contradictions it engenders, and in their sincere desire to eliminate these contradictions. Their failure to understand that this "instability" is a *necessary* feature of all capitalism and commodity economy in general brought them to *utopia*. Their failure to understand the elements of progress *inherent* in this instability makes their theories *reactionary*.*

And now we invite Messrs. the Narodniks to answer this question: Does Mr. N. —on agree with the views of scientific theory on the two points mentioned? Does he regard instability as a characteristic of the present system, and of present-day development? Does he admit the existence of elements of progress in this instability? Everybody knows that he does not, that, on the contrary, Mr. N. —on proclaims this "instability" of capitalism to be simply an abnormality, a digression, and so forth, and regards it as decadence, retrogression (cf. above: *"robs of* stability") and idealises that very economic stagnation (recall the "age-old foundations," "time-hallowed principles," and so forth) whose destruction is the historical merit of "unstable" capitalism. It is clear, therefore, that we were quite right in including him among the romanticists and that no "quotations" and "references" on his part will change *this character of his own arguments*.

We shall deal again with this "instability" later (in connection with the hostility of romanticism and Narodism to the diminution of the agricultural population to the advantage of the industrial population); at present let us quote a passage from *A Critique of Some of the Propositions of Political Economy* in which the *sentimental* attacks on money economy are examined.

---

* This term is employed in its *historico-philosophical* sense, describing only the *error* of the theoreticians who take models for their theories from *obsolete* forms of society. It does not apply at all to the personal qualities of these theoreticians, or to their programmes. Everybody knows that neither Sismondi nor Proudhon were reactionaries in the ordinary sense of the term. We are explaining these elementary truths because, as we shall see below, the Narodnik gentlemen have not grasped them to this day.

"These definite social functions" (namely, of the seller and buyer) "are no outgrowths of human nature, but are the products of exchange relations between men who produce their goods in the form of commodities. They are so far from being purely individual relations between buyer and seller that both enter into these relations only to the extent that their individual labour is disregarded and is turned into money as labour of no individual. Therefore, just as it is childish to regard these bourgeois economic roles of buyer and seller as eternal social forms of human individuality, so it is, on the other hand, preposterous to lament over them as the cause of the extinction of individuality.

"How deeply some beautiful souls are wounded by the merely superficial aspect of the antagonism which asserts itself in buying and selling may be seen from the following abstract from M. Isaac Pereire's *Leçons sur l'industrie et les finances*, Paris, 1832. The fact that the same Isaac in his capacity of inventor and dictator of the 'Crédit mobilier'* has acquired the reputation of the wolf of the Paris Bourse shows what lurks behind the sentimental criticism of economics. Says M. Pereire, at the time an apostle of Saint-Simon: 'Since individuals are isolated and separated from one another both in their labours and in consumption, exchange takes place between them in the products of their respective industries. From the necessity of exchange arises the necessity of determining the relative value of things. The ideas of value and exchange are thus intimately connected and both express in their actual form individualism and antagonism.... The determination of values of products takes place only because there are sales and purchases, or, to put it differently, because there is an antagonism between different members of society. One has to occupy himself with price and value only where there is sale and purchase, that is to say, where every individual is obliged *to struggle* to procure for himself the objects necessary for the maintenance of his existence'" (op. cit., p. 68).[70]

The question is: wherein lies Pereire's *sentimentality*? He talks only about the individualism, antagonism and con-

---

* A bank which grants loans on the security of movable property.—*Ed.*

flict inherent in capitalism, he says the very thing our Narodniks say in different keys, and, moreover, they seem
to be speaking the truth, because "individualism, antagonism and conflict" are indeed necessary attributes of exchange,
of commodity production. His sentimentality lies in
that this Saint-Simonist, carried away by his condemnation
of the contradictions of capitalism, *fails to discern behind
these contradictions* the fact that *exchange* also expresses a
special form of *social economy*, that it, consequently, *not
only disunites* (it does that only in respect of the medieval
associations, which capitalism destroys), *but also unites* men,
compelling them to enter into intercourse with each other
through the medium of the market.* It was this superficial
understanding, caused by their eagerness to "trounce" capitalism (from the utopian point of view) that gave the above-
quoted author occasion to call Pereire's criticism *sentimental.*

But why should we worry about Pereire, the long-forgotten apostle of long-forgotten Saint-Simonism? Would it
not be better to take the modern "apostle" of Narodism?

"Production ... was robbed of its popular character and
assumed an individual, capitalist character" (Mr. N. —on,
Sketches, pp. 321-22).

You see how this disguised romanticist argues: "people's
production became individual production." And as by "people's production" the author wants to imply the village
community,[71] he points to the decline of the *social* character of production, to the shrinking of the *social* form of
production.

But is that so? The "village community" provided (*if
it did provide*; but we are ready to make any concession to
the author) for organised production only in the one individual community, isolated from all the other communities. The social character of production embraced *only the
members of the one village community.*** Capitalism, however,

---

* Substituting unity along the lines of social status and social
interests of a whole country, and even of the whole world, for local
and social-estate associations.

** According to the Zemstvo statistics (Blagoveshchensky's *Combined Returns*), the average size of *a village community*, for 123 uyezds
in 22 gubernias, is 53 households, with a population of 323 of both
sexes.

gives production a social character in a whole country. "Individualism" means the destruction of social ties; but these ties are destroyed by the *market*, which replaces them by ties between *masses of individuals* who are not bound together by a village community, a social estate, a given trade, the restricted area of a given industry, etc. The tie created by capitalism manifests itself in the form of contradictions and antagonism, and *therefore*, our romanticist refuses to see this tie (although the village community, too, as a form of organisation of production never existed without the other forms of contradictions and antagonism inherent in the old modes of production).The utopian point of view transforms his criticism of capitalism, as well, into a *sentimental* one.

II
THE PETTY-BOURGEOIS CHARACTER OF ROMANTICISM

The idealisation of small production reveals to us another typical feature of romanticist and Narodnik criticism, namely, its *petty-bourgeois character*. We have seen that the French and the Russian romanticists are unanimous in converting small production into a "social organisation," into a "form of production," and *in contrasting it to capitalism*. We have also seen that this contrasting of one to the other is nothing but the expression of an extremely superficial understanding, that it is the artificial and incorrect singling out of one form of commodity economy (large-scale industrial capital) and condemnation of it, while utopianly idealising *another form of the same* commodity economy (small production). The misfortune of both the European romanticists of the early nineteenth century and of the Russian romanticists of the late nineteenth century is that they invent for themselves a sort of abstract small production existing outside of the social relations of production, and *overlook* the trifling circumstance that this small production actually exists in an environment of *commodity production*—this applies both to the small economy on the European continent in the 1820s and to Russian peasant economy in the 1890s. *Actually*, the small producer, whom the romanticists and the Narodniks place on a pedestal, is therefore a *petty bourgeois* who exists in the same antagonistic relations as every other member of capitalist society, and who also defends his interests by means of a struggle which, on the one hand, is constantly creating a small minority of big bourgeois, and on the other, pushes the majority into the ranks of the proletariat. Actually, as everybody sees and knows, there are no small producers who do not stand *between* these two opposite classes, and this middle position necessarily determines the specific character of the petty bourgeoisie, its dual character, its two-facedness, its gravitation towards the minority which has emerged from the struggle successfully, its hostility towards the "failures," i.e., the majority. The more commodity economy develops, the more strongly and sharply do these qualities stand out, and the more evident does it become that the idealisation of small production merely expresses a reactionary, *petty-bourgeois* point of view.

We must make no mistake about the meaning of these terms, which the author of *A Critique of Some of the Propositions of Political Economy* applied specifically to Sismondi. These terms do not at all mean that Sismondi *defends* the backward petty bourgeois. *Nowhere does Sismondi defend them*: he wants to take the point of view of the labouring classes in general, he expresses his sympathy for all the members of these classes, he is pleased, for example, with factory legislation, he attacks capitalism and exposes its contradictions. In a word, his point of view is exactly the same as that of the modern Narodniks.

The question is: on what grounds, then, is he described as a petty bourgeois? On the grounds that he does not understand the connection between small production (which he idealises) and big capital (which he attacks). On the grounds that he *does not see* that his beloved small producer, the peasant, is in reality becoming a petty bourgeois. We must never forget the following explanation about reducing the theories of various authors to the interests and points of view of different classes:

"Only one must not form the narrow-minded notion that the petty bourgeoisie, on principle, wishes to enforce an egoistic class interest. Rather, it believes that the *special* conditions of its emancipation are the *general* conditions within the frame of which alone modern society can be saved and the class struggle avoided. Just as little must one imagine that the democratic representatives are indeed all shopkeepers or enthusiastic champions of shopkeepers. According to their education and their individual position they may be as far apart as heaven from earth. What makes them representatives of the petty bourgeoisie is the fact that in their minds they do not get beyond the limits which the latter do not get beyond in life, that they are consequently driven, theoretically, to the same problems and solutions to which material interest and social position drive the latter practically. This is, in general, the relationship between the *political and literary representatives* of a class and the class they represent" (Karl Marx, *The Eighteenth Brumaire of Louis Bonaparte*, translated into Russian by Bazarov and Stepanov, pp. 179-80).[72]

Hence, those Narodniks who think that the sole object of referring to petty-bourgeois character is to say something exceptionally venomous, that it is simply a polemical ruse, cut a very comical figure. By this attitude they reveal their misconception of the general views of their opponents, and chiefly their misconception of the basis of *that very* criticism of capitalism with which they all "agree," and of the way in which it *differs* from sentimental and petty-bourgeois criticism. The mere fact that they strive so hard to evade the very problem of these latter forms of criticism, of their existence in Western Europe, of their relation to the scientific criticism, clearly shows *why* the Narodniks do not want to understand this difference.*

---

* For example, Ephrucy wrote two articles on the subject of "how Sismondi regarded the growth of capitalism" (*Russkoye Bogatstvo*, No. 7, p. 139), and yet *absolutely failed to understand* exactly *how* Sismondi did regard it. *Russkoye Bogatstvo*'s contributor *did not notice* Sismondi's petty-bourgeois point of view. But since Ephrucy is undoubtedly familiar with Sismondi; since he (as we shall see later) is familiar with that very representative of the modern theory who characterised Sismondi in that way; since he, too, wishes to "agree" with this representative of the new theory—his failure to understand acquires a quite definite significance. The Narodnik could not see in the romanticist what he does not see in himself.

Let us explain the above with an example. In the bibliographical section of *Russkaya Mysl*[73] for 1896, No. 5 (p. 229, et seq.), it is stated that among the intelligentsia "a group has lately appeared and is growing with amazing rapidity" which in principle is unreservedly hostile to Narodism. The reviewer points in the briefest outline to the causes and character of this hostility, and one cannot but note with appreciation that he gives quite correctly the *gist* of the point of view hostile to Narodism.* The reviewer does not share this point of view. He does not understand that the ideas of class interests, etc., should compel us to deny "people's ideals" ("simply *people*'s but not Narodnik"; ibid., p. 229), which, he says, are the welfare, freedom and consciousness of the peasantry, i.e., of the majority of the population.

"We shall be told, of course, as others have been told," says the reviewer, "that the ideals of the peasant author" (this is a reference to the wishes expressed by a certain peasant) "are petty-bourgeois and that, therefore, to this day our literature has represented and defended the interests of the petty bourgeoisie. But this is simply a bogey, and who, except those possessing the world outlook and mental habits of a Zamoskvorechye merchant's wife, can be frightened by such a bogey?..."

Strongly spoken! But let us hear what he has to say further:

"... The basic criterion, both of the conditions of human intercourse and of deliberate social measures, is not economic categories, borrowed, moreover, from conditions alien to the country, and formed under different circumstances, but the happiness and welfare, material and spiritual, of the majority of the population. And if a certain mode of life, and certain measures for maintaining and developing this mode of life, lead to this happiness, call them petty-bourgeois, or what you will, it will not alter the situation: they—this mode of life and these measures—will

---

* It sounds very strange, of course, to praise a man for correctly conveying somebody else's ideas!! But what would you have? Among the ordinary controversialists of *Russkoye Bogatstvo* and of the old *Novoye Slovo*, Messrs. Krivenko and Vorontsov, *such* a method of controversy is indeed a rare exception.

still be essentially progressive, and for that very reason
will represent the *highest ideal attainable by society under
existing conditions and in its present state*" (ibid., pp. 229-
30, author's italics).

Does the reviewer really not see that in the heat of controversy he has jumped over the problem?

Although the accusation that Narodism is petty-bourgeois is described by him with supreme severity as "simply
a bogey," he produces no proof of this assertion, except
the following incredibly amazing proposition: "The
criterion ... is not economic categories, but the happiness
of the majority." Why, this is the same as saying: the criterion of the weather is not meteorological observations,
but the way the majority feels! What, we ask, are these
"economic categories" if not the *scientific formulation* of
the population's conditions of economy and life, and moreover, not of the "population" in general, but of *definite*
groups of the population, which occupy a definite place under the *present* system of social economy? By opposing
the highly abstract idea of "the happiness of the majority" to "economic categories," the reviewer simply strikes
out the entire development of social science since the end
of the last century and reverts to naïve rationalistic speculation, which ignores the existence and the development of
definite social relationships. With one stroke of the pen
he wipes out all that the human mind, in its attempt *to
understand* social phenomena, has achieved at the price
of centuries of searching! And after thus relieving himself of all scientific encumbrances, the reviewer *believes
the problem is solved*. Indeed, he bluntly concludes: "If
a certain mode of life ... leads to this happiness, call it
what you will, it will not alter the situation." What do you
think of that? But the whole question was: *what* mode
of life? The author himself had only just said that those
who regarded peasant economy as a special mode of life
("people's production," or whatever you like to call it)
were opposed by others who asserted that it is not a special mode of life, but just the ordinary *petty-bourgeois*
mode of life, similar to that of every other kind of small
production in a country of commodity production and
capitalism. If it automatically follows from the form-

er view that "this mode of life" ("people's production") "leads to happiness," then it also automatically follows from the latter view that "this mode of life" (the petty-bourgeois mode) leads to capitalism and to nothing else, leads to the "majority of the population" being forced into the ranks of the proletariat and to the conversion of the minority into a rural (or industrial) bourgeoisie. Is it not obvious that the reviewer fired a shot into the air, and amidst the noise of the shot took as proven exactly what is denied by the second view, which is so unkindly declared to be "simply a bogey"?

Had he wanted to examine the second view seriously, he obviously should have proved one of two things: either that "petty bourgeoisie" is a wrong scientific category, that one can conceive of capitalism and commodity economy *without* a petty bourgeoisie (as indeed the Narodniks actually do, and thereby completely revert to Sismondi's point of view), *or* that this category is *inapplicable* to Russia, i.e., that here we have neither capitalism nor the prevalence of commodity economy, that the small producers do not become commodity producers, that the above-mentioned process of ousting the majority and of strengthening the "independence" of the minority is not taking place among them. Now, however, having seen that he treats the reference to the petty-bourgeois character of Narodism simply as a desire to "offend" the Narodniks, and having read the above-quoted phrase about the "bogey," we involuntarily recall the well-known utterance: "Pray, Kit Kitych!"[4] Who would offend you? You yourself can offend anybody!"

III
THE PROBLEM OF THE GROWTH
OF THE INDUSTRIAL POPULATION AT THE EXPENSE
OF THE AGRICULTURAL POPULATION

Let us return to Sismondi. In addition to his idealisation of the petty bourgeoisie, in addition to his romanticist failure to understand how, under the present social system of economy, the "peasantry" is transformed into a petty bourgeoisie, he holds an extremely characteristic view about the diminution of the agricultural population to the advantage of the industrial population. It is common knowledge that this phenomenon—one of the most striking manifestations of a country's capitalist development — is observed in all civilised countries, and also in Russia.*

Sismondi, an outstanding economist of his time, must, of course, have seen this fact. He openly records it, but fails completely to understand the necessary connection between it and the development of capitalism (to put it even more generally: between it and the division of social labour, the growth of commodity economy called forth by this phenomenon). He simply *condemns* it as a defect in the "system."

After pointing to the enormous progress made by English agriculture, Sismondi says:

"While admiring the carefully cultivated fields, we must look at the people who cultivate them; they constitute only half the number to be seen in France on an equal area. Some economists regard this as a gain; in my opinion it is a loss" (I, 239).

We can understand why the ideologists of the bourgeoisie regarded this thing as a gain (we shall soon see that *such* is also the view of the scientific critique of capitalism): in this way they formulated the growth of bourgeois wealth, commerce and industry. While hastening to *condemn* this phenomenon, Sismondi forgets to think about its causes.

"In France and in Italy," he says, "where, it is calculated, four-fifths of the population belong to the agricultural class, four-fifths of the nation will have the national bread to eat, no matter what the price of foreign grain may be" (I, 264). Fuit Troja! is what can be said of this.

---

* The percentage of the urban population in European Russia has been growing in the post-Reform period. Here we must confine ourselves merely to pointing to this most commonly known symptom, although it expresses the phenomenon *far from completely*, in that it does not include important features specific to Russia as compared with Western Europe. This is not the place to examine these specific features (the peasants' lack of freedom of movement, the existence of industrial and factory villages, internal colonisation of the country, and so forth).

There are now no countries (even the most highly agricultural) which are not entirely dependent upon *the price of grain*, i.e., upon world capitalist production of grain.

"If a nation cannot increase its commercial population except by demanding from each a larger amount of work for the same pay, it must fear an increase in its industrial population" (I, 322). As the reader sees, this is merely kind advice devoid of all sense and meaning, for here the concept "nation" is based on the artificial exclusion of the antagonisms between the classes which constitute this "nation." As always, Sismondi simply *wriggles out* of these antagonisms by means of the well-meaning wish that ... there should be no antagonisms.

"In England, agriculture employs only 770,199 families, commerce and industry employ 959,632, the other estates in society 413,316. It is truly frightful (effrayante) that such a large proportion of the population, out of a total of 2,143,147 families, or 10,150,615 persons, exists on commercial wealth. Happily, France is still far from having such an enormous number of workers depending upon luck in a remote market" (I, 434). Here Sismondi even seems to forget that this "happiness" is due entirely to the lag in France's capitalist development.

Depicting the changes in the existing system which are "desirable" from his point of view (we shall discuss these later), Sismondi says that "the result" (of reforms to suit the romantic taste) "would undoubtedly be that more than one country living merely by industry would have to successively close down many workshops, and that the urban population, which had increased excessively, would rapidly decline, whereas the rural population would begin to grow" (II, 367).

This example brings out in particular relief the helplessness of the sentimental criticism of capitalism and the impotent vexation of the petty bourgeois! Sismondi simply *complains** that things are going one way and not another. His grief at the destruction of the Eden of the rural population's patriarchal dullness and downtrodden condition is

---

* "Ultimately ... this form of Socialism" (namely the trend of petty-bourgeois criticism, of which Sismondi was the head) "ended in a miserable fit of the blues."[75]

so great that our economist does not even discern why it takes place. He therefore overlooks the fact that the increase in the industrial population is necessarily and inseverably connected with commodity economy and capitalism. Commodity economy develops to the degree that the social division of labour develops. And the division of labour means precisely that one industry after another, one form of processing the raw product after another, *separates* from agriculture, becomes independent, and consequently gives rise to an industrial population. Therefore, to discuss commodity economy and capitalism and ignore the law of the relative growth of the industrial population, means to have no notion whatever of the *fundamental* characteristics of the *present* system of social economy.

"It is in the nature of capitalist production to continually reduce the agricultural population as compared with the non-agricultural, because in industry (in the strict sense) the increase of constant capital in relation to variable capital goes hand in hand with an absolute increase, though relative decrease,* in variable capital; on the other hand, in agriculture the variable capital required for the exploitation of a certain plot of land decreases absolutely; it can thus only increase to the extent that new land** is taken into cultivation, but this again requires as a prerequisite a still greater growth of the non-agricultural population" (III, 2, 177). [76]

On this point modern theory takes a view diametrically opposite to that of romanticism with its sentimental

---

* From this the reader can judge the wit of Mr. N. —on who, in his *Sketches*, without ceremony transforms the *relative* decrease of variable capital and of the number of workers into an *absolute* one, and from this draws a host of the absurdest conclusions concerning the "shrinking" of the home market, and so forth.

** It was this condition that we had in mind when we said that the internal colonisation of Russia hindered the manifestation of the law of the greater growth of the industrial population. It is enough to recall the difference between Russia's long-settled central areas, where the industrial population grew not so much in the towns as in the factory villages and townships, and, say, Novorossiya, which has been settled in the post-Reform period, and where the towns are growing at a pace comparable with that of America. We hope to deal with this problem in greater detail elsewhere.

complaints. When we understand that something is inevitable, we naturally adopt a totally different attitude towards it and are able to appraise its different aspects. The phenomenon we are now discussing is one of the most profound and most general of the contradictions of the capitalist system. The separation of town from country, their oppositeness, and the exploitation of the countryside by the town—these universal concomitants of developing capitalism—are a necessary product of the preponderance of "commercial wealth" (to use Sismondi's term) over "territorial wealth" (agricultural wealth). Therefore, the predominance of the town over the countryside (economically, politically, intellectually, and in all other respects) is a universal and inevitable thing in all countries where there is commodity production and capitalism, including Russia: only sentimental romanticists can bewail this. Scientific theory, on the contrary, points to the *progressive* aspect given to this contradiction by large-scale industrial capital. "Capitalist production, by collecting the population in great centres, and causing an ever-increasing preponderance of town population ... concentrates the historical motive-power of society"[77] (die geschichtliche Bewegungskraft der Gesellschaft).* If the predominance of the town is inevitable, only the attraction of the population to the towns can neutralise (and, as history shows, does in fact neutralise) the one-sided character of this predominance. If the town necessarily gains itself a privileged position, leaving the village subordinate, undeveloped, helpless and downtrodden, only the influx of the village population into the towns, only this mingling and merging of the agricultural with the non-agricultural population, can lift the rural population out of its helplessness. Therefore, in reply to the reactionary complaints and lamentations of the romanticists, modern theory in-

---

* Cf. also the particularly striking characterisation of the progressive role played by industrial centres in the intellectual development of the population in *Die Lage der arbeitenden Klasse in England*, 1845.[78] That the recognition of this role did not prevent the author of *The Condition of the Working Class in England* from profoundly understanding the contradiction manifested in the separation of town from country, is proved by his polemical book against Dühring.[79]

dicates exactly how this narrowing of the gap between the conditions of life of the agricultural and of the non-agricultural population creates the conditions for eliminating the antithesis between town and country.

The question now is: what is the point of view of our Narodnik economists on this problem? Undoubtedly, that of the sentimental romanticist. Far from understanding that the growth of the industrial population is *necessary* under the present system of social economy, they even *try to close their eyes* to the phenomenon itself, like the bird which hides its head under its wing. As was to be expected, no answer was forthcoming to P. Struve's statement that Mr. N. —on, in his arguments about capitalism, commits a gross error when he asserts that there is an *absolute* diminution of variable capital (*Critical Remarks*, p. 255), and that it is absurd to contrast Russia with the West in respect of the former's smaller percentage of industrial population and at the same time to ignore the *growth* of this percentage as a result of the development of capitalism* (*Sozialpolitisches Centralblatt*,[80] 1893, No. 1). While constantly harping upon the specific features of Russia, the Narodnik economists have not even been able to present the problem of the *actual* specific features of the formation of an industrial population in Russia,** to which we briefly referred above. Such is the Narodniks' *theoretical* attitude towards this problem. Actually, however, when the Narodniks, untrammelled by theoretical doubts, discuss the conditions of the peasants in the post-Reform countryside, they admit that the peasants who are ousted from agriculture migrate to the towns and to factory areas, but they confine themselves to *bewailing* this state of affairs, just as Sismondi *bewailed* it.*** They do not notice at all either the economic

---

* Let the reader recall that *this is the mistake* made by Sismondi when he said that "happily" eighty per cent of the population of France were agricultural, as if this was a specific feature of some "people's production," and so forth, and not a reflection of lag in capitalist development.

** Cf. Volgin, *The Substantiation of Narodism in the Works of Mr. Vorontsov*. St. Petersburg, 1896, pp. 215-16.

*** In fairness, however, it must be said that Sismondi observes the growth of the industrial population in several countries, and recognises its universal nature and reveals here and there an under-

or (what is perhaps more important) the moral and educational significance of the profound change that has taken
place in the conditions of life of the masses of the population in post-Reform Russia—a process which, for the
first time, has disturbed the peasantry's settled life, their
position of being tied to their localities, given them
mobility, and narrowed the gap between the agricultural
and non-agricultural labourers, the rural and the urban
workers.* All they have derived from it is an occasion
for sentimental-romanticist lamentations.

---

standing of the fact that this is not merely some "anomaly," and so
forth, but a profound change in the people's conditions of life—
a change which admittedly has something good in it. At all events,
the following observation of his on the harmfulness of the division
of labour reveals views far more profound than those of Mr. Mikhailovsky, for example, who invented a general "formula of progress,"
instead of analysing the definite forms assumed by the division of
labour in different formations of social economy and at different
periods of development.

"Although the uniformity of the operations to which all the workers'
activities in the factories are reduced must obviously harm their
mental development (intelligence), nevertheless, it must be said
in fairness that according to the observations of the best judges,
the manufactory workers in England are superior in intelligence,
education and morals to the agricultural workers" (ouvriers des champs)
(I, 397). And Sismondi indicates the cause of this: Vivant sans cesse
ensemble, moins épuisés par la fatigue et pouvant se livrer davantage
à la conversation, les idées ont circulé plus rapidement entre eux
(Living constantly together, they are less fatigued, and having greater
opportunities of conversing with each other, ideas have spread more
rapidly among them.—Ed.). But, he adds in a melancholy tone,
aucun attachement à l'ordre établi (they display no attachment
to the established order.—Ed.).

* The forms assumed by this process are also different in the
central parts of European Russia as compared with the border regions.
It is mainly *agricultural* workers from the central black-earth gubernias and partly *nona-gricultural* workers from the industrial gubernias who migrate *to the border regions*, where they spread their knowledge of "their trades" and "implant" industry among the purely agricultural population. The migrants *from the industrial region* are *non-
agricultural* workers, part of whom scatter to all parts of Russia,
but most of whom stream into the metropolitan cities and the large
industrial centres; and this industrial current, if one may so express
it, is so strong, that it creates a shortage of *agricultural* workers, who
migrate *to the industrial gubernias* (Moscow, Yaroslavl and other
gubernias) from the central black-earth gubernias. See S. A. Korolenko, *Hired Labour, etc.*

IV
PRACTICAL PROPOSALS OF ROMANTICISM

We shall now endeavour to sum up Sismondi's point of view on capitalism (a task which, as the reader remembers, Ephrucy, too, set himself) and examine the practical programme of romanticism.

We have seen that Sismondi's merit lay in his being one of the first *to point* to the contradictions of capitalism. But in pointing to them he not only made no attempt to analyse them and explain their origin, development and trend, but even regarded them as unnatural, or mistaken digressions from the normal. He naïvely protested against these "digressions" with moralising phrases, denunciations, advice to eliminate them, and so forth, as if these contradictions did not express the *real interests* of real groups of the population occupying a definite place in the general system of social economy of the present day. This is the most outstanding feature of romanticism—to regard antagonism of interests (which is deeply rooted in the very system of social economy) as a contradiction or an error of doctrine, system, even of measures, and so forth. Here the narrow outlook of the Kleinbürger,* who stands aloof from developed contradictions and occupies an intermediary, transitional position between the two poles, is combined with a naïve idealism—we are almost ready to say a bureaucratic outlook—which attributes the existence of a social system to the opinions of men (especially of the powers that be) and not vice versa. We shall quote examples of all Sismondi's arguments of this kind.

"In forgetting men for the sake of things, has not England sacrificed the aim to the means?

"The example of England is all the more striking in that this nation is free, enlightened and well governed, and that all her misfortunes are due solely to her pursuit of a *wrong* economic line" (I, p. IX). In general Sismondi uses England as an example to frighten the Continent with—just like our romanticists, who imagine that they are contributing something new and not the oldest kind of rubbish.

---

* Petty bourgeois.—*Ed.*

"In drawing my readers' attention to England, I wanted to show ... the history of our own future, if we continue to act on the principles she has followed" (I, p. XVI).

"... The Continental countries deem it necessary to follow England in her career of manufacture" (II, 330). "There is no more astonishing, no more frightful spectacle than that presented by England" (II, 332).*

"It must not be forgotten that wealth is merely that which represents (n'est que la représentation) the pleasures and amenities of life" (here wealth in general is substituted for bourgeois wealth!), "and to create artificial wealth and thereby doom a nation to all that which actually represents poverty and suffering, means taking the name for the thing itself" (prendre le mot pour la chose) (I, 379).

"... As long as nations followed only the dictates (commands, indications) of nature and enjoyed the advantages provided by climate, soil, location and the possession of raw materials, they did not place themselves *in an unnatural position* (une position forcée), they did not seek *apparent wealth* (une opulence apparente) which for the masses becomes real poverty" (I, 411). Bourgeois wealth is only apparent wealth!! "It is dangerous for a nation to close its doors to foreign trade: this compels the nation to engage, in a way (en quelque sorte) *in false activity*, which leads to its ruin" (I, 448) **

---

* To show clearly the relation between *European* and *Russian* romanticism we shall quote, in footnotes, passages from Mr. N. —on. "We have refused to learn the lesson taught us by the course of economic development of Western Europe. We have been so dazzled by the brilliance of the development of capitalism in England, and we are so astonished by the immeasurably more rapid development of capitalism in the American States," etc. (323). As you see, even Mr. N. —on's expressions are not distinguished for their novelty! He is "astonished" by the same thing that "astonished" Sismondi at the beginning of the century.

** "... The economic path we have pursued for the past thirty years has been a wrong one" (281).... "We have too long identified the interests of capitalism with those of the national economy— an extremely fatal blunder.... *The apparent results* of the protection of industry ... *have obscured our vision* to such a degree that we have totally lost sight of the popular-social aspect ... we have lost sight of the price paid for this development, we have forgotten the aim of all production" (298)—except capitalist production!

"... Wages contain a necessary part which must sustain the life, strength and health of those who receive them.... Woe to the government that encroaches upon this part—it sacrifices everything (il sacrifie tout ensemble)—men, and hope of future wealth.... This difference enables us to understand how wrong is the policy of those governments which have reduced the wages of the working classes to the limit required to increase the net revenues of factory owners, merchants and property owners" (II, 169).*

"The time has come at last to ask: whither are we going?" (où l'on veut aller) (II, 328).

"Their separation" (the separation of the property-owning class from the working people), "the antagonism of their interests, is the result of the present-day artificial organisation which we have given human society.... The natural order of social progress did not by any means tend to separate men from things, or wealth from labour; in the rural districts the property owner could remain a tiller of the soil; in the towns the capitalist could remain an artisan; the separation of the working class from the leisured class was not absolutely indispensable for the existence of society, or for production; we introduced it for the greatest benefit of all; it devolves upon us (il nous appartient) to regulate it so that this benefit may be really achieved" (II, 348).

"Having been put in opposition to each other, the producers" (i.e., the masters and the workers) "were compelled to proceed along a path *diametrically opposed* to the interests of society.... In this constant struggle to reduce wages, the public interest, in which, however, all participate, is forgotten by all" (II, 359-60). And this too is preceded by mention of the paths bequeathed by history: "At the beginning of social life *every man possesses capital*, through which he applies his labour, and nearly all artisans live on

---

"Disdain for one's own past ... the implanting of capitalism" ... (283). ... "We ... have resorted to all means to implant capitalism"... (323). ... "We have overlooked" ... (ibid.).

* "... We have not hindered the development of the capitalist forms of production in spite of the fact that they are based upon the expropriation of the peasantry" (323).

a revenue consisting equally of profit and wages"
(II, 359).*

Enough, it seems.... We can be certain that a reader who
is familiar neither with Sismondi nor with Mr. N. —on will
find it difficult to say which of the points of view of the
two romanticists, the one in the footnote or the one in the
text, is the more primitive and naïve.

Sismondi's practical proposals, to which he devoted so
much space in his *Nouveaux Principes*, fully conform to
this.

The difference between us and Adam Smith, says Sismondi
in the very first book of his work, is that "we nearly always
call for that very governmental interference which Adam
Smith rejected" (I, 52). "The state does not rectify distribution" (I, 80).... "The legislator could ensure the poor
man some guarantees against universal competition" (I, 81).
"Production must be commensurate with social revenue, and
those who encourage unlimited production without taking
the trouble to ascertain what this revenue is, are pushing
the nation to ruin, though they think they are opening to it
the road to wealth (le chemin des richesses)" (I, 82).
"When the progress of wealth is gradual (gradué), when it
is proportionate to itself, when none of its parts develops
with excessive rapidity, it disseminates universal prosperity.... Perhaps it is the duty of governments to restrain
(ralentir!!) this movement in order to regulate it" (I, 409-
10).

Of the enormous historical importance of the development of the productive forces of society, which takes place
precisely through these contradictions and disproportions,
Sismondi has not the faintest idea!

"If the government exercises a regulating and moderating influence upon the pursuit of wealth, it can be infinite-

---

* "Instead of adhering firmly to our age-old traditions; instead
of developing the principle of a close tie between the means of production and the direct producer ... instead of increasing the productivity of its (*the peasantry*'s) labour by concentrating the means of
production in its hands ... instead of that, we have taken the *abso-*
lutely opposite path" (322-23). "We have mistaken the development
of capitalism for the development of the whole of people's production ... we *have overlooked* the fact that the development of one ... can
only proceed at the expense of the other" (323). Our italics.

ly beneficial" (I, 413). "Some of the measures to regulate trade which are nowadays condemned by public opinion, although meriting condemnation as a stimulus to industry, may, perhaps, be justified as a curb" (I, 415).

These arguments of Sismondi's already reveal his astonishing lack of historical sense: he has not the faintest idea that liberation from medieval regulation constituted the entire historical significance of the period contemporary to him. He does not realise that his arguments bring grist to the mill of the defenders of the ancien régime, who at that time were still so strong even in France, not to speak of the other countries of the West-European continent where they ruled.*

Thus, the starting-point of Sismondi's practical proposals is—tutelage, restraint, regulation.

This point of view follows quite naturally and inevitably from the whole of Sismondi's range of ideas. He lived at the very time when large-scale machine industry was taking its first steps on the European continent, when there began that sharp and abrupt change of all social relations under the influence of machines (note, under the influence of machine industry, and not of "capitalism" in general),** a change which is known in economic science as the *industrial revolution*.*** Here is how it is described by one of the first economists able fully to appreciate the profundity of the revolution which created modern European societies in place of the patriarchal semi-medieval societies:

---

* Ephrucy discerned "civic courage" in these regrets and longings of Sismondi (No. 7, p. 139). So the expression of sentimental longings calls for civic courage!! Open any high-school textbook on history and you will read that in the first quarter of the nineteenth century the West-European countries were organised on lines which the science of constitutional law designates by the term: Polizeistaat (police state.—*Ed*.). You will read that the historical task not only of that quarter, but also of the subsequent quarter of the century, was to combat it. You will understand then that Sismondi's point of view smacks of the dull-wittedness of the small French peasant of the Restoration period; that Sismondi exemplifies the combination of petty-bourgeois sentimental romanticism with phenomenal civic immaturity.

** Capitalism in England dates not from the end of the eighteenth century but from a far earlier period.

*** These words are in English in the original.—*Ed*.

"Such, in brief, is the history of English industrial development in the past sixty years" (this was written in 1844), "a history which has no counterpart in the annals of humanity. Sixty, eighty years ago, England was a country like every other, with small towns, few and simple industries, and a thin but proportionally large agricultural population. Today it is a country like *no* other, with a capital of two and a half million inhabitants; with vast manufacturing cities; with an industry that supplies the world, and produces almost everything by means of the most complex machinery; with an industrious, intelligent, dense population, of which two-thirds are employed in trade and commerce, and composed of classes wholly different; forming, in fact, with other customs and other needs, a different nation from the England of those days. The industrial revolution is of the same importance for England as the political revolution for France, and the philosophical revolution for Germany; and the difference between England in 1760 and in 1844 is at least as great as that between France, under the ancien régime and during the revolution of July."*

This was the complete "break-up" of all the old, deep-rooted relationships, whose economic basis had been small production. Naturally, with his reactionary, petty-bourgeois point of view, Sismondi could not understand the significance of this "break-up." Naturally, he first of all, and most of all, wished, urged, pleaded, demanded that this "break-up should be stopped."**

But how should this "break-up be stopped"? First of all, of course, by supporting the people's ... that is to say, "patriarchal production," the peasantry and small farming in general. Sismondi devotes a whole chapter (t. II, l. VII, ch. VIII) to the subject of "how the government should protect the population from the consequences of competition."

"In relation to the agricultural population, the government's general task is to ensure those who work (à ceux qui travaillent) a part of the property, or to support (favoriser)

---

* Engels, *Die Lage der arbeitenden Klasse in England.*[81]
** We make so bold as to hope that Mr. N. —on will not resent our borrowing this expression from him (p. 345), as we think it extremely apt and characteristic.

what we have called patriarchal agriculture in preference to all other kinds" (II, 340).

"A Statute of Elizabeth, which was disregarded, prohibited the building of *cottages** in England unless each was allotted a four-acre plot of land. Had this law been obeyed, no day labourer could have married without receiving a *cottage,** and no *cottager** would have been reduced to extreme poverty. This would have been a step forward (c'est quelque chose), but it would not have been enough; under the English climate, the peasant population would have lived in want on four acres per family. Today, most of the English cottagers have only one and a half to two acres of land, for which they pay a fairly high rent.... The law should compel ... the landlord, when he distributes his field among many *cottagers,** to give each one enough land to live on" (II, 342-43).**

The reader will see that the proposals of romanticism are absolutely *identical* with the proposals and programme of the Narodniks: they too ignore *actual* economic development, and in the epoch of large-scale machine industry,

---

* These words are in English in the original.—*Ed.*

** "Adhere to our age-old traditions;" (is it not patriotism?) "... develop our inherited principle of close connection between the means of production and the direct producers"... (Mr. N. —on, 322). "We have turned from the path we have followed for many centuries; we have begun to eliminate production based on the close connection between the direct producer and the means of production, on the close connection between agriculture and manufacturing industry, and have based our economic policy on the principle of developing capitalist production, which is based on the alienation of the means of production from the direct producers, with all its accompanying disasters, from which Western Europe is now suffering" (281). Let the reader compare this with the above-quoted view of the "West Europeans" themselves on these "disasters from which Western Europe is suffering," and so forth. "The principle ... of allotting land to the peasants or ... providing the producers with implements of labour" (p. 2) ... "the age-old foundations of the people's life" (75). ... "Hence, we have in these figures" (i.e., figures showing "the minimum amount of land needed under present economic conditions to ensure the material security of the rural population") "one of the elements for the solution of the economic problem, but only *one* of the elements" (65). As you see the West-European romanticists were no less fond than the Russian of seeking in "age-old traditions" "sanctions" for people's production.

fierce competition and conflict of interests they fatuously presume the preservation of conditions which reproduce the patriarchal conditions of the hoary past.

V
THE REACTIONARY CHARACTER OF ROMANTICISM

It goes without saying that Sismondi could not but realise *how* actual development was proceeding. Therefore, in demanding "encouragement for small farming" (II, 355), he plainly said that it was necessary "to direct agriculture along a road diametrically opposite to that which it is following in England today" (II, 354-55).*

"Happily, England possesses means for doing a great deal for her rural poor by dividing among them her vast common lands (ses immenses communaux).... If her common lands were divided up into free allotments (en propriétés franches) of twenty to thirty acres they" (the English) "would see the revival of that proud and independent class of countrymen, the *yeomanry*,** whose almost complete extinction they now deplore" (II, 357-58).

The "plans" of romanticism are depicted as very easily realisable—precisely because they ignore real interests, and this is the essence of romanticism. "Such a proposal" (to allot small plots of land to day labourers and to impose the duty of guardianship over the latter upon the landowners) "will probably rouse the indignation of the big landowners, who alone enjoy legislative power today in England; nevertheless, it is a just one.... The big landowners alone need the services of day labourers; they created them—let them, therefore, maintain them" (II, 357).

One is not surprised to read such naïve things written at the beginning of the century: the "theory" of romanticism conforms to the primitive state of capitalism in general, which conditioned such a primitive point of view. At that time there was still conformity between the actual

---

* Cf. Mr. V.V.'s Narodnik programme "to drag history along another line." Cf. Volgin, loc. cit., p. 181.

** The word is in English in the original.—*Ed.*

development of capitalism—the theoretical conception of it—and the attitude towards capitalism, and Sismondi, at all events, appears as a writer who is consistent and true to himself.

"We have already shown," says Sismondi, "the protection that this class" (i.e., the class of artisans) "once found in the establishment of guilds and corporations (des jurandes et des maîtrises).... We are not proposing that their strange and restrictive organisation should be restored.... But the legislator should set himself the aim of increasing the reward for industrial labour, of extricating those engaged in industry from the precarious (précaire) position in which they are living and, finally, of making it easier for them to acquire what they call a *status** (un état) .... Today, the workers are born and die workers, whereas formerly, the status of worker was merely the preliminary stage, the first rung to a higher status. It is this ability to advance (cette faculté progressive) that it is important to restore. Employers must be given an incentive to promote their workers to a higher status; to arrange it so that a man who hires himself to work in a manufactory shall actually start by working simply for wages, but that he should always have the hope, provided his conduct is good, of sharing in the profits of the enterprise" (II, 344-45).

It would be difficult to express the viewpoint of the petty bourgeois more strikingly! The guilds are Sismondi's ideal, and the reservation he makes about the undesirability of restoring them obviously means only that the principle, the idea of the guilds should be taken (exactly as the Narodniks want to take the principle, the idea of the village community, and not the contemporary fiscal association called the village community) and that its monstrous medieval features should be discarded. The absurdity of Sismondi's plan is not his wholesale defence of the guilds, nor his wanting to restore them in their entirety—he did not set out to do that. The absurdity lies in his making his model an *association* which arose out of the local artisans' narrow, primitive need for organisation, and wanted to apply this yardstick, this model, to capitalist society, whose organis-

---

* Author's italics.

ing, socialising element is large-scale machine industry, which breaks down medieval barriers and obliterates differences of place, origin and trade. Appreciating the need for association, for organisation in general, in one form or another, the romanticist takes as a model the association which satisfied the narrow need for organisation in patriarchal, immobile society, and wants to apply it to a totally transformed society, a society with a mobile population, and with labour socialised within the bounds not of a village community, or a corporation, but of a whole country, and even beyond the bounds of a single country.*

It is this mistake that quite justly earns for the romanticist the designation of *reactionary*, although this term is not used to indicate a desire simply to restore medieval institutions, but the attempt to measure the new society with the old patriarchal yardstick, the desire to find a model in the old order and traditions, which are totally unsuited to the changed economic conditions.

Ephrucy understood nothing of this circumstance. He understood the characterisation of Sismondi's theory as reactionary in the crude, vulgar sense. Ephrucy was abashed.... What do you mean? he argued, how can Sismondi be called a reactionary when he plainly says that he does not want to restore the guilds? And Ephrucy decided that it was

---

* An exactly similar mistake is made by the Narodniks in relation to another association (*the village community*), which satisfied the narrow need of association of local peasants linked to each other by the joint ownership of land, pastures, etc. (but chiefly by the joint rule of the landlords and bureaucrats), but which does not in any way satisfy the needs of the commodity economy and capitalism that breaks down all local, social-estate and other such barriers and introduces a profound economic antagonism of interests *within* the village community. The need for association, for organisation, has not diminished in capitalist society; on the contrary, in has grown immeasurably. But it is utterly absurd to use the old yardstick for the purpose of satisfying this need of the new society. This new society is already demanding, firstly, that the association shall not be according to locality, social estate, or other such category; secondly, that its starting-point shall be the difference in status and interests that has been created by capitalism and by the differentiation of the peasantry. Local, social-estate association, on the other hand, which links together peasants who differ sharply from each other in economic status and interests, now, because of its *compulsory nature*, becomes *harmful* for the peasants themselves and for social development as a whole.

unfair to "accuse" Sismondi of being "retrogressive," that, on the contrary, Sismondi's attitude "to the guild organisation was correct" and that he "fully appreciated its historical importance" (No. 7, p. 147), as has been proved, he says, by the historical researches of such and such professors into the good sides of the guild organisation.

Quasi-scientific writers often possess an amazing ability not to see the wood for the trees! Sismondi's point of view on the guilds is characteristic and important precisely because he links his practical proposals with them.* *That is why* his theory is described as *reactionary*. But Ephrucy begins to talk without rhyme or reason about modern historical works on the guilds!

The result of these inappropriate and quasi-scientific arguments was that Ephrucy by-passed the very substance of the question, namely: is it or is it not fair to describe Sismondi's theory as reactionary? He overlooked the very thing that is most important—Sismondi's *point of view*. "I have been accused," says Sismondi, "of being an enemy of social progress in political economy, a partisan of barbarous and coercive institutions. No, I do not want what has already been, but I want something better than the present. I cannot judge the present otherwise than by comparing it with the past, but I am far from wishing to restore the old ruins when I refer to them in order to demonstrate the eternal needs of society" (II, 433). The *wishes* of the romanticists are very good (as are those of the Narodniks). Their recognition of the contradictions of capitalism places them above the blind optimists who deny the existence of these contradictions. And it is not because he wanted to return to the Middle Ages that he was regarded as a reactionary, but because, in his practical proposals, he "compared the present with the past" and not with the future; because he "demonstrated the eternal needs of society"** *by referring* to "ruins" and not *by referring* to the trends of modern development. It was this petty-bourgeois viewpoint of Sismondi's which sharply distinguishes him from the other authors, who also demon-

---

* See above, at least the title of the chapter from which we quoted the arguments about the guilds (quoted also by Ephrucy: p. 147).
** The fact that he *demonstrated* the existence of these needs places him, we repeat, far above the narrow-minded bourgeois economists.

strated, in his time and after, the "eternal needs of society," that Ephrucy failed to understand.

This mistake of Ephrucy's was due to the very same narrow interpretation of the terms "petty-bourgeois" doctrine and "reactionary" doctrine referred to above in connection with the first of these terms. They by no means imply the selfish greed of the small shopkeeper, or a desire to halt social development, to turn back: they simply indicate the given author's *mistaken* point of view, his limited understanding and narrow outlook, which prompt the choice of means (for the achievement of very good aims) that cannot be effective in practice, and that can satisfy only the small producer or be of service to the defenders of the past. Sismondi, for example, is not at all a fanatical advocate of small *proprietorship*. He understands the need for organisation and for association no less than our contemporary Narodniks do. He expresses the wish that "half the profits" of industrial enterprises should be "distributed among the associated workers" (II, 346). He openly advocates a "system of association" under which all the "achievements of production benefit the one engaged in it" (II, 438). In speaking of the relation between his doctrine and the doctrines, then well known, of Owen, Fourier, Thompson and Muiron, Sismondi says: "I, like they, want to see association instead of mutual opposition among those who produce a given article in common. But I do not think that the means which they proposed for the achievement of this object could ever lead to it" (II, 365).

The difference between Sismondi and these authors is precisely one of *viewpoint*. It is quite natural, therefore, that Ephrucy, who does not understand this viewpoint, should completely misinterpret Sismondi's attitude to these authors.

"That Sismondi exercised too little influence upon his contemporaries," we read in *Russkoye Bogatstvo*, No. 8, p. 57, "that the social reforms he proposed were not put into effect, is due mainly to the fact that he was a long way ahead of his time. He wrote at a time when the bourgeoisie was enjoying its honeymoon.... Naturally, under these circumstances, the voice of a man who was demanding social reforms could not but remain a voice crying in the wilderness. But we know that posterity has not treated him much better. This, perhaps, is due to Sismondi's having been, as we have already said above, an author who wrote in a transitional period; although he wanted big changes, he could not completely discard the past. Moderate people therefore thought he was too radical, whereas in the opinion of the representatives of more extreme trends, he was too moderate."

Firstly, to say that Sismondi was "ahead of his time" with the reforms he proposed indicates a complete misunderstanding of the very substance of the doctrine of Sismondi, who himself stated that he compared the present with the past. One must indeed be infinitely short-sighted (or infinitely partial to romanticism) to overlook the general spirit and general significance of Sismondi's theory only because Sismondi favoured factory legislation,* and so forth.

Secondly, Ephrucy thus assumes that the difference between Sismondi and the other authors is only in the *degree of radicalness* of the reforms they proposed: they went further, but he did not entirely discard the past.

That is not the point. The difference between Sismondi and these authors is a much deeper one—it is not that some went further and others were timid,** but that they regarded the *very character* of reforms from two *diametrically opposite* points of view. Sismondi demonstrated the "eternal needs of society." So, too, did these authors. Sismondi was a utopian, he based his proposals on an abstract idea and not on real interests. So were these authors; they also based their plans on an abstract idea. But it was the *character* of their respective plans that differed entirely, because they

---

* But even on this subject Sismondi was not "ahead" of his day, for he merely approved of what was already being practised in England, but was unable to understand the connection that existed between these changes and large-scale machine industry and the progressive historical work it was doing.

** We do not wish to say that there is no difference in this respect between the authors referred to, but it *does not explain the point* and misrepresents the relation between Sismondi and the other authors: it is made to appear that they held the same point of view and differed only in the radicalness and consistency of the conclusions they drew. But the point is not that Sismondi "did *not* go" *so far*, but that he "went" *back*, whereas the other authors referred to "went" *forward*.

regarded modern economic development, which presented the question of "eternal needs," from *diametrically opposite* angles. The authors referred to anticipated the future; with the foresight of genius they divined the trend that would be taken by the "break-up" which the machine industry of that period was effecting before their eyes. They looked in the direction in which development was in fact proceeding; they, indeed, *were ahead* of that development. Sismondi, however, *turned his back* on this development; his utopia did not anticipate the future, but restored the past; he did not look forward, he looked backward, and dreamed of "stopping the break-up," that very "break-up" *from which* the authors mentioned deduced their utopias.* That is why Sismondi's utopia is regarded—and quite rightly—as reactionary. The grounds for this characterisation, we repeat once again, *are merely* that Sismondi did not understand the progressive significance of that "break-up" of the old semi-medieval, patriarchal social relations in the West-European countries which at the end of last century large-scale machine industry began to effect.

This specific viewpoint of Sismondi's can be discerned even in his arguments about "association" in general. "I want," he says, "the ownership of the manufactories (la propriété des manufactures) to be shared among a large number of medium capitalists, and not concentrated in the hands of one man who owns many millions..." (II, 365). The viewpoint of the petty bourgeois is still more strikingly reflected in the following utterance: "Not the poor class, but the day-labourer class should be abolished; it should be brought back to the propertied class" (II, 308) To be *"brought back"* to the propertied class—these words express the sum and substance of Sismondi's doctrine!

It goes without saying that Sismondi himself must have felt that his fine wishes were impracticable, he must have

---

* "Robert Owen," says Marx, "the father of Co-operative Factories and Stores, but who ... in no way shared the illusions of his followers with regard to the bearing (Tragweite) of these isolated elements of transformation, not only practically made the factory system the sole foundation of his experiments, but also declared that system to be theoretically the starting-point of the 'social revolution.'" [32]

been conscious that they were incompatible with the contemporary conflict of interests. "The task of reuniting the interests of those who associate in the same process of production (qui concourent à la même production) ... is undoubtedly a difficult one, but I do not think this difficulty is as great as is supposed" (II, 450).* The consciousness of this incompatibility of his desires and aspirations and the actual conditions and their development naturally stimulates the desire to prove that it is "not yet too late... to go back," and so forth. The romanticist tries to base himself upon the *undeveloped state* of the contradictions of the existing system, upon the *backwardness* of the country. "The nations have won a system of freedom into which we have entered" (this refers to the fall of feudalism); "but at the time they destroyed the yoke that they had borne for so long, the labourers (les hommes de peine) were not bereft of all property. In the rural districts they possessed land for a half share in the crops, were chinsh peasants (censitaires),[83] and tenant farmers (ils se trouvèrent associés à la propriété du sol). In the towns, as members of corporations and trade guilds (métiers) which they formed for mutual protection, they were independent tradesmen (ils se trouvèrent associés à la propriété de leur industrie). Only in our days, only in the most recent times (c'est dans ce moment même) is the progress of wealth and competition breaking up all these associations. But this break-up (révolution) is not yet half accomplished" (II, 437).

"True, only one nation is in this unnatural position today; only in one nation do we see this permanent contrast between apparent wealth (richesse apparente) and the frightful poverty of a tenth of the population, which is forced to live on public charity. But this nation, so worthy of emulation in other respects, so dazzling even in its errors, has, by its example, tempted all the statesmen of the Continent. And if these reflections cannot now benefit her, I shall at least, I think, render a service to mankind and to my fellow

---

* "The task which Russian society has to fulfil is becoming more and more complicated every day. Capitalism is extending its conquests day after day..." (ibid.).

countrymen by pointing to the danger of the path she is following, and by showing from her own experience that to base political economy on the principle of unrestricted competition means to sacrifice the interests of mankind to the simultaneous operation of all personal passions" (II, 368).*
That is how Sismondi concludes his *Nouveaux Principes*.

The general significance of Sismondi and of his theory was distinctly formulated by Marx in the following comment, which first outlines the conditions of West-European economic life that gave rise to such a theory (and did so exactly at the time when capitalism was only just beginning to create large-scale machine industry there), and then gives an appraisal of it.**

"The medieval burgesses and the small peasant proprietors were the precursors of the modern bourgeoisie. In those countries which are but little developed, industrially and commercially, these two classes still vegetate side by side with the rising bourgeoisie.

"In countries where modern civilisation has become fully developed, a new class of petty bourgeois has been formed, fluctuating between proletariat and bourgeoisie and ever renewing itself as a supplementary part of bourgeois society. The individual members of this class, however, are being constantly hurled down into the proletariat by the action of competition, and, as modern industry develops, they even see the moment approaching when they will completely disappear as an independent section of modern society, to be replaced, in manufactures, agriculture and commerce, by overlookers, bailiffs and shopmen.

"In countries like France, where the peasants constitute far more than half of the population, it was natural that writers who sided with the proletariat against the bourgeoisie should use, in their criticism of the bourgeois regime, the standard of the peasant and petty bourgeois, and from the standpoint of these intermediate classes should take up the

---

* "Russian society has to fulfil a great task, one that is extremely difficult but not impossible—to develop the productive forces of the population in such a form as to benefit not an insignificant minority, but the entire people" (N. —on, 343).
** Cf. quotations in *Russkoye Bogatstvo*, No. 8, p. 57, and also Mr. N. —on's article in *Russkoye Bogatstvo*, No. 6, p. 94.

cudgels for the working class. Thus arose petty-bourgeois Socialism. Sismondi was the head of this school, not only in France but also in England.

"This doctrine dissected with great acuteness the contradictions in the conditions of modern production. It laid bare the hypocritical apologies of economists. It proved, incontrovertibly, the disastrous effects of machinery and division of labour; the concentration of capital and land in a few hands; overproduction and crises; it pointed out the inevitable ruin of the petty bourgeois and peasant, the misery of the proletariat, the anarchy in production, the crying inequalities in the distribution of wealth, the industrial war of extermination between nations, the dissolution of old moral bonds, of the old family relations, of the old nationalities.*

"In its positive aims, however, this form of Socialism aspires either to restoring the old means of production and of exchange, and with them the old property relations, and the old society, or to cramping the modern means of production and of exchange, within the framework of the old property relations that have been, and were bound to be, exploded by those means. In either case, it is both reactionary and utopian.

"Its last words are: corporate guilds for manufacture; patriarchal relations in agriculture."**

We tried to prove that this description is correct as we examined each separate item of Sismondi's doctrine. Here let us merely note the curious trick employed by Ephrucy to crown all the blunders he made in his exposition, criticism and appraisal of romanticism. The reader will remember that at the very beginning of his article (in

---

* Ephrucy quotes this passage in No. 8 of *Russkoye Bogatstvo*, p. 57 (from the beginning of this paragraph).
** Cf. *Russkoye Bogatstvo*, 1894, No. 6, p. 88, article referred to. In the translation of this passage Mr. N. —on is guilty of two mistranslations and of one omission. Instead of "petty-bourgeois" and "petty-peasant" he translates "narrow-burgher" and "narrow-peasant." Instead of "cudgels for the workers" he translates "cudgels for the people," although in the original we have the word Arbeiter. (In the English translation of 1888, authorised by Engels, it is "working class."—*Ed.*) He omitted the words: "were bound to be exploded" (gesprengt werden mussten).[84]

Russkoye Bogatstvo, No. 7), Ephrucy stated that it was "unfair" and "incorrect" to include Sismondi among the reactionaries and utopians (loc. cit., p. 138). To prove this thesis Ephrucy firstly contrived to say nothing at all about the main thing—the connection between Sismondi's *point of view* and the position and interests of a special class in capitalist society, the small producers; secondly, in examining the various tenets of Sismondi's theory Ephrucy in part presented his attitude to modern theory in a totally wrong light, as we have shown above, and in part, simply ignored the modern theory and defended Sismondi with references to German scholars who "went no further" than Sismondi; thirdly and lastly, Ephrucy was pleased to sum up his appraisal of Sismondi in the following way: "Our (!) opinion of the importance of Simonde de Sismondi," he says, "we can (!!) sum up in the following words" of a German economist (*Russkoye Bogatstvo*, No. 8, p. 57), and then follows the passage indicated above, i.e., *only a part* of the characterisation given by that economist; but the part which explains the connection between Sismondi's theory and a special class in modern society, and the part where the final conclusion is drawn that Sismondi is reactionary and utopian, are omitted! More than that. Ephrucy did not confine himself to taking *a fragment* of the comment, which gives no idea of the comment *as a whole*, and thereby presenting this economist's attitude towards Sismondi in a totally wrong light; he tried, further, to embellish Sismondi, while pretending that he was merely conveying the opinion of that economist.

"Let us add to this," says Ephrucy, "that in some of his theoretical views, Sismondi is the predecessor of the most outstanding modern economists*: let us recall his views on revenue from capital and on crises, his classification of national revenue, and so forth" (ibid.). Thus, instead of *supplementing* this German economist's reference to Sismondi's merits with the same economist's reference to Sismondi's petty-bourgeois point of view, and to the reactionary character of his utopia, Ephrucy *supplements* the list of Sismondi's *merits with precisely those parts of his theory* (such as his

---

* Such as Adolph Wagner?—*K. T.*

"classification of the national revenue") *which*, in the opinion
of this same economist, contain *not a single scientific word*.

We may be told: Ephrucy may not in the least share the
opinion that the explanation of economic doctrines must
be sought in economic reality; he may be profoundly convinced that A. Wagner's theory of the "classification of
the national revenue" is the "most outstanding" theory. We
are quite willing to believe this. But what right had he to
flirt with the theory which the Narodnik gentlemen are so
fond of saying they "agree" with, when in fact, he completely misunderstood that theory's attitude to Sismondi, and
did everything possible (and even impossible) to present
this attitude in a totally wrong light?

We would not have devoted so much space to this question had it concerned only Ephrucy—an author whose name
we meet in Narodnik literature perhaps for the first time.
It is not Ephrucy's personality, nor even his views, that
are important for us, but *the Narodniks' attitude in general towards the theory of the famous German economist which,
they claim, they agree with*. Ephrucy is by no means an exception. On the contrary, his is quite a typical case, and to
prove this we have throughout drawn a parallel between
Sismondi's viewpoint and theory and Mr. N. —on's viewpoint and theory.* The similarity proved to be complete:
the theoretical views, the viewpoint regarding capitalism,
and the character of the practical conclusions and proposals of both authors proved to be *identical*. And as Mr. N.
—on's views may be described as the last word in Narodism,
we have a right to conclude that *the economic theory of the
Narodniks is but a Russian variety of European romanticism*.

It goes without saying that Russia's specific historic and
economic features, on the one hand, and her incomparably
greater backwardness, on the other, lend Narodism particularly marked distinctive features. But these distinctions
are no more than those between varieties within the same

* Mr. V. V., another Narodnik economist, is quite in accord
with Mr. N. —on on the extremely important questions referred to
above, and differs from him only in that his point of view is even
more primitive.

species and, therefore, do not disprove the *similarity* between Narodism and petty-bourgeois romanticism.

Perhaps the most outstanding and striking distinction is the effort the Narodnik economists make to disguise their romanticism by stating that they "agree" with modern theory and by *referring* to it as often as possible, although this theory sharply disapproves of romanticism and has grown up in the course of a fierce struggle against petty-bourgeois doctrines of every variety.

The analysis of Sismondi's theory is of special interest precisely because it provides an opportunity to examine the *general methods* used in wearing this disguise.

We have seen that *both* romanticism and the modern theory *indicate the same* contradictions existing in contemporary social economy. The Narodniks take advantage of this when they *point* to the fact that modern theory recognises the contradictions which manifest themselves in crises, in the quest for a foreign market, in the growth of production simultaneously with a decline in consumption, in protective tariffs, in the harmful effects of machine industry, and so on, and so forth. And the Narodniks are quite right: modern theory does indeed *recognise all these* contradictions, which romanticism also recognised. But the question is: has a single Narodnik ever asked wherein lies the difference between the scientific analysis of these contradictions, which reduces them to the different interests that spring from the present system of economy, and the utilisation of these references to contradictions merely in order to utter good wishes? No, we do not find a single Narodnik who has examined this question of the difference between the modern theory and romanticism. The Narodniks likewise utilise their references to contradictions merely in order to utter good wishes.

The next question is: has a single Narodnik ever asked wherein lies the difference between the sentimental criticism of capitalism and the scientific, dialectical criticism of it? Not one of them has raised this question of the second major difference between modern theory and romanticism. Not one of them has considered it necessary to use the present development of social and economic relations as the criterion of his theories (yet it is the application of this criterion that constitutes the chief distinguishing feature of scientific criticism).

And the last question is: has a single Narodnik ever asked wherein lies the difference between the viewpoint of romanticism, which idealises small production and bewails the "break-up" of its foundations by "capitalism," and the viewpoint of the modern theory, which takes large-scale capitalist machine production as its point of departure and proclaims this "break-up of foundations" to be progressive? (We employ this generally accepted Narodnik term. It vividly describes the process of change in social relations resulting from the influence of large-scale machine industry which *everywhere*, and not only in Russia, has taken place with an abruptness and sharpness that have astonished public opinion.) Again no. Not a single Narodnik has asked himself this question, not one of them has attempted to apply to the Russian "break-up" those yardsticks which made people acknowledge the West-European "break-up" as progressive. They all weep about the foundations, advise that this break-up be stopped, and assure us through their tears that this is the "modern theory."...

The comparison of Sismondi's theory and their "theory," which they have presented as a new and independent solution of the problem of capitalism based on the last word of West-European science and life, clearly demonstrates to what a primitive stage of the development of capitalism and public thought the origin of that theory belongs. But the point is not that this theory is old. There are quite a few very old European theories that would be very new for Russia. The point is that even *when that theory appeared, it was a petty-bourgeois and reactionary theory.*

VI

CORN TARIFFS IN ENGLAND AS APPRAISED
BY ROMANTICISM AND BY SCIENTIFIC THEORY

We shall supplement our comparison between the theory of the romanticism on the main points of contemporary economics and the modern theory with a comparison between their treatment of a certain *practical* problem. Such a comparison will be all the more interesting because, on the one hand, this practical problem is one of the biggest, most fundamental problems of capitalism, and on the other hand, because the two most outstanding exponents of these hostile theories have expressed their opinion on this subject.

We are referring to the *Corn Laws* in England and their repeal.[85] In the second quarter of the present century this problem deeply interested not only English but also Continental economists; they all realised that this was by no means a specific problem relating to tariff policy, but the general problem of Free Trade, of free competition, of the "destiny of capitalism." It was a matter of crowning the edifice of capitalism by giving full effect to free competition; of clearing the road for the completion of that "break-up" which large-scale machine industry began in England at the end of the last century; of removing the obstacles that were hindering this "break-up" in *agriculture*. It was *in this way* that the two Continental economists of whom we intend to speak viewed the problem.

In the second edition of his *Nouveaux Principes* Sismondi added a chapter specially devoted to "laws governing trade in grain" (l. III, ch. X).

First of all, he emphasises the urgency of the problem: "Half the English people today are demanding the repeal of the Corn Laws, demanding it with extreme irritation against those who support them; but the other half are demanding that they be retained, and cry out indignantly against those who want them repealed" (I, 251).

In examining the problem, Sismondi points out that the interests of the English farmers demanded corn tariffs to ensure them a *remunerating price*.* The interests of the manufacturers, however, demanded the repeal of the Corn Laws, because the manufactories could not exist without foreign markets, and the further development of English exports was being retarded by the laws, which restricted imports: "The manufactory owners added that the glut in the market was the result of these same Corn Laws; that wealthy people on the Continent could not buy their goods because they could not find a market for their corn" (I, 254).**

---

* These words are in English in the original.—*Ed.*
** One-sided as may be this explanation given by the English manufacturers, who ignore the deeper causes of crises and their inev-

"The opening of the market to foreign corn will probably ruin the English landowners and reduce all rents to an infinitely low price. This, undoubtedly, is a great calamity, but it is not an injustice" (I, 254). And Sismondi proceeds to argue in the naïvest manner that the revenues of the landowners should be commensurate with the service (sic!!) they render "society" (capitalist?), and so forth. "The farmers," continues Sismondi, "will withdraw their capital, or part at least, from agriculture."

This argument of Sismondi's (and he contents himself with this argument) reveals the main flaw in romanticism, which does not pay sufficient attention to the process of economic development that is actually taking place. We have seen that Sismondi himself points to the gradual development and growth of capitalist farming in England. But he hastens to denounce this process instead of studying its causes. It is only this haste, the desire to thrust his innocent wishes upon history, that can explain the fact that Sismondi overlooks the general trend of capitalist development in agriculture and the inevitable *acceleration of this process* with the repeal of the Corn Laws, i.e., the capitalist progress of agriculture instead of its decline, which Sismondi prophesies.

But Sismondi remains true to himself. He had no sooner approached the contradiction inherent in this capitalist process than he immediately set about naïvely "refuting" it in his endeavour to prove at all costs that the path being followed by the "English fatherland" was a wrong one.

"What will the day labourer do?... Work will stop, the fields will be converted into pastures.... What will become of the 540,000 families who will be denied work?* Even assum-

---

itability when the expansion of the market is slight, it, nevertheless, undoubtedly contains the absolutely correct idea that the realisation of the product by its sale abroad demands, *on the whole,* corresponding imports from abroad.

We bring this explanation of the English manufacturers to the notice of those economists who brush aside the problem of the realisation of the product in capitalist society with the profound remark: "They will sell abroad."

* To "prove" the unsoundness of capitalism, Sismondi forthwith makes an approximate calculation (such as our Russian romanticist, Mr. V. V., for example, is so fond of doing). Six hundred thou-

ing that they will be fit for any kind of industrial work, is there, at the present time, an industry capable of absorbing them?... Can a government be found that will voluntarily subject half the nation it governs to such a crisis?... Will those to whom the agriculturists are thus sacrificed benefit by it to any extent? After all, these agriculturists are the nearest and most reliable consumers of English manufactures. The cessation of their consumption would strike industry a blow more fatal than the closing of one of the biggest foreign markets" (255-56). The notorious "shrinking of the home market" appears upon the scene. "How much will the manufactories lose by the cessation of the consumption of the whole class of English agriculturists, who constitute nearly half the nation? How much will the manufactories lose by the cessation of the consumption of wealthy people, whose revenues from agriculture will be almost wiped out?" (267). The romanticist moves heaven and earth to prove to the manufacturers that the contradictions inherent in the development of their industry, and of their wealth, merely express their error, their short-sightedness. And to "convince" the manufacturers of the "danger" of capitalism, Sismondi dilates on the threatening competition of Polish and Russian grain (pp. 257-61). He resorts to every possible argument; he even wants to touch the pride of Englishmen. "What will become of England's honour if the Emperor of Russia is in a position, whenever he wishes, to obtain some concession or other from her, to starve her by closing the Baltic ports?" (268). Let the reader recall how Sismondi tried to prove that the "apologists of the money power" were wrong, by contending that it was quite easy to cheat when selling.... Sismondi wants to "refute" the theoretical interpreters of capitalist farming by arguing that the rich farmers cannot withstand the competition of the wretched peasants (quoted above), and in the end arrives at his favourite conclusion, evidently convinced that he has proved that the

sand families, he says, are engaged in agriculture. When the fields are converted into pastures, no more than a tenth of this number will be "wanted." ... The less the understanding of the process in all its complexity shown by this author, the more eagerly he resorts to childish "rule of thumb" calculations.

path being followed by the "English fatherland" is a "wrong one." "The example of England shows us that this practice" (the development of money economy, to which Sismondi contrasts l'habitude de se fournir soi-même, "the habit of providing for oneself") "is not without its dangers" (263). "The very system of economy" (namely, capitalist farming) "is bad, rests on a dangerous foundation, and this is what one should try to change" (266).

The concrete problem evoked by the conflict of definite interests in a definite system of economy is thus submerged in a flood of innocent wishes! But the interested parties themselves raised the issue so sharply that to confine oneself to such a "solution" (as romanticism does on all other problems) became utterly impossible.

"But what is to be done?" Sismondi asks in despair. "Open England's ports, or close them? Doom the manufacturing or the rural workers of England to starvation and death? It is, indeed, a dreadful question; the position in which the English Cabinet finds itself is one of the most delicate that statesmen can possibly face" (260). And Sismondi again and again reverts to the "general conclusion" that the system of capitalist farming is "dangerous," that it is "dangerous to subordinate the whole of agriculture to a system of speculation." But "how it is possible, in England, to take measures, effective but at the same time gradual, such as would raise the significance (remettraient en honneur) of the small farms, when one half of the nation, employed in the manufactories, is suffering hunger and the measures they demand doom the other half of the nation, engaged in agriculture, to starvation—I do not know. I think the Corn Laws should be considerably amended; but I advise those who are demanding their complete repeal to study the following problems carefully" (267)—then follow the old complaints and apprehensions about the decline of agriculture, the shrinking of the home market, and so forth.

Thus, at the very first impact with reality, romanticism suffered utter fiasco. It was obliged to issue to itself a testimonium paupertatis and itself acknowledge receipt of it. Recall how easily and simply romanticism "solved" all problems in "theory"! Protection is unwise, capitalism is a fatal blunder, the road England has taken is wrong and dangerous, production must keep in step with consumption, while industry and commerce must keep in step with agriculture, machines are advantageous only when they lead to a rise in wages or to a reduction of the working day, means of production should not be alienated from the producer, exchange must not run ahead of production, must not lead to speculation, and so on, and so forth. Romanticism countered every contradiction with an appropriate sentimental phrase, answered every question with an appropriate innocent wish, and called the sticking of these labels upon all the facts of current life a "solution" to the problems. It is not surprising that these solutions were so charmingly simple and easy: they ignored only one little circumstance—the real interests, the conflict of which constituted the contradiction. And when the development of this contradiction brought the romanticist face to face with one of these particularly violent conflicts, such as was the struggle between the parties in England that preceded the repeal of the Corn Laws, our romanticist lost his head altogether. He felt perfectly at ease in the haze of dreams and good wishes, he so skilfully composed maxims applicable to "society" in general (but inapplicable to any historically determined system of society); but when he dropped from his world of fantasy into the maelstrom of real life and conflict of interests, he did not even have a criterion of how concrete problems are to be solved. The habit of advancing abstract propositions and of reaching abstract solutions reduced the problem to the bare formula: which part of the population should be ruined—the agricultural or the manufacturing? And, of course, the romanticist could not but conclude that neither part should be ruined, that it was necessary to "turn from the path" ... but the real contradictions encompassed him so tightly that he was unable to ascend again into the haze of good wishes, and the romanticist was obliged *to give an answer*. Sismondi even gave two answers: first—"I do not know"; second—"on the one hand, it cannot but be recognised; on the other hand, it must be admitted."[86]

On January 9, 1848, Karl Marx delivered a "speech on Free Trade"* at a public meeting in Brussels. Unlike the romanticists, who declared that "political economy is not a science of calculation, but a science of morality," he took as the point of departure of his exposition precisely the plain and sober *calculation of interests*. Instead of regarding the problem of the Corn Laws as one concerning a "system" chosen by a nation or as one of legislation (as Sismondi looked upon it), the speaker began by presenting it as a conflict of interests between manufacturers and landowners, and showed how the English manufacturers tried to raise the issue as the affair of the entire nation, tried to assure the workers that they were acting in the interests of the national welfare. Unlike the romanticists, who had presented the problem in the shape of the considerations which a legislator must have in mind when carrying out the reform, the speaker reduced the problem to the conflict between the real interests of the different classes of English society. He showed that the entire problem sprang from the necessity of cheapening raw materials for the manufacturers. He described the distrust of the English workers who regarded "these self-sacrificing gentlemen, Bowring, Bright and their colleagues, as their worst enemies...."

"The manufacturers build great palaces at immense expense, in which the *Anti-Corn-Law League*[88] takes up, in some respects, its official residence; they send an army of missionaries to all corners of England to preach the gospel of Free Trade; they have printed and distributed gratis thousands of pamphlets to enlighten the worker upon his own interests, they spend enormous sums to make the press favourable to their cause; they organise a vast administrative system for the conduct of the Free Trade movement, and they display all their wealth of eloquence at public meetings. It was at one of these meetings that a worker cried out: 'If the landlords were to sell our bones, you manufacturers would be the first to buy them in order to put them through a steam-mill and make flour of them.' The English workers have very well understood the significance of the struggle between the landlords and the industrial capital-

---

* "Discours sur le libre—échange."[87] We are using the German translation: "Rede über die Frage des Freihandels."

ists. They know very well that the price of bread was to be
reduced in order to reduce wages, and that industrial profit
would rise by as much as rent fell."

Thus the very *presentation of the problem* is quite different
from that of Sismondi. The aims the speaker set himself
were, firstly, to explain the attitude of the different classes
of English society towards the problem from the angle of
their interests; and secondly, to throw light on the significance
of the reform in the general evolution of the English social
economy.

The speaker's views on this last point coincide with those
of Sismondi in that he, too, does not see in this a particular
problem, but the *general one* of the development of capitalism
in general, of "Free Trade" as a system. "The repeal of the Corn
Laws in England is the greatest triumph of Free Trade in the
nineteenth century."[89] "... By the repeal of the Corn Laws,
free competition, the present social economy is carried to its
extreme point."* Hence, the issue presents itself to these
authors as a question of whether *the further development
of capitalism is desirable* or should be retarded, whether "different paths" should be sought, and so forth. And we know
that their affirmative answer to this question was indeed the
solution of the general fundamental problem of the "destiny
of capitalism" and not of the specific problem of the Corn
Laws in England, for the point of view established here was
also applied much later in relation to other countries. The
authors held such views in the 1840s in relation to Germany,
and in relation to America,** and declared that free competi-

---

* *Die Lage der arbeitenden Klasse in England* (1845).[90] This work
was written from exactly the same point of view *before* the repeal
of the Corn Laws (1846), whereas the speech dealt with in the text
was delivered *after* they were repealed. But the difference in time
is of no importance to us: it is sufficient to compare the above-quoted
arguments of Sismondi, advanced in 1827, with this speech of 1848,
to see the complete identity of the *elements of the problem* in the case
of both authors. The idea of comparing Sismondi with a later German
economist was borrowed by us from *Handwörterbuch der Staatswissenschaften*, B. V., Art. "Sismondi" von Lippert, Seite 679. The parallel
he drew was of such thrilling interest that Mr. Lippert's exposition
at once lost all its woodenness ... that is to say, "objectivity," and
became interesting, vivacious, and even fervid.

** Cf. *Neue Zeit*,[91] the recently discovered articles of Marx in
Westphälisches Dampfboot.[92]

tion was progressive for that country; with respect to Germany one of them wrote, as late as the sixties, that she suffered not only from capitalism, but also from the insufficient development of capitalism.

Let us return to the speech we have been dealing with. We pointed to the fundamentally different point of view of the speaker, who reduced the problem to one of the interests of the different classes in English society. We see the same profound difference in his presentation of the purely theoretical problem of the significance of the repeal of the Corn Laws to the social economy. For him it is not the abstract question of which *system* England should adopt, what path she should choose (as the question is put by Sismondi, who forgets that England has a past and a present, which already determine that path). No, he forthwith presents the question on the basis of the *present-day social and economic system*; he asks himself: what *must be the next step* in the development of this system following the repeal of the Corn Laws?

The difficulty involved in this question was that of determining how the repeal of the Corn Laws would affect *agriculture*, for as regards industry its effect was clear to everybody.

To prove that this repeal would benefit agriculture as well, the *Anti-Corn-Law League** offered a prize for the three best essays on the beneficial effect the repeal of the Corn Laws would have upon English agriculture. The speaker briefly outlined the views of the three prize-winners, Hope, Morse, and Greg, and at once singled out the last-named, whose essay most scientifically and most strictly followed the principles laid down by classical political economy.

Writing mainly for big farmers, Greg, himself a big manufacturer, showed that the repeal of the Corn Laws would thrust the small farmers out of agriculture and they would turn to industry, but it would benefit the big farmers who would be able to rent land on longer leases, invest more capital in the land, employ more machines and get along with less labour, which was bound to become cheaper with the fall in the price of corn. The landlords, however, would have to be content with a lower rent because land of poorer

---

* These words are in English in the original.—*Ed.*

quality would drop out of cultivation, as it would be unable to withstand the competition of cheap imported grain.

The speaker proved to be quite right in regarding this forecast and this open defence of capitalism in agriculture as the most scientific. History has confirmed his forecast. "The repeal of the Corn Laws gave a marvellous impulse to English agriculture.... A positive decrease of the agricultural population went hand in hand with increase of the area under cultivation, with more intensive cultivation, unheard-of accumulation of the capital incorporated with the soil, and devoted to its working, an augmentation in the products of the soil without parallel in the history of English agriculture, plethoric rent-rolls of landlords, and growing wealth of the capitalist farmers.... Greater outlay of capital per acre, and, as a consequence, more rapid concentration of farms, were essential conditions of the new method."*

But the speaker, of course, did not confine himself to recognising Greg's arguments as being the most correct. Coming from the mouth of Greg, they were the reasoning of a Free Trader who was discussing English agriculture in general, and was trying to prove that the repeal of the Corn Laws would benefit the nation as a whole. After what we have said above it is evident that these were not the views of the speaker.

---

* This was written in 1867.[93] To explain the rise in rents, one must bear in mind the law established by the modern analysis of differential rent, namely, that *a rise in rent is possible simultaneously with a reduction in the price of corn.* "When the English corn duties were abolished in 1846, the English manufacturers believed that they had thereby turned the landowning aristocracy into paupers. Instead, they became richer than ever. How did this occur? Very simply. In the first place, the farmers were now compelled by contract to invest £ 12 per acre annually instead of £ 8. And, secondly, the landlords, being strongly represented in the Lower House too, granted themselves a large government subsidy for drainage projects and other permanent improvements of their land. Since no total displacement of the poorest soil took place, but rather, at worst, it became employed for other purposes—and mostly only temporarily— rents rose in proportion to the increased investment of capital, and the landed aristocracy consequently was better off than ever before" (*Das Kapital*, III, 2, 259).[94]

He explained that a reduction in the price of corn, so glorified by the Free Traders, meant an inevitable reduction in wages, the cheapening of the commodity "labour" (more exactly: labour-power); that the drop in the price of corn would never be able to compensate the workers for the drop in wages, firstly, because with the drop in the price of corn it would be more difficult for the worker to save on the consumption of bread with a view to buying other articles; secondly, because the progress of industry cheapens articles of consumption, substituting spirits for beer, potatoes for bread, cotton for wool and linen, and, by all this, lowering the worker's standard of requirements and living.

Thus we see that *apparently* the speaker establishes the elements of the problem just as Sismondi does: he *too* admits that the ruination of the small farmers and the impoverishment of the workers in industry and agriculture will be the inevitable consequences of Free Trade. It is here that our Narodniks, who are also distinguished for their inimitable skill in "citing," usually stop quoting "excerpts," and with complete satisfaction declare that they fully "agree." But these methods merely show that they do not understand, firstly, the tremendous difference in the presentation of the problem, which we indicated above; secondly, they overlooked the fact that *it is only here* that the radical difference between the new theory and romanticism *begins*: the romanticist turns from the concrete problems of actual development to dreams, whereas the realist takes the established facts as his criterion in definitely solving the concrete problem.

Pointing to the forthcoming improvement in the conditions of the workers the speaker went on to say:

"Thereupon the economists will tell you:

"'Well, we admit that competition among the workers, which will certainly not have diminished under Free Trade, will very soon bring wages into harmony with the low price of commodities. But, on the other hand, the low price of commodities will increase consumption, the larger consumption will require increased production, which will be followed by a larger demand for hands, and this larger demand for hands will be followed by a rise in wages.'

"The whole line of argument amounts to this: *Free Trade increases productive forces*. If industry keeps growing, if wealth, if the productive power, if, in a word, productive capital increases the demand for labour, the price of labour, and consequently the rate of wages, rise also. *The most favourable condition for the worker is the growth of capital. This must be admitted.** If capital remains stationary, industry will not merely remain stationary but will decline and in this case the worker will be the first victim. He goes to the wall before the capitalist. And in the case where capital keeps growing, in the circumstances which we have said are the *best* for the worker, what will be his lot? He will go to the wall just the same...." And quoting data given by English economists the speaker went on to explain in detail how the concentration of capital increases the division of labour, which cheapens labour-power by substituting unskilled for skilled labour, how the machines oust the workers, how big capital ruins the small industrialists and small rentiers and leads to the intensification of crises, which still further increase the number of unemployed. The conclusion he drew from his analysis was that Free Trade signifies nothing but freedom for the development of capital.

Thus, the speaker was able to find a criterion for the solution of the problem which at first sight seemed to lead to the hopeless dilemma that brought Sismondi to a halt: both Free Trade and its restraint equally lead to the ruin of the workers. *The criterion is the development of the productive forces.* It was immediately evident that the problem was treated from the historical angle: instead of comparing capitalism with some abstract society as it should be (i.e., fundamentally with a utopia), the author compared it with the *preceding stages* of social economy, compared the different stages of capitalism as they successively replaced one another, *and established the fact that the productive forces of society develop thanks to the development of capitalism*. By applying scientific criticism to the arguments of the Free Traders he was able to avoid the

---

* Our italics.

mistake usually made by the romanticists who, denying that the arguments have any importance, "throw out the baby with the bath water"; he was able to pick out their sound kernel, i.e., the undoubted fact of enormous technical progress. Our Narodniks, with their characteristic wit, would, of course, have concluded that this author, who had so openly taken *the side of big capital against the small producer*, was an "apologist of money power," the more so that he was addressing continental Europe and applying the conclusions he drew from English life to his own country, where at that time large-scale machine industry was only taking its first timid steps. And yet, precisely this example (like a host of similar examples from West-European history) could help them study the thing they are not at all able to understand (perhaps they do not wish to do so?), namely, that to admit that big capital is progressive as compared with small production, is very, very far from being "apologetics."

It is sufficient to recall the above-quoted chapter from Sismondi and this speech to be convinced that the latter is superior both from the standpoint of theory and of hostility towards every kind of "apologetics." The speaker described the contradictions that accompany the development of big capital much more exactly, fully, straightforwardly and frankly than the romanticists ever did. But he never descended to uttering a single sentimental phrase bewailing this development. He never uttered a word anywhere about a possibility of "diversion from the path." He understood that by means of such phrases people merely cover up the fact that they themselves are "diverting" from the problem reality confronts them with, i.e., a certain economic reality, a certain economic development and certain interests that spring from this development.

The above-mentioned fully scientific criterion enabled him to solve this problem while remaining a consistent realist.

"Do not imagine, gentlemen," said the speaker, "that in criticising freedom of trade we have the least intention of defending the system of protection." And he went on to point out that under the contemporary system of social economy both Free Trade and protection rested on the same basis, briefly referred to the "breaking-up" process of the old economic life and of the old semi-patriarchal relationships in West-European countries carried through by capitalism in England and on the Continent, and indicated the social fact that under certain conditions Free Trade *hastens* this "break-up."* And he concluded with the words: "It is in this sense alone, gentlemen, that I vote in favour of Free Trade."[96]

---

* This progressive significance of the repeal of the Corn Laws was also clearly indicated by the author of "Die Lage" *even before the repeal took place* (loc. cit., p. 179)[95] and he specially stressed the influence it would have upon the consciousness of the producers.

THE NEW FACTORY LAW[97]

Written in exile in summer 1897
Appendix written in autumn 1897
Published in pamphlet form
in Geneva in 1899

Published according
to the 1899 edition

НОВЫЙ
Фабричный Законъ

Изданіе Россійской Соціальдемократической Рабочей Партіи.

ЖЕНЕВА
Типографія „Союза Русскихъ Соціальдемократовъ"
1899

Cover of Lenin's pamphlet *The New Factory Law.*
1899

I

WHY WAS THE NEW FACTORY LAW PASSED?

On June 2, 1897, a new factory law was passed reducing working hours in mills and factories and establishing holidays. The workers of St. Petersburg have long been waiting for this law, which the government promised in 1896, after the fright it received from the mass workers' strike in the spring of that year. This mass strike at the cotton-spinning and cotton-weaving mills was followed by others, and in all cases the workers demanded shorter working hours. The government took savage reprisals against the strikers; it arrested masses of workers right and left and exiled them without trial. It also tried, in its fright, to influence the workers by silly talk about the employers' Christian love for the workers (Minister Witte's circular to the factory inspectors issued in 1895-96). But the workers only jeered at this talk, and no amount of persecution could check the movement, in which tens and hundreds of thousands of workers were involved. It was then that the government realised that it would have to yield and concede to at least some of the workers' demands. In addition to the lies and cant and savage persecution of strikers, the St. Petersburg workers received in answer to their strikes the government's promise of a law to reduce working hours. This promise was announced to the workers with unusual solemnity in special notices[98] from the Minister of Finance, which were posted up in the factories. The workers waited impatiently for the fulfilment of the promise, they expected the law to be promulgated by April 19, 1897, and were already prepared to believe that this government promise, like numerous other government statements, was a gross lie. This time, however, the government kept its promise, a law was promulgated—but *what kind* of a law we shall see further on. But first we must examine the circumstances which prompted the government to keep its promise.

Our government began to occupy itself with the problem of reducing working hours long before 1896. The problem was raised fifteen years ago: the St. Petersburg employers petitioned for a law of this kind as far back as 1883. Similar petitions were made on several other occasions by other employers, too (notably the Polish), but they were all pigeon-holed, as were a host of other projects for improving the workers' conditions. The Russian Government does not hurry to deal with such projects; they lie pigeon-holed for decades. Now when it comes to handing over several million rubles to loyal Russian landowners who "petition" for doles from the public funds, or to granting a subsidy or bonus to the "downtrodden" employers, then the Russian Government does hurry, and the wheels of the bureaucratic and ministerial machine begin to revolve at full speed, as though "greased" with "palm-oil." When matters concern the workers, however, not only are draft laws pigeon-holed for years and decades (for example, the Employers' Liability Bill has been in the "drafting stage," I think, for over ten years), but even laws already passed are not enforced, for the officials of His Imperial Majesty's Government are loath to incommode Messrs. the Employers (for example, the law of 1886, which makes it incumbent upon employers to provide hospitals for their workers, has in the vast majority of cases not been enforced to this day). The question is, what caused action on a long-standing issue to be taken so quickly on this occasion? Why was it settled at once, given priority over other measures and pushed through the Ministry and the Council of State? Why did it at once assume the form of a bill and become law? Obviously, there was some force that spurred on the officials, stirred them into action, broke down their stubborn reluctance to "pester" our native employers with new demands. This force was the St. Petersburg workers and the huge strikes they conducted in 1895-96, which, thanks to the assistance the workers received from the Social-Democrats (through the League of Struggle), were accompanied by the presentation of definite demands to the government and by the distribution of socialist proclamations and leaflets among the workers. The government realised that no amount of police persecution would break the determination of the working masses, once they had become conscious of their interests, had united for a struggle, and were led by the party of Social-Democrats, the champions of the workers' cause. The government was forced to make concessions. The workers *compelled* the government to pass the new factory law, they *won* it from their bitterest enemy, just as they did in the case of the law of June 3, 1886, passed eleven years ago, on factory rules, fines, wage rates, etc. At that time the workers' struggle was waged most vigorously in Moscow and Vladimir gubernias. It took the form of numerous strikes; then, too, the workers presented plain and precise demands to the government, and during the famous Morozov strike, conditions drawn up by the workers themselves were handed up to the inspector from the crowd. These conditions stated, for example, that the workers demanded a reduction of fines. The law of June 3, 1886, passed soon after, was a direct *answer* to the workers' demands and contained regulations governing fines.*

And so it is today. In 1896, the workers demanded a reduction of working hours, and backed their demands by huge strikes. The government *is* now *answering* this demand by promulgating a law reducing working hours. At that time, in 1886, the workers' revolts compelled the government to yield, and it tried to reduce its concessions to a minimum, to leave loopholes for the employers, to delay the introduction of the new regulations, to do the workers out of as many of their demands as possible. Today, in 1897, the government is in the same way yielding only to the workers' revolts, and in the same way is trying by all the means in its power to reduce the concessions to the workers, *to haggle*, to do them out of an hour or two, even to lengthen working hours as compared with those proposed by the employers; it is trying to give the employers the benefit of a few more holidays by not making them compulsory; it is trying to delay

---

* See pamphlet *Explanation of the Law on Fines.* (In the present volume, p. 29.—*Ed.*)

18—789

the introduction of the new system by postponing the operation of the principal regulations, pending future instructions by the ministers. Thus the laws of June 3, 1886, and of June 2, 1897—which are the principal factory acts in Russia—are both forced concessions, won by the Russian workers from the police government. Both show *how* the Russian Government treats the most legitimate demands of the workers.

II

WHAT SHOULD BE CONSIDERED WORKING TIME?

Let us examine in detail the law of June 2, 1897.* As we have said, the new law, firstly, limits the working day for all workers, and, secondly, establishes compulsory rest-days on Sundays and holidays. Before laying down rules about the amount of working time the law must first define what is meant by working time. The new law lays down the following rule: "Working time, or the number of working hours per day, shall in the case of every worker be deemed to be the time during which, according to the labour contract, he is obliged to be on the premises of the establishment and at the disposal of the manager for the performance of work." Hence, all the time that the worker spends at the factory, either according to schedule or at the manager's demand, is to be considered as working time. Whether the worker, during this time, is engaged at his actual or customary work, or whether the manager orders him to do some other job, or even to just *wait*, makes no difference: all the time the worker spends at the factory must be considered as working time. For example, in some factories, after the bell goes on Saturdays, the workers remain to clean the machines. According to the law, time spent on cleaning machines is also to be regarded as *part of working time*. Consequently, if an employer does not pay the worker for cleaning machines, it means that he is *making gratuitous use of the hired worker's working time*. Hence, if an employer who has hired a worker at piece rates compels him to wait, or to do some other job without special

---

* It comes into force in November 1898.

pay (every worker knows that this often happens), it means that the employer is *making gratuitous use of the hired worker's working time*. The workers should remember this definition of working time as laid down in the new law and, on the strength of it, resist every attempt on an employer's part to make gratuitous use of labour-power. Naturally, such a definition of working time should follow logically from the labour contract: some workers may think this so obvious that it is not worth talking about. But the government, in its anxiety to serve the capitalists, deliberately obscures a great deal of what is obvious to every worker. So here too the government has tried to leave a little loophole for those gentlemen, the employers. The law defines working time as the time the worker *is obliged under the labour contract* to be in the factory. But what if the labour contract does not specify how many hours a day the worker is obliged to be in the factory? It often happens at engineering plants, for example, that all the contract between the workers and the employer says is that the workers undertake to make a certain article (a machine part, a certain number of bolts or nuts, etc.) at a certain price; *but nothing is said* about how much time the worker has to spend on the job. Is the new law about the number of working hours per day applicable in such cases? Common sense, of course, would suggest that it is; after all, the worker is employed in the factory—how can this not be considered working time? But the "common sense" of the capitalists, and of the government that supports them, is of a special brand. According to the letter of the clause we have quoted, the law on the reduction of working hours can easily be evaded in such cases. The employer may argue that in the contract he did not *oblige* the worker to be in the factory—and there you are. And since not every employer is so smart as to see this trick, the officials of the Ministry of Finance hastened to draw the attention of Russia's merchants to this useful little loophole in the new law. The Ministry of Finance has long been issuing its own special sheet, *Vestnik Finansov, Promyshlennosti i Torgovli*[99]—one of those official periodicals which, besides publishing government decisions, do their best to magnify the achievements of the Russian capitalists and to extol the government's solicitude for the pockets of the bankers, factory owners, merchants and landowners, under the guise of solicitude for the people. Shortly after the new law was passed this sheet published an article on it (*Vestnik Finansov*, No. 26, 1897) explaining its significance at length and arguing that it was precisely the government's function to be concerned about the health of the workers. Well, it was in this article that the officials did their best to show the employers how to get round the new law. This article clearly explains that the new law cannot be applied in those cases where the labour contract says nothing about working time, for when a worker contracts to do a definite job "*he is not a hired worker, but a person who accepts an order*." Thus, it is not very hard for an employer to dispense with the inconvenient law: all he has to do is to call the worker a "person who accepts an order" and not a worker! Instead of stating that working time is deemed to be the time *a worker is in the factory* at the disposal of the employer, the law is *deliberately* worded more vaguely and speaks of the time during which the worker *is obliged under contract* to be in the factory. One would think that this amounts to the same thing, but actually, here again they have not scrupled to resort to deliberate vagueness to the workers' detriment!

III

TO WHAT EXTENT DOES THE NEW LAW REDUCE WORKING HOURS?

The law of June 2, 1897, restricts working time on day-work to 11½ hours. On Saturdays, and on the eve of holidays, it restricts it to 10 hours. Hence, the reduction of working hours under the new law is miserly. There are quite a number of workers—and in St. Petersburg they most likely form the majority—for whom this law will mean *no reduction* of working hours at all; rather the contrary, it threatens to lengthen them. The ordinary working day in St. Petersburg factories is 10 to 10½ hours. The legislative enactment of such excessive working hours clearly shows that this law was an answer to the demands of workers at the St. Petersburg cotton-spinning and cotton-weaving mills. *For these* workers, the new law does perhaps mean a reduction of working hours, since most of them worked 12 to 14 hours a day. (We shall explain later why we say "perhaps.") The law lays down a ten-hour day for artisans, and also for factories under the jurisdiction of the Ministry of War. The government, however, decided that factory workers might be made to work longer hours! Even the St. Petersburg employers petitioned the government for a reduction of the working day to 11 hours! The government decided to throw in an extra half-hour for the benefit of the Moscow employers, who compel their workers to keep going, in two shifts, right round the clock, and whom the workers apparently have not yet taught a proper lesson. The Russian Government, which boasts of its solicitude for the workers' welfare, has in fact proved to be as stingy as a petty huckster. It has proved to be more stingy than the employers themselves, who squeeze extra thousands out of the workers as a result of every extra half-hour of work. The workers can clearly see from this example that the government not only protects the interests of the employers, but protects the interests of the *worst* of them, and that it is a far worse enemy of the workers than the capitalist class. The St. Petersburg workers would have won *shorter hours* for themselves and for all Russian workers had *not the government interfered*. The united workers had forced the employers to yield; the St. Petersburg employers were prepared to concede the workers' demands; but the government forbade the employers to yield, so as not to create a precedent for the workers. Then the majority of the St. Petersburg employers realised that they would have to make concessions to the workers, and petitioned the government to reduce the working day to 11 hours. But the government protects the interests of the employers of all Russia, and not only of St. Petersburg, and since there are employers in Holy Russia who are far more stingy than those of St. Petersburg, the government, in its desire to be "fair," could not allow the St. Petersburg employers to rob the workers *too little*. The employers of St. Petersburg must not run too far ahead of those in the rest of Russia; and so the government adds a half-hour to the working day requested by the capitalists. Clearly, the workers must draw three lessons from this conduct of the government:

First lesson: Russia's advanced workers must do their utmost to draw the more backward workers into the movement. Unless the entire mass of Russian workers is enlisted in the struggle for the workers' cause, the advanced workers of the capital cannot hope to win much, even if they force *their* employers to yield; for the government is so exceedingly "fair" that it does not allow the better employers to make substantial concessions to the workers. Second lesson: the Russian Government is a far worse enemy of the Russian workers than the Russian employers are, for the government not only protects the interests of the employers, not only resorts, for this purpose, to brutal persecution of the workers, to arrests, deportations and the use of troops against unarmed workers, but what is more, protects the interests of the *most stingy* employers and resists any tendency of the better employers to yield to the workers. Third lesson: in order to win themselves *human* working conditions and an eight-hour day, for which the workers are now striving all over the world, the Russian workers must rely on the strength of their own organisation alone and steadily win one concession after another from the government. The government is, as it were, bargaining with the workers, trying to see whether it can impose an extra half-hour or so. But the workers will show that they know how to stand up for their demands. The government is, as it were, testing the workers' patience, to see whether it can get off with quite a cheap concession. But the workers will show that they have patience enough for a most stubborn struggle, since to them it is a fight for their lives, a fight to prevent the working people from being utterly downtrodden and oppressed.

IV

WHAT DOES THE LAW CONSIDER "NIGHT-TIME"
FOR THE WORKERS?

"Night-time shall mean the period between 9 p.m. and 5 a.m. when one shift operates, and between 10 p.m. and 4 a.m. when two or more shifts operate." So runs the new law. "Night" for the common people, who have to toil all their lives for others, and "night" for the fine folk, who live on the labour of others, are, according to the "law," two entirely different things. During the greater part of the year both in St. Petersburg and in Moscow it is still quite dark, still night at 4 a.m. But the Russian law lays it down that the worker must adjust his whole life to the interests of capital; the worker must believe that day-time begins *without fail* after four in the morning, even if it may still be several hours before sunrise. And if the worker does not live in the factory grounds, he has to get up at *three* o'clock, and even earlier, in order to be at the factory at four! For St. Petersburg officials the "day" begins at noon, or even at 1 p.m.; but then, officials are a special type of people.... The workers' "day" only ends at ten at night, and if the streets are quite dark when he leaves the factory, he should not be disconcerted by this: he should remember and believe that the "day" has only just ended—for so the law decrees. Why not pass a law that makes the worker's "day" begin when the factory whistle summons him to work, and end when that same whistle summons a new shift? That would be franker and fairer! In Switzerland they already have a law which defines what night-time is for the worker; but how can you expect the Swiss to be up to all the tricks devised by Russian police officials? It appears that among these terrible Swiss a working man's "night" is the same as that of other people, namely, from 8 p.m. to 5 (or 6) a.m. The only restriction on "night-work" in the new law is that workers engaged even part of the night shall not work more than ten hours. That is all. The law does not prohibit night-work. In this respect, too, the law falls short of the *petitions* of the St. Petersburg employers, who fourteen years ago (in 1883) appealed for the prohibition of night-work for adults. Consequently, the St. Petersburg workers would have won more from the employers in this respect too, *had not the government interfered* in order to protect the interests of the most retrograde employers in Russia. The government would not listen to the employers of St. Petersburg, for it did not want to offend those in Moscow, most of whom compel their workers to work at night. As usual, the government tried to mask its subservience to the interests of the *worst* employers by deceptive talk and assurances. In an article explaining the new law, *Vestnik*

Finansov, published by the Ministry of Finance, stated that in other countries (France, for instance) night-work is forbidden. But, it declared, our law cannot do this. "It is not always possible to forbid establishments to work a full twenty-four hours: a large number of industries, by their very nature, require continuous operation."

This is obviously quite a lame excuse. We are not discussing special industries which require continuous operation, but industries in general. Even under the present law continuous operation is impossible when work is done in two shifts unless overtime is worked, since day-work has been fixed at 11½ hours and night-work at 10 hours, or 21½ hours in all. That is why the new law makes special provision for industries in which continuous operation is necessary (through special ministerial regulations, of which more anon). Consequently, there was absolutely nothing to make the prohibition of night-work "impossible." We have already said that the government would have us believe that it is concerned for the workers' health. Here is what the Ministry of Finance says about night-work: "Night-work is undoubtedly more fatiguing and unhealthy and, in general, less natural than work by daylight; and it is more detrimental the longer and more systematic it is. It might seem that in view of the detrimental character of night-work, it would be better to prohibit it for adult male workers too (just as it is prohibited for women and for adolescents of both sexes in some industries, and in the case of children everywhere). But there are no grounds for this even from the standpoint of the worker's general welfare; moderate night-work is less detrimental to him than excessively long hours of day-work for the same pay." You see how skilful Russian Government officials are in throwing dust into the eyes of the people! Even their protection of the interests of the worst employers is presented as solicitude for the "worker's welfare." And how brazen is the justification invented by the Ministry: "moderate night-work," don't you see, "is less detrimental than excessively long hours of day-work for the same pay." The Ministry wants to say that the worker is driven to work at night by low wages, so low that the *worker* cannot get along without working excessively long hours. And so, the Ministry, confident that this will always be so, that

the worker will never succeed in winning better wages, cyn-
ically declares: since the worker has to toil monstrously
long hours to feed his family, is it not all the same to him
whether he works the extra hours in the day-time or at
night? Of course, if the majority of the Russian workers
go on earning the same miserable wages as at present, want
will drive them to work extra hours. But how insolent it
is to justify the sanctioning of night-work on the plea of
the worker's downtrodden condition! "The pay for the work
will be the same"—that is the main thing for the servitors
of capital—"and with the present level of wages, the worker
cannot get along without working extra hours." And bureaucrats like these, who concoct kulak arguments in the interests of the stingy employers, have the audacity to talk
about the "standpoint of the worker's general welfare."
But are they not too confident in hoping that the worker will
always be so downtrodden, that he will always agree to
this "same pay," that is, to the same beggarly remuneration for his labour? Low wages and long hours always go
hand in hand; the one is impossible without the other. When
pay is low, the worker is forced to work extra hours, and
to work at night, in order to earn enough to live on. When
working hours are excessively long, pay will always be low,
because when working long hours the worker produces less
articles per hour and of far worse quality than in a short
working day, and because the worker, crushed as he is by
excessive toil, will always remain downtrodden and powerless
under the yoke of capital. Consequently, when the Ministry,
which serves the Russian factory owners, proposes to preserve
the present preposterously low wages of the Russian workers,
and at the same time talks about the "workers' welfare," it
shows as clearly as clear can be that its phrases are sheer
cant and lies.

V

HOW DOES THE MINISTRY OF FINANCE
TRY TO PROVE THAT TO RESTRICT OVERTIME
WOULD BE "UNFAIR" TO THE WORKER?

We have referred to the new law as a law to reduce the
working day. We have said that it restricts the working
day to 11½ hours (10 hours in the case of night-work). But

actually this is not so, it is far worse. All the restrictions provided for in the law relate only to ordinary, normal, regular work, but not to *overtime*. Consequently, the employer's "right" to compel the workers to work any number of hours, even twenty-four at a stretch, *is not restricted at all*. Here is what the law says about overtime: "Overtime shall mean work performed by the worker in an industrial establishment during hours other than those in which he is obliged to work by factory rules. Overtime shall be permitted only by special agreement between the manager of the industrial establishment and the worker. The labour contract may contain stipulations only as regards such overtime work as is necessitated by the technical conditions of the industry." This is a highly important clause of the new law, and its edge is directed entirely against the workers, leaving the employer a free hand. Hitherto overtime has been regulated by custom; there has been no mention of it in any law. Now the government has *legalised* overtime. The stipulation in the law that such work shall require a "special agreement" between worker and employer is just an empty and utterly meaningless phrase. All work is done "by agreement" between the workers and the employers. The workers are not serfs (although many a Russian official would like nothing better than to turn them into such); they work for hire, that is, by agreement. There was no point in stipulating that overtime shall be done by agreement. The government - inserted that meaningless phrase into the law in order to create the impression that it wants to restrict overtime. As a matter of fact the law does not restrict it at all. Formerly the master used to say to the worker: "If you want to work overtime, all right; if not, here's your discharge!"— and now he will say the same. Only formerly it was done by custom; now it will be done with the sanction of the *law*. Formerly, an employer who dismissed a worker for refusing to work overtime could not claim the support of the law; now the law directly suggests to him how he can oppress the worker. Instead of restricting overtime, this clause of the law may easily render it more prevalent. The law even permits the employer to include the demand for overtime in the contract when "it is necessitated by the technical conditions of the industry." This reservation will cause no inconvenience to the employer at all. How is one to decide which work is "necessitated by the technical conditions of the industry," and which is not? Who will investigate it? If an employer states that the job he has given a worker to do out of hours is "necessitated by the technical conditions of the industry," how can he be refuted? Nobody will investigate it, nobody will check the employer's statement. The law has only *strengthened* the arbitrary powers of the employers by suggesting to them a *particularly reliable* way of oppressing the workers.

Now, all the employer has to do is to stipulate in the contract that the worker has no right to refuse to work overtime when "necessitated by the technical conditions of the industry," and the trick is done! Let the worker decline to work overtime—he will simply be discharged. And where (thinks the employer) will you find a worker who will attempt to prove that the work was not "necessitated by the technical conditions of the industry"! The very idea of a worker making such a complaint is ridiculous. Needless to say, there will never be any such complaints, and they would be useless if they were made. The government has therefore quite legally endowed the employers with arbitrary powers as regards overtime. How eager the Ministry of Finance is in its haste to serve the employers and to teach them how to make the widest use of overtime under the protection of the new legislation is very clearly shown by the following argument in *Vestnik Finansov*: "Overtime is also necessary in the case of rush orders, which the employers cannot possibly foresee* in industries operating for definite and brief seasons, if the owner of the establishment finds it impossible or difficult to increase the number of workers."

You see how skilfully the law is "interpreted" by the zealous lackeys of the employers installed in the Ministry of Finance! The law only speaks of overtime necessitated by technical conditions, but the Ministry of Finance hastens to consider as "necessitated" overtime due to "unforeseen" (?!)

---

* The old song! Every year Russian factories—especially those in the central regions—receive rush orders for the Nizhni-Novgorod Fair; and every year they solemnly assure all the simpletons who believe them, or who pretend to believe them, that they were unable to foresee this!...

orders, and even when the employer finds it "difficult" to increase the number of workers! Why, that is simply making fools of the workers! Any astute employer can *always* say that he finds it "difficult." Increasing the number of workers means hiring others, which means reducing the number of unemployed hanging round the factory gate, means lessening competition among workers, making them more exacting in their demands and, perhaps, having to agree to pay higher wages. It goes without saying that there is not an employer who would not consider this to be "difficult" for him. With such arbitrary powers for the employers to demand overtime, the law on the reduction of the working day is robbed of all value. There will be no reduction at all for vast numbers of workers, since they will continue to work 15 to 18 hours a day and more, remaining at the factory at night to do overtime. The absurdity of a law to reduce the working day which does not forbid (or at least restrict) overtime is so obvious that in all the preliminary drafts of the law it was proposed to restrict overtime. As far back as 1883, the St. Petersburg employers (the employers themselves!) petitioned to have overtime restricted to *one hour* a day. The government, scared by the St. Petersburg strikes of 1895-96, immediately appointed a commission to draft a bill to reduce working hours; this commission also recommended that overtime be restricted, namely, to 120 hours a year.* By rejecting every proposal to restrict overtime in any degree whatsoever, the government definitely set out to protect the interests of the worst of the employers, openly legalised the complete subjection of the workers, and made it quite clear that it intended to leave everything as it was before and to make shift with meaningless phrases. In its anxiety to serve the interests of the employers, the Ministry of Finance went so far as to try to prove that any restriction of overtime would be "unfair to the worker himself." Here are its arguments, which should give every worker food for thought. "To deprive the worker of the right to work at the factory more than a fixed number of hours a day would be

---

* Even the Ministry of Finance itself, in its interpretation of the new law, was obliged to admit that "the sanctioning of overtime seems to be inappropriate" (*Vestnik Finansov*).

difficult in practice" (Why? Because the factory inspectors are very remiss in the performance of their duties, fearing nothing so much as to offend the employers? Or because so long as the Russian worker has no rights and is inarticulate, it will be difficult to carry out any reforms for his benefit? The Ministry of Finance has unwittingly let the cat out of the bag: indeed, as long as the Russian workers, like the Russian people in general, stand disfranchised in face of a police government, as long as they have no political rights, no reforms can be effective) ... "and would be unfair to the workers: a man should not be punished for seeking the means of subsistence, for occasionally exerting his strength even above the limit beyond which his work may prove detrimental to his health." See how humane and philanthropic the Russian Government is! Bow in gratitude, Russian workers! The government is so merciful, that it "does not rob" you of the "right" to work 18 hours a day, even 24 if you like. The government is so fair that it does not want to punish you when the employer forces you to overstrain yourself at the job! In all other countries, it is the employer, not the worker, who *is punished* if work is done at the factory over and above the regular hours. Our officials have forgotten that. Indeed, how could Russian officials take the risk of *punishing* the employers! Perish the thought! We shall soon see that the employers will not be punished even if they break every clause of this new law. In all other countries, the workers, in their "search for the means of subsistence," have the right to organise unions, mutual benefit societies, to openly resist the employer, to present their demands to him, to conduct strikes. In our country this is not allowed. On the other hand, however, our workers have been granted the "right" to work any number of "extra" hours a day. Why did these humane officials forget to add that our fair government "does not rob" the Russian worker of the "right" to be sent to prison without trial, or to be beaten up by any police bashi-bazouk for every attempt to protect himself from the oppression of the capitalists?

VI
WHAT POWERS DOES THE NEW LAW GRANT THE MINISTERS?

We have already shown that on the most essential points the new law has not laid down any obligatory, hard and fast rules. The government has preferred to grant the fullest possible powers to the administration (namely, the ministers) to establish all sorts of rules and privileges in the interests of employers, to hamper the application of the new law, etc. The powers granted to the ministers by the new law are extremely broad and extensive. The ministers (namely, the Minister of Finance or the Minister of Railways, etc., in concurrence with the Minister of Internal Affairs) are "empowered" to issue detailed regulations governing the application of the new law. A host of questions relating to all the clauses of the new law in *all* and *sundry* respects are left entirely to the discretion of the ministers. The powers of the ministers are so vast that they are virtually the sole executors of the new law; if they want to, they can issue regulations which will really enforce it; or, if they want to, they can act so that the law will be scarcely enforced at all. And, indeed, see what regulations the ministers are empowered to issue "in pursuance of the present law" (that is the way the law puts it. We have already seen how smart the Ministry of Finance can be when acting "in pursuance" of the law—it will act in such a way that the workers, in its opinion, will only have to be thankful that the government does not punish them for working too much and does not "deprive them of the right" to work even 24 hours a day). We would enumerate all the various categories of these regulations if that were possible; but the fact is that, in addition to the questions enumerated in the law which are to be settled by the ministerial regulations, the law also empowers them to issue *other regulations* without any restriction. The ministers may issue regulations governing working hours. That is to say, it is not enough to have a law governing working hours; there are to be ministerial regulations for the same thing. The ministers may issue regulations concerning shifts; but, of course, they may also not, so as not to inconvenience the employers. The ministers have been empowered to issue regulations govern-

ing the number of shifts a day, meal times, etc. That is
what the *law* says: et cetera (*and so forth*); in other words,
the ministers are empowered to issue any regulations they
like. If they don't like, there will be no regulations on meal
times at all, and the employers will go on oppressing the
workers as they do now, not allowing them to go home for
dinner, and not allowing mothers to go home to feed their
children. It is left to the ministers to issue regulations governing overtime, namely, indicating when it shall be
permitted, how frequently, and what record shall be kept.
Consequently, here the ministers have a perfectly free hand.
They may even *alter* the requirements of the law, that is,
they may strengthen or *mitigate* them (the law deliberately
stipulates the right of the ministers to mitigate the requirements of the new law in respect of the employers) in three
cases: firstly, "when same is deemed necessary owing to the
character of the industry (continuity and so forth)." This
"and so forth" is also in the law, thus enabling the ministers to plead any "character of the industry" they like.
Secondly, "owing to the nature of the work (tending of
boilers or transmission belts, current and emergency repairs,
and so forth)." Here we have "and so forth" again! Thirdly,
"and in other important and exceptional cases." Further,
the ministers may determine which industries are particularly detrimental to the health of the workers (or they may
not: the law does not compel, but only authorises them to
do so ... although they had that authority before, but never
wanted to exercise it!) and to issue special regulations for
these industries. The workers now see why we said that
it is impossible to enumerate the questions left to be settled by the ministers: the law is strewn with "et ceteras" and
"and so forths." Russian laws in general may be divided into
two categories: those which grant some rights to the workers
and the common people generally, and others which prohibit something, or allow officials to prohibit it. In the
laws of the first category, even the most trivial rights of the
workers *are enumerated with the utmost precision* (even, for
example, the worker's right to absent himself from work
with good cause) and *not the least* departure is permitted on
pain of the severest penalties. In these laws you will not find
a single "et cetera" or "and so forth." In the laws of the second

category, only general prohibitions are *invariably* indicated, *without any precise enumeration*, so that the management may prohibit *anything it likes*; in these laws you will always find small but very important additions: "et cetera," "and so forth." These little phrases are striking testimony of the almighty power exercised by Russian officials over the people, and of the latter's utter rightlessness in regard to them; of the senseless and savage character of the abominable bureaucracy and red tape in which every institution of the Imperial Russian Government is steeped through and through. Any law which may be of the slightest benefit is invariably so wrapped up in red tape that its enforcement is endlessly delayed. More, the enforcement of the law is left to the complete discretion of the officials, who, as everybody knows, are ready heart and soul to "serve" any moneybag, and to play every possible dirty trick on the common people. The ministers, be it remembered, are only empowered to issue all these regulations "in pursuance of the present law"; that is, they may issue them or they may not. The law does not bind them to anything. The law does not fix any date: they may issue the regulations now, or they may do so in ten years' time. Naturally, the *few* rules enumerated in the law lose all meaning and importance: they are empty words that merely conceal the government's desire to frustrate the law in its practical application. Vast powers are granted to our ministers by practically every law affecting the life of the workers. And we understand perfectly why the government does so: it wants to be of the greatest possible service to the employers. After all, it is much easier for an employer to influence the official responsible for enforcing the law, than to influence the passage of the law itself. Everybody knows how easily our capitalist magnates gain access to the drawing-rooms of Messrs. the Ministers and there engage in pleasant conversations, how hospitably they entertain each other at dinners, what gracious little presents to the tune of tens and hundreds of thousands of rubles are made to the corrupt officials of the Imperial Government (either directly, in the shape of bribes, or indirectly, in the shape of shares to company "founders," or of honorary and lucrative posts in these companies). Consequently, the broader the rights the new law confers on the officials in respect of its enforcement, the more advantageous it is both for the *officials* and for the *factory owners*: the advantage to the officials is that they can grab more, and to the factory owners that they can more easily secure privileges and exemptions. In illustration, let us remind the workers of two cases which show what these ministerial regulations issued "*in pursuance*. of the law" lead to in practice. The law of June 3, 1886, laid it down that the fines money belongs to the workers and must be expended on their needs. The minister "pursued" this law in such a way that in St. Petersburg, for instance, it was not enforced for ten years, and when at last it began to be enforced, the whole matter was put into the hands of the employer, whom the worker has to beg for his money as though it were a dole. Second example: this same law (of June 3, 1886) lays it down that wages must be paid not less than twice a month; but the minister "pursued" the law in such a way as to give the employers the right to withhold the wages of a new worker for six weeks. Every worker now clearly understands why this time, too, the ministers have been empowered to "pursue" the law. The employers also understand this perfectly, and they have already set their machinery going. We have seen that the ministers are "empowered" to issue regulations on overtime. The employers have already begun to bring pressure to bear on the government to induce it *not to restrict* overtime. *Moskovskiye Vedomosti*, a newspaper which always zealously defends the interests of the worst employers, persistently eggs on the government to the most savage and brutal actions, and enjoys such immense influence "in high spheres" (that is, among the higher officials, ministers, etc.), has now launched a regular campaign against the imposition of restrictions on overtime. The employers have thousands of ways of exerting pressure on the government: they have their societies and associations; employers are members of numerous government commissions and boards (for example, the Factory Boards), they have personal access to ministers; they may write as much as they like in the press about their wishes and demands, and the press has tremendous influence in our times. As to the workers, they have *no* legal means of exerting pressure on the government. There is only one thing the workers can do, and that is to join forces, to spread the consciousness of their interests as members of one class among all the workers, and to put up united resistance to the government and the employers. Every worker can now see that the enforcement of the new law will depend entirely on who exerts strongest pressure on the government, the employers or the workers. It was only by struggle, by a conscious and staunch struggle, that the workers secured the *passage* of this law. Only by struggle will they be able to secure the actual enforcement of the law, and its enforcement in the interests of the workers. Without a stubborn struggle, without the staunch resistance of the united workers to every claim the employers make, the new law will remain a scrap of paper, one of those false and pretentious signboards with which our government tries to embellish the utterly rotten edifice of police tyranny and the rightless and oppressed state of the workers.

VII

HOW OUR "CHRISTIAN" GOVERNMENT CURTAILS THE WORKERS' HOLIDAYS

Besides regulations on working hours, the new law also contains a regulation concerning compulsory rest-days for factory workers on Sundays and holidays. The grovelling hacks, of whom there are so many among our Russian newspapermen and journalists, have hastened to mark this regulation by lauding our government and its humaneness to the skies. We shall presently see that actually this humane law tends *to curtail* holidays for the workers. But first let us examine the general regulations concerning Sunday and holiday rest. First of all, it should be noted that the St. Petersburg employers petitioned for the establishment of legal rest-days on Sundays and holidays fourteen years ago (in 1883). In other words, here too, the Russian Government only delayed, postponed and *resisted* reform as long as it was possible. According to the law, the list of holidays on which work is forbidden explicitly includes all Sundays and fourteen other holidays, of which we shall speak at greater length later. The law does not absolutely forbid work on holidays, but permits it on the following condi-

tions: firstly, "mutual agreement" between the employer and
the workers is required; secondly, work on a holiday is
permitted, provided it is "compensated by a week-day";
thirdly, the agreement to replace the holiday by a week-day
must be immediately reported to the factory inspector.
Hence, under the law, work on holidays must on no account
be allowed to reduce the number of rest-days, for the employer is obliged to compensate the workers for working on a
holiday by giving them a free week-day. The workers must
always bear this in mind, and also the fact that the law
demands the mutual consent of the employer and the workers for such an arrangement. In other words, the workers
may always quite legally *refuse to agree* to such an arrangement, and the employer has *no right* to compel them to do
so. In practice, of course, the employer will be able to extort
the workers' consent in the following way: he will ask the
workers one by one to agree, and each worker will be afraid
to refuse, for fear of being discharged. In doing this, the
employers will of course be acting illegally, for the law
demands the *consent of the workers*, that is, of all the workers
jointly. But how can all the workers in one factory (and
there are sometimes hundreds and even thousands of them,
working in many different places) make their common consent known? The law does not say how, and here again it
has placed in the hands of the employers another means of
oppressing the workers. The workers have only one way
of preventing such oppression: in every such case they must
demand the election of workers' deputies to convey the *general* decision of all the workers to the employer. The workers
can base this demand on the law, for the latter speaks of
the consent of all the *workers*, and all the workers cannot
speak to the employer at once. This system of electing workers' deputies will, in general, be very beneficial to the
workers, and will be useful for all kinds of other negotiations
with the employers and the office, inasmuch as it is very
difficult, and often quite impossible, for the individual
worker to present his demands, claims, etc. Further, as
regards workers of "non-Orthodox persuasion," the law "permits" that days which are not celebrated by their Church
may not be included in the list of holidays. But then there
are other holidays which are celebrated by Catholics, and

19*

not by Orthodox people. The law says nothing about this and, therefore, makes an attempt to discriminate somewhat against non-Orthodox workers. Even more marked is the discrimination against non-Christian workers: for them the law "permits" other days in the week instead of Sunday to be included in the list of holidays. Only "permits"! Our Christian government so savagely persecutes persons who do not profess the ruling religion that very likely this too is an attempt to oppress non-Christians by making the law vague. The law is indeed very obscure on this point. It should be interpreted as meaning that one day in the week must be a compulsory rest-day, and that all that is permitted is the substitution of some other day for Sunday. But the "ruling" religion only grants privileges to the "rulers"; as for the working man, it will never miss an opportunity to invent some sort of a trap for him. Let us see *which holidays* the law says must be included in the list. It is all very well talking about establishing Sunday and holiday rest; but even before this the workers did not as a rule, in the majority of cases, work either on Sundays or on holidays. The law, after all, may fix the rest-days in such a way that the total number of *compulsory* holidays may prove to be far fewer than the number of *customary* holidays. *This is exactly what our Christian government has done in the new law.* It has established 66 holidays in the year: 52 Sundays, 8 fixed holidays (January 1 and 6, March 25, August 6 and 15, September 8, and December 25 and 26) and 6 movable holidays (Friday and Saturday in Passion Week, Easter Monday and Tuesday, Ascension Day and Descent of the Holy Ghost). But how many *customary* holidays a year have there been in our factories till now? We have precise information on this score for Moscow and Smolensk gubernias, and that only for a few factories. But as the difference between the factories, and even between the two gubernias, is very small, this information is quite sufficient to enable us to form an opinion about the real value of the new law. In Moscow Gubernia, figures were collected for 47 large factories, employing a total of over 20,000 workers. It was found that in hand-operated factories, the number of holidays per year is 97, and in the machine-operated factories the number is 98. The lowest number of holidays per year is 78. These 78 holidays are celebrated at all the investigated factories *without exception*. In Smolensk Gubernia, the information relates to 15 factories, employing a total of about 5,000 to 6,000 workers. The average number of holidays per year is 86, or nearly as many as in Moscow Gubernia. The lowest number of holidays was found at one of the factories, where it was 75. Corresponding to this number of holidays per year, which is *customary* for Russian factories, is the number of holidays established for factories under the jurisdiction of the War Ministry, where 88 annual holidays are the rule. The laws of our country recognise practically the same number of days for civil servants as nonworking (87 a year). Consequently, each year the workers had the same number of *customary* holidays as other citizens. In its solicitude for the workers' health, our "Christian government" cut out a fourth of these customary holidays, 22 in all, leaving only 66 compulsory holidays. Let us enumerate the customary holidays cut out by the government in the new law. Of the fixed holidays the following have been cut out: February 2—Candlemas; May 9—St Nicholas' day; June 29—St Peter's day; July 8—the Feast of Our Lady of Kazan; July 20—St Elijah's day; August 29—St John the Baptist's day; September 14—the Feast of the Holy Cross; October 1 — the Feast of the Intercession (even this holiday the government deemed superfluous and non-compulsory. We may be certain that not a single employer will be found who will dare compel his employees to work on that day. Here again the government is protecting the interests and mean practices of the worst employers); November 21—Presentation of the Blessed Virgin, and December 6—St Nicholas' day. Thus, 10 fixed holidays have been cut out.* Further, of the movable holidays, the following have been cut out: Shrove Saturday and Wednesday of the last week of Lent, i.e., two holidays. In all, therefore, 12 holidays have been cut out from the *minimum* hitherto allowed the workers as rest-days according to prevailing custom. Our government is so fond of calling itself a "Christian" govern-

* We have enumerated only the holidays that have been observed by *all* factories till now. There are many other holidays that have been observed by the *overwhelming majority* of factories, for example, pre-Lent days, Shrove Friday; Thursday, Friday and Saturday of Easter week, and many others.

ment; when addressing the workers, the ministers and other officials sweeten their speeches with phrases about the "Christian love" and "Christian sentiments" of the employers and of the government towards the workers, etc. But as soon as action takes the place of phrases, all this hypocritical and canting talk is sent to blazes, and the government becomes a huckster trying to extort something from the workers wherever possible. The employers themselves, that is, the best of them, long long ago petitioned for the establishment of legal rest-days on Sundays and holidays. After fifteen years of procrastination, the government has at last passed a law establishing *compulsory* rest on Sundays and holidays, but while making this concession to the workers it does not miss the opportunity of injuring them by cutting out one-fourth of the customary holidays from the list of those that are compulsory. Thus, the government is behaving like a real usurer: while making one concession, it does its best to make up for it by some other extortion. With such a law, it may very easily happen that at some of the factories the employers will try *to reduce* the number of workers' rest-days and compel the workers to work on holidays which have hitherto been kept but which the law has not included in the compulsory list of holidays. To prevent their conditions from being worsened, the workers must, in this respect too, always be ready to resist every attempt to reduce the number of holidays. The law only specifies the compulsory holidays; but the workers have the right to demand others as well. Only they must see to it that all the holidays are stipulated in the rules of the factory and should place no trust in verbal promises. The workers can be sure of not being compelled to work on a holiday only when that holiday has been included in the factory rules. Just as in the case of holidays, so in the case of half-holidays, the law attempts to leave matters where they were before, and even in some respects to worsen them. The law provides for only one half-holiday—Christmas eve: on that day work must cease not later than noon. This has been the case until now at the majority of factories, and if any factory did not release the workers at noon on Christmas eve, in most cases it allowed them a half-holiday on the eve of some other big holiday. Generally speaking, one half-holiday in the year has hitherto been the rule at the majority of the factories. Further, the new law says that on Saturdays and the eve of holidays the working day is limited to ten hours, that is, 1 ½ hours less than the ordinary working day. Here, too, the law has not improved the workers' conditions, and, if anything, has worsened them: hitherto, *at nearly all the factories*, work on Saturday ceased earlier than usual. One investigator, who has collected a great deal of information on this subject and who is generally well acquainted with factory life, states that it may be safely concluded that, on the average, work on Saturdays ceases two hours before the usual time. Consequently, here, too, the law did not miss the opportunity, while converting a *customary* rest period into a *compulsory* one, to extort from the workers at least one half-hour as compensation for this concession. One half-hour a week amounts to 23 hours a year (counting 46 working weeks), that is, two days extra work for the employer's benefit.... Not a bad present for our poor, indigent employers! We may be quite sure that these knights of the moneybag will not hesitate to accept this present and will do their best to compensate themselves in this way for the "sacrifices" demanded of them by the new law (as they are fond of putting it), and, therefore, in this respect too, the workers must rely only on themselves, on the strength of their organisation. Without a stubborn struggle, the working class, in this respect too, will fail to achieve any improvement in their condition, notwithstanding the new law.

VIII

HOW IS THE OBSERVANCE
OF THE NEW LAW GUARANTEED?

How is the observance of laws guaranteed in general? Firstly, by supervision over the observance, and secondly, by punishment of infringements, of the law. Let us see how matters stand with regard to the new factory law. Supervision over the observance of laws has been entrusted to the factory inspectors. Hitherto, the regulations governing factory supervision issued in 1886 have not been extended to the whole of Russia by far, but only to a few gubernias, the most highly industrialised ones. The extension of the area of factory supervision has always followed the extension of the area of the working-class movement and of workers' strikes. On the very date that the law to reduce the working hours was promulgated (that is, June 2, 1897), another law was issued extending factory supervision to the whole of Russia and to the entire Kingdom of Poland. This extension of the factory regulations to the whole of Russia and the institution of Factory Inspection is, of course, a step forward. The workers will take advantage of this to inform a larger number of their comrades about their conditions, about the labour laws, about the attitude of the government and its officials towards the workers, etc. The application of the same rules that govern the advanced workers (of St. Petersburg, Moscow, Vladimir and other gubernias) to all factory workers in Russia will, of course, also help the working-class movement to spread more rapidly to all Russian workers. As to how far *effectively* the factory inspectors supervise the observance of the law, we shall not go into this in detail. A separate pamphlet should be written on this subject (it is so wide), and perhaps we shall find some other opportunity to discuss the question of Factory Inspection with the workers. Let us only briefly remark that so few factory inspectors are appointed in Russia that they are very rarely to be seen at the factories. The factory inspectors are completely under the jurisdiction of the Ministry of Finance, which turns them into servitors of the employers, compels them to report strikes and unrest to the police, to prosecute workers for leaving the factory even when the employer himself does not prosecute them; in a word, it turns them, in a manner of speaking, into police officials, into factory police. The employer has thousands of ways of exerting influence on the factory inspectors and of forcing them to do what he wants. The workers, however, have no means of influencing the factory inspectors, and cannot have such means as long as the workers do not enjoy the right of free assembly, the right to form their unions, to discuss their affairs in the press, and to issue workers' newspapers. So long as these rights are withheld, no supervision by officials over the employers can ever be serious and effective. But supervision alone is not enough to secure

the observance of the law. Strict penalties for non-observance
of the law must also be imposed. Otherwise, what is the good
of a factory inspector telling the employer that he is acting
wrongly? The employer will simply ignore him and go on
acting as before. That is why, when a new law is passed,
the penalties imposed on those who infringe it are always
stipulated. *The new law of June 2, 1897, reducing working
hours and establishing rest-days, however, contains no
penalties for its infringement.* The workers can see from
this how different is the government's attitude to the employers and to the workers. When a law is passed, say, forbidding the worker to leave the factory before his time is up, the
penalty in case he does leave is fixed at once, including even
so severe a penalty as arrest. For going on strike, for example,
the workers are liable, under the law, to arrest and even
imprisonment, but the employer is only fined for the infringement of the regulations which causes the strike. So in
this case, too, the requirement of the law that the employers
shall allow the workers to rest on Sundays and holidays and
not make them work more than 11½ hours a day is not supported by any penalties for its infringement. What will be
done to an employer who is guilty of infringing this law?
At the most, he may be hauled before the magistrate, who
cannot levy a fine exceeding 50 rubles, or the Factory Board
may itself impose a penalty in the shape of a fine. But will
a fine of 50 rubles deter an employer? Why, he makes far
much more than 50 rubles profit by compelling all his workers to
work a night or on a holiday! It will actually benefit the factory
owner to break the law and pay a fine. The failure of the law
to stipulate the penalty for its infringement by the employer
is a crying injustice, which plainly shows that our government is anxious to delay the enforcement of the law as long
as possible, that it does not intend to demand strict observance of the law by the employers. It happened in other
countries, too, in times long past, that a government would
pass factory laws without stipulating any penalties for
their infringement. And, in fact, such laws were not
observed at all and remained mere scraps of paper. That is
why this ridiculous custom of passing laws without ensuring
their enforcement has long been abandoned in other countries. Today the Russian Government is resorting to this

same old trick in the hope that the workers will not notice it. But this hope is unfounded. As soon as the workers become acquainted with the new law, they themselves will see to it that it is observed; they will not allow the slightest departure from it and will refuse to work until its provisions are complied with. Such supervision by the workers themselves will be far more effective than that of any factory police. Without such supervision the law will not be observed.

IX

WILL THE NEW LAW IMPROVE THE WORKERS'
CONDITION?

At first glance, it may even seem strange that we raise this question. The law reduces working hours and establishes compulsory rest-days on Sundays and holidays. Surely this is an improvement of the workers' condition? But we have already shown in detail above how vague and indefinite are the provisions of the new law, how often the law, while laying down rules to improve the workers' condition, itself frustrates those rules by leaving the employer's arbitrary power untouched, or by limiting the compulsory holidays to a number far smaller than is customary.

Let us try and calculate whether working time will be reduced by the introduction of the new law if the number of rest-days is no more than the number established by the law, that is, if the workers are given rest-days only on the compulsory holidays established by the law, and the employers succeed in compelling them to work on the other, customary holidays. Whether they succeed or not is, of course, an open question. That will depend on what resistance the workers put up. But that the employers will try to compensate themselves for the reduction in working hours by reducing the number of holidays, is beyond doubt. That the law does its utmost to assist this noble endeavour of the capitalists to oppress the workers, is also beyond doubt. Well, let us see what the effect of this would be. To compare working time under the old system with that under the new (i.e., under the law of June 2, 1897), we must take *the number of working hours per year*. Only in this way can account be taken of all the holidays and shorter working days on the eve of holidays. How many hours a year does the Russian factory worker usually work now, that is, before the operation of the law of June 2, 1897? It goes without saying that exact information on this point is not available, for it is impossible to calculate the number of working hours of every worker. We must avail ourselves of the information collected for *a few* factories, and assume that the number of hours at other factories is approximately the same as that at the factories investigated. Let us take the information collected for Moscow Gubernia. The number of working days in the year was calculated exactly in the case of 45 big factories. It was found that the total number of working days in the year at all these 45 factories together was 12,010, that is, an average of 267 working days per factory.* The number of working hours per week (as shown by data for several hundred factories) averages 74, or $12\frac{1}{2}$ hours a day. Hence, in the year there were $267 \times 12\frac{1}{2} = 3,293$ working hours, or in round numbers 3,300. In the city of Odessa, we reckoned up the figures for 54 large factories for which we have information regarding the number of working days in the year, and the number of hours. We found that the average number of working hours per year in all these factories is 3,139, or considerably less than in Moscow Gubernia. In Odessa the working day is shorter, in most cases 10½ hours, the average for these 54 factories being 10.7 hours. Hence the number of working hours per year is lower, although there are fewer holidays. Let us see how many working hours we get under the new law. First of all, let us count up the number of working days in the year. For this purpose, we must deduct from 365, firstly, 66 holidays; secondly, half a day on Christmas eve, and, thirdly, the free time the worker

---

* If the number of working days in the year is 267, the number of non-working days, holidays, must be 98. We said above that there were 89 holidays, but we arrived at this figure by taking, firstly, only machine-operated factories, and secondly, not the average number of holidays for all factories, but the number of holidays most often met with.

enjoys by ceasing work 1½ hours earlier on the eve of holidays. The number of holiday eves will be 60 (not 66, for about 6 holidays coincide with other rest-days). Hence, the reduced hours on the eve of holidays amount to $60 \times 1\frac{1}{2} = 90$ working hours, or 8 working days. Thus, in all, from the 365 days in the year, we have to deduct 74½ holidays $(66 + \frac{1}{2} + 8 = 74\frac{1}{2})$. The result is 290½ working days, or $290\frac{1}{2} \times 11\frac{1}{2} = 3,340$ working hours. Thus we find that if the number of holidays is reduced to the compulsory number established by the law, *the condition of the workers will be worsened rather than improved by the introduction of the new law*. On the whole, the number of working hours per year will remain what it was before, or will even be *increased*! Of course, this calculation is only approximate; it cannot be made with complete accuracy. But it is based on quite reliable data and clearly shows what a smart device the government has invented to oppress the workers by reducing the number of compulsory holidays as compared with the customary number. This calculation clearly shows that if the workers do not firmly stand up for one another and offer joint resistance to the employers, their condition may be worsened by the introduction of the new law! And please note in addition, that in this calculation we have taken only *day*-work, that is, *ordinary* working hours. But what about overtime? As we have seen, the law placed no restrictions on this, and we do not know whether the ministers will introduce any restrictions in the regulations which they have been "empowered" to issue. It is this absence of any restrictions on overtime which chiefly leads us to doubt whether the new law will improve the condition of the workers. If, with the reduction of the normal (ordinary) working day, the wages of the majority of the Russian workers remain as preposterously low as they are at present, *the worker will be compelled by want to consent to work overtime, and his condition will not improve*. What the worker needs is to work no more than eight hours a day, and to have time for rest, for his development, and for the enjoyment of his rights as a human being, a family man, and a citizen. What the worker needs is to get not a beggarly wage, but enough to live a decent human life, himself to enjoy the advantage of the improvements introduced in production, and not to surrender all the profit to his exploiters. If in order to earn the same pay the worker has to work the same number of hours as before, is it not all the same to him whether his excessive toil is called ordinary time or overtime? The law to reduce the working day will then remain *a dead letter, a scrap of paper*. The new law will then not affect the employers in the slightest, and will not compel them to concede anything to the working people. And the officials of the Ministry of Finance, in their servility to the capitalists, *are evidently already hinting at this*. In the same *Vestnik Finansov* article they reassure the employers by saying: "The new law, while restricting freedom of contract in the hiring of workers for ordinary jobs, does not deprive the employer of the opportunity to operate his establishment at any time of the day or night and even, in case of need" (yes, yes! our poor downtrodden employers so often experience the "need" for the unpaid labour of the Russian workers) ... "on holidays by entering into special agreements" (to work overtime) "with the workers."

You see how these lackeys bow and scrape to the moneybags! Please don't be much disturbed, Messrs. the Employers, they as much as say: you may "operate your establishment at any time of the day or night"; all you have to do is to call *overtime* what used to be considered ordinary time. *You merely have to change the name, that is all!*

The most amazing thing in this statement is the brazenness of the officials; they are convinced in advance that there will be no restriction whatever on overtime (if overtime is restricted, the employers will not be able to operate at any time of the day or night!). They are convinced in advance that their frank and cynical advice to the employers not to stand on ceremony will not reach the ears of the workers! In this, even the officials of the Ministry of Finance, we think, have excelled themselves! It will be very instructive for the workers to learn *how* officials talk to the employers and *what* advice they give them. On learning this, the workers will realise that under cover of the new law their old enemies are attacking them, in pursuit of their old striving to enslave the workers on the most *"legal grounds."*

X

WHAT IS THE SIGNIFICANCE OF THE NEW LAW?

We have now acquainted ourselves with the new law in all its details. All that remains is to discuss *what significance* this law has for the workers and the working-class movement in Russia.

The significance of the new factory law lies, on the one hand, in its being a forced concession by the government, in its having been *won* from the police government by the united and class-conscious workers. The promulgation of this law shows the *success* of the working-class movement in Russia; it shows what tremendous power lies in the class-conscious and staunch demand of the working masses. No amount of persecution, no wholesale arrests and deportations, no grandiose political trials, no hounding of the workers have been of any avail. The government set all its forces and resources into motion. It hurled itself upon the St. Petersburg workers with all the weight of the tremendous power it commands. It hounded and persecuted the workers without trial and with unparalleled ferocity in the endeavour at all costs *to knock* the spirit of protest, of struggle, *out* of the workers, *to crush* the workers' incipient socialist movement against the employers and the government. It was all to no avail, and the government was compelled to realise that no amount of persecution of individual workers would eradicate *the workers' movement* and that it would have to make concessions. This autocratic government, considered to be all-powerful and independent of the people, had to yield to the demands of several tens of thousands of St. Petersburg workers. We have seen how insignificant and ambiguous these concessions are. But this is only the first step. The working-class movement has long ago spread beyond St. Petersburg; it is growing and expanding, embracing the masses of industrial workers with growing thoroughness *all over the country*. And when all these masses, led by one party, the socialist party, present their joint demands, the government will no longer be able to get away with such an insignificant concession!

On the other hand, the significance of the new law lies in the fact that it necessarily and inevitably *gives a fresh impetus* to the Russian working-class movement. We have seen how the law tries wherever possible to leave loopholes for the employers, to leave the most important points vague and indefinite. Everywhere there is bound to be conflict between the employers and the workers over the application of this law; and this conflict will embrace a far larger area, for the law applies to the whole of Russia. The workers will be able to wage the struggle consciously and firmly, to insist on their demands, and to evade the snares which our anti-strike police laws have set for them. The introduction of new factory regulations, the change in the ordinary, regular working day in the vast majority of factories all over Russia will be of tremendous benefit: it will stir up the most backward sections of the workers; everywhere it will awaken a most lively interest in questions of factory life and factory regulations; it will provide a splendid, convenient and *lawful* opportunity for the workers to present their *demands*, to uphold *their interpretation of the law*, to uphold the *old customs* when they are more advantageous to the worker (as, for example, the *customary holidays* and the cessation of work on Saturdays not 1½ but 2 and more hours earlier), to press for more favourable terms when concluding *new agreements* on overtime, and to press for *higher pay*, so that the reduction of the working day may really benefit the workers and not be detrimental to them in any way.

APPENDIX

I

The pamphlet on the new factory law (the law of June 2, 1897) had already been written when, in the beginning of October, there were published *regulations governing the application* of this law, as endorsed by the Ministry of Finance in agreement with the Ministry of Internal Affairs on September 20, 1897. We have already spoken about the enormous importance these regulations must have for the law as a whole. This time the Ministry hastened to issue regulations before the new law came into force, because these regulations (as we shall see presently) indicate the cases in which departures from the requirements of the new law are permitted, i.e., when the employers are permitted "to operate" for longer hours than stipulated by law. If the factory owners did not urgently need these regulations, the workers, of course, would have had to wait long before they were issued. The publication of the "regulations" was soon followed by the publication of Instructions to Factory Inspectorate Officials concerning the application of the law of June 2, 1897, ostensibly for the purpose merely of *explaining* to the factory inspectors how the law should be applied; these instructions legally give the officials a perfectly free hand and are directed entirely *against the workers*, for they permit the employers to evade the law in every way. The Imperial Government is very fond of drafting laws in magnificent terms and then of permitting these laws to be evaded by substituting *instructions* for them. A detailed examination of the regulations reveals to us that this is precisely the nature of the new instructions. Let us also point out that these "instructions" are largely *copied word for word* from the article in *Vestnik Finansov* which we referred to on many occasions in the pamphlet on the new law. Thus, in the pamphlet we showed how *Vestnik Finansov* suggested a trick to the employers, namely: the newspaper explained that the new law did not apply in those cases where no mention was made of the length of the working day in the contract between the worker and the employer, since in that case, it suggested, the worker was not "a hired worker, but a person who accepts an order." This pettifogging explanation is repeated word for word in the "instructions." The regulations consist of twenty-two clauses, many of which, however, simply repeat in their entirety the clauses of the law of June 2, 1897. Let us observe that these regulations apply only to employers "who come within the jurisdiction of the Ministry of Finance"; they do not apply to mining and metallurgical plants, or to railway workshops, or to government factories. A strict distinction must be drawn between these regulations and the law itself: the regulations have been issued only *in pursuance* of the law, and the ministers who issued them may supplement and amend them, or issue new ones. The regulations deal with the following five subjects: 1) meal times; 2) Sunday and holiday rest; 3) departures from the new law; 4) shifts and 5) overtime. Let us examine the regulations on each subject in detail and show in each case how the Ministry of Finance, in its instructions, recommends that these regulations be applied.

II

Concerning meal times, the following regulations are laid down: first, that meal times do not count as part of working hours, that the worker is free during meal times; the meal times must be indicated in the factory rules; second, that meal times are obligatory only in those cases when the working day exceeds ten hours, and the meal time must not be less than of one hour's duration. This regulation does not improve the workers' condition in the least. If anything, it does the opposite. An hour's break is very little: most factories allow an hour and a half for dinner, and in some cases also half an hour for lunch. The ministers did

their best to make the break as short as possible! Quite often
the worker scarcely has time to go home to dinner in an hour.

It goes without saying that the workers will not permit
such a short break to be established and will demand a longer
one. Another reservation concerning compulsory meal hours
also threatens to encroach upon the workers' rights: according to the ministers' regulations, a break for meals is
obligatory only when the working day exceeds ten hours!
Hence, where the working day is ten hours, the employer is
entitled not to give the workers a break for meals! Again,
the workers themselves will have to see to it that the employers will not be able and will not dare to take advantage of
this right. The workers can refuse to agree to such regulations (when they are included in the factory rules) and
can demand more frequent breaks for meals. The ministers were not satisfied even with these restrictions. In a
"note" to this regulation it is added that "in cases where considerable obstacles are encountered, departures from this
requirement are *permitted*," i.e., Messrs. the Employers are
permitted to give the workers no breaks for meals at all!
The ministers permit this, but it is hardly likely that the
workers will *permit it*. Moreover, the ministers also *permit* departures when the demand for a break is recognised
as burdensome for the workers. Oh, these solicitous ministers! Our ministers thought about the "burden" which meal-
time breaks would impose upon the workers, but Messrs. the
Ministers do not say a word about the "burden" imposed upon
the workers by having to get their dinner within an hour, or
about the still greater "burden" of working *ten hours* without a break! A third regulation governing meal times requires that the worker be given the opportunity to take food
at intervals of no more than six hours. But the regulations
do not call for a *break* every six hours; what, then, is the
sense of such a regulation? How can a worker take food without a break? Messrs. the Ministers did not trouble about
that. If there is no break (the regulations say), the worker
"must be given an opportunity to take food during working
time, and the factory rules must indicate the place for
taking food." The whole of this regulation is so absurd
that one can only express astonishment! One of two
things: *either* this "place for taking food" will be indi-

cated as *one other than where the worker works*; in that case a *break* will be inevitable. Or the place will be indicated as *the one where the worker works*; in that case, what is the sense of indicating the place? If the worker has no right to interrupt his work—how can he eat *without interrupting* his work? Messrs. the Ministers regard the workers as machines: a machine can be fed with oil while it is working, why then (think our "solicitous" ministerial hangers-on of the capital) cannot the worker stuff himself with food while working? The only hope left to the workers is that such a stupid regulation could only have been invented in Russian bureaucratic offices, and will not actually be put into force. The workers will demand that the *indicated* "place for taking food" *will not be where they work*: the workers will demand a *break for meals* every six hours. This, then, is all the regulations say about meal times. The ministers have pursued the law in such a way that it can only worsen the workers' condition, unless the workers themselves stand up, and stand up together, for their rights and not for the ministerial regulations.

III

Concerning Sundays and holidays, there is only one brief regulation, namely, that on Sundays and holidays the workers must be free from work for no less than twenty-four hours at a stretch. This was *the least* that could be ordered "in pursuance" of the law governing Sundays and holidays. It could not be less. It never occurred to the ministers to give the workers longer rest periods (for example, thirty-six hours, as is the case in some other countries). As regards non-Christians, the regulations say nothing.

IV

On the subject of departures from the law, there are many regulations, very many in fact, and drawn up in great detail. Let us remind the workers that the law gave the ministers power to permit, in the regulations, departures from the law, by *extending* the requirements of the law (i.e., demanding

more for the workers from the employers) and *reducing* the requirements of the law (i.e., demanding *less* for the workers
from the employers). Let us see what the ministers have
done. First regulation. Departures from the law are
permitted in those cases where "the workers are engaged
on *continuous* operations, i.e., such operations as cannot
arbitrarily be interrupted without damage to instruments,
materials, or goods." In such cases, Messrs. the Employers
may "operate" for periods longer than that provided for in
the law. All that the regulation demands in such a case is,
firstly, that the working hours during the course of two
consecutive days should not exceed twenty-four hours
(and in the case of broken shifts—thirty hours). Why it says
twenty-four hours in two days and not twelve hours in one
day we shall see in the paragraph dealing with shifts. Secondly, the regulation demands that where operations are continuous, the worker must be freed from work four days a
month, if his working day exceeds eight hours. Thus, for
workers who are engaged on *continuous* operations, the number of rest-days is *greatly reduced*: four a month, forty-eight
a year, whereas *even* the law (with all its restricted holidays)
allows sixty-six compulsory holidays a year. What reasonable grounds did the ministers have for reducing this number
of holidays? None whatever; in any case, the *continuity of
operations* is broken even with four holidays a month, i.e.,
in any case the employers must hire other workers for the
holidays (if the operation is *indeed* continuous, i.e., if it
cannot be *interrupted*). Thus, Messrs. the Ministers cut the
workers' holidays still more *only in order* to "restrict" the
employers as little as possible, to reduce the number of
cases when *other* workers must be hired! More than that.
The "instructions" go so far as to permit the factory inspectors
to sanction factory rules which provide for *even fewer
rest-days for the workers*! The factory inspector must
merely report such cases to the Department of Commerce
and Industry. This is a very striking example, which
shows why our government is fond of meaningless laws and
detailed regulations and instructions: to alter an inconvenient regulation, it is sufficient to apply to the Department
... of Palm-Greasing!! Similarly, the factory inspector may
(according to the instructions!) permit the term continuous

to be applied to such operations as are not included in the list appended to the instructions: it is sufficient to report to the Department.... A note to this regulation says that the continuous operations must be *specially indicated* in the factory rules. "Departures from this law are only permitted insofar as they are really necessary" (this is what the ministers' regulation says). But who is to see whether they are *really* necessary or not? Nobody but the workers: they must not permit reservations regarding continuous operations to be included in the factory rules unless they are *really* necessary. Second regulation. Departures from the law are permitted in cases where the workers are engaged on auxiliary operations in various kinds of production (current repairs, tending of boilers, motors and transmission belts, heating, lighting, water supply, watch and fire service, and so forth). These departures must also be *especially indicated* in the factory rules. As regards rest-days for these workers, *the regulations do not say a word.* Again, the workers themselves must see to it that they get rest-days, i.e., must not agree to factory rules which do not provide rest-days for such workers. Third regulation. Departures from the regulations governing the length of the working day and rest on Sundays and holidays and from the factory rules are permitted in two other cases: first, in case of sudden damage to machines, tools, etc., which causes a stoppage of work in the whole factory, or in one of its departments. In such cases, the necessary *repairs* may be made regardless of the regulations. Secondly, permission is given, regardless of the regulations, to perform "temporary work in any department of the establishment in those cases when, as a consequence of fire, break-down and similar unforeseen circumstances, the work in one or another department of the establishment is reduced or entirely stopped for a time, and when that is essential for the full running of the other departments of the establishment." (In such cases, the employer must that very day report the matter to the factory inspector, who *sanctions* such work.) This last regulation shows what tremendous "solicitude" our ministers display to ensure that the employers do not expend an extra ruble. Suppose there was a fire in one department of a factory. Work is stopped. After the repairs are made the employer wants to make up for lost time. *Therefore*, the minister permits him to squeeze as much extra labour out of the workers as he likes by compelling them to work even as long as eighteen hours a day. But what have the workers got to do with it? When the employer makes more profit, does he share it with the workers, does he shorten the working day? Why, then, should the working day *be lengthened* for the workers when the employer suffers loss? Why, that means—I take the profit, but I make the workers bear the losses. If it is necessary to make up for lost time, why not hire additional workers? The "solicitude" displayed by the Russian ministers for the pockets of the employers is amazing! Fourth regulation. Departures from the new law may also be made "in other especially important and exceptional cases." (What are these cases? So many especially important and exceptional cases have been enumerated that one might think no more would be left!) Such departures are permitted in each separate case by the Minister of Finance and the Minister of Internal Affairs. Thus the employer will make a request, the ministers will grant permission, and all's well. The workers are not even asked: can the "gentry" be expected to ask the opinion of the common people? The vulgar mob must work for the capitalists and not argue about whether it is an "exceptional" case or just the ordinary lust for gain that compels the employer to go begging. Such are the ministers' regulations about departures from the new law. As we see, all these regulations indicate how and when the law may not be obeyed, how and when the law's demands on the employers for the workers' benefit may be reduced. The ministers say *not a single word* about increasing the legal demands upon the employers for the workers' benefit. Let the workers recall what was said in the pamphlet on the new factory law about the purpose for which the law gives the ministers such great powers!

V

As regards shifts, there is only one short regulation which, in cases where 18 hours' work is done in two shifts, permits an *increase* in the number of hours to 12 a day with the proviso that the working time for two weeks shall not exceed 9 hours per day for each worker. Thus, this regulation also permits *lengthening* of the working day. How many regulations have there been *to lengthen* the working day, but not one to shorten it—and there will be none! According to this regulation, the workers may be compelled to work 12 hours a day for a whole week, and the "instructions" again add that the factory inspectors may permit other departures from the law, provided they report these to the Director.... The question of shifts is also covered by the above-mentioned regulation which fixes the working time on continuous operations at *24 hours in two days*. The instructions explain why it says 24 hours in two days and not 12 hours in one day. This is said in order to leave in force the scandalous system that prevails in some factories of working a continuous *double shift with an interval of eight hours*: under this system, a worker works 16 hours one day and 8 hours the next, without ever having proper rest or proper sleep. It is difficult to imagine anything more scandalous than such shifts; but far from doing anything to restrict this scandalous system, the ministers even had the insolence to say in the "instructions" that under many circumstances such shifts are more convenient for the workers!! How solicitous the ministers are for the *convenience of the workers*!

VI

As regards overtime, the regulations at first sight appear to give the most precise directions. The limitation of overtime is the chief thing required not only in the ministerial regulations, but also in the new law as a whole. We have already spoken above about the utter vagueness of the law itself on this point, about the original intention of the Ministry of Finance not to issue any additional overtime regulations. It now turns out that the ministers have after all limited overtime, have limited it in precisely the way proposed by the commission which drafted the new law, i.e., to 120 hours a year. But, on the other hand, in his "instructions," the Minister of Finance reproduced from *Vestnik Finansov*, for the edification of the factory inspectors, all the traps and tricks *against the workers* which we quoted in the pamphlet on the new law: the "instructions," we repeat, are copied from *Vestnik Finansov*.

The first regulation concerns the point in the new law which permits the employer to include in the contract with the worker the stipulation to work such overtime as is necessitated by the technical conditions of the industry. We have already mentioned the vagueness of this. And yet, this clause of the law is of enormous importance: if the stipulation to work overtime is included in the factory rules, then overtime becomes *obligatory* for the worker, and *the entire law remains entirely unenforced in this respect*. The ministerial regulations now interpret this term in the following way: only such work may be regarded as "necessitated by the technical conditions of the industry" as is called forth "exclusively by departures from its normal course which are accidental and dependent upon the nature of the industry." Thus, for example, departures called forth by an increased influx of orders are not affected (as they are not dependent upon the nature of the industry). Departures called forth by a fire, break-down and so forth, are also not affected, because they, too, do not depend upon the nature of the industry itself. *Common sense* would suggest that this is how the regulation should be interpreted. But here the "instructions" come to the employers' aid. The "instructions" so brilliantly increase the number of cases when overtime may be made compulsory for the workers, including it in the terms of hire, i.e., in the factory rules, that *absolutely anything you like* can be classed among these cases. Indeed, let the workers recall how the law *was pursued* in the *Vestnik Finansov* article and compare the "instructions" with the latter. First, the "instructions" speak of work "necessitated by the technical conditions of the industry"—and then, imperceptibly, it substitutes another term: "work that is absolutely essential" (Is that so? But who is to judge what is essential?)—and further on the instructions give petty examples of what is "absolutely essential": it turns out that this includes those cases when the employer finds it "impossible, or difficult" (our old acquaintance!) "to increase the number of workers," when there is rush and urgent work (in seasonal work, for example);

when a print-shop has to issue a newspaper daily; when the job could not be foreseen in advance, and so forth. In short, if you want anything, ask for it. The shameless hangers-on of the capitalists in the Ministry of Finance *have pursued* the law in such a way that the employer *has the right* to include in his factory rules the demand *for any amount of overtime. And once such a demand is included in the factory rules, the whole new law goes to blazes and everything remains as before.* The workers must not permit these demands to be included in the factory rules, otherwise their conditions, far from being improved, will be worsened. This example shows the workers how the employers and government officials conspire to enslave the workers again on a legal basis. The "instructions" clearly reveal this conspiracy, this subservience of the Ministry of Finance to the interests of the capitalists.

The second overtime regulation lays down that the overtime by each worker shall not exceed 120 hours per year, but this figure *does not include*, firstly, the overtime stipulated in the contract as obligatory for the worker due to "the technical conditions of the industry," and we have just seen that the ministers have permitted this term to be applied to *any number* of cases which have nothing to do with the "technical conditions of the industry"; secondly, it does not include the overtime worked in case of fire, breakdown, and so forth, or to make up for time lost in case of a stoppage in some department.

Taken together, all these overtime regulations remind us astonishingly of the fable about how the lion shared the prey "equally" among his fellow hunters; the first portion he took by right; the second portion he took for being the king of beasts; the third for being strongest of all; and as for the fourth—whoever dared as much as stretch his paw towards it would not get away alive.[100] This is exactly how our employers will now argue about overtime. First, they will squeeze overtime out of the workers "by right," on the plea that it is "necessitated by the technical conditions of the industry," i.e., any amount of overtime, as long as it is provided for in the factory rules. Second, they will squeeze overtime out of the workers in "special cases," i.e., when they want to throw the burden of their losses

on the workers. Third, they will squeeze another 120
hours per year out of them on the grounds that they are
rich and the workers are poor. Fourth, in "exceptional cases"
they will receive special privileges from the ministers. And
then the workers may "freely" enjoy what remains out of
the 24 hours of the day after all this—bearing well in mind
that the fair government does not by any means "deprive
them of their right" to work even 24 hours a day.... *To
legalise* this squeezing of overtime out of the workers it is
ordered that the employers shall keep special *registers* of all
these forms of overtime. In one register they will record what
they squeeze out of the workers "by right"; in another register, what they squeeze out in "special cases"; in a third, what
they squeeze out by "special agreement" (not more than 120
hours per year); in a fourth, what they squeeze out of them
in "exceptional cases." Instead of an improvement in the
workers' condition, we get nothing but red tape and bureaucratic correspondence (as is always the case with all the reforms introduced by the autocratic Russian Government).
The factory policemen will visit the factories and "inspect"...
these registers (which the devil himself will not be able
to make head or tail of), and during the time that they are
free from this useful occupation they will report to the
Director of the Department of Commerce and Manufacture
suggesting new sops for the employers, and to the Department
of Police about workers' strikes. How shrewd are these
people, these hucksters and bashi-bazouks who constitute
our government! For a reasonable price they will now hire
a foreign representative who will shout at all the crossroads
of "Europe" about the laws for the workers' benefit that we
have in this country.

VII

In conclusion let us make a general survey of the ministerial regulations. Let us recall what regulations the new law
provides the ministers with. Three categories of regulations:
1) regulations to interpret the law; 2) regulations to increase
or reduce the demands made by the new law on employers;
3) regulations concerning trades especially harmful to the

workers' health. What use have the ministers made of the powers granted them by this law?

As to the first category, they have confined themselves to the most essential, to the very minimum below which they could not go. They have permitted overtime on a very wide and elastic scale—120 hours per year and, moreover, by means of the instructions have introduced such a host of exceptions that they rob the regulations of all meaning. They have done their best to cut down the workers' meal times, they have left the scandalous shift system as it was, if they have not actually made it worse.

As to the second category of regulations, the ministers *have done all they could* to reduce the demands of the new law on the employers, i.e., *they have done all they could for the employers* and *absolutely nothing for the workers*: in no single case do the regulations increase the demands of the new law upon the employers for the workers' benefit.

As to the third category of regulations (i.e., those for the benefit of the workers who are compelled to work at the most harmful occupations), the ministers have done absolutely nothing, they have said not a single word about them. All that the instructions say is that the factory inspectors may report to the Department about especially injurious trades! As far as "reporting" goes the factory inspectors could formerly also report anything they liked, only till now, for some inexplicable reason, these factory policemen "reported" about workers' strikes and about methods of terrorising the workers, and not about protecting the workers in the especially injurious trades.

From this the workers can see for themselves what they may expect from the officials of the police government. To secure an eight-hour day and the complete banning of overtime the Russian workers still have a long and stubborn struggle to wage.

ABOUT A CERTAIN NEWSPAPER ARTICLE

Issue No. 239 of *Russkiye Vedomosti* [101] (dated August 30) contains a short article by Mr. N. Levitsky entitled "Certain Problems Affecting the Life of the People." "Living in the country and being in constant contact with the people" the author "long ago came up against" certain problems affecting the life of the people, the solution of which by means of appropriate "measures" is an "urgent necessity," a "pressing need." The author expresses the conviction that his "brief remarks" on a subject of such importance "will meet with a response among those who are interested in the people's needs," and he expresses the desire to provoke an exchange of opinion on the problems he advances.

The "lofty style" in which Mr. N. Levitsky's article is written and the high-sounding words in which it abounds lead one to expect that it deals with some really important, urgent, vital problems of modern life. Actually, however, the author's proposals merely provide one more example, and an exceedingly striking one at that, of the truly Manilovian[102] fantasy to which the Narodnik journalists have accustomed the Russian public. That is why we thought it would be useful to voice our views on the problems that Mr. N. Levitsky raises.

Mr. N. Levitsky enumerates five "problems" (point by point) and he not only provides an "answer" for every "problem," but also indicates very definitely the appropriate "measure" to be taken. The first problem is—"cheap and accessible" credit, the elimination of the tyranny of money-lenders, "kulaks, and all sorts of sharks and parasites." The measure to be taken is—"to devise a simpler type of village peasants' loan and savings bank," and the author proposes that the branches of the State Bank should issue savings-bank books not to individuals, but to specially organised associations, which will make deposits and receive loans through a single treasurer.

And so the author's long "contact with the people" enabled him to draw this conclusion on the hackneyed problem of credit—"devise" a new type of loan and savings bank! Evidently the author imagines that not enough paper and ink is being wasted in this country on drafting endless "types," "models," "rules," "model rules," "normal rules," etc., etc. "Living in the country," our practical man failed to see any of the more important problems raised by the desire to replace the "kulak" by "cheap and accessible credit." We shall not, of course, discuss here the importance of credit: we take the author's aim *for granted*; we shall merely examine from the purely practical aspect the remedies he proposes with such pomp. Credit is an institution of developed commodity circulation. The question is—is it possible to establish such an institution among our peasantry, whom the countless survivals of laws and prohibitions that spring from the division of society into social estates have placed in conditions that *rule out* regular, free, extensive and developed commodity circulation? Is it not ridiculous, when speaking of the urgent and pressing needs of the people, to reduce the problem of credit to devising "rules" of a new type and to say nothing whatever about the need *to abolish* the entire mass of "rules" which hinder regular commodity circulation among the peasantry, hinder the free purchase and sale of property—real estate and personal property—hinder the peasants from moving freely from place to place and from one occupation to another, and hinder individuals from other classes and social estates from joining the peasant communities? What can be more comical than fighting "kulaks, usurers, parasites and sharks" by perfecting the "rules" of credit banks? Usury in its worst forms is most tenacious in our rural districts, and is so precisely because of the exclusiveness of the estate system there, because of the thousand fetters which shackle the development of commodity circulation— and yet our practical-minded author says not a word about these fetters, but declares that the drafting of *new* rules is the urgent problem of rural credit. In all probability the developed capitalist countries, where the rural districts have long been placed in conditions that facilitate the circulation of commodities, and where credit has been extensively developed, in all probability these countries achieved this success thanks to the multitude of "rules" drafted by benevolent officials!

The second problem is—"the helpless position of a peasant family when the head of the family dies," and also "the urgent necessity" of "safeguarding and preserving the peasant working agricultural population by all possible means and methods." As you see, the further he goes the wider and more majestic become Mr. Levitsky's "problems"! The first problem concerned a very ordinary bourgeois institution, the value of which we could only admit with very considerable reservation; but here we have a problem of such gigantic importance that "in principle" we fully admit its urgency and cannot suppress a warm feeling for the author for *raising* it. But the Narodnik's gigantic problem is matched by a "measure" of gigantic ... what is the mildest way we can put it? ... unwisdom. Listen: "... there arises the urgent need to organise and introduce compulsory (sic!) *mutual life insurance for the entire peasant population on a mass scale at the cheapest possible rates** (societies, associations, artels, etc.). And it is necessary to ascertain the role and part to be played in this business by a) private insurance companies, b) the Zemstvos, and c) the state."

Our muzhiks are so dull-witted! They give no thought to the fact that if the head of the family dies the rest will have to go begging; that if the crop fails they will starve, and that even if they have a good crop sometimes, they will have to go begging just the same on returning from abortive quests for "earnings." These stupid muzhiks have no idea that there is such a thing as "life insurance," to which many good gentlemen have long had recourse and out of which other good gentlemen (shareholders in insurance companies) make money. Starving "Sysoika"[103] has no idea that all he has to do is to join with "Mityai," who is starving like himself, in organising a mutual life insurance company (with low, very

---

* Author's italics.

low contributions!), and their families will be provided for in the event of their death. Luckily, the thinking for these dull-witted muzhiks is done by our enlightened Narodnik intelligentsia, one of whose representatives "living in the country and being in constant contact with the people," "long ago came up against" this tremendous, this astounding and stupendous "project"!

Third problem. "In connection with this problem it is necessary to raise and discuss the problem of establishing *an imperial capital fund for insuring the lives of the peasant population** on the same lines as the existing imperial food and fire funds." It goes without saying that to deal with insurance, we must discuss the question of capital. But it seems to us that our highly esteemed author is guilty here of an important omission. Is it not also "necessary to raise and discuss" the question as to which ministry and which department will be in charge of the proposed institution? Firstly, there can be no doubt that the Economic Department of the Ministry of Internal Affairs should be in charge of it. Secondly, the Zemstvo Department of the Ministry of Internal Affairs is also closely interested. Thirdly, the Ministry of Finance should also be in charge of insurance affairs. In view of this, would it not be more advisable to propose the establishment of a special Chief Administration of State Compulsory Mutual Life Insurance for the Entire Peasant Population, on the lines, say, of the *Chief State Horse-Breeding Administration*?

Fourth problem. "Further, in view of the tremendously widespread character of all sorts of artels throughout Russia, and also in view of their undoubted usefulness and importance to the national economy, the urgent need has arisen 4) of organising a separate, special *Society for the Promotion of Agricultural and Other Artels*." That artels of all sorts are beneficial to the classes of the population who organise them is undoubted. It is also undoubted that to unite the representatives of the various classes will also be of great benefit to the entire national economy. Only the author waxes far too enthusiastic when he talks about "the tremendously widespread character of all sorts of artels throughout

---

* Author's italics.

Russia." Everybody knows that, compared with any West-European country, the number of "all sorts of artels" is *incredibly, phenomenally small* in Russia.... "Everybody knows this" ... except the dreamy Manilov. The editors of *Russkiye Vedomosti*, for example, know it since they published *above* Mr. N. Levitsky's article a very interesting and highly informative item, entitled "Syndicates in France." From this article Mr. N. Levitsky might have learned how immensely "*all sorts* of artels" are developed in capitalist France (compared with non-capitalist Russia). I underline "all sorts," for it can easily be seen from this article that there are four sorts of syndicates in France: 1) workers' syndicates (2, 163 syndicates with 419,172 members); 2) employers' syndicates (1,622 with 130,752 members); 3) agricultural syndicates (1,188 with 398,048 members) and 4) mixed syndicates (173 with 31,126 members). Add up all these figures, Mr. Levitsky! You will get a total of nearly a million people (979,000) organised in "all sorts of artels." And now tell us, with your hand on your heart, are you really not ashamed of the phrase you let slip about the "tremendously widespread character of all sorts (sic!!!) of artels throughout Russia"? Do you really fail to see what a comical, sadly comical impression your article creates by the side of the bare figures of the "syndicates in France"? These poor Frenchmen, whom, evidently, the canker of capitalism has deprived of the "tremendously widespread character of all sorts of artels," would probably burst into Homeric laughter at the proposal to establish a "separate special society" ... for promoting the establishment of all sorts of societies! It goes without saying, however, that this laughter would only be a demonstration of the notorious frivolity of the French, who are incapable of understanding Russian thoroughness. These frivolous Frenchmen form "all sorts of artels," not only without first setting up "societies for the promotion of artels" but even—horribile dictu!—without first drawing up "model," "normal" rules and "simplified types" of societies of various kinds!

Fifth problem ... (the urgent need has arisen) "to publish, under the auspices of this society (or separately), *a special organ ... devoted exclusively to the study of the co-operative movement in Russia and abroad.*"... Yes, yes, Mr. Levitsky!

When a disordered stomach prevents a person from having a proper meal, he has no alternative but to read about how other people eat. But in all probability, the doctors would not allow a person who is so sick to read about the dinners other people eat, for such reading might stimulate an inordinate appetite not commensurate with the diet prescribed.... And the doctors would be quite consistent in doing so.

We have expounded Mr. Levitsky's short article in sufficient detail. The reader will probably ask whether it was worth dealing at such length with a casual newspaper article, whether it was worth devoting such a lengthy comment to it. Indeed, what importance is there in the fact that somebody (who, generally speaking, is prompted by the best intentions) happened to talk nonsense about some sort of compulsory mutual life insurance for the entire peasant population? We have heard very similar opinions expressed on analogous subjects. These opinions are, to say the least, groundless. Maybe it is an accident that our "progressive journalists" every now and again positively vomit up such phenomenally wild "projects" on the lines of "feudal socialism" that one can only shrug one's shoulders in amazement? Maybe it is an accident that organs like *Russkoye Bogatstvo* and *Russkiye Vedomosti*, which are by no means ultra-Narodnik, which always protest against the extremes of Narodism and against the conclusions drawn from Narodism à la Mr. V. V., and which are even not averse to covering up the rags and tatters of their Narodism with the bright new label of some "ethico-sociological school," that even such organs periodically, with punctilious regularity, present the Russian public now with some "educational utopia" proposed by Mr. S. Yuzhakov[104]—a scheme for compulsory secondary education in agricultural gymnasia in which indigent peasants are to pay the tuition fees by work—and now with this project of Mr. N. Levitsky's for compulsory mutual life insurance for the entire peasant population?*

It would be too naïve to put this down to accident. There is a Manilov in every Narodnik. Disdain for conditions as they really are and for economic evolution as it really is,

---

* Comparing these two fantasy-weavers of Narodnik journalism one cannot help giving preference to Mr. N. Levitsky, whose project is *a trifle cleverer* than that of Mr. S. Yuzhakov.

unwillingness to analyse the real interests of the different classes of Russian society in their inter-relationships, the habit of laying down the law *from above* about the "needs" and "destiny" of the fatherland, of boasting about the miserable survivals of medieval associations that exist in the Russian village communities and artels, together with a disdainful attitude towards the incomparably more highly developed associations characteristic of more highly developed capitalism—all these features are to be found in a greater or lesser degree in *every* Narodnik. That is why it is so edifying to watch some not over-clever, but very naïve, writer, with a fearlessness worthy of a better cause, carrying these features to their full logical development and embodying them in the dazzling picture of some "project." These projects always turn out to be dazzling, so dazzling that merely *to show* them to the reader is *to prove* how harmful contemporary petty-bourgeois Narodism is to our social thought and social development. Such projects always contain much that is comical; in most cases a superficial reading of them creates no other impression than a desire to laugh. But try to get at their real meaning and you will say: "It would all be funny were it not so sad!"[105]

Written in exile in September 1897
   Published in the magazine
   Novoye Slovo, No. 1, 1897
     Signed: K. T—n

Published according
to the text in
Novoye Slovo

THE TASKS OF THE RUSSIAN SOCIAL-DEMOCRATS[106]

Written in exile
at the end of 1897

First published in pamphlet
form in Geneva, 1898

Published according to the
text of the 1902 edition
checked with a copy of the
manuscript, the 1898 and 1905
editions, and the text in the
miscellany *Twelve Years*
by Vl. Ilyin, 1907

ПРОЛЕТАРІИ ВСѢХЪ СТРАНЪ, СОЕДИНЯЙТЕСЬ!

РОССІЙСКАЯ СОЦІАЛЬДЕМОКРАТИЧЕСКАЯ РАБОЧАЯ ПАРТІЯ.

Н. ЛЕНИНЪ.

ЗАДАЧИ РУССКИХЪ СОЦІАЛЬДЕМОКРАТОВЪ

Изданіе 2-е.

СЪ ПРЕДИСЛОВІЯМИ

АВТОРА

И

П. Б. АКСЕЛЬРОДА.

Изданіе Загран. Лиги Русск. Революціонной Соціальдемократіи.

ЖЕНЕВА
Типографія Лиги, Route Caroline, 27.
1902 г.

Cover of the second edition of Lenin's
Tasks of the Russian Social-Democrats. 1902

The second half of the nineties witnessed a remarkable increase in the work being done on the presentation and solution of the problems of the Russian revolution. The appearance of a new revolutionary party, Narodnoye Pravo,[107] the growing influence and successes of the Social-Democrats, the evolution within Narodnaya Volya[108]—all this has evoked a lively discussion on questions of programme both in study circles of socialist intellectuals and workers and in illegal literature. Regarding the latter sphere, reference should be made to "An Urgent Question" and the "Manifesto" (1894) of the Narodnoye Pravo Party, to the *Leaflet of the Narodnaya Volya Group*, to *Rabotnik* published abroad by the League of Russian Social-Democrats,[109] to the increasing output of revolutionary pamphlets in Russia, mainly for workers, and the agitation conducted by the Social-Democratic League of Struggle for the Emancipation of the Working Class in St. Petersburg around the important strikes there in 1896, etc.

At the present time (the end of 1897), the most urgent question, in our opinion, is that of the *practical* activities of the Social-Democrats. We emphasise the *practical* side of Social-Democracy, because on the theoretical side the most critical period—the period of stubborn refusal by its opponents to understand it, of strenuous efforts to suppress the new trend the moment it arose, on the one hand, and of stalwart defence of the fundamentals of Social-Democracy, on the other—is now apparently behind us. Now the *main and basic features* of the theoretical views of the Social-Democrats have been sufficiently clarified. The same cannot be said about the *practical* side of Social-Democracy, about its political *programme*, its methods, its tactics. It is in this sphere, we think, that misapprehension and mutual misunderstanding mostly prevail, preventing a complete rapprochement between Social-Democracy and those revolutionaries who in theory have completely renounced the principles of the Narodnaya Volya and in practice are either led by the very force of circumstances to carry on propaganda and agitation among the workers—nay, more: to conduct their activities among the workers on the basis of the *class struggle*—or else strive to base their whole programme and revolutionary activities on *democratic* tasks. If we are not mistaken, the latter description fits the two revolutionary groups which are operating in Russia at the present time, parallel to the Social-Democrats, namely, the Narodnaya Volya and Narodnoye Pravo.

We, therefore, think it particularly opportune to try to explain the *practical* tasks of the Social-Democrats and to state the grounds on which we consider their programme to be the most rational of the three now existing and the arguments advanced against it to be based very largely on misunderstanding.

The object of the practical activities of the Social-Democrats is, as is well known, to lead the class struggle of the proletariat and to organise that struggle in both its manifestations: socialist (the fight against the capitalist class aimed at destroying the class system and organising socialist society), and democratic (the fight against absolutism aimed at winning political liberty in Russia and democratising the political and social system of Russia). We said *as is well known.* And indeed, from the very moment they appeared as a separate social-revolutionary trend, the Russian Social-Democrats have always quite definitely indicated this object of their activities, have always emphasised the dual manifestation and content of the class struggle of the proletariat and have always insisted on the inseparable connection between their socialist and democratic tasks—a connection clearly expressed in the name they have adopted. Nevertheless, to this day you often meet socialists who have the most distorted notions about the Social-Democrats and accuse them of ignoring the political struggle, etc. Let us, therefore, dwell a little on a description of both aspects of the practical activities of Russian Social-Democracy.

Let us begin with socialist activity. One would have thought that the character of Social-Democratic activity in this respect had become quite clear since the Social-Democratic League of Struggle for the Emancipation of the Working Class in St. Petersburg began its activities among the St. Petersburg workers. The socialist activities of Russian Social-Democrats consist in spreading *by propaganda* the teachings of scientific socialism, in spreading among the workers a proper understanding of the present social and economic system, its basis and its development, an understanding of the various *classes* in Russian society, of their interrelations, of the struggle between these classes, of the role of the working class in this struggle, of its attitude towards the declining and the developing classes, towards the past and the future of capitalism, an understanding of the historical task of international Social-Democracy and of the Russian working class. Inseparably connected with propaganda is *agitation* among the workers, which naturally comes to the forefront in the present political conditions of Russia and at the present level of development of the masses of workers. Agitation among the workers means that the Social-Democrats take part in all the spontaneous manifestations of the working-class struggle, in all the conflicts between the workers and the capitalists over the working day, wages, working conditions, etc., etc. Our task is to merge our activities with the practical, everyday questions of working-class life, to help the workers understand these questions, to draw the workers' attention to the most important abuses, to help them formulate their demands to the employers more precisely and practically, to develop among the workers consciousness of their solidarity, consciousness of the common interests and common cause of all the Russian workers as a united working class that is part of the international army of the proletariat. To organise study circles among workers, to establish proper and secret connections between them and the central group of Social-Democrats, to publish and distribute working-class literature, to organise the receipt of correspondence from all centres of the working-class movement, to publish agitational leaflets and manifestos and to distribute them, and to train a body of experienced agitators—such, in broad outline, are the manifestations of the socialist activities of Russian Social-Democracy.

Our work is primarily and mainly directed to the factory, urban workers. Russian Social-Democracy must not dissipate its forces; it must concentrate its activities on the industrial proletariat, who are most susceptible to Social-Democratic ideas, most developed intellectually and politically, and most important by virtue of their numbers and concentration in the country's large political centres. The creation of a durable revolutionary organisation among the factory, urban workers is therefore the first and most urgent task confronting Social-Democracy, one from which it would be highly unwise to let ourselves be diverted at the present time. But, while recognising the necessity of concentrating our forces on the factory workers and opposing the dissipation of our forces, we do not in the least wish to suggest that the Russian Social-Democrats should ignore other strata of the Russian proletariat and working class. Nothing of the kind. The very conditions of life of the Russian factory workers very often compel them to enter into the closest relations with the handicraftsmen, the industrial proletariat scattered outside the factory in towns and villages, and whose conditions are infinitely worse. The Russian factory worker also comes into direct contact with the rural population (very often the factory worker's family live in the country) and, consequently, he cannot but come into close contact with the rural proletariat, with the many millions of regular farm workers and day labourers, and also with those ruined peasants who, while clinging to their miserable plots of land, have to work off their debts and take on all sorts of "casual jobs," i.e., are also wage-labourers. The Russian Social-Democrats think it inopportune *to send* their forces among the handicraftsmen and rural labourers, but they do not in the least intend to ignore them; they will try to enlighten the advanced workers also on questions affecting the lives of the handicraftsmen and rural labourers, so that when these workers come into contact with the more backward strata of the proletariat, they will imbue them with the

ideas of the class struggle, socialism and the political tasks
of Russian democracy in general and of the Russian proletariat in particular. It is impractical to send agitators among
the handicraftsmen and rural labourers when there is still
so much work to be done among the factory, urban workers,
but in numerous cases the socialist worker comes willy-
nilly into contact with these people and must be able to take
advantage of these opportunities and understand the general
tasks of Social-Democracy in Russia. Hence, those who accuse the Russian Social-Democrats of being narrow-minded,
of trying to ignore the mass of the labouring population for
the sake of the factory workers, are profoundly mistaken.
On the contrary, agitation among the advanced sections of
the proletariat is the surest and the only way to rouse (as
the movement expands) the entire Russian proletariat. The
dissemination of socialism and of the idea of the class struggle among the urban workers will inevitably cause these ideas
to flow in the smaller and more scattered channels. This
requires that these ideas take deeper root among the better
prepared elements and spread throughout the vanguard of
the Russian working-class movement and of the Russian
revolution. While concentrating all its forces on activity
among the factory workers, Russian Social-Democracy is
ready to support those Russian revolutionaries who, in practice, come to base their socialist activities on the class struggle of the proletariat; but it does not in the least conceal
the point that no practical alliances with other groups of
revolutionaries can, or should, lead to compromises or concessions on matters of theory, programme or banner. Convinced that the doctrine of scientific socialism and the class
struggle is the only revolutionary theory that can today
serve as the banner of the revolutionary movement, the
Russian Social-Democrats will exert every effort to spread
this doctrine, to guard it against false interpretation
and to combat every attempt to impose vaguer doctrines
on the still young working-class movement in Russia.
Theoretical reasoning proves and the practical activities
of the Social-Democrats show that all *socialists* in Russia
should become *Social-Democrats.*

Let us now deal with the *democratic* tasks and with the
democratic work of the Social-Democrats. Let us repeat,

once again, that this work is *inseparably* connected with socialist activity. In conducting *propaganda* among the workers, the Social-Democrats *cannot* avoid political problems, and they would regard any attempt to avoid them, or even to push them aside, as a profound mistake and a departure from the basic principles of international Social-Democracy. Simultaneously with the dissemination of scientific socialism, Russian Social-Democrats set themselves the task of propagating *democratic ideas* among the working-class masses; they strive to spread an understanding of absolutism in all its manifestations, of its class content, of the necessity to overthrow it, of the impossibility of waging a successful struggle for the workers' cause without achieving political liberty and the democratisation of Russia's political and social system. In conducting *agitation* among the workers on their immediate *economic* demands, the Social-Democrats inseparably link this with agitation on the immediate political needs, the distress and the demands of the working class, agitation against police tyranny, manifested in every strike, in every conflict between workers and capitalists, agitation against the restriction of the rights of the workers as Russian citizens in general and as the class suffering the worst oppression and having the least rights in particular, agitation against every prominent representative and flunkey of absolutism who comes into direct contact with the workers and who clearly reveals to the working class its condition of political slavery. Just as there is no issue affecting the life of the workers in the economic field that must be left unused for the purpose of economic agitation, so there is no issue in the political field that does not serve as a subject for political agitation. These two kinds of agitation are inseparably connected in the activities of the Social-Democrats as the two sides of the same medal. Both economic and political agitation are equally necessary to develop the class-consciousness of the proletariat; both economic and political agitation are equally necessary for guiding the class struggle of the Russian workers, because every class struggle is a political struggle. By arousing the class-consciousness of the workers, by organising, disciplining and training them for united action and for the fight for the ideals of Social-Democracy, both kinds of agitation will enable the workers to test their strength on immediate issues and immediate needs, to wring partial concessions from their enemy and thus improve their economic conditions, compel the capitalists to reckon with the strength of the organised workers, compel the government to extend the workers' rights, to pay heed to their demands and keep the government in constant fear of the hostility of the masses of workers led by a strong Social-Democratic organisation.

We have pointed to the inseparably close connection between *socialist* and *democratic* propaganda *and* agitation, to the complete parallelism of revolutionary activity in both spheres. Nevertheless, there is a big difference between these two types of activity and struggle. The difference is that in the economic struggle the proletariat stands absolutely alone against both the landed nobility and the bourgeoisie, except, perhaps, for the help it receives (and by no means always) from those elements of the petty bourgeoisie which gravitate towards the proletariat. In the democratic, *political* struggle, however, the Russian working class does not stand alone; at its side are all the political opposition elements, strata and classes, since they are hostile to absolutism and are fighting it in one form or another. Here *side by side* with the proletariat stand the opposition elements of the bourgeoisie, or of the educated classes, or of the petty bourgeoisie, or of the nationalities, religions and sects, etc., etc., persecuted by the autocratic government. The question naturally arises of what the attitude of the working class towards these elements should be. Further, should it not combine with them in the common struggle against the autocracy? After all, all Social-Democrats admit that the political revolution in Russia must precede the socialist revolution; should they not, therefore, combine with all the elements in the political opposition to fight the autocracy, setting socialism aside for the time being? Is not this essential in order to strengthen the fight against the autocracy?

Let us examine these two questions.

The attitude of the working class, as a fighter against the autocracy, towards all the other social classes and groups in the political opposition is very precisely determined by the basic principles of Social-Democracy expounded in the famous *Communist Manifesto*. The Social-Democrats support the progressive social classes against the reactionary classes, the bourgeoisie against the representatives of privileged landowning estate and the bureaucracy, the big bourgeoisie against the reactionary strivings of the petty bourgeoisie. This support does not presuppose, nor does it call for, any compromise with non-Social-Democratic programmes and principles—it is support given to an ally against a *particular* enemy. Moreover, the Social-Democrats render this support in order to expedite the fall of the common enemy, but expect nothing *for themselves* from these temporary allies, and concede nothing to them. The Social-Democrats support every revolutionary movement against the present social system, they support all oppressed nationalities, persecuted religions, downtrodden social estates, etc., in their fight for equal rights.

Support for all elements of the political opposition will be expressed in the propaganda of the Social-Democrats by the fact that, in showing that the autocracy is hostile to the workers' cause, they will also point to its hostility towards various other social groups; they will point to the solidarity of the working class with these groups on *a particular issue, in a particular task*, etc. In agitation, this support will be expressed by the Social-Democrats' taking advantage of every manifestation of the police tyranny of the autocracy to point out to the workers how this tyranny affects all Russian citizens *in general*, and the representatives of the exceptionally oppressed social estates, nationalities, religions, sects, etc., in particular; and how that tyranny affects *the working class* especially. Finally, in practice, this support is expressed in the readiness of the Russian Social-Democrats to enter into alliances with revolutionaries of other trends for the purpose of achieving certain particular aims, and this readiness has been shown in practice on more than one occasion.

This brings us to the second question. While pointing to the solidarity of one or other of the various opposition groups with the workers, the Social-Democrats will always single out the workers from the rest, they will always point out that this solidarity is temporary and conditional, they will always emphasise the independent class identity of the proletariat, who tomorrow may find themselves in opposition to their allies of today. We shall be told that "such action will *weaken* all the fighters for political liberty at the present time." We shall reply that such action will *strengthen* all the fighters for political liberty. Only those fighters are strong who rely on the *consciously recognised* real interests of certain *classes*, and any attempt to obscure these class interests, which already play a predominant role in contemporary society, will only weaken the fighters. That is the first point. The second point is that, in the fight against the autocracy, the working class must single itself out, for it is the *only* thoroughly consistent and unreserved enemy of the autocracy, *only* between the working class and the autocracy is no compromise possible, *only* in the working class can democracy find a champion who makes no reservations, is not irresolute and does not look back. The hostility of all other classes, groups and strata of the population towards the autocracy is *not unqualified*; their democracy always looks back. The bourgeoisie cannot but realise that industrial and social development is being retarded by the autocracy, but it fears the complete democratisation of the political and social system and can at any moment enter into alliance with the autocracy against the proletariat. The petty bourgeoisie is two-faced by its very nature, and while it gravitates, on the one hand, towards the proletariat and democracy, on the other, it gravitates towards the reactionary classes, tries to hold up the march of history, is apt to be seduced by the experiments and blandishments of the autocracy (for example, the "people's policy"[110] of Alexander III), is capable of concluding an alliance with the ruling classes against the proletariat *for the sake of* strengthening its own *small-proprietor* position. Educated people, and the "intelligentsia" generally, cannot but revolt against the savage police tyranny of the autocracy, which hunts down thought and knowledge; but the material interests of this intelligentsia bind it to the autocracy and to the bourgeoisie, compel it to be inconsistent, to compromise, to sell its oppositional and revolutionary ardour for an official salary, or a share of profits or dividends. As for the democratic elements among the oppressed nationalities and the persecuted religions, everybody knows and sees that the class antagonisms within these categories of the population are much deeper-going and stronger than the solidarity binding all classes within any one category against the autocracy and in favour of democratic institutions. The proletariat alone can be—and because of its class position must be—a consistently democratic, determined enemy of absolutism, incapable of making any concessions or compromises. The proletariat alone can be the *vanguard fighter* for political liberty and for democratic institutions. Firstly, this is because political tyranny bears most heavily upon the proletariat whose position gives it no opportunity to secure a modification of that tyranny—it has no access to the higher authorities, not even to the officials, and it has no influence on public opinion. Secondly, the proletariat alone is capable of bringing about the *complete* democratisation of the political and social system, since this would place the system in the hands of the workers. That is why the *merging* of the democratic activities of the working class with the democratic aspirations of other classes and groups would *weaken* the democratic movement, would *weaken* the political struggle, would make it less determined, less consistent, more likely to compromise. On the other hand, if the working class *stands out* as the vanguard fighter for democratic institutions, this will *strengthen* the democratic movement, will *strengthen* the struggle for political liberty, because the working class will *spur on* all the other democratic and political opposition elements, will push the liberals towards the political radicals, will push the radicals towards an irrevocable rupture with the whole of the political and social structure of present society. We said above that all *socialists* in Russia should become *Social-Democrats*. We now add: all true and consistent *democrats* in Russia should become *Social-Democrats*.

We will illustrate what we mean by quoting the following example. Take the civil service, the bureaucracy, as representing a special category of persons who specialise in the work of administration and occupy a privileged position as compared with the people. We see this institution everywhere, from autocratic and semi-Asiatic Russia to cultured, free and civilised England, as an essential organ of bourgeois society. The *complete lack of rights* of the people in relation to government officials and the *complete* absence of control over the privileged bureaucracy correspond to the backwardness of Russia and to its absolutism. In England powerful popular control is exercised over the administration, but even there that control *is far from being complete*, even there the bureaucracy retains not a few of its privileges, and not- infrequently is the master and not the servant of the people. Even in England we see that powerful social groups support the privileged position of the bureaucracy and hinder the complete democratisation of that institution. Why? Because it is in the interests of the proletariat alone to democratise it *completely*; the most progressive strata of the bourgeoisie defend certain prerogatives of the bureaucracy and are opposed to the election of all officials, opposed to the complete abolition of electoral qualifications, opposed to making officials directly responsible to the, people, etc., because these strata realise that the proletariat will take advantage of such complete democratisation in order to use it *against* the bourgeoisie. This is the case in Russia, too. Many and most diverse strata of the Russian people are opposed to the omnipotent, irresponsible, corrupt, savage, ignorant and parasitic Russian bureaucracy. But except for the proletariat, *not one* of these strata would agree to the complete democratisation of the bureaucracy, because all these strata (bourgeoisie, petty bourgeoisie, the "intelligentsia" in general) have some ties with the bureaucracy, because all these strata are *kith and kin* of the Russian bureaucracy. Who does not know how easy it is in Holy Russia for a radical intellectual, or socialist intellectual, to turn into an official of the Imperial Government, an official who takes comfort from the thought that he does "good" within the limits of office routine, an official who pleads this "good" in justification of his political indifference, his servility towards the government of the knout and the whip? *The proletariat* alone is unreservedly hostile to the autocracy and the Russian bureaucracy, *the proletariat* alone has no *ties* with these organs of aristocratic-bourgeois society and the proletariat alone is capable of irreconcilable hostility towards them and of waging a determined struggle against them.

When we show that the proletariat, led in its class struggle by Social-Democracy, is the vanguard fighter of Russian democracy, we encounter the very widespread and very strange opinion that Russian Social-Democracy relegates political tasks and political struggle to the background. As we see, this opinion is the very opposite of the truth. How are we to explain this astonishing failure to understand the principles of Social-Democracy that have often been expounded and were expounded in the very first Russian Social-Democratic publications, in the pamphlets and books published abroad by the Emancipation of Labour group?[111] In our view, the explanation of this amazing fact lies in the following three circumstances.

First, it lies in the general failure of the representatives of old revolutionary theories to understand the principles of Social-Democracy, accustomed as they are to base their programmes and plans of activity on abstract ideas and not on an exact appraisal of the actual classes operating in the country, classes that have been placed in certain relationships by history. This lack of realistic discussion of the *interests* which support Russian democracy can only give rise to the opinion that Russian Social-Democracy leaves the democratic tasks of Russian revolutionaries in the background.

Second, it lies in the failure to understand that when economic and political issues, and socialist and democratic activities, are united into one whole, into the single *class struggle of the proletariat*, this does not weaken but strengthens the democratic movement and the political struggle, by bringing it closer to the real interests of the mass of the people, dragging political issues out of the "stuffy studies of the intelligentsia" into the street, into the midst of the workers and labouring classes, and replacing abstract ideas by real manifestations of political oppression from which the greatest sufferers are the proletariat, and on the basis of which the Social-Democrats conduct their agitation. It often seems to the Russian radical that instead of frankly and directly calling upon the advanced workers to join the political struggle, the Social-Democrat points to the task of developing the working-class movement, of organising the class struggle of the proletariat, and thereby *retreats* from his democracy, relegates the political struggle to the background. But if this is *retreat*, it is the kind of retreat that is meant in the French proverb: "Il faut reculer pour mieux sauter!" (Step back in order to leap farther forward.)

Third, the misunderstanding arises from the fact that the very term "political struggle" means something different to the Narodovoltsi and Narodopravtsi, on the one hand, and to the Social-Democrats, on the other. The Social-Democrats understand the political struggle differently, they understand it *much more broadly* than do the representatives of the old revolutionary theories. A clear illustration of this seeming paradox is provided by the *Leaflet of the Narodnaya Volya Group*, No. 4, December 9, 1895. While heartily welcoming this publication, which testifies to the profound and fruitful thinking that is going on among the present-day Narodovoltsi, we cannot refrain from mentioning P. L. Lavrov's article, "Programme questions" (pp. 19-22), which vividly reveals the different conception of the political struggle entertained by the old-style Narodovoltsi.* "... Here," writes P. L. Lavrov, speaking of the relation .of the Narodnaya Volya programme to the Social-Democratic programme, "one thing and one thing alone is material, viz., is it possible to organise a strong workers' party under the autocracy and to do so apart from the organisation of a revolutionary party directed against the autocracy?" (p. 21, col. 2); also a little before that (in col. 1): "... to organise a Russian workers' party while autocracy reigns without at the same time organising a revolutionary party against this autocracy." We cannot at all understand these distinctions which seem to be of such cardinal importance to P. L. Lavrov. What is the meaning of "a workers' party *apart from* a revolutionary party against the autoc-

---

* P. L. Lavrov's article in No. 4 is, in fact, only an "excerpt" from a long letter written by him for *Material*.[112] We have heard that the full text of this letter and a reply by Plekhanov were also published abroad this summer (1897), but we have seen neither the one nor the other. Nor do we know whether *Leaflet of the Narodnaya Volya Group*, No. 5, in which the editors promised to publish an editorial article on P. L. Lavrov's letter, has appeared yet. See No. 4, p. 22, col. 1, footnote.

racy"?? Is not a workers' party itself a revolutionary party? Is it not directed against the autocracy? This queer idea is explained in the following passage in P. L. Lavrov's article: "A Russian workers' party will have to be organised under the rule of the autocracy with all its charms. If the Social-Democrats succeeded in doing this without at the same time organising a political *conspiracy** against the autocracy, with all that goes with such a *conspiracy*,* then, of course, their political programme would be a fit and proper programme for Russian socialists, since the emancipation of the workers by the efforts of the workers themselves would be accomplished. But this is very doubtful, if not impossible" (p. 21, col. 1). So that's the point! To the Narodovoltsi, the term political struggle is synonymous with the term political *conspiracy*! It must be confessed that in these words P. L. Lavrov has managed to bring out in bold relief the fundamental difference between the tactics in the political struggle adopted by the Narodovoltsi and by the Social-Democrats. Blanquist,[113] conspiratorial traditions are fearfully strong among the former, so much so that they cannot conceive of political struggle except in the form of political conspiracy. The Social-Democrats, however, are not guilty of such a narrow outlook; they do not believe in conspiracies; they think that the period of conspiracies has long passed away, that to reduce political struggle to conspiracy means, on the one hand, immensely restricting its scope, and, on the other hand, choosing the most unsuitable methods of struggle. Everyone will understand that P. L. Lavrov's remark that "the Russian Social-Democrats take the activities of the West as an unfailing model" (p. 21, col. 1) is nothing more than a polemical manoeuvre, and that actually the Russian Social-Democrats have never forgotten the political conditions here, they have never dreamed of being able to form a workers' party in Russia legally, they have never separated the task of fighting for socialism from that of fighting for political liberty. But they have always thought, and continue to think, that this fight must be waged not by conspirators, but by a revolutionary party based on the working-

---

* Our italics.

class movement. They think that the fight against the autocracy must consist not in organising conspiracies, but in educating, disciplining and organising the proletariat, in political agitation among the workers which denounces every manifestation of absolutism, which pillories all the knights of the police government and compels this government to make concessions. Is this not precisely the kind of activity being conducted by the St. Petersburg League of Struggle for the Emancipation of the Working Class? Does not this organisation represent the embryo of a revolutionary party based on the working-class movement, which leads the class struggle of the proletariat against capital and against the autocratic government without hatching any conspiracies, while deriving its strength from the *combination* of socialist and democratic struggle into the single, indivisible class struggle of the St. Petersburg proletariat? Brief as they may have been, have not the activities of the League already shown that the proletariat, led by Social-Democracy, is a big political force with which the government is already compelled to reckon, and to which it hastens to make concessions? Both the haste with which the law of June 2, 1897, was passed, and the content of that law clearly reveal its significance as a concession wrung by the proletariat, as a position won from the enemy of the Russian people. This concession is a very tiny one, the position won is very small, but the working-class organisation that has succeeded in forcing this concession is also not distinguished for breadth, stability, long standing or wealth of experience or resources. As is well known, the League of Struggle was formed only in 1895-96, and its appeals to the workers have been confined to hectographed or lithographed leaflets. Can it be denied that an organisation like this, if it united, at least, the biggest centres of the working-class movement in Russia (the St. Petersburg, Moscow-Vladimir, and the southern areas, and also the most important towns like Odessa, Kiev, Saratov, etc.), if it had a revolutionary organ at its disposal and enjoyed as much prestige among the Russian workers generally as the League of Struggle does among the St. Petersburg workers—can it be denied that such an organisation would be a tremendous political factor in contemporary Russia, a factor that the government would have to reckon with in its entire home and foreign policy? By leading the class struggle of the proletariat, developing organisation and discipline among the workers, helping them to fight for their immediate economic needs and to win position after position from capital, by politically educating the workers and systematically and unswervingly attacking the autocracy and making life a torment for every tsarist bashi-bazouk who makes the proletariat feel the heavy paw of the police government—such an organisation would at one and the same time be a workers' party organisation adapted to our conditions, and a powerful revolutionary party directed against the autocracy. To discuss in advance what methods this organisation will resort to in order to deliver a smashing blow at the autocracy, whether, for example, it will prefer insurrection, a mass political strike, or some other form of attack, to discuss these things in advance and to decide this question now would be empty doctrinairism. It would be akin to generals calling a council of war before they had mustered their troops, mobilised them, and undertaken a campaign against the enemy. When the army of the proletariat fights unswervingly and under the leadership of a strong Social-Democratic organisation for its economic and political emancipation, that army will itself indicate the methods and means of action to the generals. Then, and then only, will it be possible to decide the question of striking the final blow at the autocracy; for the solution of the problem depends on the state of the working-class movement, on its breadth, on the methods of struggle developed by the movement, on the qualities of the revolutionary organisation leading the movement, on the attitude of other social elements to the proletariat and to the autocracy, on the conditions governing home and foreign politics—in a word, it depends on a thousand and one things which cannot be guessed, and which it would be useless to try to guess in advance.

That is why the following argument of P. L. Lavrov's is also extremely unfair:

"If, however, they" (the Social-Democrats) "have, in one way or another, not only to group the workers' forces for the struggle against capital, but also to rally revolutionary individuals and groups for the struggle against the autocracy, the Russian Social-Democrats will *actually* be adopting the programme of their opponents, the Narodnaya Volya, no matter what they may call themselves. Differences of opinion concerning the village community, the destiny of capitalism in Russia and economic materialism are points of detail of very little importance to the real cause, either facilitating or hindering the solution of particular problems, particular methods of preparing the main points, but nothing more" (p. 21, col. 1).

It is strange to have to challenge this last proposition— that differences of opinion on the fundamental questions of Russian life and of the development of Russian society, on the fundamental problems of the conception of history, concern only "points of detail"! It was said long ago that without a revolutionary theory there can be no revolutionary movement, and it is hardly necessary to advance proof of this truth *at the present time*. The theory of the class struggle, the materialist conception of Russian history and the materialist appraisal of the present economic and political situation in Russia, recognition of the need to relate the revolutionary struggle strictly to the definite interests of a definite class and to analyse its relation to other classes —to call these great revolutionary questions "points of detail" is so colossally wrong and unexpected, coming from a veteran of revolutionary *theory*, that we are almost prepared to regard this passage as a lapsus. As for the first part of the tirade quoted, its unfairness is still more astonishing. To state in print that the Russian Social-Democrats only group the workers' forces for the struggle against capital (i.e., only for the economic struggle!) and do not rally revolutionary individuals and groups for the struggle against the autocracy, means that the author either does not know or does not want to know generally known facts concerning the activities of the Russian Social-Democrats. Or, perhaps, P. L. Lavrov does not regard the Social-Democrats who are engaged in practical work in Russia as "revolutionary individuals" and "revolutionary groups"?! Or (and this, perhaps, is more likely) by "struggle" against the autocracy he means only conspiracies against it? (Cf. p. 21, col. 2: "... it is a matter of ... organising a revolutionary *conspiracy*";

our italics.) Perhaps, in P. L. Lavrov's opinion, those who do not organise political conspiracies are not engaged in political struggle? We repeat once again: opinions like these fully correspond to the old-time traditions of the old-time Narodnaya Volya, but do not correspond at all either to contemporary conceptions of the political struggle or to contemporary conditions.

We have still to say a few words about the Narodopravtsi. P. L. Lavrov is quite right, in our opinion, when he says that the Social-Democrats "recommend the Narodopravtsi as being more frank, and are ready to support them, without, however, merging with them" (p. 19, col. 2); he should only have added: as more frank *democrats*, and *to the degree that* the Narodopravtsi act as consistent democrats. Unfortunately, this condition is more a matter of the desired future than of the actual present. The Narodopravtsi expressed a desire to free the democratic tasks from Narodism and from the obsolete forms of "Russian socialism" generally; but they themselves were still far from being freed from old prejudices, and were far from consistent when they described their party, exclusively a party for political reforms, as a "social (??!)-revolutionary" party (see their "Manifesto" dated February 19, 1894), and declared in their "Manifesto" that "the term people's rights includes the organisation of people's industry" (we are obliged to quote from memory) and thus introduced Narodnik prejudices sub rosa. Hence, P. L. Lavrov was, perhaps, not altogether wrong when he described them as "masquerade politicians" (p. 20, col. 2). But perhaps it would be fairer to regard the doctrine of Narodnoye Pravo as transitional, to the credit of which it must be said that it was ashamed of the original character of the Narodnik doctrines and openly gave battle to those most abominable Narodnik reactionaries who, despite the existence of absolute rule by the police and the upper class, have the audacity to speak of the desirability of economic and not political reforms (see "An Urgent Question," published by the Narodnoye Pravo Party). If the Narodnoye Pravo Party does not really contain anybody but ex-socialists who conceal their socialist banner for tactical considerations, and who merely don the mask of non-socialist politicians (as P. L. Lavrov assumes, p. 20, col. 2), then, of course, that party has no future whatever. If, however, the party also contains not masquerade, but real non-socialist politicians, non-socialist democrats, then this party can do no little good by striving to draw closer to the political opposition among our bourgeoisie, by striving to arouse the political consciousness of our petty bourgeoisie, small shopkeepers, small artisans, etc.—the class which, everywhere in Western Europe, played a part in the democratic movement and, in Russia, has made exceptionally rapid progress in cultural and other respects in the post-Reform period, and which cannot avoid feeling the oppression of the police government that gives its cynical support to the big factory owners, the magnates of finance and industrial monopoly. All that is needed for this is that the Narodopravtsi should make it their task to draw closer to various strata of the population and should not confine themselves to the very same "intelligentsia" whose impotence, owing to their isolation from the real interests of the masses, is admitted even in "An Urgent Question." What is needed is that the Narodopravtsi abandon all idea of merging different social elements and of pushing socialism aside in favour of political tasks, that they abandon the false shame which prevents them from drawing closer to the bourgeois strata of the population, i.e., that they not only talk about a programme for non-socialist politicians, but act according to this programme, rousing and developing the class-consciousness of those social groups and classes for whom socialism is quite unnecessary, but who, as time goes on, increasingly feel the oppression of the autocracy and the need for political liberty.

Russian Social-Democracy is still very young. It is only just emerging from its embryonic state in which theoretical questions predominated. It is only just beginning to develop its practical activity. In place of criticism of Social-Democratic theories and programmes, revolutionaries of other parties have of necessity moved on to criticism of the *practical activity* of the Russian Social-Democrats. And it must be admitted that this latter criticism differs most sharply from the criticism of theory, differs so much, in fact, that it was possible to float the comical rumour that the St. Petersburg League of Struggle is not a Social-Democratic organisation. The very fact that such a rumour appeared shows how unfounded is the accusation now current that the Social-Democrats ignore the political struggle. The very fact that such a rumour appeared shows that many revolutionaries whom the Social-Democrats' *theory* could not convince are beginning to be convinced by their *practice*.

Russian Social-Democracy is still faced with an enormous, almost untouched field of work. The awakening of the Russian working class, its spontaneous striving for knowledge, organisation, socialism, for the struggle against its exploiters and oppressors becomes more widespread, more strikingly apparent every day. The enormous progress made by Russian capitalism in recent times is a guarantee that the working-class movement will grow uninterruptedly in breadth and depth. We are apparently now passing through the period in the capitalist cycle when industry is "prospering," when business is brisk, when the factories are working at full capacity and when countless new factories, new enterprises, joint-stock companies, railway enterprises, etc., etc., are springing up like mushrooms. One need not be a prophet to foretell the inevitable and fairly sharp crash that is bound to succeed this period of industrial "prosperity." This crash will ruin masses of small owners, will throw masses of workers into the ranks of the unemployed, and will thus confront all the workers in an acute form with the problems of socialism and democracy which have long faced every class-conscious, every thinking worker. Russian Social-Democrats must see to it that when this crash comes the Russian proletariat is more class-conscious, more united, able to understand the tasks of the Russian working class, capable of putting up resistance to the capitalist class—which is now reaping huge profits and always strives to burden the workers with the losses—and capable of leading Russian democracy in a decisive struggle against the police autocracy, which binds and fetters the Russian workers and the whole of the Russian people.

And so, to work, comrades! Let us not lose precious time! Russian Social-Democrats have much to do to meet the requirements of the awakening proletariat, to organise the working-class movement, to strengthen the revolutionary groups and their mutual ties, to supply the workers with propaganda and agitational literature, and to unite the workers' circles and Social-Democratic groups scattered all over Russia into a single *Social-Democratic Labour Party*!

TO THE WORKERS AND SOCIALISTS
OF ST. PETERSBURG
FROM THE LEAGUE OF STRUGGLE

The St. Petersburg revolutionaries are experiencing hard times. It seems that the government has concentrated all its forces for the purpose of crushing the recently born working-class movement which has given such a display of strength. Arrests are being made on an unprecedented scale and the prisons are overcrowded. Intellectuals, men and women, and masses of workers are being dragged off and exiled. Almost every day brings news of ever new victims of the police government, which has flung itself in fury upon its enemies. The government has set itself the aim of preventing the new trend in the Russian revolutionary movement from gaining strength and getting on its feet. The public prosecutors and gendarmes are already boasting that they have smashed the League of Struggle.

This boast is a lie. The League of Struggle is intact, despite all the persecution. With deep satisfaction we declare that the wholesale arrests are doing their job—they are a powerful weapon of agitation among the workers and socialist intellectuals, that the places of the fallen revolutionaries are being taken by new people who are ready, with fresh energy, to join the ranks of the champions of the Russian proletariat and of the entire people of Russia. There can be no struggle without sacrifice, and to the brutal persecution of the tsarist bashi-bazouks we calmly reply: Revolutionaries have perished—long live the revolution!

So far, increased persecution has only been able to cause a temporary weakening of certain functions of the League of Struggle, a temporary shortage of agents and agitators. This is the shortage that we now feel and that impels us to call upon all class-conscious workers and all intellectuals desirous of devoting their energies to the revolutionary cause. The League of Struggle needs agents. Let all study circles and all individuals desirous of working in any sphere of revolutionary activity, even the most restricted, inform those in touch with the League of Struggle. (Should any group be unable to contact such individuals—this is very unlikely—they can do so through the League of Russian Social-Democrats Abroad.) People are needed for all kinds of work, and the more strictly revolutionaries specialise in the various aspects of revolutionary activity, the more strictly they give thought to their methods of underground work and ways of screening it, the more selflessly they concentrate on the minor, unseen, particular jobs, the safer will the whole thing be and the more difficult will it be for the gendarmes and spies to discover the revolutionaries. In advance the government has enmeshed not only the existing centres of anti-government elements, but also possible and probable ones, in a network of agents. The government is steadily developing the size and range of the activities of those of its lackeys who are hounding revolutionaries, is devising new methods, introducing more provocateurs, trying to exert pressure on the arrested by means of intimidation, confrontation with false testimony, forged signatures, planting faked letters, etc., etc. Without a strengthening and development of revolutionary discipline, organisation and underground activity, struggle against the government is impossible. And underground activity demands above all that groups and individuals specialise in different aspects of work and that the job of co-ordination be assigned to the central group of the League of Struggle, with as few members as possible. The aspects of revolutionary work are extremely varied. Legal agitators are needed who can talk to the workers in a way that *does not render* them liable to prosecution, and can say just *a*, leaving it to others to say *b* and *c*. Literature and leaflet distributors are needed. Organisers of workers' study circles and groups are needed.

Correspondents are needed who can give a complete picture of events in all factories. People are needed who will keep an eye on spies and provocateurs. People are needed who will arrange underground meeting places. People are needed to deliver literature, transmit instructions, and to arrange all kinds of contacts. Fund collectors are needed. Agents are needed to work among the intelligentsia and government officials, people in contact with the workers and factory life, with the administration (with the police, factory inspectors, etc.). People are needed for contact with the different towns of Russia and other countries. People are needed to arrange various ways of running off all sorts of literature. People are needed to look after literature and other things, etc., etc. The smaller and more specific the job undertaken by the individual person or individual group, the greater will be the chance that they will think things out, do the job properly and guarantee it best against failure, that they will consider all the details of underground work and use all possible means of hoodwinking and misleading the gendarmes, the more will success be assured, the harder will it be for the police and gendarmes to keep track of the revolutionaries and their links with their organisations, and the easier for the revolutionary party to replace, without prejudice to the cause as a whole, agents and members who have fallen. We know that specialisation of this kind is a very difficult matter, difficult because it demands from the individual the greatest endurance and selflessness, demands the giving of all one's strength to work that is inconspicuous, monotonous, that deprives one of contact with comrades and subordinates the revolutionary's entire life to a grim and rigid routine. But it was only in conditions such as these that the greatest men of revolutionary practice in Russia succeeded in carrying out the boldest undertakings, spending years on all-round preparation, and we are profoundly convinced that the Social-Democrats will prove no less self-sacrificing than the revolutionaries of previous generations. We are also aware that the preliminary period envisaged by our system during which the League of Struggle will collect the necessary information about individuals or groups offering their services and give them something to do by way of trial will be a very difficult one for many people eager to devote their energies to revolutionary work. But without this preliminary testing, revolutionary activity in present-day Russia is impossible.

In suggesting this system of work to our new comrades we are expressing a view arrived at after long experience, being deeply convinced that it best of all guarantees successful revolutionary work.

Владиміръ Ильинъ.

ЭКОНОМИЧЕСКІЕ
ЭТЮДЫ И СТАТЬИ.

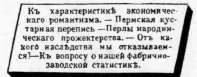

Къ характеристикѣ экономическаго романтизма. — Пермская кустарная перепись. — Перлы народническаго прожектерства. — Отъ какого наслѣдства мы отказываемся? — Къ вопросу о нашей фабрично-заводской статистикѣ.

С.-ПЕТЕРБУРГЪ.
Типо-литографія А. Лейферта. Бол. Морская, 65.
1899.

Cover of *Economic Studies and Essays*
by V. Ilyin (V. I. Lenin)

THE HANDICRAFT CENSUS OF 1894-95
IN PERM GUBERNIA
AND
GENERAL PROBLEMS
OF "HANDICRAFT" INDUSTRY [114]

Written in exile in 1897
First published in 1898 in the
miscellany *Economic Studies and
Essays* by Vladimir Ilyin

Published according to the
text in *Economic Studies and Essays* checked
with the text in the miscellany
The Agrarian Question
by Vl. Ilyin, 1908

ARTICLE ONE

(I. General Data.—II. The "Handicraftsman" and Wage-Labour.—
III. "Communal-Labour Continuity")

Perm scientific societies, assisted by the Zemstvo, have undertaken the preparation of an extensive handbook for the 1896 Exhibition in Nizhni-Novgorod under the general title: *A Survey of Perm Territory*. Enough material has been collected to fill well over three thousand pages, and the whole edition is to consist of eight volumes. As was to be expected, the work was not completed in time for the exhibition, and so far only the first volume, a sketch of the handicraft industries of the gubernia,* has been published. For the novelty, wealth and fulness of the material on which it is based, the *Sketch* is a work of outstanding interest. The material was obtained through a special *handicraft census* financed by the Zemstvo and taken in 1894-95. This was a house-to-house census, each householder being questioned individually. The information was collected by the Zemsky Nachalniks.[115] The programme of this house-to-house investigation was very broad, embracing the members of the families of master handicraftsmen, the wage-labour employed by them, agriculture, information on the purchase of raw materials, the technique of production, distribution of work according to the months of the year, sale of products, dates on which the establishments were founded, and the indebtedness of handicraftsmen. As far as we are aware, this is perhaps the first time such abun-

---

* *A Survey of Perm Territory. A Sketch of the State of Handicraft Industry in Perm Gubernia*. Published out of funds provided by the Perm Gubernia Zemstvo. Perm, 1896, pp. II +365+232 pp. of tables, 16 diagrams and a map of Perm Gubernia. Price: 1 ruble 50 kopeks.

dant information has been published in our literature. But
to whom much is given, much is required. The very wealth
of the material entitles us to demand its thorough analysis
by the investigators, but the *Sketch* is a long way from
meeting this demand. Both in the tabulated data and in
the method of grouping and analysing them there are many
gaps, which the present author has had in part to fill by
selecting material from various parts of the book and com-
puting the appropriate data.

Our purpose is to acquaint the reader with the material
of the census, the methods by which it has been analysed,
and the conclusions to be drawn from the data relative to
the *economic realities* of our "handicraft industries." We
underscore the words "economic realities," because we only
deal with what exists in reality, and why that reality is
what it is, and not something else. As to extending the conclusions drawn from the data on Perm Gubernia to "our
handicraft industries" in general, the reader will see from
what follows that such an extention is quite legitimate,
for the forms of "handicraft industry" in Perm Gubernia
are exceedingly varied and embrace *every possible* form ever
mentioned in the literature on the subject.

But there is one request we must earnestly make, namely,
that the reader draw the strictest possible distinction between two aspects of the following commentary: the study
and analysis of the actual facts, on the one hand, and the
discussion of the Narodnik views held by the authors of the
Sketch, on the other.

I

GENERAL DATA

The handicraft census of 1894-95 embraced 8,991 families
(excluding the families of wage-workers) in all uyezds of
the gubernia, or, in the opinion of the investigators, about
72 per cent of the total number of Perm handicraftsmen; other
data point to the existence of 3,484 families more. The
basic division according to type adopted in the *Sketch* is
as follows: two *groups* of handicraftsmen are distinguished
(indicated in the tables by the Roman numerals I and

II): those who have a farm (I) and those who have not (II); then three *sub-groups* of each group (Arabic numerals 1, 2 and 3): 1) those who produce for the market; 2) those who work to order for private customers, and 3) those who work to order for buyers-up. In the last two sub-groups the raw material is usually supplied by the customer or the buyer-up. Let us take a look at this method of classifying. The division of handicraftsmen into those who farm land and those who do not is, of course, a sound and necessary method. The large number of landless handicraftsmen in Perm Gubernia, frequently concentrated in industrial settlements, has led the authors to stick to this classification and to use it in the tables. We learn, for example, that 6,638 persons, or one-third of the total number of handicraftsmen (19,970 working members of families and wage-workers in 8,991 establishments) do not farm land.* This fact alone shows the fallacy of the common assumptions and assertions that the connection between handicraft industry and agriculture is universal; this connection is sometimes stressed as a specifically Russian feature. If we exclude the rural (and urban) artisans who have been wrongly classed as "handicraftsmen," we find that 2,268 of the remaining 5,566 families, or over two-fifths of the total number of industrialists working for the market, are landless. Unfortunately, even this basic classification is not adhered to consistently in the *Sketch*. Firstly, it is applied only to master craftsmen, no similar data being given for wage-workers. This omission is due to the fact that, in general, the census registered only the establishments, the owners, and ignored the wage-workers and their families. In place of these terms, the *Sketch* employs the very inaccurate expression "families engaged in handicraft industries." This is inaccurate because families whose members are employed by handicraftsmen as wage-workers are no less "engaged in handicraft industries" than the families which hire them. The absence of house-to-house information on the families of wage-workers (who constitute one-fourth of the total number of workers) is a grave omission in the census. This omission is

---

* Actually, more than one-third are landless, for the census covered only one town. But of that more anon.

highly characteristic of the Narodniks, who at once adopt the viewpoint of the small producer and leave wage-labour in the shade. Below we shall find frequent gaps of this kind in the information on wage-workers, but for the moment let us confine ourselves to the remark that although the absence of information on wage-workers' families is a common feature of the literature on handicrafts, there are exceptions. In the Moscow Zemstvo statistics one occasionally comes across systematic information on wage-workers' families, and even more so in the well-known inquiry of Messrs. Kharizomenov and Prugavin, *Industries of Vladimir Gubernia*, which contains house-to-house censuses that register wage-workers' families on a par with those of masters. Secondly, by including the mass of landless industrialists under the heading of handicraftsmen, the investigators naturally removed the grounds for the common, although absolutely incorrect, method of excluding the *urban* industrialists from this category. And, indeed, we find that the 1894-95 census includes one town—Kungur (p. 33 of the tables)—but *only one*. No explanation is given in the *Sketch*, and it remains a mystery why the census was taken for one town only, and why this particular town was chosen—whether by chance or for some sound reason. This causes no little confusion, and seriously detracts from the value of the general data. On the whole, therefore, the handicraft census repeats the usual Narodnik mistake of separating the country ("handicraftsmen") from the town, although often enough an industrial district embraces a town and the surrounding villages. It is high time to abandon this distinction, which is due to prejudice and an exaggeration of outdated divisions into social estates.

We have already referred on several occasions to rural and urban artisans, sometimes excluding them from the number of handicraftsmen, and sometimes not. The fact is that these fluctuations are characteristic of all literature on "handicraft" industries, and demonstrate the unsuitability of a term like "handicraftsman" for the purposes of scientific investigation. The generally accepted opinion is that only those who work for the market, the commodity producers, should be regarded as handicraftsmen; but in practice it would be hard to find an investigation of the handicraft industries in which artisans, that is, producers who work for private customers (2nd sub-group in the *Sketch*) are not counted as handicraftsmen. Both in the *Transactions of the Commission of Inquiry into the Handicraft Industry* and the *Industries of Moscow Gubernia* you will find artisans classed as "handicraftsmen." We consider it useless to argue about the meaning of the word "handicraft," for, as we shall see later, *there is no form of industry* (except perhaps machine industry) which has not been included under this traditional term, a term that is absolutely useless for scientific investigation. It is certain that a strict distinction must be made between commodity producers who work for the market (1st sub-group) and artisans who fulfil the orders of private customers (2nd sub-group), because of the complete difference in the social and economic significance of these forms of industry. The attempts made in the *Sketch* to obliterate this distinction (cf. pp. 13 and 177) are very unsuccessful; far more correct is the remark made in another Zemstvo statistical publication on the Perm handicraftsmen to the effect that "the artisans have very few points of contact with the sphere of handicraft industry— fewer than the latter has with factory industry."* Both factory industry and the 1st sub-group of "handicraftsmen" relate to *commodity production*, which is non-existent in the 2nd sub-group. A no less strict distinction must be made in the case of the 3rd sub-group, the handicraftsmen who work for buyers-up (and manufacturers) and who differ *essentially* from those of the first two sub-groups. It would be desirable for all investigators of so-called "handicraft" industry to adhere strictly to this division and use precise political-economic terminology, instead of assigning an arbitrary meaning to colloquial terms.

The following table shows the division of the "handicraftsmen" into groups and sub-groups:

Before proceeding to draw conclusions from these figures,

---

* *The Handicraft Industries of Perm Gubernia at the Siberian-Urals Science and Industry Exhibition in Ekaterinburg*, 1887, by Y. Krasnoperov, in three parts, Perm, 1888-89, Part I, p. 8. We shall quote from this valuable publication, briefly referring to it as *Handicraft Industries* and indicating the part and the page.

| | Group I | | | | Group II | | | | Grand total |
| | Sub-group | | | Total | Sub-group | | | Total | |
	1	2	3		1	2	3		
Number of establishments {	2,285	2,821	1,013	6,119	935	604	1,333	2,872	8,991
	37.3	46.1	16.6	100	32.6	21.0	46.4	100	—
Number of: Family workers	4,201	4,146	1,957	10,304	1,648	881	2,233	4,762	15,066
Wage-workers	1,753	681	594	3,028	750	282	844	1,876	4,904
Total	5,954	4,827	2,551	13,332	2,398	1,163	3,077	6,638	19,970
Number of establishments employing wage-workers	700	490	251	1,441	353	148	482	983	2,424

let us recall that the town of Kungur was included in Group II, which thus consists of a mixture of urban and rural industrialists. We see from the table that although there is a preponderance of agriculturists (Group I) among the *rural* industrialists and artisans, they are more backward in the development of forms of industry than those who do not cultivate the land (Group II). Among the former primitive artisanship is far more prevalent than production for the market. The greater development of capitalism among the non-agriculturists is shown by the larger proportion of establishments employing wage-workers, of the wage-workers themselves, and of handicraftsmen who work for buyers-up. It may therefore be concluded that the tie with agriculture tends to preserve the more backward forms of industry, and vice versa, that the development of capitalism in industry leads to a break with agriculture. Unfortunately, exact information on this subject is not available, and we have perforce to content ourselves with indirect indications. For example, the *Sketch* tells us nothing about the division of the rural population of Perm Gubernia into agriculturists and landless people, and so we cannot determine in which of these categories the industries are most developed. There is a similar neglect of the highly interesting question of the territorial distribution of industry (the investigators were in possession of the most exact information on this point, for each village separately), of the concentration of industrialists in the non-agricultural, factory, or trade and industrial settlements generally, of the centres of each branch of industry, and of the spread of the industries from these centres to the surrounding villages. If we add to this that the household statistics showing when the establishments were founded (see § III below) provided an opportunity to determine how the industries developed, that is, whether they spread from the centres to the surrounding villages or vice versa, whether they spread mostly among agriculturists or non-agriculturists, etc., then one cannot help regretting the inadequate analysis of the data. The only information we are able to obtain concerns the distribution of industries by uyezds. To acquaint the reader with these figures we shall group the uyezds as suggested in the *Sketch* (p. 31): 1) the five "uyezds where the proportion of handicraftsmen working for the market is largest and where, simultaneously, the development of handicraft industry is relatively high"; 2) the five "uyezds where the development of the handicraft industry is relatively weak and where the handicraftsmen working for the market predominate"; 3) the two "uyezds where it is also at a low level, but where the majority often consists of handicraftsmen who fulfil orders for private customers." Summarising the principal data for these groups of uyezds we get the following table (see p. 364).

This table enables us to draw the following interesting conclusions. The more highly rural industry is developed in a group of uyezds, 1) the smaller the proportion of rural artisans, i.e., artisan production is to a greater extent replaced by commodity production; 2) the larger the proportion of handicraftsmen who belong to the non-agricultural population, and 3) the more marked the development of capitalist relations and the larger the proportion of dependent handicraftsmen. In the third group of uyezds the rural artisans predominate (77.7% of all the handicraftsmen); in this case agriculturists predominate (only 5.7% are non-agriculturists) and capitalism is poorly developed: only 7.2% are wage-workers and only 2.7% of the handicraftsmen's families work for buyers-up, i.e., a total of only 9.9% are dependent handicraftsmen. In the second group of uyezds, on the contrary, commodity production

Groups of uyezds	Number of handicraftsmen												Percentages of handicraftsmen		Number of persons, both sexes, in families		
	Producing for the market			Producing for buyers-up			Producing for private customers			In all			Producing for the market (see footnote)	Dependent	With own farm	Farming no land	Total
	Members of families	Wage-workers	Total	Members of families	Wage-workers	Total	Members of families	Wage-workers	Total	Members of families	Wage-workers	Total					
1) Five uyezds in which handicraft industry is most highly developed	4,160	1,702	5,862	3,930 / 27.4	1,397	5,327	2,501	623	3,124 / 21.8	10,591	3,722 / 26.0	14,313 / 100	78.2	53.4	21,320 / 57.9	15,483 / 42.1	36,803 / 100
2) Five uyezds in which handicraft industry is less highly developed	1,436	904	2,340	259 / 6.3	158	417	1,077	252	1,329 / 32.5	2,772	1,314 / 32.1	4,086 / 100	67.5	38.4	7,335 / 66.2	3,740 / 33.8	11,075 / 100
3) Two uyezds in which artisan production predominates	340	59	399	56 / 2.7	—	56	1,499	88	1,587 / 77.7	1,895	147 / 7.2	2,042 / 100	22.3	9.9	5,998 / 94.3	364 / 5.7	6,362 / 100
In all	5,936	2,665	8,601	4,245 / 20.8	1,555	5,800	5,077	963	6,040 / 29.5	15,258	5,183 / 25.3	20,441 / 100	70.5	46.1	34,653 / 63.9	19,587 / 36.1	54,240 / 100

1) The first group consists of Shadrinsk, Kungur, Krasnoufimsk, Ekaterinburg and Osa uyezds; the second of Verkhoturye, Perm, Irbit, Okhansk and Cherdyn uyezds, and the third, Solikamsk and Kamyshlov uyezds.

2) By "dependent" handicraftsmen we mean: a) wage-workers and b) members of the handicraftsman's family who produce for buyers-up.

3) The number of handicraftsmen in the table differs from that given above since the figures for the uyezds given in the Sketch (pp. 30-31) differ from the totals in the appended table.

predominates and is already eliminating handicraft: only 32.5% are artisans. The percentage of handicraftsmen engaged in agriculture drops from 94.3% to 66.2%, the proportion of wage-workers increases more than fourfold—from 7.2% to 32.1%; there is an increase, although not so large, in the proportion of family workers who work for buyers-up, so that the aggregate proportion of dependent handicraftsmen is 38.4%, or nearly two-fifths of the total. Lastly, in the first group of uyezds, natural artisan production is still further eliminated by commodity production and employs only one-fifth of the total number of "handicraftsmen" (21.8%), and at the same time the number of non-agricultural industrialists increases to 42.1%; the proportion of wage-workers drops somewhat (from 32.1% to 26%), but on the other hand there is an enormous increase in the proportion of family workers dependent on buyers-up, namely, from 6.3% to 27.4%, so that the aggregate number of dependent handicraftsmen is more than half the total—53.4%. The district with the largest (absolute and relative) number of "handicraftsmen" is the one where capitalism is most developed: the growth of commodity production forces artisan production into the background, leads to the development of capitalism and to the transfer of industries to non-agriculturists, in other words, to the separation of industry from agriculture (or, perhaps, to the concentration of industries among the non-agricultural population). The reader may doubt whether it is right to regard capitalism as being more developed in the first group of uyezds, where there are fewer wage-workers than in the second, but where more handicraftsmen work for buyers-up. Domestic industry, it may be objected, is a lower form of capitalism. But we shall see below that many of these buyers-up are manufacturers who own large capitalist establishments. Here domestic industry is an *adjunct of the factory*, and signifies a higher degree of concentration of production and capital (some of the buyers-up have 200, 500, even 1,000 persons and more, working for them), a higher degree of division of labour, and, consequently, a more highly developed form of capitalism. This form is to the small workshop of the owner who employs wage-workers as capitalist manufacture is to capitalist simple co-operation.

The figures quoted are sufficient to refute the attempt of the compilers of the *Sketch* to draw a fundamental contrast between "the handicraft form of production" and "capitalist production"—an assertion which repeats the traditional prejudice of all the Russian Narodniks, headed by Messrs. V.V. and N. —on. The Perm Narodniks assume that the "basic difference" between these two forms is that under handicraft production "labour owns both the instruments and materials of production and all the fruits of labour in the shape of the produce of production" (p. 3). We are now in a position to declare quite emphatically that this is false. Even if we include artisans among the handicraftsmen *the majority of them do not fit this definition*: this applies, firstly, to the wage-workers, and they represent 25.3%; secondly, to family workers who work for buyers-up, for they own neither the materials of production nor the fruits of their labour, but are merely paid wages—and they constitute 20.8%; and, thirdly, to the family workers of the first and second sub-groups who employ wage-workers, for they own the "fruits" of other labour in addition to their own. They probably constitute about 10% (1,691 of the 6,645 establishments in the first and second sub-groups, or 25.4%, employ wage-workers; in the 1,691 establishments there are probably not less than 2,000 family workers). And so we already have $25.3\% + 20.8\% + 10\% = 56.1\%$ of the "handicraftsmen," or more than half, who do not fit this definition. In other words, even in a remote and economically backward gubernia like Perm, the "handicraftsmen" who either hire themselves out or hire others, who exploit or are exploited, *are already preponderant today*. But it would be far more correct for such a computation to exclude artisan production and to take commodity production alone. Artisan production is such an archaic form of industry that even among our native Narodniks, who have repeatedly proclaimed that backwardness is Russia's good fortune (à la Messrs. V.V., Yuzhakov and Co.), there has not been a single one who has frankly and openly risked defending it and proclaiming it a "pledge" of his ideals. Artisan production in Perm Gubernia is still very widespread as compared with Central Russia: we need only mention the dyeing industry, for instance. This is a purely artisan industry for the dyeing of peasant homespuns, which in less out-of-the-way parts of Russia have long been superseded by factory-made prints. But even in Perm Gubernia artisan production has been pushed far into the background: even in rural industry, only 29.5%, or less than one-third, of the producers are artisans. If we exclude the artisans, then, we get 14,401 persons who work for the market; of these, 29.3% are wage-workers and 29.5% family workers who work for buyers-up, in other words, 58.8% are dependent "handi-craftsmen," while another 7% or 8% are small masters employing wage-workers. Thus, about 66%, or nearly *two-thirds*, of the "handicraftsmen" have *two* fundamental *points of similarity*, and not of difference, with capitalism: firstly, they are all commodity producers, and capitalism is nothing but commodity production developed to the full; secondly, the specifically capitalist relations of the purchase and sale of labour-power apply to *a large number* of them. The compilers of the *Sketch* try hard to assure the reader that for "weighty" reasons, wage-labour in "handicraft" production has a significance all of its own. We shall examine these assurances and the examples they quote in their proper place (§ VII). Here it will be enough to mention that wherever commodity production prevails and wage-labour is not casually but systematically employed, we have all the features of capitalism. One may say that it is undevel-oped, embryonic, that it possesses specific forms, but it is a distortion of the truth to assume a "basic difference" when in reality there is a *basic similarity*.

Let us, incidentally, mention one other distortion. On p. 5 of the *Sketch* it is said that "the products of the handi-craftsman ... are made from materials that are chiefly procured locally." But the *Sketch* itself provides us with the data to check this point, it shows how the distribution of handicraftsmen engaged in processing livestock produce compares with the distribution of livestock and agricultural produce in the uyezds of the gubernia, how the dis-tribution of those who process plant products compares with the distribution of forests; and how the distribu-tion of those engaged in metal-working compares with the distribution of the pig-iron and malleable iron produced in the gubernia. This comparison shows that 68.9% of the handicraftsmen engaged in processing livestock products are concentrated in three uyezds, which account for only 25.1% of the livestock population, and only 29.5% of the cultivated area. In other words, we find that the very contrary of the above assertion is true, and the *Sketch* itself at this point declares that "the high degree of development of the industries engaged in processing livestock produce is chiefly dependent on raw materials brought from outside— for instance, in the Kungur and Ekaterinburg uyezds on the raw hides dressed by the local leather factories and handicraft tanneries, from which the material for the boot industry, the principal handicraft in these uyezds, is obtained" (24-25). Hence, handicraft industry in these parts is based not only on the large turnover of the local capitalist leather merchants, but also on semi-manufactures obtained from factory owners, i.e., handicraft industry is a sequel or adjunct to developed commodity circulation and to capitalist leather establishments. "In Shadrinsk Uyezd, the raw material brought from outside is wool, which furnishes the material for the chief industry of the uyezd—the making of felt boots." Further, 61.3% of the handicraftsmen engaged in processing plant produce are concentrated in four uyezds. Yet these four uyezds contain only 20.7% of the total forest area of the gubernia. On the other hand, in the two uyezds where 51.7% of the forest area is concentrated, there are only 2.6% of the handicraftsmen engaged in processing plant produce (p. 25). In other words, here too we find the contrary to be the case, and here too the *Sketch* states that the raw material is brought from outside (p. 26).* Hence, we observe the very interesting fact that a deep-rooted *commodity circulation* precedes the development of the handicraft industries (and is a condition for their development). This fact is very important, for it shows, firstly, that commodity economy is long established, handicraft industry being only one of its elements; it shows also how absurd it is to depict our handicraft industry as a sort of tabula rasa still "able" to take a different path. The investigators report, for example, that "handicraft industry"

---

* These two types of handicraftsmen—those processing livestock and plant produce—make up 33%+28% =61% of the total number. Metal-working engages 25% of the handicraftsmen (p. 20).

in Perm Gubernia "continues to reflect the influence of those means of communication which determined the commercial and industrial physiognomy of the area not only in the pre-railway days, but even in pre-Reform days" (p. 39). Actually, the town of Kungur was the road junction in the Cis-Urals area: through it passes the Siberian highway which connects Kungur with Ekaterinburg, with branches to Shadrinsk; another commercial highway from Kungur, that of Blago-datnaya Gora, connects the town with Osa. Lastly, the Birsk highway connects Kungur with Krasnoufimsk. "We thus find that the handicraft industry of the gubernia became concentrated in districts around the highway junctions: in the Cis-Urals area—in the uyezds of Kungur, Krasnoufimsk and Osa and in the Trans-Urals area—in the uyezds of Ekaterinburg and Shadrinsk" (p. 39). Let us remind the reader that it is these five uyezds that constitute the group that is first in its development of handicraft industry, and that 70% of the total number of handicraftsmen are concentrated in them. Secondly, this fact shows us that the "organisation of exchange" in handicraft industry, about which the handicraft friends of the muzhik chatter so frivolously, *has already been created* and by none other than the Russian merchant class itself. Later on we shall find much to confirm this. Only in the third category of handicraftsmen (those who process metal) do we find that the distribution of raw material production and its processing by handicraftsmen correspond: 70% of this category of handicraftsmen are concentrated in the four uyezds producing 70.6% of the total pig-iron and malleable iron. But here the raw material is itself a product of the large-scale metallurgical industry, which, as we shall see, has its "own views" on the "handicraftsman."

II

THE "HANDICRAFTSMAN" AND WAGE-LABOUR

Let us now summarise the data on wage-labour in the handicraft industries of Perm Gubernia. Without re-peating the absolute figures already cited, let us confine ourselves to indicating the most interesting percentages:

		Group I				Group II				To-tal
		Sub-group			In all	Sub-group			In all	
		1	2	3		1	2	3		
Percentage of establishments	Employing wage-workers	30.6	17.4	24.1	23.6	37.8	24.4	36.1	34.2	26.9
	Employing only wage-workers	1.3	1.2	0.7	1.1	1.6	1.4	0.3	1.0	1.1
	Employing six or more wage-workers	2.0	0.1	1.4	1.1	1.3	0.8	0.4	0.8	0.9
Wage-workers		29.4	14.1	23.2	22.7	31.2	29.3	27.4	28.3	24.5
Average number of workers per establishment	Family	1.8	1.5	1.9	1.6	1.7	1.4	1.6	1.6	1.6
	Wage	0.75	0.23	0.57	0.48	0.78	0.43	0.63	0.63	0.52
	Total	2.6	1.7	2.5	2.1	2.5	1.8	2.2	2.2	2.1
Percentage of establishments with three or more family workers		20.3	7.8	20.9	15.1	18.5	8.6	14.3	14.6	14.9

We thus see that the percentage of wage-workers is *higher* among the non-agriculturists than among the agriculturists, and that the difference is *chiefly* accounted for by the second sub-group: among the farming artisans the proportion of wage-workers is 14.1%, and among the non-agriculturists it is 29.3%, or over twice as high. In the other two sub-groups, the proportion of wage-workers in Group II is slightly higher than in Group I. It has already been said that this results from capitalism being less developed among the agricultural population. Of course, the Perm Narodniks, like all other Narodniks, declare this to be of advantage to the agriculturists. We shall not, at this point, enter into a controversy on the general subject of whether the under-development and backwardness of the given social and economic relations may be regarded as an advantage; we shall merely say that the figures we quote below will show that this is an advantage that gives the agriculturists low earnings.

It is interesting to note that insofar as the employment of wage-labour is concerned the difference *between the groups* is less than the difference *between the sub-groups of the same group*. In other words, the economic structure of the industry (artisans—commodity producers—workers for buyers-up) has a greater influence on the extent to which wage-labour is employed than the existence or absence of ties with agriculture. For example, the small agriculturist commodity producer is more akin to the small non-agriculturist commodity producer than to the agriculturist artisan. The proportion of wage-workers in the first sub-group is 29.4% in Group I and 31.2% in Group II, whereas in the second sub-group of Group I it is only 14.1%. Similarly, the agriculturist who works for a buyer-up is more akin to the non-agriculturist who does the same (23.2% and 27.4% wage-workers respectively) than to the agriculturist artisan. This shows us that the general prevalence of capitalist commodity relations in the country tends to reduce to one level the agriculturist and the non-agriculturist engaged in industry. This levelling process is brought out even more saliently by the data on the incomes of handicraftsmen. The second sub-group, as we have said, is an exception; but if, instead of the figures showing the percentage of wage-workers, we take the average number of wage-workers per establishment, we shall find that the agriculturist artisans are more akin to the non-agriculturist artisans (0.23 and 0.43 wage-workers per establishment respectively) than to the agriculturists in the other sub-groups. The average number of workers per establishment among the artisans of both groups is almost the same (1.7 and 1.8), whereas in the sub-groups of each group this average differs very considerably (Group I—2.6 and 1.7; Group II—2.5 and 1.8).

The average figures per establishment in each sub-group also reveal the interesting fact that the number is lowest among the artisans of both groups: 1.7 and 1.8 workers per workshop respectively. This means that production is most scattered among artisans, the individual producers are most isolated, and co-operation in production least practised. First place in this respect is held by the first sub-group of each group, that is, by the small masters who produce for the market. The number of people engaged in the workshops in these sub-groups is the largest (2.6 and 2.5 persons); here handicraftsmen with big families are the most numerous (20.3% and 18.5% have 3 or more workers in the family; the third sub-group of Group I—20.9%—is something of an exception); at the same time the employment of wage-labour is the largest (0.75 and 0.78 wage-workers per workshop); and there is also the largest proportion of big establishments (2.0% and 1.3% of establishments employ six or more wage-workers). Consequently, co-operation in production is here most wide-spread, because of the most extensive employment of wage-labour, and of members of the family (1.8 and 1.7 family workers per establishment; the third sub-group of Group I, with 1.9 persons, is something of an exception).

This latter circumstance brings us to the highly important question of the relation between family labour and wage-labour employed by "handicraftsmen," a relation which prompts us to doubt the correctness of the prevailing Narodnik doctrine that wage-labour in handicraft production merely "supplements" family labour. The Perm Narodniks support this view when they argue on p. 55 that "the identification of the interests of the handicraftsmen with those of the kulaks" is refuted by the fact that the most prosperous handicraftsmen (Group I) have the largest number of family workers, whereas "if the handicraftsman were prompted solely by the profit motive, the sole incentive of the kulak, and not by the desire to consolidate and develop his establishment with the aid of all the members of his family, we should expect the proportion of members of the family who devoted their labours to production to be smallest in this sub-group of establishments" (?!). A strange conclusion! How can any conclusion regarding the role of "personal participation in work" (p. 55) be drawn if nothing is said about wage-labour? If the prosperity of handicraftsmen with large families did not indicate kulak tendencies, we should find among them the *lowest* proportion of wage-workers, the *lowest* proportion of establishments employing them, the *lowest* proportion of establishments with a large number of workers (more than five), and the *smallest* average number of workers per establishment. Actually, however, the most prosperous handicraftsmen (first sub-group) hold *first, and not last* place *in all these respects*, and this despite the fact that they have the largest families and the

largest number of family workers, and constitute the largest proportion of handicraftsmen with three or more
family workers! Clearly, the facts point to the very opposite
of what the Narodniks would have them mean: the handicraftsman does, in fact, strive for profit, and by kulak methods; he takes advantage of his greater prosperity (one of the
conditions for which is the possession of a large family)
to employ wage-labour on a *larger* scale. Having a larger
number of family workers than the other handicraftsmen he
uses this to oust the others by hiring the *largest* number of
workers. "Family co-operation,"about which Mr. V.V. and the
other Narodniks speak so unctuously (cf. *Handicraft Industries*, I, p.14), is a guarantee of the development of capitalist
co-operation. This, of course, will seem a paradox to the
reader who is used to Narodnik prejudices; but it is a fact.
To obtain precise data on this subject, one should know not
only the distribution of the establishments according to
the number of family and of wage-workers (which is given in
the *Sketch*), but also according to the *combination* of family
and wage-labour. The house-to-house returns furnished every
opportunity of making such a combination, of calculating
the number of establishments in each category employing one,
two, etc., wage-workers and classifying them according to
the number of family workers. Unfortunately, this was not
done. In order to make up for this omission, if only partially, let us turn to the work already mentioned, *Handicraft Industries*, where we do find combined tables of establishments classified according to the number of family and
wage-workers. The tables are given for five industries,
embracing a total of 749 establishments with 1,945 workers
(op. cit., I, pp. 59, 78 and 160; III, pp. 87 and 109). In order
to analyse these data with reference to the problem we are
now considering, namely, the relation between family labour and wage-labour, we must divide all the establishments
into groups according to the total number of workers (for
it is the total number of workers which shows the size of the
workshop and the degree of co-operation in production), and
determine the role of family labour and wage-labour in
each group. Let us take four groups: 1) establishments with
one worker; 2) establishments with two to four workers;
3) establishments with five to nine workers, and 4) establish-

ments with ten or more workers. This division according to the total number of workers is all the more necessary, as the establishments with one worker and those with ten, for example, obviously represent entirely different economic types; to combine them and strike "averages" would be utterly absurd as we shall see later in the case of the figures given in the *Sketch*. Grouping the data as indicated, we get the following table:

Establishments grouped according to total number of workers	Number of establishments	Number of			Number of establishments employing wage-workers	Per cent	Number per establishment of		
		Family workers	Wage-workers	Total			Family workers	Wage-workers	Total
Establishments with 1 worker	345	343	2	345	2	0.5	0.995	0.005	1.00
" 2 to 4 workers	319	559	251	810	143	44.8	1.76	0.78	2.54
" 5 to 9 workers	59	111	249	360	53	89.8	1.88	4.22	6.10
" 10 or more workers	26	56	374	430	26	100	2.15	14.38	16.53
Total	749	1,069	876	1,945	224	29.9	1.43	1.16	2.59

These detailed figures fully confirm the proposition advanced above, which seemed so paradoxical at first glance, i.e., the larger the total number of workers in an establishment, the larger the number of family workers employed in it, and the more extensive, consequently, the "family co-operation"; but, at the same time, capitalist co-operation also increases, and does so far more rapidly. Despite the fact that they have a large number of family workers, the more prosperous handicraftsmen employ many additional wage-workers. "Family co-operation" is thus the pledge and foundation of *capitalist co-operation*.

Let us examine the data of the 1894-95 census relating to family and wage-labour. The establishments are divided according to the number of family workers as follows:

						%
Establishments with		0	family	workers	97	1.1
„	„	1	„	„	4,787	53.2
„	„	2	„	„	2,770	30.8
„	„	3	„	„	898	10.0
„	„	4	„	„	279	3.1
„	„	5 or more	„		160	1.8
				Total	8,991	100.0

The preponderance of one-man establishments should be noted: they constitute more than half the total. Even if we were to assume that all the establishments that combine family labour with wage-labour have no more than one family worker each, we would still find that 2,500 of them would be run by one man. These are the representatives of the most scattered producers, representatives of the most disunited small workshops—a disunity that is generally characteristic of the much-vaunted "people's production." Let us take a glance at the opposite pole, the largest workshops:

		%	Number of wage-workers*	Wage-workers per estab-lishment
Establishments with				
0 wage-workers	6,567	73.1	—	—
1 „ „	1,537	17.2	1,537	1
2 „ „	457	5.1	914	2
3 „ „	213	2.3	639	3
4 „ „	88	0.9	352	4
5 „ „	44	0.5	220	5
6-9 „ „	41⎬85	0.4⎬0.9	290⎬1,242	7.1⎬14.6
10 or more „	44	0.5	952	21.7
Total	8,991	100	4,904	0.5

Thus we see that the "small" establishments of the handicraftsmen sometimes attain imposing dimensions: nearly one-fourth of the total number of wage-workers is concentrated in the 85 largest establishments; on an average, each such establishment employs 14.6 wage-workers. These handicraftsmen

---

* Computed from the data in the *Sketch* (p. 54 and total number of wage-workers).

are already employers, owners of capitalist establishments.* Co-operation on capitalist lines is widely employed in them: with 15 workers per establishment, division of labour is possible on a fairly extensive scale, there is a big saving on premises and tools, of which a larger quantity and greater variety can be used. Their purchase of raw material and the sale of the product are necessarily conducted on a large scale; this considerably reduces the cost of raw material and its delivery, facilitates sales, and makes proper commercial relations possible. When we come to consider the data on incomes we shall find confirmation of this in the 1894-95 census. At the moment it will be sufficient to mention these generally-known theoretical propositions. It should, therefore, be clear that the technical and economic features of these establishments also differ radically from those of the one-man workshops, and it is really astonishing that the Perm statisticians should nevertheless have decided *to combine* them and compute general "averages" from them. It may be said a priori that such averages will be absolutely fictitious, and that the analysis of the household statistics, in addition to dividing the handicraftsmen into groups and sub-groups, should also have divided them into categories based upon the number of workers per establishment (both family and wage-workers). Unless such a division is made, there can be no question of obtaining accurate data on incomes, or on the conditions of purchase of raw material and sale of products, or on the technique of production, or on the relative status of the wage-worker and the owner of the one-man establishment, or on the relation between the big and small workshops—all of which are items of the highest importance for a study of the economics of "handicraft industry." The Perm investigators endeavour, of course, to underrate the importance of the capitalist workshops. If there are establishments with five or more family workers, they argue, that means that competition between the "capitalist" and the "handicraft

---

* The overwhelming majority of our "factories" (so called in the official statistics), actually 15,000 out of 21,000, employ less than 16 workers. See *Directory of Factories for 1890*.

form of production" (sic!) can only have significance when the number of wage-workers exceeds five per establishment, and such establishments constitute only 1% of the total. The argument is purely artificial: in the first place, establishments with five family workers and five wage-workers are a pure abstraction, resulting from an inadequate analysis of the facts, for wage-labour is combined with family labour. An establishment with three family workers will, by hiring another three workers, have more than five workers and, compared with the one-man establishments, will occupy an exceptional competitive position. Secondly, if the statisticians really wanted to investigate the question of "competition" between the various establishments, dividing them according to the number of wage-workers they employ, why did they not make use of the data of the house-to-house census? Why did they not group the establishments according to the number of workers and show the size of their incomes? Would it not have been more appropriate for statisticians who had such rich material at their disposal to make a real study of the facts, instead of treating the reader to all sorts of stuff of their own invention and hastily abandoning facts in order to "do battle" with the adversaries of Narodism?

"... From the standpoint of the supporters of capitalism, this percentage may, perhaps, be considered sufficient ground for the prediction that the handicraft form must inevitably degenerate into the capitalist form; but in this respect it does not actually represent an alarming symptom at all, especially in view of the following circumstances..." (p. 56).

Charming, is it not? Instead of taking the trouble to sift the available material for precise data *on the capitalist* establishments, the authors *combined* them with the one-man establishments and then began to controvert imaginary "predictors"!—We do not know what these "supporters of capitalism" who are so repugnant to the Perm statisticians are likely "to predict," but for our part we can only say that all these phrases merely cover an attempt to evade the facts. And the facts show that there is no special "handicraft form of production" (that is an invention of "handicraft" economists), that the small commodity producers give rise to large capitalist establishments (in the tables we found a handicraftsman employing 65 wage-workers!—p. 169), and that it was the investigators' duty to group the data in such a way that we could examine this process and compare the various establishments *insofar as they approximate capitalist enterprises*. The Perm statisticians not only failed to do this themselves, but even deprived us of the opportunity of doing so, for in the tables all the establishments in a given sub-group are lumped together so that it is impossible to separate the factory owner from the one-man producer. The compilers cover up the omission with meaningless aphorisms. The large establishments, you see, constitute only 1% of the total, so that if they are excluded, the conclusions based on the remaining 99% will not be affected (p. 56). But this one per cent, this one-hundredth part, is not commensurate with the others! One large establishment is equal to more than 15 establishments of the one-man producers who account for over 30 "hundredths" (of the total number of establishments)! This calculation relates to the number of workers. And if we take the gross output, or net income, we shall find that one large establishment is not equal to 15, but perhaps to 30 other establishments.* *One-fourth* of all the wage-workers is concentrated in this "one-hundredth" of the establishments, an average of 14.6 workers per establishment. To give the reader some idea of the significance of this latter figure, let us take the figures given for Perm Gubernia in the *Collection of Data on Factory Industry in Russia* (published by the Department of Commerce and Manufactures). As the figures vary considerably from year to year, we shall take the average for seven years (1885-91). The result for Perm Gubernia is 885 "factories and works" (as understood by the official statistics), with an aggregate output of 22,645,000 rubles and a total of 13,006 wage-workers, which gives us an "average" of 14.6 workers per factory.

---

* We shall presently give data showing the distribution of establishments according to net income. We learn that the aggregate net income of 2,376 establishments with the lowest income (up to 50 rubles)=77,900 rubles, while that of 80 establishments with the highest income=83,150 rubles. The average per "establishment," therefore, is 32 rubles and 1,039 rubles respectively.

In confirmation of their opinion that the large establishments are of no great significance, the compilers of the *Sketch* refer to the fact that very few (8%) of the number of wage-workers employed by the handicraftsmen are employed by the year, the majority being piece-workers (37%), seasonal workers (30%) and day labourers (25%, p. 51). The piece-workers "usually work in their own homes with their own implements and maintain themselves," while the day labourers are engaged "temporarily," like agricultural labourers. That being the case, "we cannot regard the relatively large number of wage-workers as unquestionable proof that these establishments are of the capitalist type" (56).... "It is our conviction that neither the piece-workers, nor the day labourers in general constitute the cadres of a working class similar to the West-European proletariat; only those who work regularly throughout the year can form these cadres."

All praise to the Perm Narodniks for their interest in the relation between the Russian wage-workers and the "West-European proletariat." The question is an interesting one, there's no gainsaying that! Nevertheless, from statisticians we would have preferred to hear statements based on fact, and not on "conviction." For, after all, the mere utterance of one's "conviction" will not always convince others.... Would it not have been better to give more facts, instead of telling the reader about the "convictions" of Mr. X or Mr. Y? How incredibly few facts on the position of the wage-workers, working conditions, working hours in the establishments of various size, the families of the wage-workers, etc., are given in the *Sketch*. If the only purpose of the argument on the difference between the Russian workers and the West-European proletariat was to hide this omission, we should have to retract our praise....

All we learn about wage-workers from the *Sketch* is their division into four categories: annual, seasonal, piece and day workers. To get some idea of these categories, we have to turn to the data scattered throughout the book. The number of workers in each category and their earnings are given for 29 industries (out of 43). In these 29 industries there are 4,795 wage-workers, earning a total of 233,784 rubles. In all the 43 industries, there are 4,904 wage-workers with aggregate earnings amounting to 238,992 rubles. Thus, our summary embraces 98% of the wage-workers and their earnings. Here, en regard,* are the figures of the *Sketch*** and of our summary:

	Number of wage-workers according to *Sketch*	%	Number of wage-workers	%	Total (rubles)	Per worker (rubles)	%***
				Figures of our summary		Their earnings:	
Annual	379	8	351	7.4	26,978	76.8	100
Seasonal	1,496	30	1,432	29.8	40,958	28.6	37
Piece	1,812	37	1,577	32.9	92,357	58.5	76.1
Day	1,217	25	1,435	29.9	73,491	51.2	66.7
Total	4,904	100	4,795	100	233,784	48.7	

In the *Sketch* summary there are either mistakes or misprints. But that is by the way. The point of chief interest is the data on earnings. The earnings of the piece-workers, of whom the *Sketch* says that "essentially, piece-work is the nearest stage on the road to economic independence" (p. 51—also, no doubt, "according to our conviction"?), are *considerably lower* than those of the worker employed by the year. If the statement of the statisticians that the master usually finds board for the annual worker, whereas the piece-worker has to find his own, is based on fact and not merely on "conviction," the difference will be even greater. The Perm master handicraftsmen have chosen a queer way to place their workers on the "road to independence"! It consists in *lowering wages....* The fluctuations in the working season, as we shall see, are not big enough to explain this difference. Further, it is very interesting to note that a day labourer's earnings equal 66.7% of an annual worker's. Hence, each day labourer is occupied on an average for about eight months in the year. Obviously, it would be far more correct to refer to this as a "temporary" diversion from industry (if the day labourers are really diverted

---

* For purposes of comparison.—*Ed.*
** P. 50. The *Sketch* does not summarise the figures for earnings.
*** The earnings of an annual worker are taken as 100.

from industry of their own accord, and not because the master does not furnish them with work), than as the "predominance of the seasonal element in wage-labour" (p. 52).

III

"COMMUNAL-LABOUR CONTINUITY"

The data collected by the handicraft census which indicate the foundation dates of practically all the establishments investigated are of great interest. Here are the general data on the subject:

Number of establish-
ments founded before 1845 640
in 1845-55 251
„ 1855-65 533
„ 1865-75 1,339
„ 1875-85 2,652
„ 1885-95 3,469

Total 8,884

Thus, we see that the post-Reform period has stimulated a big development in handicraft industry. It seems the conditions favouring this development have been and are operating with ever-growing force as time goes on, since each succeeding decade has witnessed the opening of more and more establishments. This fact is clear evidence of the intensity with which the development of commodity production, the separation of agriculture from industry, and the growth of commerce and industry in general are proceeding among the peasantry. We say "separation of agriculture from industry," for this separation begins earlier than the separation of the agriculturists from the industrialists: every enterprise which produces for the market gives rise to exchange between agriculturists and industrialists. Hence, the appearance of such an enterprise implies that the agriculturists cease to produce articles in their homes and purchase them in the market, and to make such purchases the peasant has to sell agricultural produce. The growing number of commercial and industrial establishments thus implies a growing social division of labour, the general basis of commodity economy and of capitalism.*

The opinion has been expressed in Narodnik literature that the rapid development of *small production* in industry since the Reform is not a phenomenon of a capitalist nature. The argument is that the growth of small production proves its strength and vitality, as compared with large-scale production (Mr. V.V.). This argument is absolutely false. The growth of small production among the peasantry signifies the appearance of new industries, the conversion of new branches of raw material processing into independent spheres of industry, progress in the social division of labour, the initial process of capitalist development, while the swallowing-up of small by large establishments implies a further step forward by capitalism, leading to the triumph of its higher forms. The spread of small establishments among the peasantry extends commodity economy and prepares the ground for capitalism (by creating petty masters and wage-labourers), while the swallowing-up of small establishments by manufactories and factories implies that big capitalism is utilising ground that has been prepared. The simultaneous existence of these two, seemingly contradictory, processes in one country actually has nothing contradictory in it: it is quite natural that in a more developed part of the country, or in a more developed sphere of industry, capitalism should progress by drawing small handicraftsmen into the mechanised factory, while in more remote regions, or in backward branches of industry, the process of capitalist development is only in its initial stage and manifests itself in the appearance of new branches and new industries. Capitalist manufacture "conquers but partially the domain of national production, and always rests on the handicrafts of the town and the domestic industry of the rural districts as its ultimate basis (Hintergrund). If it destroys these in one form, in particular branches, at certain points, it calls them up again elsewhere..." (*Das Kapital*, I², S. 779). [116]

---

* Consequently, if Mr. N. — on's attacks on the "separation of industry from agriculture" were not the platonic lamentations of a romanticist, he should also bewail the appearance of every handicraft establishment.

The figures showing the dates the establishments were founded are also inadequately treated in the *Sketch*: all the information given is for uyezds, and not for groups or sub-groups; nor is there any other grouping (according to size of establishment, whether located in the centre of the industry or in the surrounding villages, etc.). Although they did not analyse the census data in accordance with their own system of groups and sub-groups, the Perm Narodniks here too found it necessary to treat the reader to sermons that are amazing for their ultra-Narodnik unctuousness and ... absurdity. The Perm statisticians have made the discovery that in the "handicraft form of production" there prevails a specific "form of continuity" of establishments, namely, "communal-labour continuity," whereas the system that prevails in capitalist industry is "property-inheritance continuity," and that "communal-labour continuity organically converts the wage-worker into an independent master" (sic!), which finds expression in the fact that when the owner of an establishment dies and there are no family workers among the heirs, the industry passes to another family, "perhaps to that of a wage-worker employed in the very same establishment," and also in the fact that "community land tenure guarantees the labour industrial independence of both the owner of a handicraft industrial establishment and his wage-worker" (pp. 7, 68, et al.).

We have no doubt that this "communal-labour principle of continuity in the handicraft industries," as invented by the Perm Narodniks, will occupy a fitting place in the history of literature, alongside the sentimental theory of "people's production" propounded by Messrs. V.V., N. —on, and others. Both theories are of the same mould, both embellish and distort the truth with the help of Manilovian phrases. Everybody knows that the establishments, materials, tools, etc., of the handicraftsmen are private *property* which is transmitted by *inheritance*, and not by some sort of communal law; that the village community in no way guarantees independence even in agriculture, let alone industry, and that the same economic struggle and exploitation goes on within the community as outside it. What has been turned into the special theory of the "communal-labour principle" is the simple fact that the small master, owning very little capital, has to work himself, and that the wage-worker *may* become a master (if he is thrifty and abstemious, of course); examples of this are cited in the *Sketch* on p. 69.... All the theoreticians of the petty bourgeoisie have always consoled themselves with the fact that in small production a worker *may* become a master, and none of their ideals have ever gone beyond the conversion of the workers into small masters. The *Sketch* even makes an attempt to cite "statistical data confirming the principle of communal-labour continuity" (45). These data relate to the tanning industry. Out of 129 establishments, 90 (i.e., 70%) have been founded since 1870; yet in 1869 there were 161 handicraft tanneries (according to the "list of inhabited places"), while in 1895 there were 153. That is to say, tanneries have been transferred from some families to others—and this is regarded as the "principle of communal-labour continuity." It would be absurd, of course, to argue against this anxiety to detect some special "principle" in the fact that small establishments are easily opened and just as easily shut down, freely pass from one hand to another, and so on. Let us only add, with regard to the tanning industry in particular, that, firstly, the dates of origin of the establishments indicate that this industry developed far *more slowly* than the other industries, and that, secondly, it is absolutely useless to compare 1869 with 1895, for the term "handicraft tannery" is constantly confused with the term "leather factory." In the 1860s the overwhelming majority of the "leather factories" in Perm Gubernia (according to the factory statistics) had an output valued at less than 1,000 rubles (see the *Ministry of Finance Yearbook*, Part I, St. Petersburg, 1869. Tables and notes); in the 1890s establishments with an output of less than 1,000 rubles were, on the one hand, excluded from the list of factories, and the list of "handicraft tanneries," on the other, happened to include many establishments with an output of over 1,000 rubles, some even with an output of 5,000 rubles, 10,000 rubles and more (*Sketch*, p. 70, and pp. 149 and 150 of the tables). What is the use of comparing data for 1869 and 1895 when no definite distinction is made between handicraft and factory-type tanneries?

Thirdly, even if it were true that the number of tanneries has decreased, might this not mean that many small establishments have been closed down and that larger establishments have been gradually opened in their place? Are we to believe that such a "change" also confirms the "principle of communal-labour continuity"?

And the crowning incongruity is that all this sugary talk about the "communal-labour principle," the "guarantee of communal-labour independence," and the like, refers to the tanning industry, where the agriculturist handicraftsmen represent the purest type of petty bourgeois (see below), an industry which is highly concentrated in *three* large establishments (factories) that have been included in the list side by side with the one-man handicraft and artisan establishments. Here are the figures showing this concentration:

In all, there are 148 establishments in this industry. Workers: 267 family+172 wage-workers=439; aggregate output=151,022 rubles; net income=26,207 rubles. Among these establishments there are 3 with 0 family workers+ 65 wage-workers=65. Value of output=44,275 rubles; net income=3,391 rubles (p. 70 of the text, and pp. 149 and 150 of the tables).

In other words, in *three* establishments out of 148 ("only 2.1%," as the *Sketch* reassuringly puts it—p. 76) there is a concentration of *nearly one-third* of the total output of the "handicraft tanning industry," yielding their owners thousands of rubles of income without their taking any part in production. We shall encounter many similar incongruities in relation to other industries, too. But in describing this industry, the authors of the *Sketch* paused, by way of exception, to discuss the three establishments mentioned. With regard to one of them we are told that the owner (an agriculturist!) "is apparently occupied exclusively in commerce, having his leather shops in the village of Beloyarskoye and the city of Ekaterinburg" (pp. 76-77). This is a specimen of how capital invested in production combines with capital invested in commerce—a fact that should be noted by the authors of the *Sketch*, who depict "kulakdom" and commercial operations as something adventitious, divorced from production! In another establishment, the family consists of five males, not one of whom works at the trade: "the father is engaged in commercial operations connected with his industry, and the sons (varying in age from 18 to 53), all of them educated, have apparently taken to other and more congenial pursuits than transferring hides from one vat to another and washing them" (p. 77). The authors magnanimously concede that these establishments are "capitalist in character"—"but how far the future of these enterprises is ensured on the principle of transmission as inherited property is a question to which only the future can give its decisive answer" (76). How profound! "The future is a question to which only the future can give an answer." The sacred truth! But does it warrant a distortion of the present?

ARTICLE TWO

(IV. The Agriculture of "Handicraftsmen." — V. Large and Small
Establishments.—The Incomes of the Handicraftsmen)

IV

THE AGRICULTURE OF "HANDICRAFTSMEN"

The house-to-house census of master handicraftsmen, big
and small, provide very interesting data on the agriculture
they engage in. Here are the figures, divided according to
the sub-groups, as given in the *Sketch*:

	Per household			Percentage of households	
Sub-groups	Area cultivated (dessiatines)	Horses*	Cows*	Owning no horses	Owning no cows
1. Commodity producers	7.1	2.1	2.2	7.4	5
2. Artisans	6.2	1.9	2.1	9.0	6
3. Working for a buyer-up	4.5	1.4	1.3	16.0	13
In all	6.3	1.8	2.0	9.5	6

We thus see that the more prosperous the handicraftsmen are as industrialists, the more prosperous they are as
agriculturists. The lower they rank in production, the
lower they rank in agriculture. The handicraft census data,
therefore, fully confirm the opinion already expressed in
literature, namely, that the differentiation of the handicraftsmen in industry goes hand in hand with their differentiation as peasants in agriculture (A. Volgin, *The Substantiation of Narodism, etc.*, pp. 211, et seq.). As the
wage-workers employed by the handicraftsmen are on an
even lower (or not higher) level than the handicraftsmen who
work for buyers-up, we are entitled to conclude that the

* In the *Sketch* there is an obvious misprint in this column (see
p. 58), which we have corrected.

proportion of impoverished agriculturists among them is even higher. The house-to-house census, as we have already said, did not cover the wage-workers. At any rate, even the figures cited clearly show how ludicrous is the assertion in the *Sketch* that "community land tenure guarantees the labour industrial independence of both the owner of a handicraft industrial establishment and his wage-worker."

The absence of detailed information on the agricultural activity of the one-man producers and small and large masters is very acutely felt in the data now under examination. To fill the gap, if only partially, we must turn to the data for the separate industries; sometimes in the *Sketch* we come across information on the number of agricultural labourers employed by masters,* but no general summary is given.

Take the tanner agriculturists—131 households. They employ 124 agricultural labourers; they cultivate 16.9 dessiatines and possess 4.6 horses per household; they have 4.1 cows each (p. 71). The wage-workers (73 annual and 51 seasonal) receive 2,492 rubles in wages, or 20.1 rubles each, whereas the average wage of a worker in the tanning industry is 52 rubles. Here too, therefore, we observe the phenomenon common to all capitalist countries—the status of the agricultural labourer is lower than that of the industrial labourer. The "handicraft" tanners obviously represent the purest type of peasant bourgeoisie, and the celebrated "combination of industry with agriculture" so highly praised by the Narodniks is nothing more than the prosperous owners of commercial and industrial establishments transferring *capital* from commerce and industry to agriculture, and paying their farm labourers incredibly low wages.**

---

* It is well known that among the peasants even industrial workers are often compelled to perform agricultural work. Cf. *Handicraft Industries, etc.,* III, p. 7.

** The seasonal labourer in agriculture always receives more than half the yearly wage. But let us assume that in this case the seasonal labourers receive only half the wage of the annual worker. The wage of an annual worker will then be $\left(2{,}492 : \left(73 + \frac{51}{2}\right) \right) = 25.5$ rubles. According to the Department of Agriculture, the average wages over a period of 10 years (1881-91) for a farm labourer employed by the year in Perm Gubernia was 50 rubles with board.

Take the handicraft oil-millers. The agriculturists among them number 173. A household, on the average, cultivates 10.1 dessiatines and possesses 3.5 horses and 3.3 cows. There is no household without at least one horse and a cow. Together, they employ 98 labourers (annual and seasonal) who receive in wages a total of 3,438 rubles, or an average of 35.1 rubles each. "The refuse, or oil-cake that remains after the milling process, serves as excellent cattle feed, thanks to which it is possible to manure the fields on a larger scale. Thus the household derives a triple advantage from the industry: the income from the industry itself, the income from livestock, and a higher yield from the fields" (164). "Agriculture is carried on by them" (the oil-millers) "on a wide scale, and many of them, not contenting themselves with the community allotments they get, also rent land from the poor households" (168). The data showing the distribution of flax and hemp growing by uyezds reveal "a certain connection between the area under flax and hemp and the distribution of the oil-milling industry among the uyezds of the gubernia" (170).

Hence, the commercial and industrial enterprises in this case are those known as technical agricultural industries, the development of which is always characteristic of the progress of commercial and capitalist agriculture.

Take the flour-millers. Most of them engage in agriculture—385 out of 421. A household, on the average, cultivates 11.0 dessiatines and possesses 3.0 horses and 3.5 cows. They employ 307 workers who are also agriculturists and who receive wages totalling 6,211 rubles. Like the oil-milling industry, "flour-milling serves the millers as a means of marketing the produce of their own farms in the most profitable form" (178).

These examples, we think, should be quite sufficient to show how absurd it is to regard the term "handicraftsman agriculturist" as signifying something homogeneous and uniform. All the agriculturists we have cited are representatives of the agricultural petty bourgeoisie, and to combine these types with the rest of the peasantry, including even the ruined households, is to obscure the most characteristic features of reality.

In the concluding part of their description of the oil-milling industry, the compilers try to argue against the "capitalist doctrine" that the stratification of the peasants is capitalist evolution. This proposition, they claim, is based on the "absolutely arbitrary assertion that this stratification is a factor of most recent times and is an obvious symptom of the rapid de facto spread of the capitalist regime among the peasantry despite the existence of de jure community land tenure" (176). The compilers argue that the village community has never precluded property stratifications, but it "does not perpetuate them, does not give rise to classes"; "these transitory stratifications have not become more marked with the lapse of time, but, on the contrary, have been gradually obliterated" (177). Naturally, such an assertion, in substantiation of which the artels (of which more anon, § VII), family divisions (sic!) and land redivisions (!) are cited, can only evoke a smile. To say that the claim that differentiation of the peasantry is growing and spreading is an "arbitrary" one, means to ignore well-known facts: peasants lose their horses and abandon the land on a mass scale and this is coupled with "technical progress in peasant farming" (cf. *Progressive Trends in Peasant Farming* by Mr. V. V.); the increase in the letting and mortgaging of allotments is coupled with increased land renting; the increase in the number of commercial and industrial establishments is coupled with an increase in the number of migratory industrialists, i. e., vagrant wage-workers; etc., etc.

The house-to-house census should have provided a wealth of material on the highly interesting question of how the incomes and earnings of the agriculturist handicraftsmen compare with the incomes of the non-agriculturists. All the data on this subject are to be found in the tables, but the *Sketch* gives no summary, and we have had to compile one from the material contained in the book. This summary was based, firstly, on those given in the *Sketch* for the individual industries. All we had to do in this case was to add together the data for the various industries. But such summaries are not given in tabular form for all industries. In some cases it was clear that mistakes or misprints had crept in—which is only natural in the absence of check totals. Secondly, the summary was based on a selection of figures contained in the descriptions of certain industries. Thirdly, where neither of these sources was available, we had to turn directly to the tables (for example, in the case of the last industry: "mining"). It goes without saying that owing to this diversity in the character of the material contained in our summary, mistakes and inaccuracies were bound to have crept in. Nevertheless, we believe that although the grand totals of our summary do not coincide with the totals of the table, the deductions drawn from it may fully serve their purpose, for whatever corrections might be introduced, the average magnitudes and proportions (and it is these alone that we use for our deductions) would be but slightly changed. For example, according to the totals of the tables in the *Sketch*, the gross income per worker is 134.8 rubles, and according to our summary it is 133.3 rubles; the net income per family worker is 69.0 rubles and 68.0 rubles respectively; the earnings per wage-worker are 48.7 rubles and 48.6 rubles respectively.

Here are the results of our summary showing gross income, net income, and the earnings of wage-workers in each group and sub-group (see table on page 392).

The chief results of this tabulation are as follows:

1) The non-agricultural industrial population takes an incomparably bigger part in industry (relative to their numbers) than the agricultural population. The number of non-agriculturist workers is less than half the number of agriculturist workers. But they account for nearly half the gross output: 1,276,772 rubles out of a total of 2,655,007 rubles, or 48.1%. As regards income from production, that is, the net income of the masters plus the workers' wages, the non-agriculturists even surpass the agriculturists, accounting for 647,666 rubles out of a total of 1,260,335 rubles, or 51.4%. Consequently, we find that, while they are a minority in numbers, the non-agricultural industrialists do not lag behind the agriculturists in volume of output. This fact is of great importance when we come to judge the traditional Narodnik theory that agriculture is the "main foundation" of so-called handicraft industry.

From this, other conclusions follow naturally:

2) The gross output per non-agriculturist worker (gross income) is considerably higher than that of the agricultur-

Group	Sub-group	Number of establishments	Number of			Gross income (rubles)		Net income (rubles)		Wages (rubles)		Net income and wages combined	Number of households in debt
			Family workers	Wage-workers	Total	Total	Per worker	Total	Per family worker	Total	Per wage-worker		
I	1	2,239	4,122	1,726	5,848	758,493	129.7	204,004	49.5	74,558	43.2	278,562	225
I	2	2,841	4,249	712	4,961	383,441	77.3	186,719	43.9	34,937	49.0	221,656	93
I	3	1,016	1,878	586	2,464	236,301	95.9	91,916	48.9	20,535	35.0	112,451	304
Total for Group I		6,096	10,249	3,024	13,273	1,378,235	103.8	482,639	47.1	130,030	43.0	612,669	622
II	1	959	1,672	738	2,410	605,509	251.2	220,713	132.0	45,949	62.2	266,662	176
II	2	595	876	272	1,148	178,916	155.8	90,203	102.9	18,404	67.6	108,607	51
II	3	1,320	2,231	852	3,083	492,347	159.7	229,108	102.7	43,289	50.8	272,397	262
Total for Group II		2,874	4,779	1,862	6,641	1,276,772	192.2	540,024	113.0	107,642	57.8	647,666	489
Grand total		8,970	15,028	4,886	19,914	2,655,007	133.3	1,022,663	68.0	237,672	48.6	1,260,335	1,111

ist: 192.2 rubles as against 103.8 rubles, or nearly *twice* as much. As we shall see later, the working season of the non-agriculturists is longer than that of the agriculturists, but the difference is by no means so very great, so that the higher labour productivity of the non-agriculturists is beyond all doubt. This difference is smallest in the third sub-group— the handicraftsmen who work for buyers-up—which is quite natural.

3) The net income of the non-agriculturist masters, big and small, is *more than double* that of the agriculturists: 113.0 rubles, as against 47.1 rubles (nearly two-and-a-half times as much). This difference is to be observed in all the sub-groups, but it is the biggest in the first, among the handi-craftsmen who produce for the market. It goes without saying that this difference is least of all to be explained by the difference in the length of working periods. There can be no doubt that it is due to the fact that *the tie with the land lowers the incomes of the industrialists*; the market discounts the incomes derived by the handicraftsmen from agriculture, and the agriculturists have to content themselves with lower earnings. This is probably aggravated by the fact that the agriculturists suffer bigger losses on sales, spend more for materials and are more dependent on the merchants. In any case, it is a fact that the *handicraftsman's tie with the land reduces his earnings*. There is no need to say more about the enormous significance of this fact which throws a true light on the meaning of the "power of the soil" in modern society. We need only recall what a tremendous factor low earnings are in preserving methods of production that are primitive and entail bondage, in retarding the use of machinery, and in lowering the workers' standard of living.*

---

* On this last point (which is the first in importance) we would say that it is unfortunate that the *Sketch* furnishes no data on the standard of living of the agriculturists and non-agriculturists. But other investigators have noted that it is a common phenomenon for the living standard of the non-agriculturist industrialists to be incomparably higher than that of the "raw" agriculturists, and this is equally true of Perm Gubernia. Cf. *Reports and Investigations of Handicraft Industry in Russia* published by the Ministry of Agriculture and State Property, Vol. III, Yegunov's article. The author points to the completely "urban" standard of living in some

4) The wages of non-agriculturist wage-workers are also everywhere higher than those of agriculturists, but the difference is by no means as great as in the case of the incomes of the masters. Generally, in all three sub-groups, the wage-worker employed by the agriculturist handicraftsman earns an average of 43.0 rubles, while the wage-worker employed by the non-agriculturist earns 57.8 rubles, or one-third more. This difference *may* to a large extent (*but not entirely*) be due to the difference in the length of the working season. As to the relation between this difference and the tie with the land, we cannot form a judgement, for we have no data on agriculturist and non-agriculturist wage-workers. Apart from the length of the working season, the difference in the level of requirements, of course, also plays its part.

5) The difference between the size of the masters' incomes and workers' wages is incomparably larger in the case of the non-agriculturists than in that of the agriculturists: taking all three sub-groups, the income of a non-agriculturist master is almost double a worker's wages (113 rubles and 57.8 rubles respectively), whereas among the agriculturists the income of the master is only slightly higher— *4.1 rubles* more (47.1 and 43.0)! If these figures are astonishing, even more so are those relating to the agriculturist artisans (I, 2), where the income of the master is *less* than a worker's wages! But the reason for this will become quite clear later, when we cite data showing the tremendous difference between the size of incomes in large and small establishments. By increasing productivity of labour, the large establishments make it possible to pay wages exceeding the income of the poor, individual handicraftsmen working alone, whose "independence," in view of their subjection to the market, is quite fictitious. This vast difference between the incomes of the large and the small establishments is to be observed in both groups, but much more so in the case of the agriculturists (due to the more depressed state of

---

of the landless villages, to the endeavour of the non-agriculturist handicraftsman to dress and live "as decent people do" (European clothes, even to the starched shirt; samovar; larger consumption of tea, sugar, white bread, beef, etc.). The author draws on the family budgets contained in Zemstvo statistical publications.

the small handicraftsmen). The negligible difference between the income of the small master and the wages of the
worker clearly shows that the income of the *small* agriculturist handicraftsman who employs no wage-workers is
not higher, and often even lower than the wages of a hired
worker. As a matter of fact, the net income of the master
(47.1 rubles per family worker) is the *average* for all establishments, large and small, for both the owners of factories
and of one-man workshops. Naturally, in the case of the
big masters, the difference between their net income and the
wages of their workers is not 4 rubles, but anything from
ten to one hundred times as much, which means that the
income of the small one-man workshop is considerably below 47 rubles; in other words, this income is *not higher,
but often even lower* than the wages of a worker. Handicraft
census data on the division of establishments according to net
income (see below, § V) fully bear out this seemingly paradoxical conclusion. But these data relate to all the establishments in general, to agriculturists and non-agriculturists
alike, and that is why this deduction from the above table
is so important: we have learnt that it is the agriculturists
whose earnings are lowest, in other words, that "the tie
with the land" greatly reduces earnings.

We have already said, when discussing the difference
between the incomes of the agriculturists and the non-agriculturists, that this difference cannot be explained by the
difference in the length of the working periods. Let us now
examine the census data on this subject. One of the items
in the census programme, as we learn from the "introduction,"
was the investigation of the "intensity of production throughout the year, on the basis of the number of family members
and wage-workers engaged in production each month" (p. 14).
Since this was a house-to-house census, in other words, since
each establishment was investigated separately (unfortunately, a specimen of the house-to-house census forms is not appended to the *Sketch*), it must be assumed that information
regarding the number of workers engaged each month, or
the number of working months in the year, was gathered
in the case of each establishment. In the *Sketch* these data
are gathered in one table (pp. 57 and 58), in which the number of workers (family and wage-workers together) *engaged*

in each month of the year is given for each of the sub-groups of both groups.

The attempt of the 1894-95 handicraft census to determine with such precision how many months in the year the handicraftsmen work is highly instructive and interesting. Indeed, without such information the data on incomes and earnings would be incomplete, and the statistical calculations would be only approximate. But, unfortunately, the data on working periods have been very scantily analysed: apart from this general table,. all we are given is information on the number of workers engaged each month in only a few industries, sometimes divided according to groups, sometimes not; division according to sub-groups has not been made for any industry. The separation of the large establishments from the small would have been particularly valuable in this instance, for we have every reason to expect—both a priori and on the basis of data provided by other investigators of handicraft industry—that the working periods of the big and the small handicraftsmen are not the same. Furthermore, the table itself on page 57 is apparently not free from mistakes or misprints (for example, in the months February, August and November; columns 2 and 3 of Group II have evidently been mixed up, for the number of workers in the third sub-group is larger than in the second). Even when these inaccuracies are corrected (and the corrections are sometimes only approximate), the table gives rise to no little misgiving, which renders the use of it risky. For instance, when we examine the data in the table by sub-groups, we find that in the third sub-group (Group I) the maximum number of workers, 2,911, are engaged in December. Yet, according to the *Sketch*, the total number of workers in the third sub-group is 2,551. Similarly, in the third sub-group of Group II: maximum number of workers 3,221, actual number 3,077. On the other hand, in the sub-groups the *maxima* engaged in one of the months are *less* than the actual number of workers. How is this to be explained? Is it because information on this subject was not gathered for all the establishments? That is very likely, although there is no hint of it in the *Sketch*. In the case of the second sub-group of Group II, not only is the maximum number of workers (February) larger than the actual number

(1,882 and 1,163 respectively), but even the *average number* of workers engaged in one month (i.e., the quotient obtained by dividing the total number of workers engaged in the twelve months by 12) is *higher* than the actual number of workers (1,265 and 1,163 respectively)!! Which figure, one asks, did the registrars regard as actual: the average number of workers for the year, the average for some period (winter, say), or the number actually employed in some particular month? An investigation of the monthly number of workers engaged in the separate industries does not help to clear up the puzzle. In the majority of the twenty-three industries for which this information is furnished, the maximum number of workers engaged in any one month of the year is *less* than the actual number of workers. In the case of two industries, the maximum is *higher* than the actual number of workers: in the copper-working industry (239 and 233 respectively) and in the forges (Group II—1,811 and 1,269 respectively). The maximum is equal to the actual number of workers in the case of two industries (rope-making and oil-milling, Group II).

This being the case, we cannot use the data showing the number of workers engaged month by month for a comparison with their earnings, with the actual number of workers employed, etc. All that remains is to treat these data regardless of others, and to compare the maximum and the minimum numbers of workers engaged in each month. This is what is done in the *Sketch*, but the separate months are compared. We consider it more correct to compare winter and summer; for that will enable us to determine how far agriculture diverts workers from industry. We took the average number of workers engaged in winter (October to March) as the standard, and, applying this standard to the number of workers engaged in summer, we arrived at the number of summer working months. By adding up the number of winter and summer months we got the number of working months in the year. Let us illustrate this by an example. In the first sub-group of Group I there were 18,060 workers engaged in the six winter months, which gives us an average of (18,060: 6=) 3,010 workers in one month. In the summer, 12,345 workers were employed; in other words, the summer working season is equal to (12,345:3,010) 4.1 months. Hence, the working period in the first sub-group of Group I amounts to 10.1 months in the year.

This method of analysing the data seemed to us both the most correct and the most convenient. It is the most correct, because it is based on a comparison of winter and summer months, and hence, on an exact determination of the extent to which agriculture diverts workers from industry. That the winter months have been correctly taken is confirmed by the fact that in the October-March period the number of workers in both groups is higher than the average for the year. There is the greatest increase in the number of workers from September to October, and the greatest decrease from March to April. Incidentally, the choice of other months would have had little effect on the conclusions. We consider the method chosen to be the most suitable because it gives an exact figure for the working period which allows us to compare the groups and sub-groups in this respect.

Here are the data obtained by this method:

	Group I Sub-groups			Aver-age	Group II Sub-groups			Aver-age	For the two groups
	1	2	3		1	2	3		
Working period (months)	10.1	9.6	10.5	10.0	10.0	10.4	10.9	10.5	10.2

These figures lead us to conclude that the difference between the working periods for agriculturists and non-agriculturists is *very small*: that of the non-agriculturists is only 5% longer. The smallness of this difference gives rise to doubt as to the correctness of the figures. In order to verify them, we have made some calculations and summaries of material scattered throughout the book and have arrived at the following results:

The *Sketch* furnishes data on the monthly employment of workers in 23 of the 43 industries; the data are given according to groups in the case of 12 (13)* of them but not in the case of the remaining 10 groups. We find that in three of the industries (pitch and tar, dyeing and brick-making) the number of workers is higher in summer than in winter:

---

* There is only one group in the horn industry—Group I.

in the six winter months only 1,953 workers are engaged in all three industries as against 4,918 in the six summer months. In these industries there is a great preponderance of agriculturists over non-agriculturists, the former constituting 85.9% of the total number of workers. It was obviously quite wrong to combine these, so to speak, summer industries with the others in the grand totals for groups, as that meant combining unlike things and artificially raising the number of summer workers in all industries. There are two ways of correcting the error which results from this. The first is to deduct the figures for these three industries from the totals given in the *Sketch* for Groups I and II.* The result is a working period of 9.6 months for Group I, and of 10.4 months for Group II. Here the difference between the two groups is bigger, but still very small—8.3%. The second method of correcting the error is to combine the figures for the twelve industries for which the *Sketch* gives information on the monthly employment of workers in Groups I and II separately. This will embrace 70% of the total number of handicraftsmen, and, what is more, the comparison between Groups I and II will be more correct. We find that in the case of these twelve industries the working period in Group I is only 8.9 months, and in Group II, 10.7 months, while for the two groups together it is 9.7 months. The working period of the non-agriculturists is now 20.2% longer than that of the agriculturists. The agriculturists do not work for 3.1 months in summer, the non-agriculturists for only 1.3 months. Even if we take the maximum difference in the working periods in Groups II and I as the standard, we shall find that not only the differences in the gross output of the workers of Groups I and II, or in the net incomes of their establishments, but even the differences in the wages of agriculturist and non-agriculturist wage-workers *cannot be explained by the difference in the length of the working periods.* Consequently, the conclusion drawn above, namely, that the tie with the land reduces the handicraftsmen's earnings, remains fully valid.

---

* The distribution of the workers in these three industries between Group I and Group II is done approximately, 85.9% being taken as the standard for Group I.

We must therefore conclude that the compilers of the
Sketch are mistaken in their desire to explain the difference
between the earnings of the agriculturists and non-agriculturists by the difference in the length of the working periods.
Their mistake was due to their not attempting to express
the differences in the working periods by exact figures, and
this led them astray. For example, on page 106 of the *Sketch*
it is stated that the difference between the earnings of the
agriculturist and the non-agriculturist furriers "is chiefly
determined by the number of working days devoted to industry." Yet the earnings of the non-agriculturists in this
industry are from two to four times greater than those of
the agriculturists (65 and 280 rubles respectively per family
worker in the first sub-group, and 27 and 62 rubles in the
second sub-group), whereas the working period of the non-
agriculturists is longer by only 28.7% (8.5 months as compared with 6.6).

The fact that the tie with the land lowers earnings could
not escape the attention even of the compilers of the *Sketch*;
but they expressed it in the usual Narodnik formula
on the "superiority" of the handicraft to the capitalist
form: "by combining agriculture with industry, the handicraftsman ... is able to sell his wares cheaper than those of
the factory" (p. 4); in other words, he can manage on smaller
earnings. But where is the "superiority" of the tie with the
land, if the market already so dominates the whole of the
country's industrial life that it discounts this tie by lowering the earnings of the agriculturist handicraftsman;
if capital can take advantage of this "tie" to exert greater
pressure on the agriculturist handicraftsman, who is less
able to defend his interests, to choose a different master, a
different customer, or a different occupation? The lowering
of wages (and of industrial earnings in general) when the
worker (or the small industrialist) has a plot of land is something common to all capitalist countries, and is perfectly well known to all employers who have long ago appreciated the vast "superiority" of workers tied to the land.
Only in the decadent West do they bluntly call a spade a
spade, but in our country the lowering of wages, the
lowering of the living standard of the working population,
the delay in introducing machinery, and the perpetuation

of all sorts of bondage is referred to as the "superiority" of "people's production," which "combines agriculture with industry."...

In concluding our review of the 1894-95 census data on the working period, we cannot refrain from once again expressing our regret that the data obtained have been so incompletely analysed, nor from voicing the hope that this defect will not deter other investigators of this interesting problem. One cannot but admit that the method of investigation—determination of the number of workers employed each month—was very well chosen. Above we have given data for the working period by groups and subgroups. There was some possibility of verifying the data for the groups. But it is utterly impossible to verify the data for the sub-groups, since the book furnishes absolutely no information on the differences in the length of the working period in the various sub-groups. Therefore, in citing these data, we make the reservation that we cannot guarantee their absolute reliability; and if we draw further conclusions, it is only for the purpose of raising this question and drawing the investigators' attention to it. The most important conclusion is that the smallest difference in the working periods in Groups I and II is in the first sub-group (only 1% in all: 10.1 months and 10.0 months); in other words, it is the most prosperous handicraftsmen and the biggest and *wealthiest agriculturists* who are *least diverted from agriculture.* The difference is largest in the case of the artisans (second sub-group: 9.5 months and 10.4 months), that is, the industrialists and *middle* agriculturists least affected by commodity production. It would appear that the prosperous agriculturists are diverted so little from agriculture either because of their larger families or their greater exploitation of wage-labour in industry or their hiring of agricultural labourers, and that the artisans are most diverted from agriculture because they have been less differentiated as agriculturists, have retained patriarchal relations to a great extent, and work directly for agricultural customers who reduce their orders in the summer.*

---

* There is an exception: the dyeing industry is run entirely by artisans, and summer work is greater than winter work.

The "tie with agriculture," the census reveals, has a very marked influence on the *literacy* of the handicraftsmen;—literacy among wage-labourers has *unfortunately* not been investigated. It appears that the non-agricultural population* is *far more literate* than the agricultural, and this feature is to be observed for both men and women in all sub-groups without exception. Here are the census figures (in percentages) on this subject in extenso (p. 62):

		Group I (agriculturists)				Group II (non-agriculturists)				Both groups
		Sub-groups			Average	Sub-groups			Average	
		1	2	3		1	2	3		
"Percentage of literate persons to total"	Males	32	33	20	31	41	45	33	39	33
	Females	9	6	4	7	17	22	14	17	9
"Percentage of literate persons among those directly engaged in production"	Males	39	37	26	36	44	57	51	49	40
	Females	13	17	4	10	53	21	23	30	19
Percentage of families with literate members		49	43	34	44	55	63	50	55	47

It is interesting to note that in the case of the non-agricultural population literacy is spreading far more rapidly among the women than among the men. The proportion of literate males in Group II is 1 ½ to 2 times as great as in Group I, while the proportion of literate females is 2½ to 5³/₄ times as great.

Summarising the conclusions drawn from the 1894-95 census on the subject of "agriculture connected with industry," we may take it as demonstrated that the tie with agriculture:

1) preserves the most backward forms of industry and retards economic development;

2) reduces the handicraftsmen's earnings and income, so that the *most* prosperous sub-groups of agriculturist masters earn, in general and on the average, less than the *least*

---

* We would remind the reader that only one town (and that an uyezd centre) was here included by way of exception: only 1,412, or 29.6 per cent, of the 4,762 family workers in Group II are town dwellers.

prosperous non-agriculturist sub-groups of *wage-workers*, to say nothing of the non-agriculturist masters. The masters of Group I have very low incomes even when compared with the wage-workers of that group—sometimes they are slightly higher and sometimes even lower than the workers' wages;

3) retards the cultural development of the population whose consumption level is lower than that of the non-agriculturists and whose standard of literacy is far behind that of the latter.

These conclusions will be useful later for our assessment of the Narodnik programme of industrial policy.

4) Differentiation among the agriculturist handicraftsmen is seen to run parallel to that of the industrialists. The higher (more prosperous) categories of agriculturists constitute a pure type of peasant bourgeoisie who employ regular and day labourers to run their farms.

5) The working period of the agriculturists is shorter than that of the non-agriculturists, but the difference is very small (5% to 20%).

V

LARGE AND SMALL ESTABLISHMENTS.—THE INCOMES
OF THE HANDICRAFTSMEN

We must dwell in greater detail on the data of the 1894-95 census on *incomes* from handicrafts. The attempt to collect household data on incomes is very instructive, and it would be quite wrong to confine ourselves to general "averages" for the sub-groups (given above). We have already, on more than one occasion, referred to the fictitious nature of "averages" derived by adding together individual handicraftsmen and owners of big establishments and then dividing the total obtained by the number of the components. Let us endeavour to assemble the data contained in the *Sketch* on this subject in order to illustrate this method clearly and prove its fictitious nature and to demonstrate that in scientific investigations and in analysing house-to-house census data handicraftsmen must be grouped in categories according to number of workers (family and wage-workers) employed in the workshop, and all the census data arranged in accordance with these categories.

26*

The compilers of the *Sketch* must have noted the all too obvious fact of higher incomes in the big establishments, and tried to minimise its significance. Instead of giving precise census data on the large establishments (which they could have selected with no difficulty), they again confined themselves to general discussions, arguments and inventions against conclusions which the Narodniks find unpleasant. Let us examine these arguments.

"If in such" (big) "establishments we meet with a family income disproportionately larger than that of the small establishments, we must not lose sight of the fact that a considerable part of this income is mainly the reproduction of the value, firstly, of a certain portion of the fixed capital transmitted to the product, secondly, of the labour and expenses connected with commerce and transport which play no part in production, and, thirdly, of the value of food supplied to wage-workers who receive their board from the masters. These facts" (facts, indeed!) "limit the possibility of certain illusions arising which give an exaggerated notion of the advantages of wage-labour in handicraft industry or, what amounts to the same thing, of the capitalist element" (p. 15). That it is highly desirable in all investigations "to limit" the possibility of illusions is something which nobody, of course, doubts, but for this it is necessary to combat "illusions" by means of *facts*, facts taken from the household census, and not by citing one's own opinions, which are themselves sometimes mere "illusions." Is not, indeed, the authors' argument about commercial and transport expenses an illusion? Who does not know that these expenses per unit of product are far smaller for the big producer than the small producer,* that the former buys his material cheaper and sells his product dearer, knowing how (and being in a position) to choose time and place? The handicraft census, too, mentions these generally known facts— cf. pp. 204 and 263, for example—and one cannot but regret that the *Sketch* contains no *facts* about expenses on the purchase of raw materials and the sale of the product by

---

* It goes without saying that only handicraftsmen *in the same sub-group* can be compared, and that a commodity producer cannot be compared with an artisan or a handicraftsman who works for a buyer-up.

big and small industrialists, by handicraftsmen and buyers-up. Further, as regards the wear and tear of fixed capital, here again the authors, while combating illusions, are themselves the victims of an illusion. Theory tells us that large expenditures on fixed capital diminish the part of the value per unit of product that represents wear and tear and is transmitted to the product. "An analysis and comparison of the prices of commodities produced by handicrafts or manufactures, and of the prices of the same commodities produced by machinery, shows generally that, in the product of machinery, the value due to the instruments of labour increases relatively, but decreases absolutely. In other words, its absolute amount decreases, but its amount, relatively to the total value of the product, of a pound of yarn, for instance, increases" (*Das Kapital*, I², S. 406).[117] The census also reckoned the costs of production, which include (p. 14, point 7) "repair of tools and fixtures." What reason is there to believe that omissions in the registration of this point are to be met with more frequently among the big than among the small masters? Would not rather the contrary be the case? As to board provided for wage-workers, there are no *facts* on this point in the *Sketch* at all: we do not know exactly how many workers board with their masters, how frequent are the omissions in the census on this point, how often agriculturist masters feed their wage-workers with produce from their farms, and how often the masters entered the workers' board under expenditure on production. Similarly, no *facts* on the inequality in the length of the working period in the big and the small establishments are given. We do not deny that the working period in the big establishments is very likely longer than in the small ones, but, firstly, the differences in income are out of all proportion to the differences in the length of the working period; and, secondly, it remains to be stated that the Perm statisticians have been unable to offer a single weighty argument, based on precise data, against the precise *facts* of the house-to-house census (given below), and in support of the Narodnik "illusions."

We have obtained the data for the large and small establishments in the following way: we examined the tables appended to the *Sketch*, noted the large establishments (wherever they could be picked out, that is, wherever they were not lumped together with the mass of establishments in a general total), and compared them with the general totals given in the *Sketch* for all the establishments of *the same* group and sub-group. This question is so important that we hope the reader will not reproach us for the numerous tables we give below: in tables the facts stand out more saliently and compactly.

Felt-boot industry:

Group I Sub-group 1	Number of establishments	Number of			Gross income		Wages of wage-workers		Net income		Reference to pages of *Sketch*
		Family workers	Wage-workers	Total	Total	Per worker	Total	Per worker	Total	Per family worker	
					Rubles						
Total	58	99	95	194	22,769	117.3	4,338	45.6	7,410	75.0	P. 112 of text
Large establishments	10	14	65	79	13,291	168.0	3,481	53.5	3,107	222.0	Pp. 214, 215 and 154 of tables
Other establishments not including the large	48	85	30	115	9,478	82.4	857	28.5	4,303	41.2	

Thus, the "average" income per family worker, 75 rubles, was obtained by adding together incomes of 222 rubles and 41 rubles. It appears that, after deducting the ten large establishments* with 14 family workers, the remaining establishments show a *net income* that is *below* the wages of a wage-worker (41.2 against 45.6 rubles), while in the large establishments wages are still higher. The productivity of labour in the large establishments is more than double

---

* But these are by no means the largest establishments. From the division of establishments according to number of wage-workers (p. 113) it may be calculated that in three establishments there are 163 wage-workers, or an average of 54 per establishment. Yet these are also regarded as "handicraft establishments" and are added together with the one-man workshops (of which there are no less than 460 in the industry) to obtain general "average"!

(168.0 and 82.4 rubles), the earnings of a wage-worker nearly double (53 rubles and 28 rubles), while the net income is
five times higher (222 and 41 rubles). Obviously, no talk
about differences in the working period or any other argument can eliminate the fact that the big establishments have
the highest labour productivity* and the highest income, while
the small handicraftsmen, for all their "independence" (first
sub-group: those who work independently for the market) and
their tie with the land (Group I), earn less than wage-workers.

In the carpentry trade the "net income" of the first sub-
group of Group I "averages" 37.4 rubles per family worker,
whereas the average earnings of a wage-worker in the same
sub-group are 56.9 rubles (p. 131). It is impossible to pick out
the big establishments from the tables, but it can scarcely be
doubted that this "average" income per family worker was
obtained by combining the highly profitable establishments
employing wage-workers (who, after all, are not paid 56 rubles
for nothing) with the dwarf workshops of the small "independent" handicraftsmen, who get much less than a wage-worker.

Next comes the bast-matting industry:

Group I Sub-group 1	Number of establishments	Number of			Gross income		Wages		Net income		Reference to pages of *Sketch*
		Family workers	Wage-workers	Total	Total	Per worker	Total	Per wage-worker	Total	Per family worker	
Total	99	206	252	458	38,681	84.4	6,664	26.4	10,244	49.7	P. 151 of text
Large establishments	11	11	95	106	18,170	171.4	2,520	26.5	3,597	327.0	Pp. 95, 97 and 136 of tables
Others	88	195	157	352	20,511	58.2	4,144	26.4	6,647	34.0	

Thus, almost half the total output is concentrated in eleven
of the ninety-nine establishments. In them, productivity of
labour is more than double; the wages of the workers are also
higher; and net income is more than six times the "average"

---

* "In one of the establishments" the introduction of a wool-carding
machine was mentioned (p. 119).

and nearly ten times as high as that of the others, i.e., the smaller establishments. The latter have incomes but slightly higher than a worker's wages (34 and 26 rubles respectively).

Rope and string industry*:

Group I Sub-group 1	Number of establishments	Number of			Gross income		Wages		Net income		Reference to pages of *Sketch*
		Family workers	Wage-workers	Total	Total	Per worker	Total	Per wage-worker	Total	Per family worker	
Total	58	179	106	285	81,672	286	6,946	65.6	16,127	90.1	P. 158 of text *
Large establishments	4	5	56	61	48,912	800	4,695	83.8	5,599	1,119.0	Pp. 40 and 188 of tables
Others	54	174	50	224	32,760	146	2,251	45.0	10,528	60.5	

Thus, here too the general "averages" show a higher income for the family workers than for the wage-workers (90 against 65.6 rubles). But 4 of the 58 establishments account for *over half* the total output. In these establishments (capitalist manufactories of the pure type)** productivity of labour is almost three times the average (800 and 286 rubles) and over five times that of the remaining, i.e., smaller, establishments (800 and 146 rubles). Workers' wages are much higher in the factories than in the small masters' workshops (84 and 45 rubles). The net income of the manufacturers is over 1,000 rubles per family as compared with the "average" of 90 rubles and with the 60.5 rubles of the

---

* There is apparently a misprint or error in the table on p. 158: in Irbit Uyezd the net income is more than the 9,827 rubles shown in the total. We had to change this table according to the data in the tables appended to the *Sketch*.

** Cf. *Handicraft Industries*, pp. 46-47, as well as the description of the industry given in the *Sketch*, p. 162, et seq. It is most typical that "these employers were once real handicraftsmen and that is why they have always been fond ... of giving themselves that name."

small handicraftsmen. The income of the small handicraftsman is, therefore, lower than a worker's wages (60.5 and
65.6 rubles).

The pitch and tar industry:

Group I Sub-group 1	Number of establishments	Number of			Gross income		Wages		Net income		Reference to pages of *Sketch*
		Family workers	Wage-workers	Total	Total	Per worker	Total	Per wage-worker	Total	Per family worker	
Total	167	319	80	399	22,076	55.3	2,150	26.8	10,979	34.4	P. 189 of text
Large establishments	9	10	16	26	4,440	170.7	654	40.8	2,697	269.7	Pp. 100, 101, 137, 160, 161 and 220 of tables
Others	158	309	64	373	17,636	47.3	1,496	23.2	8,282	26.8	

Although this industry is, in general, a small one that
employs very few wage-workers (20%) we again find the
same purely capitalist phenomenon of the superiority of the
large (relatively large) establishments of the independent
handicraftsmen in the agricultural group. And yet pitch and
tar production is a purely peasant, "people's" industry! In the
large establishments labour productivity is over three times,
workers' wages about one-and-a-half times and net income
about eight times the "average"; their net income, moreover,
is ten times as high as that of other handicraft families who
earn no more than the average wage-worker, and *less than
a wage-worker in the larger establishments*. Let us note that
pitch and tar production is chiefly a summer occupation, so
that differences in the working period cannot be very great.*

---

* It may be seen from the *Sketch* that in the pitch and tar industry both the primitive method of distilling pitch *in pits* and the
more perfected *cauldron*, and even *cylindrical boiler*, methods are
employed (p. 195). The household census furnished material showing
the distribution of these different methods, but it was not utilised,
the large establishments not being treated separately.

The baking industry:

Group 1 Sub-group 1	Number of establishments	Number of			Gross income		Wages		Net income		Reference to pages of *Sketch*
		Family workers	Wage-workers	Total	Total	Per worker	Total	Per wage-worker	Total	Per family worker	
Total	27	63	55	118	44,619	378.1	2,497	45.4	7,484	118.8	P. 215 of text Pp. 68 and 229 of tables
Large estab-lishments	4	7	42	49	25,740	525	2,050	48.8	4,859	694	
Others	23	56	13	69	18,879	273		447	34.4	2,625	46.8	

Thus, here again, the averages for the entire sub-group are absolutely fictitious. The large establishments (of small capitalists) account for over half the total output, yield a net income six times the average and 14 times that of the small masters, and pay their workers *wages exceeding the incomes of the small handicraftsmen*. We do not mention productivity of labour; three or four of the large establishments produce a more valuable product—treacle.

The pottery industry. Here again we have a typical small peasant industry with an insignificant number of wage-workers (13%), very small establishments (less than two workers per establishment) and a predominance of agriculturists. And here too we get the same picture:

Group I Sub-group 1	Number of establishments	Number of			Gross income		Wages		Net income		Reference to pages of *Sketch*
		Family workers	Wage-workers	Total	Total	Per worker	Total	Per wage-worker	Total	Per family worker	
Total	97	163	31	194	12,414	63.9	1,830	59	6,657	41	P. 291 of text Pp. 168 and 206 of tables
Large estab-lishments	7	9	17	26	4,187	161.0	1,400	80.2	1,372	152	
Others	90	154	14	168	8,227	48.9	430	30.0	5,285	34.3	

Here, consequently, it is at once apparent from the "average" figures that the wage-worker's earnings are *higher* than the family worker's income. By treating the large establishments separately, we get the explanation of this contradiction, which we have already recorded in numerous instances. In the large establishments labour productivity, wages and masters' incomes are all incomparably higher, while the small handicraftsmen get less than the wage-workers *and less than half the earnings of the wage-workers in the best-organised shops.*

The brick industry:

Group I Sub-group 1	Number of establishments	Number of			Gross income		Wages		Net income		Reference to pages of *Sketch*
		Family workers	Wage-workers	Total	Total	Per worker	Total	Per wage-worker	Total	Per family worker	
Total	229	558	218	776	17,606	22.6	4,560	20.9	10,126	18.1	P. 299 of text
Large establishments	8	9	45	54	3,130	57.9	1,415	31.4	1,298	144	Pp. 46, 120, 169 and 183 of tables
Others	221	549	173	722	14,476	20.0	3,145	18.2	8,828	16.0	

Thus, here too, the "average" income of a family worker is lower than the earnings of a wage-worker. Here again it is to be explained by combining the big establishments—which are distinguished by a considerably higher labour productivity, higher payment of wage-workers, and a very high (comparatively) income—and the small establishments, the income of whose owners is about half the earnings of the wage-workers in the big establishments.

We might go on citing figures for other industries too,[*] but we think that those given are more than enough.

_____

[*] Cf. vehicle building, p. 308 of the text and pp. 11 and 12 of the tables; chest making, p. 335; tailoring, p. 344, etc.

Let us now summarise the conclusions that follow from the facts examined:

1) The combining of large and small establishments results in absolutely fictitious "average" figures, which give no conception of the real state of affairs, obscure cardinal differences, and present as homogeneous something that is heterogeneous, of mixed composition.

2) The data for a number of industries show that the large establishments (where a large number of workers are engaged) are distinguished from the average and small establishments:

   a) by an incomparably higher productivity of labour;
   b) by better payment of wage-workers, and
   c) by a far higher net income.

3) All the large establishments we have selected, without exception, employ wage-labour on an incomparably larger scale (than the average-sized establishments in the given industry), the proportion of wage-labour being substantially greater than that of family labour. The value of their output is as much as 10,000 rubles, while the number of wage-workers employed is ten and more per establishment. These large establishments, therefore, represent capitalist workshops. The census data consequently reveal *the prevalence of purely capitalist laws and relations* in the celebrated "handicraft" industry; they reveal the absolute superiority of the capitalist workshops, based on the co-operation of wage-workers, over the one-man workshops and small workshops in general—a superiority both in productivity of labour and in remuneration for labour, even of wage-workers.

4) In the case of a number of the industries the earnings of the small *independent* handicraftsmen prove to be no higher, and often even lower, than the earnings of wage-workers ~in the same industry. This difference would be even greater if to the wage-workers' earnings were added the value of the board received by some of them.

We have dealt with this last conclusion separately because the first three concern phenomena that are universal and inevitable under the laws of commodity production, whereas the last does not contain phenomena that are everywhere inevitable. We accordingly formulate this concept as follows: because of lower labour productivity in small establishments and the defenceless position of their owners in the market (especially in the case of agriculturists), it is possible that the earnings of an independent handicraftsman may be lower than those of a wage-worker—and the facts show that this very often is the case.

The validity of our calculations is beyond question, for we have taken a number of industries, not choosing them at random, but taking all those where the tables allowed us to deal with the large establishments separately; we have not taken individual establishments, but all those of the same kind, and in every case compared with them several large establishments in different uyezds. But it would be desirable to express the phenomena described in a more general and more precise form. Fortunately, the *Sketch* contains material that enables us to satisfy this desire *in part*. This is the material on the *division of establishments according to net income*. In the case of certain industries, the *Sketch* indicates how many establishments have a net income of up to 50, 100, 200 rubles, etc. It is these data that we have combined. We find that there are data available for 28 industries,* embracing 8,364 establishments, or 93.2% of the total number (8,991). In all, in these 28 industries there are 8,377 establishments (income figures are not given for 13 establishments), with 14,135 family and 4,625 wage-workers, or 18,760 in all, which constitutes 93.9% of the total number of workers. Naturally, from these data covering 93% of the handicraftsmen we are fully entitled to draw conclusions regarding all of them, for there are no grounds for assuming that the remaining 7% differ from these 93%. Before presenting our summary, it is necessary to make the following remarks:

1) In thus classifying the material, the compilers of the *Sketch* have not always strictly adhered to uniform and identical headings for the groups. For example, they have "up

---

* These data are also available for the lace-, lock- and accordion-making industries, but we omit them, as they do not record establishments according to the number of family workers.

to 100 rubles," "less than 100 rubles," and sometimes even "100 rubles each." The top and bottom limits of the category are not always indicated, that is, sometimes the classification begins with the category "up to 100 rubles," sometimes with that of "up to 50 rubles," "up to 10 rubles," and so on; sometimes the classification ends with the category "1,000 rubles and over," sometimes the categories "2,000 to 3,000 rubles" and others are introduced. None of these inaccuracies is of any serious importance. We have unified all the categories contained in the *Sketch* (there are fifteen of them: up to 10, up to 20, up to 50, up to 100, up to 200, up to 300, up to 400, up to 500, up to 600, up to 700, up to 800, up to 900, up to 1,000, 1,000 and over, and 2,000 to 3,000 rubles), and we have eliminated all minor inaccuracies and misunderstandings by assigning them to one or another of these categories.

2) The *Sketch* only indicates the *number of establishments* in certain income categories, but does not indicate the *income* of all the establishments in each category. Yet it is these latter figures that we need most. We have therefore assumed that the aggregate income of the establishments in any category is determined with sufficient accuracy by multiplying the number of establishments by the average income, that is, by the arithmetical mean of the maximum and minimum of the given category (for example, 150 rubles in the case of the 100 to 200 ruble category, etc.). Only in the case of the lowest two categories (up to 10 rubles and up to 20 rubles) have the maximum incomes (10 rubles and 20 rubles respectively) been taken instead of the averages. Verification has shown that this method (one generally permissible in statistical calculations) yields results that approximate very closely to reality. For instance, the aggregate net income of the handicraft families in these 28 industries, according to the *Sketch*, amounts to 951,653 rubles, while according to our approximate figures, based on the income categories, it amounts to 955,150 rubles, an excess of 3,497 rubles=0.36%. Consequently, the difference or error is less than 4 kopeks in 10 rubles.

3) From our summary we learn the average income per family (in each category), but not per family worker. To

determine the latter, another approximate calculation had to be made. Knowing the division of families according to the number of family workers (and separately—according to the number of wage-workers employed), we assumed that the lower the income of a family, the smaller its size (i.e., the smaller the number of family workers per establishment) and the fewer the establishments employing wage-workers. On the contrary, the higher the income per family, the larger the number of establishments employing wage-workers and the larger the family, that is, the number of family workers per establishment is larger. Obviously, this assumption is the most favourable for anyone who might want to contest our conclusions. In other words, *whatever* other assumption was made, it would only help to reinforce our conclusions.

We now give a summary showing the division of the handicraftsmen according to the income of their establishments.

Category (rubles)	Number of establishments	Average income per establishment (Approximately)	Income of all establishments (Approximately)	Category (rubles)	Number of establishments	Average income per establishment (Approximately)	Income of all establishments (Approximately)
Up to 10	127	10	1,270	Up to 600	40	550	22,000
" " 20	139	20	2,780	" " 700	38	650	24,700
" " 50	2,110	35	73,850	" " 800	22	750	16,500
" " 100	3,494	75	262,050	" " 900	20	850	17,000
" " 200	1,414	150	212,100	" " 1,000	17	950	16,150
" " 300	602	250	150,050	1,000 and over	19	1,500	28,500
" " 400	208	350	72,800	2,000-3,000	2	2,500	5,000
" " 500	112	450	50,400				
All establishments					8,364	—	955,150

These data are too detailed and have therefore to be combined under simpler and clearer headings. Let us take five income categories of handicraftsmen: a) poor, with incomes of up to 50 rubles per family; b) in straitened circumstances, with incomes of 50 to 100 rubles per family; c) medium, with incomes of 100 to 300 rubles per family; d) well-to-do, with incomes of 300 to 500 rubles per family, and e) affluent, with incomes of over 500 rubles per family.

According to the data showing the incomes of establishments we shall add to these categories a rough division of establishments according to the number of family and wage-workers they employ.* We get the following table (see p. 417).

These data lead to very interesting conclusions, which we shall now enumerate, taking the handicraftsmen category by category:

a) Over one-fourth of the families (28.4%) come under the category of *poor*, with an average income of about 33 rubles per family. Let us assume that this is the income of only one family worker, that all in this category are one-man producers. In any case the earnings of these handicraftsmen are *considerably lower* than the average earnings of wage-workers employed by handicraftsmen (45.85 rubles). If the majority of these one-man producers belong to the lower (3rd) sub-group, that is, work for buyers-up, this means that the "masters" pay those who work at home less than wage-workers employed in the workshop. Even if we assume that the working period of this category is the shortest, their earnings are nevertheless at the poverty level.

b) Over two-fifths of the total number of handicraftsmen (41.8%) belong to the group of families in straitened circumstances, who have an average income of 75 rubles per family. Not all of these are one-man establishments (the previous category was assumed to consist solely of

---

* The 8,377 establishments in the 28 industries are divided according to the number of family and wage-workers as follows: no family workers—95 establishments; 1 worker—4,362; 2 workers—2,632; 3 workers—870; 4 workers—275; 5 workers and over—143. The establishments employing wage-workers number 2,228, and are divided as follows: 1 wage-worker—1,359; 2 workers—447; 3 workers—201; 4 workers—96; 5 workers and more—125. The wage-workers total 4,625, and their aggregate wages total 212,096 rubles (45.85 rubles per worker).

Categories of handicraftsmen according to size of income	Number		Net income		Average income		Rough division of families										
							According to number of family workers						According to number of wage-workers				
	Families	%	Rubles	%	Per family	Per family worker (approx.)	1	2	3	4	5 or more	0	1	2	3	4	5 or more
a) Poor	2,376	28.4	77,900	8.2	32.7	32.7	2,376	—	—	—	—	—	—	—	—	—	—
b) In straitened circumstances	3,494	41.8	262,050	27.4	75.0	50	1,986	1,508	—	—	—	—	—	—	—	—	—
c) Medium	2,016	24.1	362,150	37.9	179.6	72.0	—	1,124	870	22	—	—	1,359	392	—	—	—
d) Well-to-do	320	3.8	123,200	12.9	385.0	100.0	—	—	—	253	67	—	—	55	201	64	—
e) Affluent	158	1.9	129,850	13.6	821.8	348	—	—	—	—	76	82	—	—	—	32	125
Total	8,364	100	955,150	100	114.2	67.5	4,362	2,632	870	275	143	82	1,359	447	201	96	125

one-man producers): about half the families have two family workers each, and hence the average earnings per family worker are only about 50 rubles, *i.e.*, *not more, or
even less, than the earnings of a wage-worker employed by
a handicraftsman* (apart from wages, amounting to 45.85
rubles, part of the wage-workers also receive their board).
*Thus, judged by their earnings, seven-tenths of the total num-
ber of handicraftsmen are on a par with, and some even
at a lower level than, the wage-workers employed by handicraftsmen.* Astonishing as this conclusion is, it fully conforms to the facts quoted above on the superiority of large
establishments over small. The low income level of these
handicraftsmen can be judged by the fact that the average wage of an agricultural labourer employed by the year in
Perm Gubernia is 50 rubles, in addition to board.* Consequently, the standard of living of seven-tenths of the "independent" handicraftsmen is no higher than that of agricultural labourers!

The Narodniks, of course, will say that these earnings
are only supplementary to agriculture. But in the first place,
has it not been established long ago that only a minority
of the peasants are able to derive enough from agriculture
to maintain their families, after land redemption payments,
rent and farm expenses are deducted? And please note that
we are comparing the handicraftsman's earnings with the
wages of a farm labourer who receives his board from his
master. Secondly, seven-tenths of the total number of handicraftsmen must also include non-agriculturists. Thirdly,
even if it turns out that agriculture covers the maintenance
of the agriculturist handicraftsmen of these categories,
the drastic effect of the tie with the land in reducing earnings still remains beyond all doubt.

Another comparison: in Krasnoufimsk Uyezd, the average earnings of a wage-worker employed by a handicraftsman are 33.2 rubles (p. 149 of the tables), while the average
earnings of a person employed at "his own" works, that
is, of an ironworker from among the former possessional[118]
peasants, are estimated by the Zemstvo statisticians at

---

* The cost of board is 45 rubles per annum, according to the
figures—average for 10 years (1881-91)—of the Department of
Agriculture. (See S. A. Korolenko, *Hired Labour*, etc.)

78.7 rubles (*Material for a Statistical Survey of Perm Gubernia. Krasnoufimsk Uyezd. Zavodsk District*, Kazan, 1894), or over twice as much. And it is a generally known fact that the wages of ironworkers from among the former possessional peasants are always lower than wages of "free" workers in the factories. One can, therefore, see that reduced consumption, a miserable standard of living, is the price paid for the celebrated "independence" of the Russian handicraftsman "based on an organic tie between industry and agriculture"!

c) In the category of "medium" handicraftsmen we have included families with incomes of 100 to 300 rubles, or an average of about 180 rubles per family. They constitute almost one-fourth of the total number (24.1%). Absolutely, their income is very, very low: counting two-and-a-half family workers per establishment, it amounts to about 72 rubles per family worker—a very inadequate sum, and one which no factory worker would envy. Compared, however, with the incomes of the mass of handicraftsmen this sum is fairly high! It appears that even this meagre "sufficiency" is only secured at the expense of others: the majority of the handicraftsmen in this category employ wage-workers (roughly about 85% of the masters employ wage-labourers, and the average for the 2,016 establishments is over one wage-worker per establishment). Hence, in order to fight their way out of the mass of poverty-stricken handicraftsmen, this category, under the existing commodity-capitalist relations, have to win a "sufficiency" for themselves from others, have to engage in economic struggle, to squeeze out the mass of the small producers still further and become petty bourgeois. Either poverty and the lowering of their standard of living to the nec plus ultra, or (*for a minority*) the building-up of their (absolutely very meagre) welfare at the expense of others—such is the dilemma with which commodity production confronts the small producer. Such is the language of facts.

d) The category of well-to-do handicraftsmen embraces only 3.8% of the families, those with an average income of about 385 rubles, or about 100 rubles per family worker (assuming that under this heading come masters with 4 or 5 family workers per establishment). Such an income, about double the earnings of a wage-worker, is already based on a considerable employment of wage-labour: all the establishments in this category employ an average of about 3 wage-workers per establishment.

e) The affluent handicraftsmen, those with an average income of 820 rubles per family, constitute only 1.9% of the total. This category partly includes establishments with 5 family workers, and partly establishments with no family workers at all, that is, those based exclusively on wage-labour. On an average, this amounts to about 350 rubles of income per family worker. The high incomes of these "handicraftsmen" accrue from the large number of wage-workers employed, averaging about 10 persons per establishment. * These are already small manufacturers, owners of capitalist workshops, and to include them among the "handicraftsmen," together with the one-man establishments, rural artisans and even domestic producers who work for manufacturers (and sometimes, as we shall see below, for these same affluent handicraftsmen!) only testifies, as we have already remarked, to the utter vagueness and haziness of the term "handicraft."

In concluding our examination of the census data on handicraftsmen's incomes we must make the following remark. It might be said that the concentration of incomes in the handicraft industries is not very high: 5.7% of the establishments account for 26.5% of the total income, and 29.8% for 64.4%. Our reply to this is that, firstly, even this degree of concentration shows how totally unsuitable and unscientific are sweeping arguments about "handicraftsmen," and "average" figures relating to them. Secondly, we should not lose sight of the fact that these data *do not include buyers-up*, with the result that the income division is highly inaccurate. We have seen that 2,346 families and 5,628 workers work for buyers-up (third sub-group); consequently, here it is the buyers-up who get the principal income. Their separation from the mass of the producers is absolutely artificial and entirely unwarranted. Just as it would

---

* Of the 2,228 establishments employing wage-workers in these 28 industries, 46 employ 10 wage-workers or more—a total of 887, or an average of 19.2 wage-workers per establishment.

be wrong to describe the economic relations in large-scale factory industry without mentioning the size of the manufacturers' incomes, so is it wrong to describe the economics of "handicraft" industry without mentioning the incomes of the buyers-up—incomes obtained from the same industry in which handicraftsmen are also engaged, and constituting part of the value of goods produced by handicraftsmen. We are therefore entitled, in fact we are obliged, to conclude that the actual distribution of incomes in handicraft industry is far more uneven than was shown above, for the categories which include the largest industrialists of all have been omitted.

ARTICLE THREE

(VI. What Is a Buyer-Up?—VII. "Gratifying Features" of Handicraft
Industry.—VIII. The Narodnik Programme of Industrial Policy)

VI
WHAT IS A BUYER-UP?

Above we called the buyers-up the biggest of the industrialists. From the ordinary Narodnik viewpoint, this is
heresy. It is customary to depict our buyers-up as individuals who take no part in production, who are extraneous
and alien to industry itself, and depend "solely" on exchange.

This is not the place to dwell in detail on the theoretical
fallacies contained in this view, which is based on a failure
to understand the general and principal groundwork, foundation, or background of present-day industry (handicraft
industry included)—namely, *commodity economy*, of which
merchant capital is an essential component, and not a casual and incidental adjunct. Here we must stick to the facts
and figures of the handicraft census, and our task will now
be to examine and analyse the data on buyers-up. A circumstance favouring this examination is the fact that handicraftsmen who work for buyers-up have been put into a separate
sub-group (the third). But this advantage is outweighed by
the great number of omissions and uninvestigated factors,
which rather seriously complicates our inquiry. No data are
available on the number of buyers-up, on large buyers-up
and small, on their ties with the well-to-do handicraftsmen
(ties of origin, ties between the commercial operations of
the buyer-up and production in his workshop, etc.), on the
business of the buyer-up. The Narodnik prejudice of treating the buyer-up as extraneous prevented most investigators of handicraft industry from examining business done
by buyers-up, although this is obviously a prime and prin-

cipal question for the economist. A careful and detailed study should be made of the *business* methods of the buyer-up, how his capital is built up, how this capital operates in the purchase of raw material and the sale of the product, what are the conditions (social and economic) in which capital operates in these spheres, what expenses he incurs in organising purchases and sales, how these expenses vary according to the amount of merchant capital and the volume of purchases and sales, and what conditions sometimes induce the buyer-up to process the raw material partly in his own workshops and then to give out the semi-finished product to domestic workers for further processing (the final finishing process sometimes being done by the buyer-up himself), and sometimes to sell the raw material to small industrialists, in order, later, to buy their wares in the market. A comparison should be made between the cost of production of an article turned out by a small handicraftsman, by a large producer in a workshop where several wage-workers are employed, and by a buyer-up who gives out material to be worked up by domestic workers. The unit of investigation should be each *enterprise*, that is, each separate buyer-up, and it is necessary to determine the amount of his turnover, the number of persons working for him in his workshop or workshops, or in their own homes, the number of workers he employs to acquire raw materials, to store them and the finished product, and to sell the latter. A comparison should be made between the technique of production (number and quality of implements and fixtures, *division of labour*, etc.) used by the small master, the workshop owner who employs wage-workers, and by the buyer-up. Only such an *economic investigation* can give an exact scientific answer to the questions: what is a buyer-up, what is his significance in the economic process and in the historical development of the forms of industry under commodity production. The absence of such information in the conclusions of the house-to-house census, which made a detailed study of all these questions for each handicraftsman, cannot but be regarded as a serious omission. Even if it was impossible (for some reason or another) to register and investigate the business of each buyer-up, much of this information could have been drawn from the household data on handicraftsmen who work for buyers-up. Instead, we find nothing in the *Sketch* but hackneyed Narodnik phrases, such as: the "kulak" is "essentially alien to production itself" (p. 7)—the kulak category being extended to include both buyers-up and owners of assembly workshops, on the one hand, and usurers, on the other; "wage-labour is governed not by its technical concentration, as in the case of the factory (?), but by the monetary dependence of the handicraftsmen ... one of the forms of kulakism" (309-10); "the source of the exploitation of labour ... lies in the function of exchange, and not in the function of production" (101); or what we often meet with in the handicraft industries is not the "capitalisation of production," but the "capitalisation of the process of exchange" (265). Of course, we have no intention of accusing the *Sketch* investigators of originality: they simply borrowed wholesale the maxims scattered so profusely in the works of, say, "our well-known" Mr. V. V.

In order to judge the true value of such phrases, we have only to remember, for example, that in one of our principal industries, textiles, the "buyer-up" was the immediate forerunner, the father, of the big manufacturer engaged in large-scale machine production. All our textile industries began with supplying yarn to be worked up by handicraftsmen at home; this, in other words, was work for the "buyer-up," for the "kulak," who, while possessing no workshop of his own ("was alien to production"), "merely" supplied the yarn, and took the finished goods. Our good Narodniks did not even attempt to investigate the origin of these buyers-up, their genealogical connections with the owners of small workshops, their role as organisers of the buying of raw materials and the selling of products, the role of their capital in concentrating means of production, in gathering together masses of scattered small handicraftsmen, in introducing division of labour, and in creating the elements of what is not only large-scale production but which is also becoming machine production. Our good Narodniks confined themselves to whining and complaining about this "deplorable," "artificial," etc., etc., phenomenon; they consoled themselves with the belief that this was not the "capitalisation" of production, but "merely" of the process of exchange, and talked sentimentally about "different paths for the fatherland." Meanwhile

these "artificial" and "unsubstantial" "kulaks" kept on following their old path, continued to concentrate capital, to "gather together" means of production and producers, to extend
their purchases of raw materials, to further the division of production into separate operations (warping, weaving, dyeing,
finishing, etc.) and to transform scattered, technically backward *capitalist manufacture*, based on hand labour and servitude, into *capitalist machine industry*.

An exactly similar process is now taking place in the bulk
of our so-called "handicraft" industries; and the Narodniks
in just the same way shun an investigation of realities as
they develop, in just the same way replace a discussion of
the origin of existing relations and their evolution by a discussion of what *might* be (*if* what is were not), in just the
same way console themselves with the thought that so far
these are "merely" buyers-up, and in just the same way idealise and paint in rosy colours the worst forms of capitalism—
worst in technical backwardness, economic imperfection,
and the social and cultural conditions of the working masses.

Let us turn to the data of the Perm handicraft census.
Wherever necessary, we shall endeavour to make good the
above-mentioned omissions by drawing upon *Handicraft
Industries of Perm Gubernia, etc.*, a book to which we have
already referred. Let us first of all pick out the industries
which account for the bulk of the handicraftsmen employed
by buyers-up (third sub-group). For this purpose we shall
have to turn to our own summary, which (as already mentioned) does not coincide with the *Sketch* figures.

Industry	Number of families working for buyers-up		
	Group I	Group II	Total
Bootmaking	31	605	636
Felt-boot	607	12	619
Ironworking	70	412	482
Bast-matting	132	10	142
Carpentry and joinery	38	49	87
Vehicle-building	32	28	60
Tailoring	4	42	46
Total for 7 industries . . .	914	1,158	2,072
Total number of handicrafts- men in third sub-group . . .	1,016	1,320	**2,336**

Thus, about nine-tenths of the handicraftsmen working for buyers-up are concentrated in these seven industries. It is to these industries that we shall turn first.

Let us begin with the bootmaking industry. The overwhelming majority of the bootmakers who work for buyers-up are in Kungur Uyezd, the centre of the leather industry in Perm Gubernia. A large number of handicraftsmen work for leather manufacturers: on p. 87 of the *Sketch* mention is made of 8 buyers-up, who have 445 establishments working for them.* All these buyers-up have been leather goods manufacturers "for ages," and their names may be found in the *Directory of Factories* for 1890 and 1879, and in the notes to the *Ministry of Finance Yearbook*, Issue I for 1869.[119] The leather goods manufacturers cut out the leather and in this form distribute it to the "handicraftsmen" to be sewn. The lasting is done separately, by several families, who work to the order of the manufacturers. Generally speaking, a whole number of "handicraft" industries are connected with the leather goods factories, that is, a whole series of operations are done in the home. These include 1) dressing of hides and skins; 2) sewing of uppers; 3) gluing of leather clippings into boards for stiffeners; 4) making of screws for boots; 5) making of brads for boots; 6) last making; 7) preparation of ash for the tanneries; 8) making of "tan" (from willow bark). The scrap and waste of the leather industry are used by the felt and glue-making industries (*Handicraft Industries*, III, pp. 3-4, et al.). In addition to detailed division of labour (i.e., division of the production of an article into several operations performed by different persons), a commodity division of labour has arisen in this industry: each family (sometimes even each street in a handicraft village) produces one kind of footwear. There is an amusing point we must mention—in *Handicraft Industries, etc.*, the "Kungur leather industry" is declared to be a "typical expression of the idea of the organic connection between factory and handicraft industry to their mutual advantage" (sic!) ... the factory entering into a

---

* These include two buyers-up (Ponomaryov and Fominsky) who have 217 establishments working for them. Altogether, there are 470 bootmaking establishments working for buyers-up in Kungur Uyezd.

correct (sic!) association with handicraft industry, with the object, in its own interests (exactly!), of developing and not reducing ... its capacity (III, p. 3). For example, Fominsky, the manufacturer, was awarded a gold medal at the 1887 Ekaterinburg Exhibition not only for the excellent quality of his leather, but also for his "extensive operations, *which furnish work for the surrounding population*" (ibid., p. 4, author's italics). Indeed, of the 1,450 persons he employed, 1,300 were domestic workers. Of the 120 persons employed by Sartakov, another manufacturer, 100 were domestic workers, etc. Hence the Perm manufacturers vie very successfully with the Narodnik intellectuals in implanting and developing handicraft industries....

The organisation of the bootmaking industry in Krasnoufimsk Uyezd (*Handicraft Industries*, 1, pp. 148-49) is in every way analogous; the leather goods manufacturers also stitch leather boots, partly in their workshops, partly by giving the work out to domestic workers. One of the biggest of the owners of a leather and boot establishment employs about 200 regular workers.

We are now in a position to form a fairly clear idea of the economic organisation of the bootmaking and of many other allied "handicraft" industries. They are nothing but *branches* of large capitalist workshops ("factories," according to the terminology used in our official statistics), performing nothing but *detailed operations* in the large-scale capitalist manufacture of leather goods. The entrepreneurs have organised the buying of materials on a broad scale, have set up factories for tanning the hides, and have established a whole organisation for the further processing of the leather based on the division of labour (as the technical condition) and wage-labour (as the economic condition): some of the operations (such as cutting out leather for boots) are performed in their workshops, others are performed by "handicraftsmen" who work for them in their homes, the employers determining the amount of output, the rates of payment, the kind of goods to be made, and the quantity of each kind. They have also organised the wholesale marketing of the product. Obviously, in scientific terminology this is nothing but *capitalist manufacture*, in part already passing into the higher form of *factory* industry (inasmuch as machines and machinery are used in production: the big leather factories have steam engines). To single out parts of this system of manufacture as a separate "handicraft" form of production is a patent absurdity, which only obscures the basic fact that wage-labour prevails in the leather goods production and bootmaking and that the *entire* trade is under the sway of big capital. Instead of comical arguments on the desirability of a "co-operative organisation of exchange" in this industry (*Sketch*, p. 93), it would not be amiss to make a detailed study of its actual organisation, a study of the conditions which make it preferable for the manufacturers to give out work to be done in the home. The manufacturers undoubtedly find it more profitable, and we shall understand why if we bear in mind the low earnings of the handicraftsmen in general, and in particular of the handicraft agriculturists and those of the third sub-group. By giving out material to be worked up at home, the employers lower wages, economise on premises, partly on implements, and on supervision, evade the not always welcome demands made on manufacturers (they are not manufacturers but merchants!), get workers who are more scattered, disunited, and less capable of self-defence, and also unpaid taskmasters for these workers—"middlemen," "subcontractors" (as they are called in our textile industry under the system of giving out yarn to be used in the home)—in the shape of those handicraftsmen they employ and who, *in their turn, employ wage-workers* (it was found that the 636 families who make boots for buyers-up employ 278 wage-workers). We have already seen from the general table that these wage-workers (in the third sub-group) receive the lowest wages of all. And this is not surprising, for they are subjected to double exploitation: exploitation by their own employer who squeezes his "own little profit" out of the workers, and exploitation by the leather goods manufacturer who gives out material to the small masters. We know that these small middlemen, who are well familiar with local conditions and with the personal characteristics of the workers, are particularly prolific in inventing different forms of extortion, in practising bondage hiring, the *truck system*,[120] etc. The excessive working hours in these workshops and

---

* These words are in English in the original —*Ed*.

"handicraftsmen's huts" are common knowledge, and one cannot help regretting that the 1894-95 handicraft census has furnished practically no information on subjects so important for the study of our native *sweating system*,* with its host of middlemen who intensify the pressure on the workers and its utterly shameless and unrestricted exploitation.

On the organisation of the felt-boot industry (the second largest as regards the absolute number of families working for buyers-up) the *Sketch*, unfortunately, gives practically no information whatever. We have seen that in this industry there are handicraftsmen who employ dozens of wage-workers, but whether they give out work to be done at home, get part of the operations done outside their workshops,** was not made clear. Let us only note a fact mentioned by the investigators, that the sanitary conditions in the felt-boot industry are extremely unsatisfactory (*Sketch*, p. 119; *Handicraft Industries*, III, 16)—intolerable heat, excessive dust, stifling atmosphere. And this in the cottages the handicraftsmen live in! The natural result is that they are unable to stand more than fifteen years of this work and end as consumptives. I. I. Molleson, an investigator of workshop sanitary conditions, says: "The chief contingent of felt-boot makers consists of workers between the ages of 13 and 30. They are nearly all easily recognisable by their pallor, dull complexion, and their languid and *sickly appearance*" (III, p. 145, author's italics). The practical conclusion drawn by this investigator is: "It should be made incumbent on the employers to build workshops (felt-boot) of much larger size, so as to provide a specified constant volume of air per worker"; the "workshops should be designed exclusively for work, and it should be strictly forbidden to allow workers to sleep in them at night" (ibid.). In other words, the sanitary inspectors demand the building of factories for these handicraftsmen and the prohibition of work in the home. One cannot help hoping that this recommendation will be acted

---

* These words are in English in the original.—*Ed.*

** The felt industry in the Arzamas and Semyonov uyezds of Nizhni-Novgorod Gubernia is organised on those lines. See *Transactions of the Commission of Inquiry into Handicraft Industry* and the *Material* of the Nizhni-Novgorod Zemstvo Statistical Department.

upon, for it would promote technical progress by eliminating a host of middlemen and would pave the way for the regulation of working hours and working conditions; in a word, it would eliminate the most crying abuses in our "people's" industry.

Among the buyers-up in the bast-matting industry is a merchant named Butakov, who, we learn from information for 1879, had a bast-matting factory in the town of Osa, which employed 180 workers.* Has this manufacturer to be regarded as "alien to production itself," just because he has found it more profitable to give out the work to be done at home? It would also be interesting to know in what way the buyers-up who have been thrown out of the list of handicraftsmen differ from those "handicraftsmen" who, having no family workers, "purchase bast and give it out to craftsmen to make into matting and sacks on their own looms" (*Sketch*, 152)—a striking illustration of the confusion into which the investigators have been led by Narodnik prejudices. The sanitary conditions in this industry will also not bear criticism—overcrowding, filth, dust, damp, foul smells and long working hours (12 to 15 a day), all of which turns the centres of the industry into veritable "hotbeds of famine typhus," ** of which, in fact, there have been frequent outbreaks.

On the organisation of work for buyers-up in the ironworking industry, we again learn nothing from the *Sketch* and are again obliged to turn to *Handicraft Industries, etc.*, which contains a very interesting description of this industry in Nizhni-Tagil. The manufacture of trays and other articles is divided among several establishments: *forging, tinning*, and *decorating*. Some of the handicraft masters have establishments of all these kinds, and are consequently manufacturers of the pure type. Others perform one of the operations in their own workshops and then give out the articles to handicraftsmen for tinning and decorating in their homes. Here, consequently, the uniformity of the economic organisation of the industry—both when the work is given out to be done in the home and when several detail

---

* *Directory of Factories for 1879*. The matting makers working for buyers-up are mostly concentrated in Osa Uyezd.
** *Sketch*, p. 157.

workshops belong to one master—stands out very clearly.
The handicraftsmen who act as buyers-up, giving out work
to be done at home, are among the biggest masters (of whom
there are 25) who have organised the most profitable purchase of raw material and the marketing of the product on
a large scale; these twenty-five handicraftsmen (and they
alone) take their goods to the fair or have their own shops.
In addition to them, the big "manufacturer traders" are also
buyers-up; they exhibited their wares at the Factory Department of the Ekaterinburg Exhibition. The author of
the book classes them under "factory-handicraft (sic!)
industry" (*Handicraft Industries*, I, pp. 98-99). Thus, on
the whole, we get a very typical picture of capitalist manufacture, interwoven in the most diverse and fantastic ways
with small establishments. In order to demonstrate clearly
how little the division of industrialists into "handicraftsmen" and "manufacturers," into producers and "buyers-up,"
helps us to understand these complex relations, let us take
the figures given in this book and show the economic relations in the industry in a table:

Independent production for the market					Production for buyers-up			
Estab-lish-ments	Family workers	Wage-workers	Total	Total output (thou-sand rubles)	Estab-lish-ments	Fami-ly work-ers	Wage-work-ers	Total
A. "Factory-handicraft industry"								
?	?	?	?	60+7	a) 29	51	39	90
("manufacturer traders")					b) 39	53	79	132
B. "Handicraft industry"					68	104	118	222
25	(handicraftsman buyers-up)			95+30				
16	88	161	249	8				
				163+37				
				200,000	rubles = total output of the entire Nizhni-Tagil industry			

a) Handicraftsmen dependent on others for marketing.
b) Handicraftsmen dependent on others for both marketing and production.

And now we shall be told that the buyers-up, like the usurers, are "alien to production itself," that their domination merely implies the "capitalisation of the process of exchange," and not the "capitalisation of production"!

Another highly typical instance of capitalist manufacture is the chest-making industry (*Sketch*, pp. 334-39; *Handicraft Industries*, I, pp. 31-40). It is organised as follows: a few big proprietors who own workshops employing wage-workers purchase the materials, *partly* manufacture the goods in their own workshops, but mainly give out material to small detailed workshops, subsequently assembling the various parts of the chest in their own workshops and sending the finished article to market. Division of labour—the typical condition and technical basis of manufacture—is widely employed in production: the making of a complete chest is divided into ten or twelve detailed operations each performed by different handicraftsmen. Thus, the organisation of the industry consists in combining detail workers (Theilarbeiter, as they are called in *Das Kapital*) under the command of *capital*. Why capital prefers to give out work to be done at home rather than employ wage-workers in a workshop is made quite clear by the data provided in the 1894-95 handicraft census on the establishments of the Nevyansk Factory, Ekaterinburg Uyezd (one of the centres of the industry), where, *side by side* with assembly workshops, we also meet with detail handicraftsmen. Hence a comparison between the two is quite possible. Here are comparative figures given in a table (on p. 173 of the tables):

Chest-makers of Nevyansk Factory	Group	Sub-group	Number of establishments	Number of			Gross income		Wages		Net income	
				Family workers	Wage-workers	Total	Total	Per worker	Total	Per wage-worker	Total	Per family worker
"Buyers-up"	II	1	2	1	13	14	5,850	418	1,300	100	1,617	808.5*
"Handi-craftsmen"	II	3	8	11	8	19	1,315	70.3	351	44	984	89.4

* Per establishment.

Before examining this table, we must say that if we had taken the data for the entire first and third sub-groups (*Sketch*, p. 335) and not for the Nevyansk Factory alone, the conclusions would have been the same. The gross income in the two sub-groups obviously cannot be compared, for the same material passes through the hands of various detail workers and through the assembly workshops. But the data for incomes and wages are characteristic. We find that the wages of hired workers in the assembly workshops are higher than the incomes of the dependent handicraftsmen (100 rubles and 89 rubles respectively), notwithstanding the fact that the latter exploit wage-workers in their turn. But the wages of these latter are *less than half* those of the workers in the assembly workshops. Why, then, should our employers not prefer "handicraft" industry to factory industry, when the former yields them such substantial "advantages"! We find a fully analogous organisation of production for the buyers-up in the vehicle-building industry (*Sketch*, p. 308, et seq.; *Handicraft Industries*, I, p. 42, et seq.)—the same assembly workshops, whose owners are "buyers-up" (and work-distributors, work-givers) in relation to the handicraftsmen who make the parts, and the earnings of the wage-worker in the workshop are again higher than the income of the dependent handicraftsman (not to mention his wage-worker). These higher wages are recorded for both agriculturists (Group I) and non-agriculturists (Group II). In the cabinet-making industry, the buyers-up are the furniture shops in the city of Perm (*Sketch*, 133; *Handicraft Industries*, II, 11) that supply the handicraftsmen with models when placing orders, and in this way, incidentally, have "gradually improved the technique of production."

In the tailoring trade, the ready-made clothing shops in Perm and Ekaterinburg give out material to be made up by handicraftsmen. As we know, an exactly similar organisation of the tailoring and dressmaking industry also exists in other capitalist countries, in Western Europe and America. The difference between the "capitalist" West and Russia, with her "people's industry," is that this state of affairs

is called the Schwitz-system* in the West and means are
sought to combat this worst of all systems of exploitation;
the German tailors, for example, demand that the masters
should build factories (that is, are "artificially implanting
capitalism," as the Russian Narodnik would put it)—whereas
in our country this "sweating system" is benignly called
"handicraft industry" and its superiority to capitalism is
argued and discussed.

———

We have now examined all the industries in which the
vast majority of handicraftsmen employed by buyers-up are
engaged. What are the results of our review? We have become convinced of the absolute unsoundness of the Narodnik
contention that the buyers-up, and even the assembly workshop masters, are mere usurers, elements alien to production, and so on. Despite the above-mentioned inadequacy
of the *Sketch* data, despite the absence in the census programme of questions about the business conducted by the
buyers-up, we have succeeded in establishing, for most of
the industries, intimate ties between the buyers-up and production—even their direct participation in production,
"participation" as owners of shops which employ wage-workers. Nothing could be more absurd than the opinion that
working for buyers-up is merely the result of some abuse,
of some accident, of some "capitalisation of the process of exchange" and not of production. The contrary is true: working
for a buyer-up is *a special form of production*, a special organisation of economic relations in production—an organisation which has directly sprung from small commodity
production ("petty people's production," as it is customary
to call it in our lofty literature), and which to this day is
connected with it by a thousand threads; for it is the most
prosperous petty masters, the most go-ahead "handicraftsmen,"
who lay the basis for this system by extending their operations through supplying work to domestic workers. Work
for buyers-up is directly associated with the capitalist work-

———

* Sweating system.—*Ed.*

shop employing wage-workers, and often just constitutes an extension of it or one of its departments; it is simply an *adjunct of the factory*, understanding this latter expression in the generally accepted and not the scientific sense. In the scientific classification of forms of industry in their successive development, work for buyers-up belongs to a considerable extent to *capitalist manufacture*, since 1) it is based on hand production and on the existence of many small establishments; 2) it introduces division of labour between these establishments and develops it also within the workshop; 3) it places the merchant at the head of production, as is always the case in manufacture, which presupposes production on an extensive scale, and the wholesale purchase of raw material and marketing of the product; 4) it reduces those who work to the status of wage-workers engaged either in a master's workshop or in their own homes. These features, as we know, are typical of the scientific conception of manufacture as a special stage in the development of capitalism in industry (see *Das Kapital*, I, Kapitel XII).[121] This form of industry, then, already implies the deep-going rule of capitalism, being the direct predecessor of its last and highest form—large-scale machine industry. Work for the buyer-up is consequently a backward form of capitalism, and in contemporary society this backwardness has the effect of seriously worsening the conditions of the working people, who are exploited by a host of middlemen (the *sweating system**), are disunited, are compelled to content themselves with the lowest wages and to work under the most insanitary conditions and for extremely long hours, and—what is most important—under conditions which render public control of production extremely difficult.

———

We have now concluded our review of the 1894-95 handicraft census data. This review has fully confirmed the statement made above regarding the utter meaninglessness of the term "handicraft industry." We have seen that this

---

* These words are in English in the original.—*Ed.*

28*

term has been used to cover the most diverse forms of industry, we might even say: *practically every form of industry known to science*. And, indeed, the term has been made to include patriarchal artisans who work for private customers using the customers' own materials and receiving remuneration sometimes in kind, sometimes in cash. Further, it has been made to include representatives of an entirely different form of industry—the small commodity producers who work together in families. It has been made to include owners of capitalist workshops who employ wage-workers, and also these wage-workers themselves, who sometimes number several dozen to an establishment. It has been made to include manufactory owners who possess capital in considerable quantity and command a whole system of detail workshops. It has likewise been made to include workers employed at home for capitalists. In all these subdivisions, both agriculturists and non-agriculturists, peasants and town dwellers have equally been regarded as "handicraftsmen." The confusion is by no means peculiar to this particular investigation of the Perm handicrafts. Not at all. It is to be met with *whenever* and *wherever* anything is said or written about "handicraft" industry. Anybody who is familiar, for example, with the *Transactions of the Commission of Inquiry into Handicraft Industry* knows that it, too, classes all these categories as handicraftsmen. And it is a favourite method of our Narodnik economists to lump together this endless variety of forms of industry, to call this jumble "handicraft," "people's" industry, and—risum teneatis, amici!*—*to contrast* this meaningless hodge-podge with "capitalism," with "factory industry." This admirable method, which testifies to the remarkable profundity and erudition of its initiator, was, if we are not mistaken, "theoretically justified" by Mr. V. V., who on the very first pages of his *Essays on Handicraft Industry* takes the official figures for the number of "factory" workers in Moscow, Vladimir and other gubernias, compares them with the number of "handicraftsmen," and finds, of course, that "people's industry" in Holy Russia is developed to a far greater extent than "capitalism." But our "authoritative" economist

---

* Restrain your laughter, friends!—*Ed.*

very wisely remains silent on the fact, established time and again by investigators,* that the overwhelming majority of these "handicraftsmen" *also work for manufacturers*. The compilers of the *Sketch*, faithful to Narodnik prejudices, have used the same method. Although the total annual output of "handicraft" industry in Perm Gubernia amounts to only 5 million rubles,** and that of "factory" industry to 30 million rubles, "the number of persons employed in factory industry amounts to 19,000 and in handicraft industry, to 26,000" (p. 364). The classification, you see, is almost touching in its simplicity:

a) Factory workers 19,000
b) Handicraftsmen 26,000

Total 45,000

Naturally, such a classification offers endless scope for reflections on the "possibility of a different path for the fatherland"!

But it is not for nothing that we have before us the data of the handicraft household census which investigated the forms of industry. We shall attempt to give a classification that *corresponds* to the census data (of which the Narodnik classification is a sheer mockery) and to the various forms of industry. We shall apply the percentages revealed by the census for 20,000 workers, to the higher figure of 26,000 derived by the authors from other sources.

---

* If nothing more, see Mr. Kharizomenov's article, "The Importance of Handicraft Industry," in *Yuridichesky Vestnik*,[122] 1883, Nos. 11 and 12, which contains a summary of the statistical material then available.

** Not to mention the curious way in which this figure was arrived at. For instance, the largest component is the flour-milling industry (1,200,000 rubles), arrived at by including the total value of the grain ground by the millers! In the tables and in the description given in the *Sketch*, only the gross income of 143,000 rubles was taken (see p. 358 and note). The bootmaking industry accounts for 930,000 rubles, a substantial part of which consists of the turnover of the Kungur *factory owners*; and so on, and so forth.

A. Commodity Production.

Number of workers

I. Workers capitalistically employed.

(1) "Factory" workers (averaging, according to statistics for the seven years, 1885-91, 14.6 workers per establishment)   19,000
42.2%

(2) Wage-workers employed by "handicraftsmen" (25% of total).

(One-fourth of these are employed in establishments averaging 14.6 workers per establishment) 6,500
14.4%   30,700
68.2%

(3) Workers engaged at home in the employ of buyers-up, i.e., working members of handicraftsmen's families in the third sub-group—20%.

. (Many of these work *for the same employers* as the workers under items 1 and 2)   5,200
11.6%

II. Small commodity producers, i.e., handicraftsmen's families in the first sub-group—30%.

(About one-third of these employ wage-workers) 7,800
17.4%

B. Artisan Production.

Rural (and partly urban) artisans, i.e., handicraftsmen's families in the second sub-group—25%.

(A small proportion of these also employ wage-workers) 6,500
14.4%

Total   45,000
100%

We are fully aware that there are errors even in this classification: it does not include factory owners, but does include handicraftsmen who employ dozens of wage-workers; some manufactory owners have been included accidentally, but not specified, while others have not been included, having been discarded as "buyers-up"; it includes urban artisans of one town, but not of eleven other towns, and so on. At any rate, this classification is based on the census *data* on *forms of industry*, and the errors mentioned are errors in these data, and not errors of classification.* In any case, this classification gives an accurate idea of the real state of affairs, it explains the real social and economic relations of the various participants in industry, and, consequently, their status and their interests—and such an explanation is the supreme task of any scientific economic investigation.

VII

"GRATIFYING FEATURES" OF HANDICRAFT INDUSTRY

We might be accused of one-sidedness, of accentuating only the dark sides of handicraft industry, were we to pass over in silence the facts mentioned in the *Sketch* which are intended to stress its "bright side" and "gratifying features."

We are told, for example, that wage-labour in handicraft industry has a character of its own, for here the wage-worker lives in "close contact" with the master, and "may" himself become a master. The "gratifying feature" here, then, is the benign wish to turn all workers into small masters!** Incidentally, not all—only some, for "the tendency to exploit the labour of others is undoubtedly characteristic of all men in general, including the handicraftsman" (*Sketch*, p. 6). This sentence is simply inimitable for the naïveté with which "all men" are without further ado identified with the petty bourgeois! It is not surprising that those who look at the world through petty-bourgeois spectacles should discover such remarkable truths. On p. 268, a small factory employing

---

* The objection may be raised that the wage-workers employed by artisan handicraftsmen (20% of the wage-workers employed by handicraftsmen) should be classed under artisan and not commodity production. But here labour-power is itself a commodity, and its purchase and sale is an essential feature of capitalism.

** Not a word is said as to how this "close contact" reacts on the system and correctness of payment, the methods of hire, the enslavement of the worker, the *truck system* [these words are in English in the original.—*Ed.*], and so on.

eight wage-workers and with an output of 10,000 rubles is proclaimed to be "by its labour situation (sic!) a handicraft enterprise in the strict sense of the term." On pp. 272-74, we are told how another small manufacturer (employing seven wage-workers and five apprentices, and with an output of 7,000 rubles) erected a blast furnace on a site rented from a village community and applied to the Handicraft Bank for a loan of 5,000 rubles with which to erect a furnace, explaining that his "whole enterprise is of purely local interest, inasmuch as the ore will be mined on community allotments by the local peasants themselves." The bank refused the loan for purely formal reasons. And the *Sketch* uses this as a peg on which to hang an attractive picture of the conversion of this enterprise into a co-operative: "this will undoubtedly please the employer, as one who has at heart the interests of the fellow community members around him and not only those of the industry." The enterprise "embraces numerous labour interests of the fellow community members, who will be mining ore and felling timber and carrying them to the factory." "Householders will deliver ore, charcoal, etc., to the factory, just as the womenfolk deliver milk to the public cheese factory. Of course, this presupposes a more complex organisation than that of a public cheese factory, especially if the local skilled and unskilled labourers are employed in running the business itself, that is, smelting iron from ore." How idyllic! Manual labourers ("fellow community members") will "deliver" ore, fuel and the rest "to the factory," just as peasant women deliver milk to the cheese factory! We will not deny that the Handicraft Bank can (if its bureaucratic organisation does not prevent it) perform the same sort of service as other banks in developing commodity production and capitalism, but it would be very sad indeed if it were at the same time to develop the pharisaism and Manilov chit-chat of loan-seeking employers.

So far we have seen how enterprises employing large numbers of wage-workers have been proclaimed "handicraft" on the ground that their owners work themselves. But for pettybourgeois people this condition would be rather restrictive, and so the *Sketch* endeavours to expand it: it appears that an enterprise which "is conducted solely with the help of wage-labour" may also be a handicraft enterprise, provided that its "success" depends upon the owner's "personal participation" (p. 295), or even if the owners "are obliged to confine their participation to the various worries involved in running the industry" (p. 301). Our Perm Narodniks are making splendid "progress," are they not? "Personal labour"— "personal participation"—"various worries." Mein Liebchen, was willst du noch mehr?*[123] Wage-labour in the brick industry, it appears, yields "special advantages" (302) to the wage-labourers, whom the brick kilns provide with "supplementary earnings"; yet the owners of these kilns often experience "a shortage of money for the hire of workers." The *Sketch* concludes that such owners should be granted credit facilities by the Handicraft Bank, "assigning such enterprises, according to a note to Article 7, point 3 of the Handicraft Bank Statutes, to specially deserving cases" (p. 302). Not very well put, but very impressive and portentous! "In conclusion," we read at the end of the description of the brick industry, "we find sufficient grounds for declaring that among the peasants in the brick industry the interests of masters and wage-workers have so much in common that although no artels have been formally registered in this industry, actually there is a strong tie of companionship between the masters and their wage-workers" (305). We would refer the reader to the statistical picture of these "ties of companionship" given above. It is also a curious fact—as a specimen of the confusion existing in Narodnik economic concepts— that the *Sketch* defends wage-labour and paints it in rosy colours by asserting that the kulak is not a master employing wage-workers, but an owner of money capital who "exploits labour in the person of the master handicraftsman and his wage-workers" (!), and at the same time launches into the most irrational and immoderate defence of the kulaks: "kulakism, in whatever gloomy colours it may be painted, is so far a necessary wheel in the exchange mechanism of handicraft production.... Kulakism should undoubtedly be regarded as a blessing insofar as the successes of the handicraft industry are concerned, when compared with a situation under which the handicraftsman would be without work were

---

* What more would you have, my dear?—*Ed.*

there no kulak or no finances available" (p. 8).* How long
will this "insofar" last? If it were said that merchant and usury
capital is a necessary factor in the development of capitalism, a necessary wheel in the mechanism of a *poorly developed* capitalist society (such as ours), that would be true. Thus
interpreted, the word "insofar" would mean: *insofar* as the
innumerable restrictions on freedom of industry and freedom
of competition (especially among the peasantry) continue to
preserve the most backward and most pernicious forms of capitalism in our country. Only we fear that this interpretation
will not be to the liking of the Perm or any other Narodniks!

Let us now go over to the artels, those most direct and most
important expressions of the alleged community principles
which the Narodniks insist on finding in the handicraft industries. It will be interesting to examine the handicraft *household* census data for the entire gubernia, a census whose
programme specifically included the registration and study
of artels (p. 14, point 2). We are accordingly in a position not
only to acquaint ourselves with the various types of artels,
but also to learn how widespread they are.

Take the oil-milling industry. "Domestic artels in the
strict sense of the term": in the villages of Pokrovskoye
and Gavryata, two oil-mills are owned by five brothers, who
have separated to form individual households, but who use
the mills in turn. These facts are of "profound interest,"
for "they throw light on the contract conditions of communal-
labour continuity in the handicraft industries." Obviously,
such domestic "artels are an important precedent to the spreading of factory-type industries among the handicraftsmen on co-
operative lines" (pp. 175-76). So then, the artel, in the strict
sense of the term, as a precedent to co-operation and, as an

---

* We find the same idea expressed in *Handicraft Industries*,
I, p. 39, et. seq., in a controversy with the newspaper *Dyelovoi Korrespondent*,[124] which said that the kulaks (masters of assembly workshops in the chest-making industry) should not be included in the
Handicraft Section. "Our entire handicraft industry," we read in
reply, "is in bondage to private capital, so that if only those handicraftsmen who trade in their own goods were included in the Handicraft Section it would be as empty as an eggshell." A highly significant admission, is it not? Using the data of the census, we have shown
above the meaning of this "bondage to private capital" which holds
the handicraft industries in its grip.

expression of the communal principle, consists in *property held in common by unseparated heirs*!! If that is so, then obviously the true palladium of the "communal principle" and "co-operation" is Roman civil law and Volume X of our code,[125] with its institutions of the condominium, i.e., property held in common by heirs and non-heirs!

"In the flour-milling industry ... the peasants' artel spirit of enterprise found most vivid expression in peculiar domestic forms." Many of the mills are jointly used by associations or even by whole villages. Use of the mills: the most widespread method is by rotation; then comes division of the net proceeds into shares proportionate to the expenses incurred by each partner; in "such cases the associated owners very rarely take part themselves in production which is usually done by wage-labour" (p. 181; the same is true of the pitch-boiling artels—p. 197). Truly an amazing peculiarity, and an amazing display of the artel principle—the common property of petty owners who jointly hire workers! On the contrary, the fact that the handicraftsmen use the mills, pitch-boiling plants and smithies *in rotation* testifies to the astonishing disunity of the producers, whom even common property cannot induce to work co-operatively.

"One of the forms of artel organisation" is the "artel smithies" (239). With the object of economising fuel, the master smiths jointly operate one smithy, hiring one labourer to work the bellows (economy in workers!) and renting both the premises and the hammer from the smithy owner in return for a special payment. And so, the hiring out of articles that are the private property of one person to others for money is "artel organisation"! Verily, Roman law fully deserves to be called the code of "artel organisation"!... "In the artel organisation ... we find fresh evidence of the absence of class crystallisation in production among the handicraftsmen—evidence of the same merging of different strata of agriculturists and handicraftsmen that we observed in the case of the artel flour mills" (239). And after this, there are malicious persons who still dare to speak of the differentiation of the peasantry!

Hitherto, therefore, we have not had a single instance of handicraftsmen *combining* to buy raw materials or to market the product, not to mention combination in production itself! Nevertheless, such combinations exist. The Perm Gubernia handicraft household census registers *as many as four of them*. They were *all* formed with the help of the Handicraft Bank—three in the vehicle-building trade, and one in the production of agricultural machines. One of the artels employs wage-labour (two apprentices and two hired "auxiliary" workers). In another, two partners use a smithy and a workshop belonging to a third partner, for which he receives special payment. They buy raw material and market the product in common, but they work in separate workshops (except in the case of the smithy and workshop rented for cash). Together, these four artels embrace 21 family workers. The Perm Handicraft Bank has functioned for several years. Let us assume that it will now "unite" (for the renting of a neighbour's smithy) not 20, but 50 family workers *a year*. All the 15,000 handicraft family workers will then be "united" in "artel organisations" in exactly 300 years. And when that job is done, they will begin "to unite" the handicraftsmen's wage-workers.... And the Perm Narodniks exult: "These cardinal economic conceptions, evolved by the independent workings of the handicraftsmen's minds, serve as a firm pledge of the economic progress of industry among them, based on labour's independence of capital, for these facts speak not only of an elemental, but of a fully conscious aspiration of the handicraftsmen for labour independence" (p. 333). Have mercy, gentlemen! It is impossible, of course, to picture Narodism without Manilovian phrase-mongering, but, after all, there's a limit to everything! *Not one* of the artels, as we have seen, expresses the "principle of labour's independence of capital": they are all artels of masters and small masters, many of them employing wage-workers. There is no co-operation in these artels; even the joint purchase of raw materials and sale of the product is ridiculously rare and embraces a surprisingly insignificant number of masters. It may be safely said that there is no capitalist country in the world where a register of nearly 9,000 small establishments, with 20,000 workers, would reveal *such astonishing dispersion and backwardness* of the producers; where among the latter one would find only a score or so cases of *property owned in common*, and *less than a dozen* cases of three to five owners uniting to buy raw materials and sell the product! Such dispersion would be the *surest indication of unrelieved economic and cultural stagnation*, if we did not, fortunately, see that capitalism is day by day uprooting patriarchal handicraft, with the parochialism of its small self-sufficing proprietors, and breaking down the small local markets (on which small production depends), replacing them by the national and the world market, *compelling* the producers, not only of a village like Gavryata, but of a whole country, and even of several countries, to enter into association with each other, forming associations that are no longer merely of masters, big and small, and confronting them with far wider problems than that of buying timber or iron more cheaply, or selling nails or carts more profitably.

VIII
THE NARODNIK PROGRAMME OF INDUSTRIAL POLICY

Since practical recommendations and measures are always connected with what is considered to be "gratifying" and promising in reality, one knows a priori what wishes for the handicraft industry would be expressed in the *Sketch* since it has reduced all "gratifying features" to drawing a rose-coloured picture of wage-labour in petty economy and an exalted notion of the extremely scanty and one-sided associations of small proprietors. These wishes, a rehash of the usual Narodnik recipes, amaze one by their contradictory character, on the one hand, and by their inordinate exaggeration of commonplace "measures," converted by phrase-mongering into solutions of great problems, on the other. At the very beginning of the *Sketch*, in the introduction, before the census data are even dealt with, we meet with verbose statements about the "task of handicraft credit" being "to overcome (sic!) the money shortage," about the "co-operative organisation of exchange between production and consumption" (p. 8), about "spreading artel organisations," establishing handicraft warehouses, technical advice bureaus, technical schools, and the like (p. 9). These statements recur in the book over and over again. "The economics of the industry must be so reorganised as to place the handicraftsmen in possession of money; or, to put it more plainly, to emancipate the handicraftsman from the kulak" (119). "The task of our time" is to effect "the emancipation of the handicraftsman by means of credit," etc. (267). "Exchange processes must be rationalised," measures must be adopted "to implant rational principles of credit, exchange and production in peasant farming" (362); what is needed is the "economic organisation of labour" (sic!!—p. 363), "the rational arrangement of the economics of the national economy," and so on, and so forth. All this, as we see, is the familiar Narodnik panacea, tacked on to the census data. And, as though in final confirmation of their Narodnik orthodoxy, the compilers did not fail to condemn money economy in general, and for the reader's edification inform him that artisan production "performs a valuable service to the national economy, by affording it the opportunity to avoid the conversion of natural economy into money economy." "The national economy is vitally interested in demanding that the raw materials it produces be worked up on the spot, as far as possible without the intervention of money in the exchange processes" (p. 360).

Here we have the Narodnik programme expounded with a fullness and frankness that leave nothing to be desired! We say the "Narodnik programme," for we are interested, not in what distinguishes the compilers of the *Sketch* from other Narodniks, but, on the contrary, in what they have in common. What interests us is the practical Narodnik programme for the handicraft industries in general. It is easy to see that the main features of this programme are saliently stressed in the *Sketch*: 1) condemnation of money economy and sympathy for natural economy and primitive artisan production; 2) various measures for the encouragement of small peasant production, such as credits, technical developments, etc.; 3) the spreading of associations and societies of all kinds among the masters, big and small—raw material, warehousing, loan-and-savings, credit, consumers' and producers' societies; 4) "organisation of labour"—a current phrase in all and sundry Narodnik good intentions. Let us examine this programme.

To take first the condemnation of money economy: as far as industry is concerned, it is already of a purely Platonic character. Even in Perm Gubernia, artisan production has already been forced far into the background by commodity production, and is in such a pitiful state that we find the

Sketch itself talking about the desirability of "emancipating the handicraftsman from dependence," in other words, of abolishing the artisan's dependence on the private customer "by seeking means of extending the marketing area beyond the local consumption demand" (p. 33). In other words, condemnation of money economy in theory and a desire to convert artisan production into commodity production in practice! And this contradiction is by no means peculiar to the *Sketch*, it is characteristic of all Narodnik projects: however much they may kick against commodity (money) economy, realities driven out of the door fly in at the window, and the measures they advocate only serve to develop commodity production. Credit is an illustration of this. In their plans and proposals the Narodniks cannot dispense with commodity economy. The *Sketch*, for example, does not even hint that the proposed reforms should not be based on commodity economy. On the contrary, all it wants is rational principles of *exchange*, the co-operative organisation of *exchange*. Commodity economy remains, and is only to be reformed on *rational* lines. There is nothing new in this utopia; it had many an eminent exponent in the old economic literature. Its theoretical unsoundness was disclosed long ago, so that there is no need to dwell on the subject here. Instead of uttering absurd phrases about the necessity of "rationalising" economy, would they not do better first "to rationalise" their notions of the *existing* economy, of the socio-economic relations existing among that extremely variegated and dissimilar mass of "handicraftsmen" whose destinies our Narodniks wish to decide so bureaucratically and frivolously from above? Has not actual life shown us time and again that Narodnik practical measures, concocted in accordance with supposedly "pure" ideas on "organisation of labour," etc., lead in practice to nothing but encouragement and support for the "enterprising muzhik," the small manufacturer or the buyer-up and all the representatives of the petty bourgeoisie in general? This is not fortuitous, it is not because individual measures are imperfect or unsuitable. On the contrary, given the general basis of commodity economy, it is the petty bourgeois above all and before all who inevitably and necessarily make use of credits, warehouses, banks, technical advice and the like.

But, it may be objected, if that is so, if the Narodniks in the practical measures they suggest, unconsciously and involuntarily serve to develop the petty bourgeoisie, and, hence, capitalism in general, why should their programme be attacked by people who on principle regard the development of capitalism as a progressive process? Is it reasonable to attack practical and useful programmes because their ideological integument is wrong, or, to put it mildly, debatable, for surely nobody will deny the "usefulness" of technical education, credits and of producers' societies and associations?

These are not imaginary objections. In one form or another, in one connection or another, they are constantly to be heard in the replies to the arguments levelled against the Narodniks. We shall not dwell here on the point that even if such objections were justified, they do not in the least refute the fact that the dressing-up of petty-bourgeois projects as the most exalted social panaceas is in itself a cause of grave social harm. We intend to put the question on the practical footing of the vital and immediate needs of the times, and to judge the Narodnik programme from this *deliberately* narrowed viewpoint.

Although many of the Narodnik measures are of practical value in serving to develop capitalism, nevertheless, taken as a whole, they are 1) supremely inconsistent, 2) lifelessly doctrinaire, and 3) paltry compared with the actual problems with which developing capitalism confronts our industry. Let us explain. We have shown, firstly, how inconsistent the Narodniks are as *practical* men. Side by side with the measures indicated above, which are usually described as a liberal economic policy, and which have always been inscribed on the banners of bourgeois leaders in the West, the Narodniks contrive to cling to their intention of *retarding* contemporary economic development, of *preventing* the progress of capitalism, and of *supporting* small production, which is being bled white in the struggle against large-scale production. They advocate laws and institutions which restrict the freedom of the mobilisation of land and freedom of movement, and which retain the peasantry as a closed social estate, etc. Are there, we ask, any reasonable grounds for *retarding* the development of capitalism and big industry? We have seen from the census data that the notorious "inde-

pendence" of the handicraftsmen is no guarantee that they
will not be subordinated to merchant capital, to exploitation
in its worst form; that *actually* the condition of the vast
bulk of these "independent" handicraftsmen is often *more
wretched* than that of the handicraftsmen's wage-workers,
and that their earnings are astonishingly low, their working
conditions (from the standpoint of sanitation and hours)
highly unsatisfactory, and production scattered, technically
primitive and undeveloped. Are there, we ask, any reasonable grounds for perpetuating the police laws which reinforce
the "tie with the land," and *forbid* the breaking of a tie that
appeals so strongly to the Narodniks?* The data of the
1894-95 "handicraft census" in Perm Gubernia are clear proof
of the utter absurdity of artificial measures to tie the peasants
to the land. All these measures do is reduce their earnings,
which, wherever the "tie with the land" exists, are less than
half those of the non-agriculturists; they lower the standard
of living, increase the isolation and disunity of producers
scattered throughout the villages and render them more defenceless than ever against the buyer-up and subcontractor. At
the same time, the fact that the peasants are tied to the land
hinders the development of agriculture, without, however,
being able to prevent the rise of a rural petty-bourgeois
class. The Narodniks avoid raising the question: should the
development of capitalism be retarded or not? They prefer to
discuss "the possibility of different paths for the fatherland."
But anybody who begins to talk about immediate practical
measures thereby adopts the *existing path*.** Do whatever
you like "to drag" the fatherland on to a different path!
Such efforts will arouse no criticism (except the criticism

---

* The *Sketch*, too, speaks very enthusiastically of the advantages
of the village community and of the harm of the "freedom to
mobilise" landed property, which, it claims, would result in the
emergence of a "proletariat" (p. 6). This contrasting of the community with freedom to dispose of land is an excellent illustration of
the most reactionary and noxious feature of the "community." It
would be interesting to know whether there is a single capitalist
country in which a "proletarian" earning from 33 to 50 rubles a year
would not be classed as a *pauper*?

** And that this existing path is the development of capitalism
has not, as far as we know, been denied by the Narodniks themselves,
either by Mr. N. —on, or by Mr. V. V., or by Mr. Yuzhakov, etc., etc.

of laughter). But do not defend that which artificially *retards* present-day development, do not drown the problem of removing the obstacles from the existing path in talk about a "different path."

Here is another thing that should be borne in mind when judging the Narodniks' practical programme. We have already seen that the Narodniks try to formulate their ideas as abstractly as possible, to present them as the abstract demands of "pure" science or "pure" justice, and not as the real needs of real classes having definite interests. Credit—that vital need of every master, big and small, in capitalist society— is presented by the Narodnik as a sort of element in the system of the organisation of labour; masters' associations and societies are depicted as the embryonic expression of the idea of co-operation in general, of the idea of "handicraft emancipation," etc., whereas everybody knows that all such associations actually pursue aims which have nothing in common with such lofty matters, but are simply connected with the size of these masters' incomes, with the growing strength of their position and with their increasing profits. To thus convert commonplace bourgeois and petty-bourgeois wishes into a sort of social panacea only *emasculates* them, robs them of their vitality, of the guarantee of their urgency and practicability. The Narodnik endeavours to present the urgent needs of each proprietor, buyer-up, or merchant (credits, associations, technical assistance) as general questions towering above individual interests. The Narodnik imagines that he is thereby enhancing their significance, exalting them, whereas actually he is only converting a vital matter that *interests* certain specific groups of the population into a philistine wish, into armchair speculation, bureaucratic "reflections on the benefits" of things. Directly connected with this is a third circumstance. Not realising that such practical measures as credits and artels, technical assistance, etc., reflect the needs of developing capitalism, the Narodnik is unable to voice the general and fundamental needs of this development, and instead proposes paltry, casually selected, half-measures which in themselves are incapable of exerting any serious influence and are inevitably doomed to failure. Had the Narodnik openly and consistently adopted the standpoint of an exponent of the needs of social development along

capitalist lines, he would have been able to note *the general
conditions, the general demands* of this development, and he
would have seen that, given these general conditions (the
chief of them, in the present case, being freedom of industry),
all his petty projects and measures would be achieved automatically, that is, by the activities of the interested parties
themselves, whereas, by ignoring these general conditions
and proposing nothing but practical measures of an utterly
incidental character, he' is only beating about the bush. Let
us, by way of illustration, take the question of the freedom
of industry. On the one hand, it is so much the general and
fundamental question of questions concerning industrial
policy, that an examination of it is particularly appropriate.
On the other hand, the specific conditions of the Perm area
furnish interesting corroboration of the cardinal importance
of this question.

The metallurgical industry, as we know, is the major
feature of the economic life of the area and has laid a very
specific impress on it. Both the history of the area's colonisation and its present condition are closely connected
with the needs of the Urals iron industry. "Generally speaking, the peasants were settled in the Urals in order to furnish hands for the ironmasters," we read in the letter of Babushkin, a resident of Nizhniye Sergi, quoted in the *Transactions of the Commission of Inquiry into Handicraft
Industry*.* And these artless words very faithfully depict the
tremendous part played by the ironmasters in the life of the
area, their significance as landlords and factory owners combined, accustomed to undivided and unrestricted rule, as
monopolists who base their industry on possessional rights
and not on capital and competition. The monopoly basis of
the Urals metallurgical industry has been reflected in law,
in the well-known Article 394 of Volume VII of the Code of
Laws (Mining Statute), an article about which so much has
been and is still being written in literature on the Urals.
This law, promulgated in 1806, provides, firstly, that the
sanction of the mining authority shall be required for mining
towns to open any factory and, secondly, forbids the
opening in the ironworks area of "any manufactory or

---

* Part XVI, pp. 594-95. Cited in *Handicraft Industries*, I, p. 140.

factory whose operation chiefly depends on the action
of fire, necessitating the use of coal or wood." In 1861 the
Urals ironmasters particularly insisted on the inclusion of
this law in the terms governing the emancipation of the peasants, and Article 11 of the regulations for ironworkers reiterates the same prohibition.* The report of the Board
of the Handicraft Industrial Bank for 1895 states, among
other things, that "most numerous of all, however, are complaints against the ban imposed by officials of the Department
of Mines and the possessional works owners on the *opening*
of fire-using establishments within the areas under their jurisdiction, and against all sorts of restrictions on the operations
of the metal trades" (*Sketch*, p. 223). Thus, the traditions of
the "good old days" have been preserved intact in the Urals
to this day, and the attitude towards small peasant industry
in this region fully harmonises with the "organisation of
labour" which ensured the ironmasters a supply of factory
workers tied to their locality. These traditions are very
strikingly illustrated in the following report in *Permskiye
Gubernskiye Vedomosti*,[126] No. 183, 1896, quoted in the
Sketch and rightly referred to there as being "highly
eloquent." Here it is: "The Ministry of Agriculture and
State Property requested the Urals ironmasters to discuss
the possibility of the ironworks taking measures to encourage
the development of handicraft production in the Urals.
The ironmasters informed the Ministry that the development
of handicraft industry in the Urals would be detrimental to
big industry, for even today, when handicrafts are poorly
developed in the Urals, the population are unable to furnish

---

* See *Handicraft Industries*, I, pp. 18-19.—*Sketch*, pp. 222,
223, and 244.—Yegunov's article in Volume III of *Reports and
Investigations of Handicraft Industry in Russia* published by the Ministry of State Property and Agriculture. In publishing Yegunov's article, the Ministry, in a comment, makes the reservation that the author's
views "substantially differ from the opinion and information of the
Department of Mines." In Krasnoufimsk Uyezd, for example, as
many as 400 smithies were closed down under these laws. Cf. *Transactions of the Commission of Inquiry into Handicraft Industry*,
Part XVI, article by V. D. Belov, "Handicraft Industry in the Urals and
Its Connection with Metallurgy." The author relates that the
handicraftsmen, fearing to incur the severity of the law, hide their
machines. One handicraftsman built a furnace *on wheels* to cast iron-
ware, so as to make it easier to hide (op. cit., p. 18)!

the works with the required number of hands*; if the population were to find jobs that could be done at home, the ironworks would risk being brought to a complete standstill"
(*Sketch*, p. 244). This report evoked the following exclamation
from the compilers of the *Sketch*: "Of course, freedom of industry is a prime and essential condition of all industry, whether
large, medium or *small*.... In the name of freedom of industry,
all its branches should be legally equal. ... The metal-working
handicraft industries of the Urals should be freed from all
exceptional fetters imposed by the ironmasters to restrict
their *natural* development" (ibid. Our italics). Reading this
heartfelt and perfectly just defence of "freedom of industry,"
we were reminded of the story about the metaphysical
philosopher who delayed climbing out of a pit while he pondered over the nature of the rope that had been thrown
him. At last he decided: "It is nothing but a rope"![127] In
the same way, the Perm Narodniks ask disdainfully about
freedom of industry, freedom of capitalist development, freedom of competition: What is freedom of industry?—Simply
a bourgeois demand! Their aspirations soar much higher; it is
not freedom of competition they want (what a low, narrow,
bourgeois aspiration!), but "organisation of labour."... But
these Manilovian dreams have only to come "face to face"
with prosaic and unadorned reality, and that reality immediately smells of such an *"organisation of labour"* that the
Narodnik forgets all about the "harmfulness" and "danger"
of capitalism, about the "possibility of different paths for
the fatherland," and calls for *"freedom of industry."*

We repeat, we regard this desire as fully justified and consider that this view (shared not only by the *Sketch*, but by
practically every author who has written on this subject)
does credit to the Narodniks. But ... what is one to do? It
is impossible to say a word in praise of the Narodniks without
immediately following it up with a big "but"—but we have
two important remarks to make in this connection.

---

* Let us explain for the benefit of the reader that our iron industry
statistics have repeatedly shown that the number of workers
employed in proportion to output is considerably higher in the Urals
than in the Southern or Polish iron districts. Low wages—the result of the workers being tied to the land—keeps the Urals at a
much lower technical level than the South or Poland.

First. We can be sure that the overwhelming majority of the Narodniks will indignantly deny the correctness of our identifying "freedom of industry" with "freedom of capitalism." They will say that the abolition of monopolies and of the survivals of serfdom is "simply" a demand for equality, that it is in the interest of the "entire" national economy in general and of peasant economy in particular, and not of capitalism at all. We know that the Narodniks will say this. But it will be untrue. Over a hundred years have elapsed since the days when "freedom of industry" was regarded in this idealistic abstract way, as a fundamental and natural (cf. the word italicised in the *Sketch*) "right of man." Since then the demand for "freedom of industry" has been advanced and achieved in a number of countries, and everywhere this demand has expressed the discrepancy between growing capitalism and the survivals of monopoly and regulation, everywhere it has served as the watchword of the advanced bourgeoisie, and everywhere it has resulted in the complete triumph of capitalism, and nothing else. Theory has since fully explained the absolute naïveté of the illusion that "freedom of industry" is a demand of "pure reason," of abstract "equality," and has shown that freedom of industry is a capitalist issue. The achievement of "freedom of industry" is by no means a "legal" reform only; it is a profound economic reform. The demand for "freedom of industry" is always indicative of a discrepancy between the legal institutions (which reflect production relations that have already outlived their day) and *the new production relations*, which have developed in spite of the old institutions, have outgrown them and demand their abolition. If the order of things in the Urals is now evoking a general cry for "freedom of industry," it means that the traditional regulations, monopolies and privileges that benefit the landlord ironmasters are restricting *existing economic relations*, *existing* economic forces. What are these relations and forces? These relations are the *relations of commodity economy*. These forces are the forces of *capital*, which guides commodity economy. We have only to remember the "confession" of the Perm Narodnik quoted above: "Our entire handicraft industry is in bondage to private capital." And, even without this confession, the handicraft census data speak quite eloquently for themselves.

Second remark. We welcome the defence of freedom of industry by the Narodniks. But we make this welcome contingent on its being *conducted consistently*. Does "freedom of industry" merely consist in abolishing the ban on the opening of fire-using establishments in the Urals? Does not the fact that the peasant has no right to leave his village community, or to engage in any industry or pursuit he likes, constitute a far more serious restriction on "freedom of industry"? Does not the absence of freedom of movement, the fact that the law does not recognise the right of every citizen to choose any town or village community in the country as his place of domicile, constitute a restriction on freedom of industry? Does not the peasant community, with its social-estate exclusiveness—the fact that members of the trading and industrial class cannot enter it—constitute a restriction on freedom of industry? And so on, and so forth. We have enumerated far more serious, more general and widespread restrictions on freedom of industry, restrictions that affect all Russia, and the entire mass of the peasantry most of all. If "large, medium and small" industries are to have equal rights, should not the small industries be granted the same right to alienate land as is enjoyed by the large industries? If the Urals mining laws are "exceptional fetters, restricting natural development," do not collective responsibility, the inalienability of allotments and the special social-estate laws and regulations governing trades and occupations, migration and transfer from one social estate to another, constitute "exceptional fetters"? Do they not "restrict natural development"?

The truth is that on this question, too, the Narodniks have betrayed the half-heartedness and two-facedness that are characteristic of every Kleinbürger ideology. On the one hand, the Narodniks do not deny that in our society there are a host of survivals of the "organisation of labour" whose origin dates back to the days of apanage rights, and which are in crying contradiction to the modern economic system and to the country's entire economic and cultural development. On the other hand, they cannot help seeing that this economic system and development threaten to ruin the small producer, and, fearful for the fate of this palladium of their "ideals," the Narodniks try to drag history back, to halt development, beg and plead that it be "forbidden," "not allowed," and cover up this pitiful reactionary prattle with talk about "organisation of labour," talk that can only sound as a bitter mockery.

The chief and fundamental objection we have to make to the *practical* Narodnik programme for modern industry should now, of course, be clear to the reader. Insofar as the Narodnik measures are part of, or coincide with, the reform which, since the days of Adam Smith, has been known as *freedom of industry* (in the broad sense of the term), they are progressive. But, firstly, in that case, they contain nothing specifically "Narodnik," nothing that gives special support to small production and "special paths" for the fatherland. Secondly, this favourable side of the Narodnik programme is weakened and distorted by the substitution of partial and minor projects and measures for a general and fundamental solution of the problem—freedom of industry. Insofar, however, as Narodnik aspirations run counter to freedom of industry and endeavour to retard modern development, they are reactionary and meaningless, and their achievement can bring nothing but harm. Let us illustrate this by examples. Take credit. Credit is an institution of most developed commodity circulation, of the most developed, nation-wide turnover of commodities. Wherever achieved, "freedom of industry" inevitably leads to the formation of credit institutions as commercial enterprises, to the breaking-down of the peasants' social-estate exclusiveness, to their mingling with the classes which make most frequent resort to credit, to the independent formation of credit societies by interested persons, and so on. On the other hand, what value can there be in credit measures conferred on the "muzhiks" by Zemstvo officials and other "intellectuals" if the laws and institutions keep the peasantry in a condition which *precludes the possibility* of a proper, developed commodity circulation, in a condition in which *labour service* is far easier, far more practicable, attainable and workable than property responsibility (the foundation of credit)? Under these conditions, credit measures will always be something adventitious, an alien growth planted in absolutely uncongenial soil; they will be still-born, something only dreamy intellectual Manilovs and well-meaning officials could give birth to, and which the real *traders in*

money capital will always jeer at. So as to make no unfounded
assertion, let us quote the opinion of Yegunov (in the article
mentioned above) whom nobody can suspect of—"materialism." Speaking in reference to handicraft warehouses, he
says: "Even under the most favourable local conditions, a
stationary warehouse, and the only one in the whole uyezd
at that, never can and never will replace a perpetually mobile
and personally interested trader." In reference to the Perm
Handicraft Bank, we are told that in order to obtain a loan
the handicraftsman must hand in an application to the bank
or its agent and name his guarantors. The agent comes, veri-
fies his statement, gathers detailed information about his
business, etc., "and this whole pile of documents is sent, at the
handicraftsman's expense, to the head office of the bank."
If it decides to grant the loan, the bank sends (through the
agent, or through the volost administration) a bond for signature, and only when the borrower has signed it (his signature
being certified by the volost authorities) and sent it back to the
bank, does he receive his money. If an artel applies for a loan,
a copy of the articles of association is required. It is the function of the agents to see that loans are expended for the specific purposes for which they have been granted, that the
business of clients is run on sound lines, etc. "Obviously, in
no way can it be said that handicraftsmen can *easily obtain*
bank loans; it may be safely said that the handicraftsman
will far more readily turn to the local moneyed man for a loan
than submit to all the trying formalities we have described,
pay postage, notary's and local government fees, patiently
wait all the months that elapse between the moment the need
for the loan arises and the day it is granted, and put up with
supervision for the whole period of the loan" (op. cit., p. 170).
The Narodnik view on some sort of anti-capitalist credit is
just as absurd as the incongruous, clumsy and useless attempts (using wrong methods) to get done by "intellectuals"
and officials things that have everywhere and always
been the business of traders.

Technical education. There is hardly need, we think, to
dwell on this subject ... except to remind the reader of the
project, worthy of "eternal memory," of our well-known
progressive writer, Mr. Yuzhakov, to implant agricultural
gymnasia in Russia, at which poor peasant men and women

would *work off* the cost of their education by serving, for example, as cooks or laundresses.* ... Artels: but who does not know that the chief obstacle to their spreading is the traditions of the very same "organisation of labour" which has found expression in the Urals mining laws? Who does not know that wherever freedom of industry has been introduced in full it has always led to an unparalleled blossoming and development of all sorts of societies and associations? It is very comical at times to see our Narodniks trying to represent their opponents as enemies of artels, associations, etc., in general. The boot, of course, is on the other foot! The fact is that if you want to look for the idea of association and for the means of implementing it, you must not look back, to the past, to patriarchal artisan and small production, which are the cause of the extreme isolation, disunity and backwardness of the producers, but forward, to the future, towards the development of large-scale industrial capitalism.

We are perfectly aware of the haughty contempt with which the Narodnik will regard this programme of industrial policy that is being opposed to his own. "Freedom of industry"! What an old-fashioned, narrow, Manchester School** bourgeois aspiration! The Narodnik is convinced that for him this is an überwundener Standpunkt,*** that he has succeeded in rising above the transient and one-sided interests on which this aspiration is based, that he has risen to a profounder and purer idea of "organisation of labour." ... Actually, however, he has only *sunk* from progressive bourgeois ideology to reactionary petty-bourgeois ideology, which helplessly vacillates between the desire to accelerate modern economic development and the desire to retard it, between the interests of small masters and the interests of labour. On this question, the latter coincide with the interests of big industrial capital.

---

* See next article.

** There will be some, no doubt, who think that "freedom of industry" precludes such measures as factory legislation, etc. By "freedom of industry" is meant the abolition of all *survivals of the past* that hinder the development of capitalism. But factory legislation, like the other measures of modern so-called Socialpolitik, *presupposes* an advanced development of capitalism and, in its turn, *furthers* that development.

*** Discarded viewpoint.—*Ed.*

GEMS OF NARODNIK
PROJECT-MONGERING

(S. N. YUZHAKOV, EDUCATIONAL PROBLEMS. JOURNALISTIC ESSAYS.—SECONDARY-SCHOOL REFORM.—SYSTEMS AND AIMS OF HIGHER EDUCATION.—GYMNASIUM TEXT-BOOKS.—THE PROBLEM OF UNIVERSAL EDUCATION. — WOMEN AND EDUCATION. ST. PETERSBURG, 1897, PP. VIII + 283. PRICE 1 RUBLE 50 KOPEKS.) [128]

Written in exile at the end of 1897 First published in 1898 in the miscellany *Economic Studies and Essays* by Vladimir Ilyin

Published according to the text in *Economic Studies and Essays*

I

Under the above title Mr. Yuzhakov has published a collection of his articles that appeared in *Russkoye Bogatstvo* in the years 1895-97. The author believes that his articles "embrace the most important of these problems," i.e., "educational problems," and, "taken together, constitute a sort of review of the most timely and urgent, but still inadequately satisfied needs of our intellectual culture." (Preface p. V.) On page 5, it is once more stressed that the author in, tends to dwell "chiefly on problems of principle." But all these phrases merely show Mr. Yuzhakov's predilection for a broad sweep of thought, or rather, not so much of thought as of the pen. Even the title of the book is too broad. As a matter of fact—as can be seen from the list of articles in the subtitle to the book—the author does not deal with "educational problems" at all, but solely with the problem of the schools, and only of the secondary and higher schools at that. Of all the articles in the book, the most practical one is that on the textbooks used in our gymnasia. The author goes into a detailed examination of the current textbooks of the Russian language, geography and history, and demonstrates their utter worthlessness. This article would make the more interesting reading if it, too, were not made irksome by the author's usual verbosity. We intend to draw the reader's attention to only two of the articles in the book, one on the reform in secondary education, and the other on universal education, for these articles really do touch upon problems of principle and are very typical for an explanation of the favourite ideas of *Russkoye Bogatstvo*. The Grineviches and Mikhailovskies are reduced to digging in the muck-heap of Russian

doggerel for examples of preposterously stupid conclusions
drawn from a hostile doctrine. We, however, do not need
to engage in such dreary excavations for the same purpose:
we have only to turn to the magazine *Russkoye Bogatstvo*—
and to only one of its undoubted "pillars" at that.

·II

Section II of the article "Principles of Reform in Secondary
Education" has been entitled by Mr. Yuzhakov "Aims of
Secondary Education. Class Interests and Class Schools"
(see Contents). The theme, as you see, is of absorbing interest, promising as it does to explain one of the cardinal problems, not only of education, but of social life in general,
a problem, moreover, that is the source of one of the major
disagreements between the Narodniks and the "disciples." [129]
Let us then see what conception this contributor to *Russkoye Bogatstvo* has of "class interests and class schools."

The author quite rightly says that the formula, "the school
should prepare a man for life," is quite meaningless, and that
the question is what is needed for life, and "who needs it"
(6). "Who needs secondary education?—means: in whose interests, for whose benefit and advantage is education given
to secondary-school pupils?" (7). A splendid formulation of
the question, and we would give' our heartfelt praise to the
author if ... if all these preludes did not later prove to be
just empty talk: "It may be to the benefit and advantage
of the state, the nation, of some particular social class,
or of the individual who is being educated." Here the
muddle begins: we have to conclude that a class-divided
society is compatible with a non-class state, with a non-
class nation, with individuals standing outside of classes!
We shall soon see that this is by no means a slip of Mr.
Yuzhakov's pen, that he actually does hold this absurd
opinion. "If class interests are kept in mind when drawing up the school curriculum, there can of course be no
question of one general type of state secondary school. In
that case the educational establishments are necessarily
of the social-estate type, providing not only instruction, but
also education in the wider sense, for they not only have to
impart an education adapted to the special interests and

aims of the estate, but also social-estate habits and a social-estate esprit de corps" (7). The first conclusion to be
drawn from this harangue is that Mr. Yuzhakov does not
understand the difference between estates and classes, and
therefore hopelessly muddles these quite different concepts.
The same misunderstanding is revealed in other parts of the
article (see p. 8, for example), and this is all the more surprising as Mr. Yuzhakov in this same article comes very close
to the essential distinction between these concepts. "It
should be borne in mind," Mr. Yuzhakov informs us on page
11, "that often (although not necessarily) political, economic
and religious organisations sometimes constitute legal privileges, sometimes the actual prerogatives of special groups
of the population. In the first instance we have estates, in
the second classes." Here *one* of the differences between
class and social estate has been correctly noted, namely,
that what distinguishes classes from one another is not legal
privileges, but actual conditions, and that, consequently,
classes in modern society presume *legal equality*. And
there is another difference between social estates and classes
which Mr. Yuzhakov apparently does not ignore: "... And at
that time" (i.e., after the abolition of serfdom) "... we renounced the feudal and social-estate structure of national
life, and with it the system of exclusive social-estate schools.
Today, the introduction of the capitalist process is dividing
the Russian nation, not so much into estates, as into economic classes..." (8). Here another distinction between estates
and classes in European and Russian history is correctly indicated, namely, that the social estates are a feature of feudal,
and classes of capitalist society.* If Mr. Yuzhakov had given
even a little thought to these distinctions, and had not surrendered himself so easily to the sway of his agile pen and his
Kleinbürger** heart, he would have written neither the
above-quoted tirade, nor the rest of the twaddle, such as that
class curricula in schools are bound to mean one curriculum
for the rich and another for the poor, that in Western Europe

---

* Social estates presuppose the division of society into classes,
being themselves one of the forms of class distinction. When we speak
simply of classes, we always presume the non-estate classes of capitalist society.

** Petty bourgeois.—*Ed.*

class curricula are a failure, that class schools presume class exclusiveness, and so on and so forth. All this shows as clearly as can be that despite the promising title, despite his high-flown phrases, Mr. Yuzhakov has no conception of the nature of class schools. It is, most worthy Mr. Narodnik, that education is organised in one and the same way, and is equally accessible to all the *wealthy*. It is this last word alone that explains the nature of class schools, as distinct from social-estate schools. It is therefore the purest nonsense on Mr. Yuzhakov's part to say, as he did in the above-mentioned tirade, that where the schools follow class interests "there can be no question of one general type of state secondary school." Just the opposite: class schools— if adhered to consistently, that is, if they are freed of every survival of the social-estate system—necessarily presume one general type of school. Full legal *equality*, full equality of rights for all citizens, with education fully equal and accessible to all the wealthy—these constitute the essence of class society (and, consequently, of class education). Estate schools demand that the pupils shall belong to a given social estate. The class school knows no estates, it only knows citizens. Of all pupils it demands *one thing only*, namely, that they should pay for their education. A difference in curricula for rich and poor is by no means essential for class schools, since those who have not the wherewithal to pay for tuition, for textbooks and for the pupil's maintenance during the whole tuition period are simply barred by the class school from secondary education. The class school by no means presumes class exclusiveness: on the contrary, unlike social estates, classes always leave the road quite free for the transfer of individuals from one class to another. The class schools do not close their doors to anybody who has the means to pay for tuition. To say that in Western Europe "no success attends these dangerous programmes of semi-education and of the class moral and intellectual segregation of the various sections of the people" (9) is an utter perversion of the truth; for everybody knows that, both in the West and in Russia, the secondary schools are essentially class schools and serve the interests of only a very small part of the population. In view of the incredible confusion of ideas betrayed by Mr. Yuzhakov, we even think it worth while to give the follow-

The house in Shushenskoye village in which Lenin lived in exile

ing supplementary explanation for his benefit: in modern society, even the secondary schools which charge no tuition fees are nonetheless class schools, for the cost of maintaining the pupil for seven or eight years is immeasurably greater than the tuition fee, and is only within the reach of a very small minority. If Mr. Yuzhakov is anxious to be a practical adviser to contemporary reformers of the secondary schools, if he wants to treat the problem from the angle of present-day realities (as he does), he should only speak of the substitution of class schools for estate schools—*only* of that, or else remain entirely silent on this ticklish question of "class interests and class schools." And even so, these problems of principle have very little in common with the substitution of modern languages for the classical languages, which Mr. Yuzhakov recommends in this article. Had he confined himself to this recommendation, we would have had no objection, and would have even been ready to forgive him his unrestrained rhetoric. But since he has *himself* raised the question of "class interests and class schools," let him bear the responsibility for all his absurd utterances.

Mr. Yuzhakov's utterances on this theme are by no means confined to what has already been said. Faithful to the fundamental ideas of the "subjective method in sociology," Mr. Yuzhakov, having touched on the subject of classes, rises to a "broad point of view" (12, p. 15), so broad, that he can superbly ignore class differences; so broad that it enables him to speak, not of individual classes (fie, how narrow!), but of the nation in general. This magnificent "broadness" of view is attained by the hackneyed method of all moralists, big and small, and by the Kleinbürger moralists in particular. Mr. Yuzhakov sternly condemns this division of society into classes (and its reflection in education), holding forth with supreme grandiloquence and incomparable fervour on the "danger" (9) of this thing; on the point that "the class system of education in all its shapes and forms is fundamentally hostile to the interests of the state, the nation and the individuals to be educated"* (8); on the "inexpediency and

---

* One or the other, most worthy Mr. Kleinbürger: either you are talking about a society that is divided into classes, or about one that is not. In the first case, there can be no such thing as non-

danger from both the state and the national standpoint" (9) of class curricula in schools; on the point that historical examples illustrate only "that exceptionally anti-national development of the class system and class interests of which we have spoken, and which has already been admitted as dangerous to the national welfare and to the state itself" (11); on the point that "the class system of administration has been abolished in one form or another everywhere" (11); on the point that this "dangerous" division into classes arouses "antagonism between the various groups of the population" and gradually obliterates "the sense of national solidarity and national patriotism" (12); on the point that "broadly, correctly and far-sightedly understood, the interests of the nation as a whole, of the state, and of individual citizens in general should not be mutually contradictory (at least in the modern state)" (15), and so on and so forth. This is all sheer cant, empty phrase-mongering, which obscures the very essence of contemporary reality with the senseless "aspirations" of the Kleinbürger, aspirations that imperceptibly find their way into the description of things as they are. To find an analogy for the sort of outlook which gives rise to such phrase-mongering we have to turn to the exponents of that "ethical" school[130] in the West which was the natural and inevitable expression of the theoretical cowardice and political perplexity of the bourgeoisie there.

We, however, shall confine ourselves to comparing the following little fact with this magnificent eloquence and lofty-mindedness, this remarkable perspicacity and far-sightedness. Mr. Yuzhakov touched on the subject of social-estate and class schools. As regards the first, precise statistics are available—at least as far as male gymnasia, progymnasia and modern schools are concerned. Here are the figures, which we have borrowed from a publication of the Ministry of Finance: *Productive Forces of Russia* (St. Petersburg, 1896, Part XIX, Public Education, p. 31):

---

class education. In the second case, there can be neither a class state, nor a class nation, nor individuals who do not belong to one of the classes. And in both cases the phrase is meaningless and only expresses the innocent wish of a Kleinbürger who timidly closes his eyes to the most prominent features of contemporary reality.

"The division of students according to social estate (as percentages of the total number) may be seen from the following table:

Children of	In the male gymnasia and progymnasia of the Ministry of Public Education			In modern schools		
	1880	1884	1892	1880	1884	1892
Hereditary and life nobles and officials	47.6	49.2	56.2	44.0	40.7	38.0
Clergy	5.1	5.0	3.9	2.6	1.8	0.9
Urban estates . .	33.3	35.9	31.3	37.0	41.8	43.0
Rural estates (including non-Russian and minor officials)	8.0	7.9	5.9	10.4	10.9	12.7
Foreigners	2.0	2.0	1.9	3.0	4.8	5.4
Other estates . . .	2.0	Included in previous		3.0	Included in previous	
	100.0	100.0	100.0	100.0	100.0	100.0"

This table shows clearly how incautious Mr. Yuzhakov was when he said that we had immediately and resolutely (??) "renounced social-estate schools." On the contrary, the social-estate system prevails in our secondary schools to this day, even if 56 per cent of the students in the gymnasia (not to mention the privileged educational establishments for the nobility, etc.) are sons of nobles and officials. Their only serious rival is the urban estates, who now predominate in the modern schools. The proportion of the rural estates—especially if we bear in mind their vast numerical superiority over the other estates—is altogether insignificant. This table, therefore, clearly shows that anybody who sets out to discuss the character of our contemporary secondary schools should be perfectly clear in his own mind that it is only estate and class schools that are in question, and that insofar as "we" actually do renounce estate schools, it is exclusively in the interests of class schools. It goes without saying that we do not by any means intend to claim that the question of superseding the estate schools by class schools, and of improving the latter, is of no importance or concern to those classes that do not and cannot enjoy the advantages of secondary education: on the contrary, it is not a matter of unconcern to them either, for the estate system lays a particularly heavy burden on them both in life and in school, and the superseding of estate schools by class schools is only one of the links in the general and all-round Europeanisation of Russia. All we want is to show how Mr. Yuzhakov distorted the facts, and that actually his supposedly "broad" point of view is immeasurably inferior even to the bourgeois view on the question. Incidentally, on the subject of the bourgeois views. Mr. A. Manuilov simply cannot understand why P. B. Struve, who so explicitly revealed the one-sidedness of Schulze-Gävernitz, nevertheless "propagates his bourgeois ideas" (*Russkoye Bogatstvo*, No. 11, p. 93). Mr. A. Manuilov's failure to understand this is solely and exclusively due to his failure to understand the fundamental views not only of the Russian, but of all the West-European "disciples," and not only of the disciples, but of the teacher as well. Or perhaps Mr. Manuilov will deny that one of the fundamental views of the "teacher"—views that run like a scarlet thread through all his theoretical, literary and practical activities—is an ineradicable hatred of those lovers of "broad points of view" who with the help of sugary phrases obscure the class division of modern society? Or that another of his fundamental views is a firm recognition of the progressiveness and preferability of frank and consistent "bourgeois ideas" as compared with the ideas of those Kleinbürger who are so anxious to retard and halt capitalism? If this is not clear to Mr. Manuilov, let him ponder, say, over the writings of his fellow magazine contributor, Mr. Yuzhakov. Let him imagine that, on the subject now of interest to us, we see alongside Mr. Yuzhakov a frank and consistent exponent of "bourgeois ideas," who upholds the class character of the contemporary school, seeking to prove that nothing better could be imagined, and striving to eliminate the estate schools completely and to make the class schools more widely accessible (in the sense referred to above). Really, such ideas would be far superior to those of Mr. Yuzhakov's: attention would be drawn to the contemporary school's real needs, namely, to the abolition of its social-estate exclusiveness, and not to the vague "broad point of view" of the Kleinbürger. A frank elucida-

tion and defence of the one-sided character of the contemporary school would present a proper picture of reality,
and by its very one-sidedness would help to enlighten the
minds of the other side.* Mr. Yuzhakov's "broad" effusions,
on the contrary, only help to pervert social consciousness.
Lastly, as to the practical side of the matter ...but Mr. Yuzhakov does not go one jot beyond the limits of the class school,
not only in this article, but also in his "utopia," which we
shall now proceed to consider.

III

Mr. Yuzhakov's article dealing with "the problem of universal education" (see the title of the book) is called: "An
Educational Utopia. A Plan for Universal Compulsory Secondary Education." The very heading shows that this highly
edifying article of Mr. Yuzhakov's promises a lot. But, actually, Mr. Yuzhakov's "utopia" promises even far more. "Nothing less, dear readers, without concession or compromise..."
—is the way the author begins his article.—"A complete
gymnasium education for the entire population of both sexes,
compulsory for all, and involving no expenditure by the state,
Zemstvo or people—such is my grand educational utopia"
(201)! The worthy Mr. Yuzhakov evidently thinks that the
crux of the matter is that of "expenditure"; on this same page
he repeats that universal elementary education entails expenditure, but that universal secondary education, according to
his "plan," entails no expenditure at all. But not only does

---

* We are fully aware that it is very, very hard for *Russkoye Bogatstvo* contributors to understand an argument of this character.
That again is due to their failure to understand not only the "disciples," but also the "teacher."

Here, for example, is how one of the "teachers" sought, as far
back as 1845, to prove that the English workers gained from the
repeal of the Corn Laws. This repeal, he wrote, involves the farmers'
transformation into "Liberals, i.e., conscious bourgeois," and this
growth of class-consciousness on the one side necessarily involves a
similar growth of class-consciousness on the other (F. Engels, *The
Condition of the Working Class in England in 1844.* New York,
1887, p. 179).[131] How is it that you, gentlemen contributors to
Russkoye Bogatstvo, just bow and scrape before the "teachers," but
do not expose them for "propagating bourgeois ideas"?

Mr. Yuzhakov's plan entail no expenditure: it promises something far more than secondary education for the entire people. In order to give an idea of the full scope of what the *Russkoye Bogatstvo* contributor promises, we must anticipate and quote the author's own triumphant exclamations after he has set forth his plan in full and stands back to admire it. Mr. Yuzhakov's plan is to combine gymnasium education with the productive labour of the "gymnasium students," who are to maintain themselves: " ...The cultivation of the school land... will ensure abundant, palatable and wholesome food for the entire younger generation from birth to graduation from the gymnasium and also for the young people working off the cost of their education" (about this institution of the Yuzhakov Zukunftsstaat,* more anon) "and for the whole staff of administrators, teachers and managers. Furthermore, they will all be supplied with footwear, and clothes will be made for them. In addition, the school land will yield about 20,000 rubles, to wit, 15,000 rubles from surplus milk and spring wheat ... and about 5,000 rubles from the sale of skins, bristle, feathers, and other by-products" (216). Just think, reader, the *entire* younger generation to be maintained until graduation from the gymnasium, that is, until the ages of 21-25 (p. 203)! Why, that means maintaining *half* the country's total population.** The maintenance and education of scores of millions—that is real "organisation of labour" for you! Mr. Yuzhakov, evidently, was seriously annoyed with the wicked people who asserted that the Narodnik projects for the "organisation of labour" are nothing but the empty twaddle of empty windbags, and so he decided to annihilate these wicked people completely by publishing a full "plan" for this "organisation of labour"—to be achieved "without any expenditure." ... But even that is not all: "...In the process, we enlarged the task; we had this same organisation assume the cost of maintaining the entire child population; we took care to ensure dowries for young people about to be married—one that is quite good for the countryside; we found it

---

* State of the future.—*Ed.*
** According to Bunyakovsky, for every thousand inhabitants in Russia there are 485 between the ages of 0 and 20 years, and 576 between the ages of 0 and 25 years.

possible out of the same funds to appoint in every gymnasium,
that is, in every rural area, a doctor, a veterinary surgeon, a
trained agronomist, a trained gardener, a technologist and six
artisans, no less (who will raise the level of culture and satisfy the corresponding requirements of the whole locality)....
And the financial and economic problems involved in realising these aims will all be solved by the adoption of our
plan...."* How disgraced those evil tongues will now be
that insinuated that the celebrated Narodnik "we" was a
"mysterious stranger," a Jew with two skull-caps, and the like!
What unseemly slander! Henceforth a mere reference to Mr.
Yuzhakov's "plan" will be enough to prove the almighty
power of this "we" and the feasibility of "our" projects.

Maybe the reader will have his doubts about this word:
feasibility? Maybe the reader will say that by calling his
creation a utopia, Mr. Yuzhakov eliminated the question
of feasibility?—That would be so if Mr. Yuzhakov himself
had not made highly substantial reservations about the word
"utopia," and if he had not repeatedly stressed the feasibility
of his plan throughout his essay. "I make bold to think," he
says at the very beginning of his article, "that this plan for
universal secondary education will seem a utopia only at
first glance" (201).... What more do you want?... "I make
even bolder to assert that education on these lines for the entire population is far more feasible than universal elementary
education, which has nevertheless already been realised in
Germany, France, England and the United States, and is
very near to being realised in several of the gubernias of Russia" (201). Mr Yuzhakov is so convinced of the feasibility
of his plan (apparently, after having said that "plan" is a more
appropriate word than utopia is), that he does not neglect
even the most minor "practical conveniences" in the elaboration of that plan, deliberately preserving, for example, the system of two gymnasia, for boys and girls, in deference to the
"prejudice prevailing on the European continent against
coeducation," and insistently stresses that his plan would
"make it possible to leave the established curricula of the
male and female gymnasia undisturbed, and would provide

---

* P. 237. Both eloquent lines of dots in this effusion belong to
Mr. Yuzhakov. We would not have dared to omit a single letter.

16**

more lessons, and, therefore, higher remuneration, for the teaching staffs."... "All this is of no mean importance, given the desire not to confine it to a mere experiment, but to achieve really universal education" (205-06). There have been many utopians in the world who vied in the attractiveness and elegance of their utopias, but hardly one of them will be found to have betrayed so much solicitude for the "established curricula" and the remuneration of teaching staffs. We are convinced that future generations will long continue to point to Mr. Yuzhakov as a truly practical and truly business-like "utopian."

Obviously, in view of these promises of the author, his plan for universal education deserves the most careful examination.

IV

The principle from which Mr. Yuzhakov proceeds is that the gymnasium should at the same time be an agricultural establishment and ensure its own maintenance by the summer labour of its pupils. That is the fundamental idea of the plan. "That this idea is a correct one, can scarcely be doubted" (237), Mr. Yuzhakov opines. And we agree with him that this is indeed a correct idea; only, it should not necessarily be tacked on to the "gymnasia," or to the possibility of making them "pay" by their pupils' labour. The correct idea is that an ideal future society cannot be conceived without the combination of education with the productive labour of the younger generation: neither training and education without productive labour, nor productive labour without parallel training and education could be raised to the degree required by the present level of technology and the state of scientific knowledge. This thought was already expressed by the great utopians of the past; and it is fully shared by the "disciples," who for this reason, incidentally, do not object in principle to female and juvenile labour in industry, regard attempts to completely forbid such labour as reactionary, and only insist on the proper hygienic conditions being created for it. Mr. Yuzhakov is therefore wrong when he says: "I only wanted to suggest the idea" (237).... The idea was suggested long ago, and we hesitate to believe (until the contrary is demonstrated) that Mr. Yuzhakov could have been unfamiliar with it. What this *Russkoye Bogatstvo* contributor wanted to suggest, and did suggest, was an absolutely independent *plan for implementing* this idea. Only in this sense is it to be regarded as original, but here its originality goes as far ... as the Pillars of Hercules.

If universal productive labour is to be combined with universal education, then obviously the duty of sharing in productive labour should be laid upon *all*. That, one would think, is self-evident. But no, it appears not. Our "Narodnik's" solution of the matter is that the duty of physical labour should indeed be established as a general principle; *but not for all, only for people without means.*

The reader may think we are joking? Not a bit of it! "The purely urban gymnasia for people of means who are prepared to pay the full cost of education in money, might be preserved in their present form" (229). On page 231 "people of means" are classed without more ado as "categories of the population" not liable to compulsory education in the "agricultural gymnasia." Thus, in our Narodnik's opinion, compulsory productive labour is not a condition for general and all-round human development, but simply a means of paying the cost of gymnasium education. That is how he puts it. At the very beginning of his article, Mr. Yuzhakov discusses the problem of the winter workers needed by the agricultural gymnasia. The most "logical" of all, in his opinion, is the following method of ensuring winter workers for the gymnasia. The pupils of the junior classes do not work, and consequently receive their maintenance and tuition free, paying nothing towards the expenditures incurred by the school. "That being so, is it not his direct duty to work off these expenditures at the end of the course? This duty, carefully thought out and firmly established for everybody *who is unable to pay the cost of tuition*, will assure the gymnasium farm the necessary contingent of winter workers and an additional contingent of summer workers.... Regarded theoretically, this is very simple, comprehensible and quite incontrovertible" (205, our italics). Mercy on us, what could be "simpler"? Pay if you have the money, work if you have not!—every shopkeeper will agree that nothing could be more "comprehensible." And how wonderfully practical it all is! Only— where does the "utopia" come in? And why does Mr. Yuzhakov, by such plans, besmirch the grand fundamental idea which he intended to make the basis of his utopia?

Labour service performed by students without means is the basis of Mr. Yuzhakov's whole plan. True, he admits another method of acquiring winter workers—by hire,* but gives it a secondary place. Labour service, however—for three years (and if necessary even for four)—is to be compulsory for all who are not called up for military service, in other words, for two-thirds of the male students and for all the girls. "This system alone," Mr. Yuzhakov bluntly declares, "furnishes the key to the problem of universal education—and secondary, not just elementary, education at that" (207-08). "A small contingent of regular workers, who have remained on at the gymnasium altogether, and have identified their lives with it (!?), will supplement these labour forces of the gymnasium farm. Such are the potential, and by no means utopian, labour resources of our agricultural gymnasium" (208). And, it goes without saying, that with no shortage of things to be done, they will also do other jobs: "Auxiliary personnel for kitchen and laundry, as well as postmen, may easily be selected from among the three-year workers who have been graduated from the gymnasium" (209). The gymnasia will need tradesmen: tailors, bootmakers, carpenters, etc. Of course, "assistants may be supplied them from among those performing their three years' labour service" (210).

What will these farm-hands (or agricultural gymnasium students? I really don't know what to call them) receive in return for their labour? Everything required for their subsistence—"abundant and palatable food." Mr. Yuzhakov calculates it all to a nicety, on the basis of the rations "usually allowed an agricultural labourer." True, he "does not propose to feed the gymnasium on these lines" (210), but he nevertheless retains these rations, for after all the students will also

---

* "A gymnasium farm, directed by an experienced and trained manager, equipped with all modern improvements and supplied with a contingent of skilled and educated workers, should be a profitable undertaking and justify the hire of the necessary contingent of workers, some of the more deserving (sic!) of whom might be given a share in the proceeds. To a certain extent this method would probably have to be practised, especially in regard to landless peasants graduated from this gymnasium" (204).

gather potatoes, peas and lentils from their land, will sow hemp and sunflower for vegetable oil, and in addition, on non-fast days will receive half a pound of meat and two glasses of milk each. Don't think, reader, that Mr. Yuzhakov just touches lightly on this question, only by way of illustration. No, he has it all calculated down to the last detail—the number of calves, yearlings and two-year-olds, the maintenance of the sick, feed for poultry, and all the rest. He has forgotten neither the kitchen swill, nor the animal entrails, nor the vegetable peelings (212). Nothing is overlooked. Furthermore, clothes and footwear may be made in the gymnasium itself. "But cotton goods for underwear, bed linen, table linen and summer clothes, and more substantial material for winter clothing, and skins—if only sheepskin—for winter top clothes will, of course, have to be bought. Naturally, the teachers and other personnel and their families will have to provide their own materials, although they may be granted the services of the workshops. Properly speaking, for the students and three-year workers, this expenditure may, without stinting, be calculated at 50 rubles a year, or about 60,000 rubles for the whole establishment annually" (213).

We are positively beginning to be thrilled by the practical sense of our Narodnik. Just imagine: "we," "society," are instituting organisation of labour on such a grand scale, we are endowing the people with universal secondary education; and all this without any expenditure whatever, and with such immense moral advantages! What a splendid lesson it will be to "our" present agricultural labourers—who, in their ignorance, rudeness and boorishness, refuse to work for less than 61 rubles a year with board*—when they see labourers with a gymnasium education working for 50 rubles a year! We may be sure that even Korobochka[132] herself will agree with Mr. Yuzhakov that the theoretical basis of his plan is thoroughly "comprehensible."

---

* According to the Department of Agriculture and Rural Industry, the average annual wage of an agricultural labourer employed by the year in European Russia is 61 rubles 29 kopeks (average for the ten years 1881-91), plus board, valued at 46 rubles.

V

How will the economy of the gymnasia be run, and how will they be administered? The economy, as we have already seen, will be mixed: part natural and part cash economy. Mr. Yuzhakov, of course, goes very thoroughly into this important question. On page 216, he calculates minutely, item by item, that each gymnasium will need 160,000 to 170,000 rubles in cash, so that for all the 15,000 to 20,000 gymnasia, a sum of about 3,000 million rubles will be required. Well, of course, they will sell agricultural produce and receive money in return. Our author is so provident as to take account of the general conditions of modern commodity-capitalist economy! "Gymnasia situated in the vicinity of towns or railway stations, on lines not remote from large centres, would be of an entirely different type. Vegetable and fruit growing, dairy farming and handicrafts may well replace field cultivation" (228). Trade, as we see, will be on no mean scale. Who is to run it, the author does not say. It is to be presumed that the pedagogical councils of the gymnasia will also act in part as commercial councils. Sceptics may want to know what is to happen if schools go bankrupt, and whether they are able to engage in trade at all. But that, of course, would be unwarranted cavilling: if uneducated merchants can carry on trade, can success be doubted if representatives of our intellectual society get down to the job?

The gymnasia will naturally require land for their farms. Mr. Yuzhakov writes: "I think ... that if this idea is destined to be put to practical test, for experimental purposes the first of these agricultural gymnasia should be granted plots of 6,000 to 7,000 dessiatines each" (228). For a population of 109 million—20,000 gymnasia—about 100 million dessiatines would be required. But it should not be forgotten that only 80 million persons are engaged in agricultural labour. "It is only their children who should be put through the agricultural gymnasia."

Then, various categories of the population,* amounting

---

* Here is a full list of these categories of fortunates who are to be exempted from the agricultural gymnasia: "people of means, people undergoing correction, Mahommedan girls, non-Russians belonging

to nearly another 8 million, will have to be excluded, which will leave 72 million. They will need only 60 million to 72 million dessiatines. "And that, of course, is a lot" (231). But Mr. Yuzhakov is not dismayed. After all, the state, too, has lots of land; only it is not very conveniently situated. "For example, in Northern Polesye there are 127,600,000 dessiatines, and here, especially if, where necessary, a system of exchanging private and even peasant land for state land were adopted with the object of placing the former at the disposal of the schools, it would very likely not be difficult to supply our agricultural gymnasia with land gratis. The situation is equally good" ... in the south-east (231). Hm ... "good"! So send them off to Archangel Gubernia! True, hitherto it has served more as a place of exile, and the state forests there for the most part have not even been "opened up"— but that's a detail. As soon as gymnasium students in the charge of learned teachers are sent there they will cut down all these forests, clear the ground, and implant civilisation!

And in the central region a system of land redemption might be arranged; after all, not more than about 80 million dessiatines are required. Issue a "guaranteed loan," the payments on which, it need scarcely be said, to be apportioned among the "gymnasia receiving free land" (232)— and the trick's done! Mr. Yuzhakov assures us that there is no need to be alarmed at the "immensity of the financial operation. It is neither a chimera nor a utopia" (232). "Actually speaking," it will be "a gilt-edged mortgage." We should say so! But, once again, why talk about a "utopia"? And

---

to small nationalities, members of fanatical sects, the blind, deaf and dumb, idiots, insane, chronic inebriates, the diseased, and criminals" (231). We read this list with a clutch at the heart. Heavens, we thought, shall we manage to get at least our own kith and kin included in the list of exempted!—Under the first category, perhaps?—but no, our means will scarcely allow that. Well, we might manage with a little cunning to get the womenfolk classed as Mahommedan girls; but what about the males? The only hope is the third category. Mr. Yuzhakov's fellow contributor to the magazine, Mr. Mikhailovsky, as we know, has already simply classed P.B. Struve as a non-Russian national, so perhaps he will be gracious enough to class us also at least as "non-Russians belonging to small nationalities," and so exempt our kith and kin from the agricultural gymnasia!

does Mr. Yuzhakov seriously think that our peasants are so downtrodden and ignorant as to give their consent to such a plan?? There are the redemption payments to be made for the land, and the "payments on the loan to cover inauguration expenditures," * and to maintain the entire school, and to pay the salaries of all the teachers, and, to cap it all, in return for all this (in return for having hired paid teachers?), to perform labour service for a trifle of three years each! Isn't this going it a little too strong, Mr. Enlightened "Narodnik"? When, in 1897, you reprinted your creative effort that had appeared in *Russkoye Bogatstvo* in 1895—did you think where your characteristic Narodnik fondness for financial operations and instalment schemes would lead you? Let us recall, dear reader, that what he promised was universal education "involving no expenditure by the state, Zemstvo or people." And our financial genius really does not demand a single ruble from state or Zemstvo. But what about "the people"—or, more precisely, the *peasants without means*?** It is with their money that the land is bought, and the gymnasia inaugurated (for it is they who pay interest on and the redemption of the capital employed for the purpose), and it is they who pay the teachers and maintain all the gymnasia. And labour service in addition. What for? Because—our inexorable financier answers—you paid nothing for your education and maintenance in the junior classes (204). But, firstly, the non-working ages include only the "preparatory and first two gymnasium classes" (206)—and then come the semi-workers. And, secondly, these children, after all, are maintained by their elder brothers, who also pay the teachers for the tuition of the young. No, Mr. Yuzhakov, such a plan would be absolutely *unfeasible* not only in our day, but even in Arakcheyev's time,[133] for it is indeed a *feudal* "utopia."

Mr. Yuzhakov has very little to say about the administration of the gymnasia. It is true that he enumerates the teaching staff in great detail and appoints a salary for each, a "comparatively small" one (for they get free quarters, mainte-

---

* P. 216—10,000 rubles per gymnasium.
** Since those with means are excluded. Mr. Yuzhakov himself suspects that "a certain proportion of the agricultural population, too, will prefer to send their children to urban secondary schools that charge fees" (230). We should think so!

nance of their children and "half the expenditures on clothing")—50 rubles per annum, you might think? No, a little
more: "the head-master, head-mistress and chief agronomist
2,400 rubles each, the inspector," etc., according to rank,
descending the hierarchic ladder down to 200 rubles for minor
employees (214). Not a bad career, you see, for those representatives of educated society who have "preferred" the fee-charg-
ing urban schools to the agricultural gymnasia! Pay attention
to this "half the expenditures on clothing," which the teachers are guaranteed. According to our Narodnik's plan, they
are to enjoy the services of the workshops (as we have already
seen), in other words, the right to have their apparel sewn or
repaired by the "gymnasium pupils." How solicitous Mr.
Yuzhakov is—for the welfare of the teachers! However, he is
also solicitous for the welfare of the "gymnasium students"—
just as a good farmer is solicitous for the welfare of his
cattle: they have to be fed, watered, housed and ... coupled.
Listen to this:

"If ... marriage is allowed between young people who
have completed the course and remain at the gymnasium for
another three years ... this three-year stay will be far less
onerous than military service" (207). "If marriage is allowed"!! That is, it may not be allowed? But in that case, worthy Mr. Progressivist, a new law would be required *to restrict* the civic rights of the *peasants.* But need we be surprised
at this "slip of the pen" (?) on Mr. Yuzhakov's part, when all
through his "utopia," amidst the most minute examination of
teachers' salaries, labour service by the pupils, etc., it never
once occurred to him that it might not be amiss—at any
rate in the "utopia"—to allow a certain share in admin-
istering the "gymnasium" and in managing the farm
to the "pupils" themselves, who, after all, maintain the
whole establishment and are graduated from it at from
23 to 25 years of age; that they are not only "gymnasium
pupils," but also *citizens*. Our Narodnik forgot all about
this trifle! But on the other hand, he went very thoroughly
into the problem of "pupils" guilty of bad conduct. "A fourth
type" (of gymnasium) "would have to be instituted for students who have been expelled from the ordinary schools for
bad conduct. Since it is obligatory for the whole younger generation to undergo a course of secondary education, it would

be irrational to release students from it on the ground of bad conduct. In the upper classes, this might be a direct temptation and stimulus to bad conduct." (Believe it or not, that is what is printed on page 229!!) "The institution of special gymnasia for students expelled for bad conduct would be a logical complement to the whole system." They would be called "corrective gymnasia" (230).

Is it not incomparable,' this "educational utopia" in the Russian taste, with its corrective gymnasia for ruffians who may be "tempted" by the prospect of obtaining "release" — from education!?

VI

The reader perhaps has not forgotten a certain project for the direction of industry which was rightly described as a revival of mercantilism,[134] as a project for a "bourgeois-bureaucratic-socialist organisation of home industry"[135] (p. 238). To describe Mr. Yuzhakov's "plan" an even more complex term is required. It has to be called a *feudal-bureaucratic-bourgeois-socialist* experiment. A rather clumsy, four-storeyed term—but what would you have? The plan itself is clumsy. But, on the other hand, this term *accurately* conveys all the characteristic features of Mr. Yuzhakov's "utopia." Let us begin the examination from the fourth storey. "One of the chief features of the *scientific* conception of socialism is the planned regulation of social production," quite rightly remarks the author just quoted.* This feature is to be found in the "utopia," since the enterprise of tens of millions of workers is to be organised in advance according to one general plan. The bourgeois character of the utopia is beyond doubt: firstly, according to Mr. Yuzhakov's "plan," the secondary school *remains a class school.* And this after all the pompous phrases poured out by Mr. Yuzhakov "against" the class school in his first article!! One school for the rich, another for the poor; if you have money, pay for tuition—if you have not, work! More: the schools for the rich, as we saw, are to retain their "present form." In the present secondary schools of the Ministry of Public Education, for example, the tuition fees cover only 28.7% of the total expenditures; 40.0% is sup-

---

* *Novoye Slovo*, April 1897. Review of Home Affairs.

plied by the treasury; 21.8% by donations from individuals, institutions and societies; 3.1% is derived from interest on capital, and 6.4% from other sources (*Productive Forces*, Section XIX, p. 35). Mr. Yuzhakov, therefore, *has accentuated* the class character of the secondary schools *as compared with what now exists*: according to his "plan," the rich will pay only 28.7% of the cost of their tuition, while the poor will pay the *total* cost of theirs, and perform labour service into the bargain! Not bad for a "Narodnik" utopia! Secondly, the plan envisages the hire of winter workers by the gymnasia, especially from among landless peasants. Thirdly, the distinction between town and country—that foundation of the social division of labour—is retained. Since Mr. Yuzhakov is introducing the planned organisation of social labour, since he is devising a "utopia" for the combination of education and productive labour, the retention of this distinction is absurd, and shows that our author has not the slightest conception of the subject he has undertaken to discuss. Not only did the "teachers" of the present-day disciples criticise this absurdity in their writings, but so did the old utopians, and even our great Russian utopian.[136] But that is nothing to Mr. Yuzhakov! Fourthly—and this is the major reason for calling this "utopia" a bourgeois one—*side by side* with attempting the planned organisation of social production, it proposes to retain commodity production. The gymnasia will produce for the *market*. Consequently, social production will be governed by the laws of the market, to which the "gymnasia" will also have to submit! But that is nothing to Mr. Yuzhakov! Where do you get the idea, he will no doubt say, that production will be governed by certain laws of the market? Sheer nonsense! Production will be governed by the orders of the worthy directors of the agricultural schools, and not by the laws of the market. Voilà tout. Of the purely bureaucratic structure of Mr. Yuzhakov's utopian gymnasia we have already spoken. The "Educational Utopia," it is to be hoped, will do a useful service by showing the Russian reading public the full profundity of the "democracy" of our contemporary Narodniks. The feudal feature in Mr. Yuzhakov's "plan" is the labour service to be rendered by the poor in return for tuition. Had this sort of project been drafted by a consistent bourgeois, it would have contained neither a first nor a second storey, and it would have been far superior to this Narodnik utopia, and far more useful. Labour service is the economic essence of the serf system. In capitalist society, a man who has no means has to sell his labour-power in order to buy the means of subsistence. In feudal society, a man who has no means has to perform labour service in return for the means of subsistence he receives from his lord. Labour service necessarily means that the one who performs it is compelled to work, has fewer rights; it involves what the author of *Das Kapital* called "ausserökonomischer Zwang"* (III, 2, 324). Hence, in Russia as well, inasmuch as labour service still survives, a necessary complement to it is the peasant's inferiority in respect of civic rights—the fact of his being tied to the land, corporal punishment, and the right to assign him to compulsory labour. Mr. Yuzhakov does not understand this connection between labour service and inferiority of rights, but the shrewd sense of a "practical" man suggested to him that, since the gymnasium students will have to perform labour service, it will not be amiss to introduce corrective gymnasia for those who dare try to avoid education; and that adult "student" workers should be kept in the position of little schoolboys.

It would be interesting to know why our utopian needed the first three storeys of his creation? Had he left only the fourth, not a word of objection could have been raised, for, after all, the man himself told us frankly and in advance that he was writing a "utopia"! But here his Kleinbürger nature betrayed him. On the one hand, a "utopia" is a good thing, but, on the other, teachers' salaries for our worthy intellectuals are not a bad thing either. On the one hand, we have "no expenditure for the people," but, on the other—no, friend, just you pay the interest and return the debt in full, and do three years' labour service in the bargain! On the one hand, we have grandiloquent declamations on the danger and harm of class division, while, on the other, a purely class "utopia." Such perpetual vacillations between the old and the new, such curious claims to reach above one's own stature, that is, to rise superior to all classes, are the essence of every Kleinbürger outlook.

* * *

* Other than economic pressure.

Are you familiar, reader, with Mr. Sergei Sharapov's *The Russian Farmer. Some Thoughts on the Organisation of Farming in Russia on New Lines* (free supplement to the magazine *Sever*[187] for 1894), St.Petersburg, 1894? We would strongly recommend *Russkoye Bogatstvo* contributors in general, and Mr. Yuzhakov in particular, to acquaint themselves with it. The first chapter is entitled: "Moral Conditions for Russian Farming." Here the author rehashes ideas very much akin to those of "Narodism"—that Russia and the West differ radically, that pure commercial calculation prevails in the West, and that there masters and workers are not preoccupied with moral questions. Here, in Russia, on the contrary, thanks to the allocation of land to the peasants in 1861 "their existence has acquired an aim entirely different from that in the West" (8). "Our peasant who has obtained land has acquired an independent aim in life." In a word, sanction was given to people's production—as Mr. Nikolai —on put it far more plainly. The landlord in our country—Mr. Sharapov goes on to develop his idea—is interested in the peasant's welfare because this peasant cultivates the landlord's estate with his own implements. "His" (the landlord's) "calculations include not only the profit he personally derives from his enterprise, but also a *moral*, or rather a *psychological, element*" (12, author's italics). And Mr. Sharapov declares with fervour (not inferior to that of Mr. Yuzhakov's) that capitalism in our country is impossible. What is possible, and necessary, in our country is not capitalism, but an "alliance of lord and muzhik" (the title of chapter II of Mr. Sharapov's book). "Economy should be based on a close solidarity between lord and muzhik" (25): it is the duty of the lord to spread enlightenment, and of the muzhik—well, the duty of the muzhik, of course, is to work! And so he, Mr. Sergei Sharapov, "after repeated and painful mistakes," at last established on his own estate the "said alliance between lord and muzhik" (26). He introduced a rational crop rotation, etc., etc., and concluded a contract with the peasants, under which the latter receive meadows, pasture and arable from the landlord, and also seed for so many dessiatines, etc. The peasants, on their part, undertake to do all the work on the landlord's farm (to cart manure, spread phosphates, plough, sow, reap, carry the sheaves to "my barn," thresh, etc., etc., so many dessiatines of each crop), and over and above this to pay, at first 600 rubles, then 800, 850, 1,100, and finally 1,200 rubles (i.e., an annual increment). These sums are payable in instalments—coinciding with the dates of payment of interest into the Nobles' Bank (36, et seq.). It goes without saying that the author is a "convinced supporter of the village community" (37). We say, "it goes without saying," because such farms would be impossible without laws that tie the peasants to their allotments and that secure the peasant community's exclusiveness as a social estate. Mr. Sharapov is guaranteed the due receipt of payments from the peasants by the existence of a "prohibition on the sale of produce without his consent, which makes it incumbent on them to store everything in my barns" (36). Since it would be extremely difficult to exact payment from the poor peasants, Mr. Sharapov has arranged to receive it from the rich peasants: these rich peasants themselves select a group of weaker ones, form an artel and place themselves at the head of it (38), and pay the landlord with great promptitude, inasmuch as they can always get back what is due from the poor peasants when they sell the produce (39). "It is very hard for many of the poor peasants, especially those with small families, to work for me. It is a very big strain on them, but evasion is out of the question, for the peasants would refuse to accept the cattle of a defaulting householder into the herd. Nor would I, the peasants would insist on that, and willy-nilly the poor peasant has to work. That, of course, is compulsion in a way, but do you know what the effect is? A year or two of renting land, and the poor peasant has paid off his arrears of taxes, has redeemed his things from pawn, finds himself in possession of money, begins to rebuild his cottage and—lo and behold! he has ceased to be a poor peasant" (39). And Mr. Sharapov "points with pride" to the fact that "his" peasants (he keeps referring to them as "my peasants") are flourishing, that he is spreading enlightenment, introducing clover, phosphates, and so on, whereas "left to themselves, the peasants would have done nothing" (35). "All the work, moreover, has to be done at my orders and instructions. I decide on the time for sowing, manuring and reaping. All summer, serfdom is practically restored—except, of course, that there is no manhandling and no floggings in the stable" (p. 29).

As you see, Mr. Sharapov, the blunt squire, is a little more outspoken than Mr. Yuzhakov, the enlightened publicist. But is there much difference between the types of farming on the estate of the former and in the utopia of the latter? In both cases the whole essence lies in labour service; in both cases we have *compulsion*, either by the pressure of the rich men who dominate the "village community," or the threat of being consigned to a corrective gymnasium. The reader may object that Mr. Sharapov runs his farm for profit, whereas the officials in Mr. Yuzhakov's utopia do so from zeal for the common good. One moment. Mr. Sharapov says outright that he farms from moral motives, that he surrenders half the proceeds to the peasants, and so on; and we have neither the reason nor the right to believe him less than Mr. Yuzhakov, who, after all, also provides his utopian teachers with by no means utopian "lucrative posts." And if some landlord follows Mr. Yuzhakov's advice and lets his land be used as an agricultural gymnasium, and receives interest from the "students" for payment into the Nobles' Bank (a "gilt-edged mortgage," in Mr. Yuzhakov's own words), the difference will practically disappear. Of course, a tremendous difference in "educational problems" still remains—but, heavens, would not Mr. Sergei Sharapov prefer to hire educated labourers at 50 rubles than uneducated ones at 60 rubles?

And so, if Mr. Manuilov does not understand even now why the Russian (and not only the Russian) disciples consider it necessary, in the interests of labour, to support consistent bourgeois people and consistent bourgeois ideas, as *against* those survivals of the past which are responsible for farms like Mr. Sharapov's and "utopias" like Mr. Yuzhakov's, then, we must confess, it is difficult even to argue with him, for we are evidently talking different languages. Mr. Manuilov presumably reasons on the lines of the celebrated recipe of the celebrated Mr. Mikhailovsky: take what is good from here and from there—like Gogol's young lady,[138] who wanted to take the nose from one suitor and stick it above the chin of another. To us, however, it seems that such reasoning is nothing but the Kleinbürger's comic effort to rise superior to the definite classes that have fully evolved in our midst and that have assumed quite a definite place in the process of historical development going on before our eyes. The "uto-

pias" naturally and inevitably engendered by such reasoning
are, however, no longer comic, but harmful, especially when
they lead to utterly unbridled bureaucratic inventions. For
quite understandable reasons this phenomenon is to be met
with in Russia with particular frequency; but it is not
confined to Russia. Not for nothing did Antonio Labriola,
in his excellent book *Essais sur la conception matérialiste
de l'histoire* (Paris, Giard et Brière, 1897), say in reference
to Prussia, that the pernicious forms of utopia against which
the "teachers" fought half a century ago have now been supplemented by one other: "a bureaucratic and fiscal utopia,
a utopia of cretins" (l'utopie bureaucratique et fiscale,
l'utopie des crétins. Page 105, note).

VII

In conclusion, let us revert once more to educational
problems, but not to Mr. Yuzhakov's book, which has that
title. It has already been remarked that this title is too
broad, for educational problems are by no means identical
with questions of schooling; education is not confined to schooling. Had Mr. Yuzhakov really dealt with "educational problems" from the standpoint of principle, and examined the
relations between the various classes, he could not have avoided the part played by Russia's capitalist development in the
matter of educating the labouring masses. This problem was
touched upon by another *Russkoye Bogatstvo* contributor, Mr. Mikhailovsky, in No. 11, 1897. Writing in reference
to the statement by Mr. Novus[139] that Marx did not fear,
and rightly so, to speak of the "idiocy of rural life,"[140] and
considered it one of the merits of capitalism and of the bourgeoisie that they had "rescued" a considerable part of the
population from this "idiocy," Mr. Mikhailovsky says:
"I do not know where Marx used this coarse (?) expression"
—a characteristic confession that he is not acquainted with
one of Marx's cardinal writings (*Manifesto*)! But what
follows is even more characteristic: "... but it has long been
known that there is no need to break furniture even if Alexander the Great was a hero. Generally speaking, Marx was unfastidious in his expressions, and, of course, to imitate him in

this respect would be, to say the least, unwise. But even so, I am certain" (hear, hear!) "that this expression was simply a boutade on Marx's part. And if the generation that worried so much, along with Mr. Zlatovratsky, over the intricate problems of rural life suffered much woe in vain, no less—though different—is the woe of the generation being educated in a spirit of contempt for the 'idiocy of rural life'" (p. 139)....

It is highly characteristic of Mr. Mikhailovsky that, having proclaimed his agreement with Marx's economic doctrine time and again, he is so utterly ignorant of this doctrine as to express the "certainty" that the words of Marx quoted by Novus were due simply to his being carried away, simply to an unfastidious choice of expressions, and were simply a boutade! No, Mr. Mikhailovsky, you are grievously mistaken. These words of Marx are no boutade, but an expression of one of the most cardinal and fundamental features of his whole outlook, both theoretical and practical. These words clearly express a recognition of the *progressive nature* of the diversion of the population from agriculture to industry, from country to town, one of the most characteristic features of capitalist development, that is to be observed both in the West and in Russia. In my article, "A Characterisation of Economic Romanticism," I have already had occasion to show how important is this view of Marx's, which has been adopted by all the "disciples," and how sharply contradictory it is to absolutely all romantic theories, ranging from those of old Sismondi to those of Mr. N. —on. There I pointed out (p. 39[141]) that. this view is also quite definitely expressed by Marx in *Das Kapital* (I. Band, 2-te Aufl., S. 527-28[142]), and by Engels in his *Condition of the Working Class in England.* To this might be added Marx's *Der Achtzehnte Brumaire des Louis Bonaparte* (Hamb. 1885. Cf. S. 98[143]).* Both these

---

* Mr. Novus could not have guessed, of course, that Mr. Mikhailovsky was so ignorant of the works of Marx, or else he would have quoted the passage in full: Die Bourgeoisie hat das Land der Herrschaft der Stadt unterworfen. Sie hat enorme Städte geschaffen, sie hat die Zahl der städtischen Bevölkerung gegenüber der ländlichen in hohem Grade vermehrt und so einen bedeutenden Theil der Bevölkerung dem Idiotismus des Landlebens entrissen. (The bourgeoisie has subjected the country to the rule of the towns. It has created enormous cities, has greatly increased the urban population as compared

writers expressed their views on this subject at such length, repeated them so often on the most varied occasions, that it could only have occurred to a man who is absolutely unfamiliar with their teachings to declare that the word "idiocy" in the passage quoted is simply a piece of "coarseness" and a "boutade." Lastly, Mr. Mikhailovsky might also have recalled the fact that all these writers' followers have expressed themselves on a large number of practical issues in the spirit of this doctrine, advocating, for example, complete freedom of movement, and protesting against plans to endow the worker with a plot of land or a house of his own, and the like.

Further, in the tirade we have quoted, Mr. Mikhailovsky accuses Novus and his supporters of educating the present generation "in a spirit of contempt for the idiocy of rural life." *This is not true.* The "disciples" would, of course, be deserving of censure if they were "contemptuous" of rural inhabitants, crushed as they are by want and ignorance, but Mr. Mikhailovsky could not prove a single one of them guilty of such an attitude. While speaking of the "idiocy of rural life," the disciples at the same time point the way out of this state of affairs opened up by the development of capitalism. Let us repeat what we said above in the article on economic romanticism: "If the predominance of the town is necessarily so, only the attraction of the population to the towns can neutralise (and, as history shows, does in fact neutralise) the one-sided character of this predominance. If the town necessarily gains for itself a privileged position, only the influx of the village population into the towns, only this mingling and merging of the agricultural with the non-agricultural population can lift the rural population out of its helplessness. Therefore, in reply to the reactionary complaints and lamentations of the romanticists, the modern theory indicates exactly how this narrowing of the gap between the conditions of life of the agricultural and of the non-agricultural population creates the conditions for eliminating the distinction between town and country."*

---

with the rural, and has thus rescued a considerable part of the population from the idiocy of rural life.—*Manifesto of the Communist Party.—Ed.*)

* See p. 229 in this book.—*Ed.*

This is not a contemptuous attitude towards the "idiocy of rural life" at all, but a desire to find a way out of it. The only "contempt" that follows from these views is towards the doctrines which recommend "seeking paths for the fatherland," instead of seeking a way out along the *existing* path and its further course.

The difference between the Narodniks and the "disciples" as to the significance of the process of diversion of population from agriculture to industry is a difference in solving the *practical issues* connected with this process, and not only in theoretical principles and in assessing the facts of Russian history and realities. The "disciples" naturally insist on the need for abolishing all the antiquated restrictions on peasant travel and migration from the countryside to the towns, whereas the Narodniks either openly uphold these restrictions, or cautiously avoid the subject altogether (which in practice amounts to the same thing). This example, too, might have helped Mr. Manuilov to understand the, to him, astonishing fact that the "disciples" express their solidarity with spokesmen of the bourgeoisie. A consistent bourgeois will always stand for the abolition of these restrictions on movement—and as far as the worker is concerned, his most vital interests demand their abolition. Hence, solidarity between them is quite natural and inevitable. On the other hand, the agrarians (big and small, down to the enterprising muzhik inclusive) find this process of diversion of population to industry a disadvantage, and zealously try to retard it, having Narodnik theories to back them.

To conclude: on this great question of the diversion of the population from agriculture by capitalism, Mr. Mikhailovsky betrayed a complete misunderstanding of Marx's teachings, and avoided the issue of the difference between the Russian "disciples" and the Narodniks both on the theoretical and practical aspects of the question, with the help of meaningless phrases.

THE HERITAGE WE RENOUNCE[144]

Written in exile at the end of 1897
First published in 1898 in the miscel-
lany *Economic Studies and Essays* by
Vladimir Ilyin

Published according to the
text in the miscellany

Referring, in *Russkoye Bogatstvo*, No. 10, 1897, to a comment by Mr. Minsky on the "dialectical materialists," Mr. Mikhailovsky says: "He" (Mr. Minsky) "must know that these people do not acknowledge any continuity with the past and emphatically renounce the heritage" (p. 179) — that is, the "heritage of the 1860-70s," which Mr. V. Rozanov solemnly renounced in 1891 in *Moskovskiye Vedomosti* (p. 178).

Mr. Mikhailovsky's statement about the "Russian disciples" is a falsehood. True, he is not the only, and not the independent, author of the falsehood that "the Russian disciples renounce the heritage"—it has been reiterated for quite a long time now by practically all the representatives of the liberal-Narodnik press when fighting the "disciples." As far as we remember, when Mr. Mikhailovsky began his fierce war on the "disciples" he had not yet invented this falsehood but others had done so before him. Later he, too, chose to seize upon it. The further the "disciples" developed their views in Russian literature, the more minutely and thoroughly they set forth their opinions on a number of issues, both theoretical and practical, the more rarely did one find the hostile press objecting in substance to the fundamental tenets of the new trend, to the view that Russian capitalism is progressive, that the Narodnik idealisation of the small producer is absurd, that the explanation of trends of social thought and of legal and political institutions must be sought in the material interests of the various classes of Russian society. These fundamental tenets were hushed up, it was—and still is—thought best to say nothing about them, but fabrications to discredit the new trend were concocted with all the greater fertility. One of these fabrications—"shabby fabrications"—is the modish phrase that "the Russian disciples renounce the heritage," that they have broken with the best traditions of the best, the most progressive section of Russian society, that they have severed the democratic thread, etc., etc., and all the many other ways in which this is expressed. The fact that such phrases are so widely used prompts us to undertake a detailed examination and refutation of them. In order that our exposition may not appear unsupported, we shall begin by drawing an historico-literary parallel between two "essayists of the countryside," chosen in order to describe the "heritage." Let us say in advance that we shall confine ourselves exclusively to economic and social questions, that of the "heritage," we shall examine only these, leaving aside philosophical, literary, aesthetic and other problems.

I

ONE REPRESENTATIVE OF THE "HERITAGE"

Thirty years ago, in 1867, *Otechestvenniye Zapiski*[145] began publishing a series of essays by Skaldin, under the title *In the Backwoods and in the Capital*. The essays appeared over a period of three years, 1867-69. In 1870 the author gathered them together in a single volume bearing the same title.* A perusal of this book, now almost forgotten, is extremely instructive from the angle of the subject under discussion, i.e., the relation in which the representatives of the "heritage" stand to the Narodniks and the "Russian disciples." The title of the book is inaccurate. The author himself was conscious of this, and he explains in a foreword that his theme is the attitude of the "capital" to the "countryside," in other words, that his book is a series of social essays on rural conditions, and that he does not propose to

---

* Skaldin, *In the Backwoods and in the Capital*, St. Petersburg, 1870 (p. 451). We have not been able to obtain copies of *Otechestvenniye Zapiski* for this period and have used only the book.

speak of the capital specifically. Or rather, he might have proposed to do so, but does not find it expedient: ὡς δύναμαι — οὐ βούλομαι, ὡς δὲ βούλομαι — οὐ δύναμαι (for I will not write as I may, and may not write as I will), Skaldin says, borrowing the words of a Greek writer to explain the inexpediency.

Let us give a brief exposition of Skaldin's views.

We shall begin with the peasant Reform[146]—that initial point from which all who wish to expound their general views on economic and social problems must, even to this day, inevitably begin. Very much space is devoted to the peasant Reform in Skaldin's book. He was perhaps the first writer who—on a broad basis of fact and a detailed examination of all aspects of life in the countryside—systematically showed the poverty-stricken state of the peasants *after* the Reform, the deterioration of their conditions, the new forms of their subjection, economic, legal and in daily life—the first, in a word, to show all that has since been elucidated and demonstrated in such detail and thoroughness in numerous investigations and surveys. Today all these truths are no longer new. At that time they were not only new, but aroused distrust in liberal society, which feared that behind these references to the so-called "defects of the Reform" lurked a condemnation of it and concealed support for serfdom. Skaldin's views are the more interesting because he was a contemporary of the Reform (and even perhaps had a hand in it. We have no historical or literary information or biographical data about him at our disposal). Consequently, his views are based on direct observation both of the "capital" and the "countryside" of the time, and not on an armchair study of printed material.

What first of all strikes the contemporary reader, who is accustomed to the Narodniks' sickly gushing over the peasant Reform, is the extreme *sobriety* of Skaldin's views on the subject. He looks at the Reform without any illusions or idealisation; he sees it as a transaction between two parties, the landlords and the peasants, who until then had used the land in common on definite terms and now had divided it, the division being accompanied by a change in the legal status of both parties. The factor which determined the mode of division and the size of the share of each party was their

respective interests. These interests determined the ambitions
of both parties, while the fact that one of them was able to
have a direct hand in the Reform itself, and in the practical
working-out of the various questions connected with its implementation, determined, among other things, that party's dominant position. That is how Skaldin understands the Reform.
He dwells in particular detail on the principal question of the
Reform, the allotments and land redemption payments,
reverting to it time and again in the course of his essays.
(Skaldin's book is divided into eleven essays, each of them
self-contained, their form reminding one of letters from
the countryside. The first essay is dated 1866, and the last,
1869.) It goes without saying that on the subject of the so-
called "land-poor" peasants, there is nothing in Skaldin's
book that is new to the contemporary reader, but at the end
of the sixties his testimony was both new and valuable.
We shall not, of course, recapitulate it, but shall only remark
on that feature of his description of the facts which distinguishes him—to his advantage—from the Narodniks. Skaldin does not talk about "land poverty," but about the "excessive amount of land cut off from the peasants' allotments"
(p. 213, also p. 214 and many other places; cf. title of the
third essay), and says that the largest allotments established
by the Regulations[147] proved to be smaller than those
they had before (p. 257), incidentally citing some extremely
characteristic and typical opinions of peasants on this aspect of the Reform.* Skaldin's explanations and proofs of
this fact are very circumstantial, forceful and even vehement
for a writer who as a rule is extremely moderate and temper-
ate, and whose general outlook is undoubtedly bourgeois.
The fact, then, must have been too starkly evident, if such
a writer as Skaldin speaks of it so emphatically. Skaldin also
speaks very emphatically and circumstantially of the severe
burden of the payments, and supports his statements with

---

* "'Our land has been so trimmed down by *him*'" (author's italics) "'that we can't live without this cut-off land; he has surrounded
us on all sides with his fields and we have nowhere to pasture our
cattle; so you have to pay for your allotment, and on top of that
you have to pay for the cut-off land, just as much as he asks.'" "'How
does that better us?' said one literate and experienced muzhik, a
former quit-renter. 'We are paying the same quit-rent as before,
though our land has been trimmed down.'"

many facts. "Inordinate taxation," reads a sub-title to the third essay (1867), "is the chief cause of their" (the peasants') "poverty," and Skaldin shows that taxation is higher than the peasants' returns from the land, and he cites from the *Proceedings of the Commission on Taxation* data relative to the incidence of taxation of the upper and lower classes in Russia which show that 76% of the taxation falls on the lower classes and 17% on the upper, whereas in Western Europe the correlation is everywhere incomparably more favourable to the lower classes. A sub-title to the seventh essay (1868) reads, "Excessive money dues are one of the chief causes of poverty among the peasants," and the author shows that the new conditions of life at once demanded money, money and more money of the peasant, that the Regulation made it a principle to compensate the landlords for the abolition of serfdom as well (252), and that the amount of the quit-rent was based "on sworn information supplied by the landlords, their stewards and village elders, that is, on absolutely arbitrary data not deserving of the slightest credence" (255), in consequence of which the average quit-rents computed by the commissions were higher than the existing average quit-rents. "Added to the burden of quit-rent borne by the peasants was the loss of land which they had used for centuries" (258). "Had the redemption price of the land not been assessed on the basis of the capitalised amount of the quit-rents, but on the basis of its actual value at the time of the emancipation, the redemption could have been paid off very easily and would not even have required the assistance of the government, or the issue of credit certificates" (264). "Redemption, which was designed by the Regulation of February 19 to make things easier for the peasants and to consummate the work of improving their conditions, in reality often has the effect of putting them into even more straitened circumstances" (269). We cite these excerpts—which, in themselves, are of little interest and are in part out-of-date—in order to show how energetically the peasants' interests were defended by a writer who was hostile to the village community and whose opinions on a whole number of questions were those of a true member of the Manchester School. It is very instructive to note that nearly all the useful and non-reactionary precepts of

Narodism fully coincide with those of this Mancunian. It goes without saying that, such being Skaldin's opinion of the Reform, he could not possibly sentimentally idealise it in the way the Narodniks did, and still do, when they say that it sanctioned people's production, that it was superior to the West-European peasant reforms, that it made a tabula rasa of Russia, and so on. Skaldin did not and could not say anything of the kind; further, he said plainly that in our country peasant Reform was less advantageous, less beneficial to the peasants than in the West. "The question will be put plainly," he wrote, "if we ask ourselves why the beneficial consequences of the emancipation in our country are not growing with the steady speed with which they did, say, in Prussia or Saxony in the first quarter of the present century" (221). "In Prussia, and throughout Germany, the peasants paid not for the redemption of their allotments, which had long been recognised as their property by law, but for the redemption of their compulsory services to the landlords"(272).

Let us now pass from the economic to the legal aspect of the Reform, as Skaldin sees it. Skaldin is a bitter foe of collective responsibility, of the passport system, and of the patriarchal power of the peasant "community" (and of the urban community) over its members. In the third essay (1867) he insists on the abolition of collective responsibility, the poll tax and the passport system, on the necessity for an equitable property tax, and on the replacement of passports by free and permanent certificates. "In no other civilised country is there a tax on internal passports" (109). We know that this tax was only abolished in 1897. In the title to the fourth essay, we read: "arbitrary actions of village communities and urban dumas in sending out passports and levying taxes on absentee payers."... "Collective responsibility is a heavy burden which efficient and industrious husbandmen have to bear on account of idlers and wastrels" (126). Skaldin is disposed to attribute the differentiation of the peasantry, which was already to be observed at that time, to the personal qualities of those who get on or go under. He describes in detail the difficulties peasants living in St. Petersburg experience in obtaining or prolonging passports, and repudiates those who would retort that "thank God, all this multitude of landless peasants have not been registered in the towns, have not increased the numbers of propertyless town-dwellers" (130).... "This barbarous collective responsibility..." (131). ... "Can people placed in such a position be called free citizens? Are they not the same old glebae adscripti?*" (132). The peasant Reform is blamed. "But is the peasant Reform to blame for the fact that the law, having released the peasant from his bond to the landlord has devised nothing to deliver him from his bond to his community and place of registration?... Where are the attributes of civil liberty, if the peasant is not free to decide either his place of domicile or manner of occupation?" (132). Skaldin very accurately and aptly calls our peasant a "settled proletarian" (231).** In the heading to the eighth essay (1868) we read: "the fact that the peasants are tied to their communities and allotments prevents improvement of their conditions.... It is an obstacle to the development of outside industries." "Apart from the ignorance of the peasants and the burden of progressively mounting taxation, one of the causes retarding the development of peasant labour and, consequently, of peasant prosperity, is the fact that they are tied to their communities and allotments. The tying of the labourer to one place and the shackling of the rural community in unbreakable fetters—this in itself is an extremely unfavourable condition for the development of labour, private enterprise and small landed property" (284). "Bound to their allotments and communities, and unable to apply their labour where it would be more productive and of greater advantage to themselves, the peasants are, as it were, frozen in that congested, herdlike, unproductive form of life in which they emerged from serfdom" (285).

---

* Peasants in the Roman Empire were bound to definite plots of land which they could not abandon however unprofitable their cultivation might be.—*Ed.*

** Skaldin very circumstantially demonstrates the correctness not only of the first, but also of the second part of this definition (proletarian). He devotes much space in his essays to a description of the peasants' dependent status and their poverty, to a description of the hard lot of the agricultural labourer, to a "description of the 1868 famine" (heading of the fifth essay) and of the diverse forms of peasant bondage and humiliation. There were people in the sixties, as there are in the nineties, who sought to hush up or deny the existence of famine. Skaldin passionately opposes them. It would of course be superfluous to give detailed excerpts on this point.

Skaldin, consequently, regards these aspects of peasant life from the purely bourgeois standpoint, but in spite of that (and, perhaps, because of it), his assessment of the harm caused to all social development and to the peasants themselves by the fact that the latter are tied down is very accurate. And it causes particular harm (let us add) to the lowest sections of the peasantry, the rural proletariat. Skaldin says very aptly: "the concern of the law that the peasants shall not remain without land is admirable; but it should not be forgotten that the concern of the peasants themselves on this score is incomparably greater than that of any legislator" (286). "Apart from the fact that the peasant is bound to his allotment and his community, even his temporary departure to earn something elsewhere involves considerable difficulty and expense, owing to collective responsibility and the passport system" (298). "For many peasants, in my opinion, a way out of their difficult situation would be opened if ... measures were taken to make it easier for peasants to give up their land" (294). Here Skaldin is expressing a wish that runs sharply counter to the Narodnik projects, which all tend in the very opposite direction, namely, to perpetuate the village community, to make the allotments inalienable, etc. There has been ample evidence since then to show that Skaldin was perfectly right: the fact that the peasant remains tied to the land, and that the peasant community is an exclusive social estate only worsens the position of the rural proletariat and retards the country's economic development, while being unable in any degree to protect the "settled proletarian" from the worst forms of bondage and subjection, or from the decline of his wages and living standards to the very lowest level.

The reader may have already seen from the above-quoted excerpts that Skaldin is a foe of the village community. He objects to the community and to land redistribution because he favours private property, enterprise and so on (p. 142, et seq.). To the defenders of the village community Skaldin retorts that "the ancient common law" has outlived its day. "In all countries," he writes, "as the rural dwellers came into contact with a civilised environment, their common law lost its primeval purity and became subject to corruption and distortion. The same is to be observed in our country: the power of the community is gradually being turned into the power of the village exploiters and rural clerks and, instead of protecting the person of the peasant, is a heavy burden upon him" (143)—a very true observation, corroborated by endless facts in these thirty years. In Skaldin's opinion, "the patriarchal family, communal ownership of the land and common law" have been irrevocably condemned by history. "Those who would preserve these venerable monuments of past centuries for us in perpetuity, show thereby that they are more capable of being carried away by an idea than of penetrating into realities and grasping the irresistible march of history" (162), and to this correct observation Skaldin adds hot Manchester School philippics. "Community land tenure," he says elsewhere, "places every peasant in slavish subjection to the whole community" (222). Therefore, Skaldin's unreserved hostility to the village community from the purely bourgeois standpoint is combined with his consistent defence of the peasants' interests. Hostile though he is to the village community, Skaldin does not advance foolish projects for forcibly abolishing the community and forcibly introducing some other, similar system of land ownership, such as are usually concocted by the present-day opponents of the village community, who favour gross interferences in the peasants' life and attack the village community from anything but the standpoint of the peasants' interests. Skaldin, on the contrary, strongly protests against being classed with the believers in "forcible abolition of communal land tenure" (144). "The Regulation of February 19," he says, "very wisely left it to the peasants themselves ... to pass ... from communal to family tenure. Indeed, none but the peasants themselves can properly decide the best time for such passage." Consequently, Skaldin is opposed to the village community only for the reason that it hampers economic development, prevents the peasant from withdrawing from the community and giving up his land, that is, for the same reason that the "Russian disciples" are opposed to it today; this hostility has nothing in common with defence of the selfish interests of the landlords, with defence of the survivals and the spirit of serfdom, with advocacy of interference in the life of the peasants. It is very important to note this difference, because the present-day

Narodniks, who are accustomed to seeing enemies of the village community only in the camp of *Moskovskiye Vedomosti* and the like, very willingly pretend to be oblivious to *any other* kind of hostility to the village community.

Skaldin's general opinion about the causes of the peasants' distressed condition is that they are all survivals of serfdom. Describing the famine of 1868, he remarks that the serf-owners pointed to it with malicious glee, ascribing it to the dissoluteness of the peasants, to the abolition of the landlords' tutelage, and so on. Skaldin heatedly refutes these views. "The causes of the impoverishment of the peasants," he says, "*were inherited from serfdom* (212), and are not the result of its abolition; they are the general causes which keep the majority of our peasants at a level bordering on that of the proletariat"—and he repeats the above-quoted opinions of the Reform. It is absurd to attack the family division of the land: "Even if divisions do injure the peasants' material interests for a while, they save their personal freedom and the moral dignity of the peasant family, that is, those higher human blessings without which no civil progress is possible" (217), and Skaldin rightly points to the real reasons for the campaign against land divisions: "many landlords highly exaggerate the harm caused by divisions, blaming them, as well as drunkenness, for all the consequences of the various causes of the peasants' poverty, which the landlords are so unwilling to recognise" (218). To those who say that much is being written today about the peasants' poverty, but that formerly it was not so and that therefore the peasants' conditions must have deteriorated, Skaldin replies that: "In order to form a judgement of the results of the peasants' emancipation from the landlords' power, by comparing the peasants' present with their former condition, it would have been necessary, while serfdom still prevailed, to trim down the peasants' allotments as they have been now trimmed down, and to tax the peasants with all the duties which have appeared since the emancipation, and then see how the peasant serfs would have borne such conditions" (219). It is a supremely characteristic and important feature of Skaldin's views that he reduces *all* the causes of the deterioration in the peasants' condition to survivals of serfdom, to its legacy of labour service, quit-rent, cut-off land, and the peasants' lack of rights, and immobility. Skaldin not only does not see that the causes of the peasants' impoverishment might be found in the very structure of the new socio-economic relations, in the very structure of the post-Reform economy; he absolutely refuses to entertain the thought, being profoundly convinced that the complete abolition of all these survivals of serfdom would usher in an era of universal well-being. His views, in fact, are negative: remove the obstacles to the free development of the peasantry, remove the shackles bequeathed by serfdom, and everything will be for the best in this best of possible worlds. Skaldin writes: "Here" (i. e., in relation to the peasantry) "there is only one course the government can follow: *to eliminate* steadily and unflaggingly *the causes* which have reduced our peasants to their present state of dullness and poverty and which do not allow them to rise to their feet" (224, my italics). Highly characteristic in this respect is the reply given by Skaldin to those who defend the "community" (that is, binding the peasants to the village communities and allotments) on the ground that, without it, "a rural proletariat will emerge." "This objection," Skaldin says, "falls to the ground when we remember what boundless tracts of land lie idle in our country from lack of hands to cultivate them. If the law did not hamper the natural distribution of manpower, the only people who would be real proletarians in Russia would be the professional beggars or the incorrigibly vicious and dissipated" (144)—the typical view of the eighteenth-century economists and "enlighteners," who believed that abolition of serfdom and all its survivals would usher in a reign of universal well-being on earth. The Narodnik would no doubt look down on Skaldin with disdain and say that he was simply a bourgeois. Yes, of course, Skaldin was a bourgeois, but he was a representative of the progressive bourgeois ideology which the Narodniks have replaced by one that is petty-bourgeois and, on a whole number of points, reactionary. And this "bourgeois" had a better idea than the Narodnik of how to defend those practical and real interests of the peasants which coincided, and coincide now, with the requirements of social development generally!*

* And vice versa, all the progressive practical measures that we find the Narodniks advocating are, in substance, *fully bourgeois,*

To complete our account of Skaldin's views, let us add that he is opposed to the system of social estates, advocates a single court of justice for all of them, sympathises "theoretically" with the idea that the volost authorities should not be constituted on the basis of social estates, is an ardent advocate of public education, especially general education, favours local self-government and Zemstvo institutions, and believes that land credits, especially small, should be widely available, for there is a strong desire among the peasants to buy land. Here, too, Skaldin is a true "Mancunian": he says, for instance, that Zemstvo and municipal banks are "a patriarchal or primitive form of bank" and should give way to private banks, which are "vastly superior" (80). The land might be endowed with value "through the stimulation of industrial and commercial activity in our provinces" (71), and so on.

To sum up. In outlook, Skaldin may be called a bourgeois enlightener. His views are very reminiscent of those of the eighteenth-century economists (correspondingly refracted, of course, in the prism of Russian conditions), and he reflected the general "enlightenment" character of the "heritage" of the sixties quite vividly. Like the West-European enlighteners and the majority of the literary representatives of the sixties, Skaldin was imbued with a violent hostility to serfdom and *all its* economic, social and legal products. That was the first characteristic feature of the "enlightener." The second characteristic feature common to all the Russian enlighteners was ardent advocacy of education, self-government, liberty, European forms of life and all-round Europeanisation of Russia generally. And the third characteristic feature of the "enlightener" was his defence of the interests of the masses, chiefly of the peasants (who, in the days of the enlighteners, were not yet fully emancipated or only in process of being emancipated), the sincere belief that abolition of serfdom and its survivals would be followed by universal well-being, and a sincere desire to help bring this about. These three features constitute the

---

that is, they conduce to the capitalist line of development, and no other. Only petty-bourgeois people could concoct the theory that extension of peasant land tenure, tax reduction, resettlement, credits, technical progress, marketing arrangements and suchlike measures would serve the interests of so-called "people's production."

essence of what in our country is called "the heritage of the sixties," and it is important to emphasise that *there is nothing whatsoever of Narodism in this heritage*. There are quite a number of Russian writers whose views are characterised by these features and who have never had anything in common with Narodism. Where the outlook of a writer bears these features, he is always recognised by everyone as having "preserved the traditions of the sixties," quite irrespective of what his attitude to Narodism may be. Nobody, of course, would think of saying that Mr. M. Stasyulevich, for instance, whose jubilee was recently celebrated, had "renounced the heritage" —merely because he was an opponent of Narodism or was indifferent to the questions advanced by Narodism. We have taken Skaldin* as an example precisely because, while he was *undoubtedly* a representative of the "heritage," he was at the same time a confirmed enemy of those ancient institutions which the Narodniks have taken under their protection.

We have said that Skaldin was a bourgeois. Ample proof of this description has been given above, but it must be observed that this word is often understood very incorrectly, narrowly and unhistorically, it being associated (*without distinction of historical period*) with a selfish defence of the interests of a minority. It must not be forgotten that at the time when the eighteenth-century enlighteners (who are by general consent included among the leaders of the bour-

---

* It might perhaps be objected that Skaldin is not typical of the sixties because of his hostility to the village community and because of his tone. But it is not a question of the village community alone. It is a question of the views common to all the enlighteners, which Skaldin shared. As to his tone, it really is not typical in its calm reasonableness, moderation, emphasis on gradualness, etc. It was not without reason that Engels called Skaldin a *Liberalkonservativ*.[148] However, the selection of a representative of the heritage with a more typical tone would, firstly, be inconvenient for various reasons, and might, secondly, give rise to misunderstanding when comparing him with the present-day Narodniks.[149] Because of the very character of our task, the *tone* (contrary to the proverb) *does not make the music*, and Skaldin's untypical tone serves to bring out his "music," that is, the substance of his views, more distinctly. And it is only the substance that interests us. It is only on the basis of the substance of writers' views (and not of their tone) that we intend to draw the comparison between the representatives of the heritage and the present-day Narodniks.

geoisie) wrote, and at the time when our enlighteners of the forties and sixties wrote, *all* social problems amounted to the struggle against serfdom and its survivals. At that time the new socio-economic relations and their contradictions were still in embryo. No selfishness was therefore displayed at that time by the ideologists of the bourgeoisie; on the contrary, both in the West and in Russia, they quite sincerely believed in universal well-being and sincerely desired it, they sincerely did not see (partly could not yet see) the contradictions in the system which was growing out of serfdom. It is not for nothing that Skaldin in one part of his book quotes Adam Smith: we have seen that both his views and the character of his arguments in many respects repeat the theses of that great ideologist of the progressive bourgeoisie.

And so, if we compare Skaldin's practical suggestions with the views of the present-day Narodniks, on the one hand, and with the attitude to them of the "Russian disciples," on the other, we shall find that the "disciples" will always support Skaldin's suggestions, since the latter reflect the interests of the progressive social classes, and the vital interests of social development generally along the present, i. e., capitalist, path. The things that the Narodniks have changed in Skaldin's practical wishes, or in his presentation of problems, are *a change for the worse*, and are rejected by the "disciples." It is not against the "heritage" that the disciples "hurl themselves" (that is an absurd fabrication), but against the romantic and petty-bourgeois additions to the heritage made by the Narodniks. To these additions we shall now pass.

II

NARODISM'S ADDITION TO THE "HERITAGE"

From Skaldin, let us pass to Engelhardt. His *Letters from the Countryside* are likewise essays on the social aspects of rural life, so that in substance and even in form his book very much resembles that of Skaldin's. Engelhardt is much more talented than Skaldin, and his letters from the country are incomparably more lively and imaginative. The lengthy disquisitions of the serious author of *In the*

Backwoods and in the Capital are not to be found in
Engelhardt's book, which, for its part, is replete with deft
delineation and imagery. It is not surprising that Engelhardt's book enjoys the steady sympathy of the reading public,
and only recently appeared in a fresh edition, while Skaldin's book is almost completely forgotten, although it was
only two years after its publication that *Otechestvenniye
Zapiski* began printing Engelhardt's letters. There is therefore no need for us to acquaint the reader with the contents
of Engelhardt's book, and we shall confine ourselves to a
brief exposition of two aspects of his views: first, views that
are characteristic of the "heritage" in general, and common
to Engelhardt and Skaldin in particular; and, second, views
that are specifically Narodnik. Engelhardt is *already a Narodnik*, but his views still contain so much that is common to
all the enlighteners, so much that has been discarded or altered by contemporary Narodism, that one is at a loss how
to class him—with the representatives of the "heritage" in
general, without the Narodnik tinge, or with the Narodniks.
What makes Engelhardt akin to the former is, primarily,
the remarkable sobriety of his views, his plain and direct
descriptions of realities, his relentless exposure of all
the bad sides of the "foundations" in general, and of the peasantry in particular—of those very "foundations," the false
idealisation and embellishment of which is an essential
component of Narodism. Engelhardt's very feebly and timidly expressed Narodism is therefore in direct and crying
contradiction to the picture of rural *realities* that he paints
with such talent, and if some economist or sociologist were
to base his opinions of the countryside on Engelhardt's
facts and *observations*,* he would find it impossible to draw
Narodnik conclusions from such material. Idealisation of
the peasant and his village community is one of the essen-

---

* Incidentally, this would be not only extremely interesting
and instructive, but also perfectly legitimate on the part of an economic investigator. If scientists trust the data of questionnaires—
the answers and opinions of numerous proprietors, who all too often
are biassed and ill-informed, have not developed a consistent outlook
or intelligently thought out their views—why not trust the observations gathered for a full eleven years by a man with splendid powers
of observation, who is unquestionably sincere and has made a superb
study of what he is talking about.

17*

tial components of Narodism, and Narodniks of all shades, from Mr. V. V. to Mr. Mikhailovsky, have given full rein to this effort to idealise and embellish the "community." There is not the slightest trace of such embellishment in Engelhardt. As against the fashionable talk about the communal spirit of our peasantry, the current contrasting of this "communal spirit" to the individualism of the town, the competition of capitalist economy, etc., Engelhardt is absolutely relentless in exposing the amazing *individualism* of the small farmer. He shows at length that our "peasants in matter of ownership have the keenest possible sense of property" (p. 62, 1885 ed.), that they cannot tolerate "gang work," hate it from narrowly selfish and egoistic motives: in gang work each is "afraid of doing more than the others" (p. 206). This fear of doing more work than others goes to comical (or, rather, tragicomical) extremes; the author, for instance, tells of women living under one roof and bound by ties of common residence and kinship, each of whom washes only her particular part of the table at which they eat, or who milk the cows in turn, each getting milk for her *own* child (for fear that others may hide some of the milk) and preparing porridge for her own child separately (p. 323). Engelhardt brings out these features in such detail, and corroborates them with such a mass of examples, that there can be no question of their being exceptional instances. One or the other: either Engelhardt is a worthless observer who deserves no credence, or the tale about the communal spirit and communal virtues of our muzhik are sheer imagination, which transfers to *economic practice* features abstracted from the form of *land tenure* (and from this form of landholding there are additionally abstracted all the fiscal and administrative aspects). Engelhardt shows that in his economic activity the muzhik aims at becoming a kulak. "There is a definite dose of the kulak in every peasant," he says (p. 491), "kulak ideals prevail among the peasants."... "I have said time and again that individualism, egoism, the urge to exploit are strongly developed among the peasants."... "Each prides himself on being a pike and strives to swallow the tiddler." Engelhardt demonstrates superbly that the trend among the peasantry is not towards the "communal" system, not towards "people's production," but towards the most or-

dinary petty-bourgeois system inherent in all capitalist societies. He describes and proves incontrovertibly the tendency of the well-to-do peasant to launch into trade (363), to
loan grain in return for work, to buy the labour of the poor
muzhik (pp. 457, 492, etc.)—or, in economic language, the
conversion of enterprising muzhiks into a rural bourgeoisie.
"If," says Engelhardt, "the peasants do not adopt the artel
form of economy and each continues to conduct his own farm
in isolation, then, even if there is an abundance of land,
there will be both landless peasants and farm labourers
among the peasant tillers. Further, I believe that the difference in status among the peasants will be even wider than
it now is. Despite communal ownership of the land, side by
side with the 'rich,' there will be many virtually landless farm
labourers. What benefit is it to me or my children if I have
the right to land, but neither the capital nor the implements
with which to cultivate it? It is like giving a blind man land
and saying—eat it!" (p. 370). With a sort of melancholy iro-
ny, the "artel form of economy" figures forlornly in this passage as a pious and innocent wish which, far from following
from the facts about the peasantry, is directly repudiated
and ruled out by them.

Another feature which makes Engelhardt akin to the
representatives of the heritage without any Narodnik tinge
is his belief that the chief and fundamental cause of the
distressed condition of the peasantry is the survivals
of serfdom and the reglementation characteristic of it. Do
away with these survivals and this reglementation, and all
will be well. Engelhardt's absolute hostility to reglementation and his caustic scoffing at all attempts to confer
happiness on the muzhik through reglementation from above,
are in the sharpest contrast to the Narodniks' faith in "the
reason and conscience, the knowledge and patriotism of
the ruling classes" (the words of Mr. Yuzhakov, in *Russkoye Bogatstvo*, 1896, No. 12, p. 106), to their fantastic
projects for "organising production," etc. Let us recall Engelhardt's sarcastic denunciation of the rule that vodka
should not be sold at flour-mills, a rule intended for the
muzhik's "good"; or the disgust with which he speaks of the
obligatory order issued by several Zemstvos in 1880 forbidding the sowing of rye before August 15, of that gross in-

terference by armchair "scientists"—also actuated by consideration for the muzhik's good—in the farming of "millions of peasant proprietors" (424). Referring to such rules and orders as those forbidding smoking in pine forests, pike fishing in spring, cutting birch for the May festival, bird-nest pillaging and so on, Engelhardt sarcastically remarks: ..."solicitude for the muzhik is and always has been the principal concern of intellectual minds. Who lives for himself? Everybody lives for the muzhik!... The muzhik is stupid, he cannot manage his own affairs. If nobody looks after him, he will burn down all the forests, kill off all the birds, denude the rivers of fish, ruin the land, and himself die out" (398). Do you think, reader, that this writer could have had any sympathy for laws so dear to the hearts of the Narodniks, as, say, those forbidding alienation of allotments? Could his pen have written anything like the phrase of one of the pillars of *Russkoye Bogatstvo* quoted above? Could he have shared the view of Mr. N. Karyshev, another pillar of the same journal, who flung the reproach at our gubernia Zemstvos (in the nineties!) that they "find no room" "for regular large and substantial expenditure on the organisation of agricultural labour"?*

Let us mention another feature which makes Engelhardt akin to Skaldin: his unconscious attitude to many purely bourgeois aspirations and measures. Not that Engelhardt tries to gild the petty bourgeois or to concoct excuses (à la Mr. V. V.) for not applying this designation to any particular entrepreneur—far from it. As a practical farmer, Engelhardt is simply infatuated with every progressive innovation, every improvement in farming methods, and completely fails to realise that the social form of these improvements is the most effective refutation of his own theory that capitalism is impossible in our country. Let us recall, for instance, how delighted he was with the success he achieved on his farm thanks to the introduction of the *piece-rate system of paying* his workers (for flax scutching, threshing, etc.). Engelhardt does not even suspect that the substitution of piece rates for time rates is one of the most

---

* *Russkoye Bogatstvo*, 1896, No. 5, May. Mr. Karyshev's article about gubernia Zemstvo expenditure on economic measures. P. 20.

widespread methods by which a developing capitalist economy heightens the intensification of labour and increases the rate of surplus-value. Another example. Engelhardt scoffs at the programme of *Zemledelcheskaya Gazeta*[150]: "discontinuation of leasing fields for cycle cultivation[151]; farming based on employment of labourers; introduction of improved machines, implements and cattle breeds and of multi-field system; improvement of meadows and pastures, etc., etc." "All this, however, is nothing but general talk!" Engelhardt exclaims (128). Yet it was this programme that Engelhardt adopted in his own practical farming; he achieved technical progress on his own farm precisely by basing it on the employment of farm labourers. Or again: we know how frankly and faithfully Engelhardt exposed the real tendencies of the enterprising muzhik; but that did not prevent him from asserting that "it is not factories that are needed, but *small*" (Engelhardt's italics) "rural distilleries, oil mills," etc. (p. 336), that is, what is "needed" is that the rural bourgeoisie should go in for agricultural industries—which has always and everywhere been one of the major indications of agricultural capitalism. Here we have the influence of the fact that Engelhardt was not a theoretician but a practical farmer. It is one thing to argue that progress is possible without capitalism, and another thing to farm yourself. Having set himself the aim of conducting his farm on rational lines, Engelhardt *was compelled*, by virtue of surrounding circumstances, to strive for this by purely capitalistic methods and to leave aside all his theoretical and abstract misgivings concerning the "employment of farm labourers." In the field of theory Skaldin argued like a typical member of the Manchester School, completely failing to realise both that his arguments were of just this character, and that they corresponded to the needs of Russia's capitalist evolution. In the field of practice Engelhardt was compelled to act as a typical Mancunian, despite his theoretical protest against capitalism and his desire to believe that his fatherland was following a path of its own.

Engelhardt did believe this, and it is this that induces us to call him a Narodnik. He had already clearly perceived the *real* trend of economic development in Russia, and sought *to explain away* the contradictions of this develop-

ment. He endeavoured to prove that agricultural capitalism was impossible in Russia, that "there is no Knecht
in our country" (p. 556)—though he himself refuted in the
greatest detail the story that our workers are expensive,
and himself showed how miserably he paid his cattleman,
Pyotr, who with his family, after their keep, had only
6 rubles a year left "with which to buy salt, vegetable oil,
clothing" (p. 10). "Yet even he is envied, and if I turned him
off, fifty others would immediately be found eager to take
his place" (p. 11). Speaking of the success of his farm, and of
the skilful way his workers handle the plough, Engelhardt triumphantly exclaims: "And who are these ploughmen?
Ignorant, unconscientious Russian peasants" (p. 225).

Though his own farming experience and his exposure of
the peasant's individualism refuted all illusions concerning the "community spirit," Engelhardt not only "believed"
that the peasants could adopt an artel form of economy, but
expressed the "conviction" that such would indeed be the
case, and that we, the Russians, would accomplish this great
feat and introduce a new mode of farming. "It is this that
constitutes the exceptional character, the specific nature of
our economy" (p. 349). Engelhardt the realist turns into
Engelhardt the romanticist, who replaces the complete lack of
"exceptional character" in his own methods of farming, and in
the peasants' farming methods as he observed them by "*faith*"
in a future "exceptional character"! From this faith it is only a
stone's throw to the ultra-Narodnik features which—though
very few—one finds in Engelhardt, to a narrow nationalism
bordering on chauvinism ("We'll give Europe a drubbing," and
"in Europe, too, the muzhik will be on our side" (p. 387)—said
Engelhardt to a landlord with whom he was discussing the
prospect of war), and even to idealisation of labour service!
Yes, this selfsame Engelhardt who devoted so many superb pages of his book to describing the downtrodden and
degraded condition of the peasant who has taken a loan of
money or grain to be paid off in work and is compelled to toil
almost for nothing in the very worst conditions of personal
dependence*—this selfsame Engelhardt goes to the length

---

* Remember the picture of the village elder (i.e., the landlord's
steward) summoning a peasant to work when the latter's own grain

of saying that "it would be a good thing if the doctor" (he was talking of the benefit of and need for doctors in the countryside. *V. I.*) "had a farm of his own, so that the muzhik could pay for the treatment with his labour" (p. 41). Comment is superfluous.

—All in all, comparing the above-enumerated good features of Engelhardt's outlook (i.e., those he has in common with the representatives of the "heritage" without any Narodnik tinge) with the bad (i.e., the Narodnik features), we have to admit that the former unquestionably predominate in the author of *Letters from the Countryside*, while the latter are an extraneous and accidental admixture, as it were, which has drifted in from without and is at odds with the general tone of his book.

III

HAS THE "HERITAGE" GAINED FROM ASSOCIATION WITH NARODISM?

"But what do you understand by Narodism?" the reader will probably ask. "The meaning attached to the concept 'heritage' was defined above, but no definition of the concept 'Narodism' has been given."

By Narodism we mean a system of views which comprises the following three features: 1) *Belief that capitalism in Russia represents a deterioration, a retrogression.* Hence the urge and desire to "retard," "halt," "stop the break-up" of the age-old foundations by capitalism, and similar reactionary cries. 2) *Belief in the exceptional character of the Russian economic system in general, and of the peasantry, with its village community, artel, etc., in particular.* It is not considered necessary to apply to Russian economic relationships the concepts elaborated by modern science concerning the different social classes and their conflicts. The village-community peasantry is regarded as something higher and

---

is already overripe and spoiling, and he is compelled to go merely because, if he does not, the volost authorities will "take his pants down."

better than capitalism; there is a disposition to idealise the "foundations." The existence among the peasantry of contradictions characteristic of every commodity and capitalist economy is denied or slurred over; it is denied that any connection exists between these contradictions and their more developed form in capitalist industry and capitalist agriculture. 3) *Disregard of the connection between the "intelligentsia" and the country's legal and political institutions, on the one hand, and the material interests of definite social classes, on the other.* Denial of this connection, lack of a materialist explanation of these social factors, induces the belief that they represent a force capable of "dragging history along another line" (Mr. V. V.), of "diversion from the path" (Mr. N. —on, Mr. Yuzhakov, etc.), and so on.

That is what we mean by "Narodism." The reader will consequently see that we use this term in its broad sense, just as all the "Russian disciples" use it when opposing a whole system of views, and not individual representatives of this system. Among these individual representatives there are differences, of course, and sometimes important ones. Nobody ignores these differences. But the afore-mentioned views are common to all the most diverse representatives of Narodism, from—well, Mr. Yuzov, let us say, to Mr. Mikhailovsky. To these objectionable features of their views, the Yuzovs, Sazonovs, V. V., etc., add others, which are not shared, for instance, either by Mr. Mikhailovsky or by other contributors to the present-day *Russkoye Bogatstvo.* To deny these differences between the Narodniks in the narrow sense and the Narodniks in general would, of course, be wrong; but it would be wronger still to ignore the fact that the *fundamental* socio-economic views of all Narodniks coincide on the afore-mentioned major points. And since it is these fundamental views that the "Russian disciples" reject, and not only "deplorable deviations" from them in a worse direction, they are obviously fully entitled to employ the term "Narodism" in its wider meaning. Not only are they entitled to do so; they cannot do otherwise.

Turning to the fundamental views of Narodism outlined above, the first thing we must note is that the "heritage"

has absolutely no part in them. There are a whole number of
undeniable representatives and guardians of the "heritage"
who have nothing in common with Narodism, who do not
pose the question of capitalism at all, who do not believe in
the exceptional character of Russia, the peasant community,
etc., and who do not regard the intelligentsia and our legal
and political institutions as a factor capable of "diversion from the path." Above we named in illustration the
editor and publisher of *Vestnik Yevropy*,[152] who might be
accused of anything save violation of the traditions of the
heritage. On the other hand, there are people whose views
resemble the afore-mentioned fundamental principles of
Narodism, yet who plainly and frankly "renounce the heritage"—we might mention, for example, the same Mr. Y. Abramov to whom Mr. Mikhailovsky refers, or Mr. Yuzov.
The Narodism which the "Russian disciples" battle against
did not even exist when the heritage was (to use a legal term)
"bequeathed," that is, in the sixties. Germs, rudiments of
Narodism existed, of course, not only in the sixties, but in
the forties and even earlier*—but it is not the history of
Narodism that concerns us here. We repeat, what is important for us is to establish that the "heritage" of the sixties,
in the sense outlined above, has nothing in common with
Narodism, i.e., that there is nothing in common in the substance of their views, that they pose different problems. There
are guardians of the "heritage" who are not Narodniks,
and there are Narodniks who "have renounced the heritage." Of
course, there are also Narodniks who guard the "heritage,"
or who pretend to do so. That is why we speak of a connection between the heritage and Narodism. Let us see what
has been the effect of this connection.

First, Narodism made a big *step forward* compared with
the heritage *by posing* for the attention of society problems which the guardians of the heritage were partly (in
their time) not yet able to pose, or partly did not, and do
not, pose because of their inherent narrowness of outlook.
In *posing* these problems the Narodniks performed a great
historical service, and it is quite natural and understanda-

---

* Cf. Tugan-Baranovsky's *The Russian Factory* (St. Petersburg,
1898).

33*

ble, that, having offered a solution (whatever it may be worth) for these problems, Narodism *thereby* occupied a foremost place among the progressive trends of Russian social thought.

But the solution of these problems proposed by Narodism proved to be worthless, to be based on backward theories, long ago discarded in Western Europe, on a romantic and petty-bourgeois criticism of capitalism, on a disregard for the cardinal facts of Russian history and reality. So long as the development of capitalism in Russia and of its inherent contradictions was still very weak, this primitive criticism of capitalism could hold its ground. But Narodism is absolutely incapable of measuring up to the contemporary development of capitalism in Russia, the contemporary state of our knowledge of Russian economic history and reality, the contemporary demands made on sociological theory. Once progressive, as the first to pose the problem of capitalism, nowadays Narodism is a *reactionary* and *harmful* theory which misleads social thought and plays into the hands of stagnation and Asiatic backwardness. Today the reactionary character of its criticism of capitalism has even lent Narodism features that make it *inferior* to the outlook which confines itself to faithful guardianship of the heritage.* That this is so we shall now endeavour to prove by analysing each of the three basic features of the Narodnik outlook mentioned above.

The first feature—the belief that in Russia capitalism represents a deterioration, a retrogression. Very soon after the problem of capitalism in Russia had been posed, it became clear that our economic development was capitalistic, and the Narodniks proclaimed this development a retrogression, a mistake, a deviation from the path supposedly prescribed by the whole history of the nation's life, from the path supposedly hallowed by age-old foundations, and so on and so forth. The enlighteners' ardent faith in this course of social development was replaced by distrust

---

* I have already had occasion to remark above in the article on economic romanticism that our opponents display remarkable short-sightedness in regarding the terms *reactionary* and *petty-bourgeois* as polemical abuse, when they have a perfectly definite historico-philosophical meaning. (See p. 217 of the present volume.—*Ed.*)

of it; historical optimism and cheerfulness were replaced by pessimism and dejection founded on the fact that the farther matters proceeded as they were proceeding, the harder and more difficult would it be to solve the problems raised by the new development; appeals were made to "retard" and "halt" this development; the theory was advanced that Russia's backwardness was her good fortune, and so forth. All these features of the Narodnik outlook, far from having anything in common with the "heritage," flatly contradict it. The belief that Russian capitalism represents a "deviation from the path," a deterioration, etc., leads to a misrepresentation of Russia's whole economic evolution, to a misrepresentation of that "change-over" which is taking place before our eyes. Carried away by their desire to retard and stop the break-up of the age-old foundations by capitalism, the Narodniks display an amazing lack of historical tact, they forget that *antecedent* to this capitalism there was nothing but the same exploitation combined with countless forms of bondage and personal dependence, which burdened the position of the labourer, nothing but routine and stagnation in social production and, hence, in all spheres of social life. Contending against capitalism from their romantic, petty-bourgeois angle, the Narodniks throw all historical realism overboard and always compare the *reality* of capitalism with a *fiction* of the pre-capitalist order. The "heritage" of the sixties with their ardent faith in the progressive character of the existing course of social development, their relentless enmity directed wholly and exclusively against the relics of the past, their conviction that these relics had only to be swept clean away and everything would go splendidly—this "heritage," far from having any part in the aforementioned views of Narodism, runs directly counter to them.

The second feature of Narodism is belief in Russia's exceptionalism, idealisation of the peasantry, the village community, etc. The doctrine of Russia's exceptionalism induced the Narodniks to seize upon out-dated West-European theories, prompted them to regard many of the achievements of West-European culture with amazing levity: the Narodniks reassured themselves with the thought that, if we lacked some of the features of civilised humanity, "we are destined," on the other hand, to show the world new modes of economy, etc. Not only was the analysis of capitalism and all its manifestations given by progressive West-European thought not accepted in relation to Holy Russia; every effort was made to invent excuses for not drawing the same conclusions about Russian capitalism as were made regarding European capitalism. The Narodniks bowed and scraped to the authors of this analysis and—calmly continued to remain romanticists of the same sort as these authors had all their lives contended against. Again, this doctrine of Russia's exceptionalism, which is shared by all the Narodniks, far from having anything in common with the "heritage," runs directly counter to it. The "sixties," on the contrary, desired to Europeanise Russia, believed that she should adopt the general European culture, were concerned to have the institutions of this culture transferred to our anything but exceptional soil. Any doctrine that teaches that Russia is exceptional is completely at variance with the spirit and the tradition of the sixties. Even more at variance with this tradition is Narodism's idealisation and over-embellishment of the countryside. This false idealisation, which desired at all costs to see something specific in our rural system, something quite unlike the rural system in every other country in the period of pre-capitalist relations, is in naked contradiction to the traditions of the sober and realistic heritage. The wider and more deeply capitalism developed, the more distinctly did the countryside display the contradictions common to every commodity-capitalist society, the more and more glaringly did the antithesis stand out between the Narodniks' honeyed talk about the peasant's "community spirit," "artel spirit," etc., on the one hand, and the actual division of the peasantry into a rural bourgeoisie and a rural proletariat on the other; and the more rapidly did the Narodniks, who continued to look upon things with the eyes of the peasant, change from sentimental romanticists into ideologists of the petty bourgeoisie, because in modern society the small producer changes into a commodity producer. Their false idealisation of the countryside and romantic dreams about the "community spirit" led the Narodniks to adopt an extremely frivolous attitude towards the peasants' real needs arising from the existing course of economic development. In theory one might talk to one's heart's content about the strength of the foundations, but in practice every Narodnik sensed very well that the elimination of the relics of the past, the survivals of the pre-Reform system, which to this day bind our peasantry from head to foot, would open the way to precisely the capitalist course of development, and no other. Better stagnation than capitalist progress— this, essentially, is every Narodnik's attitude to the countryside, although of course not every Narodnik would venture to say so frankly and bluntly, with the naïve forthrightness of a Mr. V. V. "Tied to their allotments and communities, and unable to apply their labour where it would be more productive and of greater advantage to themselves, the peasants are, as it were, frozen in that congested, herd-like, unproductive form of life in which they emerged from serfdom." That is how one of the representatives of the "heritage" saw it from his characteristic "enlightener's" standpoint.[153] "Better that the peasants remain frozen in their routine, patriarchal form of life, than clear the way for capitalism in the countryside"— that, essentially, is how every Narodnik sees it. Indeed, probably not a single Narodnik would venture to deny that social-estate exclusiveness of the peasant community, with its collective responsibility and its ban on the sale of land and on the right to refuse an allotment, stands in the sharpest contradiction to contemporary economic *realities*, to contemporary commodity-capitalist relations and their development. To deny this contradiction is impossible, but the whole point is that the Narodniks are mortally afraid of this presentation of the question, of this contrasting of the legal status of the peasantry with economic realities and the present course of economic development. The Narodnik is stubbornly determined to believe in a non-existent non-capitalist development which is a figment of his romantic imagination, and therefore ... and therefore he is prepared to retard the present development, which is proceeding along capitalist lines. The Narodnik's attitude to such problems as the social-estate exclusiveness of the peasant community, collective responsibility, and the peasant's right to sell and give up his allotment, is not only one of extreme caution and fear for the fate of the "foundations" (the foundations of routine and stagnation); more than this, the Narodnik falls so low that he even welcomes the police rule forbidding the peasants to sell land. To such a Narodnik, one might retort in the words of Engelhardt: "The muzhik is stupid, he cannot manage his own affairs. If nobody looks after him, he will burn down all the forests, kill off all the birds, denude the rivers of fish, ruin the land and himself die out." Here the Narodnik quite definitely "renounces the heritage," becomes a reactionary. And note that with the progress of economic development, this destruction of the social-estate exclusiveness of the peasant community increasingly becomes an imperative necessity for the rural proletariat, while the inconveniences arising therefrom for the peasant bourgeoisie are not at all considerable. The "enterprising muzhik" may easily rent land on the side, open an establishment in some other village, and travel on business wherever he likes and whenever he likes. But for the "peasant" who lives chiefly from the sale of his labour-power, being tied to his allotment and community is an enormous restriction on his economic activity, makes it impossible for him to find a better employer, and compels him to sell his labour-power only to local purchasers, who invariably pay less and seek all sorts of ways and means of reducing him to bondage. Having surrendered to the sway of romantic dreaming and set himself the aim of maintaining and preserving the foundations despite the course of economic development, the Narodnik, without himself observing it, had slipped down this inclined plane until he found himself side by side with the agrarian, who yearns with all his heart and soul for the preservation and consolidation of the "peasant's tie with the land." It is worth recalling, for example, that this social-estate exclusiveness of the peasant community has bred specific methods of hiring workers: factory and farm owners send out agents to the villages, especially those heavily in arrears, to hire labourers on the most advantageous terms. Fortunately, the development of agricultural capitalism, by breaking down the "settled state" of the proletarian (such is the effect of the so-called agricultural outside employments), is gradually substituting free hire for this form of bondage.

Another, and perhaps no less striking corroboration of our contention that the present-day Narodnik theories are pernicious, is to be found in the common tendency among the Narodniks *to idealise labour services.* We have already given an example of how Engelhardt, consummating his Narodnik fall from grace, went so far as to say that "it would be a good thing" to develop labour services in the countryside! We find the same thing in Mr. Yuzhakov's famous project for agricultural gymnasia (*Russkoye Bogatstvo*, 1895, No. 5).* In serious economic articles in the same journal, a fellow contributor of Engelhardt's, Mr. V. V., indulged in similar idealisation when he declared that the peasant had scored a victory over the landlord, who had supposedly wanted to introduce capitalism; but the whole trouble was that the peasant undertook to cultivate the landlord's land in return for land received from him "on lease"—in other words, was restoring the very same mode of economy as existed under serfdom. These are some of the most glaring illustrations of the Narodniks' reactionary attitude to problems concerning our agriculture. In less glaring form, you will find this idea advocated by every Narodnik. Every Narodnik says that capitalism in our agriculture is pernicious and dangerous, because capitalism, you see, substitutes the farm labourer for the independent peasant. The *reality* of capitalism (the "farm labourer") is contrasted to the *fiction* of the "independent" peasant: and this fiction is based on the peasant ownership of means of production in the pre-capitalist era, the fact being modestly ignored that the peasant has to pay double their value for these means of production; that these means of production serve for the performance of labour service; hat the living standard of this "independent" peasant is so low that in any capitalist country he would be classed as a pauper; and that added to the hopeless poverty and intellectual inertness of this "independent" peasant is the personal dependence that inevitably accompanies pre-capitalist forms of economy.

The third characteristic feature of Narodism—disregard of the connection between the "intelligentsia" and the

---

* See pp. 73-80 and 459-89 of the present volume.—*Ed.*

country's legal and political institutions, on the one hand, and the material interests of definite social classes, on the other—is bound up indissolubly with the previous ones: only this unrealistic attitude to sociological problems could have bred the doctrine that Russian capitalism is a "mistake," and that "diversion from the path" is possible. This Narodnik view, too, bears no relation to the "heritage" and traditions of the sixties; on the contrary, it *runs directly counter to these traditions*. A natural corollary to this view is the Narodniks' attitude to the numerous survivals of the pre-Reform reglementation of Russian life, an attitude which the representatives of the "heritage" could not possibly have shared. To illustrate this attitude, we shall take the liberty of borrowing the excellent, remarks of Mr. V. Ivanov in his article "A Shabby Fabrication" (*Novoye Slovo*, September 1897). The author refers to Mr. Boborykin's novel *A Different Way*, and exposes his misconception of the dispute between the Narodniks and the "disciples." Mr. Boborykin makes his hero, a Narodnik, reproach the "disciples" for supposedly dreaming of "a barrack regime with the intolerable despotism of reglementation." Mr. V. Ivanov observes in this connection that:

"Far from saying that the 'dream' of their opponents was the intolerable despotism of 'reglementation,' they" (the Narodniks) "*cannot and will not say so as long as they remain Narodniks*. The substance of their dispute with the 'economic materialists' *in this respect* is that, in the opinion of the Narodniks, the remaining survivals of the old reglementation may serve as the basis for its further development. The intolerableness of the old reglementation is veiled from their eyes, on the one hand, by their conviction that the very 'peasant soul (single and indivisible) is evolving' towards reglementation, and, on the other, by their belief in the existing or coming moral beauty of the 'intelligentsia,' 'society,' or the 'leading classes' generally. They accuse the economic materialists of being infatuated not with 'reglementation,' but, on the contrary, with the West-European system, which is based on freedom from reglementation. And the economic materialists really do assert that the survivals of the old reglementation, which sprang from a natural form of economy, are daily becoming more 'intolerable' in a country that has passed over to a money economy, entailing countless changes both in the actual status and in the mental and moral complexion of the various sections of its population. They are therefore convinced that the conditions necessary for the rise of a new and beneficial 'reglementation' of the country's economic life cannot develop out of the survivals of a reglementation which was adapted to a natural economy and serfdom, and can only evolve in such an atmosphere of wide and comprehensive freedom from the old reglementation as exists in the advanced countries of Western Europe and America. That is how matters stand with the question of 'reglementation' in the dispute between the Narodniks and their opponents" (pp. 11-12, loc. cit.). This attitude of the Narodniks to "the survivals of the old reglementation is, perhaps, their most flagrant departure from the traditions of the "heritage." The representatives of this heritage were, as we have seen, distinguished by their ineradicable and fierce aversion for every survival of the old reglementation. Consequently, in this respect the "disciples" are incomparably closer to the "traditions" and "heritage" of the sixties than the Narodniks are.

In addition to the highly important error of the Narodniks mentioned above, their lack of sociological realism impels them to a specific manner of thinking and reasoning about social affairs and problems which might be called narrow intellectual self-conceit or, perhaps, the bureaucratic mentality. The Narodnik is always dilating on the path "we" should choose for our country, the misfortunes that would arise if "we" directed the country along such-and-such a path, the prospects "we" could ensure ourselves if we avoided the dangers of the path old Europe has taken, if we "take what is good" both from Europe and from our ancient village-community system, and so on and so forth. Hence the Narodnik's complete distrust and contempt for the independent trends of the various social classes which are shaping history in accordance with their own interests. Hence the amazing levity with which the Narodnik (forgetting the conditions surrounding him) advances all sorts of social projects, from the "organisation of agricultural

labour" to the "communalisation of production" through
the good offices of our "society." "Mit der Gründlichkeit der
geschichtlichen Action wird also der Umfang der Masse
zunehmen, deren Action sie ist"*—these words express one
of the profoundest and most important precepts of that historico-philosophical theory which our Narodniks will not
and cannot understand. As man's history-making activity
grows broader and deeper, the size of that mass of the population which is the conscious maker of history is bound to
increase. The Narodnik, however, always regarded the population in general, and the working population in particular, as the object of this or that more or less sensible measure,
as something to be directed along this or that path, and
never regarded the various classes of the population as independent history-makers on the existing path, never asked
which conditions of the present path might stimulate (or,
on the contrary, paralyse) the independent and conscious
activity of these history-makers.

And so, although Narodism, by *posing* the question of
capitalism in Russia, made a big step forward compared
with the "heritage" of the enlighteners, the *solution* of the
question it offered has proved so unsatisfactory, because
of its petty-bourgeois outlook and sentimental criticism of
capitalism, that on a number of cardinal questions of social
life it *lags behind* the "enlighteners." Narodism's association
with the heritage and traditions of our enlighteners has
proved in the end to be a *drawback*: the new questions
with which Russian social thought has been confronted
by Russia's post-Reform economic development, Narodism
has not solved, confining itself to sentimental and reactionary lamentations over them; while Narodnik romanticism
has obscured the old questions already posed by the enlighteners, thus retarding their full solution.

---

* Marx, *Die heilige Familie*, p. 120. Quoted from Beltov, p. 235.
("With the thoroughness of the historical action, the size of the mass
whose action it is will therefore increase." Marx, *The Holy Family*. [154]—
Ed.)

IV

THE "ENLIGHTENERS," THE NARODNIKS, AND THE "DISCIPLES"

We may now sum up the results of our comparisons. Let us endeavour to give a brief description of the relationship in which each of the trends of social thought enumerated in the sub-title stands to the others.

The enlightener believes in the present course of social development, because he fails to observe its inherent contradictions. The Narodnik fears the present course of social development, because he is already aware of these contradictions. The "disciple" believes in the present course of social development, because he sees the only earnest of a better future in the full development of these contradictions. The first and last trends therefore strive to support, accelerate, facilitate development along the present path, to remove all obstacles which hamper this development and retard it. Narodism, on the contrary, strives to retard and halt this development, is afraid of abolishing certain obstacles to the development of capitalism. The first and last trends are distinguished by what may be called historical optimism: the farther and the quicker things go as they are, the better it will be. Narodism, on the contrary, naturally tends to historical pessimism: the farther things go as they are, the worse it will be. The "enlighteners" never posed questions concerning the character of post-Reform development and confined themselves exclusively to warring against the survivals of the pre-Reform system, to the negative task of clearing the way for a European type of development in Russia. Narodism posed the question of capitalism in Russia, but answered it in the sense that capitalism is reactionary, and therefore could not wholly accept the heritage of the enlighteners: the Narodniks always warred against people who in general strove to Europeanise Russia from the standpoint of a "single civilisation"; warred against them not only because they, the Narodniks, could not confine themselves to these people's ideals (such a war would have been just), but because they did not want to go so far in the development of this, i.e., capitalist, civilisation. The "disciples" answer the question of capitalism in Russia in the sense that it is progressive, and they therefore not only can, but must, accept the heritage of the enlighteners in its entirety, supplementing it with an analysis of the contradictions of capitalism from the standpoint of the propertyless producers. The enlighteners did not single out any one class of the population for special attention; they not only spoke of the people in general, but even of the nation in general. The Narodniks were desirous of representing the interests of labour, but they did not point to any definite groups in the contemporary economic system; actually, they always took the standpoint of the small producer, whom capitalism converts into a commodity producer. The "disciples" not only take the interests of labour as their criterion, but in doing so point to quite definite economic groups in the capitalist economy, namely, the propertyless producers. By the nature of their aims, the first and last trends correspond to the interests of the classes which are created and developed by capitalism; Narodism, by its nature, corresponds to the interests of the class of small producers, the petty bourgeoisie, which occupies an intermediate position among the classes of contemporary society. Consequently, Narodism's contradictory attitude to the "heritage" is not accidental, but is a necessary result of the very nature of the Narodnik views: we have seen that one of the basic features of the enlighteners' views was the ardent desire to Europeanise Russia, but the Narodniks cannot possibly share this desire fully without ceasing to be Narodniks.

We have in the end arrived at the conclusion which we have repeatedly indicated above in particular instances, namely, that *the disciples are much more consistent and faithful guardians of the heritage than the Narodniks*. Far from renouncing the heritage, they consider it one of their principal duties to refute the romantic and petty-bourgeois fears which induce the Narodniks on very many and very important points to reject the European ideals of the enlighteners. But it goes without saying that the "disciples" do not guard the heritage in the way an archivist guards an old document. Guarding the heritage does not mean confining oneself to the heritage, and the "disciples" add to their defence of the general ideals of Europeanism an analysis of the contradictions implicit in our capitalist development, and an assessment of this development from the specific standpoint indicated above.

V

MR. MIKHAILOVSKY ON THE "DISCIPLES'" RENUNCIATION OF THE HERITAGE

Let us, in conclusion, return to Mr. Mikhailovsky and examine his statements on the subject under consideration. Not only does Mr. Mikhailovsky declare that these people (the disciples) "do not acknowledge any continuity with the past and emphatically renounce the heritage" (loc. cit., 179); he also affirms that "they" (together with other persons of the most diverse trends, up to and including Mr. Abramov, Mr. Volynsky and Mr. Rozanov) "hurl themselves against the heritage with the greatest fury" (180). To which heritage is Mr. Mikhailovsky referring? To the heritage of the sixties and seventies, the heritage which *Moskovskiye Vedomosti* solemnly renounced and renounces (178).

We have already said that if it is a question of the "heritage" that has fallen to the people of today, then one must distinguish between *two heritages*: one is the heritage of the enlighteners in general, of the people who were absolutely hostile to the whole pre-Reform order, who stood for European ideals and for the interests of the broad mass of the population. The other heritage is Narodism. We have already shown that to confuse these two different things would be a gross error, for everyone knows that there have been, and still are, people who guard the "traditions of the sixties" but have nothing in common with Narodism. All Mr. Mikhailovsky's observations are founded wholly and exclusively upon a confusion of these totally different heritages. And since Mr. Mikhailovsky must be aware of this difference, his sally is not only absurd, but definitely slanderous. Did *Moskovskiye Vedomosti* hurl itself against Narodism specifically? Not at all: it hurled itself no less, if not more, against the enlighteners in general, and

Vestnik Yevropy, which absolutely abhors Narodism, is in its eyes no less an enemy than the Narodnik *Russkoye Bogatstvo*. *Moskovskiye Vedomosti* would, of course, disagree on many points with the Narodniks who most emphatically renounce the heritage—Yuzov, for example—but it would hardly hurl itself against him with fury, and in any case, it would praise him for that which distinguishes him from the Narodniks who desire to guard the heritage. Did Mr. Abramov or Mr. Volynsky hurl himself against Narodism? Not at all. The former is himself a Narodnik; and both hurled themselves against the enlighteners in general. Did the "Russian disciples" hurl themselves against the Russian enlighteners? Did they ever renounce the heritage which enjoins unreserved hostility to the pre-Reform way of life and its survivals? Far from hurling themselves against it, they denounced the Narodniks for desiring to maintain some of these survivals out of a petty-bourgeois fear of capitalism. Did they ever hurl themselves against the heritage which enjoins European ideals generally? Far from hurling themselves against it, they denounced the Narodniks because on many very important issues, instead of espousing general European ideals, they concoct the most arrant nonsense about Russia's exceptional character. Did they ever hurl themselves against the heritage which enjoins concern for the interests of the labouring masses of the population? Far from hurling themselves against it, they denounced the Narodniks because their concern for these interests is inconsistent (owing to their confirmed tendency to lump together the peasant bourgeoisie and the rural proletariat); because the value of their concern is diminished by their habit of dreaming of what might be, instead of turning their attention to what is; because their concern is extremely circumscribed, since they have never been able properly to appraise the conditions (economic and other) which make it easier or harder for these people to care for their own interests themselves.

Mr. Mikhailovsky may not agree with these denunciations —being a Narodnik, he certainly will not agree with them— but to assert that certain people "furiously" attack the "heritage of the sixties and the seventies," when, actually, they "furiously" attack *only Narodism*, and attack it for having failed to solve the new problems posed by post-Reform history *in the spirit of this heritage and without contradicting it*—such an assertion is a direct misrepresentation of the truth.

Mr. Mikhailovsky most amusingly complains that the "disciples" readily confuse "us" (i.e., the *Russkoye Bogatstvo* writers) with the "Narodniks" and other persons who have no connection with *Russkoye Bogatstvo* (p. 180). This curious attempt at dissociation from the "Narodniks," while at the same time preserving all the basic views of Narodism, can evoke nothing but laughter. Everyone knows that all the "Russian disciples" employ the words "Narodnik" and "Narodism" in the broad sense. That there are quite a number of different shades among the Narodniks has not been forgotten or denied by anybody: in their books neither P. Struve nor N. Beltov, for instance, "confused" Mr. N. Mikhailovsky with Mr. V. V., or even for that matter with Mr. Yuzhakov; that is, they did not gloss over the differences between them, or ascribe the views of one to the other. P. B. Struve even expressly drew attention to the difference between Mr. Yuzhakov's views and those of Mr. Mikhailovsky. It is one thing to confuse different views; it is another to generalise and class in one category writers who, despite their differences on many questions, are at one on the fundamental and principal points, points which the "disciples" oppose. What is important for the "disciple" is not to show the worthlessness of the views which distinguish, for instance, a Mr. Yuzov from the other Narodniks, but to refute the views *common to Mr. Yuzov and Mr. Mikhailovsky and all the Narodniks in general*—that is, their attitude to Russia's capitalist evolution, their discussion of economic and social problems from the standpoint of the small producer, their failure to understand social (or historical) materialism. *These features* are the common property of a whole trend of social thought which has played a big historical role. This broad trend contains the most varied shades: right and left flanks, people who have sunk to nationalism and anti-semitism, etc., and people who are not guilty of these things; people who have been contemptuous of many of the behests of the "heritage," and people who have striven their utmost (that is, the utmost possible to a Narodnik) to guard these behests. Not one of the "Russian disciples" has denied these differences of shade; not one of them has Mr. Mikhailovsky been able to convict of ascribing the views of a Narodnik of one shade to a Narodnik of another shade. But since we oppose the fundamental views *common* to all these different shades, why should we be expected to speak of partial differences within the general trend? That, surely, is an absolutely senseless demand! Long before the appearance of the "disciples," our literature had noted many times that writers who were far from unanimous on everything held common views on Russian capitalism, the peasant "community," the almighty power of so-called "society," and not only noted it, but praised it as a happy peculiarity of Russia. Again, in its broad sense, the term "Narodism" was employed in our literature long before the appearance of the "disciples." Not only did Mr. Mikhailovsky contribute for many years to a journal along with the "Narodnik" (in the narrow sense) Mr. V. V., but the outlook of both bore the same fundamental features mentioned above. Though, both in the eighties and the nineties, he objected to some of Mr. V. V.'s conclusions, and denied the correctness of his excursions into the field of abstract sociology, Mr. Mikhailovsky, both in the eighties and the nineties, made the reservation that his criticism was not directed against Mr. V. V.'s economic works, that he was at one with his basic views on Russian capitalism. Consequently, if the pillars of *Russkoye Bogatstvo*, who have done so much to develop, reinforce and disseminate the views of Narodism (in the broad sense), now think that they can escape the criticism of the "Russian disciples" simply by declaring that they are not "Narodniks" (in the narrow sense), that they constitute a quite specific "ethico-social school"—such subterfuges, of course, can only expose to justified ridicule people who are so brave and at the same time so diplomatic.

On p. 182 of his article, Mr. Mikhailovsky also levels the following phenomenal argument against the "disciples." Mr. Kamensky venomously attacks the Narodniks[155]; that, you see, "indicates that he is angry, which he is not entitled (sic!!) to be. We, the 'subjective oldsters,' as well as the 'subjective youngsters,' can permit ourselves this weakness without being guilty of self-contradiction. But the representatives of a doctrine which 'prides itself on its inexorable objectivity' " (the expression of one of the "disciples") "are in a different position."

What is this?! If people insist that views on social phenomena must be based upon an inexorably objective analysis of *realities* and the real course of development, then it follows that they are not entitled to be angry?! Why, this is utter twaddle, the sheer gibberish! Have you not heard, Mr. Mikhailovsky, that the famous work on *Capital* is considered to be one of the finest specimens of inexorable objectivity in the investigation of social phenomena? It is precisely the inexorable objectivity of the work that is regarded by many scientists and economists as its principal and basic defect. Yet rarely will you find in a scientific work so much "feeling," so much heated and passionate polemical attacks on representatives of backward views, on representatives of the social classes which, in the author's convinced opinion, are hampering social development. A writer who shows with inexorable objectivity that the opinions of Proudhon, say, are a natural, understandable and inevitable reflexion of the views and sentiments of the French petit bourgeois, nevertheless "hurls himself" against that ideologist of the petty bourgeoisie with tremendous passion and fiery wrath. Does Mr. Mikhailovsky believe that Marx is here guilty of "self-contradiction"? If a certain doctrine demands of everyone taking part in public life an inexorably objective analysis of realities and of the relationships between the various classes arising from these realities, by what miracle can the conclusion be drawn from this that they must not sympathise, are "not entitled" to sympathise with one or another class? It is ridiculous in this connection even to talk of duty, for no living person *can help taking the side* of one class or another (once he has understood their interrelationships), can help rejoicing at the successes of that class and being disappointed by its failures, can help being angered by those who are hostile to that class, who hamper its development by disseminating backward views, and so on and so forth. Mr. Mikhailovsky's nonsensical sally only shows that he still fails to grasp the very elementary distinction between determinism and fatalism.

34*

"'Capital is coming'!—that is certain," writes Mr. Mikhailovsky,—"but (sic!!) the question is, how shall we greet it" (p. 189).

Mr. Mikhailovsky makes a great discovery, points to a "question" to which the "Russian disciples" have evidently given no thought whatever! As though it were not on this question that the "Russian disciples" have parted ways with the Narodniks! One can "greet" the capitalism developing in Russia only in two ways: one can regard it either as progressive, or as retrogressive; either as a step forward on the right road, or as a deviation from the true path; one can assess it either from the standpoint of the class of small producers which capitalism destroys, or from the standpoint of the class of propertyless producers which capitalism creates. There is no middle way.* Consequently, if Mr. Mikhailovsky denies the correctness of the attitude to capitalism which the "disciples" insist on, it means that he accepts the Narodnik attitude which he has many a time expressed quite definitely in his earlier articles. He has not made any additions or amendments to his old views on this subject, and continues to remain a Narodnik. But nothing of the kind! He is not a Narodnik, heaven forbid! He is a representative of an "ethico-sociological school."...

"Let no one talk," Mr. Mikhailovsky continues, "of those future (??) benefits which the further development of capitalism will (?) bring."

Mr. Mikhailovsky is no Narodnik. He only reiterates all the Narodniks' errors and fallacious methods of argument. How many times have the Narodniks been told that this talk of the "future" is wrong, that it is not a question of "future," but of actual progressive changes already taking place in the pre-capitalist relationships—changes which the development of capitalism in Russia is bringing (not, will bring). By transplanting the question to the "future,"

---

* We say nothing, of course, of the greeting given it by those who do not consider it necessary to be guided by the interests of labour, or to whom the very generalisation denoted by the term "capitalism" is incomprehensible and unintelligible. However important such trends of thought may be in Russian life, they have nothing whatever to do with the dispute between the Narodniks and their opponents, and there is no point in bringing them into it.

Mr. Mikhailovsky in point of fact takes for granted the very assertions which the "disciples" contest. He takes it for granted that in reality, in what is taking place under our eyes, the development of capitalism *is not bringing* any progressive changes into the old socio-economic relations. This is what constitutes the Narodnik view, and it is against this that the "Russian disciples" argue and demonstrate that the contrary is true. There is not a book put out by the "Russian disciples" which does not affirm and demonstrate that the replacement of labour service by wage-labour in agriculture, and the replacement of what is called "handicraft" industry by factory industry, is a real phenomenon which is taking place (and, moreover, at a tremendous speed) now, under our eyes, and not merely "in the future"; that this change is in all respects progressive, that it is breaking down routine, disunited, small-scale hand production which has been immobile and stagnant for ages; that it is increasing the productivity of social labour, and thereby creating the possibility of higher living standards for the working man; that it is also creating the conditions which convert this possibility into a necessity—namely, by converting the "settled proletarian" lost in the "backwoods," settled physically and morally, into a mobile proletarian, and by converting Asiatic forms of labour, with their infinitely developed bondage and diverse forms of personal dependence, into European forms of labour; that "the European manner of thought and feeling is no less necessary (note, necessary. *V. I.*) for the effective utilisation of machines than steam, coal, techniques,"* etc. All this, we repeat, is affirmed and demonstrated by every "disciple," but, presumably, does not apply to Mr. Mikhailovsky "and company"; all this is only written against "Narodniks" who are "not connected" with *Russkoye Bogatstvo. Russkoye Bogatstvo*, you see, is an "ethico-sociological school," whose essence is that it serves up the old rubbish under a new guise.

As we observed above, the purpose of this article is to refute the allegation so widespread in the liberal-Narodnik press that the "Russian disciples" abjure the "heritage,"

---

* The words of Schulze-Gävernitz in an article on the Moscow-Vladimir cotton industry in *Schmollers Jahrbuch*, [156] 1896.

break with the best traditions of the best section of Russian society, and so forth. It is not without interest to observe that, in reiterating these hackneyed phrases, Mr. Mikhailovsky in point of fact says exactly the same thing as was said much earlier and much more emphatically by a "Narodnik" "not connected" with *Russkoye Bogatstvo*—Mr. V. V. Are you familiar, dear reader, with the articles which this writer contributed to *Nedelya*[157] three years ago, at the close of 1894, in reply to P. B. Struve's book? If you are not, I must confess that, in my opinion, you have lost absolutely nothing. The basic idea of these articles·is that the "Russian disciples" are breaking the democratic thread which runs through all the progressive trends of Russian social thought. Is this not exactly what Mr. Mikhailovsky says, only in somewhat different terms, when he accuses the "disciples" of renouncing the "heritage," against which *Moskovskiye Vedomosti* hurls itself with fury? Actually, as we have seen, the inventors of this allegation blame others for their own sins when they assert that the "disciples'" irrevocable break with *Narodism* signifies a break with the best traditions of the best section of Russian society. Is it not the other way round, sirs? Does not such a break signify that these best traditions are being *purged of Narodism*?

NOTES

[1] The obituary, "Frederick Engels," written by Lenin in the autumn
of 1895, was published in *Rabotnik* (*The Worker*), No. 1-2, that
appeared not earlier than March 1896.

The miscellany *Rabotnik* was published at irregular intervals
outside of Russia by the League of Russian Social-Democrats in
the years 1896-99 and it was edited by the Emancipation of Labour group. Its actual initiator was Lenin, who in 1895, while
abroad, reached an agreement with G. V. Plekhanov and P. B.
Axelrod on the editing and publication of the miscellany by the
group. On his return to Russia Lenin did much to secure financial
support for the publication, and to ensure the receipt of articles
and correspondence from Russia. Before his arrest in December
1895, Lenin prepared the "Frederick Engels" obituary and several
items of correspondence, which he sent to the editors of *Rabotnik*.
Some of these appeared in Nos. 1-2 and 5-6 of the miscellany.

Altogether there were six issues of *Rabotnik* in three volumes,
and ten numbers of *Listok "Rabotnika."*

p. 15

[2] Lenin's epigraph to the article "Frederick Engels" is taken from
N. A. Nekrasov's poem "In Memory of Dobrolyubov."

p. 19

[3] Frederick Engels, *Prefatory Note to "The Peasant War in
Germany."* Marx and Engels, *Selected Works*, Vol. I, Moscow,
1958, p. 652.

p. 21

[4] The *Deutsch-Französische Jahrbücher* (*German-French Yearbooks*)
appeared in Paris in the German language, edited by K. Marx and
A. Ruge. Only the first issue, a double number, appeared in
February 1844.

The magazine ceased publication chiefly because of differences
of principle between Marx and Ruge, who was a bourgeois radical.

p. 24

⁵   Frederick Engels, "Umrisse zu einer Kritik der Nationalöko-
     nomie." Marx, Engels, *Werke*, Band 1, Dietz Verlag Berlin, 1956,
     S. 499-524.   p. 24

⁶   *The Communist League* — the first international organisation of the
     revolutionary proletariat. Preparatory to the foundation of the
     League, Marx and Engels did much to weld together the social-
     ists and the workers of all lands both ideologically and organisa-
     tionally. In the early part of 1847, Marx and Engels joined the se-
     cret German society The League of the Just. At the beginning of
     June 1847, a League of the Just congress took place in London,
     at which it was renamed The Communist League, while its
     former hazy slogan "All Men Are Brothers" was replaced by the
     militant internationalist slogan of "Working Men of All Countries,
     Unite!"
          The aims of The Communist League were the overthrow of the
     bourgeoisie, the abolition of the old bourgeois society based on
     class antagonisms, and the establishment of a new society in
     which there would be neither classes nor private property. Marx
     and Engels took part in the work of the Second Congress of the
     League, which was held in London in November and December
     1847, and on its instructions wrote the League's programme—
     Manifesto of the Communist Party — which was published in
     February 1848. The Communist League played a great historical
     role as a school of proletarian revolutionaries, as the embryo of
     the proletarian party and the predecessor of the International
     Working Men's Association (First International); it existed until
     November 1852. The history of the League is contained in the arti-
     cle by F. Engels "On the History of the Communist League"
     (Marx and Engels, *Selected Works*, Vol. II, Moscow, 1958,
     pp. 338-57).

                                                                   p. 24

⁷   *Neue Rheinische Zeitung* appeared in Cologne from June 1, 1848,
     until May 19, 1849. The managers of this newspaper were K. Marx
     and F. Engels, and the chief editor was Marx. As Lenin put
     it, the newspaper was "the best, the unsurpassed organ of the revo-
     lutionary proletariat"; it educated the masses, roused them to fight
     the counter-revolution and its influence was felt throughout Ger-
     many. From the first months of its existence, the *Neue Rheinische
     Zeitung*, because of its resolute and irreconcilable position, and of
     its militant internationalism, was persecuted by the feudal-mon-
     archist and liberal-bourgeois press, and also by the government.
     The deportation of Marx by the Prussian Government, and the
     repressive measures against its other editors were the cause of the
     paper ceasing publication. About the *Neue Rheinische Zeitung* see
     the article by Engels "Marx and the *Neue Rheinische Zeitung*
     (1848-1849)." Marx and Engels, *Selected Works*, Vol. II, Moscow,
     1958, pp. 328-37.

                                                                   p. 24

⁸ Frederick Engels, *Herr Eugen Dühring's Revolution in Science (Anti-Dühring)*.

p. 25

⁹ The Russian edition of F. Engels' *Socialism: Utopian and Scientific*, a pamphlet consisting of three chapters from his *Anti-Dühring*, appeared under this title in 1892. Marx and Engels, *Selected Works*, Vol. II, Moscow, 1958, pp. 116-55.

p. 25

¹⁰ Frederick Engels, *The Origin of the Family, Private Property and the State*. Marx and Engels, *Selected Works*, Vol. II, Moscow, 1958, pp. 170-327.

p. 25

¹¹ Frederick Engels, *Ludwig Feuerbach and the End of Classical German Philosophy*. Marx and Engels, *Selected Works*, Vol. II, Moscow, 1958, pp. 358—402.

p. 25

¹² Frederick Engels' article "The Foreign Policy of Russian Tsarism" appeared in two issues of the *Sotsial-Demokrat* (*The Social-Democrat*).

Sotsial-Demokrat—a literary and political review, published by the Emancipation of Labour group in London and Geneva in the years 1890-92. Four issues appeared. It played a big part in spreading Marxist ideas in Russia. G. V. Plekhanov, P. B. Axelrod, and V. I. Zasulich were the chief figures associated with its publication.

p. 25

¹³ Frederick Engels, *The Housing Question*. Marx and Engels, *Selected Works*, Vol. I, Moscow, 1958, pp. 546-635.

p. 25

¹⁴ Lenin refers to Frederick Engels' article "On Social Relations in Russia," and the postscript to it, contained in the book *Frederick Engels on Russia*, Geneva, 1894.

p. 25

¹⁵ *Volume IV of "Capital"* is the designation given by Lenin, in accordance with the view expressed by Engels, to Marx's *Theories of Surplus-Value* written in the years 1862-63. In the preface to Volume II of *Capital* Engels wrote: "After eliminating the numerous passages covered by Books II and III, I intend to publish the critical part of this manuscript as Book IV of *Capital*" (*Theories of Surplus-Value*) (Karl Marx, *Capital*, Vol. II, p. 2). Engels, however, did not succeed in preparing Volume IV for the press and it was first published in German, after being edited by Kautsky, in 1905 and 1910. In this edition the basic principles of the scientific publication of a text were violated and there were distortions of a number of the tenets of Marxism.

The Institute of Marxism-Leninism of the C.C. of the C.P.S.U. is issuing a new (Russian) edition of *Theories of Surplus-Value* (Volume IV of *Capital*) in three parts, according to the manuscript of 1862-63 (Karl Marx, *Theories of Surplus-Value* [Volume IV of *Capital*]). Part I appeared in 1955 and Part II in 1957.

p. 25

[16] The letter from F. Engels to I. F. Becker dated October 15, 1884.

p. 26

[17] *International Working Men's Association* (First International)— the first international organisation of the proletariat, founded by K. Marx in 1864 at an international workers' meeting convened in London by English and French workers. The foundation of the First International was the result of many years of persistent struggle waged by K. Marx and F. Engels to establish a revolutionary party of the working class. Lenin said that the First International "laid the foundation of an international organisation of the workers for the preparation of their revolutionary onslaught on capital," "laid the foundation for the proletarian, international struggle for socialism" (V. I. Lenin, *The Third International and Its Place in History*. See present edition, Vol. 29).

The central, leading body of the First International was the General Council, of which Marx was a permanent member. In the course of the struggle against the petty-bourgeois influences and sectarian tendencies then prevalent in the working-class movement (narrow trade unionism in England, Proudhonism and anarchism in the Romance countries), Marx rallied around himself the most class-conscious of the General Council members (F. Lessner, E. Dupont, G. Jung, and others). The First International directed the economic and political struggle of the workers of different countries, and strengthened their international solidarity. A tremendous part was played by the First International in disseminating Marxism, in linking-up socialism with the working-class movement.

When the Paris Commune was defeated, the working class was faced with the problem of creating, in the different countries, mass parties based on the principles advanced by the First International. "As I view European conditions," wrote Marx in 1873, "it is quite useful to let the formal organisation of the International recede into the background for the time being" (Marx to F. A. Sorge. September 27, 1873). In 1876 the First International was officially disbanded at a conference in Philadelphia.

p. 26

[18] Marx and Engels, *Manifesto of the Communist Party*, and Karl Marx, *General Rules of the International Working Men's Association*. Marx and Engels, *Selected Works*, Vol. I, Moscow, 1958, pp. 32 and 386.

p. 27

[19] The pamphlet *Explanation of the Law on Fines Imposed on Factory Workers* was written by Lenin in the autumn of 1895. It was printed in 3,000 copies in December of that year at the Lahta Press

in St. Petersburg. This printshop was an illegal one belonging to the Narodnaya Volya group, which at that time had established relations with the St. Petersburg League of Struggle for the Emancipation of the Working Class, and printed the latter's publications. The original of the pamphlet was burned, like all others, after being set up in type.

For purposes of secrecy fictitious information was printed on the cover. For example, it was stated that the pamphlet was published by A. Y. Vasilyev's book warehouse in Kherson, that it was printed at K. N. Subbotin's Press, Ekaterinoslav St., on premises belonging to a certain Kalinin; that it was on sale in all bookshops in Moscow and St. Petersburg. The title-page contained the inscription: "Permitted by the Censor. Kherson, November 14, 1895." In 1897 the pamphlet was re-issued in Geneva by the League of Russian Social-Democrats Abroad.

It had a wide circulation, as is shown by the fact that according to reports of the Police Department, copies of it were found in the years 1895-1905 during searches and arrests in St. Petersburg, Kiev, Yaroslavl, Ivanovo-Voznesensk, Kazan, Sormovo, Nizhni-Novgorod, Orekhovo-Zuyevo, Saratov, Krasnoyarsk, Perm, and other Russian towns.

p. 29

[20] *Novoye Vremya (New Times)*—a daily newspaper that appeared in St. Petersburg from 1868 to 1917. It belonged to different publishers at different times and repeatedly changed its political line. At first it was moderately liberal, but in 1876, when A. S. Suvorin began to publish it, it became an organ of reactionary circles among the aristocracy and bureaucracy. From 1905 it became an organ of the Black Hundreds. Following the February bourgeois-democratic revolution in 1917, it gave the fullest support to the bourgeois Provisional Government's counter-revolutionary policy and conducted a furious campaign of slander against the Bolsheviks. It was closed down by the Revolutionary Military Committee of the Petrograd Soviet on October 26 (November 8, new style), 1917. Lenin called *Novoye Vremya* a typical example of the venal press.

p. 37

[21] *Moskovskiye Vedomosti (Moscow Recorder)*—one of the oldest Russian newspapers, originally issued (in 1756) as a small sheet by Moscow University. In the 1860s its line became monarchist-nationalist, reflecting the views of the most reactionary sections of the landlords and the clergy. In 1905 it became one of the leading papers of the Black Hundreds, and continued to appear until the October Revolution in 1917.

p. 37

[22] *Instructions to Factory Inspectorate Officials*. These contained a list of the duties of factory inspectors. Endorsed by the Minister of Finance S. Y. Witte, they were published in June 1894.

p. 51

[23] *Council of State*—a legislative-consultative body in tsarist Russia, whose members were appointed by the tsar. It consisted in the main of big landowners and tsarist dignitaries.

p. 51

[24] *Ostsee gubernias*—the name given in tsarist Russia to Estland, Courland and Lifland gubernias of the Baltic region. They now constitute the territory of the Latvian and Estonian Soviet Socialist Republics.

p. 67

[25] *"Gymnasium Farms and Corrective Gymnasia"* was written in the autumn of 1895 in answer to S. N. Yuzhakov's article "An Educational Utopia. A Plan for Universal, Compulsory Secondary Education," published in *Russkoye Bogatstvo (Russian Wealth)* for May 1895.

Lenin severely criticised the plan advanced by Yuzhakov, who proposed compulsory secondary education in agricultural high schools (gymnasia), the poorer students having to cover the cost of their tuition by labour service, and showed its reactionary character. At the end of 1897, when in exile in Siberia, Lenin returned to this subject in the article "Gems of Narodnik Project-Mongering" (see pp. 459-89 of this volume).

The article was published over the signature of K. T—in on November 25 (December 7), 1895, in the *Samarsky Vestnik (Samara Herald)*.

The newspaper *Samarsky Vestnik* appeared in Samara (now the city of Kuibyshev) from 1883 to 1904. From the end of 1896 to March 1897 it was controlled by the "legal Marxists" (P. P. Maslov, R. Gvozdyov [R. E. Zimmerman], A. A. Sanin, V. V. Portugalov and others). In the 1890s it published occasional articles by Russian revolutionary Marxists.

p. 73

[26] *Russkoye Bogatstvo (Russian Wealth)*—a monthly magazine published in St. Petersburg from 1876 to the middle of 1918. In the early 1890s it became the organ of the liberal Narodniks, and was edited by S. N. Krivenko and N. K. Mikhailovsky. The journal advocated reconciliation with the tsarist government and waged a bitter struggle against Marxism and the Russian Marxists.

In 1906 it became the organ of the semi-Cadet "Popular Socialist" Party.

p. 73

[27] *Zemstvo*—the name given to the local government bodies introduced in the central gubernias of tsarist Russia in 1864. They were dominated by the nobility and their powers were limited to purely local economic problems (hospital and road building, statistics, insurance, etc.) Their activities were controlled by the provincial Governors and the Ministry of Internal Affairs, which could pre-

vent the implementation of any decisions disapproved by the government.

p. 74

[28] The leaflet *"To the Working Men and Women of the Thornton Factory"* was written after November 7(19), 1895, in connection with a strike of about 500 weavers that broke out on November 6(18) against bad conditions and the new oppressive measures introduced by the factory management. The strike was directed by the St. Petersburg League of Struggle for the Emancipation of the Working Class. Before the strike broke out, the League of Struggle issued a leaflet, written by G. M. Krzhizhanovsky, containing the weavers' demands, but so far it has not been possible to find a copy of it.

Lenin's leaflet was issued several days later and circulated in the factory when the strike was over. The facts about the workers' conditions were carefully collected by Lenin himself.

The leaflet was mimeographed, and in the spring of 1896 was reprinted abroad in No. 1-2 of the *Rabotnik* miscellany.

p. 81

[29] *Noils*—short-staple combings separated from the long wool fibres by carding.

p. 82

[30] *Schmitz*—a measure of 5 arshins (about 11½ feet) used in fixing weavers' rates.

p. 82

[31] *"Bieber"* and *"Ural"*—names of sorts of woollen cloth.

p. 84

[32] *"What Are Our Ministers Thinking About?"*—an article Lenin intended for the newspaper *Rabocheye Dyelo (The Workers' Cause)*. An issue of the paper was prepared by the St. Petersburg League of Struggle for the Emancipation of the Working Class by agreement with the Narodnaya Volya group. The first issue of *Rabocheye Dyelo* was prepared and edited by Lenin, who wrote all the main articles, including the leading article "To the Russian Workers," "What Are Our Ministers Thinking About?", "Frederick Engels," and "The Yaroslavl Strike in 1895." Articles were also written by other members of the St. Petersburg League of Struggle, G. M. Krzhizhanovsky, A. A. Vaneyev, P. K. Zaporozhets, L. Martov (Y. O. Zederbaum), and M. A. Silvin. Lenin wrote the following regarding the first issue of *Rabocheye Dyelo* in his *What Is To Be Done?*:

"This issue was ready to go to press when it was seized by the gendarmes, who, on the night of December 8, 1895, raided the house of one of the members of the group, Anatoly Alexeyevich Vaneyev, and so the original *Rabocheye Dyelo* was not destined to see the light of day. The leading article in this issue (which perhaps in some thirty years' time some *Russkaya Starina* [*The Russian Antiquary*] will unearth in the archives of the Police Department) described the historical tasks of the working class in Russia, and regarded the achievement of political liberty as the most important. This issue also contained an article entitled 'What Are Our Ministers Thinking About?' which dealt with the breaking-up of the elementary education committees by the police. In addition, there was some correspondence, not only from St. Petersburg, but from other parts of Russia, too (for example, a letter about the assault on the workers in Yaroslavl Gubernia)" (see present edition, Vol. 5, *What Is To Be Done?*, chapter II).

With the exception of a copy of the article "What Are Our Ministers Thinking About?", discovered in January 1924 in the Police Department records on the League of Struggle, the manuscripts of these articles have not yet been found.

p. 87

[33] *Stepan Razin* and *Yemelyan Pugachov* were the leaders of extensive peasant revolts in Russia in the seventeenth and eighteenth centuries.

p. 90

[34] The "*Draft and Explanation of a Programme for the Social-Democratic Party*" were written by Lenin while in prison in St. Petersburg. The "Draft Programme" was written in December 1895, some time after the 9th (21st) of that month. The "Explanation of the Programme" was written in June-July 1896. The reminiscences of N. K. Krupskaya and A. I. Ulyanova-Yelizarova show that the text was written in milk between the lines of some book. Lenin's original text was evidently first developed and then copied.

In the Archives of the Institute of Marxism-Leninism of the C.C. of the C.P.S.U. there are three copies of the "Draft Programme." The first one, found among Lenin's personal papers for the period of 1900-04, was written by an unknown hand in invisible ink between the lines of S. Chugunov's article "The Human Cervical Vertebra from the Viewpoint of the Theory of Evolution" in issue No. 5, 1900, of the magazine *Nauchnoye Obozreniye*. There is no heading to this copy. The pages are numbered in pencil in Lenin's handwriting and were placed in an envelope with the inscription, also in Lenin's handwriting: "Old (1895) Draft Programme."

The second copy was also found among Lenin's personal papers for the period 1900-04; it was typed on tissue paper and headed: "Old (1895) Draft Programme for the Social-Democratic Party."

The third copy, found in the Geneva archives of the R.S.D.L.P., consists of 39 sheets of hectographed text. As distinct from the other two copies, this one contains not only the "Draft Programme," but also an "Explanation of the Programme," which together constitute one integral whole.

p. 93

35 *Nauchnoye Obozreniye (Science Review)*—a journal that appeared in St. Petersburg from 1894 to 1903, at first weekly, then monthly. It had no definite line, but "to be in the fashion" (Lenin's expression) allowed Marxists to use its columns. It published several letters and articles by Marx and Engels, and also three articles by V. I. Lenin: "A Note on the Question of the Market Theory," "Once More on the Theory of Realisation," "Uncritical Criticism."

p. 93.

36 *Land redemption payments* were established by the Regulation Governing Redemption by Peasants Who Have Emerged from Serf Dependence..., adopted on February 19, 1861. The tsarist government compelled the peasants, in return for the allotments assigned to them, to pay redemption to the landlords amounting to several times the real price of the land. When the purchase deal was concluded, the government paid the landlords the purchase price, which was considered a debt owed by the peasants, to be repaid over a period of 49 years. The instalments to be paid annually by the peasants were called land redemption payments. These were an intolerable burden on the peasants and caused their ruin and impoverishment en masse. The peasants formerly belonging to landlords alone paid nearly 2,000 million rubles to the tsarist government, whereas the market price of the land that the peasants received did not exceed 544 million rubles. In view of the fact that the adoption of the redemption scheme by the peasants did not take place at once, but dragged on until 1883, the redemption payments were only to have ended by 1932. However the peasant movement during the first Russian revolution, in 1905-07, compelled the tsarist government to abolish the redemption payments as from January 1907.

p. 98

37 *Collective responsibility* was a compulsory measure making the peasants of each village community collectively responsible for timely and full payments and for the fulfilment of all sorts of services to the state and the landlords (payment of taxes and of land redemption instalments, provision of recruits for the army, etc.). This form of bondage, which was retained even after serfdom had been abolished, remained in force until 1906.

p. 98

38 The copyist apparently could not decipher several words following the word "refused." The hectographed notebook continues as follows: "[blank]*... the rule of irresponsible officials than any interference by society in government affairs, the more readily does it present the opportunity ... [blank II]."

p. 112

39 Lenin refers to the circular to factory inspectors issued by Minister of Finance S. Y. Witte following the strikes in the summer and autumn of 1895. Comments on the circular are given on pp. 123-24 of this volume.

p. 116

[40] Lenin wrote the leaflet *"To the Tsarist Government"* in prison at a date previous to November 25 (December 7), 1896. It was mimeographed by the League of Struggle for the Emancipation of the Working Class.

The leaflet was a reply to S. Y. Witte's circular addressed to factory inspectors, and to the report of the 1896 summer strikes in St. Petersburg published on July 19 (31), 1896, in issue No. 158 of *Pravitelstvenny Vestnik (Government Herald)*.

p. 122

[41] Lenin called the strikes that took place in May-June 1896 "the famous St. Petersburg industrial war." They were caused by the employers' refusal to pay the workers in full for holidays on the occasion of the coronation of Nicholas II. A strike that broke out at the Russian Cotton-Spinning Mill (Kalinkin) rapidly spread to all the main cotton-spinning and weaving mills of St. Petersburg. For the first time the proletariat of that city undertook a struggle against their exploiters on a broad front, embracing over 30,000 workers, who struck work under the leadership of the St. Petersburg League of Struggle for the Emancipation of the Working Class. The League issued leaflets and manifestoes calling on the workers to stand solidly and steadfastly in defence of their rights; it published and distributed the strikers' main demands, which included the 10½-hour working day, increased rates, and payment of wages on time. The St. Petersburg strikes gave an impetus to the working-class movement in Moscow and other Russian towns, and forced the government to speed up the review of the factory laws and the issue of the law of June 2 (14), 1897, by which the working day at factories and mills was reduced to 11½ hours. The strikes, as Lenin subsequently wrote, "ushered in an era of steady advance in the working-class movement, that most powerful factor in the whole of our revolution."

p. 123

[42] *Pravitelstvenny Vestnik (Government Herald)* — a daily newspaper, official organ of the tsarist government; appeared in St. Petersburg from 1869 to 1917.

p. 124

[43] *The League of Struggle for the Emancipation of the Working Class,* organised by Lenin in the autumn of 1895, consisted of about twenty Marxist workers' circles in St. Petersburg. The entire work of the League was based on the principles of centralism and strict discipline. The League was headed by a central group consisting of V. I. Lenin, A. A. Vaneyev, N. K. Zaporozhets, G. M. Krzhizhanovsky, N. K. Krupskaya, L. Martov (Y. O. Zederbaum), M. A. Silvin, V. V. Starkov, and others. The entire work of the League was, however, under the direct leadership of five members of the group headed by Lenin. The League was divided into several district organisations. Such front-rank class-conscious workers as I. V. Babushkin, V. A. Shelgunov connected the groups with the facto-

ries, where there were organisers in charge of gathering information and distributing literature. Workers' study-circles were established in the big plants.

For the first time in Russia the League set about introducing socialism into the working-class movement, effecting a transition from the propagation of Marxism among small numbers of advanced workers attending study-circles to political agitation among the broad masses of the proletariat. It directed the working-class movement, and linked up the workers' struggle for economic demands with the political struggle against tsarism. A strike was organised in November 1895 at the Thornton woollen mill. It was under the leadership of the League that the famous St. Petersburg textile workers' strike, involving over 30,000 workers, took place in the summer of 1896. The League issued leaflets and pamphlets, and prepared the ground for the issue of the newspaper *Rabocheye Dyelo* (*The Workers' Cause*). The League publications were issued under V. I. Lenin's editorship. The League's influence spread far beyond St. Petersburg, workers' study-circles having united, on its initiative, into similar Leagues in Moscow, Kiev, Ekaterinoslav and other cities and parts of Russia.

Late in the night of December 8 (20), 1895, the tsarist government dealt a severe blow to the League by arresting a considerable number of its leading members, headed by Lenin.

An issue of *Rabocheye Dyelo* ready for the press was also seized. The League replied to the arrest of Lenin and the other members by issuing a leaflet containing political demands, in which reference was made for the first time to the existence of the League.

While in prison Lenin continued to lead the work of the League, helped it with his advice, got coded letters and leaflets smuggled out of prison, wrote the pamphlet *On Strikes* and the "Draft and Explanation of a Programme for the Social-Democratic Party."

The League was significant, as Lenin put it, because it was the first real rudiment of a revolutionary party which had the support of the working-class movement and directed the class struggle of the proletariat.

p. 127

[44] The essay "*A Characterisation of Economic Romanticism*" was written by Lenin while in exile in Siberia in the spring of 1897. It appeared in four issues (Nos. 7-10) of the "legal Marxist" magazine *Novoye Slovo* (*New Word*) for April-July 1897, over the signature K. T—n. It was included later in the miscellany entitled *Economic Studies and Essays* by Vladimir Ilyin which appeared in October 1898 (though the date given on the cover and the title-page is 1899). Early in 1908 it appeared, slightly amended and abridged, along with other items in *The Agrarian Question* by Vl. Ilyin. The parts of it omitted in this miscellany were section three, chapter II, "The Problem of the Growth of the Industrial Population at the Expense of the Agricultural Population," and the end of section five, chapter II, "The Reactionary Character of Romanticism." A postscript was added to chapter I.

When preparing the editions legally published in 1897 and 1898, Lenin was compelled for censorship reasons to substitute the term "modern theory" for "Marx's theory" and "the well-known German economist" for "Marx," "realist" for "Marxist," the word "paper" for *Capital*, and so on. In the 1908 edition Lenin either altered a considerable number of these expressions in the text or added the necessary footnotes. In the second and third Russian editions of the *Collected Works*, the corrections were given in footnotes. In the present edition the corrections have been introduced into the text.

p. 129

[44] *Novoye Slovo* (*New Word*)—a monthly scientific, literary and political journal, published originally in St, Petersburg from 1894 by the liberal Narodniks. In the early part of 1897 it was taken over by the "legal Marxists" (P. B. Struve, M. I. Tugan-Baranovsky, and others). *Novoye Slovo* published two of Lenin's articles when he was in exile in Siberia—"A Characterisation of Economic Romanticism" and "About a Certain Newspaper Article." The journal also carried the writings of G. V. Plekhanov, V. I. Zasulich, L. Martov, A. M. Gorky, and others. In December 1897 it was closed down by the tsarist government.

p. 129

[46] *V. V.* (pseudonym of V. P. Vorontsov) and *N.—on* (pseudonym of N. F. Danielson) were ideologists of liberal Narodism of the 1880s and 1890s.

p. 134

[47] Lenin refers to MacCulloch's polemical article "Mr. Owen's Plans for Relieving the National Distress," published anonymously in 1819 in *The Edinburgh Review* (Vol. XXXII), to which Sismondi replied.
The Edinburgh Review or Critical Journal was a scientific, literary and political journal that appeared from 1802 to 1929.

p. 149

[48] Karl Marx, *Capital*, Vol. II, Moscow, 1957, p. 373; Vol. III, Moscow, 1959, p. 821.

p. 151

[49] Karl Marx, *Capital*, Vol. II, Moscow, 1957, pp. 351-523.

p. 152

[50] In the 1897 and 1898 editions Lenin referred to M. I. Tugan-Baranovsky's *Industrial Crises*, Part II. In the 1908 edition Lenin introduced a change by referring instead to his own book *The Development of Capitalism in Russia*, which appeared in 1899 (see present edition, Vol. 3).

p. 152

[51] Karl Marx, *Capital*, Vol. II, Moscow, 1957, p. 391.

p. 154

[52] Karl Marx, *Capital*, Vol. III, Moscow, 1959, p. 245.

p. 156

[53] Karl Marx, *Capital*, Vol. II, Moscow, 1957, p. 316.

p. 169

[54] *Katheder-Socialists*—representatives of a trend in bourgeois political economy of the 1870s and 1880s who, under the guise of socialism, advocated bourgeois-liberal reformism from university chairs (*Katheder* in German). The fear aroused among the exploiting classes by the spread of Marxism in the working-class movement and the growth of that movement brought Katheder-Socialism into being; it united the efforts of bourgeois ideologists to find fresh means of keeping the working people in subjugation.

Among the Katheder-Socialists were A. Wagner, G. Schmoller, L. Brentano, and V. Sombart who asserted that the bourgeois state is above classes, can reconcile mutually hostile classes, and can gradually introduce "socialism" without affecting the interests of the capitalists but at the same time taking the demands of the working people as far as possible into consideration. They suggested the legalisation of police-regulated wage-labour, and the revival of the medieval guilds. Marx and Engels exposed Katheder-Socialism, showing how essentially reactionary it was. Lenin called the Katheder-Socialists the bed bugs of "police-bourgeois university science" who hated Marx's revolutionary teachings. In Russia the views of the Katheder-Socialists were advocated by the "legal Marxists."

p. 174

[55] Marx and Engels, *On Britain*, Moscow, 1953, p. 119.

p. 180

[56] Karl Marx, *Capital*, Vol. I, Moscow, 1958, p. 642.

p. 180

[57] Karl Marx, *Capital*, Vol. I, Moscow, 1958, p. 643.

p. 180

[58] The quotations referred to were taken from the estimation of Sismondi's petty-bourgeois socialism given in the *Manifesto of the Communist Party* (see Marx and Engels, *Selected Works*, Vol. I, Moscow, 1958, p. 57). N. F. Danielson used them in his article "Something About the Conditions of Our Economic Development" in *Russkoye Bogatstvo*, No. 6, 1894.

p. 199

[59] *Zur Kritik*—initial words of the title of Marx's *Zur Kritik der politischen Ökonomie*. Lenin cites passages from P. P. Rumyantsev's Russian translation of this book published in 1896 (K. Marx, *Zur Kritik der politischen Ökonomie*, Moskau-Leningrad, 1934, S. 49).

p. 199

[60] Karl Marx, *Critique of the Gotha Programme*. Marx and Engels, *Selected Works*, Vol. II, Moscow, 1958, pp. 24-25.

In the 1897 and 1898 editions Lenin, in view of the censorship, did not refer directly to Marx, but to Struve. In the 1908 edition, however, he referred to Marx's *Critique of the Gotha Programme*. This correction has been made in the present edition.

p. 203

[61] Karl Marx, *Capital*, Vol. III, Moscow, 1959, pp. 856, 860, 861.

p. 204

[62] Lenin refers to Narodnik polemical articles directed against the Marxists: N. F. Danielson, "An Apology for Money Power as a Sign of the Times," published under the pseudonym Nikolai —on in *Russkoye Bogatstvo*, No. 1-2, 1895; V. P. Vorontsov, "German Social-Democratism and Russian Bourgeoisism," published under the pseudonym V. V. in the newspaper *Nedelya (Week)*, Nos. 47-49, 1894.

p. 204

[63] Karl Marx, *Poverty of Philosophy*, Moscow, p. 55.

p. 205

[64] Karl Marx, *Capital*, Vol. III, Moscow, 1959, p. 819.

p. 205

[65] G. V. Plekhanov (N. Beltov), *The Development of the Monist View of History*, Moscow, 1956, p. 60.

p. 207

[66] Karl Marx, *Theorien über den Mehrwert*, Bd. I, Hb. 2, S. 304, 1923. For pages cited here see pp. 309 and 313.

p. 207

[67] *"Progressive" publicist of the late nineteenth century* is an ironical reference to the liberal Narodnik S. N. Yuzhakov. An extract from his article "Problems of Hegemony at the End of the Nineteenth Century," published in *Russkaya Mysl (Russian Thought)*, Nos. 3-4, 1885, was quoted by P. B. Struve.

p. 211

[68] Karl Marx, *The Poverty of Philosophy*, Moscow, pp. 167-68.

Because of the censorship Lenin substituted the word "writers" for "socialists" (in the German original—*Sozialisten*).

p. 213

[69] Karl Marx, *The Poverty of Philosophy*, Moscow, p. 74.

p. 216

[70] Karl Marx, *Zur Kritik der politischen Ökonomie*, Moskau-Leningrad, 1934, S. 85.

p. 218

[71] The *village* (land) *community* (*obshchina* or *mir*) in Russia was the communal form of peasant use of the land, characterised by compulsory crop rotation, and undivided woods and pastures. Its principal features were collective responsibility, the periodical redistribution of the land with no right to refuse the allotment given, and prohibition of its purchase and sale.

The Russian village community dates back to ancient times, and in the course of historical development gradually became one of the mainstays of feudalism in Russia. The landlords and the tsarist government used the village community to intensify feudal oppression and to squeeze land redemption payments and taxes out of the people. Lenin pointed out that the village community "does not save the peasant from turning into a proletarian; actually it serves as a medieval barrier dividing the peasants, who are as if chained to small associations and to categories which have lost all 'reason for existence'" (V. I. Lenin, *The Agrarian Question in Russia Towards the Close of the Nineteenth Century*. See present edition, Vol. 15).

The problem of the village community aroused heated arguments and brought an extensive economic literature into existence. Particularly great interest in the village community was displayed by the Narodniks, who saw in it the guarantee of Russia's socialist evolution by a special path. By tendentiously gathering and falsifying facts and employing so-called "average figures," the Narodniks sought to prove that the community peasantry in Russia possessed a special sort of "steadfastness," and that the peasant community protected the peasants against the penetration of capitalist relations into their lives, and "saved" them from ruin and class differentiation. As early as the 1880s G. V. Plekhanov showed that the Narodnik illusions about "community socialism" were unfounded and in the 1890s Lenin completely refuted the Narodnik theories. Lenin made use of a tremendous amount of statistical material and countless facts to show how capitalist relations were developing in the Russian village, and how capital, by penetrating into the patriarchal village community, was splitting the peasantry into two antagonistic classes, the kulaks and the poor peasants.

In 1906 tsarist minister Stolypin issued a law favouring the kulaks that allowed peasants to leave the community and to sell their allotments. This law laid the basis for the official abolition of the village community system and intensified the differentiation among the peasantry. In nine years following the adoption of the law, over two million peasant families withdrew from the communities.

p. 219

[72] Karl Marx, *The Eighteenth Brumaire of Louis Bonaparte*. Mar and Engels, *Selected Works*, Vol. I, Moscow, 1958, p. 275.

p. 22

[73] *Russkaya Mysl (Russian Thought)*—a monthly literary and polit ical journal published in Moscow from 1880 to 1918; up to 190 it was liberal Narodnik in trend. In the nineties, during the po lemic between the Marxists and the liberal Narodniks, the editor of the journal, while adhering to the Narodnik outlook, occasion ally allowed articles by Marxists to be published in its columns Items by the progressive writers A. M. Gorky, V. G. Korolenko D. N. Mamin-Sibiryak, G. I. Uspensky, A. P. Chekhov, and oth ers, were published in the journal's literature section.

After the 1905 Revolution, *Russkaya Mysl* became the orga of the Right wing of the Cadet Party, and was edited by P. B. Stru ve. It was closed down in the middle of 1918.

p. 22

[74] *Kit Kitych*—the nickname of Tit Titych, a rich merchant, one o the characters in A. N. Ostrovsky's comedy *Shouldering Anoth er's Troubles*. Lenin gives this epithet to the capitalist money bags.

p. 22

[75] Marx and Engels, *Manifesto of the Communist Party. Selected Works*, Vol. I, Moscow, 1958, p. 57.

p. 22

[76] Karl Marx, *Capital*, Vol. III, Moscow, 1959, p. 622.

p. 228

[77] Karl Marx, *Capital*, Vol. I, Moscow, 1958, p. 505.

p. 229

[78] Marx and Engels, *On Britain*, Moscow, 1953, pp. 1-336.

p. 229

[79] Frederick Engels, *Anti-Dühring*, Moscow, 1954, pp. 402-14.

p. 229

[80] *Sozialpolitisches Centralblatt (Central Social-Political Sheet)* — organ of the Right wing of German Social-Democracy. First ap peared in 1892.

p. 230

[81] Marx and Engels, *On Britain*, Moscow, 1953, pp. 49-50.

p. 237

[82] Karl Marx, *Capital*, Vol. I, Moscow, 1956, pp. 503-04.

In the 1897 and 1898 editions, because of the censorship, Lenin replaced the words "social revolution" (*der sozialen Revolution*) by the words "social transformation." In the 1908 edition Lenin translated the words as "social revolution." This correction has been made in the present edition.

p. 245

Chinsh peasants—those entitled to the hereditary possession of the land in perpetuity, and who had to pay an almost fixed quit-rent, known as *chinsh*. In tsarist Russia, the *chinsh* system operated mainly in Poland, Lithuania, Byelorussia, and the Black Sea littoral of the Ukraine.

p. 246

Marx and Engels, *Manifesto of the Communist Party. Selected Works*, Vol. I, Moscow, 1958, p. 57.

p. 248

The Corn Laws, which were introduced in England in 1815, established high tariffs on imported corn, and at times prohibited corn imports. They enabled the big landowners to increase grain prices on the home market and to secure enormous rents. They also strengthened the political position of the landed aristocracy. There was a fierce and protracted struggle between the big landowners and the bourgeoisie over the Corn Laws which ended in their repeal in 1846.

p. 253

"On the one hand, it cannot but be recognised, on the other hand, it must be admitted"—an ironical expression used by M. Y. Saltykov-Shchedrin in his stories "The Diary of a Provincial in St. Petersburg" and "Funeral."

p. 257

Karl Marx, *The Poverty of Philosophy*, Moscow, pp. 234-53.

p. 258

The Anti-Corn-Law League (this term is in English in the original) was founded in 1838 by the textile manufacturers Cobden and Bright. Its headquarters were in Manchester, the centre of the Free-Trade movement.

The Anti-Corn-Law League, as its name indicates, fought to secure the repeal of the Corn Laws, and stood for Free Trade, demagogically asserting that it would improve the workers' standard of living, although reduced corn prices could only result in reduced wages for the workers and increased profits for the capitalists. The conflict over this issue between the industrial bourgeoisie and the landed aristocracy ended in the repeal of the Corn Laws in 1846. Marx's views on the anti-Corn-Law movement are given in his speech "On Free Trade" (see Appendix to *The Poverty of Philosophy* by Karl Marx, Moscow, pp. 234-53).

p. 258

[89] Karl Marx, *The Poverty of Philosophy*, Moscow, p. 234.

p. 259

[90] Marx and Engels, *On Britain*, Moscow, 1953, p. 303.

p. 259

[91] *Die Neue Zeit* (*New Times*)—theoretical journal of German Social-Democracy. Appeared in Stuttgart from 1883 to 1923. Prior
to October 1917 was edited by K. Kautsky, then by H. Cunow. In
1885-95, articles by K. Marx and F. Engels appeared in its columns. Engels frequently made suggestions to the editors of *Die
Neue Zeit*, and severely criticised them for departing from Marxism. The journal also published articles by F. Mehring, P. La-
fargue, G. V. Plekhanov, and other leading figures of the international working-class movement. In the late 1890s the journal made
a practice of publishing articles by revisionists. During the First
World War (1914-18) the journal adopted a centrist, Kautskian
position in support of the social-chauvinists.

p. 259

[92] The articles mentioned by V. I. Lenin are: "The Anti-Kriege Circular" by K. Marx and F. Engels, and chapter IV, Vol. II of *German Ideology*, both of which appeared in *Das Westphälische Dampfboot* for July 1846 and August-September 1847, while extracts
from them were reprinted in Nos. 27 and 28 of *Die Neue Zeit*, 1895-
96 (MEGA, Erste Abteilung, Band 6, S. 10, 11, 12, 13; Band 5,
S. 500, 501, 502).

Das Westphälische Dampfboot (*Westphalian Steamer*)—a monthly magazine, organ of one of the trends of petty-bourgeois German, or "true," socialism; was edited by O. Lüning in Bielefeld
and Paderborn (Germany) from January 1845 to March 1848.

p. 259

[93] Karl Marx, *Capital*, Vol. I, Moscow, 1958, pp. 677-78.

p. 261

[94] Karl Marx, *Capital*, Vol. III, Moscow, 1959, p. 709.

p. 261

[95] Marx and Engels, *On Britain*, Moscow, 1953, pp. 302-03.

p. 265

[96] Karl Marx, *The Poverty of Philosophy*, Moscow, p. 253.

For censorship reasons Lenin changed (or excluded) words
from the section of Marx's "On Free Trade" cited here. Thus, he translated the words "hastens the social revolution" as "hastens this
'break-up'" and the phrase "in this revolutionary sense alone" as
"in this sense alone."

p 265

[97] Lenin wrote the pamphlet *The New Factory Law* in the summer of 1897 while in exile in Siberia, and the supplement in the autumn of the same year. Judging from P. B. Axelrod's preface to the first edition of Lenin's pamphlet *The Tasks of the Russian Social-Democrats*, the manuscript of the pamphlet appeared abroad only in autumn 1898. It was printed in 1899 in Geneva by the Emancipation of Labour group at the press of The League of Russian Social-Democrats.

p. 267

[98] Lenin refers to the notices that appeared at the beginning of January 1897 in all St. Petersburg spinning and weaving mills introducing the 11½-hour working day as from April 16 (28), i.e, shortly before May Day (April 19), the day of the international solidarity of the working people of all countries.

p. 271

[99] *Vestnik Finansov, Promyshlennosti i Torgovli* (*Finance, Industry and Trade Herald*)—a weekly journal published by the Ministry of Finance in St. Petersburg from November 1883 to 1917 (until January 1885 it was called *Ukazatel Pravitelstvennykh Rasporyazheny po Ministerstvu Finansov* [*Record of Government Instructions—Ministry of Finance*]). Government regulations, economic articles and reviews were published in its columns.

p. 275

[100] Lenin paraphrases I. A. Krylov's fable "The Lion's Share."

p. 313

[101] *Russkiye Vedomosti* (*Russian Recorder*)—a newspaper published in Moscow from 1863 onwards; it expressed the views of the moderate liberal intelligentsia. Among its contributors in the 1880s and 1890s were the democratic writers V. G. Korolenko, M. Y. Saltykov-Shchedrin and G. I. Uspensky. It also published items written by liberal Narodniks. In 1905 it became the organ of the Right wing of the bourgeois Cadet Party. Lenin said that *Russkiye Vedomosti* was a peculiar combination of "Right-wing Cadetism and a strain of Narodism." In 1918 it was closed down together with other counter-revolutionary newspapers.

p. 316

[102] *Manilov*—a character in Gogol's *Dead Souls*, typifying the weak-willed, hollow dreamer and inert windbag.

p. 316

[103] *Sysoika* —one of the chief characters in F. M. Reshetnikov's *Poliipovtsi*, typifying the ignorant and rightless poor peasant who is weighed down by want and unbearable toil.

p. 318

[104] See Note 25.

p. 321

[105] Lines from M. Y. Lermontov's poem "To A. O. Smirnova."

p. 322

[106] The pamphlet *The Tasks of the Russian Social-Democrats* was written by Lenin in exile (Siberia) at the close of 1897, and was first published in 1898 by the Emancipation of Labour group in Geneva. It circulated widely among Russia's advanced workers. According to Police Department data for the years 1898-1905, copies of the pamphlet were discovered during searches and arrests made in St. Petersburg, Moscow, Smolensk, Kazan, Orel, Kiev, Vilno, Feodosia, Irkutsk, Archangel, Sormovo, Kovno and other towns.

The original manuscript of the pamphlet has not been found but there is a copy made by some unknown hand. In 1902 a second edition of it appeared in Geneva, and in 1905 a third edition, each with a preface by V. I. Lenin. The pamphlet was also included in the miscellany: Vl. Ilyin, *Twelve Years*, published in November 1907 (the cover and title-page of which are dated 1908). The 1902, 1905 and 1907 editions do not contain the leaflet "To the St. Petersburg Workers and Socialists from the League of Struggle" included in the copy of the manuscript, and as a supplement to the first edition of the pamphlet. The leaflet was published in all the previous editions of the *Collected Works* and is also included in the present edition. The copy made from the manuscript contains several slips of the pen. Inaccuracies also appeared in the first edition of the pamphlet, which was published abroad by the Emancipation of Labour group, but these were corrected by Lenin in the subsequent editions.

p. 323

[107] *Narodnoye Pravo* (People's Right)—an illegal organisation of Russian democratic intellectuals founded in the summer of 1893, its initiators including O. V. Aptekman, A. I. Bogdanovich, A. V. Gedeonovsky, M. A. Natanson, and N. S. Tyutchev who had formerly belonged to the Narodnaya Volya. The Narodopravtsi, as the members of the party were called, set themselves the aim of uniting all opposition forces to fight for political reforms. Their organisation issued two programme documents, "Manifesto," and "An Urgent Question." In the spring of 1894 the group was broken up by the tsarist government. Lenin's estimation of the Narodnoye Pravo as a political party will be found in his *What the "Friends of the People" Are and How They Fight the Social-Democrats* (see present edition, Vol. I) and on page 344 of the present volume. Most of the Narodopravtsi subsequently joined the Socialist-Revolutionary Party.

p. 327

[108] *The Narodnaya Volya* (People's Will) group (Narodovoltsi) came into existence in St. Petersburg in the autumn of 1891 with its own programme. Its original membership included M. S. Olminsky (Alexan-

drov), N. L. Meshcheryakov, Y. M. Alexandrova, A. A. Fedulov, and
A. A. Yergin. Pamphlets and *Rabochy Sbornik (Workers' Miscellany)*, and two issues of *Letuchy Listok (The Leaflet)* were published illegally by the group's press. In April 1894 the group was
broken up by the police, but soon renewed its activities. At that
period it was in process of abandoning Narodnaya Volya views for
Social-Democracy. The last issue of *Letuchy Listok*, No. 4, that
appeared in December 1895, clearly bore traces of Social-Democratic influence. The group established contact with the St. Petersburg League of Struggle for the Emancipation of the Working
Class, used its press to issue several of the League's publications,
for example, Lenin's *Explanation of the Law on Fines Imposed on
Factory Workers* (see pp. 29-72 of the present volume), and nego-
tiated with the League about the joint publication of the newspaper
Rabocheye Dyelo. It was intended to use the group's press to issue
Lenin's pamphlet *On Strikes*, which was smuggled out of
prison in May 1896. But the suggestion fell through in view of the
police discovery and destruction of the press, and the arrest of
members of the group in June 1896. The group then went out of
existence, and some of its members (P. F. Kudelli, N. L. Meshcheryakov, M. S. Olminsky, and others) later became active figures in the Russian Social-Democratic Labour Party, although the
majority joined the Socialist-Revolutionary Party.

p. 327

[109] *The League of Russian Social-Democrats Abroad* was founded in 1894
in Geneva, on the initiative of the Emancipation of Labour group,
and had its own press where it printed revolutionary literature. At
first the Emancipation of Labour group guided the League and edited its publications. The League issued the *Rabotnik* miscellanies
and the *Listki "Rabotnika,"* and published Lenin's *Explanation of
the Law on Fines Imposed on Factory Workers* (1897), Plekhanov's
New Drive Against Russian Social-Democracy (1897), etc. The First
Congress of the R.S.D.L.P., held in March 1898, recognised
the League as the Party's representative abroad. As time proceeded,
the opportunist elements—the "economists,". or so-called "young"
group, secured the upper hand in the League. At the First Congress
of the League held in Zurich in November 1898, the Emancipation
of Labour group announced their refusal to edit League publications, with the exception of No. 5-6 of *Rabotnik* and Lenin's
pamphlets *The Tasks of the Russian Social-Democrats* and *The New
Factory Law*, which the group undertook to publish. From then
on the League published *Rabocheye Dyelo*, a magazine of the "economists." The Emancipation of Labour group finally broke with the
League and left its ranks in April 1900, at the League's Second Congress held in Geneva, when the Emancipation of Labour group
and its supporters left the Congress and established an independent
Sotsial-Demokrat organisation. In 1903 the Second Congress
of the R.S.D.L.P. adopted a decision to disband the League.

p. 327

[110] This passage refers to the policy pursued by N. P. Ignatyev, Minister of Internal Affairs in 1881-82, which was intended, as Lenin put it, "to bamboozle" the liberals; by playing at democracy it was hoped to hide the fact that the government of Alexander III had gone over entirely to the side of reaction. Part of the policy was the calling of conferences of "knowledgeable people" which included Marshals of the Nobility, representatives of the Zemstvo Administrations and similar people to discuss problems relating to a reduction in land redemption payments, the proper organisation of migration, and local government reform. A suggestion was even made to convene a so-called Zemsky Sobor, to be attended by a crowd of three thousand strong. All these devices, however, ended in Ignatyev's resignation, followed by a period of "unbridled, incredibly senseless and brutal reaction" (see *What the "Friends of the People" Are and How They Fight the Social-Democrats*, present edition, Vol. 1).

p. 335

[111] *The Emancipation of Labour group* was the first Russian Marxist group. It was founded in Geneva by G. V. Plekhanov in 1883, and included P. B. Axelrod, L. G. Deutsch, Vera Zasulich, and V. N. Ignatov.

The group did much to spread Marxism in Russia. It translated such Marxist works as *Manifesto of the Communist Party* by Marx and Engels, *Wage-Labour and Capital* by Marx, and *Socialism: Utopian and Scientific*, by Engels, etc., published them abroad and organised their distribution in Russia. Plekhanov and his group seriously undermined Narodism. In 1883 Plekhanov drafted a programme for the Russian Social-Democrats and in 1885 made another draft. The two drafts were published by the Emancipation of Labour group and marked an important step towards the establishment of a Social-Democratic Party in Russia. Plekhanov's *Socialism and the Political Struggle* (1883), *Our Differences* (1885), *The Development of the Monist View of History* (1895) played a considerable part in disseminating Marxist views. The group, however, made some serious mistakes. It clung to remnants of Narodnik views, underestimated the revolutionary role of the peasantry, and overestimated the part played by the liberal bourgeoisie. These errors were the germs of the future Menshevik views held by Plekhanov and other members of the group. The group played a great part in imbuing the Russian working class with revolutionary class-consciousness but it had no practical ties with the working-class movement. Lenin pointed out that the Emancipation of Labour group "only theoretically founded the Social-Democracy and took the first step in the direction of the working-class movement." The group established ties with the international labour movement, and represented Russian Social-Democracy at all congresses of the Second International from the first held in Paris in 1889 onwards.

At the Second Congress of the R.S.D.L.P held in August 1903, the Emancipation of Labour group announced its dissolution.

p. 338

[112] Lenin refers to collections of articles entitled *Material for a History of the Russian Social-Revolutionary Movement*, published in Geneva in the years 1893-96 by the Group of Old Narodnaya Volya Members (P. L. Lavrov, N. S. Rusanov, and others). In all, four collections appeared in five volumes (seventeen were originally planned).

p. 339

[113] *Blanquism*—a trend in the French socialist movement headed by the outstanding revolutionary and prominent representative of French utopian communism, Louis-Auguste Blanqui (1805-81).

The Blanquists denied the class struggle, and awaited "mankind's emancipation from wage slavery by a conspiracy of a small minority of intellectuals and not by the class struggle of the proletariat" (V. I. Lenin, *Results of the Congress*. See present edition, Vol. 10). They did not take account of the concrete situation requisite for the victory of an uprising and showed their disdain for ties with the masses, substituting the actions of a clandestine handful of conspirators for the activity of a revolutionary party.

p. 340

[114] The article *"The Handicraft Census of 1894-95 in Perm Gubernia and General Problems of 'Handicraft' Industry"* was written by Lenin when in exile in Siberia in August and September 1897, not later than the 7th (19th) of the latter month. The material contained in this article was used by him in his book *The Development of Capitalism in Russia*.

The article was first published in 1898 in the miscellany *Economic Studies and Essays*, and reprinted in 1908 in the miscellany *The Agrarian Question*.

p. 355

[115] In 1889 the tsarist government introduced the administrative post of Zemsky Nachalnik in order to increase the power of the landlords over the peasants. The Zemsky Nachalniks were appointed from among the local landed nobility, and were given enormous power, not only administrative but also juridical, over the peasants, including the right to have peasants arrested and flogged.

p. 357

[116] Karl Marx, *Capital*, Vol. I, Moscow, 1958, p. 748.

p. 382

[117] Karl Marx, *Capital*, Vol. I, Moscow, 1958, p. 390.

p. 405

[118] By a decree of Peter I issued in 1721 merchant factory owners were given the right to purchase peasants for work in their factories. The feudal workers attached to such enterprises under the possessional right were called "possessional peasants."

p. 418

[119] The *Ministry of Finance Yearbook*, Issue I, St. Petersburg, 1869, p. 225.

p. 426

[120] The *truck system*—the system of paying the workers wages in the shape of goods and foodstuffs from the employer's shop. This system was additional exploitation of the workers, and in Russia, was particularly widespread in the areas where handicraft industry flourished.

p. 428

[121] Karl Marx, *Capital*, Vol. I, Moscow, 1958, pp. 336-68.

p. 435

[122] *Yuridichesky Vestnik* (*The Legal Messenger*)—a monthly magazine, bourgeois-liberal in trend, published in Moscow from 1867 to 1892.

p. 437

[123] Lenin quotes from Heine's poem "Du hast Diamanten und Perlen..." ("Thou hast diamonds and pearls").

p. 441

[124] *Dyelovoi Korrespondent* (*Business Correspondent*)—a commercial and industrial newspaper that appeared in Ekaterinburg (now Sverdlovsk) from 1886 to 1898. Its columns contained informative items, announcements, articles on economic problems, and reviews.

p. 441

[125] Vol. X, part I, of the *Code of Laws of the Russian Empire*.

p. 442

[126] *Permskiye Gubernskiye Vedomosti* (*Perm Gubernia Record*)—an official paper that appeared weekly, and then daily, in Perm from 1838 to 1917.

p. 452

[127] Cf. I. I. Khemnitser's fable "The Metaphysician," in which the metaphysician is the embodiment of empty theorising.

p. 453

[128] The article "*Gems of Narodnik Project-Mongering*" was written at the close of 1897 during Lenin's exile in Siberia. He wrote it for *Novoye Slovo*, being unaware that the government had closed that magazine down in December 1897.

In 1898 Lenin included the article in his miscellany *Economic Studies and Essays*.

p. 459

[129] The "*disciples*"—the term used in the 1890s as a legal way of referring to the followers of Marx and Engels.

p. 462

[130] In this passage Lenin refers to the historico-ethical school in political economy that grew up in Germany in the 1870s. This school attached great importance to ethical (moral) principles in economic life. Its exponents were G. Schmoller, L. Brentano and other Katheder-Socialists.

p. 466

[131] Marx and Engels, *On Britain*, Moscow, 1953, p. 303.

p. 469

[132] *Korobochka*—a character in N. V. Gogol's *Dead Souls*. A petty landlady, tight-fisted, pettifogging and stupid, she was "block-headed," to use Gogol's expression. The name Korobochka has become an epithet indicating petty miserliness and stupidity.

p. 475

[133] Lenin refers to the period of absolute police despotism and gross licence of the military associated with the name and activity of A. A. Arakcheyev, the powerful favourite of Paul I and Alexander I. Characteristic of the Arakcheyev regime were the brutal measures employed against the revolutionary movement of the oppressed masses and against all free thinking.

Arakcheyev was particularly notorious for having established military settlements designed to cheapen the cost of maintaining the army. Besides fulfilling their military duties, the settlers had to maintain themselves by farmwork. Unparalleled brutality, rigorous discipline, and regulation of the settlers' lives down to the smallest details prevailed in the military settlements.

p. 478

[134] *Mercantilism*—a system of economic views and the economic policy current in a number of European states from the fifteenth to the eighteenth century to assist the accumulation of capital and the development of commerce. The advocates of mercantilism identified the nation's wealth with money, their opinion being that the public wealth is contained exclusively in money in the shape of precious metals. The states that adhered to the mercantile system tried to regulate trade in such a way as to ensure that exports exceeded imports. With this aim, they pursued a policy of protecting home industry by regulating the import of foreign goods through the imposition of tariffs, the granting of subsidies to the manufactories, and so forth. The mercantilist economic policy helped to intensify the exploitation of the working people.

p. 480

[135] This was the expression used by P. B. Struve to describe the plan suggested by Guryev, a member of the Scientific Committee of the Ministry of Finance, in an article "Current Problems of our Country's Life," signed P. B. (see *Novoye Slovo*, No. 7, April 1897, p. 238).

p. 480

[136] By the great Russian utopian is meant N. G. Chernyshevsky (1828-89), the great Russian revolutionary democrat, scholar, writer and literary critic. One of the outstanding predecessors of Russian Social-Democracy, Chernyshevsky was the ideological inspirer and leader of the revolutionary-democratic movement in Russia in the 1860s. A utopian socialist, he considered the transition to socialism possible through the medium of the peasant community. At the same time, as a revolutionary democrat "he was able to exert a revolutionary influence on all the political events of his day, overcoming all the obstacles and obstructions of the censorship and advocating the idea of a peasant revolution, the idea of a mass struggle to overthrow all the old authorities" (V. I. Lenin, "The 'Peasant Reform' and Proletarian-Peasant Revolution." See present edition, Vol. 17). Chernyshevsky wrathfully exposed the feudal character of the "peasant" Reform of 1861, and called on the peasants to revolt. In 1862 he was arrested by the tsarist government and was confined to the Peter and Paul Fortress, where he spent nearly two years, after which he was sentenced to seven years' penal servitude and to permanent exile in Siberia. He was only allowed to return from exile towards the end of his life. To the end of his days Chernyshevsky was a passionate fighter against social injustice, against all manifestations of political and economic oppression.

Chernyshevsky's services in developing Russian materialist philosophy were tremendous, his views being the summit of pre-Marxist materialist philosophy. His materialism was of a revolutionary and active character. He vigorously criticised idealist theories, and tried to refashion Hegelian dialectics in the materialist spirit. Magnificent specimens of a dialectical approach to the study of reality are to be found in Chernyshevsky's writings on political economy, aesthetics, art criticism, and history.

Marx made a study of Chernyshevsky's works, had a very high opinion of them, and called Chernyshevsky a great Russian scholar. Lenin wrote of him that he was "the only really great Russian writer who, from the fifties up to 1888, succeeded in keeping to the level of an integral philosophic materialism.... But," continued Lenin, "due to the backwardness of Russian life, Chernyshevsky was unable to, or rather, could not, rise to the heights of the dialectical materialism of Marx and Engels" (V. I. Lenin, *Materialism and Empiriocriticism.* See present edition, Vol. 14).

Chernyshevsky's literary and critical works exerted tremendous influence on the development of Russian literature and art. His novel *What Is To Be Done?* (1863) helped to politically educate more than one generation of revolutionaries in Russia and other countries.

p. 481

[137] *Sever (North)*—a weekly literary and art journal that appeared in St. Petersburg from 1888 to 1914.

p 483

[138] *Gogol's young lady*—Agaphia Tikhonovna, a character in Gogol's comedy *Marriage*.

p. 485

[139] *Novus*—a pseudonym of P. B. Struve.

p. 486

[140] Marx and Engels, *Manifesto of the Communist Party. Selected Works*, Vol. I, Moscow, 1958, p. 38.
     Further on Lenin quotes this passage in greater detail (see footnote to p. 487 of the present volume).

p. 486

[141] Lenin refers here to page 39 of the magazine *Novoye Slovo*, No. 9, June 1897, which contains a passage from his essay "A Characterisation of Economic Romanticism" (see p. 229 of the present volume).

p. 487

[142] Karl Marx, *Capital*, Vol. I, Moscow, 1958, pp. 504-06.

p. 487

[143] Karl Marx, *The Eighteenth Brumaire of Louis Bonaparte*. Marx and Engels, *Selected Works*, Vol. I, Moscow, 1958, p. 334.

p. 487

[144] The article *"The Heritage We Renounce"* was written at the close of 1897 when in exile in Siberia. In 1898 it was published in the miscellany *Economic Studies and Essays*.

p. 491

[145] *Otechestvenniye Zapiski (Fatherland Notes)*—a literary-political magazine that began publication in St. Petersburg in 1820. From 1839 it became the best progressive journal of its day. Among its contributors were V. G. Belinsky, A. I. Herzen, T. N. Granovsky, and N. P. Ogaryov. Following Belinsky's departure from the editorial board in 1846, the importance of *Otechestvenniye Zapiski* began to diminish. In 1868 the journal came under the direction of N. A. Nekrasov and M. Y. Saltykov-Shchedrin. This marked the onset of a period in which the journal flourished anew, gathering around itself the revolutionary democratic intellectuals of Russia. When Nekrasov died (in 1877), the Narodniks gained dominant influence in the journal.
     Otechestvenniye Zapiski was continually harassed by the censors, and in April 1884 was closed down by the tsarist government.

p. 494

[146] *The "peasant Reform" of 1861*, which abolished serfdom in Russia, was effected by the tsarist government in the interests of the serf-owning landlords. The Reform was made necessary by the entire course of Russia's economic development and by the growth of a mass movement among the peasantry against feudal exploitation. In

its form the "peasant Reform" was feudal, but the force of economic development that had drawn Russia on to the capitalist path gave the feudal form a capitalist content, and this content became "the more evident the *less* land was filched from the peasants, the *more fully* the land of the peasants was separated from that of the landlords, the *less* the tribute" (i.e., redemption) "paid to the feudalists" ("The 'Peasant Reform' and Proletarian-Peasant Revolution." See present edition, Vol. 17). The "peasant Reform" marked a step towards Russia's transformation into a bourgeois monarchy. On February 19, 1861, Alexander II signed a Manifesto and Regulations for the peasants, who had been freed from feudal dependence. In all, 22,500,000 serfs, formerly belonging to landowners, were "emancipated." Landed proprietorship, however, remained. The peasants' lands were declared the property of the landlords. The peasant could only get a land allotment according to the standard established by law (and even then by agreement with the landlord), and had to redeem it, that is, pay for it. The peasants made their redemption payments to the tsarist government, that had paid the established sums to the landlords. Approximate estimates show that after the Reform, the nobility possessed 71,500,000 dessiatines of land and the peasants 33,700,000 dessiatines. The Reform enabled the landlords to cut off and appropriate one-fifth or even two-fifths of the lands formerly cultivated by the peasants.

The Reform merely undermined, but did not abolish, the old corvée system of farming. The landlords secured possession of the best parts of the peasants' allotments (the "cut-off lands," woods, meadows, watering places, grazing grounds, and so on), without which the peasants could not engage in independent farming. Until the redemption arrangements were completed the peasants were considered to be "temporarily bound," and rendered services to the landlord in the shape of quit-rent or corvée service.

The Russian revolutionary democrats, headed by N. G. Chernyshevsky, criticised the "peasant Reform" for its feudal character. V. I. Lenin called the "peasant Reform" of 1861 the first mass act of violence against the peasantry in the interests of nascent capitalism in agriculture—the landlords were "clearing the estates" for capitalism.

For material 'on the 1861 Reform, see F. Engels' article "Socialism in Germany" (*Die Neue Zeit*, Jg. X, Bd. I, 1891, H. 19) and V. I. Lenin's "The Fiftieth Anniversary of the Downfall of Serfdom," "The Jubilee," "The 'Peasant Reform' and Proletarian-Peasant Revolution" (see present edition, Vol. 17).

p. 495

[147] The Regulations of February 19, 1861, were legislative acts on the abolition of serfdom in Russia.

p. 496

[148] Engels describes Skaldin as a moderate conservative in his article

"Soziales aus Russland" ("On Social Relations in Russia").
Marx and Engels, *Selected Works*, Vol. II, Moscow, 1958, p. 58.

p. 505.

[149] When speaking of the ideological "heritage" of the 1860s Lenin
was compelled, for censorship reasons, to make reference to Skaldin. Actually Lenin considered Chernyshevsky to be the principal
representative of this "heritage." In a letter to A. N. Potresov dated
January 26, 1899, from exile in Siberia, Lenin wrote: "... nowhere,
however, do I suggest accepting the heritage from Skaldin. There
can be no doubt that it should be accepted from other people.
I think that the footnote on p. 237" (p. 505 of the present volume),
"in which I had Chernyshevsky in mind and explained why it
was not convenient to take him for purposes of comparison, will
make it easier for me to defend myself (against possible attacks by
opponents)."

p. 505

[150] *Zemledelcheskaya Gazeta (Agricultural News)*—organ of the Ministry of State Properties (from 1894—of the Ministry of State Properties and Agriculture); appeared in St. Petersburg from 1834 to
1917.

p. 511

[151] *Cycle cultivation*—an enslaving form of labour-service rendered
to the landlord by the peasant as rental for land obtained from him.
The landlord lent the peasant land or made him a loan in cash or
kind for which the peasant undertook to cultivate a "cycle" using
his own implements and draught animals: this meant cultivating
one dessiatine of spring crops and one of winter crops, occasionally supplemented by reaping a dessiatine of crops.

p. 511

[152] *Vestnik Yevropy (European Messenger)*—a monthly historico-political and literary magazine, bourgeois-liberal in trend. Appeared
in St. Petersburg from 1866 to 1918. The magazine published
articles directed against the revolutionary Marxists. The magazine's editor and publisher until 1908 was M. M. Stasyulevich.

p. 515

[153] These words are from Skaldin's book, *In the Backwoods and in the
Capital*, St. Petersburg, 1870, p. 285.

p. 519

[154] Marx and Engels, *The Holy Family*, Moscow, 1956, p. 110.

p. 524

[155] N. Kamensky was one of the pseudonyms used by G. V. Plekhanov.
The article referred to is his "Materialist Conception of History,"
published in 1897 in issue No. 12 (September) of *Novoye Slovo*.

p. 530

[156] *Schmollers Jahrbuch*—its full title is *Jahrbuch für Gesetzgebung, Verwaltung und Volkswirtschaft im Deutschen Reich (Legislative, Administrative and Economic Yearbook for the German Empire)*— a magazine dealing with political economy, published from 1877 onwards by the German bourgeois economists and Katheder-Socialists, F. Holtzendorf and L. Brentano, and from 1881 by G. Schmoller.

p. 533

[157] *Nedelya (Week)*—a liberal-Narodnik political and literary newspaper. Appeared in St. Petersburg from 1866 to 1901. Was opposed to fighting the autocracy, and advocated the so-called theory of "minor matters," i.e., appealed to the intelligentsia to abstain from revolutionary struggle and to engage in "cultural activity."

p. 534

THE LIFE AND WORK
OF
V. I. LENIN

Outstanding Dates
(1895-1897)

1895

February 18 or 19 (March 2 or 3, new style)	Lenin participates in a meeting of members of Social-Democratic groups in various Russian towns held in St. Petersburg. The problems discussed are: the transition from Marxist propaganda in narrow study circles to political agitation among the masses and the publication of popular literature for workers.
April	Lenin's *The Economic Content of Narodism and the Criticism of It in Mr. Struve's Book* is published in the miscellany *Material for a Characterisation of Our Economic Development* under the pseudonym of K. Tulin. The miscellany was seized by the tsarist censors and almost the entire edition was burned.
April 25 (May 7)	Lenin goes abroad to establish contact with the Emancipation of Labour group, and to acquaint himself with the West-European working-class movement.
May	While in Switzerland Lenin makes the acquaintance of members of the Emancipation of Labour group (G. V. Plekhanov and others), and arranges for regular contacts with them, and for the publication abroad of the miscellany *Rabotnik.*
End of May-June (June-beginning of July)	Lenin lives in Paris. Becomes acquainted with Paul Lafargue.
July	Lenin takes a cure at a Swiss sanatorium.
Latter half of July-beginning of September (first half of August-middle of September)	During his stay in Berlin, Lenin works in the public library, acquaints himself with Marxist literature, and attends workers' meetings.

July 22 *(August 3)*	Lenin attends a Social-Democratic meeting held in the Niederbarnim suburb of Berlin.
September 7(19)	Lenin returns to Russia, carrying with him a portmanteau with a false bottom containing illegal Marxist literature.
Between 7 and 29 of September (September 19 and October 11)	Lenin visits Vilno, Moscow and Orekhovo-Zuyevo, where he establishes contact with members of local Social-Democratic groups, and gets their agreement to support the miscellany *Rabotnik* then being published abroad.
September 29 (October 11)	Lenin returns to St. Petersburg.
Autumn	Lenin founds the League of Struggle for the Emancipation of the Working Class in St. Petersburg.
November	Lenin sends abroad a series of items dealing with the working-class movement in Russia, for publication in the *Rabotnik* miscellany.
Not before November 7 (19)	The St. Petersburg League of Struggle issues the leaflet written by Lenin entitled "To the Working Men and Women of the Thornton Factory."
November 25 (December 7)	Lenin's article "Gymnasium Farms and Corrective Gymnasia" is published in the newspaper *Samarsky Vestnik*.
November- beginning of December (November- middle of December)	Lenin prepares the publication of the first issue of the illegal newspaper *Rabocheye Dyelo*, organ of the St. Petersburg League of Struggle; he writes the leading article "To the Russian Workers," the article "What Are Our Ministers Thinking About?" and others. He edits the whole issue.
December 3 (15)	The publication of Lenin's pamphlet *Explanation of the Law on Fines Imposed on Factory Workers* is begun.
December 8 (20)	Meeting of the leading group of the League of Struggle, headed by Lenin, at which the first issue of *Rabocheye Dyelo*, prepared for the press, is discussed.
In the night of December 8-9 (20-21)	Lenin and other members of the St. Petersburg League of Struggle are arrested. During the search and arrest of A. A. Vaneyev, the police seize the material for the first issue of *Rabocheye Dyelo*, then ready for the press. Lenin is remanded under arrest.
December 21 (January 2, 1896)	Lenin's first interrogation in prison.
End of the year	Lenin drafts a programme for the Social-Democratic Party.

1896

1896
While in prison, Lenin · establishes contact with members of the St. Petersburg League of Struggle who escaped arrest, helps the League with advice and instruction, and has pamphlets and leaflets written by him smuggled out.

Beginning of January
While in prison Lenin begins preparations for his book *The Development of Capitalism in Russia*.

Not before March
Lenin's obituary "Frederick Engels," written in 1895, is published in the miscellany *Rabotnik*, No. 1-2.

March 30 (April 11)
Lenin's second interrogation in prison.

May 7 (19)
Third interrogation.

May 27 (June 8)
Fourth interrogation.

Summer
Lenin writes an explanation of the programme for the Social-Democratic Party.

Before November 25 (December 7)
The St. Petersburg League of Struggle issues a leaflet "To the Tsarist Government," written by Lenin while in prison.

1897

January 29 (February 10)
The tsarist government issues an order exiling Lenin to East Siberia under police surveillance for three years.

February 13 (25)
Lenin is informed of his sentence to exile in East Siberia.

February 14 (26)
Lenin is released from remand imprisonment and allowed to remain in St. Petersburg until the evening of February 17 (March 1).

February 14-17 (February 26-March 1)
Lenin has a meeting in St. Petersburg with the other "old" League of Struggle members who have been released before being sent into exile and with "young" members. At a meeting of "old" and "young" League members Lenin severely criticises the "economism" trend that is beginning to appear among the "young" members.

February 17 (March 1)
Lenin leaves St. Petersburg for exile in Siberia via Moscow.

February 18-22 (March 2-6)
On his way to exile a halt is made in Moscow, where Lenin has permission to stay for a while with his mother. He stays two days longer than allowed by the police.

February 22 (March 6)
Lenin leaves Moscow for Siberia, where he is to live in exile.

March 4 (16)	Lenin arrives in Krasnoyarsk.
March 9-April 30 (March 21-May 12)	While in Krasnoyarsk Lenin studies problems relating to Russia's economic development, using for this purpose books in the private library of G. V. Yudin, a local merchant.
April-July	Lenin's *Characterisation of Economic Romanticism* is published in *Novoye Slovo*, issues 7-10.
April 30 (May 12)	Lenin leaves Krasnoyarsk via Minusinsk for the village of Shushenskoye, the place to which he has been exiled.
May 6 (18)	Lenin arrives in Minusinsk.
May 8 (20)	Lenin arrives in the village of Shushenskoye, Minusinsk Province, Yenisei Gubernia.
Summer and autumn	Lenin writes his pamphlet *The New Factory Law* and the appendix to it.
September 27-28 (October 9-10)	Lenin travels to Minusinsk, where he makes the acquaintance of exiled members of the Narodnaya Volya and Narodnoye Pravo organisations.
September 29-October 4 (October 11-16)	From Minusinsk Lenin arrives in the village of Tesinskoye, where he spends five days among exiled Social-Democrats.
November	Lenin leaves Shushenskoye village and visits Minusinsk "without permission."
Second half of the year	Lenin writes the pamphlet *The Tasks of the Russian Social-Democrats* and the articles "The Handicraft Census of 1894-95 in Perm Gubernia and General Problems of 'Handicraft' Industry," "Gems of Narodnik Project-Mongering," and "The Heritage We Renounce."
1897	While in exile, Lenin maintains contact with the leading bodies of the working-class movement in Russia and with the Emancipation of Labour group abroad, and also corresponds with Social-Democrats in other places of exile; he continues preparations for his book *The Development of Capitalism in Russia*. Lenin gives legal advice to the peasants of Shushenskoye village and the surrounding region, and enjoys great prestige among them.